A Commanding Presence

Arma amens capio; nec sat rationis in armis

Arms I seize, distraught; though there is
little sense in taking arms

Virgil, *Aen*. ii, 314

A COMMANDING PRESENCE

WELLINGTON IN THE PENINSULA, 1808–1814

LOGISTICS · STRATEGY · SURVIVAL

by

Ian Robertson

SPELLMOUNT

British Library Cataloguing in Publication Data:
A catalogue record for this book is available
from the British Library

ISBN 978 1 86227 374 0

First published in the UK in 2008 by
Spellmount Limited
Cirencester Road, Chalford
Stroud, Gloucestershire. GL6 8PE

Tel: 01453 883300
Fax: 01453 883233
E-mail: enquiries@spellmount.com
Website: www.spellmount.com

Spellmount Limited is an imprint of NPI Media Group

1 3 5 7 9 8 6 4 2

Typesetting and origination by NPI Media Group
Printed in Great Britain

Contents

List of Maps

and in the latter half of the colour section:

The base material for these, with the exception of Map 7, has been supplied by Data Spain © 2006

List of Illustrations

Note. In the interest of displaying as much detail as possible, several of the illustrations have been deliberately cropped, dispensing with superfluous areas of foliage, sky, etc.

Monochrome plate section following page 128

Colour plate section following page 224

Preface and Acknowledgements

The many battles fought by Wellington have always excited interest and controversy, and always will;[1] but it is still not generally realised that – apart from the brief Waterloo campaign – a high proportion of the fighting on land between British and French troops during the Napoleonic period took place in Portugal and Spain: thus the war – a series of campaigns and sieges extending from August 1808 until April 1814 – became known as the 'Peninsular War', although the culminating campaign progressed through south-western France as far as Toulouse.

My interest was prompted by my marriage to a Basque, whose parents now lie in the cemetery of Sare, a village through which part of the battle of the Nivelle was fought. At that time – now fifty years ago – although contemporary narratives might still be acquired inexpensively and with comparative ease, there was little of consequence in print concerning that war, and I was able to commission, edit – indeed largely rewrite – *Wellington in the Peninsula,* the first volume of Jac Weller's trilogy, devoted to those campaigns which have continued to engage my interest ever since.

It is a large subject – Sir Charles Oman's magisterial history, published between 1902 and 1930, ran to seven substantial volumes – and it had been written about repeatedly before that time, and also since then. The present work does not pretend to present an 'authoritative' interpretation of that long-drawn-out confrontation, but rather to provide an approach to the Contest from an untypical perspective, placing several important but frequently neglected elements or features of it in their proper context, notably those applying when the armies were not engaged in actual fighting, which was some ninety per cent of the time!

While major battles may provide significant hooks on which to hang the sequence of events – and are thus given adequate notice – that less emphasis is given to detailed description of tactics, is intentional;[2] nor have Orders of Battle been tabulated.

Likewise, partly in an attempt to keep its extent within reasonable limits, comparatively less detail is given in the last three chapters then in the first fourteen, for I have written extensively already on the battles in the Pyrenees and the final phase of the war in *Wellington invades France*.[3] This is not to suggest that those critical last ten months were not as essential to an understanding of the war, which certainly did not stop abruptly at the frontier, nor did the intensity of the confrontation tail off in any way, as some have assumed.[4]

When the Duke later remarked: 'I made a computation of all the men I lost in Spain – killed, prisoners, deserters, everything – it amounted to 36,000 men in six years', he added that it would have been infinitely greater had not sufficient attention been given to the army's 'regular subsistence', a vital contribution to his eventual success which had been inadequately examined. In this study I have endeavoured to give proper emphasis to the immense practical difficulties faced by the Commissariat Department in their perennial struggle to provision and sustain the Allied army as an effectual fighting force. Imposed on him by the physical features and climatic conditions peculiar to the Peninsula, Logistical problems – among a complex mix of other pressures and issues – materially affected Strategic decisions, and it was Wellington's commanding presence that enabled them to be resolved. Very rarely was he caught off his guard, or found in a precarious situation, due to a error of judgement.[5]

By focusing on these, among others topics, may well induce military historians to devote due attention to the less sanguinary but equally absorbing aspects of that formidable conflict, for fighting actual battles, which took up so small an amount of the army's time, was only part of a far wider scene. The struggle against the elements during an often bitterly cold winter was such that few encounters could take place during that interminable period, and some insight is provided into how Wellington's men, both officers and the rank and file, occupied themselves during those tedious months of inaction when not recuperating from the last campaign, or training and preparing for the next.[6]

By the spring of 1814, having thrashed the French at Vitoria and crossed the Pyrenees into France, a high proportion of Wellington's officers and men, whether British, members of the King's German Legion or the Chasseurs Britanniques, or the troops of their Portuguese allies, had already been exposed to six long years of marching and fighting under a blistering sun, or lashed by driving rain and freezing winds. Having personal experience of the extremes and vagaries of the climate of the Peninsula over a number of years, I can only confirm that the very severe physical conditions which the contesting armies had to endure should never be underestimated. The imagination must be well stretched in this enervated twenty-first century to appreciate properly the stamina and fortitude required to survive either the strenuous course of a summer campaign or the tedium of winter, under cover in cantonments: one had to be very tough, both physically and morally.

When describing the background to these campaigns, in many cases I have also preferred to draw quite heavily on the graphic narratives of participants, although aware that anecdotes should be treated with caution. Many, writing with immediacy, provide first-hand evidence of what was taking place around them even if they were unable to appreciate either the importance or otherwise of the events they experienced, or the precise part they were playing in the often extended theatre of war. Naturally, from their subjective viewpoint, often they might not 'see the wood for the trees', yet the trees – when visible on those windswept plains, or dense in the Pyrenees – were a vital and intrinsic part of the landscape.

Both Captains Joseph Moyle Sherer and Thomas Henry Browne may be aptly quoted here. As the former stressed: '... it is not my intention to offer a professional view of the progress and conduct of the war, or to enter at all upon a regular detail of movements and positions [but] ... to draw a picture of *campaigning*'. Browne admitted that his journal would not possibly 'detail all that passed in the different divisions of the army', his observations 'being confined to what could be picked up in the hurry and bustle of continued marching and counter marching, at the Head Quarters of the army, to which I was attached on the Staff of the Adjutant General. I had neither leisure nor inclination to collect the materials for book making at any future time, and am only induced to transcribe in a somewhat enlarged shape the little memoranda I made in a rough book of notes, from the pleasure I derive in retracing scenes, which at that period were so deeply interesting to me ...'

The Private Journal of Judge-Advocate Larpent is another valuable account, the more so because written by an intelligent civilian at Headquarters in the company of the better-informed staff officers and in direct contact with Wellington himself. It is also bracingly free of military rhetoric, for what he wrote were private letters without future publication in view, and his pages abound with incidents and comments on subjects which public history passes as beneath its notice.

Naturally, these narratives are of variable quality – not all authors were literate or articulate – and only a proportion of them were jotted down at the time of the events described; many were composed in later years, when dulled memories were jolted by the publication of Napier's great *History*, a mine of information from which they could pillage and pad out their own memoirs; and to give another example: on more than one occasion – notably when describing incidents during Moore's arduous retreat to Corunna, which they both experienced – Commissary Schaumann has very obviously plagiarised Adam Neale's *Letters*, published eighteen years before the completion of his own '*Diary*'. As Oman explains in his indispensible *Wellington's Army*, when excusing their occasional inaccuracies: 'The strength of men's memories differs, so does their appreciation of the relative values of a dramatic narrative as compared with a photographic record of personal experiences. But in a general way we must allow that every year that elapses between the event and the setting down of its narrative on paper decreases progressively the value of the record.' He reiterated that 'Failing memory, the love of a well-rounded tale, a spice of autolatry (evident in the narratives of Robert Blakeney and Sir Harry Smith, for example), and an appreciation of the picturesque, have impaired the value of many a veteran's reminiscences.' Again, 'One or two of the most readable narratives frankly mix up the sequence of events, with a note that the exact dating can not be reconstructed,' while although they may be 'admirable evidence for the way in which the rank and file looked on a battle, a forced march, or a prolonged shortage of rations ... we must not trust them overmuch as authorities on the greater matter of war?' A few very slight editorial liberties have been taken when quoting, only to ease the flow of a sentence, but not all errors in spelling have been corrected.

The following chapters will reflect an anglocentric view, for with rare exceptions, comparatively little survives from the pens of either officers or the rank and file of Wellington's Allies, on which one may rely. In *A Hand-Book for Travellers in Spain* (1845), Richard Ford – who rarely minced his words – when commenting on their military authorities, opined that 'The generality of French authors on the war in Spain desire to palliate the injustice of the invasion, the terrorism with which it was carried out, and to explain away defeats sustained; they seem to be written solely to conciliate French readers at the expense of truth and history, nay facts are occasionally so de-naturalized that an Englishman often supposes that the accounts must have reference to some totally distinct campaign and results.'

Academic historians are apt to insinuate that most new descriptions of the Peninsular War, other than their own, are superfluous; that they are not sufficiently 'revisionist'; cavilling that they are merely a derivative litany of Wellington's victories, to which the contribution of his Allies is belittled; or castigating them as being a combination of cultural prejudice, political partisanship, and national myth, written with no proper understanding of the wider historical issues, nor taking recent historiography into consideration, etc. While there may well be some truth in this, it should be recognised also that with such an extensive canvas to cover, it is unrealistic to expect a comprehensive portrayal of a complex period and subject which will satisfy every demand.

This is not an elaborated thesis. I have not attempted to investigate either the numerous manuscript sources preserved in public, regimental, and private libraries and archives, among them those of the National Army Museum in Chelsea, the Wellington Papers in the University of Southampton, the George Murray Papers in the National Library of Scotland, and in the Royal Engineers' Museum at Chatham, to mention a few only, or such valuable repositories of material as the *Journal of the Society for Army Historical Research* (JSAHR), although well aware that they contain rich veins to be tapped.

Political developments which effected Wellington's strategic decisions are mentioned only *en passant*: their complexities have been admirably explained in Rory Muir's *Britain and the Defeat of Napoleon*, to which the reader should refer. Both Richard Glover's *Peninsular Preparation*, and Stephen Ward's *Wellington's Headquarters*, have provided a great deal of invaluable information concerning the army at the time and the complexities of its organisation and administration, while the care of the wounded has been professionally described in Martin Howard's *Wellington's Doctors*

As Antony Brett-James was well aware when compiling his inimitable *Life in Wellington's Army*, one can only adequately cover a proportion of those complementary topics of importance or interest, and which in themselves deserve further investigation. To mention a few at random: the duties of buglers and drummers; regimental colours; recruitment and training; the treatment, transportation, and detention of prisoners;[7] any technical information about weapons, whether swords or sabres, small arms, or artillery, their manufacture, and their ammunition; the fabrication of uniforms; the function of the Horse Guards in the daily administration of the British Army; the distribution of honours and decorations, etc; let alone the immense cost of carrying on a protracted war. Sensibly, I am leaving it to more knowledgable pens to cover several related subject requiring specialist attention.[8]

In the selection of illustrative material, the emphasis has been on reproducing those drawings made by artists accompanying the armies. Far too many battle scenes that were depicted, both at the time and since, were the result of artistic license in a most fanciful form, displaying imaginary scenes, idealised, attractive, and impressive maybe – they are legion, and still frequently embellish what are professed to be historical studies – but, having little semblance to the reality, are entirely misleading.

Plans of battlegrounds are not included, as not being relevant to the problems of logistics or strategy, but the maps provided have been drawn to emphasize contour in the often rugged and convoluted regions traversed by the confronting armies, a vital factor too frequently neglected by cartographers commissioned to show the lie of the land over which they were manoeuvring, fighting, or merely subsisting. Too often, when these isolating mountain ranges have been indicated in any way, they have resembled furry caterpillars. Sections of some contemporary maps have also been reproduced if only to show what was available, and how unreliable many of them were!

Most topographical names in the text are spelt in the form printed on recent Portuguese, Spanish, and French Geographical Institute maps, except when occurring in quotations: thus inconsistencies will be found, although an attempt has been made to standardise them. As Oman warned his readers in 1930, 'Certain names of Basque villages are never written with the same letters by any two persons who have occasion to mention them,' and they have proliferated in recent decades, many reverting to what are claimed to be earlier place-names.

The author and publisher apologise for any omissions when requesting permission to use or quote from what may be copyright material, and would be grateful to be notified of any corrections that should be incorporated in a future edition

Among those to whom the author must record his thanks for information, advice, or assistance, let alone moral support, are Michael Ayrton, Thomas Bean, Sue Bradbury, George Caldwell, Robert Cooper, Michael Crumplin, Gareth Glover, Arthur Harman, Martin Howard, Rory Muir, and Jamie Wilson; while among those who have been forthcoming about their recent investigations, even if in some cases they have been too late to have been incorporated into this study, are Andrew Bamford, Huw Davies, Guy Dempsey, Bryan McMillan, and Zeta Moore: see the Bibliography, particularly the addendum.

I am also under an obligation to a number of military book publishers,[9] notably Richard Brown (Ken Trotman Ltd)[10] Charles Hewitt (Pen & Sword Books Ltd)[11] Lionel and Michael Leventhal (Greenhill Books Ltd),[12] the Naval and Military Press, John Lewis (Leonaur Ltd),[13] Eileen Hathaway (Shinglepicker Publications),[14] Mark S. Thompson (MST Publishing), Jamie Wilson (Spellmount Ltd),[15] and Buglehorn Publications, for commissioning new books on the Peninsular War, and/or for reissuing many reprints of rare or long unavailable narratives and diaries of the period, many of which, but by no means all, are listed in the Bibliography. Among other publishers are: Army Records Society and Sutton Publishing,[16] Heinemann,[17] Michael Joseph,[18] Longmans,[19] Oxford University Press,[20] and Michael Russell.[21]

Jon Parker (info@cortijo-andalucia.com) has supplied cartographical base material, which has allowed us to give a better conception of peninsular terrain, while I am much obliged to Tom Chidlaw for his perseverance in providing the effective finished product.

While maps issued by Michelin are reliable for most practical purposes, readers requiring more detail will find them reproduced in maps published by the National Geographical Institutes of Spain, Portugal, and France, although they should not expect that every place mentioned in this volume will be found, for many villages and hamlets may not have survived the passing of time. The construction of dams will have caused changes in the channel, rapidity, and height of rivers, and it is virtually impossible to trace with precision many of the tracks traversed by troops two centuries ago, which do not necessarily follow the same paths as those of the slender web of earlier highways, the surface of which might be compared with some primitive main roads of the Peninsula traversed by the author in the late 1950s.

1 The future Duke of Wellington was known as Sir Arthur Wellesley until after the battle of Talavera, when he was elevated to the Peerage as Viscount Wellington. Earl from 18 February 1812, and Marquess six months later, but was usually styled 'the Peer' or just Lord Wellington until created Duke on 3 May 1814.

2 Notable are those on Bussaco by both Chambers, and Horwood; and Muir's *Salamanca*.

3 Greenhill Books, 2004.

4 This is contrary to the notion of some British historians, who have implied that the terminal campaign was more part of the invasion of France that forced Napoleon to abdicate than a natural extension of the contest in the Peninsula. One has even described Wellesley's withdrawal to the Portuguese frontier after the carnage of Talavera as abandoning his faithful allies to their own devices, a speciously dismissive appraisal of relentlessly sustained British intervention on their behalf.

5 With hindsight, he had left himself open to criticism for not insisting at a much earlier period that the authorities supplied him with a proper siege train and a full complement of sappers and miners, or with a higher proportion of cavalry. He made occasional miscalculations, among them in underestimating his opponent's capacity to rally and return to the fray so rapidly, both at the confrontation at Fuentes de Oñoro after their ruinous retreat from the Lines, or in the wake of such signal defeats as Vitoria.

6 One may aptly repeat here what Wellington told his friend Samuel Rogers: that when one visitor to Headquarters asked to see the Army, directions were given that 'he should be conducted through ours. When he returned, he said, "I have seen nothing – nothing but here and there little clusters of men in confusion; some cooking, some washing, and some sleeping." "Then you have seen our Army," I said.'

7 See Oman's *Wellington's Army*, pp. 19-21, and 31-32; and *Inside Wellington's Peninsular Army*, pp.275-303.

8 Notable among recent titles are *Inside Wellington's Peninsular Army*, by Rory Muir, Robert Burnham, Howie Muir, and Ron McGuigan; and Guy Dempsey's *Albuera 1811: the Bloodiest Battle of the Peninsular War* (both from Pen & Sword); Michael Crumplin's *Men of Steel: Surgery in the Napoleonic Wars* (Quiller Press); and the two volumes by the late Clive Lloyd: *A History of Napoleonic and American Prisoners of*

War, 1756–1816: Hulk, Depot and Parole, although not a formal history of the subject, and the complementary volume, *The Arts and Crafts of Napoleonic and American Prisoners of War* (published by the Antique Collectors' Club)

[9] For the titles concerned, see the Bibliography under the following authors:

[10] Glover (Bridgeman, Carter, Kinloch, and Pierrepoint)

[11] Douglas, Glover (Bingham), Hunt, Mollo

[12] Glover (Griffith & Philips), Schaumann,

[13] Nicol, Blakeney, Leach, Surtees, Tomkinson

[14] Cooke, Costello, Harris, Lawrence

[15] Cocks, Fletcher (Keep, Mills), Howard, Lawrence

[16] Browne, Gordon

[17] Hennel

[18] Aitchison, Wheeler

[19] Wheatley

[20] Bragge, Ward

[21] Colville

Chronology

The main Allied actions or movements are printed in bold. Some months are deliberately left vacant to emphasise the spread of time when no important fighting was taking place.

1807

July 31–30 Sept.	The Copenhagen expedition
Oct. 18	French troops invade Spain
Nov. 30	The French vanguard, commanded by Junot, enter Lisbon
Dec.	

1808

Jan. 8	Another French army crosses into Spain and start to occupy several towns in Biscay and Navarre
Feb. 10	French troops enter Catalonia; Barcelona occupied on 29th
Mar. 23	Madrid occupied by the French under Murat
Apr.	
May 2	(El Dos de Mayo): Insurrection in Madrid, followed by uprisings throughout Spain
June 15–13 Aug.	First French siege of Zaragoza
July 12	Wellesley in temporary command of an expeditionary force to the Peninsula
14	Spanish defeated at Medina de Rioseco (north-east of Valladolid)
19	Dupont, discomforted at Bailén, surrenders to the Spanish under Castaños on the 22nd
24–16 Aug.	Second French siege of Gerona

Aug. 1	**Landing starts of the British expeditionary force at the mouth of the Mondego**
17	Combat of **Roliça** (south of Obidos)
21	Junot defeated at **Vimeiro** (north-west of Torres Vedras)
30	The Convention of Cintra signed, by which French forces in Portugal are to be repatriated
Sept. 20	Wellesley, recalled, sails for England
Oct. 6	Sir John Moore in command at Lisbon
26	Moore's troops start their advance towards the Spanish frontier
29	Spanish under Blake dispersed at Zornosa (a hamlet between Durango and Bilbao)
Nov. 6	Napoleon in person reaches Vitoria on his march towards Madrid
10 –11	Blake defeated at Espinosa de los Monteros (north of Medina de Pomar).
13	Moore's vanguard enters Salamanca
22	Baird's units reach Astorga
23	Moore concentrated at Salamanca
23	Spanish defeated at Tudela (north-west of Zaragoza)
Dec. 3	Hope's units join up with Moore's
4	Napoleon occupies Madrid
20–20 Feb.	Second French siege of Zaragoza
21	British cavalry combat at Sahagún (south-east of León)
22	Napoleon leads troops across the Guadarrama range north-west of Madrid in an attempt to encircle Moore.
24	Moore commences his retreat into Galicia
27	Minor cavalry actions near Mayorga (north-east of Benavente)
29	Delaying action near Benavente (north of Zamora)

1809

Jan. 1	Soult is left in pursuit of Moore, while Napoleon returns to France
11	Moore's vanguard reaches Corunna
13	Spanish defeated at Uclés (south-east of Tarancón)

16	Moore is mortally wounded at **Corunna**; British army evacuated
Feb. 20	Zaragoza capitulates to the French
Mar. 29	Spanish defeated at Medellín (east of Mérida)
29	Soult occupies Oporto
Apr. 23	Wellesley again commanding in Portugal
May 11	Action at Grijó, on approaching Oporto
12	**Passage of the Douro**. Wellington wrests Oporto from Soult, who retreats north-east in confusion
21–3	Battle of Aspern–Essling, forcing Napoleon to withdraw from Vienna
24–11 Dec.	Third, and main, siege of Gerona
June 10	Bridge at Alcantara broken. Victor retired up Tagus valley
15	Spanish, under Blake, beaten at Maria, and Belchite (18th)
July 3	Wellesley enters Spain west of Plasencia
5–6	Napoleon defeats the Austrians at Wagram
27/8	Pyrrhic victory at **Talavera**, after which the British are forced to retire towards Portugal. Shortly after, Wellesley is created Viscount Wellington
28–9 Dec.	The Walcheren Expedition, at the mouth of the Scheldt
Aug. 11	Spanish defeated at Almonacid (south-east of Toledo)
Sept.	
Oct.	Commencement of the building of defensive works north of Lisbon, later known as 'The Lines of Torres Vedras'
18	French discomforted by the Spanish at Tamames (east of Ciudad Rodrigo)
Nov. 19	Spanish defeated at Ocaña (south-east of Aranjuez)
28	Spanish defeated at Alba de Tormes (south-east of Salamanca)
Dec.	

1810

Jan.	
Feb. 1	Seville occupied by the French.
5	Cadiz invested by the French
Mar 19	Action at Barba del Puerco (east of Almeida)

21	French invest Astorga
Apr. 22	Astorga surrenders
May 28	Masséna reaches Salamanca
June	Ciudad Rodrigo invested
July 10	Masséna takes Ciudad Rodrigo, and later advances on Portugal
24	Combats on the Côa (west of Ciudad Rodrigo)
28	Almeida falls to the French
Aug.	
Sept. 27	Masséna defeated at **Busaco**
Oct. 10	Masséna reaches and is frustrated by The Lines of Torres Vedras
Nov.17	Masséna withdraws to Santarém and its vicinity
Dec.	

1811

Jan. 11–23	Soult besieges and takes Olivenza, then invests Badajoz
Feb. 19	Spanish defeated at the Gebora (just north of Badajoz)
Mar. 3	Masséna's army starts their retreat from Santarém
5	Graham defeats Victor at **Barrosa**, near Chiclana (south-east of Cadiz)
10	Soult captures Badajoz
15	Action at Foz de Arouce (south-east of Coimbra)
25	Cavalry affair at Campo Mayor (north-west of Badajoz)
Apr. 3	Combat at **Sabugal** (south-east of Guarda)
22–3	Wellington reconnoitres Badajoz, and orders Beresford to prepare to besiege the fortress
May 3–5	Masséna defeated at **Fuentes de Oñoro** (west of Ciudad Rodrigo)
6–12	Badajoz invested, but siege raised
10	Escape of the French garrison from Almeida
11	Affair at Barba del Puerco
16	Beresford defeats Soult at **La Albuera** (south-east of Badajoz)
25	Cavalry affair at Usagre (north-west of Llerena)
27	Badajoz re-invested and besieged
June 10	Failure of assault determined Wellington to turn siege into blockade

13	Wellington offers battle on the Caia (east of Elvas)
July	
Aug.	
Sept. 25	Action at **El Bodón** (south of Ciudad Rodrigo)
28	Wellington offers battle on the upper Côa
Oct. 25	Spanish defeated at Sagunto (north of Valencia)
28	French surprised and scattered by Hill at **Arroyomolinos de Montánchez** (north-east of Merida)
Nov.	
Dec. 21–4 Jan.	French besiege Tarifa
26	Spanish defeated at Valencia; Blake surrenders to Suchet on 8 Jan.

1812

Jan. 8–19 Jan.	Wellington invests and recaptures **Ciudad Rodrigo**
Feb.	
Mar. 16	Wellington again besieges **Badajoz**, stormed on 6 April
Apr. 11	Cavalry affair at Villagarcía (north-west of Llerena)
May 19	Hill's action at **Almaraz** (north-east of Trujillo)
June 1	Spanish defeated at Bornos (north-east of Arcos de la Frontera)
11	Cavalry affair at Maguilla (north-west of Llerena)
14	Napoleon invades Russia
17	America declares war on Britain
July 17–18	Combat on the Guarena: Castrejon and Castrillo (some distance north-east of Salamanca)
22	Marmont defeated at **Salamanca**
23	Cavalry affair at Garcia Hernández (north-east of Alba de Tormes)
Aug. 11	Combat at Majadahonda (west of Madrid) during the advance on Madrid
12	The Allies enter Madrid; Wellington declared Marquess on 18th
27	Soult evacuates Seville, which is occupied by Skerrett
31	Leaving Madrid, Wellington advances on Burgos
Sept. 19	**Burgos besieged**

Oct. 4	Soult and King Joseph converge west of Hellín (south of Albacete)
12	Napoleon retreats from Moscow
22	Raising the siege of Burgos, Wellington retires south-west to the Portuguese frontier
23	Cavalry affair at Venta del Pozo (south-west of Burgos)
Nov. 2	The French re-occupy Madrid after it is evacuated by Hill's rearguard
Dec.	

1813

Jan.	
Feb. 14	Joseph first hears of the debâcle in Russia
Mar. 23	Joseph based in Valladolid, having evacuated Madrid
Apr. 13	The French dispersed by Murray at Castalla
May 22	Wellington commences offensive operations
30	**Passage of the Esla** west of Zamora
June 2	Cavalry affair at Morales (east of Toro)
3–12	Sir John Murray's abortive siege of Tarragona
4	*Armistice of Pleiswitz* signed between the Northern Allies and Napoleon, extending truce until 20 July
21	Joseph and Jourdan defeated at **Vitoria**
25	Pamplona blockaded, surrendering on 31 Oct.
26	The action at Tolosa (south of San Sebastian)
28	San Sebastian invested
29	*The Treaty of Reichenbach*: Austria agrees to re-enter the war if Napoleon does not agree to peace terms
July 1	Napoleon, at Dresden, learns of the defeat at Vitoria
11	Soult returns to command French facing Wellington
22	Soult starts counter-offensive in the Pyrenees
25	First assault on San Sebastian fails: simultaneous actions at **Maya**, and **Roncesvalles**
28–30	Soult defeated at **Sorauren** (north of Pamplona) and near Lizaso (further north-west)
Aug. 1–2	Soult retreats down the Bidasoa valley: actions at Sumbilla, the bridge of Yanci, and Echalar

12	Austria declares war on France, news of which reaches Wellington on 3 Sept.
26–27	Napoleon defeats the Allies at Dresden
30	French under Vandamme defeated at Kulm, report of which reached Wellington on 15 Sept.
31	Spanish troops repulse Soult at San Marcial. **San Sebastián** stormed, the citadel surrendering on 8 Sept.
Sept. 3	Wellington hears of the rupture of the Armistace of Pleiswitz
Oct. 7	**Passage of the Bidasoa**: Wellington sets foot in France
16–19	Napoleon defeated at Leipzig
Nov.10	General advance into France at the battle of the **Nivelle**
Dec. 8	Wellington receives confirmation of French defeat at Leipzig
9–10	Soult's counter-offensive thwarted at the battle of the **Nive**
11	Fernando VII signs the Treaty of Valençay, and re-enters Spain on 24 March
13	Hill defeats Soult at **St Pierre**; Bayonne invested
17	Graham's expeditionary force lands in Holland

1814

Jan.	
Feb. 15	Combat at Garris (north-west of St Palais)
26	Hope crosses the bridge of boats west of Bayonne, now surrounded
27	Soult defeated at **Orthez**
Mar. 2	Combat at Aire
8	Beresford detached towards Bordeaux, occupied on the 12th
8–9	British failure at Bergen-op-Zoom
20	Combat near Tarbes
24	Soult's troops enter Toulouse
25	Marmont and Mortier defeated at Fère-Champenoise (east of Sézanne)
31	Marmont signs *Capitulation of Paris* and Allied troops enter Paris

Apr. 10	Battle of **Toulouse**, Soult retreating east during the ensuing night
12	Wellington receives news of Napoleon's abdication (on the 6th)
14	**The sortie from Bayonne**
15	*Treaty of Fontainebleau* signed. Napoleon leaves for Elba on the 28th
27	Bayonne formally surrenders
30	Wellington leaves Toulouse for Paris
May 3	Wellington created Duke
14	Wellington returns to Toulouse
17	Wellington leaves Toulouse for Madrid, remaining there from the 24th until 8 June
30	*The Treaty of Paris* signed
June	Start of the dispersal of Allied troops near Bayonne
13	Wellington resigns command of Spanish forces
14	Wellington's Farewell to his troops near Bordeaux
23	Wellington reaches Dover after five years and two months absence from Britain
July	
Aug. 8	Wellington leaves for Paris as Ambassador
Sept	Last British troops sail for England
Oct.	
Nov.	
Dec. 24	End of the American War

1815

Jan. 24	Wellington leaves Paris to attend the 'Congress of Vienna'
Feb. 26	Napoleon escapes from Elba
Mar. 7	News of the escape reaches Vienna
20	Napoleon enters Paris
29	Wellington leaves Vienna
Apr. 5	Wellington reaches Brussels
May	
June 16	Battles of **Quatre Bras** and **Ligny**
18	Napoleon defeated at **Waterloo**

Glossary and Abbreviations

abatis or **abattis**, a defensive work formed of felled trees with their branches facing outwards, usually placed a short distance in front of field-works.
Adjutant-General or **A.G.**, senior officer responsible for administration, communicating orders, providing returns and states, etc., with his Deputy (D.A.G.), Assistants (A.A.G.), and Deputy-Assistants (D.A.A.G.).
afrancesados (lit. frenchified), either Spaniards sympathizing with the French and their Revolutionary tenets (among the more prominent of whom were many cultured and liberal-minded persons, anticipating the end of the malign influence of the Roman Catholic Church and the parasitic nobility), or merely collaborators.
alcalde, mayor or local magistrate in Spain.
Artillery, Royal (R.A.), of which the Officer Commanding, representing the Ordance Department, was responsible for providing all arms and ammunition, and acted as artillery advisor to the C-in-C. A civilian subordinate acted as Inspector of the Field Train Department. A British field or horse artillery battery or 'brigade' usually consisted of five 6-pounders and one 5.5-inch howitzer, although both 3-pounders and 9-pounders were used also. The 6-pounders were an efficient and easily-handled arm, weighing almost 1,650 lbs including the carriage, while the 9-pounder weighed 1,760 lbs, and the howitzer 1,125 lbs. The latter were particularly effective at close range, projecting as much canister as a double-charged gun. The common shot was a solid round iron ball. Canister consister of a number of smaller cast-iron balls within a sheet metal can, which disintegrated on discharge and spread the shot evenly over a large area. In addition was the **shrapnel** shell (named after its inventor, Henry Shrapnell, R.A., 1761–1842), otherwise known as 'spherical case shot', adopted by the army c.1804, which was a projectile consisting of a spherical case filled with carbine balls, and later by musket-balls mixed with gunpowder fused to explode approximately 50 yards above and 100 yards in front of a target, over which the shot would shower. It was effective up to a range

of 1,000 yards. The French had no equivalent to it. *See also* under Congreve rocket. It was not until 1811 that Colonel Alexander Dickson, in charge of Wellington's artillery, was able to command an adequate battering-train of modern iron guns, shipped out from England, with which to replace the obsolete Portuguese brass 24-pounders, no two of which had the same bore. At Ciudad Rodrigo, 2,754 rounds of 24-pound shot were fired in 2 days, which as a mule could only carry eight rounds, was – according to Dickson – almost 360 mule loads. At Badajoz, 2,523 barrels of powder weighing 90 pounds each (requiring about 1,200 mules), 18,832 rounds of solid shot for 24-pounders and 13,029 rounds for the 18-pounders (some 3,590 mule loads) – not taking into account grape and case shot or howitzer shells – were expended. Additional transport was required also to supply huge amounts of fodder daily in order to keep these working mules on their feet.

banquette, an earthen platform, raised behind a parapet, from which men could stand and fire.

bastion, a section of fortifications formed at the angle of two walls, and extending beyond the main defences.

battering train, the guns, ammunition and equipment required to besiege a place.

bivouac, a temporary improvised shelter against the elements, or camping in the open, without tents, also referred to as hutting; see cantonments.

breach, a gap made in a rampart or wall by gunfire or an exploded mine, to allow troops to break in: 'practicable' meaning that it was by then in a state to be entered without an undue amount of climbing.

breastwork, a 4-5 foot high protective wall.

bridgehead or ***tête de pont***, fortifications designed to defend the far end of a bridge or pontoon; sometimes on both banks.

bridges, of which there were a variety, among them floating, flying, and pontoon, or 'of boats'. The former might be formed by a pontoon, barge, or raft or two moored to both banks by cables, and which would be hauled across, or with a strong current and properly steered, would be swept to either side of the river. At the 'bridge' of Vila Velha, a vital crossing-point of the Tagus, only a company or two, or up to twenty horses, could be ferried over at a time, according to Leach. See Pontoons.

caçadores (hunters), Portuguese light infantrymen, armed with rifles.

caisson, a chest containing explosives or, more usually, a wagon conveying ammunition.

canister or **case shot**, a projectile formed by a thin metal tube filled with lead musket balls, fired from guns at short range and at a low trajectory over attacking troops, scattering over a wide area and often causing widespread casualties. It is frequently confused with grapeshot; *see* below.

cantonments, lodgings or quarters assigned to troops, or in which they were billeted; more permanent than a bivouac.
capataz, head driver of a mule train.
casemate, a bomb-proof vault built below a rampart to protect men and ammunition. It was sometomes loopholed.
casualties. An indiscriminate reckoning of the total number of dead, wounded, and missing in an action, and frequently misleading. Many wounded later died, while many referred to in returns as 'missing' might either be dead but not found, or men straying from the scene of action who may have later reported for duty, while a proportion of the wounded might be either malingerers or slightly wounded and soon back among the effectives. Most returns listed officers and rank and file separately.
chasseurs, French light infantry, or ***à cheval***, cavalry.
chaussée, a paved highway or trunk-road, of which at this period there were few and far between; almost all others were furrowed, knee-deep in mud, and well-nigh impassable during wet weather and throughout the winter.
chevaux-de-frise, literally 'horses of Friesland', because this form of barrier was invented by the Frisans, who had no cavalry. These were usually constructed by setting large nails, swords, bayonettes, and other sharp objects into heavy beams, placed within a breach, and providing an additional hazard to assaulting troops.
Commissariat, a civilian department responsible to the Treasury, and headed by a Commissary-General in the Peninsula. (Senior officers were not included in the Army List until 1812.) The Store Department was responsible for depots, and provisioning the Army: the regular supply of food and liquor to troops, and of forage to the cavalry, the transport and issue or distribution of which (together with clothing and necessaries), was regulated by Commissaries (later under the titles: Deputies, Assistants, Deputy-assistants, and Commissary Clerks). There was a separate Accounts Department. Each infantry brigade and cavalry regiment had their own commissariat officers. See also S. G. P. Ward's *Wellington's Headquarters*.
Congreve Rocket, an inaccurate projectile, invented in 1805 by Colonel Sir William Congreve (1772–1828), in which Wellington had little confidence, for its trajectory was unpredictable, although the loud hiss effectively frightened troops encountering them for the first time, notably at the crossing of the Adour late in 1813. The 32-pounders had a range of 3,000 yards, while the more portable 12-pounders out-ranged field artillery.
Cortes, the Spanish Parliament.
counterscarp, the abrupt nearer side to the glacis of an excavated ditch, often of brick or stone construction, to make its descent more difficult.
covertway, an area between the glacis and ditch surrounding fortifications,

along which troops could pass from one position to another while being protected by a palisade, not actually 'covered'.

cuirassiers, French heavy cavalrymen protected by metal breast- and back-plates.

curtain wall, a wall joining two projecting bastions.

demilune; *see* ravelin.

depots. In the Peninsula, there were base and forward depots, established by the Commissariat, where provisions, clothing, candles, and a variety of other stores were assembled prior to onward transmission to military units.

diseases, etc. Among those prevalent in the Peninsula were *typhoid* (bacterial infection causing fever), *typhus* (spread by body louse), *dysentery* (bacterial infection affecting bowels), and *malaria* (fever caused by mosquito bite); 'Walcheren fever', from which many men who had taken part on the expedition to the Dutch coast in 1809 suffered, was a relapsing fever, probably caused by a combination of the above. 'Hospital gangrene' was another virulent epidemic: for all these, *see* Howard, *Wellington's Doctors.*

ditch, a deep trench (about 16 feet), usually at least five times as wide, encircling defensive works, its outer supporting wall being designated a counterscarp. The excavated earth could be used to make a parapet. If filled with water, the ditch formed a moat.

dragoons, medium-weight cavalrymen.

earthworks or **fieldworks**, any form of temporary fortifications (or a trench) providing shelter from enemy fire, direct or enfilading.

effectives, the total number of men available at any one time and place in a fit state to engage the enemy, after having deducted the sick and wounded.

embrasures, openings in the flank of fortifications, through which guns might fire and enfilade.

enfilade, gunfire from a position directed against the flank of approaching troops or their earthworks.

Engineers, Royal (R.E.), of which the Officer Commanding, who acted as consultant over matters of siegecraft and defence, was the storekeeper of engineering equipment for bridge-building and construction of pontoons, etc. See also Royal Staff Corps. In his *Narrative*, Londonderry remarked: 'Ours was, perhaps, the only army in Europe which possessed no corps of sappers or miners, nor any body of men peculiarly trained to carry on the more intricate details of a siege. We had, it is true, what was termed the regiment of the royal military artificers; that is to say, a battalion of carpenters, blacksmiths, stonemasons, and other handicraftsmen; but not one of these had ever seen a mine; and as to a sap, they were probably incapable of understanding the very meaning of the word ... We had no pontoons or pontooners ... and our intrenching tools consisted simply of the most common description of spades, bill-hooks, and pick-axes.' At Badajoz, however competent Colonel Richard Fletcher, the chief engineer, and his officers, may have been, there were still only 169 men of the line attached to the department to act as overseers, 48 carpenters, 48 miners, and 25 rank and file of the corps of artificers.

escalade, to assault fortifications by means of ladders rather than by making a breach in the walls.

fascines, bundles of brushwood or small branches, roped together, to revet and support the earthen walls of trenches, or when constructing a battery.

'Forlorn Hope', a group of volunteers formed to assault a breach, which would advance ahead of the main body of troops.

frise, a line of sharpened stakes set into the lower slope of a rampart, partly to ensure that the outworks are not taken by surprise.

gabions, cylindrical, open-ended, wickerwork baskets, about three feet high, filled with earth, placed above ground to provide cover for men approaching siege-works.

garrochista, cattle-herder, armed with a lance.

gendarmes, in this context, military police.

glacis, the gentle exterior slope of defensive works, extending beyond a parapet and/or ditch, constructed to ensure an uncluttered target area over which approaching troops had to cross.

grapeshot, often confused with that of canister, is a heavier shot (usually nine golf-ball-sized projectiles) tightly encased in a canvas cylinder and fired from cannon, designed to break spars and foul rigging in naval engagements, and comparatively infrequently used on land.

grenade, a 2½ inch hollow iron ball charged with powder with a short fuse, lit and thrown to explode near an enemy.

grenadiers, historically, men throwing grenades; usually the heavier-weight company in a battalion, often forming assault troops.

guerrilla (lit. 'little war'), a partisan, or member of a band of irregular troops (a *partida*) acting independently of formal armies.

horn-work, an outwork of two demi-bastions connected to the main work by parallel wings.

Horse Guards, the building in Whitehall, London, then containing the offices of the Commander-in-Chief and his staff, the Military Secretary throughout much of the Peninsular War period being Colonel Henry Torrens. For the ramifications of this administrative body, *see* S.G.P. Ward's *Wellington's Headquarters*.

Hospitals. The Inspector-General of Hospitals, as representing the Medical Board, the Purveyor's Department, and the Apothecary-General, was responsible for all medical matters and arrangements.

howitzer, a short-barrelled mobile gun projecting a common shell at low velocity but at a high angle; unlike a mortar, it was supported by trunnions and pivoted from the middle of its barrel.

hussar, a light cavalryman, originally referring to those of Hungarians.

invest, to; a preliminary action to isolate a town to be besieged from receiving any reinforcements or supplies.

jäger, a 'Hunter'; the German equivalent of a skirmisher.

Judge-Advocate-General, lawyer responsible for the legal control of courts martial, of whom there was only his deputy present in the Peninsula, D.J.A.G. Francis Larpent.

juiz de fora, local civilian magistrate in Portugal.

junta, an administrative committee set up in emergencies on a municipal, provincial or national level.

K.G.L., the King's German Legion, a formation of largely Hanoverian-officered troops serving with the British army after Napoleon's invasion of Hanover in 1803.

league, an imprecise measure of distance, varying in different countries; in Spain, roughly 4 miles.

Légère or *ligne*, French terms for light infantry.

lunette, works on either side of a ravelin, larger than a redan, and with two faces and two flanks.

magazine, a bomb-proof arsenal storing arms, powder and ammunition; also a store for provisions.

meseta, the high-lying central plateau of the Iberian peninsula.

Military Secretary (in the Peninsula), the confidential assistant to the C-in-C, partly over financial business and officers' appointments.

miqueletes, Spanish (or rather Catalan) term for their irregular 'home guard', sometimes spelt *migueletes*; also known as ***somaténes***.

mine, an aperture or tunnel excavated below fortifications, in which gunpowder was placed to explode, weakening or destroying the walls.

mortar, a large-bore cannon mounted to fire combustible material at a high elevation.

musket. The great majority of the British infantry were armed with the Tower or Brown Bess flint-lock musket, ranging from 9lb 11oz to 10lb 8oz in weight and with a 39 or 42-inch smooth-bore barrel, on the muzzle of which a bayonet might be mounted. The ammunition for one shot – a round leaden bullet – was contained in a paper cartridge (60 of which, in a waterproof pouch, were normally carried per man, plus another 60 in his knapsack), and it highest practical rate of fire was three times in a minute (if already loaded). 200 yards was about the limit at which it could kill or seriously wound, but it was most effective when at a range of less than 160 yards, or in volleys at massed troops at 100 yards, but its accuracy when aimed at a single target was limited to 75

yards. Much of its effect depended on the care and correctness with which it was loaded, but it could not be relied on to fire in damp or wet weather.
ordnance, piece of; any gun, mortar or howitzer. They were classified by the weight of the solid shot they fired: i.e. a 24-pounder howitzer threw a shot weighing 24 lbs.
Ordnance Department, responsible for the storage and distribution of all forms of arms, ammunition, gunpowder, etc.; regrettably, their close-fisted Storekeepers in the Peninsula were often reluctant to supply any material unless the requisite order was made by the appropriate officer; *see* S.G.P. Ward's *Wellington's Headquarters*.
ordenança, irregular forces called out to supplement the uniformed militia in the defence of Portugal.
palisade, a fence of stakes, about 9 feet long, set into the ground, often close to the crest of a glacis, and protecting the covered way between that point of the counterscarp of a defensive ditch.
parallel/s, a deep and wide trench or trenches dug at the approaches to a besieged place, from which troops excavating a sap could be supported. They were usually zig-zag in plan, partly to evade enfilading fire, and two or three (or more) in number.
parapet, a thick protective wall of earth raised above the crest of a rampart, usually with a ledge behind it to prevent the earth – if hit by enemy fire – from falling into and filling the adjacent ditch.
partida, a Spanish term for a guerrilla band.
Paymaster-general, or rather his Deputy, acted as the Army's banker and was ostensibly responsible for the Military Chest.
picquets, piquets, or pickets, a small outposts of troops – infantry or cavalry – placed to guard against surprise attack, by day or night, from which a vedette might be advanced.
pontoons were, ideally, 21 feet in length, 3 feet 11 inches wide, and 2 feet 1 inch thick, and were usually carried on a two-wheeled carriage, and with its equipment weighted approximately 1,200 pounds. A serious flaw in their construction was that their top was open, nor enclosed, allowing them occasionally to fill with water and sink. For details, see pp. 262-70 in Robert Burnham's chapter on Bridge Building in *Inside Wellington's Peninsular Army*. Occasionally, empty wine-casks served the purpose when there were no other material at hand with which a bridge might be constructed.
Provost marshal, head of military police, assisted by his provost guard.
puerto, a door or a mountain pass.
Quartermaster-General (Q.M.G.), senior officer responsible for overseeing the movement, quartering, equipping, and supplying of troops, with his Deputy (D.Q.M.G.), Assistants (A.Q.M.G.), and Deputy-assistants (D.A.Q.M.G.).

Headquarters usually had their separate quartermaster.
ravelin; also demi-lune, a work beyond a curtain wall, usually of two walls set at an angle, or triangular in construction, providing a position from which the approaching enemy would receive flanking fire.
redan, a simple form of field-work of two faces forming a salient angle.
redoubt, a defensive work detached from the main fortifications of a town.
revetment, a wall of brick or stone supporting the side of a rampart or ditch.
ricochet fire, round shot fired at a low angle, the bounding trajectory of which on hard ground, or off a hard surface, would cause great havoc among massed troops.
rifle. At 9½lbs, it was slightly lighter in weight than a musket, and designed by the London gunsmith Ezekiel Baker, it was extremely accurate up to 150 yards, still dangerous between 200 and 300 yards, and could hit a massed target such as a square of infantry or cause casualties among troops on the march at a range of 500 yards. However, the grooving in the 30-inch barrel made the ramming down of the bullet a stiffer operation and thus it took longer to load and fire: approximately one minute. It could fire a 'carbine' size cartridge also, and at a faster rate. The Baker rifle was first issued with a triangular bayonet 18 inches in length, later replaced by a 24 inch long, flat, single-edged, sword bayonet. According to Baron Marbot, the British infantryman were the only troops which regularly practised firing at targets using live ammunition, and thus were far more accurate than the French; nor did the French *tirailleurs* have rifles, merely smooth bore weapons, as Napoleon had withdrawn rifles from the Republican army, and they were thus at a distinct disadvantage when it came to making an accurate shot at longer range. The three Light Infantry regiments trained in the use of the rifle by Moore at Shorncliffe in 1803–4 were the 43rd, 52nd, and 95th. It was not until February 1816 that three three battalions of the latter regiment were formally styled The Rifle Brigade.
rockets; *see* Congreve.
round-shot, a solid metal ball between 3 and 4.25 inches in diameter. Cannon were categorized by the weight of shot they fired, which in the Napoleonic period ranged from 6-, 8- or 9-pounders to the 12-pounders, the heaviest used in the field.
Royal Engineers; see Engineers.
Royal Staff Corps (R.S.C.), a separate organisation to the Royal Engineers, and controlled by the Q.M.G., it was largely responsible for the construction and repair of temporary bridges, but its officers also surveyed extensive areas and provided maps, while they were frequently landed with a variety of other tasks not undertaken by the Engineers. There was a certain amount of rivalry between the two bodies.
Royal Wagon Train, or Field Train; *see* wagons.

sap, a trench, approached by parallels, and usually covered to protect the sappers from the garrison's fire, excavated close to defensive walls, from which they could be undermined or mined. The insidious burrowing operations of sappers were usually directed by an engineer.
saucisson, a long sausage-like waterproof canvas tube, packed with powder, used for firing a mine.
semaphore; *see* telegraph.
shrapnel, a projectile composed of 1-ounce lead carbine balls and later by musket-balls mixed with gunpowder, fired from cannon as well as from howitzers, with the length of fuse calculated to explode in mid air just short of a target, over which the shot would shower. This type of shell, invented by Henry Shrapnell (1761–1842) of the Royal Artillery, was improved and adopted by the army in about 1804.
sierra, mountain range, ***serra*** Portuguese; a ***serranía*** is a mountainous district.
spherical case shot; the official name for shrapnel.
squares, forming; a roughly square (or oblong) formation, having a frontage of approximately 100 feet, into which infantry would deploy for defence when in expectation of a cavalry charge. Each side might be anything from four to six ranks in depth, of which those on the outer would be kneeling, holding their muskets (butts on the ground) at an angle, making a bristling hedge of sharp bayonets, against which attacking cavalry would steer clear rather than collide, usually swerving round the sides of the square. In the hollow centre of the tightly-packed formation stood sergeants and officers, exhorting their men to hold their fire and keep steady. Well-disciplined troops – even those without experience of battle, as in the case of some Portuguese brigades at La Albuera – could thus remain holding the enemy at bay, their inner ranks keeping up regular fire, once the cavalry were within effective range. Although the sight of massed cavalry bearing down on a square was one that was likely to make the bravest man flinch, rarely did one break in the face of a charge, although if a horse was mortally wounded in its close proximity, there was the danger that it might collapse into its ranks – as happened to a French square at Garcia Hernández – and cause confusion, of which advantage could be taken. A square, or squares – in which case they formed at some distance from each other – was vulnerable to artillery, both from round-shot and more so from canister, being a dense target; and if remaining so formed, should a line of infantry be supporting the cavalry attack, only a comparatively small proportion of their muskets would be able to reply, but this dangerous situation was not one in which they found themselves very frequently.
telegraph, a system of visual communication from one area to another made by varying the position of flags or balls on the yard-arms of masts placed on conspicuous heights.

terreplein, a level emplacement for a battery of guns, behind a protective rampart.
tirailleurs; tiradores, the French and Spanish terms for infantry skirmishers or sharpshooters.
vales, a paper receipt or promise to pay for food, forage, or supplies, when cash was unavailable.
vedette, a mounted sentry usually placed on high ground beyond an outpost to observe and give notice of enemy movements; *see* picquet.
voltigeurs, French skirmishers, often of small stature, advancing with cavalry and able to leap behind a rider if necessary.
wagons. The Royal Wagon Train, formed in 1799, consisted largely of *spring wagons*, which being unsuitable for carrying heavy loads on the execrable roads of the Peninsula, became increasingly used for transporting the wounded. By 1810, only three each were attached to each regiment, which was ridiculously inadequate. Although their springs were strong, this caused them, in the words of George Simmons, to 'dance up and down in an awful manner,' and worse than the fitful movement of the bullock cars. The French ambulance system was far superior.

1

October 1807 to September 1808: From Junot's invasion to The Convention of Cintra: Roliça and Vimeiro

Revolutionary armies, commanded by Napoleon and his marshals, were still masters of extensive areas of mainland Europe during the first few years of the 19th century, although Nelson's victory at Trafalgar in October 1805 dashed French pretentions to controlling the sea. Entangled in Napoleon's web of alliances, Spain had already allied itself to France and in this battle her fleet was also largely destroyed.

In June 1807, after signing the peace treaty with Russia at Tilsit, Napoleon attempted to intimidate Portugal into severing her connection with Britain, for – apart from Sweden – she was its remaining continental ally, still a loophole in his devious design to bring recalcitrant Britain to heel. On 19 July, their minister in Paris was curtly informed that Portugal must close its ports to British shipping and seize all British goods in the country, otherwise they would risk Napoleon's ire, a threat followed up on 12 August by both French and Spanish ambassadors in Lisbon insisting that if she failed to submit to such demands and actively ally herself with France, this might well precipitate hostilities, although war was not declared specifically.

The country had been menaced with invasion much earlier, but as young Robert Southey had remarked with percipience when writing from the Portuguese capital in November 1800 to his friend William Taylor: 'Before a French army could reach Lisbon, the whole species would be embarked, and here the property is kept in chests ready at a moment's alarm. The multitude of ships always in the Tagus would take off the more valuable merchandize. Plunder therefore cannot allure the French here; the remaining bales of cotton would not pay their soldiers, nor the sugar-casks sweeten their lemonade. Besides, provisions are scarce both here and in Spain; a hostile army could not subsist six weeks. If, however, the French should choose to take possession of Lisbon in order to distress England, the blow would speedily recoil; a fleet would block the Tagus, and famine speedily drive them over the Pyrenees.'

By late August the British government learnt of Napoleon's threat, and immediately agreed to send military aid to her 'oldest ally' as soon as possible, although this would take time: indeed, eleven months passed before an expeditionary force disembarked in Portugal. There was a better chance here than anywhere else of establishing a firm foothold on mainland Europe, which it was hoped might revitalise militant opposition to Napoleonic aggression. To thwart any such intended landing, the French would have to invade Portugal and occupy Lisbon, an objective facilitated by the Spanish agreeing to allow some 25,000 troops to traverse the country. On 12 October 1807, Napoleon directed Clarke, his Minister of War, to dispatch a courier to Bayonne with orders to General Junot, commanding the Army of the Gironde assembling there since late July, to march into Spain within 24 hours of their receipt.

On the 18th, Junot's vanguard crossed the frontier, commenced the laborious ascent through the western foothills of the Pyrenees, and advanced south-west across the high-lying Castilian *meseta* on the first stage of their gratuitous invasion. Their march was fairly leisurely, for it was not until 12 November that they reached Salamanca, having noted and sketched discreetly all fortified places and defensible positions they passed. Orders were then received to push ahead rapidly by a more direct route than that down the Mondego valley, for should there be any resistance, this was likely to be at the Portuguese frontier fortress of Almeida. This other road climbed south from Ciudad Rodrigo over the Puerto de Perales to Alcántara; from there they could march down the Tagus valley via Abrantes to Lisbon. But what looked straight-forward enough on a map, was in fact a rough track traversing a granitic wilderness without resources, on which, being impassable to wheeled vehicles, all their guns except six had to be abandoned. Under torrential rain, thousands of the infantry scattered in the search for sustenance in what was virtually a desert, suffering dreadful privations and then 'went missing'; the cavalry was practically dismounted, over half the horses perishing in the cold. It was not until 30 November that the vanguard, dwindled to a mere 1,500 famished men, in tatters, limped into and seized Lisbon, being virtually unopposed.[1]

It was several months before Junot had built up a creditable force, mustering 15,000 men, by which time opposition was growing, notable in Oporto, where a provisional *junta* had been established under its patriotic bishop. Before long, 5,000 well-equipped troops had been assembled to combat the invader, and envoys had been sent to London to enlist support. By mid June 1808, the capital was in ferment, making Junot's position increasingly uncomfortable. Leaving small garrisons in the fortresses of Almeida and Elvas, he withdrew most other detached corps towards the capital, which allowed the proliferation of insurrectionary *juntas* elsewhere. By mid July there were some 24,000 troops under Junot's command concentrated west of the lower reaches of the Tagus and in the vicinity of Lisbon. Active attempts were made, notably by General Loison, to subdue other areas, but his unwarranted brutality – notably in quelling a revolt at Evora led by General Leite in late July – had merely galvanized resistance. Rather than have his more isolated units picked off relentlessly by bands of armed peasants, Loison choose to remain within easy reach of the main French concentration.

Naïvely, Spain, when allowing his troops to traverse the highway to Portugal, never suspected that Napoleon had designs on itself; but with the door to the Peninsula open, French units had been infiltrating constantly, those commanded by Marshal Murat, Napoleon's brother-in-law, occupying Madrid on 23 March, 1808. The Royal family – weak-willed Carlos IV, his domineering wife, Maria Luisa, and Manuel Godoy, her lover – was decoyed to Bayonne and taken prisoner. The king was then forced to abdicate in favour of his son, Fernando (who remained in captivity in France for the duration of the war, then imminent), and Joseph Bonaparte, Napoleon's elder brother, was proclaimed king in his stead. But on 2 May (*el Dos de Mayo*), once realising that they had been tricked, the population of Madrid rose up in almost unanimous – and briefly, energetic – revolt, as dramatically depicted by Goya. Although this insurrection was ruthlessly suppressed in the capital and some few other towns, within weeks most of the country was 'up in arms'; but ill-equipped, badly-organised, and worse-led, individual Spanish armies suffered severely whenever attempting to put up a fight.[2] After their débâcle at Bailén, the French abandoned Madrid and concentrated north of the river Ebro. They could no longer afford to ignore either the presence of other Spanish 'armies', or the more resourceful guerrilla bands then roving the country, harrying their extended lines of communication, effectively isolating smaller units, and interrupting the flow of supplies unless provided with strong escorts. Large numbers were pinned down in countering their activities.

* * *

Spanish patriots, sailing from the Asturias to seek British military intervention on their behalf, an appeal that was supported by positive assurances that Spanish armies and supplies would be available with which to prosecute the war, reached London on 8 June. And so it was agreed that troops already assembled in Ireland to attack and occupy Spanish possessions in America, which might otherwise fall into French hands, would be diverted from their initial destination to either the north coast of Spain, or to Portugal.

Enjoying the confidence of Castlereagh, a thirty-nine-year-old Lieutenant-general, Sir Arthur Wellesley, was chosen to command this expeditionary force.[3] He was given discretionary orders to land his troops wherever seemed most favourable and take whatever action he thought fit,[4] but he had been given only an imprecise idea of what the military situation might be on *terra firma*. The Spaniards had estimated Junot's army as numbering hardly 15,000 men (over 10,000 short of the total). Wellesley would soon discover to what extent he should rely on all unsubstantiated reports or fanciful figures his Allies chose to give him.

Support was not long in reaching the Peninsula. On 12 July – within five weeks of the Asturian deputies' reception in London – a British fleet weighed anchor in the Cove of Cork,[5] Wellesley sailing ahead in the *Crocodile*. On landing at Corunna on the 20th, he reported home that although the Galicians were grateful to receive any financial subsidy England could provide, they had no need of any auxiliary troops, overweeningly confident that Spanish armies, in spite of a minor recent setback, could defeat the French unaided.[6] Thus assured, while the first transports were entering Vigo bay to await orders, Wellesley sailed on to confer with the *Junta* at Oporto, by now the executive authority in un-occupied Portugal. Promising supplies and reinforcements once the British had landed, the Portuguese *Junta* also confirmed that the Spanish had minimised what had been a severe defeat at Medina de Rioseco on 14 July. Nearer the truth was the welcome news, received by Wellesley on 1 August, of Dupont's capitulation at Bailén nine days earlier.

Wellesley then conferred with Admiral Sir Charles Cotton, commanding naval units off the coast and protecting the transports, apropos the most convenient beach on which the troops might disembark. Mondego Bay was chosen, for Fort Catalina, guarding the fishing-port of Figueira da Foz, already in the hands of students from Coimbra, had been occupied by British marines on 7 July. Here, at the mouth of the Mondego, some 100 miles north of the Tagus estuary, the slow process of landing took place during the first week of August. The animated scene, as the troops were rowed through the pounding surf, was graphically described by several participants, among them Sergeant Norbert Landsheit (20th Light Dragoons): '... several boats were upset, and out of the infantry corps, which landed first, some men were lost, though I believe the casualties were not numerous ... We were directed to stand upright in the boats, with bridle in hand, and prepared, in case of accident, to spring into the saddle; a judicious precaution ... One punt capsized upon the surf, but no lives were lost, because the horses sometimes swimming, sometimes wading, carried their riders ashore. We then formed upon the beach, and carrying each man his three days' provisions, ready cooked, pushed forward to a village, the name of which I have forgotten.'

Jonathan Leach (95th regiment) recollected otherwise: 'Although the weather was perfectly calm, I never remember to have experienced more motion in a gale of wind, than we felt during the six days spent at this anchorage. The long and heavy swell made the yards of the ship at times almost touch the water, as she rolled from side to side, which caused some awful breakages amongst our wine-glasses and crockery-ware ... The disembarkation of the whole army followed as rapidly as the boats could accomplish it; and the process of passing the bar of sand, on which there is, even in the finest weather, a dangerous surf running, was effected, I believe, without any thing more serious than some wet jackets.'

Leach well remembered that while awaiting further orders, the troops

> were beset with a host of padres, friars, and monks, of all ages, each carrying a huge umbrella of the most gaudy colour imaginable; intended, no doubt, to protect their complexions, which vied with those of our chimney sweeps. These gentry welcomed us with *vivas*, and protested that, with our assistance, every Frenchman in Portugal should speedily be annihilated. Our visitors were not confined to the male sex; for some olive beauties, with sparkling eyes and jet black hair, were induced to take a peep at us; and, before we parted, some of the more favoured of us were presented with flowers and fruit from the hands of these damsels.
>
> Keeping our right towards the sea, we marched several miles over an uninterrupted plain of white sand, hot enough almost to have dressed a beef-steak, into which we sank ankle deep at every step. The troops having been on board ship so many weeks, were much fatigued with this their first day's march. We encamped near the village of Lavaos, where the whole of the army assembled as soon as the disembarkation was effected. Here we remained upwards of a week, during which several

regiments, that had been some time before embarked, under General Spencer's command, landed and joined us.

Although their heavier baggage remained in the transports, the troops were carrying a mass of equipment. Rifleman Benjamin Harris (95th), formerly a cobbler, had found the heat of the August sun exhausting, and wondered at the strength he possessed to endure it, for 'being a handicraft, I marched under a weight sufficient to impede the free motions of a donkey; for besides my well-filled kit, there was a greatcoat rolled on its top, my blanket and camp kettle, my haversack, stuffed full of leather for repairing the men's shoes, together with a hammer and other tools (the lapstone I took the liberty of flinging to the devil) ship-biscuit and beef for three days. I also carried my canteen filled with water, my hatchet and rifle, and eighty rounds of ball cartridge in my pouch …'

While encamped, the troops were delighted to receive provisions from the local peasantry and representatives of the *Junta*, for their meagre rations were one pound of biscuits and one pound of meat a day, and if the latter was salty, wine; the soldier's wives received half-rations, but no wine. Harris and his companions 'regaled themselves upon oranges, grapes, melons, and figs … an abundance of delicacies which many had never before tasted. Amongst other presents a live calf … we feasted like a company of aldermen!' Leach was likewise impressed by Portuguese hospitality, for 'they were presented with pigs, sheep, poultry, cart-loads of fruit, vegetables, and wine, the arrival of which at camp was highly acceptable; but the squeaking of pigs – the bleating of sheep – the various and discordant notes of geese, ducks, fowls, and turkeys – with the diabolical groaning of the carts, the wheels of which are never greased in Portugal, created a concert of vocal and instrumental music as no description could do justice to. The first first week after our disembarkation was employed in landing provisions, ammunition, and stores, and in making the necessary preparations for our advance on Lisbon.'

The first few days were spent organising the very rudimentary Commissary-General's Department, disgracefully neglected by the those responsible for equipping the expeditionary force, and that included James Pipon. In addition to a small Irish wagon train which had landed, numerous carts, together with 300 bullocks and carters, some 500 mules, either provided or requisitioned, were placed under the control of the Department. Regrettably, most of the slender staff appeared to be unfamiliar with the work entailed: they would have to learn the hard way, and from scratch. Among their duties was to pay promptly for all supplies and services provided: this should help to ensure regular provisioning and forage. Wellesley's experience in India had demonstrated to him how vital a competent commissariat was to the success of any campaign, although it took time and endless correspondence with London for this to sink into the minds of the hide-bound civilian authorities: it was enough to make any commander despair. He could not emphasise sufficiently to Castlereagh that 'the existence of the army depends upon the commissariat, and yet the people who manage it are incapable of managing anything out of a counting-house.'[7]

Now about 13,500 strong, they approached Leiria,[8] there reinforced by 1,600 Portuguese light troops or *Caçadores*, and cavalry commandeered by Wellesley from General Bernardino Freire's army of 6,000 raw levies. These had been entrusted to Colonel Trant, an enterprising Englishman in the Portuguese service,[9] for Wellesley had found Freire unco-operative (to the extent of demanding rations for his own men from the scant provisions collected for the British force), and left the bulk of his men in the vicinity to await instructions.[10] Until equipped with British muskets and bayonets, many of them were only armed 'with fowling-pieces, *escopetas*, carbines, and other such deadly engines.' They had not impressed Colonel Leslie (29th): 'The poor fellows had little or no uniform, but were merely in white jackets, and large broad-brimmed hats turned up at one side, some having feathers and others none, so that they cut rather a grotesque appearance.'

Conflicting reports were received as to the whereabouts and strength of Junot's combined forces, for the Portuguese, unlike the Spanish, were inclined to exaggerate numbers, when referring to those of the enemy. Several officers, acting as scouts, reported that General Delaborde's units, estimated at 6,000, were near Obidos, on the Lisbon road, while it was believed that he might be joined by Loison, with another 9,000, advancing across country from Abrantes, further east. Wellesley determined to attack the former before they united. The march south under a blistering sun was resumed, the magnifient abbey of Batalha being skirted to approach that at Alcobaça, entered on the 14th. Leach remembered

> large pine woods, growing on an arid, white, sandy, soil, occasionally varied by uncultivated heaths, with here and there a vineyard, [which] constituted the chief features of the country through which we passed … to Lyria … which had, a short time before, been visited by a considerable French force, detached from Lisbon to levy contributions … Here they

> were guilty of atrocities which exceeded belief. The town bore every mark of recent depredation, plunder, and excess of all kinds. The walls of a convent, into which I went with some other officers, were covered with blood and brains in many places ...
>
> On the 15th ... after a long march, a party of French cavalry and infantry were found near the town of Obidos, where there is a Moorish castle. Four companies of ours and the 60th regiment instantly attacked and obliged them to retire. In the ardour of pursuit, our people pushed on a considerable distance from any support, and were met by a superior body of the enemy ... A sharp skirmish ensued, in which we lost some few in killed, wounded, and missing.

Lieut. John Cox (95th) recorded that 'the enemy opened a fire of musketry from a windmill on rising ground,' and that they then 'dashed ... after them like young soldiers [until] brought up by a body of French cavalry ...', while the action was described by Harris as one in which the French skirmishers 'immediately commenced operations by raining a shower of balls upon us as we advanced ... I never heard such a tremendous noise as the firing made on this occasion ... Being overmatched, we retired to a rising ground, or hillock, in our rear, and formed there all round its summit, standing three deep, the front rank kneeling. In this position we remained all night, expecting every moment that the whole host would be upon us.'

Roliça

Wellesley had his entire force under arms an hour before dawn on the 17th, having received intelligence that Loison was now only a few hours' march away, near Rio Maior. Before advancing towards the French position immediately north of the village of Roliça, beyond which rose a horseshoe-shaped line of low hills, he divided the army into three columns, the central one being of 9,000 men. Their scarlet lines made a dazzling display, but Delaborde was too experienced and wary a general to take the bait for, as part of a wide pincer movement, Wellesley had sent Trant's column circling to the west behind the hills, while Ferguson, with two and a half brigades, a troop of cavalry and six guns, was deployed similarly to the east – from which direction Loison threatened; and after some sharp skirmishing in his front, Delaborde retired deliberately behind a cavalry screen to a stronger position along the main ridge of hills.

This was cleft by steep-sided gullies, up one of which Colonel the Hon. George Lake (29th), with misplaced enthusiasm impulsively led his men, to find themselves penned behind the enemy front; many casualties, including Lake himself, were suffered as they scrambled out of the ravine under a rain of fire from both flanks. The whole line finally swarmed to the summit, beyond which Delaborde, awaiting Loison's imminent arrival,[11] put up a stiff resistance until his position became untenable, before skilfully withdrawing behind his cavalry.

Their pursuit into more open country was not pressed, and Wellesley's brigades bivouacked in line of battle facing south and east, next morning being marched south-west towards the shallow estuary of the Maceira, for transports bringing expected reinforcement had been sighted offshore. Protected by two headlands, its sandy bay was convenient for their disembarkation and one unlikely to be disturbed by the few French still occupying Peniche,[12] a fortified harbour due west of Obidos. Not far inland lay the village of Vimeiro, commanded by two ridges and a lower, flat-topped hill, the whole providing an eminently defensible position on which Wellesley deployed his troops.

It had been decided in London that a force of this size (an additional 4,000 men, among them Sir Harry Burrard), should be commanded by a general senior in rank to young Wellesley who, although showing promise, was a mere 'sepoy general'. It was no welcome news to Wellesley that Burrard, who had not seen action for a decade, would be superseding him, and it was with misgivings that he rowed out to confer with his superior, whom he found reluctant to engage the enemy until the impending arrival of General Sir John Moore with a further 15,000 men.[13] By the time Burrard had landed next morning (the 21st), the fight was on: very sensibly, he chose not to interfere.

With 16,300 British infantry and Trant's 2,000-odd Portuguese, Wellesley considerably outnumbered Junot, who would be approaching with 10,300 infantry and 700 artillerymen, but he was at a distinct disadvantage as far as cavalry was concerned, for his 240 mounts would be opposed by some 1,950.

It is not the intention in this study to describe either battles or tactics in any detail, but it may be helpful to explain briefly what happened when a defensive line was confronted by an attacking column, as it did on this first major action in the war, and on several ensuing occasions.[14]

Vimeiro

Wellesley's patrols had been aware during the previous night that the French were approaching in force. Sergeant Landsheit remembered hearing the rumble of wheels and the sound of iron hoofs crossing a wooden bridge, and 'a dull heavy noise, like the tread of many feet over a soft soil,' before withdrawing the vedettes and trotting back to report to the advanced picquets. Soon after dawn, rising clouds of dust stirred up by Junot's columns traversing thinly wooded country and the glint of bayonets in the sun were observed far more to the east than south-east, necessitating an immediate change in the British front. The brigades on Vimeiro hill were re-deployed: behind a heavy skirmishing line armed with rifles, awaited five battalions, three disposed in a two-deep line, extending along the reverse slope of the flat hill-crest; the other two, together with 12 guns, were placed further back in support.

It was here that the French made their initial attack, repeating tactics which had served them well on so many fields during the Revolutionary wars, surging forward in two parallel columns about 400 yards apart, shielded by *tirailleurs*, supported by field artillery, their flanks protected by cavalry. The impact of such a formation was one which few continental armies could withstand, but when advancing against a disciplined line, it had a dangerous weakness. Because of its structure – approximately 30 men broad and 42 ranks in depth – only 200 of the 1,200 men usually composing it were able to return the fire of 900 muskets in line opposing them, which at the range of just over 100 yards would be delivering its first murderous volley into this compact mass.

An equally devastating discharge by the artillery, including howitzers carrying the newly-designed shrapnel shell – which did not require such precise aiming as did round shot, but even at long range could inflict heavy damage – was trained likewise on this large target, already harassed by riflemen. In Leach's words: 'In spite of the deadly fire which several hundred riflemen kept up on them, they continued to press forward with great determination, until the old 50th regiment received them with a destructive volley, following it instantly with a most brilliant and decisive charge with the bayonet, which broke and sent back, in utter dismay and confusion, and with great loss, this column, which a short time before was all confidence and exultation.'

While there may not have been confusion in the British ranks, the encounter was bewildering if not unnerving. As Harris described it: 'I myself was very soon so hotly engaged, loading and firing away, enveloped in the smoke I created, and the cloud which hung about me from the continued fire of my comrades, that I could see nothing for a few minutes but the red flash of my own piece amongst the white vapour clinging to my very clothes ... until some friendly breeze of wind clears the space around, a soldier knows no more of his position and what is about to happen in his front, or what *has* happened (even amongst his own companions) than the dead lying around.'

A second column was unable to reply to the withering fire from the two-deep line of Anstruther's 43rd, to the east of Fane's, both flanks of which had wheeled inward to envelope it. Panic-striken, the French turned tail and fled, leaving seven of their guns to be captured. Meanwhile, a third force, further north, assuming that Wellesley's skirmishers on the hillside were the main defending line in retreat, drove them up the ridge, only to be met by a line of some 3,000 muskets waiting behind the hill-crest. The French, breathless from the strenuous climb, collapsed completely when met by their disciplined volleys, and before long the country to the east was covered by retreating stragglers and wounded.

Yet another column, identified as grenadiers, found itself the target of three battalions, and was brought to a halt by the converging fire of 2,000 muskets, and likewise disintegrated. A second brigade, accompanied by General Kellermann, had veered north along lower ground to approach the village of Vimeiro, but its flank was exposed to Acland's riflemen, ordered down the ridge-slope by Wellesley, and to the fire of two guns. On reaching the village, they were met by the second line of Anstruther's brigade and, after confused hand-to-hand fighting, chose to retire rather than get cut off, only to run the gauntlet between Acland's and Fane's units.

Elsewhere, two similar attacks were similarly beaten, the first of 3,000 strong in three columns under General Solignac, when confronted by Ferguson's units: seven light companies in skirmishing order exposed to view on the hill-crest, with a main line just behind, supported by a third: some 5,780 men altogether. Solignac had assumed that the British line was formed by skirmishers only but, on reaching the crest, they were met by a thunderous volley at short range, and after two minutes broke, fleeing headlong downhill. The second attack, commanded by General Brennier, in which he was wounded and taken prisoner, although numerically stronger, likewise found itself defeated by superior fire-power.

Although the infantry were able to repulse these assaults, the cavalry displayed an inherent failing. Colonel Charles Taylor's Light Dragoons, flanked by the Portuguese contingent, were champing at the bit, awaiting orders to attack the retreating grenadiers. Landsheit well remembered Wellesley shouting 'Now, Twentieth, Now!', while his staff gave them a cheer,

> the sound of which was still in our ears, when we put our horses to their speed. The Portuguese likewise pushed forward, but through the dust which entirely enveloped us, the enemy threw in a fire, which seemed to have the effect of paralysing altogether our handsome allies. Right and left they pulled up, as if by word of command, and we never saw more of them till the battle was over. But we went very differently to work. In an instant we were in the heart of the French cavalry, cutting and hacking, and upsetting men and horses in the most extraordinary manner possible, till they broke and fled in every direction, and then we fell upon the infantry. It was here that our gallant Colonel met his fate. He rode that day a horse, which was so hot that not all his exertions would suffice to control, and he was carried headlong upon the bayonets of the French infantry, a corporal of whom shot him through the heart ... Though scattered, as always happens, by the shock of a charge, we still kept laying about us, till our white leather breeches, our hands, arms, and swords, were all besmeared with blood.

Given their head, the cavalry had galloped both out of control and out of the range of any supporting artillery, found themselves attacked by a regiment of dragoons, and were badly mauled by a more experienced and disciplined enemy. It was the first of many times during the war that they appeared to treat such actions as steeple-chases – were to run amoke, in this case with 20% casualties. Wellesley was to use this arm with caution in future: nor was it easy for him to find a commander capable of keeping them under a tight rein.

When questioned, Brennier confirmed that if other attacks had been broken, then no more could be mounted: indeed, they had suffered a crushing blow. It was still only midday, and the moment to turn pursuit into rout; but Burrard, perhaps piqued by his junior's success, for which he could claim no credit, pulled rank. Oblivious to remonstration, stubbornly he disallowed any further advance until the arrival of Moore's contingent (which earned him the epithet of 'optuse pig' from Schaumann), and ordered all units to return to their bivouacs. Many were the protestations, both then and later.[15] Burrard may have shrunk from the responsibility of taking any positive decision, knowing that within hours he would himself be superseded as commander of British forces in Portugal in the person of Sir Hew Whitefoord Dalrymple.[16]

Once the fighting was over, with many others, Harris prowled about the battlefield in the hope of finding some spoil to be picked up from the dead and dying strewn around.[17] He left a bundle of gold and silver crosses found on one Frenchman, fearing the wrath of Heaven for touching such plunder, but had no scruples about carrying off a handful of coins hidden in the lining of another's coat. As valuable were the shoes of an officer of the 50th, already stripped of his uniform. Before long, 'the roll being called', Harris and his companions were ordered to lie down and rest after their exertions, but he soon rose to continue his search for loot.

On seeing a French officer running towards him, pursued by half a dozen horsemen, Harris held up his hand, calling to them not to hurt him, to no avail, for 'one of the horsemen ... cut him down with a desparate blow, when close beside me, and ... wheeling round, as he leaned from his saddle, passed his sword through his body. I am sorry to say there was an English dragoon amongst these scoundrels; the rest, by their dress, I judged to be Portuguese cavalry. Whether the Frenchman thus slaughtered was a prisoner trying to escape, or what was the cause of this cold-blooded piece of cruelty, I know not, as the horsemen immediately galloped off without a word of explanation; and feeling quite disgusted with the scene I had witnessed, I returned to my comrades, and again throwing myself down, was soon as fast asleep as any there.'

There were bloated bodies to bury under a blazing sun. According to Schaumann, for several days 'the stench of half-buried corpses of men and horse was appalling', while rapacious vultures hovered over the battlefield. Capt. Harry Ross-Lewin remembered the churchyard at Vimeiro littered with heaps of amputated legs, and seeing a large dish full of severed hands. Harris, who had been carrying the wounded there, described two long tables having been placed end to end, and 'upon them were laid the men whose limbs it was found necessary to amputate. Both French and English were constantly lifted on and off these tables ... the surgeons with their sleeves turned up, and their hands and arms covered with blood, looked like butchers in the shambles. I saw as I passed at least twenty legs lying on the ground, many of them being clothed in the long black gaiters then worn by the infantry of the line ... not having time to take off the clothes, they merely ripped the seams and turned the cloth back, proceeding with the operation as fast as they could.' Many of the wounded were able to stagger to the improvised hospital by themselves. Harris turned to assist one, 'faint with loss of blood ... his face being completely encrusted with the blood which had flowed during the night, and had now dried. One eyeball was knocked out of the socket, and hung down on his cheek.'

Adam Neale, one of the surgeons, commented that in general the French 'appeared to be more desparately wounded than our men; many of them being shot in both legs, besides being stabbed in the trunk', and he was not alone in confirming 'that the carnage caused by the lately invented Shrapnell shells was prodigeous.' Noticing that the 'armed Portuguese peasantry' had been been putting an end to many of the wounded French, he put a guard on the cottage where some lay indiscriminately with the British. The wife of a non-commissioned officer of the 71st, whose leg had been amputated, assisted him there by distributing some warm gruel to 'the unfortunate sufferers, who, parched with thirst during the long day, had scarcely been able to procure a drop of water ...' Neale went on to supervise the embarkation of the more severely British wounded, to find that already 'a number of our sailors, with lanthorns in their hands, [were] busily employed ... It was highly gratifying to me to witness the very attentive and humane manner in which this service was performed by these kind honest-hearted tars; who, during the whole of a very cold night, were wading nearly up to the middle in the wash of the sea. Fortunately the surf was moderate; and owing to their great exertions, by ten o'clock this morning [23 August] I had seen the last of my charge sent off to the hospital ships appropriated for their reception.'

Harris records that when debating the course of the battle with his surviving companions, the subject came up as to how

> a man loses or gains caste with his comrades' by his behaviour, the officers too being closely observed and commented upon, for 'the men are very proud of those who are brave in the field, and who are kind and considerate to the soldiers under them. An act of kindness done by an officer has often during the battle been the cause of his life being saved. ... I know from experience, that in *our* army the men like best to be officered by gentlemen, men whose education has rendered them more kind in manners than your coarse officer, sprung from obscure origin, and whose style is brutal and overbearing. ... those whose birth and station might reasonably have made them fastidious under hardship and toil have generally borne their miseries without a murmur; whilst those whose previous life ... might have prepared them for the toils of war have been the first to cry out and complain of their hard fate.'[18]

General Dalrymple, who landed on the 22nd, was prejudiced against any advice which might be offered, certainly distaining that of an officer twenty years his junior, for Wellesley was urging a rapid advance towards Santarém, which would cut off any French retreat to the north-east, and hem them in between the coast and the Tagus. While 'the Gentlemen' – as Wellesley called them, ironically – were nervously debating what action should be taken, the alarm was given that a further attack was imminent: great was their relief to learn that it was only a squadron of cavalry escorting Kellermann, with a flag of truce, to propose an armistice which would enable the French 'to get out of the mousetrap' (as Kellermann was said to have muttered). Both Junot and his army were thoroughly demoralised, nor could he expect any support from units still in Lisbon: they would have enough on their hands in holding down its populace once news of the defeat reached the capital.

But even in negotiating a document suspending hostilities, previous to that which became known as 'The Convention of Cintra', the senior generals displayed their pusillanimity by submitting to French demands, which were that they would be prepared to evacuate Portugal if, together with their small arms and the spoil of conquest, they were transported back to France *in British ships*.[19] There was no reason why Junot's army, thoroughly defeated, should not have been forced to surrender unconditionally and made prisoner; nor were the isolated garrisons at Elvas and Almeida in any position to come to their relief. No clause was included which might restrict the French from fighting again – not that it could have been enforced; indeed once re-armed, they were back in Spain within three months.[20] By acceding to these provisions, the two 'gentlemen' were 'honourably' ending their own unedifying careers.

Meanwhile, Moore's troops were approaching Lisbon, reached on 9 September.[21] His contingent had entered Mondego Bay on 21 August (the day Vimeiro had been fought), two days later receiving an order from Burrard to re-embark any units already landed, and sail south to Maceira Bay. It was here on the 28th that August Schaumann, a deputy assistant commissary in the King's German Legion, with his portmanteau under his arm, descended

> into one of the flat-bottomed boats supplied by the men-o'-war. Preceeded by two sloops, we rowed rapidly towards the rocky, sandy shore of the bay, which the huge breakers had converted into a sheet of raging foam.

> The men sat four by four in the thwarts, all pressing closely together, with their packs and muskets between their legs. None of the officers were allowed to take more than a valise with him …
>
> With beating hearts we approached the first line of surf, and were lifted high up into the air. We clung frantically to our seats, and all of us had to crouch quite low … There were twenty to thirty British sailors on the shore, all quite naked, who, the moment the foremost breakers withdrew, dashed like lightning into the surf, and after many vain efforts … at last succeeded in casting a long rope to us, which we were able to seize. Then with a loud hurrah, they ran at top speed through the advancing breakers up the beach, dragging us with them, until the boat stuck fast … Finally … each of them took a soldier on his back and carried him thus on to the dry shore.[22]
>
> The tumult on the shore was interesting … officers, both military and naval, shouting and directing the landing; guns, wagons, some of which were being fitted together, mountains of ship's biscuits, haversacks, trusses of hay, barrels of meat and rum, tents, some of which were already up, and dragoons busy catching and saddling their horses.

The cavalry experienced a different problem from those that had previously landed, for some 'horses, dashing helter-skelter into the surf from the reeling vessels bringing them from the transports would then swim to shore … galloped wildly along it, to and fro, snorting, panting, neighing, and biting and kicking one another, to the great danger of all those gathered on the beach; and then they would roll over on the sand'. Although they seemed in good condition, owing to the much longer sea voyage, during which they had been standing, they had lost the use of their legs, and the moment a trooper attempted to mount one of them, it 'folded up its back legs like a dog, or rather dropped his hind-quarters on the ground.'

Schaumann, made a clerk in the British Commissariat shortly after, was not impressed by Commissary-General Rawlings, 'a puffed up and very uncivil fellow, who had set up a large marquee on the beach, and provided himself with all his London camp equipment, consisting of camp chairs of red morocco, small mahogony tables, a silk camp bed with steel springs, a canteen of silver knives, forks and spoons, and a costly apparatus for his personal ablutions … [but who] would not hear of our making up our beds with a little of the hay that had been landed, although two of his own goats were standing up to their bellies in it.' Naturally, Schaumann and his fellow commissaries 'made hay' as soon as 'the brute Rawlings' was asleep.

Schaumann described one of the bullock-carts which lumbered down to the shore to be loaded. These unwieldy vehicles, on which the Commissariat had to rely so long, consisted of 'rough planks nailed on to a massive pole or shaft. At right angles to the shaft, and under the planks, two blocks of semi-rounded wood were fixed, having a hole in the centre, and through these holes the axle was fitted. It was a live axle fixed firmly to the wheels', which as it was never greased, emitted 'a terrible squeaking and creaking',[23] without which music – so the drivers assured him – the animals 'would stand stock still and refuse to move …' These docile draught bullocks were

> harnessed by means of a wooden yoke … fastened behind their horns and attached to the axle by leather straps, there being a peg in the front of the axle for that purpose. However, they are shod with a kind of iron shoe, and in this way manage to drag a load of about half a ton up hill and down dale along the roughest mountain roads with the greatest ease. The wheels are solid, massive, and have no spokes, and are the most skillfully designed for resisting the terrible shocks and jerks they get … [while] the Portuguese bullock-drivers, with their tawny faces, their long black hair, their big three-cornered hats, their naked brown and hairy legs, cut picturesque figures. They wore a sort of blanket over their shoulders with a hole in it for their heads, and carried poles six feet long … at the end of which is a spike, with which he goads the bullocks on by striking them over their shoulders.

Some days later, the long line of the Commissariat train entered Torres Vedras, where Schaumann joined his colleagues in the church, where 'at a long table in front of the high altar … they were writing by the light of four huge wax candles stuck in richly chased gilt altar candlesticks. It was a beautiful church, all draped and decorated with crimson cloth fringed with gold.' One night, when escorting the carts of the Irish train, he noticed that one Irishmen had lagged behind after they'd passed a peasant's cottage, from which, within minutes 'the piteous bleats of a goat and the loud cackling of poultry' confirmed what was taking place, for 'The goat's throat had been cut in a twinkling … and it had been hung on to one of the carts in order to be skinned on the march. The turkeys did not fare any better, and were plucked as we went along. I attempted to point out to the fellows how disgraceful their behaviour had been, but as the Irish are a notoriously bloodthirsty and predatory crowd, my remarks made not the slightest impression on them, more particularly as I was not a commissioned officer.'

After traversing Mafra and Sintra, Schaumann was placed in charge of a stores department set up just west of Lisbon, 'to receive supplies, distribute rations and fodder to the troops, keep account of everything, and repair to the town every evening to report'. 'Supplies had arrived so plentifully from the provision ships lying in the harbour, that a veritable mountain of salt fish, oats, hay, straw, ship's biscuit, rum and wine had accumulated in one of the large barns of the farm' in which he was billeted. At four next morning the quartermasters of seven regiments, among whom were the servants of Moore's, Hill's, and Sir William Bentinck's staffs, were there to fetch their rations and fodder. Schaumann's company consisted of 'peasants, ill-bred quartermasters, blaspheming soldiers, bullocks, donkeys and mules! My wild bullocks, which we killed for meat, also caused me much anxiety; for although they were shut up in a garden surrounded by a wall five feet high, they nevertheless used sometimes to jump this height like stags, and charging into the bivouacs, would send the tents, the huts, the sentry boxes and camp kettles all flying, or they would escape into the open country, or, after being surrounded by me and my men, supported by the military, would be shot at and killed at the end of a regular hunt. A couple of them once overthrew an English sentry, although he was standing with bayonet fixed.'

Neale had attended a 'sumptuous repast' given by Junot shortly before his departure, and was much surprised 'by the light and disrespectful manner' in which one of his aides had spoken of his talents as those of 'a *bon officier de cavalerie, mais rein d'autre*', while 'it did not require a very discerning eye to discover that most of them [Junot's contingent] had been exalted to situations which they were ill qualified to fill [although] there were among them one or two young men, who had been emigrants, and possessed altogether engaging manners.'[24]

By 15 September, when the first division of Junot's army embarked, most of the British troops, previously bivouacked, were placed under canvas in the vicinity of the capital.[25] On that same day, Schaumann received orders to move to Queluz, and here, for the next two months, twenty bullocks were slaughtered daily: 600 in all, but 'their blood and entrails, which soon became putrid in the great heat, created the most appalling stench, not to mention clouds of blow-flies, which were so thick that every surface was black with them. In the end I had pits dug, in which to bury this offal'. Provisions arrived during the afternoon and evening in hundreds of vehicles requisitioned by the Portuguese government, among them hackney carriages, the superstructures of which had been removed. Imagine the framework piled with 'half a dozen barrels of salt fish and bundles of hay and wood ... rocking about, the whole drawn by two large pack mules ridden by a fellow wearing a collar, a gallooned hat, and a powdered pigtail': a comical sight indeed.

Before long, 'with the heat, the cold nights, the eating of fruit and the drinking of young wine, the health of the army became so much impaired that typhus and dysentery broke out and spread rapidly, affecting even the inhabitants of villages close to the camp.' Meanwhile, 'a huge hospital was installed in one of the wings of the castle,[26] not far behind and below our stores depot, and separated from it only by a long ditch which was used as a latrine by the dysentery patients, and was not 500 yards away. Infection was bound to occur, and I, too, got dysentery; but great as was my pain and unspeakable as was my exhaustion, I stuck to my duty, and was soon cured by an English doctor by means of opium pills and thick rice water.'

On 20 September Wellesley embarked on the *Plover* sloop of war, landing at Plymouth on 4 October. Moore, although the first to congratulate him on his military successes, had declined Wellesley's offer to write to London to impress upon the Cabinet the urgency of replacing 'the Gentlemen' by Moore, should their project of advancing into Spain be put into effect. However, this was not necessary. Britannia sickened when details of the disgraceful terms of the Convention of Cintra reached London, for they would appear to have been dictated by the vanquished, even if it enabled Portuguese territory to be cleared entirely of the French for several months without further bloodshed.[27] Recalled to face an enquiry, Dalrymple was discreetly retired; Burrard was exonerated and remained in command at Lisbon until replaced by Cradock. Wellesley, who had signed the armistice 'to oblige Sir Hew', was exonerated. As he wrote to Castlereagh on 6 October: 'I do not consider myself responsible in any degree for the terms in which it was framed, or for any of its provisions.'

Some 20,000 French under arms, and 3,500 wounded, had to be evacuated. 500 had deserted, preferring to serve in British ranks. Those embarking had to be protected by British bayonets from the fury of the Lisbon mob, from which few stragglers lingering in purlieus of the capital were likely to escape, for the '*canaille* proclaimed war to the knife against every Frenchman, of whatever trade or profession,' as an officer named Wilkie remarked,[28] having saved a merchant and barber, long resident there, from the vengeful mob, only by threatening to shoot anyone attempting to force his way into the guard-room in which they had sought refuge.

General Beresford and Lord Proby, as joint Commissioners, did their best to ensure that the French did not – in violation of the treaty – smuggle on board any items other than their arms and *personal* property.[29] Junot, who had already packed off to Paris priceless books from the Royal Library, attempted to load five Danish vessels with plunder 'under the name of private baggage'! – and they were forced to disgorge any valuables,[30] which were then put into store to await the claims of those from whom they had pillaged.

Harris, together with Lieut. William Cox (95th) and Leach, had been among the first to venture into the capital, where at first they found considerable resentment among the French encamped in its squares, but according to the Leach, before long the 'best possible understanding existed between the soldiers of the two armies, who were to be seen drinking, carousing, shaking hands, and walking arm in arm …' In general, the French officers had behaved very civily also towards the former foes, reserving their grossest epithets for their 'friends' the Portuguese, whose city, 'which swarms with monks, friars, and ecclesiastics of all ages … is filled with every species of filth and dirt, in spite of the measures taken by the French to prevent it.' As Wilkie confirmed, whatever faults may have been laid at their door, they had at least 'made the people clean the streets, have watchmen at night, and they killed hundreds of these dogs [half-wild packs prowling the streets] – the greatest nuisance in the place.' He well remembered also their triumphant march from Queluz to Belém and thence to Rocio Square, in central Lisbon, near which his regiment was quartered in a convent the French had just vacated, passing below the 'balconies and windows of all the better houses … filled with Portuguese ladies in their best attire, hailing us with continuous *vivas*, and showering down garlands and flowers. Guns were firing, and bells ringing as we marched along the streets with flying colours, and bands and drum in full activity. It was one of those exciting hours that compensate the soldier for weeks of privation and fatigue.'

Indeed, in Leach's words, 'there was such a combination of *vivas*, sky-rockets, ringing of bells, singing, dancing, screeching, crying, laughing, old and young embracing in the streets, added to the curses and execrations uttered by the populace against their late masters, as must render every attempt at description hopeless.' Unfortunately, Leach himself was soon to contract a fever, reducing him 'to a mere skeleton': bed-ridden, he was unable to take part in the subsequent advance. He was not alone, for both the 40th and 82nd Regiments were 'rather sickly'.

The Estrela convent, conveniently close to Neale's billet, had been converted into a general hospital. From here, he explored the quays at Belém where rose the 'most superb' Jeronimite monastery of Santa Maria, in the library of which a 'St Jerome' by Dürer caught his attention,[31] while nearby was a cabinet of natural history, among other curiosities: but Neale had little time at his disposal for sight-seeing. Pack animals for his baggage had to be purchased, for the greater part of the army was about to march, in the wake of which his department followed on 27 October.

Three weeks earlier, on the 6th, Sir John Moore received a despatch from Castlereagh confirming that he was to replace Dalrymple as commander of the British forces in Portugal, his assignment being to employ his troops in the North of Spain and 'to co-operate with the Spanish armies in the expulsion of the French from that kingdom.'

Moore had found 'everything in the greatest confusion' in Lisbon, and he was not alone in chafing, for there was 'very general discontent.' There were numerous problems to be resolved. Although several regiments encamped nearby were reporting sick, Moore, a humane commander, was not easily fooled. He gave his opinion in a General Order that it was 'owing to their own intemperance that so many ... are rendered incapable of marching against the Enemy.' Having stated this, he felt confident that he needed to say no more to ensure their sobriety. This was not always so easy. Some troops would go to extraordinary lengths to get drink; and as Wellington later observed to Stanhope: 'The Irish Catholic soldiers used to make use of their signs of the cross to get *aguardiente* [spirits] in the villages; for the country people, seeing from this that they were brethren in faith, used to bring out their stores more readily.'

Moore also attempted to disencumber his army of 'soldier's wives'.[32] He would have liked to ship them all home; but although his officers did their best to persuade the troops to part with them, this could not be enforced. Many had infants in arms and more at heel, and some were even advanced in pregnancy, but no matter; they would still insist on following, carrying their impedimenta, on what was expected to be a long and hazardous march, and little could be done about it. As the war progressed, the tougher and more vitiated they became.

Capt. Thomas Browne (23rd; then D.A.A.G.) thoroughly disapproved: as he wrote months later, after the battle of Salamanca:

> The character of the women ... who in spite of orders, threats, & even deprivation of rations, had forced themselves in numbers, (from the

dêpots in the rear, appointed for them), to the sides of their Husbands, now began to exhibit a fearful and melancholy change. All ideas of conduct or decency had disappeared – plunder & profligacy seemed their sole object, & the very Soldiers their Husbands evidently estimated them in proportion to their proficiency in these vices. They covered ... the ground of the field of battle when the action was over, & were seen stripping & plundering friend & foe alike. It is not doubted that they gave the finishing blow to many an Officer who was struggling with a mortal wound; & Major Offley ... , who lay on the ground, unable to move, but now dead, is said to have fallen a victim to this unheard of barbarity. The daring & enterprize of these creatures ... is not to be described. They had no hesitation in engaging themselves three or four deep to future Husbands, & according to the activity and mischief, of each, was the number of candidates for her hand, in case of disaster to her lawful Lord; & one of them has been heard to reply to a Soldier, who offered himself, as successor to her then Commanding Officer: 'Nay, but thou'rt late, as I'm promised to John Edwards first, & to Edward Atkinson next, but when they two be killed off, I'll think of thee.'

Meanwhile, General Anstruther, then at Almeida, had warned Moore of the lamentable state of the Portuguese roads, hardly one of which did not have 'very bad steps; these are generally in or near villages, of which the streets are almost universally narrow, rocky, and full of short turns impracticable for carriages of any sort ...', merely confirming what the Portuguese had admitted: 'that even in their own country they would be at a loss to indicate any road that was practical for artillery.'

What passed for paved highways in the Peninsula were very few and far between. Little had changed by the time, years later, when in conversation with Stanhope, Wellington had remarked later that 'in Portugal the only road at all deserving of the name was from Lisbon to Pombal. From Lisbon to Elvas it was most detestable, often only the dry bed of a rivulet.'[33] When asked what the Portuguese did when they were full, he replied: 'Stay at home, I believe ... But I have been obliged more than once to give orders at the villages that the large stones and fragments might be picked out of the rivulets, so that the troops might march on these roads.'

Too often they were little more than dusty, dislocating tracks in summer, quagmires in winter, and virtually impossible in wet weather.[34] Had any notice been taken of the descriptions published during the previous half century by every single British traveller experiencing the lamentable condition of all forms of communication in the Peninsula, and also the lack of transport, or even by French prisoners who might have traversed them prevously, had they been cross-questioned, this would have been no surprise. But it was not only total ignorance of the condition of the roads that was apparent. Few seem to have appreciated the fact that the country through which the army intended to march was one of the most fragmented in Europe, much of it a high-lying plateau or *meseta*, divided up by roadless mountain ranges and furrowed by fast-flowing rivers spanned by few bridges.[35] Indeed, with the exception of the valleys of the Ebro and Guadalquivir, down which ran roads of variable quality, many stretches of other important rivers – among them the Duero (Douro in Portugal), Tagus, and Guadiana, and their tributaries – ran in deep, rocky, gorges. No roads of any sort ran along their banks, while few could be used for transport by boats except near their mouths: they were more a hindrance to communication that help.[36] Some, foaming torrents in winter, in summer might be forded at certain points, but the trickle of a meandering rivulet might dry up entirely, leaving a sandy bed or *rambla* – less rutted than the nearest road, often providing a more convenient line of march. As the French were learning to their cost, once through the Pyrenees (only traversed with ease at either end), if making for Madrid, an invading army had to cross several desolate mountain chains, isolating one province from another, by roads threading tortuous defiles – perfect sites for guerrilla ambuscades – when not climbing to easily defended passes or *puertos*. While intervening plains, comparatively well populated, might be able to provide food and fodder to a ravenous army, little sustenance could be found in more mountainous areas, and it was a lengthy and laborious process, necessitating wagon-trains and convoys of pack-mules to transport accumulated supplies and forage over these ranges. On re-entering less barren districts, the troops would be obliged to disperse yet again in their perennial search for provisions: the old saying that 'in Spain large armies starve, and small armies get beaten' was one frequently found to be only too true.

No wonder that Moore was 'hypochondriacal', in the words of Schaumann, who reported also that the Portuguese had been declaring with one voice: 'Do not trust the Spaniards and their promises; for all they tell you about ample stores and large armies are sheer lies; all they wish to do is to lure you into their country, claim your victories as their own, hardly mention the help you have given them, and not even thank you. If things go wrong, they will vanish in a twinkling, and return to their homes, and leave you to your fate in the heart of

Spain, surrounded by your enemies, and exposed to every possible privation.[37] Furthermore, the year is too far advanced, and the rainy season will hurry you on too much and do you a lot of damage.'

This, in spite of whatever the 'credulous English Minister', John Hookham Frere, may have said to the contrary. Sir William Bentinck, the British military agent in Madrid, had been left entirely in the dark, not being informed beforehand about the state of the roads or what arrangements had been made to supply the troops: and nothing had been done in either respect, while his superiors in London talked of marching into Spain as if it was 'going into Hyde Park ...'

1 Forewarned of their approach, the Prince Regent, Dom João, the Portuguese royal family and court, together with several thousand of the administrative hierarchy and hangers-on, had just set sail in a scratch fleet for Brazil, escorted by a British flotilla, leaving the country to the mercy of the French.

2 As at Medina de Rioseco on 14 July, when they lost over 3,000 men, including some 1,200 taken prisoner; French casualties were just over 400. Admittedly, only eight days later, their forces were fortuitously successful at Bailén, when an entire French corps of 20,000 men commanded by General Dupont, having sacked Cordoba, capitulated to General Castaños. In Dupont's defence, it should be emphasised that of the troops at his disposal, only one battalion consisted of veterans and that most of his units were made up of undrilled conscripts: Swiss mercenaries in the Spanish service who had been compelled to transfer their allegiance, Paris municipal guards, etc., certainly not the 'picked men' referred to by Napoleon on learning of the disaster. This 'victory' gave the Spanish an inflated idea of their military strength. Subsequently, Wellington was of the opinion that Dupont had taken fright, which he would not have done had the confrontation taken place later in the war, when the French 'had seen more of the Spanish Generals and learnt to despise them. They would have cut their way through.' According to Lady Holland, always ready with informed gossip, in Dupont's baggage was found 'an immense quantity of plate from churches, and spoons, forks, and even buckles beat down into a mass,' while his mistress 'stole at Cordova cambric to make herself three hundred shifts.'

3 After Talavera, when created Viscount, known as Lord Wellington. He had served his apprenticeship in India, where he had landed early in 1797 as Colonel of the King's 33rd Foot, and this had provided him with invaluable experience in the field: his successes at Seringapatam, Assaye, Argaum, and Gawilghur had already added lustre to his name, even if these campaigns seemed remote and peripheral to the principal contest now taking place in Europe. Since his return to England in 1805, and partly due to family influence, he had held the post of Chief Secretary for Ireland. In August 1807 he had commanded a brigade at Kiöge during the Copenhagen expedition, and Parliament had thanked him for his part in bringing the recalcitrant Danes to heel.

4 Initially, only 9,000 men; but he would soon receive a reinforcement of some

4,500 troops already in the vicinity of Cadiz under General Sir Brent Spencer. For details of this and of Moore' command, see Chapter 2, by Ron MacGuigan, in *Inside Wellington's Peninsular Army.*

5 The fleet consisted of some 70 ships: 29 troop transports; 21 cavalry transports; 9 ordnance vessels; a hospital ship, and several victuallers (three packed with oats), storeships, etc.

6 It took some time before the British authorities became fully aware of the unreliability and deviousness of the Spanish Juntas in general. Charles Vaughan, writing to Lord Holland from Lugo in 1 September on that of the Asturias, had remarked of them that 'For reasons at present unknown,' they had not kept their promises; indeed ' The people of the Asturias seem to be less capable of laying aside their provincial prejudices than any other Spaniards. The English Government has, I think, been too lavish of supplies to that province. It ought to be remembered that nothing passes those mountains that once finds its way into them, and that arms and ammunition which must have been intended for the service of Spain in general have been exclusively appropriated by the Asturias to themselves.'

7 In contrast to the dilatory and muddled improvisation of the British Commissariat at this stage in the war, it is instructive to refer to the fact that some time prior to his Marengo campaign in 1800, Napoleon had already calculated the number of mules required to carry eight days' rations for 50,000 men, established dumps of every kind of supply that such a force would need on their advance, and secured by purchase or requisition all the necessary means for the transportation of such provisions.

8 It was at Leiria that Lieut.-Colonel Wilkie 'first saw a specimen of the enemy in the shape of four Swiss soldiers in scarlet, who were left behind by mistake in the prison;' and here he also learnt 'the French method of picking a lock, by putting the point of the bayonet into the keyhole, and then firing the musket with ball.'

9 'Sir' Nicolas Trant (1769–1839). Wellington referred to him after his death – a little unfairly, but probably accurately enough – as 'a very good officer, but as drunken a dog as ever lived'.

10 Several months later, Freire, fleeing before Soult's advance on Oporto, was recognised and held in protective custody at Braga, where a group of *ordenança* broke into the gaol and murdered him for his cowardice; not to be confused with the Spanish General Manuel Freire, who had commanded Spanish units at San Marcial, and later at Toulouse.

11 Had he been correctly informed of Loison's position, Wellesley might have intercepted his combination with Junot, now well on the way from Lisbon with the main army, or at least force him to make a long detour before doing so. Unfortunately, Wellesley had not been supplied with any map covering the Vimeiro area, although he had had the forethought to bring out with him a military survey of the vicinity of Lisbon, made in 1799 by General Sir Charles Stuart, and might have hoped to encounter Junot nearer the capital.

It would have been hazardous to have attacked Lisbon directly by sea, the banks of the Tagus estuary having been fortified by the French, who had also appropriated eight Russian warships lying at anchor there, and they could not be relied on to remain neutral. Any landing closer to the city would have risked being attacked before the expeditionary force had completely disembarked.

12 General D'Urban, when inspecting Peniche sixteen months later, noted that

nearly 100 heavy guns were still in position there and – perhaps with Corunna in mind – had suggested that it was perfect 'for the Embarkation of the British army, should it ever be necessary to do so in the Face of the Enemy'.

13 In the event, these troops, which had taken part in the abortive Baltic expedition, did not land until the 25th.

14 The subject is discussed in some detail by Brent Nosworthy in Chapter 10 of *Modern Studies of the War* ... (a supplementary volume to Greenhill's reprint of Oman's *History*, edited by Paddy Griffith.)

15 D'Urban, when visiting the battleground several months afterwards, maintained that it could 'never be sufficiently lamented that the British Army did not immediately march on Torres Vedras, – they would have infallibly preceded the Enemy, would have placed themselves between him and Lisbon, upon most favourable Ground, and from the confusion and dismay which prevailed in his Army, would have, without doubt, completed his destruction. The want of Cavalry alone appears to have saved the Right Column of the French from annihilation.'

16 Aged 58, he had sailed in from Gibraltar, where he had commanded the garrison.

17 The total British losses at Vimeiro were 720 men, of which 131 were killed, 534 wounded, and 51 missing: those of the French, about 2,000, including some 350 taken prisoner. Casualties at Roliça had been approximately 485 and 600 respectively.

18 Harris elsewhere emphasised, when referring to sergeant-majors, 'that command does not suit ignorant and coarse-minded men; and ... tyranny is too much used even in the brief authority which they have. A soldier ... is driven often to insubordination by being worried by these little-minded men for the veriest trifles, about which a gentleman never thinks of tormenting him. The moment the severity of the discipline of our army is relaxed, in my opinion, farewell to its efficiency, but for our men to be tormented about trifles (as I have seen at times) is often very injurious to a whole corps.

19 The only British material gain, apart from Junot's artillery, was 23 waggons of powder, shot, and shells, stores of all descriptions, and 20,000 rounds of musket ammunition.

20 Junot also accompanied Masséna's invasion of Portugal in the Autumn of 1810.

21 Already on the 1st, when writing home, Moore had declared, apropos Dalrymple: 'We are none of us satisfied with our Chief, who tho' as a man not without sense, is in no respect equal to the situation in which he has been placed. This is so marked, and is an opinion so universal, that I think it must have reached home, and must cause his removal.'

22 Not all were so lucky. Several boats turned turtle in the breakers, and men were drowned and washed up on the beach, where they were laid face downwards, with a hole dug below their heads, but 'although they were covered with hot sand and rubbed with it, it was impossible to rescusitate them,' which is not altogether surprising.

23 They still emit a piercing shriek when turning on their wooden journals.

24 Neale was given to understand that 'nothing could exceed the jealousy and hatred which existed between the different French general officers, especially Junot and Laborde, which is easily accounted for. Laborde was lieutenant-colonel of the regiment in which Junot served as a sergeant, at the commencement of the Revolution.'

[25] Junot – indignant that a mere frigate and not a line of battleship had been put at his disposal – had sailed two days earlier.

[26] He is possibly referring to the Royal Palace at Queluz.

[27] Canning proposed that the word humiliation should in future be spelt with a 'Hew'.

[28] Later Lieut-Colonel Wilkie, when contributing to Maxwell's *Peninsular Sketches*.

[29] Lieut-Colonel Lord John Proby, later 2nd Earl of Carysfort.

[30] Neale testified that they had also melted down and minted much of their spoil, and as the export of specie (money in the form of coins rather than notes) was permitted by an article in the Convention, by converting church-plate into French crowns and Napoleon *d'or*, they thus eluded detection, an example of Gallic finesse rarely surpassed.

[31] It now hangs in the Museu de Arte Antiga, Lisbon.

[32] It was then common practice, as endorsed by a General Order of 15 April 1807, that 'Women only in the proportion of Six to every Hundred Men will be permitted to embark. They should be carefully selected, as being of good Character and having the inclination and ability to render themselves useful; it is very desirable that those who have children should be left at home.' Among a variety of other occupations, they would be cooking, attending the wounded, laundrying and repairing uniforms, while on active service. Many would be widowed during the course of a campaign, some repeatedly, but few remained without a partner for long.

[33] River beds, when dry, were known as *ramblas.*

[34] George Ticknor, the American historian of Spanish literature, when first visiting the country a decade later, before any form of 'diligence service' had been set up, remarked that 'There was no travelling in Spain. Between Barcelona and Madrid, in a journey of thirteen days, we met only a few muleteers, a few carts, and one single coach like our own, only half a dozen in all; and yet the road was the main highway between the capital and one of the principal cities of the kingdom'; but it had long been so. Major William Dalrymple, travelling in the Peninsula while on leave from the Gibraltar garrison in 1774, setting out from Ponferrada for Galicia, had remarked on the road being 'very bad' after having 'travelled on a new road for about two miles, which is intended to be carried to the sea,' adding: 'And here I must observe, that except at La Carolina in the Sierra Morena, and for a few leagues about Madrid, I have never seen any made [ie surfaced] roads. There are no heavy carriages in the country I have passed, otherwise it would be impossible, particularly in winter, for them to travel. Left the Camino Real [the Royal Road], and came into an abominable road, but extremely pleasant on the banks of a most refreshing stream, the mountains rising on each side of us … began to ascend the mountain, the road like steps of stairs.'

[35] This will be obvious to anyone studying a modern contoured map, but at the time only the grossly inadequate provincial maps of Spain by Tomas Lopéz (published in 1765 onwards), Cassini's extensive series covering France, many up-dated between 1798 and 1812), or those of the État-Major were available and to hand. Few of them gave little more than a very rough representation of the terrain, as with Mentelle and Chanlaire's map (published by *Stockdale* on 13 October 1808), or Arrowsmith's map of 1809, based on Roussel and La Blottière's of the Pyrenees (1730), with addition from López and Topino de

San Miguel's work – unfortunately the latter's chart of the coast stopped at the French frontier, and did not cover St Jean-de-Luz or Bayonne. Even Cassini's could not be relied upon; nor that of the Peninsula by Jasper Nantiat, published by Faden on 1 January 1810, one which deserved 'to be burned by the public hangman,' in the opinion of General Graham.

36 The construction of dams has caused some earlier beds to change, while variations in their levels and velocities have made it difficult to ascertain the exact position of former fords.

37 A paragraph from General Dumouriez's *An Account of Portugal, as it appeared in 1766*, translated into English in 1797 – containing several chapters of interest concerning their army, few of which can have been read by the British military establishment of the time – may be aptly quoted here, although written when the Portuguese expected to be invaded by their neighbour rather than by the French: 'The Portuguese soldier is obedient, patient, robust, lively, and dextrous; but he is, at the same time, idle, filthy, and disposed to find fault with every thing; but he is capable, when properly attended to, of doing credit to his character. His aversion to the Spaniards should be encouraged, but he should be made to comprehend, that he cannot gain any advantage over the superior numbers of that nation, but by superior discipline. The mutual contempt which these nations entertain for each other, arises from their ignorance, and their presumption. It is very extraordinary, when it is their mutual interest to know each other, that their reciprocal aversion should operate so powerfully as to prevent any useful communication between them. Hence it is that a war between Spain and Portugal, will consist of little more than groping about in the dark, because neither the one nor the other have maps, or guides, or spies.'

2

October 1808 to February 1809: Moore's advance into Spain, and his death at Corunna

Schaumann records that on 9 October 'an order suddenly appeared that we were to hold ourselves in readiness. This brightened the spirits of the army, and roused its fighting ardour, for the long spell of idleness in camp had made everybody rather ill-tempered.' Troops began to move off ten days later, at the rate of a division a day.[1] At the eleventh hour, Schaumann was informed that he had been appointed commissary to the 32nd Regiment, with orders to escort a convoy of 200 bullock carts, laden with ammunition.[2] It was no use complaining that he had 'no office, no assistant, no map, no statistical and topographical description of the country'. A few days later he was summoned to appear before Sir John Moore himself, who asked how everything was going, what he thought of the spirit of the Portuguese troops he had met en route, and of their provisioning, and what were the the methods of victualling the regiments in these parts (presumably referring to Portuguese logistic procedures). Unfortunately, Schaumann does not tell us what he answered.

Leaving some 10,000 men – including invalids and malingerers – in Lisbon, under the command of General Sir John Cradock, Moore led approximately 22,000 into Spain, where he would be joined by General Sir David Baird, with 8,000 infantry and 3,000 cavalry commanded by General Sir Henry Paget,[3] who was sailing from Falmouth for Corunna:[4] the two forces would eventually converge on Salamanca.

William Jacob, when visiting Cadiz in the following September, by which time some improvement in the initial disorganization of the Spanish administration might have been expected, had commented that 'Complaints of inactivity, selfishness, inability, and intriguing spirit of the members of the [Supreme] Junta [at Cadiz] are universal.'[5] For example, while an arms factory had been established, after 'more than fourteen months since the commencement ... not a single musquet

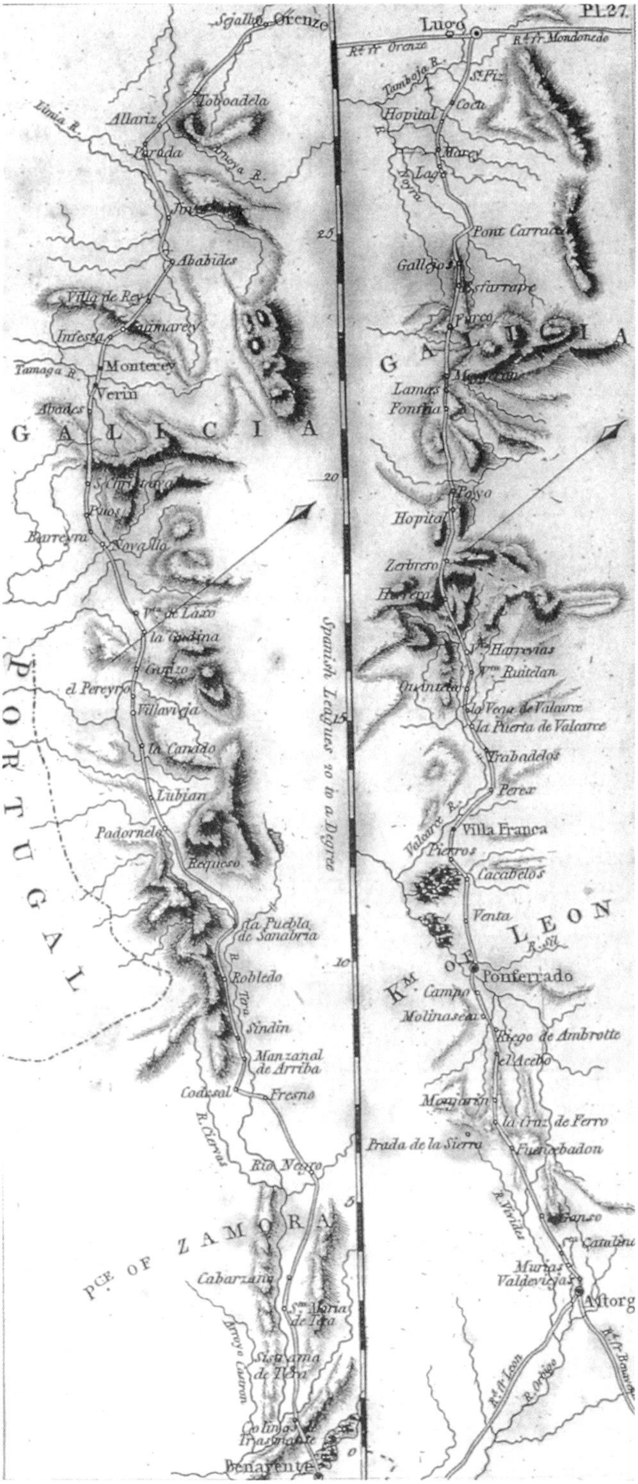

Two itineraries, one of whch shows the road between Astorga and Lugo, from Alexander de Laborde's *A View of Spain; comprising a descriptive itinerary of each province,* etc. (1809). The original French edition was published in 1807 as *Itinéraire descriptif de l'Espagne.*

has yet been produced. They are erecting a handsome building, when plenty of others might have been appropriated to the purpose ...'

Moore had divided his army into four. Two brigades under Beresford were ordered to Almeida via Coimbra and Celorico by what proved to be the least bad road;[6] on which the others (with one battery only) would converge, marching via Abrantes and Guarda. Moore followed in the wake of the latter. General Edward Paget, having separated from General Sir John Hope at Elvas, had crossed the Tagus by the Roman bridge at Alcántara, and then the Puerto de Perales to Ciudad Rodrigo. It was not until 13 November that Moore's vanguard entered Salamanca,[7] but another ten days passed before his rearguard caught up.

Leaving units in Catalonia out of his calculations, Moore had reckoned that there were only about 80,000 French troops in Spain, little suspecting that during the first week of November Napoleon himself had entered the Peninsula from Bayonne at the head of several veteran corps: 250,000 bayonets and sabres altogether, his vanguard reaching Madrid only days later. Between 31 October and 23 November, every Spanish army ranged along the line of the Ebro, with whom Moore had been invited to co-operate, was being defeated or dispersed in detail by Marshal Jourdan.

Meanwhile, Moore, misguidedly believing both Portuguese and Spaniards – utterly ignorant of the lie of their own land – who had advised him that artillery would find it impossible to traverse a more direct road,[8] had sent Hope, with 3,000 infantry, 1,000 cavalry, and 24 guns, from Elvas to Almaraz and up the Tagus valley almost to the gates of Madrid. It was not until 28 November that Hope's rearguard had crossed the Guadarrama pass (north-west of the Spanish capital); and providentially, unaware that only two days earlier a troop of Napoleon's Polish light horse,[9] supported by infantry, had forced the Puerto de Somosierra, and scattered some 12,000 Spanish troops attempting to defend it.[10] The latter had then proceeded to pillage every place through which, precipitately, they had fled.

Among those following Moore's army was Adam Neale. He had skirted the right bank of the Tagus, at Punhete (now Constância) crossing the Zêzere to reach hill-top Abrantes in torrential rain. On passing to the opposite bank, he had pressed east through 'forests of magnificent cork-trees [while] the valleys are covered with the strawberry tree, the aromatic cistus, great quantities of myrtles, honeysuckles, and wood-roses.' The countryside was attractive enough, but Neale found the weather 'particularly unpleasant, from the want of glass in the windows; you must, therefore, either permit the rain to beat into the room where you sit, or close the folding doors of the windows, which are intended to serve as shutters, leaving open a small wicket about eight inches square, to admit a few rays of light. In some rooms you find a trellis-frame or *jalousies*, which answers the purpose rather better, admitting more light, while it excludes the moisture.' Many officers, he had noticed, had brought their wives with them: 'what a situation for women!'

After Nisa, the road deteriorated. 'The wains employed in carrying our ammunition were broken down in all directions. A sergeant of the royal artillery, with a party of men, had been left to bring them on, but had found great difficulty in procuring oxen and waggons'. Neale descended steeply to the narrows of the Tagus at Vila Velha (merely a few miserable hovels, but an important place of communication throughout the war), there ferried over in a flat-bottomed boat. The road ahead was strewn with shattered wheels and disabled carriages which, cutting into a nearly perpendicular strata of 'granitic schistus, with veins of quartz,' had formed ruts 'at least three or four feet deep.' Robert Blakeney described the hazards of hauling ahead the six light six-pounder guns, the first of which was conveyed across with 'two drag-ropes attached, and to resist its rapidity while being trailed downhill these ropes were held by as many soldiers as the short and frequent turning of this zigzag descent would permit; yet the resistance was scarcely sufficient to preserve the guns from rolling over the precipice. This in a great measure arose from Captain Wilmot having opposed locking any of the wheels, alleging that by doing so the carriages would suffer materially ... [it] was excessively laborious ... and not unattended with danger. Several men who could not get clear of the ropes on suddenly coming to the sharp turns were absolutely dragged through the walls which flanked the road ... I can attest that there was not one soldier of the 28th Light Company who had heels to his shoes after the drag.' To cross the Tagus itself, 'the horses of two or three guns [were] harnessed to one gun at a time, and in this manner passed the remainder of the guns in succession across the stream, cheered by the whole of the men during the entire operation, which lasted a considerable time ... the soldiers [gave] what assistance lay in their power, in case of meeting obstacles in the bed of the river. The horses were immersed above their bellies and the men up to their middles; yet Captain Wilmot never quitted the stream, crossing and re-crossing until all the [six] guns were safely landed.'

Schaumann, traversing the same road, was incensed to find no brandy in Vila Velha, which might have cheered both the troops and bullock-drivers, the excuse being that the French had plundered the place already. Once shelters were found, rations distributed, and fires lit, he joined Colonel Hinde, the major, the adjutant, and the paymaster over a glass of mulled wine. They were calmly sitting and smoking their cigars when the sergeant-major burst in to report that the whole regiment, including the guard and picket, was 'dead drunk,' for the local authority had prevaricated, and in their search for water, ten casks of strong brandy had been discovered by some men, with which camp kettles had been rapidly filled. Naturally, those caught distributing it red-handed were placed under arrest, to be severely flogged next morning.

Passing through Castelo Branco, the rain-lashed route ran north to Guarda, where the regiments were cantoned in convents. The first Spanish village entered was Fuenteguinaldo, on the road to Ciudad Rodrigo. Many commented on the differences noticed when crossing from Portugal. Schaumann felt that although the houses were 'kept extremely clean,' and the natives wore 'a national dress which is at once dramatic and picturesque,' they were disobliging in comparison to their friendly neighbours: 'Everyone here is grave, monosyllabic, and gloomy;' and when shown to his billet, not a soul asked whether he wanted anything to eat or drink. For Blakeney, both were equally generous, the difference being that Portuguese hospitality may have been due to 'some obligation ... not unmixed with gratitude,' which the taciturn Spaniards were too proud to admit.

* * *

A month earlier, on 14 October, Lady Holland with her hispanophile husband and their entourage had disembarked at Corunna, intending to take the road to Madrid. Her *Journal* records that even before they had landed, Admiral de Courcy, the naval commander there, on coming aboard to welcome them, 'confirmed the stories we had heard of the unwillingless of the Spaniards too receive our troops.' Most of General Baird's contingent had sailed in on the previous day, but they were not given formal permission to disembark until the 26th. At least, the Junta agreed to lend Baird some 92,000 dollars in hard cash while awaiting the arrival of a consignment of coin from London, for most Spaniards, anticipating prompt payment, were reluctant to accept British Government bills.

Quartermaster William Surtees was soon to experience the defectiveness of the commissariat, for 'the gentleman sent forward to provide our two battalions with food, was so utterly unacquainted with his business, that he was actually afraid to make an attempt to issue provisions,' with the excuse that he did not understand the system of weights and measures used by the Spanish who had been baking bread for them.[11] The accommodation provided on their progress through Galicia was Spartan:[12] officers might find lodging in private houses or cells of monasteries, but the rank and file had no alternative but to lie on straw in the corridors 'as close as pigs in a sty, which was indeed necessary to keep each other warm,' a plight 'not to be complained of, as clean straw, and shelter overhead in that country, are no contemptible quarters.'

Baird's conduct in setting off for Astorga with three brigades of infantry without a word to Lord Paget, surprised Lady Holland, but secretiveness and irresolution appear to be traits of his character.[13] Paget's mounts, landing between the 7th and 12th of November, were in a parlous state, as she confirmed on the 19th (the Hollands were then on the road to Lugo, there being turned back): 'The horses, after 7 weeks confinement on a ship … plunged into the sea to be swum ashore in a state of fever, have of course suffered severely, especially in their feet; besides the change of food from oats and hay to chopped straw and maize has effected their health. Seventeen were left at Betanzos.[14] For want of horses to convey it forward, a large train of artillery were left waiting there, although 'a commissary has been employed above a month to procure the means …' In Lady Holland's opinion, 'the service would be greatly benefited by the dismissal of the whole *commissariat*; the artillery lags behind, and the men are distressed frequently for want of provisions. No army can endure privation from food and no one is more liable to it than the English, entirely from the ignorance and unskilful management of the commissaries. Between Coruña and Lugo a number of men were 36 hours totally unprovided with food, and for two days another division had not received their ratio of wine.' She went on to comment that on 25 November De Courcy, 'Under the strictest seal of secrecy … revealed some very unpleasant circumstances' to her.[15]

Paget admitted to the Hollands that not only was he apprehensive of the possible lack of proper forage for his mounts, but thought it probable that the French would attempt to prevent the junction of the two British armies.[16] While in theory it was rash to have divided them, in the field it was often impossible to keep them together, due to the duplicity and time-serving propensities of Spanish *juntas*, repeatedly displaying their incapacity to provide the supplies promised.[17]

Major Edwin Griffith (15th Hussars), had not been impressed on disembarking at Corunna by 'the *general appearance* of the natives,' and as for the women, they 'have sallow complexions, bad legs & worse teeth; the men are equal in point of *beauty* with the addition of a discontented & suspicious look, & both dress very ill. So much for the Dons & Donnas at present. I *hope* they may *improve* upon acquaintance but *fear* I can *never like them*. I *live* on shore but *sleep* onboard my ship in preference to a lousy, filthy, buggy, Spanish bed which I must turn into as soon as she quits the harbour.'

On reaching Salamanca, Moore complained to Bentinck that the Junta of Galicia had promised Baird 'every thing, but give nothing; and after waiting day after day for carts, which they had promised to procure for the carriage of stores, his Commissary was at last obliged to contract for at an exorbitant price, and then got them.'

From Astorga, D'Urban sent a message to Corunna telling Colonel Robert Craufurd that he must not expect any mules, the Governor having commandeered them all for the Spanish armies. It is not known whether or not D'Urban informed Moore, when meeting him on 12 November, that the road between Becerrea and Villafranca allowed 'no passage for an Army but in one Column ... and the Country, however beautiful, affords no subsistence to be depended upon.' On the following day D'Urban reached Almeida, where Anstruther ordered him to investigate the country on both banks of the Côa, remarking: ''tis just possible that this may become the Winter Quarters of the Army, and 'tis right therefore that its resources, Roads of communication both with Portugal and Spain, and its natural features of defence should be at least generally known to him.' This he did, reporting back on 3 December, when told that orders had been sent to Baird to retire on Corunna. D'Urban was then instructed 'to mark out Cantonments for the whole Army within the line of the Côa ...', while five days later he was ordered to reconnoitre both banks of the Agueda, and then the district south of Castelo Branco and between Alcántara and Abrantes, and 'to order a strong working Party of the Companies of the Buffs at C. Branco to repair such parts of the Road to Villa Velha' as he then thought necessary.[18] At Castelo Branco, D'Urban met Colonel Rufane Donkin, Murray's D.Q.M.G., 'who, with many Staff Officers [was] engaged in making a very extensive reconnaissance of the Tagus and its Banks,' all of which implies that it was Moore's original intention to fall back upon Portugal, not on the Galician coast.[19]

* * *

Neale was one of many concerned about the scrape in which they were in, writing from Salamanca on 26 November: 'since my arrival here, I have witnessed so much apparent apathy and indifference, that I feel the most serious apprehension of the result. Indeed I cannot help, at times, asking myself if I am really in the midst of Spain. The beings I see muffled up in long cloaks, sauntering here in listless indolence under the piazzas, are so different from the bold impassioned race, which the heated imagination had been contemplating ... you would imagine the country was in a state of profound peace; no energy, no bustle, no alacrity.' An Irishman, Dr O'Leary, who had lived thirty-five years among them, had warned a friend of Neale's not to trust the Spaniards too much, although he believed that they meant well, adding:

> as to their army ... I have watched its progress, and know it well: when they have muskets, they generally want cannon; if they have powder, they are often without flints; if they are well fed, then they are naked; if they get shoes, they want a loaf of bread; if the soldiers would fight, the officers are unwilling; and when the generals wish to have an engagement, the men are sure to run away. In short, my dear countryman, such is the Spanish army, and what, in the name of wonder, can I expect from them now? Only this: that they will leave you to your fate, to get back to your ships as fast as you can; and you can think yourselves very fortunate, if in the way they do not put their knives into your men, whom they already denominate a pack of miserable heretics; and curse for their unasked assistance, in entering their magnificent country.

Such was the unenviable position in which Moore had hardly anticipated finding himself, however sceptical some of his superiors in London may have been when surveying the rosy picture presented by both the Spaniards and their own political representative, John Hookham Frere. Moore's situation looked simple enough on a map,[20] but the military establishment can have had scant knowledge of the rough terrain through which his forces were to march, of the severe climate in the elevated, frost-bound, Castilian *meseta* or the snow-clad Galician mountains at that season. On a scorching summer day, a lone rider cantering across a plain would raise a cloud of dust seen for miles; but in winter, lashed by freezing rain, a dry *rambla* could turn into a raging torrent within a few hours; while in toiling up mountain roads, men would have their boots sucked off their feet in what had rapidly become a morass.

Moore's predicament was far more serious than he realised. Any idea of withdrawal aroused great indignation among the Spaniards, both civil and military, who maintained resolutely that Madrid would resist to the end, insisting that if only Moore would attack their main line of communication, the French would be obliged to fall back to protect it, allowing the whole of the south of Spain to rally: nothing could then stop them from expelling the intruder. Moore was less sanguine, becoming increasingly aware that retreat would be inevitable; but on the other hand, now that Hope's units had joined his (which they had done on 3 December), such a stroke against the enemy flank might possibly be effective.

Baird, even more out of humour with the Spaniards than Moore, and all for retiring before it was too late, had been instructed to withdraw to the coast (his vanguard having reached Villafranca by 6 December), when the order was countermanded. Writing from León on 30 November, La Romana, the only Spanish general within reach, suggested to Moore that they co-operated, as he now commanded a considerable force. This was most encouraging, [21] for, as he replied (6 December): 'Since my arrival in Spain, I have been put in no communication with any of the Spanish Armies, and have been kept perfectly in the dark with respect to their movements, the plans of their Generals, or their Government – and during the time my army was on its march to assemble and unite itself, I have been left exposed without the least support, [concluding]: My wish is to unite with you; and to undertake with you such operations as we may judge best for the support of Madrid, and the defeat of the Enemy.'

On the 11th, Moore set out from Salamanca for Toro, where, as Neale had noticed, although the locals had been collecting with loud shouts around a house in which some prisoners were lodged, hardly a week had elapsed since 'they permitted a party of ten or twelve French dragoons to parade through their streets, and then depart without a single shot having been fired at them, although there are at least six thousand inhabitants in the place. So much for the courage of the natives.' Yet when another cavalry patrol entered and remained several hours in nearby Tordesillas, which Lord Proby was reconnoitering, although everyone knew he was hiding there, not a soul betrayed him, all testifying their satisfaction on his reappearance, declaring that though they had no arms they would rather have died than have allowed him to be taken.

Ever since leaving Salamanca, Neale had been astonished by the want of comfort and misery in which the peasantry lived:

> Their clothes and linen ragged and threadbare; their persons shockingly filthy; houses nearly unfurnished; and their food consisting almost entirely of an execrable mess, called *gaspacho*, which they eat thrice a day. This is a mixture of vinegar, garlick, lamp-oil, and Cayenne pepper, mixed with boiling water, poured over a dishful of bread. Once a week (on Sundays that is) they allow themselves, as a rarity, a bit of bacon or a sausage ... Their chief fuel consists of chaff or chopped straw, thrown over a few twigs; and, as they are unacquainted with the luxury of a pair of bellows, they are obliged to be eternally on their knees, blowing up the embers, if they happen to have any pot or jar on the fire; for they have almost no cooking utensil that is not of earth. Now and then you see a copper ladle, which is scoured very bright, and hung against the wall for an ornament. Knives, forks, and spoons are rare articles.

Neale followed the cavalry north-east towards Mayorga. Although it was snowing heavily, the natives of several mud-built villages turned out to stare at the troops as they passed, regarding them 'with a degree of stupid wonder, without speaking, huzzaing, or giving any external token, either of satisfaction or discontent. When asked the road, they slowly disengaged their arms from the drapery of their cloaks, and pointed or waved their hands in the direction, but never offered to assist our guides.'

Madrid had fallen to the French on 4 December, but six days passed before Moore was aware of this news, and then only after John Waters, scouting near Valdestillas (south of Valladolid), secured a dispatch addressed to Soult confirming that Napoleon already occupied the capital.[22] Fortuitously, on the 13th another dispatch was intercepted, stating that not only were enemy units marching west towards Badajoz to cut off his retreat on Lisbon, but that Marshal Soult, with a comparatively weak force of 12,000 men, was intending to advance on Benavente from his position on the river Carrión, north-west of Palencia.

Three days later, Moore received a dispatch from the Supreme Junta to the effect that La Romana, near León, would be joining him with 14,000 'picked men' of his force of 22,000; he therefore ordered La Romana – who, in the event, could only muster about 7,000 or 8,000 effectives – to move against Soult. Baird was ordered to march towards Mayorga, on which Moore converged, their forces uniting on the 20th.

Sahagún

Henry Paget, learning that two regiments of Soult's dragoons were stationed at Sahagún (north-east of Mayorga), hoped to surprise them by a night advance through thick snow. At daybreak, although outnumbered, they charged into the French deploying east of the town on the alarm having been raised. Capt. Alexander Gordon (15th Hussars) described the shock as terrible:

> Horses and men were overthrown, and a shriek of terror, intermixed with oaths, groans, and prayers for mercy, issued from the whole extent of their front. Our men, although surprised at the depth of their ranks, pressed forward until they had cut their way quite through the column. In many places the bodies of the fallen formed a complete mound of men and horses, but very few of our people were hurt. Colonel Grant, who led the right centre squadron, and the Adjutant who attended him ... were both wounded – the former slightly on the forehead, the latter severely in the face. It is probable neither of them would have been hurt if our fur caps had been hooped with iron like those of the French Chasseurs,[23] instead of being stiffened with pasteboard ... [while the] appearance of their heavy dragoons was extremely martial and imposing; they wore brass helmets of the ancient Roman form, and the long black horsehair streaming from their crests as they galloped had a very fine effect. Having rode together nearly a mile, pell-mell, and slashing each other ... I overtook and halted those who were the farthest advanced in the pursuit.

The French were dispersed and a deal of plunder collected, 'as the prisoners were well supplied with many trinkets and ingots of silver, the produce of plate stolen ... and melted to render it more portable.[24] Many of their valises contained fans and parasols – rather extraordinary articles of equipment for a winter campaign. General Debelle lost his baggage and horses; we also got possession of the papers belonging to the staff ...'

From Sahagún, Moore's intention, after resting his troops for 48 hours, was to attack Soult main force between Carrión and Saldaña, but intelligence was received during the early evening of the 23rd that a massive French concentration, led by Napoleon in person, was moving against him. Without procrastination, orders were countermanded, and his leading brigades, already tramping east on frozen roads, found themselves inexplicably turned back.[25] By then, the British commanders were amply disillusioned concerning the Spanish nation and character. On that same day Paget was prompted to pen a private letter to Lord Holland from Sahagún, disabusing him of his misplaced optimism:

> *Tis not worth saving*: Such ignorance, such deceit, such apathy, such pusillanimity, such cruelty, was never both united. There is not one army that has fought at all. There is not one general who has exerted himself, there is not one province that has made any sacrifice whatever. There is but one town [Zaragoza] in all Spain that has shown an atom of energy. We are treated like enemies. The houses are shut against us. The resources of the country are withheld from us; we are roving about the country in search of Quixotic adventures to save our own honor, whilst there is not a Spaniard who does not skulk and shrink within himself at the very name of a Frenchman. I am with an army the finest in the world in numbers, enthusiastic, equal to every exertion, burning to engage. I have been one of the most strenuous advisors to advance and to take our chance. But why have I done so? For my own sake, for that of my comrades in arms, for the honor of the British army, not, believe me, not in the smallest degree for the Spaniards.

Informed that Moore had quitted Salamanca, Napoleon announced: 'Moore is the only General now worthy to contend with me. I shall move against him in person'. Next day, the 22nd, he led 50,000 men and 150 guns over the Guadarrama pass in a blizzard, intent on capturing the insignificant British army entire: his generals could finish off any residual Spanish resistance at leisure. But by the time he had reached Tordesillas (67 miles south of Sahagún) on the 26th, the bird had flown. On facing Benavente, Napoleon, thoroughly frustrated, and to save face, ordered Soult to carry on the pursuit: he had far more urgent matters to attend to in Paris.

The Retreat

Moore had made his decision, however incomprehensible it may have been to his troops. A rapid retreat was now the only possible way to extricate his army from its perilous position. He should have followed the dictates of his intuition earlier, and ignored both the specious Spanish promises, and Frere's provocative dispatches. Baird, with 7,000 men would march west and cross the Esla by ferry at Valencia de Don Juan,[26] while Hope and Fraser's divisions were ordered south-west towards the Castrogonzalo bridge, spanning the Esla near Benavente. Two light brigades under Edward Paget, would form the rearguard, reinforced by Henry Paget's hussars. At Mayorga, half way to Benavente, the latter dispersed enemy cavalry in another successful action, taking 100 prisoners.[27] Skirmishing took place throughout the evening of the 27th and next day near the Castrogonzalo bridge, where Craufurd's brigade had taken up defensive positions to keep the increasing body of French cavalry at bay while working parties were preparing to demolish it.[28]

Benavente was ransacked: Spanish property could no longer hope to be respected by their Allies, aggravated by the fact that its inhabitants had stubbornly refused them provisions. Men of the 52nd, benumbed with cold, were denied wine by the prior of the convent in which they were billeted; but Lieut. Love was not easily imposed upon.[29] As Schaumann had acidly commented on entering the castle:

> What the English soldier cannot see any purpose in does not interest him. Everywhere bayonets and nails were stuck into the beautifully decorated walls, and knapsacks and cartridge boxes were hung upon them. In the large fireplaces, decorated with marble, there burned huge fires, kept alive with broken pieces of antique furniture, either gilt or artistically carved; and the same thing was going on in the courtyard, where the walls were all black with smoke. On these fires stood a number of camp kettles. The soldiers' wives were washing their things and hanging them just where they chose. A good deal was wantonly destroyed, and every corner was scoured for hidden treasure. The English soldier, who was now quite well aware that he had been lured into this country and into a parlous position by the Spaniards under false pretences, and that they had been left in the lurch ... set about burning everything out of revenge. It was a good thing, though, that he wreaked his vengeance on inanimate objects, and not on the inhabitants … The officers ... enraged by their men's lust of destruction and desecration, seemed crushed with grief, and did all in their power to limit the damage ... but the numbers were too much for them, and the hidden corners too numerous … Besides, insubordination was already apparent … and in spite of all the discipline, it was impossible to stop it in an army which already felt that it was retreating from a country it hated.[30]

The broken bridgehead had not deterred the cavalry of the Imperial Guard from plunging into the river, only to be thrust back by Paget's hussars, leaving 55 casualties and 70 prisoner, among them General

Lefebvre-Desnoëttes.[31] On reaching the far bank, they received several rounds of well-directed shrapnel by Downman's horse-battery as a parting shot. 'The sword work during this cavalry *mêllée* is said to have been terrible,[32] and our Germans [the 3rd Hussars K.G.L.] are believed to have been mad with rage,' reported Schaumann: 'Most of the enemy's wounded had their arms cut off, and in many cases their upper limbs hung from their shoulders merely by a shred of their uniforms.'

While this carnage was taking place, Schaumann was busy distributing rations from the depot: 'opening cases, boxes and barrels, and laying out their contents – salt meat, biscuits, boots, shirts, collars, stockings, or the most magnificent English woollen blankets. Scarcely had we done this than almost the whole army came along, regiment by regiment, and each man was allowed to take what he liked and as much as he could carry.' While the bulk of the remaining stores were burned and casks of rum poured away, the peasantry gathered round to snatch what they could. Leaving the rabble to amuse themselves, 'eating, drinking, raving, shouting, quarrelling and destroying', Schaumann crept away softly 'like a fox from a dovecot', fed his horse, rested briefly, and galloped off towards La Bañeza, there starting a routine which was to keep him fit:

> I kept my great coat tightly rolled up the whole day on my saddle, and let the rain soak me as much as it liked. Then when I came under shelter, I opened my valise, put on my only dry suit of clothes, some woollen socks – for I had thrown away all superfluous things in order to lighten my poor horse's load – and a pair of slippers, and rolling myself in my cloak which had kept dry, I got close up to the fire, and was able to laugh at the others ... Finally, I would hang my wet clothes before the fire, produce some chocolate, and cook it with wine and a little pimento and sugar ... eat a few ship's biscuits, and lay myself in my horse blankets on the bare ground and sleep splendidly. On the following morning I would take my dry clothes off, and would often put my other clothes on when they were still either wet or damp, for if one moves about in them it does not hurt one.

At dawn he was told to take in charge a herd of bullocks and drive them ahead: students escaping from Salamanca and joining the retreat could lend a hand; and absurd it was to see them running behind them with their black gowns flying in the air. Before long, the cattle, confined all night in corrals, ran off the stone highway to graze on what had the appearance of a green meadow, in fact a marsh, into which they sank either head or buttock-first; and nothing could stop the whole troop charging in likewise. When called to their aid, the men of an infantry division marching past merely laughed as they drew their knives and 'proceeded to cut from the haunches of these beasts whose hindquarters were uppermost ... large steaks and fillets of beef,' to the accompaniment of fierce bellowing. Schaumann needed little convincing that his duties had come to an end: unable to endure the 'harrowing sight,' he rode hastily away.

Moore retired north-west through Astorga, where accumulated stores were destroyed, although some arms were transferred to La Romana's virtually destitute troops, recently brushed aside by Soult at Mansilla de las Mulas (south-east of León), where they had left the Esla bridge intact.[33] In full retreat, they had swarmed into the town, already choked with British regiments converging on it.

Casks of rum were staved in, that they might not fall into the hands of the enemy. Although sad to see this waste, Surtees was disgusted by his companions 'determined not to lose all,' for when their contents ran 'in streams down the gutters, some of these brutes deliberately took off their greasy caps, and laving up the rum and mud together, drank, or rather ate, the swinish mixture.'[34] Blakeney refers to his regiment, which had just marched in to add to the chaos, as containing a 'band of ventriloquists who could imitate any species of bird or animal'. A soldier named Savage, on entering a room, would crow like a cock, and then place his ear to the keyhole of any locked doors leading off it. His crowings were often answered by others, revealing the existence of concealed poultry. Throughout the night these ventriloquists were loudly bleating, cackling, cooing, and lowing, their talents bringing animals of all descriptions 'frisking to their feet.' In his search for forage, Schaumann found the floor of a house 'full to the ceiling with rye', to the disappointmernt of the cavalry's quartermasters, for unlike oats or barley, rye purges horses: nevertheless, after some hesitation, it was scooped up into sacks from the street, although thousands of bushels, scorned by the horses, were trampled over and wasted.

On the first day of 1809, Moore with his rearguard crossed the Manzanal pass north-west of Astorga. Rain had given way to flurries of snow on the flank of Monte Teleno, and from then on the weather deteriorated rapidly. Schaumann, riding ahead, recorded that 'in the mountains we came upon glaciers or roads which were so deep in snow and ice that the horses could not stand, and we were obliged to dismount. I passed by a number of glowing bivouac fires which, flaring up now and then, illuminated the wild, desolate, wintry scene ... The sausage I had had for supper made me feel dreadfully thirsty; and my horse, too, badly wanted a drink. But there was no water; everything was frozen hard. Both of us therefore ate the snow. I slept while walking, for the road was too steep and slippery to ride, and it was too cold to sit in the saddle.'

William Verner (7th Hussars) described their mounts as becoming jaded and unable to carry their riders, partly for want of shoes, and that on one morning 'there were no fewer than sixty left behind for this cause, the greater number of which were shot. One of my horses lost a shoe; by the greatest good fortune it was picked up. I always carried spare nails in the top of my cap; the difficulty was to get the shoe put on as none of our farriers were to be found.'

At Bembibre, the wine-vaults were too much of a temptation to those 'seeing in' the New Year. Hundreds of men, women and children were soon lying insensibly drunk in its snow-covered, wine-stained, streets. Any capable of getting to their feet were herded together by Paget's rearguard and sent forward, but little could be effected with men incapable of standing, let alone marching. Many showed their resentment at *not* being ordered to turn on the enemy by running riot and pillaging. Flogging ceased to have any deterrent effect. Blakeney described 'every door and window [being] broken, every lock and fastening forced. Rivers of wine ran through the houses and into the streets, where lay fantastic groups of soldiers (many with their firelocks broken), women, children, runaway Spaniards and muleteers, all apparently inanimate, except when here and there a leg or arm was seen to move, while the wine oozing from their lips and nostrils seemed the effect of gunshot wounds ... some lay senseless, others staggered ... savage roars ... were mingled with groans ...' Stragglers and those remaining in a state of stupifaction were indiscriminately butchered, regardless of sex, by the French dragoons hanging around the bedraggled skirts of the retreating army.

At Cacabelos, the Light Brigades of Craufurd and Alten (3,500 men), peeled off to make their way west to Vigo. Partly threading the valleys of the Sil and Miño, they pushed on through Orense – where provisions awaited them.[35] Surtees described their 'toilsome' cross-country march 'over high and inaccessible mountains, deeply covered with snow'; their shoes 'were nearly all worn out ... many travelling barefoot; and clothes ... ragged and filthy in the extreme,' although perhaps less so than in some of La Romana's units, who 'in their best days, are more like an armed mob.'

Once at Vigo, even those who had been 'shuffling along with sore and lacerated feet like so many lame ducks, now made an attempt to dance for joy ...' The convoy set sail on 21 January. Harris, stumbling down to the shore, using his rifle as a crutch, was one of the last to embark.[36] As he recollected it: 'Fearful of being left half blind in the lurch, I took off my cap, and placed it on the muzzle of my rifle as a signal, for I was totally unable to call out. Luckily Lieutenant Cox, who was aboard the boat, saw me, and ordered the men to return, and making one more effort, I walked into the water, and a sailor stretching his body over the gunwale, siezed me as if I had been an infant, and hauled me on board. His words were characteristic of the English sailor, I thought: "Hollo there, you lazy lubber!" he said, as he grasped hold of me, "who the hell do you think [you] is to stay humbugging [us] all day for such a fellow as you?"

* * *

On the 3rd, a spirited rearguard action took place near the bridge at Cacabelos, where Paget had taken up a strong defensive position, protected by hedges and stone walls, near which General Colbert, incautiously pushing forward his skirmishers, was shot through the head by Tom Plunkett of the 95th; their infantry were held up long enough for the main body of Moore's troops to extract itself from Villafranca.[37] Schaumann had found the town so crowded that he 'could hardly turn round in the place, and many regiments had to bivouac', but

> most of the mules and draft-bullocks and pack-horses seemed only to have lasted out up to this point, and now fell down and died ... The rations came to an end, but, amid the chaos that reigned, could ...[not] have been distributed. Fresh troops were always streaming in, the stores depots were also violently raided, and the commissaries were no longer able to perform their duties. In the end Villafranca was literally plundered, and the drunkenness which prevailed ... led to the most shameful incidents. Down by the river the artillery destroyed all their stores, and lighting big fires burnt all their ammunition waggons, which they broke up for the purpose. They also threw all their ammunition into the river. Several hundred horses, which could go no further, were led to the same spot and shot. Day and night we could hear the sound of pistol fire. Everything was destroyed. Discipline was at an end, and the officers were no longer heeded.

Any hams still hanging in the chimney smoke of his billet soon vanished. Although he had put aside a sausage to sustain him on the retreat, he awoke next morning to find that the *Jägers* lodged below, setting off well before dawn, had robbed him of it, together with his biscuits, one of his pistols, a bottle of rum, and his gloves, in addition to several things belonging to an officer of the 3rd Hussars sharing his room.[38]

As the snow-bound track ascended steeply along the flank of the narrowing Valcarse, conditions became progressively worse, exposure taking an increasing toll. Schaumann remembered entering a defile, into which

> all marched higgledy-piggledy or rather pushed each other forward through the darkness in one compact mass. Never shall I forget the heartrending cries of some wounded men, when their cart broke down, and they were deposited in a shed on the road and left behind ... [By dawn] many of the soldiers, worn out with hunger and fatigue, had fallen out of the ranks during this rapid march, and had flung themselves down in despair in the midst of the mud and filth on the side of the road ... he who still had something to eat, that he ate in secret, and then continued marching onward; the misery of the whole thing was appalling – huge mountains, intense cold, no houses, no shelter or cover of any kind, no inhabitants, no bread. Every minute a horse would collapse beneath its rider, and be shot dead. The road was strewn with dead horses, bloodstained snow, broken carts, scrapped ammunition, boxes, cases, spiked guns, dead mules, donkies and dogs, starved and frozen soldiers, women and children.[39]

Colonel Thomas Graham was able to save himself only by clinging to bushes when his mount stumbled over an edge during one wild night,[40] and many were flung down by violent gusts of freezing wind. At an earlier stage, Harris had seen the wife of a soldier named William McGuire lying in the snow when overtaken by labour who, much to his surprise, caught up with the regiment next morning, carrying their son in her arms; but many of the women and children perished in the rigours of the retreat. Schaumann saw one poor women 'sink up to her waist in a bog, whereupon, the mud and slime preventing her from rising, she fell, and the whole column marched over her.' Anyone unable to keep up, fell victim to the French.

On crossing the watershed Puerto de Pedrafita do Cebreiro, the road snaked across the hills, beyond Nogales [As Nogais] descending above the Rio Navia to reach what both Neale and Schaumann described as a three-arched bridge resembling an aqueduct uniting the sides of a deep ravine. Neale's hasty sketch[41] shows 'an engineer-officer, directing the operation of a party of pioneers and artificers, digging a mine for the destruction of the centre arch,' but although the sappers had 'bored two holes into the centre … preparing to blow it up', the operation failed. Finding the torrent being forded, Paget ordered back his men, in danger of being outflanked, which allowed an enemy column to cross 'in perfect order.' Blakeney described the heated altercation between Paget and the paymaster-general, who had demanding bullocks to replace his jaded beasts dragging ahead the 'treasure of the army,' on whom Paget had rounded: 'Pray, sir, do you take me for a bullock-driver or a muleteer …,' the tirade ending with 'ought to be hanged.' The kegs of specie, too heavy to carry, were disposed of by being hurled down adjacent precipices and dashed to pieces.[42]

On approaching Lugo, the troops requisitioned a train of fifty bullock-carts lumbering towards them loaded with stores and clothing intended for La Romana's army, including shoes, which were rapidly distributed. The Galician *Junta*, knowing perfectly well that the British were in retreat, had nevertheless sent it forward, oblivious to the fact that it could have fallen directly into enemy hands. Moore now sent word to Admiral Sir Samuel Hood (who had superseded De Courcy) to the effect that Corunna was now his destination, being closer than Vigo, from which the awaiting transports should sail north.

On the 6th, Paget's rearguard entered Lugo, where Moore, taking up a position with his right flank touching the unfordable river Miño, beat off a tentative attack by Soult's vanguard; but then, knowing that he would soon be outnumbered, they slipped away during a night of drenching rain after shooting foundered horses, destroying stores, and leaving bivouac fires burning.[43]

To emphasise the total breakdown in communications then evident, one paragraph only from D'Urban's *Journal* should be interposed here, written up on 8 January near Ciudad Rodrigo, after he had been shadowing the movements of Marshal Lefevre's Corps marching north from Placencia via the Puerto de Baños towards Salamanca: 'God knows for what reason, but the whole British Corps at Castello Branco have retreated to Abrantes, and this day a French officer, Aide-de-Camp to Marshal Berthier, has been brought in, and his arrival opens our eyes to events so unforeseen, and so unexpected, that if his account were not perfectly connected and circumstantial I should refuse all credit to it. The British Army has retreated to beyond Astorga, even beyond the Plain of El Vierzo, for the French advance posts were at Pontferrada upon the 3rd of this month! Great Heavens!'

D'Urban remained with Sir Robert Wilson's units near the Portuguese frontier, where the French were still weak.[44] On 24 January, he confirmed that letters had just been received from Cradock (unaware of Moore's movements except from reports), who had called back a brigade advancing on Almeida.[45] This had left Wilson unsupported and isolated in his attempts to sustain local resistance, although his troops might hold out in the Sierra de Francia, south of Salamanca. While space precludes any detailed narration of D'Urban's activities, one may mention that he met General Cuesta at Jaraicejo (north-east of Trujillo) on 7 March to discuss defensive measures in the area, in view off Victor's probably advance down the Tagus valley.[46] D'Urban conferred with Cradock on 10 April, and four days later accepted the post of Q.M.G. to Beresford, then stationed at Tomar. Wellesley landed at Lisbon twelve days later: see Chapter 3.

* * *

According to Graham, it was on the final stretch of the retreat on Corunna that the troops became thoroughly demoralized: 'very disorderly, the officers negligent: the whole army, with few exceptions, such as the Reserve, disorganized in the most disgraceful manner.' Stragglers were numerous: not too surprising, for Schaumann described their feet as 'swollen, frostbitten, and bleeding, from walking over roads which consisted chiefly of granite, quartz, or deep mud.' However, the weather improved, the countryside became more cultivated and food more plentiful on approaching Betanzos, where Paget's division fought their penultimate delaying action while more *materiel,* also intended for La Romana but never distributed, was destroyed. With no enemy dragoons in their immediate rear, Blakeney sensed that the troops

> showed a strong inclination to straggle anew … but a strong piquet was now sent to meet them … prick them forward and compel them to close upon the division. A guard was thrown across the road at the entrance to our position, through which all the stragglers must pass. Each man … had his pack and haversack taken off and closely searched; and all the money found upon them which it was fully ascertained could have been acquired by robbery only was collected in a heap and distributed among the men who never swerved from their colours … Brass candlesticks

> bent double, bundles of common knives, copper saucepans hammered into masses, every sort of domestic utensil which could be forced into their packs, were found upon them without any regard as to value or weight ... On this day upwards of fifteen hundred robust marauders, heavily laden with plunder, passed through the rearguard ...

On 11 January, after blowing up the bridge spanning the Mero at El Burgo – one of the few successful demolitions effected during the retreat – the vanguard tramped into Corunna; but it was not until the evening of the 14th that Hood's transports anchored in the bay and the embarkation commenced. As William Green, a private in the 95th, among the rearguard, recalled: 'We made fires and cooked our meat, took off our belts, sponged out our rifles, got a fresh supply of ammunition, took off our jackets and found plenty of vermin on our bodies, which in some cases had found their way into flesh as well as appearing outside. As knapsacks and razors were all thrown away, some of the older men had beards like Jews, not having shaved since the commencement of the retreat.'

Moore still commanded 14,800 men (including 1,800 of Leith's brigade, which had not yet seen action), and 9 six-pounders, but no effective cavalry to speak of. It was estimated that Soult might muster approximately 15,500 infantry, 4,500 cavalry, and 40 guns, but his troops were exhausted and – until finding half-destroyed provisions at Betanzos – had even less in their stomachs. Moore doubted whether Soult would be in any state to mount an attack until 16 January, which would give him time to embark those too wounded or prostrated by the march to fight; to discipline and re-animate his troops; and to feed, shoe and re-equip them from the depot, before placing them in defensive positions beyond the narrow neck of the peninsula on which Corunna stood: this should ensure an uninterrupted embarkation. All supplies and equipment impossible to carry away would be destroyed; seaward batteries were disarmed or spiked; those to landward, strengthened.[47]

Moore surveyed the future battleground on the 12th. Not having men enough to occupy the dominating heights of Peñasquedo further south, he had little alternative but to deploy them along a range of nearer but lower hills, among them Monte Mero, strewn with granite boulders, which would provide protection to his skirmishers.

Lieut. Basil Hall, coming ashore from the *Endymion* frigate, was pained to see the plight of the troops:

> Soldiers lay scattered about, wearied and dispirited, ragged in their dress and many of them sickly or rather broken down in appearance by the fatigue of the retreat. Most of their chins had been untouched by a razor for some days, perhaps weeks, while their hands and faces seemed rather less familiar with soap and water than with the smoke of their muskets and the charcoal of their cooking fires. The muskets were piled in pyramids along the ridge amongst the men, who were stretched on the ground fast asleep, not in any precise order, but within a few yards of the summit of the ridge. Many were sitting on the grass which covered the ground and looking in silence, with very wistful eyes, towards the ships. I asked one of the officers whether he thought anything could rouse the men up. In reply he said, with a very expressive smile and a slight nod of his head, 'You'll see by and by, Sir, if the French choose to come over'.

On the 13th, Schaumann was attending to the demands of three hussar quartermasters when suddenly the town was rocked by a violent explosion:[48] '... my windows flew open into our faces in a thousand pieces, the doors sprang open, the slates rolled from the roof, while I, who had been rocking myself in my chair and talking, was flung backwards by the gust of hot air that poured in at the window. Even the quartermasters, who believed a bomb had fallen in the room and burst, ducked under the table ... Pulling ourselves together, we stared at each other in dumb amazement, when the streets were suddenly filled with piteous cries. The whole population, particularly the women ... dashed out of their houses with despair written on their faces, and shouting like maniacs ...' As William Napier recalled: 'The earth trembled for miles, the rocks were torn from their bases, the agitated waters of the harbour rolled the vessels as in a storm, a vast column of smoke and dust, with flames and sparks, arose perpendicularly and slowly to a great height, where it burst, and then a shower of stones and fragments of all kinds, descending with a roaring sound, killed many persons who had remained too near the spot'.[49]

Once the dust had settled, Schaumann felt it was time to freshen himself up, and buy boots and socks, for his clothes were 'torn and caked with hard mud, my shirt hanging through my breeches, and my decayed socks are showing through my boots'. That he had a spare shirt was providential, for he had noticed that the majority of officers had lost everything. When not on duty, he haunted cafés and confectioners' shops, his evenings being spent 'laughing and joking in the company of ladies, and ... [in] drinking bouts with other officers.' This, despite of the 'pestilential stench of decomposition', for the 'artillery and cavalry horses [were] so weak, worn out, and lame,[50] that some of them dropped dead … their putrefying bodies, swollen by rain and sun, and bursting in places, are lying under the colonnades in front of the public buildings in the market place, on the quays about the harbour, and in the streets … the discharge of pistols, which are adding to their numbers, continues incessantly … Many of the cavalry officers … could not bring themselves to kill their horses … and they allowed them to run free.[51] And these noble animals, many of which are genuine blood horses, now roam about the town and eat the cabbage leaves they find in the gutters and in the refuse heaps. One of these poor brutes followed the boat which bore its master … to the transports, and twice swam like a dog from the shore to the ship; but it could not be taken on board.'

Moore's last communication – more like a private letter – written shortly before the battle, was eventually delivered to Castlereagh by his half-brother General the Hon. Charles Stewart,[52] who could also give a first-hand account of the tribulations the army had experienced. In it, he reiterated:

> ... had I followed my own opinion as a military man, I should have retired with the army from Salamanca. The Spanish armies were beaten; there was no Spanish force with which we could unite ... I was satisfied that no efforts would be made to aid us ... I was sensible, however, that the apathy and indifference of the Spaniards would never have been believed; that, had the British been withdrawn, the loss of the cause would have been imputed to their retreat; and it was necessary to risk this army to convince the people of England, as well as the rest of Europe, that the Spaniards had neither the power, nor the inclination, to make any efforts for themselves. It was for this reason that I marched to Sahagun. As a diversion it succeeded: I brought the whole disposable force of the French against this army, and it had been allowed to follow it, without a single movement made...to favour its retreat ... The people of the Gallicias, though armed, made no attempt to stop the passage of the French through their mountains. They abandoned their dwellings at our approach, drove away their carts, oxen, and every thing that could be of the smallest aid to the army. The consequence has been that our sick have been left behind; and when our horses and mules failed, which on such marches, and through such a country, was the case to a great extent, baggage, ammunition, stores, and even money, were necessarily destroyed or abandoned ...

Corunna

At about one o'clock on the 15th, according to Schaumann,

> the sound of sharp firing could be heard coming from the direction in which the armies stood, and the noise attracted a large number of people, who collected on the quays. From the windows of the house it was almost possible to get a view of the battlefield. At two o'clock the gunfire grew more fierce,[53] and it was quickly followed by the most terrific musketry fire, which veiled the heights and adjacent valleys with clouds of smoke. All the roofs, windows, balconies and ships' masts became black with spectators ... and I ran out of town in order to watch the fighting from the Santa Lucia height. It looked terrible. The whole valley was clouded with powder smoke, through which shone the flash of the guns and muskets ... Again and again we were able to see the English regiments quite plainly charging the French at the point of the bayonet, and with a loud cheer forcing them to run uphill under the protection of their guns.

Although one French attack had driven the British back through Elvina, supported by two battalions of Guards, Bentinck was able to retain hold of the neighbouring hill. The enemy cavalry had made little headway, hampered by a tangle of granite walls, and was held in check by Fraser.

It was at this point, as the sun was already sinking on that short winter day that Moore, watching the progress of the battle with Colonel Graham from a position of vantage north-west of Elvina, was hurled from his saddle by a round shot, which 'carried away his left shoulder and part of his collar-bone, leaving the arm hanging by the flesh'.[54] Graham galloped off to seek surgeons, while Hope was informed that the command had devolved on him. Moore was then carried further to the rear in a litter, soon blood-soaked, and laid on a mattress in what had served as the headquarters house; but the wound was mortal. Among his last few words to those gathered about him as life ebbed away were: 'You know I always wanted to die this way', and 'Are the French beaten?' As dusk fell, Major Colborne entered, to confirm that Lahoussaye's cavalry, attempting to break through the British right, had been brought to a halt by Paget, and that the enemy had been beaten at every point. Moore could only murmur: 'I hope my Country will do me justice.'

By six the firing had ceased. Unable to penetrate their centre or turn either of the British flanks, there was no point in prolonging the battle into the night: Soult retired, allowing his adversaries to re-assemble on the ground that they had formerly occupied. It was left to Hope to spike his few remaining guns and station strong picquets, while the troops, by brigades, left the field progressively, covered by Beresford's rear-guard nearer the town defenses. Schaumann recalled how the various units were about to enter the awaiting sloops when they were raked by fire from the hill of Santa Lucia.

> In a moment a man-o'war of seventy-four guns opened its portholes, and returning the French fire, bombarded the heights until the very harbour shook ... [but] with no effect, for the French were securely entrenched behind the rocks and only had to fire blindly among us in order to be sure of hitting at least one of our ships. All the transports immediately cut their anchors and began to get under way. They ran into each other, and damaged and smashed one another's bowpits, rigging and yards. Five ships which attempted to escape between the island of St Antonio and the Citadel got into such terrible confusion that one of them ran up on a bank ...was stranded, and had to be abandoned by its crew and blown up. Most of the transports sailed out of the harbour and made for the open sea, so that only the men-o'-war remained, and they had to take many thousands of troops on board.

Meanwhile, the 32nd was marched to adjacent rocky bay, where after floundering in the spray and forced to jettison their baggage, they were 'grasped by the mighty fists of the sailors, who were leaning overboard, and seized and dragged like sheep' to the safety of a three-master, where they were packed like sardines. The last to embark, next day, were units of Fraser's Division: by then the rest of the convoy was well out at sea, sailing for home.

Drinking water was in short supply, but Schaumann remembers 'a pailful of porridge or gruel, with a large lump of butter floating on the top of it' being left to be besieged by them next morning, followed at midday by 'peas and salt meat, with a portion of rum, which looked quite black, and at night we had a little hard cheese and some ship's biscuit.' They drove away care, forgetting their privations 'by playing cards in the cabin, where two or three whist parties were constantly engaged, or by going on deck and teasing a monkey belonging to the captain'. Their ship was luckier than many, for the wind was favourable, before which they drove direct to Portsmouth.

Some 28,000 men of Moore's original force of 33,000 were landed at harbours along the south coast of England, many belatedly, for many transports had been scattered by storms.[55] Blakeney described the 28th Regiment, part disembarking at Portsmouth, and part at

Plymouth, as presenting 'an appearance of much dirt and misery. The men were ragged, displaying torn garments of all colours; and the people of England, accustomed to witness the high order and unparalleled cleanliness of their national troops … and never having seen an army after the termination of a hard campaign, were horror-struck …'[56]

While the retreat was to cause widespread controversy in London, at least a high proportion of the entire British Army had been saved to fight again after what has been well-described as 'the Dunkerque of its day'. Whatever may have been the mistakes attributed to Moore and his officers, few could cavil at his courage and resource when extricating his men from the deplorable situation in which they were to find themselves, grossly ill-advised by both the military and civil authorities of his Allies, let alone Frere.

1 One officer has recorded that that all officers had to leave their baggage (which in his case included his books and drawings), together with their camp beds, in a warehouse at Lisbon, where they were subsequently destroyed in a fire.

2 The transport of the reserve ammunition was the responsibility of Richard Henegan, having been supplied by the Portuguese authorities with fifteen boats with which to convey it up the Tagus to Abrantes. However, due to their 'clumsy negligence, or want of proper information', they were unable to proceed beyond Santarem, where after running aground in the shallows, he was obliged 'to lay a forcible embargo on every small boat' plying the river, their peasant owners being obliged to discharge their cargoes on the banks. Onto 'one hundred and ninety-eight small craft … after tedious labour, the transfer of the Ordnance stores was effected by the thirty-second regiment, which had been selected to escort this valuable convoy' on to Abrantes. From there, it was shifted onto 'bullock wains'. On reaching Castelo Branco, by which time half the waggons had broken down, the 32nd was replaced by six companies of the Buffs, and it was not until 26 December that the convoy limped into Ciudad Rodrigo.

3 Later Marquess of Anglesey and Earl of Uxbridge.

4 To transport Moore's contingent to Corunna by sea was inadvisable in that stormy season; and it was highly unlikely that the Junta of Galicia could provision their combined forces.

5 Such litanies were all too frequent. Lord Londonderry later commented that 'On public and official reports, no confidence whatever could be placed,' while the 'supineness or treachery of the Supreme Junta became every day more conspicuous; and the duplicity of all the authorities with whom we were necessitated to confer, rose, at last, to a height which nothing could justify … Corps put down by the juntas as twenty or thirty thousand men, proved, when inspected by [our own] officers, to muster eight or ten; and of these ... perhaps one-half, or nearly one-half, might be provided with muskets.' In the summer of 1808 the Spanish regular cavalry, reputed to number 14,440 troopers, had only 9,526 mounts between them.

[6] Q.M.G. George Murray had sent officers ahead, several weeks earlier, to report on the condition of every route between Lisbon and the frontier, particularly those which were practical for artillery. There is evidence that, among others on his staff, Lieut.-Colonel Rodolphe de Willermin and Capt. Pierrepoint had been hard at work copying maps, and by 28 October had examined and reported on the roads between Coimbra and Almeida.

[7] General Blake had been defeated in the Cantabrian Mountains at Espinosa de los Monteros only two days previously, and some of his units later joined La Romana's troops. Capt. Birch R.A., who had been with Blake, reported that they had then been in great straights, without supplies for five days, their food being whatever they could find – 'wild goats and animals they could catch in the mountains' – and that this want of provisions contributed as much to their being forced to disband and disperse as to their reverse in the face of superior numbers. In his enthusiasm, Walter Savage Landor had taken part in these operations before returning to England in disgust at their failure.

[8] Although, many years later, Wellington is said to have agreed that, given the information concerning the state of Portuguese roads, Moore was quite right to have sent Hope on his roundabout route at the beginning of the campaign, but had he been commander-in-chief, in view of his experience in India and dealing with natives, he would have made certain that any information fed to him by both Spaniards and British representatives was correct before relying on it in any way. And yet, had there not been a convenient road, how would Almeida have been supplied with guns previously.

[9] Despite assertions to the contrary, the Poles had not yet been supplied with lances.

[10] As the crow flies, the Somosierra pass lies only 40 miles north-east of the Puerto de Guadarrama.

[11] Lady Holland found the bread, 'except at Santiago, quite execrable … gritty from a mixture of sand and filth, heavy and brown,' and the salt 'brown and foul.' She also refers to countrywomen on the roadside, bringing ready boiled potatoes to sell the troops as they passed, and went on to describe the mutton as 'nauseous', but beef, pork, fish, and fruit as excellent, and the 'common wine very palatable, light, and wholesome.' D'Urban, riding from Corunna, until reaching Villafranca del Bierzo, had found 'no subsistence to be depended upon', after which the bread was of superior quality to any he had met with in England.

[12] Although Benjamin D'Urban, Baird's A.Q.M.G., writing on 15 October, refers to him being 'determined to disembark the horses and three of the waggons, altogether 850 empty wood houses were inspected and approved of,' but we are left in the dark as to what happened to the latter; and were they prefabricated? The horses must refer to those of his Staff, for the Cavalry, due to some mismanagement, had been shipped last, arriving three weeks after the infantry.

[13] As D'Urban wrote on 20 October: 'I was not in his [Baird's] confidence and as my opinion was never asked, of course I never ventured to obtrude it …', and although he had 'suggested the necessity (before the Army disembarked) of ensuring sufficient dêpots, upon the different routes …so that the General might feel his movements perfectly independent of the promises of the Junta, which I should myself feel no inclination to confide in,' adding that although 'he had not at any time spoken to me on the subject … it was my wish to send forward some officers of the Department to reconnoitre the routes, and

estimate the probable resources of the Army, if he would be pleased to give me timely notice when and how he intended to move.' Unfortunately, two days later, D'Urban was informed that the Horse Guards had made an error in sending him out with Baird in the first place, which was disappointing although no great surprise. The position had 'become in an especial degree irksome from the instant I could no longer avoid feeling that the General did not treat me as a Confidential Staff Officer.' D'Urban then wrote to General Anstruther and Q.M.G. Colonel George Murray, before setting out for Moore's Headquarters (where he was to explain Baird's delay in advancing his troops), in the hope of being given a post 'in some shape with the active Army.' Before leaving Corunna, he told Baird's Military Secretary that he was unable to explain what obstacles caused the delay, as he had '*never been told*,' while – as far as he knew – nothing had yet been done 'to form independent Magazines, and all stood still.'

[14] The Hollands were awoken here by the strong smell of fire and finding their room full of smoke, due to the mindless behaviour of muleteers in the stable below, who, wanting a light, had lit *straw* torches, although aware that in and about the house stood 36 loaded ammunition waggons! What could one expect of such bumpkins ? These waggons had been mentioned also by young Fitzclarence (the eldest son of the Duke of Clarence – later William IV – and Mrs Jordan, who was a cornet in the 10th Hussars), whom the Hollands met near Lugo on 22 November, when he had 'complained of the want of assistance from the Juntas who had not furnished them with cattle or guides.' Major Edwin Griffith had also noticed that 'when there is occasion to go for fuel or straw after dark a wisp of the latter is carried flaming in the hand at the imminent risk of setting fire to their whole property in order to save a farthing a week in a rush light.'

[15] He had received secret instructions from Baird, nervous about being isolated, directing him to choose a safe place from which troops might be embarked, and that the admiral had fixed on Vigo in preference to Corunna, which was commanded by forts, and had taken measures accordingly. By 2 December there were 140 transports under convoy at Vigo (where one 50-gun ship struck a rock, the captain having used a century-old chart and refused the assistance of the pilot sent aboad, according to the ubiquitous Lady Holland), and about 32 remaining at Corunna. That same night news reached Corunna via Sir Charles Vaughan, carrying dispatches to England, of the Spanish defeat at Tudela.

By 1 January, according to Captain Capel at Vigo, there were then 11 warships and 200 transports. (Eventually, the Hollands made their way via Vigo to Oporto, and thence to Lisbon, entered during the first week of January. By 30 January they were in Seville, remaining in Andalusia until late June before returning to Lisbon, and sailing home.)

[16] These, as Canning had emphasised to Frere on 9 December, were 'not merely a considerable part of the disposable force of this country. It is, in fact, the British army ... [and] must be kept together under its own commanders, must act as one body for some distinct object, and on some settled plan [and] should not again be left, as that of Sir J. Moore and Sir D. Baird have recently been, in the heart of Spain ...'

[17] Wellesley had soon realised that the Spanish authorities could not be relied on in any way, and took appropriate action by reorganising the Commissary Department thoroughly: Moore had little time in which to do so. As Alexander

Gordon remarked in a letter sent from Lugo to his brother Lord Aberdeen on 17 November: 'We can only act on the defensive, without the Spaniards, and I fear unless things wear a more favourable aspect with them we must retreat. How could ministers send us here without knowing any thing of the state of the Country but believing every favourable report sent, and taking for Gospel the whole of the accounts in the Spanish papers of which perhaps one third is founded on fact.' This opinion was reiterated the following week: 'How miserably, how despictably do Ministers appear, in having gulped down that was said with respect to Spain and sent us here to be *sacrificed* because they would not send proper people to find out the real truth. We have seen nothing of that firm Noble spirited People we were told of. No nothing but a miserable, slow, inactive lying set, not worth fighting for.'

18 Anstruther was telling D'Urban on that same day (the 12th) what he would do 'if the French got possession of Madrid,' not yet aware that Napoleon had entered it eight days earlier!

19 To give some idea of the stamina required by such officers, between 20 November and 6 January D'Urban had ridden 720 miles, followed between 6 March and 14 April by another 560 miles. Including stretches ridden on post-horses and mules, in the five months since setting out from Corunna, he covered a total distance of 2,168 miles in an entirely strange country and during an inclement season.

20 Perhaps more so on the imperfect and frequently misleading maps of the period: see p.160–1.

21 At least La Romana appeared to want to collaborate, even if belatedly, although Wellington's own opinion of his military capacities – as later recorded by Stanhope – were summed up as: 'a good-natured, excellent man ... very clever too – knew all about the literature and poetry of his country ... but ... I never in my whole life saw a man who had acted at all with troops understand so little about them,' apparently the general opinion: Alexander Gordon, writing in December 1810, only a few weeks prior to La Romana's belated death, had commented that while he was 'an excellent scholar …in every respect a most excellent fellow, but no soldier.'

22 The Spaniards, unable to make more than a token resistance, had never thought of informing their Allies of their surrender; and yet it is also a reflection on Moore's intelligence service that it was only by Water's chance discovery that he was alerted to his critical situation.

23 The design of cavalry headgear would appear to have been a constant headache, as when five years later, Edwin Griffith (15th Hussars), complained 'Our large sad chacos [sic] have been in wear ever since we left Lisbon [six months earlier]: they are heavy, hideous, unbecoming, unserviceable, villainous affairs altogether. The tenth have not got theirs yet, yet the regt looks very well in the old worn out black ones.'

24 Several narratives, including that of Major Griffith's, confirm that that gold and silver objects, largely taken from churches, were melted down into ingots of about 1 inch square and 6 or 8 inches long.

It is recorded that when recovering the wounded, it was found that some of the French, already stripped by the locals, for fear that they may not have been quite dead, had also been stabbed repeatedly; but at least one trooper of the 15th Hussars had been seen to split the skull of a French dragoon rising from the ground to surrender.

25 Harris noticed a dragoon spurring furiously ahead to deliver a dispatch to Craufurd, then in command of the brigade, 'who turned round in his saddle the moment he had read a few lines, and thundered out the word 'to halt!' A few minutes more and we were all turned to the right-about, and retracing our steps of the night before – the contents of that epistle serving to furnish our men with many a surmise during the retrograde movement.'

26 Neale followed in his wake with the wounded, their covered spring-waggons fording the Esla, after which two ferry-boats remaining on the rising river there were scuttled. They veered north-west only to find Astorga crowded with the sick of La Romana's army, so the convoy pressed ahead to Manzanal, beyond which the road became knee-deep in snow.

27 Writing on the 28th from Benavente to Major-General the Hon. John Brodrick at Corunna, Moore admitted that it was not his wish to engage in battle unless compelled to, but 'rather to save the army, to protract, and give time to the Spanish to rally, if they can ...': by then, he should have realised that this was highly unlikely.

28 Harris remembered Craufurd, wrapped in his great-coat, but like himself drenched to the skin by the downpour, clambering up the hill-slope where he and another rifleman had concealed themselves to get a better view of the enemy, bringing a tot of rum and ordering them, once they got the word, to descend and file across the planks spanning the still unbroken arch of the bridge, which would then be blown up.

29 Reconnoitering the premises, he noticed an outhouse wall showing signs of recent construction, so tying a rope round his body, he dropped through a skylight and, finding a log, rammed and breached the wall to reveal a large vat. While the wine was being issued to the shivering soldiers, the fat prior suddenly appeared through a trap door, laughingly requesting one drink before all was consumed, at which he was thrust head first into the vat, saved the fate of the Duke of Clarence only by the arrival of officers from whom Blakeney heard the anecdote.

30 Major Griffith, on witnessing these excesses, commented that, in extenuation, the troops had been 'exasperated by the numerous instances of perfidy that the Spaniards daily exhibited.' They considered themselves as having been 'sent to Spain as auxiliaries but on their arrival found themselves principals; the natives so far from receiving them as their deliverers, treated them with a jealousy and indifference that soon created disgust; the rations of bread, meat & wine ... for which they were regularly & scrupulously paid the full value, were furnished and delivered in an ungracious manner; and they practised every species of fraud & imposition on our men to a scandalous and infamous degree.'

31 He was sent to England, but escaped in 1811 by breaking his parole.

32 Lieut. Heise had seen one Frenchman 'lying on the ground who had the whole of his head cut off horizontally above the eyes at one blow, and many others with heads split in two ... and one man who rode by with outspread arms who had received a diagonal blow across the face which had cut his mouth wide open so that his jaw, as far back as the tongue, hung down over his chest, and you could see his gullet.'

33 This allowed Soult, commanding 25,000 infantry and 6,000 cavalry, to enter León unopposed on the 31st, shortly reinforced by 10,000 men under Marshal Ney.

34 One of the many dodges 'adopted by some of our bibbers,' according to Surtees, was to borrow each other's clothes: 'that is, a 43rd man would borrow

a rifleman's jacket, and vice versa, and go away and steal, or in some other illegal mode obtain, a camp-kettle full or two; and when the owner came to point out the person who had robbed him, of course he could not be found.'

35 The track probably followed led west to La Rua, and then ascended across the hills via Puebla de Trives and Castro Caldelas; and after Orense, through Ribadavia, A Caniza, and Ponteareas.

36 Inevitably, some, missing the boats, made their way south to the comparative safety of Portugal (at least until Soult marched on Oporto); others joined local guerrilla bands.

37 Moore still had some 15,500 men with him.

38 As Schaumann later wrote, apropos many officers having complained about the defective rationing of the army at this period: 'Situated as we were … it was impossible, even with the best will in the world, to relieve our privations; for the cause of our suffering lay in the fact that we were a large army, all pursuing the same narrow road through the mountains, and could not avail ourselves of the resources which would have lain to our left and right had we been marching in three or four separate and parallel columns over roads covering a larger area of the country. Even if, owing to the special care of the commissaries in Corunna, provisions had been sent out and deposited at various places along the road – as, for instance, at Villafranca – these measures would have proved nugatory owing to the impatience and unbridled state of the foremost troops, who, in their masses, and with the wildest tumult and noise, literally stormed the stores depots … towards the end, the men even used to fight among themselves and kill one another, and one frequently saw a regular battle fought over the *débris* …

39 Schaumann saw a 'soldier's wife had sought shelter beneath a cart, but she too was lying lifeless; and the tragic part of it was that her child, who was still alive, was wimpering and trying to find nourishment at her frozen breasts! One or two officers had the child taken from her, and wrapping it in a blanket, carried it away.'

40 Graham was not designated Maj.-General until after the campaign, when it was back-dated.

41 He depicts five arches, not three.

42 The 'military chest' had contained about £25,000 in silver dollars, much of which, when the snow had melted, must have fallen into the hands of the local peasantry, however undeserving, for as Schaumann complained: 'The apathy with which the inhabitants of this mountain country, who are usually so warlike, have witnessed our misery, is revolting. They were to be seen in large armed hordes, far away from us in the mountains, and deliberately turning away when, in view of their familiarity with the passes and other conditions, they might have been very useful to us, and have covered our retreat'. Not only did they give us no assistance, 'but they took good care to remove all cattle and all food-stuffs out of our way, emptied and locked their houses, vanished, and, in addition, murdered and plundered our own men who fell out.' In their defence, Leith Hay had commented that it one could hardly 'expect that the peasantry were to rush from their houses, and supply the wants of our soldiers with the only provision that they possessed for their own families – who might in consequence be left … to starve …'

43 Neale, taking a last look at the 'mouldering walls of Lugo, which frowned over the glowing embers of our artillery-waggons,' was aware that these fires were being 'kindled to deceive the enemy, who, it appears, did not discover this *ruse*

de guerre before morning,' the 9th, by which time the army was well on the road north-west towards Guitiriz and the coast. The fact that any waggons had been hauled that far was little short of miraculous.

44 Unsuccesfully. The Junta of Ledesma, for example, 'were determined not to defend themselves, prepared to receive the French with open arms, and are in short in the French interest.' A résumé of Wilson's character and achievements in the Peninsula, notably in keeping Lapisse occupied throughout February and March, is found on pp. 253-62 of volume II of Oman's *History.*

45 No notice was taken of his 'repeated suggestion' to Cradock that the Portuguese force west of Alcántara should march east towards the Tietar valley and threaten Victor's right and rear. After the debâcle of Medellín (see following note), D'Urban was ordered to Lisbon, first making a long detour to Seville on his own initiative to acquaint Frere of the military situation, of which he was 'utterly ignorant.'

46 In the event, Cuesta was forced out of a strong position near Mesas del Ibor (on the dominating south bank of the Tagus, south-east of Almaraz) without making any resistance, his right being turned, and retired towards Medellín (on the Guadiana east of Merida), where, despite receiving reinforcement, he was soundly thrashed by Victor on 29 March. Cuesta himself was ridden over by his fleeing cavalry, D'Urban himself, with Cuesta's nephew, pulling him out 'from under the horses' feet, bruised and nearly senseless ...'

47 Corunna's streets were 'crowded with persons of both sexes, and of every rank and age, occupied in contributing to the defence of the ramparts, by mounting the guns, and distributing the shot and ammunition', and as Neale went on to comment: 'Had we met with half as much zeal and good-will in other parts of Spain, our affairs would have borne a very different aspect. Most of us have lost the whole of our horses, mules, and baggage. For my own part, I have nothing left but the clothes on my back, and am even obliged to the kindness of an acquaintance for a change of linen.' That the inhabitants were friendly is endorsed by Schaumann, who remarked that 'Several officers who have been with General Spencer in Cadiz say that the people there are just as liberal and enthusiastic as they are here. Everybody, young and old, rich and poor, alike – aye, even the women and girls – are busy on the ramparts helping to throw up entrenchments. Whole troops of young and beautiful girls go in procession with baskets on their heads, carrying ammunition into the forts and batteries, and it looks wonderfully fine.'

48 The cause of this blast had been the destruction of two adjoining magazines, containing almost 4,000 barrels of gun-powder provided by England for the use of the Spanish (but never distributed), the detonation of which shattered all the characteristic *miradores* or glazed balconies of the town. But, as Major Edwin Griffith remarked: 'none of the shops have glazed windows & very few houses; they are closed with shutters only, so you must either be exposed to all the inclemency's of the weather, or suffer a total deprivation of daylight.'

49 William Napier, then a Captain in the 43rd, was the future historian of the war. Together with his two brothers – Charles, the eldest, a Major in the 50th, and George, also a Captain and one of Moore's aides – survived the retreat.

50 Edwin Griffith was strongly critical of Lord Paget command of the cavalry during the retreat. It was not for any lack of courage on his part – 'tho 'courage alone is a very vulgar quality unless regulated by wisdom & *judgement*' – but, together with the rest of the Staff, he seemed to think that they never could

do enough: 'we were constantly marching, counter marching, and harassed in every way to such a degree, that if the main object had been to kill all the horses as soon as possible they could not have taken a more effectual method for the purpose.' Consequently, 'the horses were knocked up before the retreat commenced … & what there were remaining were in such a dreadful state that the French might doubtless have annihilated them if they had made an attack …'

51 Capt. Humphreys had been ordered to superintend the destruction of no less than 400 mounts. One of the main causes of foundering was 'not for want of shoes, but want of hammers and nails to put them on', as Napier later emphasised.

52 Later Adjutant-General to Wellington, the 3rd Marquess of Londonderry.

53 As Basil Hall described it: 'At the first discharge the whole of the British troops, from one end of the line to the other, started to their feet, snatched up their arms and formed themselves with as much regularity as if they had been exercising in Hyde Park. Before, a silence had reigned over the field – now there was a loud hum and occasionally a loud shout and many a burst of laughter, in the midst of which could be heard a peculiar click, click as the bayonets were fixed.

54 Capt. Hardinge, who was with him, in describing his fall, remarked that 'The blood flowed fast; but the attempt to stop it with my sash was useless, from the size of the wound', while, when raising him up to place him in a blanket to remove him to the rear, 'his sword, hanging on the wounded side, touched his arm, and became entangled between his legs. I perceived the inconvenience, and was in the act of unbuckling it from the waist, when he said, in his usual tone and manner, in a very distinct voice, "It is as well as it is. I had rather it should go out of the field with me".

55 Only two transports failed to reach the Channel ports, being wrecked on the Cornish coast. Oman reckoned that in the whole campaign British losses were 3,800 killed in action or had died during the retreat, or in hospital, while about 2,200 had been taken prisoner during the retreat. It has been estimated that of this total, losses at Corunna itself were in the region of 800 or 900 men, and those of Soult probably about the same, although they may well have reached a much higher figure, for the British were firing from new muskets, using fresh ammunition just issued from their magazines, while the weapons of their adversary were worn.

56 Of the survivors, some 6,000 were sick enough to require immediate medical attention. In the detailed accounts made at Portsmouth and Plymouth respectively by Dr James McGrigor and surgeon Richard Cooper, it is recorded that the most frequent causes of illness and death were dysentery and typhus, the death rate of 26% from the former being double that from typhus. Of the 241 deaths at Plymouth, only 25 were caused by wounds, while most of the others were from these diseases. As McGrigor remarked: 'The sick and healthy being mixed together indiscriminatly [on the transports], it was no matter of wonder that the number of cases of fever landed in the last stage of typhus was great; in fact, it was enormous and it excited great alarm at Portsmouth and in the neighbouring country when an account of the mortality came to be noised abroad.'

3

March to May 1809: The Douro (or Oporto) campaign

Apart from making a brief visit to Ireland since his return from Lisbon, Wellesley had remained in London, where although many 'croakers' were of the opinion that it would be far better to leave the Peninsula to its fate, his brief experience there convinced him otherwise. He disputed Moore's view that it was impossible to defend Portugal once Spain had caved in. Hardly any Portuguese territory now remained in enemy occupation, and they had maintained their spirit of resistance. This was less evident among the apathetic Spaniards: the defeats of their generals, and the duplicity and time-serving propensities of their *juntas*, too frequently failing to provide either the troops or the ample supplies promised, had caused any confidence in them to cool.

Among several lessons learnt during Wellesley's few weeks there was that he had to be entirely self-reliant as far as the acquisition of food and forage was concerned: a competent Commissary and Intelligence services were as fundamental to success on a Peninsular battlefield as well-armed and disciplined troops. Had Moore been sufficiently aware of these problems and in a position to take appropriate action, his resulting campaign might have been less disastrous, although it is arguable that the end result may not have been so very different.

Wellesley's military reputation remained high.[1] He retained the confidence of Castlereagh, for whom, on 7 March, while kicking his heels, he drew up a 'Memorandum' reiterating the reasons for his conviction that it would be in the Peninsula that Britain could prosecute the war against France most effectively. On 2 April Wellesley was formally nominated Commander-in-Chief in Portugal; but it was stipulated in his brief that he should not extend any campaign into Spain. By the 22nd he had landed at Lisbon to supersede General Sir John Cradock, who had concentrated most of the troops at his disposal in its vicinity. These now numbered about 16,000.[2]

The populace remained enthusiastic, although apprehensive as to whether their Allies would remain to protect them, or abandon them, for upwards of 500 women attached to the army had already been sent back to England. Any such doubts should have evaporated shortly after, when additional British troops disembarked, among them, on 15 April, William Tomkinson (16th Light Dragoons), the regiment's 640 horses having all survived the eight-day passage from Falmouth. Robert Semple, an English merchant visiting Lisbon – where he had seen engravings of the battle of Vimeiro in every shop – observed that Lisbon pullulated with volunteers, 'whose arms, equipment, and movements, were most varied and whimsical. The greater proportion carried pikes; some were armed with fowling-pieces, some with bayonets screwed on poles, some with small-swords, with daggers, with pistols, or with a single pistol. Here and there in their ranks were seen halberds and pikes of curious and ancient workmanship ... At the word of command, some turned to the right and others to the left, some parts of the line advanced while others remained stationary ... every thing was ridiculous, except their cause ...'

Semple travelled on to Seville, via Badajoz (where fortifications were being repaired and outworks erected) and La Albuera – not yet a name to remember – 'a place containing about one hundred and fifty houses, mostly very miserable ones ... an old church, with a tolerably handsome front, seemed to be the only object of the smallest interest.' All along the road he had met parties of armed men, and was cheered with repeated cries of 'Viva l'Inglaterra.'

It was later, while quartered in Seville, that Private William Lawrence (40th) got 'in a fine scrape,' having absented himself without leave from guard duty for 24 hours, for which he found himself facing a drumhead court-martial, and sentenced to 400 lashes.[3] As he recalled:

> Had I been sentenced to be shot, I would not have despaired more. The guards bought me to the square of the convent where my sentence was to be carried out and where the regiment was assembled to witness my punishment. The judgement was read over me by the colonel[4] and I was ordered to strip. Hardened by that time, I did so without the help that was offered and was lashed to the halberds. The colonel gave the order for the drummers to commence. Each drummer gave me 25 lashes in turn. I bore it well but, by the time I had received 175, I became so enraged with pain that I pushed the halberds. They were only planted on stones and did not stand firm so I moved them right across the square amid the laughter of the regiment.

> The colonel, judging that I had had sufficient, ordered 'the sulky rascal down.' Indeed I was sulky for, although the blood ran down my trousers, I had not given vent to a single sound. I was unbound and the corporal hove my shirt and jacket over my shoulders, then conveyed me – a miserable spectacle – to the hospital.
>
> Perhaps the flogging was a good thing in preventing me from committing greater crimes, which might have earned me even more severe punishments. Nevertheless, it was a great trial for me. A lot of that kind of punishment could have been abandoned by the army. It is hard to believe that 400 lashes could be ordered on a man, as young as I, one who had undergone all the privations of a most bloody war, for a first offence, which could have been overlooked or dealt with by a severe reprimand.[5]
>
> I was in hospital for about three weeks. When I came out – still in a very marked state, of which I bear remembrances on my back to this day – I was transferred from the Light to into the Grenadier company.

Major-general William Carr Beresford had also sailed to Lisbon in March, where he was invested by the Portuguese Regency with the rank of Field Marshal,[6] and given the assignment of reorganising the Portuguese regular army. He had the advantage of speaking Portuguese, having commanded the garrison in Madeira after its occupation by British troops in December 1807. Although somewhat of a martinet, during ensuing months he drastically reformed their entire military establishment, cutting out a deal of 'dead wood'; while this caused resentment among a minority of officers, it had a reinvigorating effect on the rank and file, which were to prove themselves surprisingly reliable during future campaigns.[7] Already, several battalions contained a number of British officers seconded from Cradock's units to the Portuguese establishment. Others were later encouraged to volunteer for this duty by receiving a step up in promotion: lieutenants becoming captains, and captains majors. D'Urban was commenting in the following December that he had 'never seen an English brigade move with more steadiness and precision.'[8] Indeed, they had been well drilled and trained, and some 20,000 were to be paid, clothed and equipped from England. Meanwhile, while awaiting additional British troops to arrive after the losses sustained during the previous campaign, they made up a good proportion of the number under arms.[9] Further discipline would be imparted by incorporating one Portuguese battalion in each British brigade.[10] Another general innovation was the per manent attachment of a company of riflemen to every infantry brigade, increasing the percentage of light troops in each by between 33 and 50, and improving their mobility. At a later date, several brigades would be combined to form autonomous Divisions which, commanded by officers of experience, could act independently whenever necessary.

The local commissariat was also rudely awakened from its *siesta*, for it was essential that the army was well-fed and supplied in every respect. Ox-carts were reserved for them as their primary form of transport; officers' private baggage would have to be carried on mule or horseback. The British Commissariat had to be self-sufficient, for while hostile forces might survive by living off the country, they could not afford to alienate the Portuguese peasantry, already sufficiently distressed by the cruel marauding they had experienced while under French occupation. At this period, the Allied Army totalling approximately 26,000 men, with 4,000 mounts, had still only a minimal number of commissaries responsible for keeping them supplied with food, drink, and forage.[11]

In spite of losses comparable to those of Moore's, having reorganized and partially re-equipped his forces, Soult had advanced into northern Portugal. The store of 2,500 undestroyed English greatcoats discovered at Corunna would not have gone very far to keep them snug that winter; more valuable were the 20,000 muskets, newly imported from England and handed over by Admiral Melgarejo to Soult at Ferrol, together with several ships of the line in the harbour, which anyone but a traitor would have scuttled or burned before surrendering.[12]

On 29 March Soult assaulted and sacked Oporto, when 5,000 Portuguese regular troops, together with the militia and armed citizens, were massacred, while thousands fleeing from the French were drowned also when the bridge of boats tethered to both banks of the Douro gave way under the press of people (or was deliberately broken by those who had already escaped). In addition to over thirty merchant vessels laden with wine, stores of English ammunition and *materiél*, the French captured 200 pieces of artillery.

Those of Soult's units extending further south occupied only the land within the range of their muskets, for the Portuguese hovered on their heels: those straggling from their battalions were picked off soon enough. It was estimated that he commanded 20,000 altogether (in fact 24,000), of which 10,000 infantry and 1,200 cavalry were at Oporto; but he had already decided to evacuate northern Portugal at leisure. He felt insecure and isolated there, only in fragile communication with Ney, whose 17,000 men were tied down within Galicia attempting to suppress subversives belatedly showing resistance.

An army commanded by Marshal Victor (keeping a weather eye on Cuesta's army, which he had scattered at Medellín as recently as 29 March) was said to be extended along the Madrid road north-east of Mérida, while a smaller force under General Lapisse was operating in the vicinity of Ciudad Rodrigo, in tenuous contact with Victor and Soult. Disregarding Ney, between them they would outnumber British forces by over two to one.

Wellesley deduced that if he attacked Soult separately, he might well be able to eject him from Portugal before turning on Victor and company; but speed and surprise was essential. Having made his decision, its implementation soon took effect; while within a fortnight of landing at Lisbon he was also persuading London to modify his instructions, permitting him to advance into Spain against Victor should it be expedient.

General Alexander Mackenzie, with a total of 12,000 men,[13] would remain near Abrantes to prevent any French flying column approaching Lisbon from that direction. Should Victor advance south of the Tagus, Mackenzie would hold the line of that river, then in flood; if Victor threatened further north, then the Zêzere could be defended. Wellesley would be receiving early intelligence of any such moves from his outposts or those of his Allies, notably from units of the Loyal Lusitanian Legion, an independent force hovering near the frontier, resourcefully commanded by General Sir Robert Wilson. Wilson was a law unto himself, too inclined to ignore orders from his superiors if he thought them unlikely to prove as effective as his own schemes.

Meanwhile, other units were being marched north towards Coimbra. When writing on 26 April from Leiria, Captain William Stothert described the 3rd Foot Guards as having been quartered at the abbey of Batalha during the previous night, and that 'an excellent dinner was served up to the officers in the refectory: the Prior himself, with several of the monks, attended during the repast. After dinner, they were conducted to see the body of John the Second, which was still in tolerable preservation, although the monarch had been dead upwards of three hundred years.'[14]

The arrival of Wellesley at Coimbra 'was announced by the firing of rockets; and the bells of the different churches immediately commenced a peal of joy,' the town being 'brilliantly illuminated' that night. Ensign John Aitchison (likewise in the 3rd Foot Guards), experienced a feeling of exhilaration, '...for with the whole of the army in Portugal I feel more confidence in the Commander-in-Chief than I should under any other officer in the service', nevertheless, 'Reverses must be expected ...' Headquarters was established in the monastery of Santa Cruz. Stothert, among others, apparently reconnoitred the convent of Sta Clara, on the south bank of the Mondego, where the nuns, 'much pleased with the visits of the British officers at the gate ... sought to amuse them by the spontaneous exertion of their talents in singing and music.' He found several of them 'handsome, and would be thought so even in England.'

On 6 May Wellesley reviewed his assembled troops at Coimbra, including Portuguese units, which increased the number of his effectives to 18,881 infantry (including a 3,095-strong K.G.L. brigade), 3,134 cavalry, and 994 artillery, but only 39 engineers, and a mere 67 responsible for the wagon train. Beresford (with 5,800 men, only 1,875 British among them) then set off north-east towards Viseu with the intention of preventing Soult from moving east from Oporto to unite with Lapisse or Victor. He crossed the Douro north of Lamego on the 10th, next day entering Amarante, spanning the Tâmega in mountainous country 30 miles east of Oporto as the crow flies.

Next day, the main body recommenced their progress up the highway towards Oporto.[15] With the intention of turning the flank of any hostile force impeding Wellesley's advance, Hill's Division (almost 4,400 men), taking advantage of a small fleet of *moliceiros* (seaweed-harvesting vessels) collected in the vicinity of Aveiro, was ferried a brigade at a time through lagoons further to the west and landed at Ovar. A minor cavalry action took place at Albergaria-a-Nova, near the river Vouga, after which the French withdrew rapidly to concentrate at the village and monastery of Grijó, expecting Wellesley to attack them frontally. Before long, they realised that their flanks were in danger of being turned, both by Hill's advance and by a thrust to their east by a Portuguese battalion, and gave way, with two squadrons of Light Dragoons in pursuit. By dawn on 12 May, together with any other units remaining south of the Douro, they had crossed to Oporto and blown up the (replaced) bridge of boats, the only means of traversing the lower reaches of the river, then in spate.

The Passage of the Douro

While aware that British troops were approaching, having neglected to leave outposts beyond the south bank, Soult had little idea of how close they were. Taking the precaution of moving all lighters and other river craft to the north bank, he complacently assumed that the

Douro itself was sufficient defence against any possible attack. He reckoned that if an attempt was made to dislodge him, it would be by an amphibious landing near the river mouth with those same boats which he had heard Hill had used, and so posted his picquets facing west. The eastern suburbs had been left virtually undefended; at least no patrols were visible to Wellesley, who on reaching the cliff-top convent of N.S. da Serra do Pilar, inconspiciously surveyed the city rising steeply from the quays opposite him, while keeping the main body of his troops hidden to the south of this commanding height.

He noticed what appeared to be an unoccupied building within a walled enclosure at no great distance east of the city. It stood within range of his artillery, but due to the configuration of the ground, was probably out of sight from Soult's main position. While ordering forward his guns, he was informed that at the village of Avintes, 4 miles upstream, a scuttled but only slightly damaged ferry-boat was being baled out and repaired. General Sir John Murray was thus ordered to use this to pass over part of his K.G.L. Brigade and a squadron of the 14th Light Dragoons, with which to oppose any attempt by Soult to escape east.

Meanwhile, a barber, who had rowed across unnoticed during the night and hidden his skiff on the south bank below Wellesley's post of vantage, was persuaded to collect four undamaged wine barges lieing unguarded on the far bank and, assisted by other boatmen, these were unobtrusively conveyed over. John Waters, ever resourceful, while supervising this operation, confirmed that the building that had been observed – in fact a seminary – was empty.[16] Within minutes, at about 10.30, the order to cross was given, but cautiously – for each barge could hold thirty men only – and it would take an hour to ferry over enough to make a substantial foothold. Scrambling up the steep far bank, the first platoon secured the seminary gate and began to fortify the enceinte by piling earth behind the walls to serve as a banquette. One barge was sighted by General Foy, who ordered an investigation, but an hour passed before Soult realised what was afoot and had taken any serious counter-measures, by which time 600 men had established themselves in this providential stronghold.

The first gun to unlimber and direct its fire against the building was immediately put out of action and its gunners killed by a shrapnel shell from the south bank, and their advancing infantry, finding themselves the vulnerable target of Wellesley's artillery, soon gave up the attack. A second attempt was checked by effective musketry fire from the garden wall, windows, and roof of the seminary, which continued to receive reinforcements.[17] The Portuenses required no encouragement in the ensuing confusion to row across their now unguarded boats, in which the Brigade of Guards and the 1/29th were ferried over, swarmed into the upper town, and took in flank those units struggling to impede egress from the seminary.

Soult sensed that the game was up: it was impossible to stem the tide or make a leisurely withdrawal. Hospitably leaving his dinner in the Palácio das Carrancas for Wellesley and his staff, Soult scurried away with his demoralised troops already streaming east precipitately. It was not until Wellesley sent forward General Charles Stewart with a squadron of the 14th Light Dragoons, that any attempt was made to intercept the headlong retreat, for Murray, contrary to orders, had allowed his K.G.L. infantry to remain passive, with the excuse that the troops flying across his front were too strong to be attacked.[18] The rear-guard might easily have been cut off; but only 300 were captured in the ensuing action, in which Foy was wounded and Delaborde taken prisoner, although he escaped in the scuffle.[19]

Rallied by Beresford's presence, General Silveira's Portuguese contingent held the east bank of the Tâmega at Amarante, obliging Loison to seek another escape route (north-west towards Guimarães). On 23 April, the French, carrying fire-brands, had penetrated as far as a wooden barrier on the bridge at Amarante, but a sudden downpour stopped the fire from taking hold, and they were forced back. Having plundered the place, and indiscriminately slaughtered its surviving inhabitants, Loison left the town in flames.[20]

Soult would have had an easier retreat north, rather than east towards where he assumed Loison would be, had not the latter kept him in ignorance both of his own movements and of the fact that the route north-east was blocked. Beresford, anticipating orders from Wellesley, sent Silveira across country towards Salamonde (between Braga and Chaves), where a bridge spanned the Cávado, while he counter-marched towards the Douro, there turning north-east to make a forced march on Chaves. It then started to pour, a drenching rain continuing for several days. Colonel Hugh Gough, with the 87th Regiment, then acting as the rearguard, described the fording of the Tâmega, where the water-level had rapidly risen to above their middles.

> One officer and 14 Privates were carried down by the Stream, but were providentially saved by the Exertions of the Mounted Officers. Two Companies were unable to pass. Here the misfortunes of the Brigade commenced. The whole of the Men's Bread, which was made of Indian Corn,

> got wet and was destroyed. Several thousand Rounds of Ammunition were rendered unserviceable, without a possibility of replacing it. A Number of Firelocks, Caps and Shoes were lost ... The Night turned out as Dark as it was possible. The Men were obliged to move in Indian files, and grope their way – no torches being provided, and the Rain preventing lighted Straw from being of Service. As there was no road, many Men lost the Column, several fell into pits, excavated by the falling of the Waters, Numbers lay down in the River from fatigue and hunger, and the greater part of the Brigade lost their shoes.

Leaving Trant in command at Oporto, Wellesley led his forces in two columns towards Braga, reached on the afternoon of the 15th. The 7th Fusiliers, searching for shelter from the elements, entered a church in its vicinity, where, within minutes, as Sgt John Spencer Cooper remembered, 'the band had possession of the altar, and the big drummer of the pulpit. Fires were wanted, and fires were made. Smash went the forms, down came the priest's stalls. The crashing of wood, the bawling and swearing of hundreds in the blinding, choking smoke that completely filled the edifice, were awful,' and pandemonium ensued as darkness set in, until 'a box of large wax candles used at the altar was found. Many of these were distributed and lighted in different parts of the church, and the scene was complete and fit for Hogarth's pencil.'

Soult, having united with Loison and Lorges (sent ahead to round up any isolated French garrisons in the region), was now in full retreat north-east through the rugged terrain of the Minho, destroyed or jettisoned all his wheeled transport, baggage, and surviving artillery, hamstrung his lame mounts and mules, and murdered the Portuguese guides forced to accompany him, lest they should be of use to his pursuers. Even the military chest, containing almost 50,000 Portuguese silver coins, was scattered over the wild banks of the Sousa by the expedient of placing it next to powder waggons to be exploded by the rearguard.[21]

The Allies, already delayed by having had to ferry all their guns, ammunition, baggage and provisions across the Douro at Oporto before continuing the pursuit, were at a disadvantage when trying to intercept the retreating enemy, for, as Wellesley explained, 'if an army throws away all its cannon, equipments, and baggage, and everything which can strengthen it, and can enable it to act together as a body; and abandons all those who are entitled to its protection, but add to its weight and impede its progress; it must be able to march by roads through which it cannot be followed, with any prospect of being overtaken, by an army which had not made the same sacrifice.'

By making forced marches, Soult had reached the Ponte Nova at Salamonde in advance of Silveira's troops, where the local peasants, not wishing to destroy their only way across the Cávado torrent, had removed the planking only. The local *Ordenança* defending the far bank, were surprised and bayonetted by a party of French traversing the remaining cross-beams in single file during the night. Their sappers rapidly repaired the bridge with tree trunks and boards torn from neighbouring huts, and within hours 20,000 infantry, 400 cavalry, and all their surviving pack-animals were across. Young Lieut. Henry Fitzclarence[22] described the rocky bed of the Cávado as being literally choked with men and horses, sumpter mules and baggage, which 'fell into the hands of the grenadiers and light companies of the Guards. These active-fingered gentry found that fishing for boxes and bodies out of the stream produced pieces of plate, and purses and belts full of gold money. Amid the scenes of death and desolation arose the shouts of the most noisy merriment.'

On the 16th, a brisk action took place at the 'Saltador' bridge,[23] a single span over the Miserela, a tributary of the Cávado, while Soult's rearguard, which suffered heavily, was crossing. Two days later, the relics of his army, leaving a trail of smoking villages and wreckage behind them, were clambering helter-skelter over the trackless frontier range of the Serra de Gerês towards Orense in Galicia. Part of Beresford's column had advanced through Chaves towards Monterrey (overlooking Verín) to cut the road leading east towards the plains of León, but the pursuit was given up at Allariz, no great distance south of Orense, with Allied units returning to Chaves on the 21st.

Schaumann, now attached to the 14th and 20th Light Dragoons and keen to resume his duties despite privations suffered under during Moore's retreat, caught up with them at Ruivães, beyond the Saltador bridge, where he bivouacked. It was a distressing scene: '... even the crockery had been taken from the houses of a neighbouring village, and ... brought into the field. The beds and the mattresses lay in rows in the mud. The drawers from the various articles of furniture had been used as mangers. Wardrobes had been transformed into bedsteads and roofs for the huts; all the glass and cutlery lay in fragments on the ground. The chairs, staircases and window frames had been used partly for fuel for the kitchen fires, and partly to feed the huge bonfires which had been lighted when the French had withdrawn. The unfortunate inhabitants stood all around lamenting their plight.'

Although the British often showed scant respect for churches, the French would wilfully desecrate them as a matter of course. Several prisoners had been locked up in one chapel, and Schaumann described how a well-dressed man at the head of a band of peasants offered ten gold florins to the English sergeant guarding the French to give them up. He does not record whether the bribe was accepted, only commenting that the cruelties perpetrated by the Portuguese against any who who fell into their hands were horrific, however they might wish to justify them; for, 'in addition to nailing them up alive on barn doors, they had stripped many of them, emasculated them, and then placed their amputated members in the victims' mouths – a ghastly sight!'

Soult lost 4,000 men in the retreat, and virtually all the equipment and *materiél* of his entire force. Wellesley was well-satisfied: his casualties during the chase were only 300, together with some 200 sick and stragglers. Certainly Moore had been avenged.[24] To continue the pursuit any further would be impractical, taking him too far from lines of communication and supply. He had also received a dispatch from Mackenzie: Victor had crossed into Portugal and reached Castelo Branco. After passing the night of the 18th in the walled hill-town of Montalegre, Wellesley rode south ahead of his exhausted troops to confer with Mackenzie, leaving them to follow in easy stages, while Silveira's men remained to guard the frontier.[25]

As he had suspected, Mackenzie had been exaggerating, for the French incursion across the Tagus in mid May at Alcántara was merely a reconnaissance in force.[26] The massive Roman bridge there had resisted destruction by Colonel William Mayne, attempting to defend it with a brigade of Sir Robert Wilson's Lusitanian Legion, but it was not until 10 June that he was able to return to there and blow up one span. Already, in mid April, the village of Alcántara had been sacked by Lapisse, where even the non-combatants were butchered, mutilated, or raped, and then – as a parting shot – burned on a pyre together with pigs and dogs!

On retiring from the Castelo Branco, Marshal Victor had turned south to occupy Mérida, but on the news of Soult's ejection from Oporto reaching Madrid on 10 June – three weeks after the event – he had been ordered by Joseph Bonaparte and Marshal Jourdan to retire into the Tagus valley, nearer the capital and in communication with General Sebastiani, who commanded some 22,000 men in the vicinity of Madridejos (50 miles south-east of Toledo). Together with the garrison at Madrid, the combined strength of the French in the area would soon be in the region of 50,000, more than Wellesley would care to face alone.

However, General Cuesta, despite of his defeat at Medellín, still mustered a force said to be 28,000 infantry and 6,000 cavalry in the vicinity of Talavera in the Tagus valley. If General Venegas, located somewhere south of Madridejos with almost 30,000 men, could keep Sebastiani occupied in La Mancha without involving himself in a pitched battle, then there was every likelihood that an Anglo-Spanish army might defeat Victor.

Wellesley had been in communication with Cuesta, proposing co-operation, and once the army, fatigued by the rapidity of recent operations, had been re-equipped and reorganised, he intended to support him. He was also in need of 20,000 pairs of shoes – at this period, an infantry shoe was a shoe,[27] with no difference between left or right! – and hoped the late arrival of a consignment from Lisbon would not delay his departure.

Another interminable problem – one which was to dog Wellesley constantly throughout the war – was the lack of specie or hard cash, now needed urgently, as substantial bills for supplies received were overdue, while two months pay was already due to his men; substantial numbers of Portuguese muleteers, bullock-drivers, carters, shepherds, among others, had to be kept contented: they could hardly be expected to accept *vales* (a paper promise to pay) or Treasury bills. The army's regular requirements in the field had to be paid for; yet despite repeated badgering, arrears were beginning to accumulate, as they continued to do so, inexorably. Wellesley, when intemperately accusing the government for their lack of support for and apparent indifference to the campaign in Spain that he anticipated would transpire, does not seem to have appreciated that it was precisely the extra expense it would inevitable incur, that the government was keen to avoid.[28]

He was preoccupied also by the undisciplined state of some regiments during his recent campaign, the rank and file robbing the peasantry of food, often with violence, and continuing to do so even when receiving full rations in their cantonments.[29] Not being one to mince his words, we find him writing: 'the army behave terribly ill: they are a rabble who cannot bear success any more than Sir John Moore's army could bear failure.' However, he was 'endeavouring to tame them,' partly by increasing the number of his assistant-provost-marshals.

There were several logistical problems to be resolved before the army was in any way self-sufficient, but in view of repeated assurances by his Spanish allies that they would keep him well-supplied, it would seem sensible to unite with Cuesta even if a specific plan of action had still to be agreed.[30] Before setting out, Wellesley ensured that his left flank was defended by Wilson's Lusitanian Legion; further north-west, Beresford commanded Portuguese army units, while Silveira's troops were still in evidence. Between them, they would keep a watch on any possible but unlikely offensive movements on the part of either Soult, now at Zamora, or Ney, who had withdrawn from Galicia into León, while a force commanded by Marshal Mortier might threaten from this direction also.

1 Among those in the cabinet who recognised his qualities was Canning, who in a private letter to Frere dated 19 April, wrote: 'In Wellesley … you will find everything you can wish – frankness – temper – honesty – quickness – comprehensiveness – and military Ability – not only eminent beyond any other military Commander that could be chosen – but perhaps possessed by him alone, of all our Commanders, in a degree that qualifies for great undertakings.'

2 Cradock, the ineffectual and desponding commander at Lisbon since 14 December, had precipitatedly withdrawn all outlying troops from as far afield as Almeida and Oporto, the presence of which could have menaced Soult's advance on that city in March, to cantonments near the capital, where they remained inactive for over three months in the expectation that, inevitably, they would be evacuated.

General Alan Cameron, who had been commanding at Oporto, when writing to Cradock on 16 January, refers to having collected 'several detachments of recovered men belonging to Sir J. Moore's army, whom I found scattered in all directions, without necessities, and some of them committing every possible excess …,' who were to form the basis of two Battalions of Detachments, later brigaded with the 29th and 97th Foot.

3 Chapters 14 of Oman's *Wellington's Army*, and 7 of Richard Glover's *Peninsular Preparation* (1963) are informative on flogging.

4 Probably James Kemmis.

5 Lawrence, then aged 18, had not long returned from the disastrous Buenos Aires expedition.

6 It was not the first time that British officers had been invited to reanimate their army: several had been reasonably successful in doing so during the 1760s under the English-born German, Count Wilhelm von Schaumburg Lippe-Bückeburg. General Dumouriez reported later that compared with their demoralised condition previously, the Portuguese cavalry and infantry could manoeuvre well and were in a tolerable state of discipline, and that the former could even leap hedges and ditches in squadrons. Although this estimate of their capacities was subscribed to by Professor Link, writing in 1797, he could not help remarking that the Portuguese officers were not sufficiently respected: the fact that 'commanders of fortresses who reside in Lisbon ... have at most seen their forts once in their lives, and generals ... never with their regiments, [did] not much contribute to this improvement.'

7 Very rarely, as at Majadahonda, did they let down their commanders.

8 He had been A.Q.M.G. to General Baird at Corunna in the previous October, but took no part in the Moore's disastrous campaign. In the following April he was nominated Beresford's Q.M.G.

[9] For organisational details, see Chapter 2, by Ron MacGuigan, of *Inside Wellington's Peninsular Army.*

[10] Except in the 1st Division. A separate, entirely Portuguese Division, was also established, in March 1810, commanded by John Hamilton.

[11] With the growth of the Allied Army, the number of commissariat officers increased to a higher proportion, partly due to the fact that additional cavalry had added to their activities.

[12] The French were unable to turn this to their advantage, as few vessels were in a seaworthy state; nor was there any material at hand with which to carry out repairs, a situation not untypical of Spanish arsenals at any time. Captain Hotham, in the *Defiance* (74), with two frigates, was keeping a close watch on both Ferrol and Corunna and, when they were evacuated by Ney in June, British marines were landed to put out of action any remaining guns defending the ports, which were regarrisoned by Spanish troops. British seamen were later landed with essential stores and material to supervise the re-equipping of the majority of the warships, which were removed by late Autumn, some to strengthen Allied naval forces off Cadiz.

[13] 4,500 British (including 1,400 cavalry and 6 six-pounder) and 7,425 Portuguese (together with five cavalry squadrons and 18 guns).

[14] More likely that of João (John) I (d. 1433), married to Philippa of Lancaster, and the founder of the abbey. Leach admitted to having cut off a button from the royal robes, when the embalmed body had been exposed by troops during the retreat from Busaço in 1810. He was not the only one to indulge in such proclivities: When at, the Escorial in August 1812, Capt. John Dobbs admitted to entering the Panteón de los Infantes and taking 'two silk buttons off John of Austria's dress,' adding 'what became of them, I cannot tell.'

[15] It comprised some 11,850 infantry, predominantly British, including five battalions only which had served with him at Vimeiro, but the majority were supplied by 'second battalions' from the home establishment, as few veterans of the Corunna campaign were yet in a fit state to return, together with 1,400 cavalry under General Sir Stapleton Cotton, and 24 guns. They were formed into seven brigades, but their brigadiers were directly responsible either to Edward Paget, Sherbrooke, or Hill, a provisional arrangement which later developed into the system of Divisions.

[16] Waters, a colonel in the Portuguese service, and previously employed by Messrs Warre, the Port wine shippers, knew the area intimately.

[17] Edward Paget, commanding at the Seminary, lost his right arm in this action, and was unable to return to the Peninsula until the Autumn of 1812.

[18] It is recorded that although most of the Allied troops had been kept well away from the Port wine stores, some K.G.L. gunners had much appreciated the contents of one they discovered: twenty of them drank 41 bottles at a sitting!

[19] As one officer in the 29th recalled: 'They made no fight. Every man seemed running for his life, throwing away their knapsacks and arms … all begging for quarter and surrendering with great good humour." In addition to prisoners, French losses were 300 killed and wounded, but Soult also abandoned some 1,500 men in Oporto's hospital, and a deal of equipment, including no less than 70 guns. Wellesley's casualties totalled 123 men (23 killed, 98 wounded, and two missing).

[20] Colonel Hugh Gough (87th) had never been 'a witness to such a scene of Misery and horror as here presented itself. Every house and public Building

... with the Exception of a Monastery, that covered the passage of the Bridge, a Chapel and about 5 detached houses, were burnt to the ground, with hundreds of its late Inhabitants lying dead in the Streets.'

21 Following in their wake, Wellesley saw 'many persons hanging in the trees by the sides of the road, executed for no reason ... excepting that they have not been friendly to the French invasion ...'

22 Later the 1st Earl of Munster.

23 There were two vital single-arched bridges that Soult had to cross to escape: that known as the Ponte Nova, spanning the Cávado not far north of Salamonde, and that further north-east over the Miserala. L'Evêque drew both, calling one the 'Saltador' – the leaper, and the other the Miserela bridge, but it would seem that the latter was also known as the 'Saltador'.

24 News of Wellesley's success had reached London on 25 May. Despite it being slighted by Lord Grey as 'nothing more than an affair of a rear-guard, and is ridiculously magnified,' Castlereagh reluctantly gave Wellesley permission to enter Spain, if essential, but at his own responsibility.

25 The main force counter-marched to Braga, and thence south via Oporto, Coimbra, and Tomar. Beresford's units traversed Vila Real, Lamego, Guarda, and Castelo Branco to converge on Abrantes, which the vanguard of the those with the least distance to cover entered on 11 June.

26 In view of this threat, the remaining Allied troops in the vicinity of Lisbon were reinforced by Admiral Berkeley landing all his marines and providing a flotilla of flatboats armed with carronades, which might resist any possible crossing of the Tagus, which although shallow, was found to be navigable as far as Abrantes, some 90 miles upstream, of which the Commissariat later took full advantage, as providing a more rapid form of transport to that base than by land.

27 Capt. Browne has recorded that whenever the men lacked shoes and were foot sore, while waiting to be properly shod, they would to cut out of the fresh hide of a recently killed bullock 'as much as would cover their feet & bind above the Ancles, the fleshy side inwards – then stiched it up, & wore it as long as it would last together ...' The muddy tracks and sodden fields traversed had made havoc with shoes.

Marc Isambard Brunel, after seeing the lacerated feet of survivors from the Corunna campaign, due to the shoddy footwear previously supplied by unscrupulous manufacturers having rapidly disintegrated, designed a machine to sew stronger boots and shoes and set up a manufactory at Battersea, manned by disabled soldiers. Impressed by their quality, Castlereagh persuaded him to expand production, the government buying them at 6s 6d. a pair; but, with the advent of peace, contracts were peremptorily cancelled, causing Brunel financial embarrassment, although eventually, due to the intervention of the Duke of York, the 80,000 pairs left on his hands were sold to the army at a discount.

28 A provisional £230,000 in specie reached Lisbon on 15 June, but not Headquarters at Abrantes for another ten days, only two days prior to Wellesley leaving the place on the first stage of his advance into Spain.

29 John Spencer Cooper was one of the first to admit that no sooner was the day's march ended, than the men turned out to steal pigs, poultry, wine, etc. One evening, after halting, a wine store was broken open, and much was carried off. On finding this out, the owner ran and brought an officer of the 53rd, who

caught one of our company, named Brown, in the act of handing out the wine in camp kettles. Seizing Brown by the collar, the officer shouted, 'Come out you rascal, and give me your name.' 'Brennan', he replied before knocking the officer down and making his escape, and was never found out. Major George Bingham, also with the 53rd, refers to the ill-secured cellars at Cantanhede, passed on the march south, which 'our people broke, and committed great excesses', which he deplored, as until then they 'had behaved ourselves very well; but our men are so harassed by incessant marching without appearing to derive any benefit from it, or without any prospect of its termination, that they are become careless and do not mind what becomes of them.'

30 Some officers, among them Major Bingham, considered the plan to be 'hazardous' ; that there was a likelihood that they would be outnumbered, and 'the farther we advance, the farther we get from our resources, and the more difficulty it will become, to make any retrograde movement; and I am afraid our faithful allies would be ready to turn against us.'

4

June to August 1809: The Talavera campaign

On 28 June Wellesley's 16,600 infantry, separated into four Divisions, together with almost 3,000 cavalry, and 5 batteries of artillery, set out from Abrantes by divergent routes towards Castelo Branco, crossing into Spain at Zarza la Mayor (west of Coria) on 3 July.[1] Reinforcements from Lisbon were expected to catch up with them. Problems over transport were met early in their progress, with bullock-carts breaking down or their Portuguese drivers, pressed into service, absconding, frequently taking their draught animals. Replacements for both had to be found at short notice, by compulsion if necessary.[2] On one occasion, thirty carts carrying medical stores were abandoned by their owners: after this episode, all such equipment was ordered to be carried on muleback.[3]

Schaumann, advancing with K.G.L. brigades of the 1st Division on the tortuous road leading north-east through the hills, remarked that it was the same one that Junot had used when invading Portugal in the late Autumn of 1807. They passed 'herds of goats grazing on the heights all round, while in the valleys you could see a plough drawn by bullocks, laboriously tearing up the parched ground. It was a picture of beautiful contrasts, a wild, and at the same time, cultivated landscape ... The inhabitants were obliging and friendly, but complained bitterly of having been robbed of all they possessed ...[and] we were shown with great triumph pieces of clothing and arms belonging to French soldiers, who, having fallen into the hands of the peasants one by one, had been miserably murdered.'

At Coria, Schaumann attended 'a bull fight, for the Spaniards liked to amuse themselves by taking the bullocks which were to be slaughtered for the British troops, and goading them to fury in a large square ... A large doll of rags and straw, with feet made of lead so that it could not fall over, was placed in the middle of the arena, and this was tossed into the air again and again by the infuriated animals …' Some provisions were supplied at Plasencia, but no means of transporting them. As they were seldom given forage, the dragoons rode into the fields each evening, each returning with 'two sheafs of barley on his horse's back', for which the Spaniards 'never forgot to claim requisition receipt notes' from Schaumann, who scathingly remarked that although they troops usually bivouacked in the open at that season, whenever obliged to seek some form of shelter, grudgingly provided, the Spaniards would hardly offer them a glass of water.

The Allied commanders had agreed to rendez-vous on the 10th at Almaraz, where the Roman bridge was an important crossing point on the Tagus. Although its wider span had been destroyed by Victor after his troops had retired up the valley, this had been repaired after a fashion by Cuesta, whom it was hoped might have assembled there the carts, waggons, provender, etc. he had promised.

On the 17th, the Allied army, approaching from Plasencia in columns, crossed the Tiétar not far north of its confluence with the Tagus,[4] the wide valley of which was here bounded to the north by the long line of the Sierra de Gredos, rising to almost 2,600m at the Pico Almanzor. Few could imagine that this barrier range, shimmering in the heat, was capped with snow for much of the year. Two days later, Schaumann and his companions in the Commissariat camped on the banks of the Tiétar after they had bathed, but during the night, not far from his bed, a dragoon 'was stung in the arm by a scorpion or a viper. There was a great to-do, and a doctor was fetched. If I remember rightly, the poor devil had to have his arm amputated because the wound festered in the great heat.'

Wellesley's party had gone ahead, escorted by a squadron of Spanish hussars, well mounted and equipped, but, as Londonderry observed, 'we were not long in discovering that they had been selected to do this duty ... simply because their appearance was superior to that of any other corps in the Spanish army.'[5] The escort then lost its way, and by the time they reached Cuesta's Headquarters, where he awaiting them, it was already dusk. His troops had been under arms for four hours already. By the wavering light of blazing torches their swarthy visages and the flashing and rattling of their arms as Wellesley passed down their lines were indeed spectacular; but he was not reassured by what he saw, nor by Cuesta, who treated him with suspicion and who, after the review, had to be lifted into his coach.[6]

General Stewart described the troops, with a few exceptions, as 'remarkably fine men,' but the majority were indifferently equipped, being noticeably deficient in shoes; and it was 'easy to perceive ... from the attitude in which they stood, as well as from the manner in which they held their arms, that little or no discipline prevailed among them ... in the aggregate, they were little better than bold peasantry, armed partially like soldiers, but completely unacquainted with a soldier's duty.'[7] The same criticism applied to their cavalry and artillery, while it was evident that the majority of their senior officers were 'incapable of bearing the fatigues or surmounting the difficulties of one hard campaign.'[8] Nor was Colonel Leslie impressed by the Spanish 'Volunteers', some of whom 'had belts, others none. They had no pouches, but a broad belt of soft leather, in which were placed a row of tin tubes, each holding a cartridge, with a fold of leather to cover them, fastened round the waist.'

The two armies converged on Oropesa, some 20 miles west of Talavera, where they paraded for inspection by Wellesley on the 21st, before continuing their march, parallel to each other. Schaumann noticed Spanish soldiers on both sides of the road, 'mixed up with women, mules and carts, who had doubtless fallen out of the ranks on the flimsiest pretext, and were now standing round large kitchen fires, comfortably smoking cigarettes and staring and yawning at us. It was a sight that gave us but a poor impression of the discipline and courage of our beloved allies.' At Oropesa, John Cooper was quartered in a convent 'close to a vault in which the dead friars were interred,' where 'one of the company, named John Clapham, wanting to cook his dinner, sought for some fuel, but finding none ... entered the vault, and throwing a friar out of his coffin, he smashed it, cooked his mess, and dined like a respectable man. Whether the ejected friar felt angry at such treatment, 'tis not for me to say, certain it was that in the dead of night a terrible uproar was made that roused the whole convent. The men started up, seized their arms, and rushed out, crying, 'What's the matter?' Some said, 'The French are coming,' and 'twas long before the hubbub subsided. However, Mr Clapham and the friar were blamed for the panic, guilty or not. The real cause was never found out.'

Once at Talavera, Schaumann found quarters in the house of 'a literary man,' as was apparent from the 'large library of dusty books bound in pigskin,' left behind when he had fled. Opposite stood a storehouse from which regular rations were distributed to Spanish regiments, leaving their Allies hungry.[9] This was more than he could stomach, so with little compunction, he ordered his party to ride out to 'way-lay and raid the Spanish convoys, force their escorts to take flight, and then bring back to the bivouac in triumph as much as they wanted.'

He had a greater triumph a day or so later, when all commissaries had been instructed to deliver everything they had collected to a central depot. Schaumann had set off with a corporal and twelve dragoons to reconnoitre the far bank of the Tagus. After a luckless hour or two they rested at the foot of some desolate hills, while one of them, an Irishman, clambered to a height, lay flat, placed one end of the ramrod of his pistol on the ground, the other end to his ear, and listened.

> He had not lain there long, when suddenly he sprang to his feet, and swore by St Patrick that he had heard the lowing of cattle and the clanging of cow-bells on the other side of the hills. At this we all raced up the hill as if we were storming a fort ... [after] a quarter of an hour, we beheld a very narrow valley entirely surrounded by hills, and in the midst of it ... a quantity of all kinds of cattle – bullocks, cows, calves, pigs, about 6,000 sheep and goats, a wooden shed, a well, and also some dogs and a few herdsmen armed with long firelocks. As we approached the dogs attacked us savagely, and the herdsmen seemed thunderstruck. I got my dragoons to surround them, and riding up to them alone, with my pistol in my hand, told them that they must follow me with all their cattle to English headquarters, where their herd would be properly valued, and where they would be paid to the last penny in good money. I added a word or two of explanation and comfort, and told them to have patience – which is the Spanish expression for making the best of a bad job ... Night was falling when we returned to the bridge at Talavera. About forty Spanish troopers, who had just watered their horses, rode into the midst of my sheep ...and seizing one or two of them by the fleece, lifted them without ceremony on to their saddles, and wanted to make off ... but we put them to flight at the point of the sword ... We had hardly entered the first streets ... when I saw a women standing at the door of her house, contemplating the cattle with amazement. Then she uttered a piercing shriek and wildly tore her hair ... In a moment I was surrounded by hundreds of such furies, and ultimately a number of threatening men, all of which stormed me with prayers and curses, and begged me to spare their cattle – Lord Jesus, the cattle of the town of Talavera!

At last, the herd careered into the Commissary-General's capacious courtyard, where Schaumann found him disputing with the Lisbon purveyor Senhor Sampaio about the non-arrival of bullocks.[10] After being complimented on for having extricated them both 'from an appalling dilemma,' Schaumann turned away and fled, first 'commending both the crowd waiting down-stairs and besieging the staircase, and the lowing and bleating cattle tightly squeezed into the courtyard, to the Commissary-General.' It was all part of the day's work.

It was while in Talavera that Schaumann, from what he had seen of them, made a general condemnation of Spanish generals, invariably parading 'in uniforms covered with gold lace, surrounded by immense staffs,' and although 'usually of good family,' they were 'both head-strong and conceited ... think nothing of disregarding orders from a higher authority; and altogether there is about them too much talk, too much church-going, and cigar-smoking. They have three big meals a day, and their sleep after luncheon is to them the principal concern of their lives.' The rest of the Spanish officers were little better, being

> mostly ignorant and ill-mannered. It is impossible to find a gentleman among them ... They are chiefly concerned with their uniforms, the cuffs of which reach to their elbows, their enormously large hats, their long Toledo swords, which they do not wear at their sides but carry under their arms, and with loafing about public walks and cafés ... Even the Spanish ladies do not hesitate to take exception to the ill-breeding, coarseness and arrogance of their own military men. '*Son brutos*', they would say. As the majority of Spanish officers hail from the lower orders, and feel themselves drawn to common and ordinary associates, they have no notion of inspiring respect among their subordinates . One frequently sees officers hobnobbing quite familiarly with their men, drinking out of the same glass, or smoking the same cigar in turns. There is, therefore, not much discipline.

He was not alone in his opinion. Surtees, among others, thought likewise, that they 'appeared utterly unfit and unable to command their men. Those who had the means, seemed to think of nothing else but dressing like apes or mountebanks, and intriguing with the women. It was really absurd and ludicrous to see the strange figures they generally made of themselves ...' Those who were mounted 'would caper and prance about the streets like so many fools, riding with their legs at full stretch, and the toe of the boot (if they had one) just touching the stirrup...' Surtees admitted that 'they were not all alike, but the majority ... were the most haughty, and ... contemptible creatures in the shape of officers, that I ever beheld.'

Victor's army had retired behind the Alberche, which entered the Tagus just east of Talavera. An opportunity of defeating him before he received reinforcements was wasted by Cuesta's obstinate last-minute refusal to carry out the agreed joint plan, which was to attack him on the 23th. Victor retired on the following day, not realising until then that, in addition to the Spaniards, he had the whole British army opposing him. Wellesley, understandably frustrated, told Cuesta in no uncertain terms that in view of his vacillation, he could not consider embarking on any further combined operations until assured that the British army – by now on half-rations – would be properly supplied with food and transport with which to bring it forward. As he remonstrated in a letter to Frere: '... I have never seen an army so ill-treated ... It is ridiculous to pretend that this country cannot supply our wants ... This is a rich country in corn, in comparison with Portugal ... The Spanish army has plenty of everything, and we alone, upon whom everything depends, are actually starving.' In fact, the Spanish themselves were also short of provisions, but they were more used to privations, and habituated to being short-changed by their own administration.[11]

Perversely, on the 24th Cuesta decided to attack alone – he would drive Victor as far as Madrid – only to have his own troops thrust back in disorder, for by then, as was evident to Wellesley, Victor had been reinforced not only by part of the Madrid garrison, accompanied by Joseph Bonaparte and Jourdan, but also by Sebastiani's units, for Venegas had done nothing in the way of delaying, as instructed, their probable convergence. Seeing Cuesta's troops swarm back towards Talavera faster than they had pressed forward so precipitately, was enough to confirm in Wellesley's mind that it would be most ill-advised to let them take up a stand with their backs to the Alberche, as was now the Spaniard's intention.[12] It was only on the morning of the 27th July, after Wellesley, who had misgivings about the Spanaird's capacity to maneouvre, had actually pleaded with him, that Cuesta consented to post his infantry either behind the surviving walls of Talavera or align them in the rear of improvised fieldworks.

The alarm being given that a battle was imminent, Schaumann, when riding to the front to view the action, noticed 'an old-fashioned coach drawn by six gaily-comparisoned mules' standing on a wooden bridge. 'A man of about seventy years old, in brown clothes and a bob-tailed wig, who, if he had not carried so many orders, might have been taken for an old German shopkeeper, descended from it accompanied by several officers, crossed the bridge, inspected it, noted that there was a hole in it, and then sat down on the steps of an iron cross standing by the roadside. The officers of his staff stood around him and smoked cigarettes. It was Don Gregorio de la Cuesta, the Spanish Commander-in-Chief!'

According to William Napier, when describing the Spanish positions, these consisted of a slightly sunken road leading north from the town, and 'ditches, mud walls, breastworks and felled trees' immediately west of the Portiña – a stream flowing into the Tagus here – as far as the Pajar de Vergara, a hillock further north: there, 'they could not be attacked seriously, nor their dispositions be even seen; thus one-half of the line of battle was rendered impregnable, yet held by the worst troops.'[13] British units extended this line towards and across the Cerro de Medellín, a ridge to the east of which stood the lower Cerro de Cascajal. Other hills – the Sierra de Segurilla – rose further north.

Wellesley had initially crossed the Alberche with two divisions to support Cuesta (having so recklessly advanced further east), but then retired to a position near the Casa de Salinas, standing among olive groves and *encinas* (evergreen oaks), its towers providing a convenient lookout post. But he had to descend rapidly when a line of *tirailleurs,* advancing furtively through the trees, followed by General Lapisse's infantry,[14] surprised part of Colonel Donkin's brigade, resting with muskets stacked. Assistant Surgeon Brooke remembered 'eating under a tree without an idea the enemy could be less than three miles distant, when the most tremendous firing came driving towards us. In an instant musket as well as cannon balls were flying about in every direction. The soldiers were surprised; some regiments had not loaded their firelocks. The [skirmishers] retreated upon us with the enemy after them. One British regiment fired on another. A slight confusion took place which gave advantage to the French and caused much bloodshed.' Fortunately, Wellesley was at hand to bring the enemy to a halt and lead back the companies of the 5/60th and Mackenzie's brigade, which had covered Donkin's precipitate retreat, but nevertheless casualties were 440, among them 70 killed. On reaching the Portiña brook, he deployed these units among the rest of his divisions.

It is not the intention to describe in any detail the course of the ensuing battle, which fell into two distinct parts, the first main combat taking place in the vicinity of the Pajar de Vergara and Cerro de Medellín.

Talavera

Victor had sent some of his dragoons ahead of the main force, which warily approached the southern end of the Allied position. Imagining that these squadrons, still trotting around out of range in their front, were about to fall on them, the entire Spanish line fired one deafening volley and turned tail: an astonishing sight.[15] As Wellesley described it in his dispatch to Castlereagh, barely concealing his profound disgust: 'Nearly two thousand of them ran off ... not 100 yards from where I was standing, who were neither attacked, nor threatened with an attack, and who were frightened only by the noise of their own fire ...' In spite of this extraordinary performance, the temporary gap in the Spanish lines was soon filled,[16] but by now it was growing dark, and once picquets were posted, Wellesley's troops, having been on their feet for several hours, settled down for the night, many on empty stomachs.

The 7th K.G.L.'s picquets were taken by surprise and suffered losses in an sudden midnight attack on the Medellín,[17] in stemming which Hill was almost taken prisoner. When at dawn his positions were heavily bombarded, Wellesley ordered his men to lie flat, preferable behind the crest, which soon was enveloped by a protective cloud of smoke, to await the inevitable attack of enemy columns,[18] three of which were soon approaching. This was followed by an artillery duel at long range, then by a lull, an informal truce in which the adversaries collected their wounded and slaked their thirst in the muddy Portiña, for the sun was now high in the sky and the suffocating heat unbearable. Oman referred to it as being 'the first example of that amicable spirit which reigned between the hostile armies all through the war, and which in its later years developed into that curious code of signals ... by which French and English gave each other notice whenever serious work was intended, refraining on all other occasions from unnecessary outpost bickering or sentry-shooting,' a habit to which the Spanish were addicted.

Capt. Sillery (R.A.) had a problem, for he was suffering from diarrhoea, a bout of which attacked him when his battery shortly came under fire. Not wishing to go to the rear (should it be said that he was afraid), having warned a fellow officer, he 'then deliberately walked a hundred yards or so in front of the brigade, and disembarrassing himself of part of his clothing, yielded to the irresistable necessity of the case, after readjusting his dress, and calmly putting on his sword and sash, he returned leisurely to his post. The transaction excited a great deal of mirth, notwithstanding the heat of the action.'

At about 1.00 p.m. the British lines immediately south of the Medellín were raked by another cannonade from no less than 80 guns. Three enemy columns then issued from a thinly wooded area into the open, where they were met with destructive artillery fire, the southernmost also receiving volleys from the Spanish troops still in position there.

Wellesley's right flank, anchored on the Pajar de Vergara, was defended by Alexander Campbell's Division with a battery of 3-pounders and four 12-pounders appropriated from the Spaniards, which after momentarily giving way under heavy fire, reformed and counter-attacked, before which the French melted away, leaving six guns behind them. These were immediately put out of action, being of no use, the British balls being too large for their bore.

While Campbell's line were thus engaged, two 12-battalion divisions, commanded by Lapisse and Sebastiani, some 15,000 men, largely veterans, were seen advancing between the Pajar and the Medellín on a front of about 1,500 yards.[19] Opposing this powerful attack was Sherbrooke's Division of 6,000 men in a single two-deep line, probably divided into twelve crescent-shaped groups directly facing the head of each enemy column. Every single British musket could fire a succession of steady rolling volleys: but only about 1,300 of the French were able to fire back. Each column was brought to a stand before they had a chance to deploy into line, and the head of each disintegrated. One after the other, the battalions retreated, with Sherbrooke's men, stabbing with their bayonets, in pursuit. Although Cameron's Brigade stopped short not far east of the Portiña and reformed, three others swarmed out of control, to find themselves facing a second line of columns, between which the survivors of the first attack found shelter. The tide of battle almost turned, for the British centre would have been left virtually unmanned, had not Wellesley, in anticipation, ordered the strong 1/48th down from the Medellín, and Mackenzie's brigade to move obliquely north to reinforce it. Through these four battalions, totalling some 3,000 men – all that could be spared to fill the rent – Sherbrooke's men, badly mauled, streamed back and reformed. They had to hold off at least 10,000 men under Sebastiani. At this moment of crisis, what was indeed a 'thin red line' closed up, awaiting the order to fire. At a range of only 50 yards, the head of the advancing column was met by a devastating volley, repeated inexorably every 15 seconds from each of the 80 half companies.[20] The northernmost division, its commander killed, broke first; while that to the south was charged in flank by Cotton's cavalry, but only briefly pursued, as French dragoons were seen massed not far to their rear.

Meanwhile, in the contingency that Victor might attempt to turn his left flank, Wellesley had already placed batteries on the Medellín to rake any approach from the north-east, with strong cavalry units deployed in the valley between it and the hills further north.[21] These were ordered to attack the French infantry now advancing over what appeared to be a level plain, which would force them to form square and provide a more vulnerable artillery target.

The ensuing encounter was another example of irrepressible cavalry running amok, although in this case an excuse might be found. In perfect order, the 23rd Light Dragoons, when increasing their pace, careered directly into a *barranco* – the precipitous bank of a *rambla* (the dry bed of a tributary rivulet of the Portiña) – concealed from them by high grass, and dust kicked up by the foremost mounts. It would not have been a serious obstacle if approached at a controlled speed, but it was a hazard at almost a gallop, unless on a mount as superior as that of Colonel Elley's, which cleared the gully, seen too late for him to have stemmed the charge. The first rank ran full tilt into it, followed by some of the second, which added to the chaos as men and mounts sought to struggle out, and many were the necks and limbs broken in the crush. Some 170 surviving sabres scrambled up the far bank, rallied and charged ahead, swerving between the infantry squares that had formed, only to run directly into a brigade of *chasseurs*. Outnumbered by five to one, and on spent mounts, they had no chance: the regiment lost half its strength in 15 minutes, including three officers and 105 men, most of them wounded, being taken prisoner. Most of the K.G.L. cavalry, coming up further to their left, were able to leap the *rambla*,[22] but made little impression on the squares and, on coming under fire from supporting squares, and after suffering casualties, were ordered to retire, as did the French: by now, both sides had had enough.

Although there was no evidence of any further assault on his lines, Wellesley was in no position to take the offensive. During the remaining few hours of daylight his wounded were collected together, but already a number had been burnt alive, unable to crawl away from fires started among long dry grass and stubble, caused by smouldering wadding fanned by the wind, and little could be done to stop it. Wellesley set about redeploying his men and posting picquets, although it was unlikely that Victor would mount another night attack: indeed, as dawn broke, the plain to the east was seen to be deserted: the French had preferred to retire discreetly. Losses had been horrfic in this Pyrrhic victory, described later by Wellington as a 'murderous' battle – 'two days of the hardest fighting I have ever been party to.'[23] It was about 6.00 that morning that the vanguard of Robert Craufurd's Light Brigade entered Talavera, and was posted east of the town. In a vain attempt to reach the battlefield in time, they had made a prodigious forced march under a blistering sun towards the distant rumble of guns: but see below.

Simmons, who noticed that at every opportunity the Spaniards had stripped naked all the wounded and dying, 'which gave admission to the attacks of myriads of pernicious flies and the heat of the burning sun,' soon found himself 'collecting the dead bodies and putting them into large heaps mixed with faggots and burning them. The stench from so many dead was volatile and offensive beyond conception, as the heat of the weather was very great.' Leach wondered which was worse: the 'unsufferable stench of the hundreds of dead bodies of men and horses still unburied,' or the smell of the blazing funeral pyres. To Schaumann, it presented a shocking spectacle: 'Corpses lay thickly about ... particularly on the hill which our troops had so bravely defended ... it looked as if several battalions were merely sleeping there. Our own men could be distinguished by their red coats, and fifty paces off could be seen the blue and grey uniforms of the enemy ... A number of French wounded who had been left behind cried plaintively to us for help, and begged us to move them away so that the Spaniards could not cut their throats,' although everything possible was being done to put a stop to such brutality.[24] In addition to the 'dead and wounded horses, weapons of all kinds, broken carts, ammunition wagons, chests, harness, shakos, light dragoon helmets, grenadier busbies, shreds of clothing, ammunition pouches [were] scattered all over the ground.' He came across some men of the 23rd Dragoons placed in a barn near the *rambla*: 'all young and fine-looking fellows – lying dead in three rows ... carried thither for burial.'

On returning to his quarters, Schaumann found it ransacked by the Spaniards: 'All our boxes and cases had been burst open, and their contents strewn over the ground, robbed, broken or hacked to pieces; our beds had been cut open and the feathers and horsehair had been shaken out and stolen, and our bookcase lay in the middle ... We waded knee-deep in feathers and plunder of every description ... broken crockery, pots, books, and written records. It was only with great pains that we were able to find a saucepan in which to prepare our usual breakfast ... We made a fire out of an armchair, a few histories of the saints bound in pigskin, and a number of crusty old legal authorities.'

Leach, having lent his mount to a brother officer, saw him returning to the bivouac

> *not* on horseback, but on foot, and with a face longer than my arm ... [for] a rascally Portuguese or Spanish boy, to whose care he had entrusted my charger ... whilst he went into a shop, had disappeared with it ... this was a serious mishap. The *prad* [then a slang term for a horse] was

> a capital one; and the saddle, bridle, and cloak affixed to the saddle, the *valise*, containing all the articles of toilet, a blanket under the saddle, and the various *et ceteras*, which ... constituted the sole comfort of campaigners, were not to be replaced for love or money on the plains of Talavera. Instead ... of having a chestnut quadruped to carry me ... and having the benefit of a cloak and blanket at night in the bivouac, (our tent was thrown away ... in consequence of the death, by starvation and fatigue, of my baggage mule) I had the felicity to tramp from the Tagus to the Guadiana, no trifling distance either, and to stretch myself at the foot of a tree every night, with no covering but the sky and a green jacket.

And on an empty stomach: 'I do not believe that more than one day's allowance of bread was issued from the 29th of July to the evening of the 2nd of August, nor were the rations of wine, spirits, and meat, forthcoming either'. Everyone scrambled 'for whatever was eatable or drinkable, at any price.' Schaumann himself 'had subsisted only on water, chocolate, biscuit, and a little wine.'[25]

But it was not only the lack of promised supplies that caused Wellesley to order his sadly depleted and famished army to march west as rapidly as it could on 3 August. Intelligence had reached him that Mortier, with 15,000 men, was threatening his line of retreat to Portugal. Already, on the 30th, French units had crossed the Puerto de Baños, on the road from Salamanca, for in spite of Cuesta's assurance that it was adequately defended, the two regiments sent there had never arrived, while the militia stationed at the pass had fled, not that they could have done much to stop the French advance down the steep descent. This allowed Mortier's force, which it was not yet realised was only the van of a far larger corps (50,000 men, commanded by Soult, whose powers of recuperation were remarkable) to enter Plasencia the following day, while reports were coming in that enemy cavalry was already at Navalmoral, close to Almaraz on the Tagus.

After a deal of haggling, Cuesta agreed to remain at Talavera to hold in check any possible re-approach by Victor, while Wellesley would march against Mortier, leaving his more seriously wounded to the tender mercy of its civilian population: he lacked all means of carrying them away. But Wellesley had not reckoned that the day after his troops had marched out of Talavera, Cuesta was to do likewise.[26] According to Capt. Charles Boothby (R.E.), who was among the 1,500 British wounded, several surgeons had been left to attend to those of both sides, and the re-occupying French, in gratitude, had allowed them to go wherever they wished. Wellesley could trust the French to treat them well, although he could not answer for the safety of any of their wounded left unguarded, such were the vindictive propensities of the Spanish population in general.[27] Stothert records that Wellesley received accounts of the wounded through the courtesy of Mortier, by then in command, who had 'placed sentries over the quarters of the officers and hospitals, to prevent any of their property being pillaged,' and had even 'advanced money to some out of his own pocket.'

Craufurd's advance

It is convenient to interpose here some description of Craufurd's march from Lisbon with 3,000 men of the Light Brigade, consisting of the first battalions of the 43rd, 52nd, and 95th Regiments, which had cast anchor at Lisbon on 28 June. Leach, who had been there before, having fought at Vimeiro, found little improvement, for although the 'country houses and convents on the sides of most picturesque hills, thickly planted with vines; the legions of wind-mills near Belem; and finally, the city itself, form altogether so enchanting a picture ... How sadly is a stranger disappointed when he lands and traverses the dirty, rascally streets of this priest-ridden city, and wades ... through one uninterrupted accumulation of disgusting filth ...' Simmons found it 'very offensive to the nose of an Englishman,' adding: 'I went to see several churches, which afforded me some amusement and excited my pity, to see a people, through ignorance and gross superstition, duped by a set of worthless priests under the plea of religion. I dined at an English hotel, and afterwards went to the opera. The dancing was too indelicate to give pleasure; at least I felt it so, [but the] Portuguese ladies seemed to enjoy the performance with great rapture ...'

Much of Leach's time was 'busily employed ... in purchasing horses, mules, donkeys, pack-saddles, cigars, and various other odds and ends indispensable in campaigning ... [until] at about midnight on 2 July, the tide serving to take us up the river, we were put into flat-bottomed boats and launches, and the tedious operation of towing us against the current commenced. After 24 hours ... every man's legs terribly cramped by being crammed so tight into the boat,' they went ashore at Valada. The croaking of innumerable frogs did not spoil his sleep, for that had been impossible the previous night, when they had remained sitting upright in the boats. It was Simmons's first night in a bivouac, where 'Hungry, wet, and cold, and without any covering, we lay down by the side of the river. I put one hand in my pocket and the other on my bosom, and lay shivering, and thinking of the glorious life of a soldier, until I fell fast asleep.' The first short stage of their long march commenced next morning.[28] At Santarém, where they halted for two days while waiting 'until the whole of the Brigade and the baggage animals ... arrived,' Simmons 'got a billet upon a blacksmith, and found his family very kind. They brought me fruit, wine, and cakes, but, as I do not understand a word of the language properly, everything was done by signs.' Both Simmons and Leach refer to having reconnoitred the convents, with the inmates of which Leach described having

> had a deal of chit-chat, although the close iron gratings which separated us from our inamorata obscured them in great measure from view. That they were all blessed with sparkling black eye, I am ready to swear; the rest was left to the imagination. By means of the *wirligig* concern in which various matters find their way out of and into the convent, these fair ladies presented us with preserved fruits, nosegays, and all sorts of fine things, in return for which certain little notes, or love-letters, written in villainously bad Portuguese, were transmitted by the same mode of conveyance to them. They appeared much interested as to the result of the campaign in which we were about to take part; and two of them, who were heartily tired of their unnatural prison, declared to myself and a brother-officer, that they were ready and willing to make their escape, with our assistance, and to share our fortunes in the 'tented field.'

No halt was made at Abrantes, where they crossed the Tagus by a bridge of pontoon boats and, after bivouacking, continued the march through Niza, re-crossing at Vila Velha by a flying bridge – above which hovered eagles and vultures – to approach Castelo Branco. Here the 95th halted for two days to let the other two regiments catch up. To ensure that there was no lagging behind, Craufurd issued disciplinary standing orders, at first unpopular; among them, as Costello recorded, that no man

> was allowed to fall out of the ranks on any pretext whatever, without a pass from the officer of his company. Thus it was that frequently, when almost dying of thirst, we were obliged to pass untasted, springs of the finest water. ...[Skulkers] were instantly tried by a drum-head court-martial, and punished accordingly; If the General found a man who had fallen out without a pass, he would take his ramrod and ride off. Often you would see him ride into camp with a dozen ramrods, and the

> adjutant of each regiment was then ordered to find the men who had none, each of whom would receive two dozen lashes. Strange as it may appear, Craufurd maintained a popularity among the men who, on every other occasion, found him to be their best friend. We afterwards learnt that all this apparent severity was considered absolutely essential to the great purpose General Craufurd had in view – dispatch.

The weather being intolerably hot, they often set off 'soon after midnight, and were thereby able ... to finish the day's work by eight or nine in the morning, and to rest during the heat of the day'; but Leach admitted to being 'one of those restless beings who after a night spent in marching, could not sleep in the bivouac during the day.' Although the Riflemen were considered the lightest troops in the service, Costello remembered each having to carry a great weight:

> There was knapsack and straps, two shirts, two pairs of stockings, one pair of shoes, ditto soles and heels, three brushes, a box of blacking, razor, soap-box and strap, and also at the time, an extra pair of trousers. There was a mess-tin, centre-tin and lid, haversack and canteen, great-coat and blanket, a powder-flask filled, a ball bag containing thirty loose balls, a small wooden mallet used to hammer the ball into the muzzle of our rifles, belt and pouch – the latter containing fifty rounds of ammunition – sword belt and rifle, besides other odds and ends that at all times are required for a service soldier. Also, each squad had to carry four bill-hooks, weighing 6lbs each, so that every other day each man had to carry it. Thus we were equiped with from 70-80lbs weight,[29] in the melting month of July. Not content with the above, the General gave strict orders for each man to have his canteen filled with water every morning before commencing the day's march.

Coria was reached on the 22nd, where Simmons entered the cathedral to hear 'some sacred music played upon the organ by a blind man': Leach thought it a fine building, but 'too much gingerbread work in the interior.' The arduous march was continued east via Galisteo and Malpartida – leaving Plasencia to the north – beyond the Tietar pressing on through Navalmoral, where half a pound of bread was distributed, the first they had seen since leaving Coria. That evening, the 27th, 'vague rumours' reached them of an impending battle, and next morning an express arrived 'directing the brigade to make the least possible delay in joining the army'. By noon, according to Leach, they entered Oropesa,

> where General Crawford considered a short halt indispensibly necessary. He then directed the commanding officers of regiments to select and leave [there] such men as were thought incapable of enduring the forced march which he determined to make, and not to halt until he reached the British army … as the distant but unceasing cannonade plainly announced … We soon met *wounded* Spanish soldiers, and Spanish soldiers *not wounded*, bending their course in a direction from the field of battle. I wish I could assert with equal truth that this retrogression was confined to our Spanish allies; but … I regret to say, that stragglers from the ranks of the British army, some without a wound, were also taking a similar direction to the rear. As they passed our column they circulated … reports of a most disheartening nature: 'The British army was utterly defeated, and in full retreat;' 'Sir Arthur Wellesley was wounded;' and, by others, 'he was killed.' In short, all was suspense and uncertainty. One thing was , nevertheless, certain – that the cannonade continued without cessation.
>
> We pressed forward until ten o'clock at night, when, having reached a pool of stagnant water near the road, in which cattle had been watered during the summer, and where they had constantly wallowed, a halt was ordeed for an hour or two. Those who have never been in similar situations may be inclined to doubt my veracity when I state, that the whole brigade, officers and soldiers, rushed into this muddy water, and drank with an eagerness and avidity impossible to describe.
>
> Leach was convinced that had Crauford foreseen that he would be arriving 'a *few hours too late* for Talavera' by giving his brigade two days rest at both Santarém and Castelo Branco rather than one, he would have 'pushed on *pêle-mêle*, without a single halt' to reach the battlefield.[30]

Retreat

The vanguard of Wellesley's famished army had regained Oropesa by noon. And ravenous, as Simmons commented, because 'our Spanish friends infested every road for miles and robbed the peasantry who were bringing bread and vegetables to us for sale, so that they were completely prevented from rendering us any assistance.' Meanwhile, Cuesta had been handed a captured dispatch – passed on to Wellesley with commendable promptness – confirming that the troops at Plasencia were none other than the combined Corps of Ney, Mortier, and Soult, with the latter in command.[31]

With his direct route into Portugal cut, Wellesley had no alternative but to turn due south at Oropesa to cross the Tagus at El Puente del

1. *Above and below:* Henri L'Evêque, 'British troops disembarking in Mondego Bay, August 1808'

2. 'Streets like steps' (at or near Mogadouro)

3. Farm carts near Bragança, displaying solid wheels: little has changed!

4. A *rambla* or dry river bed; the Ponsul at Idanha-a-Velha

5. Adam Neale, 'On the retreat to Corunna'

6. Louis Bacler d'Albe, 'Stuck in the mud: French troops fording a river'

7. A *barco rabelo* on the Douro

8. Henri L'Evêque, 'Royal Naval vessels on the Tagus opposite Alhandra, among them a gunboat' (left foreground)

9. Santarém seen from a British advance post, the Tagus on the right (published by Edward Orme)

10. Part of the imposing remains of Fort Conception, which resisted destruction

11. Young ladies of Sabugal in their finery, ready to attend a local ball. Note also the substantial granite walls of the district

12. Thomas Rowlandson, 'Learning to Smoke and drink Grog', from *The Military Adventures of Johnny Newcome*

13. Louis Bacler d'Albe, 'Guerrilla ambush'

14. Louis Bacler d'Albe, 'French blockhouse between Tolosa and Ernani'

15. Louis Bacler d'Albe, 'A house fortified by the French on the Valladolid road'

16. Francisco Goya, 'Stripping the dead', from *The Disasters of War*

17. The Dos Casas brook at Fuentes de Oñoro half a century ago

18. Thomas St Clair, 'Pombal in flames when evacuated by Masséna's troops' (11 March 1811)

19. Thomas St Clair, 'The 3rd Division being ferried across the Tagus at Vila Velha' (20 May 1811)

20. Part of Wellington's residence and Headquarters at Freineda during two winters, as it is today

21. Marching French prisoners into Salamanca after the battle (published by Edward Orme)

22. The ruined castle at Benavente prior to partial demolition in 1897, the tower (left) now part of a *parador*

23. The conventual dependencies within the *mata* or forest at Busaço in about 1870, before the erection of the palace adjacent, now a hotel

24. Robert Batty, 'Pack mules being unloaded at Irún'

25. Robert Batty, 'Captured French hutted encampment near Urrugne, together with Allied tents'

26. Imaginative portrayal of Marshal Beresford disarming a Polish Lancer at Albuera, from Jenkins' *Martial Achievements*

27. François-Joseph Heim, 'The French besieged at Burgos'; note the gabions in the foreground

28. Early nineteenth-century view of the harbour at Pasajes

29. Louis Bacler d'Albe, 'French wounded leaving Spain'

Arzobispo. Schaumann described the hazardous progress, as over the bridge poured 'a throng consisting of the most motley assortment of infantry, artillery, baggage, wounded, mules, bullocks, donkeys, women, and vehicles of all kinds, among them, of course, the ungreased bullock carts; and members of three nations, English, Spanish and Germans, squeezed, crushed and cursed one another …'

Next night they encountered a huge herd of merino sheep, which were promptly slaughtered and broiled over the bivouac fires. Many legs of mutton were seen next day held aloft on bayonets as they army continued their slow progress across trackless hills towards Jaraicejo,[32] there meeting the highway via Trujillo and Mérida to Badajoz. The Tagus should secure them from a French crossing in force, for Crauford's units had been sent ahead to Almaraz to forestall any attempt they might make there. Wellesley had meanwhile reconstituted the depleted 3rd Division, by incorporating the Light Brigade, the whole commanded by Craufurd.

It was no surprise to learn that Cuesta, ordered to hold the bridge at Arzobispo at all costs, had allowed French cavalry to ford the river a short distance upstream during the afternoon of the 8th: his guards were having their *siesta*! And when their infantry had rushed the bridge, Bassecourt's corps of 6,000 Spaniards – 'supposed to be the best' in Cuesta's army – immediately ran away,[33] leaving behind them not only the 16 guns defending the crossing, but also another 14 captured at Talavera and handed over to them by Wellesley. It was more usual for the Spaniards to appropriate. Wellesley had seen 'English horses with short tails in possession of many of the Spanish troops ... [and] on the morning of the 29th, when our officers and soldiers were engaged in collecting the wounded and in burying the dead, the arms and accoutrements of both were collected and carried away by the Spanish troops ...'[34] In the same long letter to his brother Richard, he had remarked that their infantry invariably jettisoned their arms and equipment and even discarded their uniforms, later re-assembling 'in a state of nature,' while their cavalry – 'in general well-clothed, armed, and accoutred, and remarkable well mounted ... [would] make no scruple of running off, and after an action are to be found in every village, and in every shady bottom within fifty miles of the battle.'

However, Cuesta's main force was out of immediate danger, having occupied an almost impregnable site overlooking the Tagus near Mesa de Ibor. By the 10th, Wellesley's army was bivouacking in a defensible position dominating the valley not far below the Puerto de Miravete, which providing a panoramic view north over the area from which the enemy might approach. But the heat was grilling,[35] so intense, wrote Schaumann, 'that our eyelids smarted; the ink thickened on our pens as fast as we wrote, and our skins, burnt by the sun, peeled off our noses and upper lips. Shaving and washing, and particularly drying ourselves with a coarse towel, became extremely painful. Every soldier stuck an olive leaf or a piece of paper on his under lip to prevent it from bursting.

By the 11th of August Headquarters were at Jaraicejo, not far from Trujillo, where a depot was forming, and it was not until the following day that rations of spirits were delivered to the troops.[36] On the 20th, Crauford's units, now composing the rearguard, retiring south-west from Almaraz, were given permission to requisition for themselves 'any animals in the shape of cattle, sheep, or pigs, which could be found,' and, wrote Leach,

> never do I remember having seen orders so promptly obeyed. A most furious attack was instantly made on a large herd of pigs ... The screeches and cries of those ill-fated swine, as they met their death at the point of the bayonet, the sword, or sergeant's pike, and the rapidity with which they were cut up into junks, with the hair on, and fried on the lids of camp-kettles, or toasted at the fire on a pointed stick, to allay the cravings of hunger of some thousands of half-famished soldiers, was quite incredible, and, I must add, truly ludicrous. As neither bread, salt, nor vegetables were to be procured, it must be confessed that the repast was a singular one, although it was eaten with the greatest *goût*, and washed down with some water from a rivulet hard by.

At midnight the retreat was resumed, but after thirteen hours the only provisions they could find in those deserted sierras were 'now and then a large, coarse description of pea, parched to a cinder by the sun, and an occasional God-send of wheat, found in ungleaned fields near the line of march.' Another long trudge brought them to the bridge of Almaraz, one arch of which lay in ruins.

The 3rd Division remained encamped here for a fortnight, keeping a weather eye open, should Soult's troops on the far bank attempt to ford the Tagus. They survived on 'an exceedingly coarse kind of flour, mixed with bran and chopped straw ... moistened with water, and made into a sort of pan-cake ... baked on a camp-kettle lid,' supplemented from time to time by 'antiquated goats' taken by surprise, and the honey and combs of hives they stumbled on: at least they had unlimited spring water. 'We slept in the open air, and this was the mode', as John Cooper explained: 'The great coat was inverted, and our legs were thrust into the sleeves; one half was put under us, and the other half above. The knapsacks formed our pillows. Thus arranged, with forage cap pulled over our ears, we bid good night to the stars, and rested as we could. As the river ran close by the foot of the hill on which we were bivouaced, we frequently went down to it, pulled off our shirts, washed them with or without soap, knocked them well on the flat stones, and then hung them on the rocks or bushes, picked off the vermin, and when dry, put them on again.'

One day, Schaumann was standing in the shade, 'supervising foraging operations',

> when a soldier bearing upon his shoulder a stolen bee-hive wrapped in his cloak ... breaking through a hedge with his booty ... ran panting into almost the arms of a general and his staff who happened to be riding down from the village [Deleitosa]. "Halt, scoundrel!" the general roared with rage. "What have you stolen there? Provost Marshal, arrest that man at once, and make an example of him. Sir Arthur has forbidden all plundering on pain of death." The soldier, as if thunderstruck, contemplated the general for a moment, and looked paralysed with fear. In a second, however, he recovered himself, flung the hive violently down, tore his cloak away from it, and quickly took to his heels. Meanwhile, however, the bees, outraged by the treatment they had received, swarmed angrily over the general, his staff, the provost marshal and his assistants. They even reached my foraging party, and we were all obliged to gallop away at top speed. But the soldier, whose presence of mind I admired, came off scot free. It was one of the funniest scenes I have ever witnessed.

On another day, being assisted by 'a few tame cows placed in front of them ... and mounted Spaniards [*garrochistas*] who carried long lances and had dogs with them,' Schaumann was ordered to take a herd of wild black bulls from a corral and divide them among troops bivouacked nearby. Their destination was reached as night fell, but the campfires startled the creatures. Giving dreadful snorts, they

> ploughed up the ground with their horns, and raised their tails in the air. I retreated on to the nearest rock. At last, by dint of much coaxing, my assistants succeeded in calming the brutes and getting them to move on again ... when, unfortunately, the bugles sounded the 'lights out'. Hardly had the bugles ceased when the whole of my corps ... rushed snorting and bellowing through the bivouacs, overturning camp kettles, huts,

> and even one or two horses belonging to the 14th and 16th Dragoons, and then disappeared into the darkness and gloom. All this created a most horrible tumult, and the Spaniards with their dogs galloped *ventre à terre* after the fugitives. I gave up everything for lost; but to my intense surprise, I was informed at midnight that the bulls had been brought back and were shut up in a corral …

That wasn't the end of Schaumann's predicaments, for when the commissaries arrived next morning to collect their rations, still 'on the hoof', although four 'heavy dragoons were stationed before the door of the corral, holding thick staves crosswise in front of it', once he had received a receipt note for ten of them and the door was opened, 'the whole herd, mad with hunger, would make a dash for it': instead of ten, fifteen would break through and career off, the commissary and his butchers in frantic pursuit, cursing and swearing, to kill the brutes wherever they were caught.[37]

Schaumann described the bivouacs themselves as being 'full of vermin; there were large green lizards, eighteen inches long, that lived in the hollows of trees; spiders, mosquitoes, scorpions, snakes, ants and flies. All our clothes and linen suffered accordingly.' The worst of these bivouacs was that the pools of water near them 'were full of leeches, which clung inside the nostrils of the horses and the mouths of the men'.

Another hazard was fire. Due to carelessness while cooking, the dry grass frequently caught alight, spreading before the hot wind for miles, 'and would creep like gigantic snakes in long lines over hill and dale, making a terrible fine spectacle.' In one such conflagration, Colonel Arentschildt, commanding the 1st Hussars, lost his tent and all his baggage; in another, the survivors of the 23rd Dragoons 'lost over 100 saddles ... and all their cartouche pouches were blown into the air,' after which disaster the unit was disbanded.

Although an occasional flock of sheep or herd of wild bulls might fall into their hands, the army was still half-starved. Carts full of equipment were left stranded, their bullocks having been slaughtered for food and 'soldier's wives, who as a rule went about decently clad, and were most faithful to their husbands, now rode round hungrily in rags on starved donkeys, and gave themselves to any one who wanted them in exchange for half a loaf of bread. Sick and wounded poured in daily, looking famished and cadaverous. Many of them had had nothing but water for three days. The whole army was suffering from fever and dysentery. The horses grew ever thinner and more debilitated, and suffered from a bleeding at the hoof in the region of the coronet, [and] owing to the hardness and heat of the dry ground their hoofs grew brittle and cracked.'[38]

Meanwhile, Craufurd's units had veered due west, passing Cáceres on 23 August, and re-crossed the frontier below hill-top Marvão, 'on the summit of a dark isolated mountain, which frowns over the road at its base' to approach Castelo de Vide through a valley 'abounding in the largest and most luxuriant chestnut-trees.' Here, while resting for a week, 'such good use was made of a certain fluid called "confession wine"' in its cellars 'that not a thoroughly sober individual could have been found in the whole division by nine o'clock that night': so confessed Leach.

While Craufurd's Division was retiring, additional reinforcements had left Lisbon on 28 July, among them the 34th Regiment, commanded by General Catlin Crawford. They had also followed the route via Santarém and Abrantes, but before reaching Nisa, news of Talavera reached them, and a halt was ordered. Capt. Joseph Moyle Sherer records how they all gathered round their bivouac fires 'to listen, to conjecture, and to talk about this glorious, but bloody, event,' regretting that that had not been able to share in the honours of such a day. Although their march was continued as far as Zarza la Mayor, they were then instructed to retrace their steps to Nisa, remaining there a fortnight. On 7 September they moved south to Portalegre and the main area of the army's concentration, and later towards Elvas. Sherer still had a very romantic idea of campaigning. Bivouacs were a novelty to him, but rarely as ideal as that one he described as having been marked out in advance of its occupation. This, whenever possible, would have been

> on the edge of a wood, and near a river or stream. The troops are halted in open columns, arms piled, picquets and guards paraded and posted, and, in two minutes, all appears at home. Some fetch large stones to form fire-places; others hurry off with canteens and kettles for water, while the wood resounds with the blows of the bill-hook. Dispersed, under the more distant trees, you see the officers; some dressing, some arranging a few boughs to shelter them by night; others kindling their own fires; while the most active are seen returning from the village, laden with bread, or, from some flocks of goats, feeding near us, with a supply of new milk. How often, under some spreading cork-tree, which offered shade, shelter, and fuel, have I taken up my lodging for the night; and here, or by some

> gurgling stream, by bosom fanned by whatever air was stirring, made my careless toilet, and sat down with men I liked and esteemed, to a coarse, but wholesome meal, seasoned by hunger and by cheerfulness. The rude simplicity of this life I found most pleasing ... The inconvenience of one camp taught me to enjoy the next; and I learned ... that wood and water, shade and grass, were luxuries.

Sherer went on to remark that whenever they 'remained a week or a fortnight stationary, the sutlers who followed the army overtook and opened their temporary shops in the towns near us, or in our very camps; and thus we were often well, though dearly, supplied with many comforts, such as tea, sugar, brandies, wines, segars, &c. In these sort of camps, we felt two serious wants, I allow; books, and the society of women. It is true that in the Peninsula we never enjoyed either the one or the other in perfection; yet in quarters we could often procure a few odd volumes of Latin or French, which served to beguile, and often usefully to occupy our time; and for female society you frequently met with agreeable and interesting girls in your billet.'

It was at Portalegre that Sherer found Crauford's Brigade: the regiments composing it 'very fine, and in the highest possible order.' During their time there, 'we used to frequent the gates of two nunneries, and all the sisters seemed flattered by our attentions. A military band was often brought down to the outer court of their sacred prisons, for their amusement, and some of our officers would sit for hours in the convent parlours, talking with the nuns [guarded by] a double row of thick gratings, so contrived that you could only shake hands ...'

Leach, who appeared to have a penchant for nuns, had caught sight of 'some tolerably fair specimens of Portuguese beauty' in the convents, and confirmed that their proximity offered some consolation at least for the lack of decent female company. Wellington himself was not averse to visiting them, as on the occasion at Viseu when 'Dan Mackinnon' had insinuated himself into their confidence. Together with other officers, Wellington had entered their 'parlour', where the ladies sang. As the Duke recalled to Stanhope: 'they were amazed at seeing one of the nuns, as it seemed, suddenly turn head over heels, and her petticoats falling about her head display the boots and trousers of an officer! Lord Allen afterwards tried to get in, and the superior complained to the Duke, who promised to reprimand his lordship. '"But what", he added, "shall I say to Mackinnon?" Oh, as to Mackinnon, she said, we cannot help his coming in – we must make up our minds to him; but pray speak to Lord Allen. Mackinnon was very good-looking.'[39]

The Rifle Brigade remained in the area of Portalegre and Campo Maior for three months, which for Leach, among others 'addicted to field-sports', provided with 'a fair allowance of generous wine, several cigars (to prevent infectious disease),[40] the persecution of red-legged partridges, quails, etc., or a gallop with the wire-haired greyhounds of the country across the plains ... gave rare sport,' and kept them fit. Excursions were made towards Alburquerque, where the forests contained wild boars, and red dear, apart from wolves and foxes; while the various regiments were frequently marched to the river Caia to bathe.

1 In their wake followed 122 heavily-laden carts together with additional draught-bullocks, reluctantly supplied by their peasant owners. Due to them frequently breaking down, an order, loosely interpreted, was later issued that no cart should carry more cargo than 600 lbs.

2 That 56 out 65 of the carts carrying ammunition for the 1st Division were able to reach as far as Castelo Branco, was remarkable. Another problem met with later was caused by the mutual antipathy of the Portuguese and Spanish drivers, who would only cross their common frontier under duress.

3 John Aitchison remarked on 'the small supply, nay, *extreme deficiency* of medical stores,' which showed that Wellesley 'entertained no apprehension of a reverse.'

4 Although the Tiétar was fordable in several places, Wellesley ordered Capt. Alexander Tod (Royal Staff Corps) to construct a temporary bridge close to that of pontoon which the French had destroyed, which would facilitate the advance of both waggons and artillery. Twenty pine trees in the vicinity were soon cut down, and a local inn and its outhouses demolished for the beams and rafters they contained, and the bridge completed within 24 hours. The reader is referred to Robert Burnham's absorbing chapter in *Inside Wellington's Peninsular Army* for details of this and other more complex bridging operations, in addition to Howard Douglas's *Essay*.

5 Although one officer on Wellesley's Staff noticed that many horsemen were 'devoid of covering for the legs or feet, and the naked toe was seen, peeping through a sandal, touching the stirrup.'

6 Cuesta suspected that Wellesley might be given overall command of Spanish troops.

7 As Surtees noted on another occasion: 'Nothing could exceed the hardy and robust appearance of the men in general; and had they been clothed, appointed, and disciplined like either their enemies or their allies, there could not have been a finery soldiery.' And as John Aitchison reflected: 'The men composing the Spanish army are remarkably fine and I am yet persuaded that if they were well officered they would fight. But they have no example shown them – their officers are miserable beyond conception and they are always the first to desert.' For an idea of the lamentable state of the Spanish forces, see the earlier chapters of Esdaile's *The Spanish Army in the Peninsular War*.

8 One member of Wellesley's entourage commented that 'These not only did not look like soldiers, but not even like gentlemen; and it was difficult, from their

mean and abject appearance, particularly among the infantry, to guess from what class of society they could have been taken.'

9 George Bingham had commented that the Junta had promised 40,000 rations, instead of which they provided only 6,000, and that the army had just killed the last bullocks they had brought with them from Portugal. However, he understood that four day's bread was expected up from Palencia, 'in which case on its arrival, we shall push on to Madrid, which is only four days march from this; but there again we shall not be better off than we are here, we cannot stay here, and to fall back is nearly as bad, as we have eat up the country behind us.'

10 For Sampaio, see footnote 11 on p.333.

11 Four months earlier, D'Urban had commented that 'Infinite rascalities' were being practised: Cuesta had 'discovered that the person entrusted with establishing the Post from Merida to Ciudad Rodrigo and who had reported that he had done so, has not, but had pocketed the money which the being charged with that service put into his hands and absconded'; on another occasion 'some villains who had the charge of furnishing forage for all Cuesta's Cavalry, either from being his enemies, or treacherous, or both, so managed matters that the horses had no substinence for 6 or 7 days.'

12 Cuesta's force, 'The Army of Estremadura', was said to amount to 28,000 men.

13 The Portiña was condemned by John Cooper as a small rivulet, 'dry in many places, but where there were pools, black, ugly-looking snakes were plentiful. Of this water we had to drink.'

14 Lapisse's men had unexpectedly crossed by fords obscured by smoke from a 'French bivouac, consisting in neatly built huts, full of furniture taken from Talavera,' which had been set alight by Mackenzie's men before abandoning the far bank of the Alberche.

15 Admittedly, two of the four battalions had never seen action previously; the others, brought up to strength with recruits, had hardly recovered from their defeat at Medellín four months earlier.

16 Later, Cuesta proposed shooting 200 of the fugitives, a figure reduced after remonstration, but he insisted on making an example of 25 unfortunate men chosen at random from the regiments concerned. Cooper saw them, 'dressed in white, and attended by several popish priests … marched to the front of our regiment and shot.'

17 Regrettably, in the darkness, some of the young inexperienced troops, principally from the second battalions of regiments which had embarked at Corunna, and draughts from the militia, unaware that picquets were posted in their front, fired on them, until stopped by their officers. Several men were killed in the friendly fire, among them Colonel John Ross (Coldstream Guards).

18 Their appearance differed from those encountered at Vimeiro, being much broader – c. 60 men across and 24 ranks deep – but this did not enable them to absorb any better the punishing fire with which they were met, and one after the other they broke and made for the rear, suffering some 1,300 casualties in this action alone, compared to about 750 British.

19 They were composed of two lines of 12 battalions in columns, each 30 men broad and 15 ranks deep, with an interval of 120 yards between each column: a second line of columns followed some 500 yards to the rear.

20 Ensign Aitchison commented that 'to one not having seen the ground ... it is very difficult to convey a clear idea of the whole affair in writing,' one in which he witnessed courage which few unless they had seen it, would credit, notably when our men, lying in ranks, 'were exposed to a tremendous cannonade, with shots and shells falling in every direction,' for there was not the least motion except in the immediate vicinity of the spot where a cannon shot or shell fell, when the mutilated corpses were removed to the rear, for 'they would then lie down as if nothing had occurred and remain in the ranks, steady as before.' And so they lay 'till the French came within 40 yards. They then rose, gave the enemy a volley, and repulsed them with the bayonet. This coolness on our part staggered the resolution of the enemy ... [whose] every attack was repulsed with prodigious slaughter.'

21 This area is now partly submerged by a reservoir, the waters of the Portiña having been dammed between the Medillín and the Cerro de Cascajal.

22 'non-existent ... into which the 23rd Light Dragoons supposedly crashed,' as one Spanish military historian has insinuated, as if it had been necessary for Napier to have invented such an obstacle as an excuse for the charge having miscarried.

23 In round figures, his total casualties were 5,360 men (over 800 killed, including two generals; the rest wounded or missing) over one quarter of the 20,600 engaged. French losses were heavier – 7,270 – but were a lower proportion of the troops involved.

24 George Bingham, who had fainted with fatigue and heat at the close of the action, ended his letter dated the 29th: 'At his moment the Spaniards are murdering the wounded Frenchmen in the woods in our front. I must hasten to prevent them.'

25 Writing after the battle, Bingham had commented: 'The Spanish Army is in so disorganised a state, the under officers such poltroons, the superior such traitors, I am afraid one day or other they will lead us into a scrape, from which it will be difficult to extricate outrselves. We are now without a day's provision in advance, without magazines and (notwithstanding what you may hear in England) with a population very lukewarm on our behalf. This ought to have been foreseen before we left Portugal.'

26 In his defence, had he not retreated, he would have been in grave danger of being caught between Soult's units and Victor's. Victor had in fact advanced west again, and the cavalry of the two forces met between Talavera and Oropesa on the 7 August.

27 The French often depended on the local Spanish to perform administrative duties and act as nurses, but this left their wounded vulnerable to vengence and being given a *coup de grâce* with impunity, although less likely when the hospitals were staffed by nuns.

28 This would commence at about 2.0 in the morning. Simmons refers to 'marching every day in this manner, halting occasionally for half an hour, so that we manage to get to our destined place about eleven o'clock in the forenoon, which is generally upon a piece of ground shaded with trees. There we rest till one or two the next morning and start as before ...my feet never blister ...'

29 This may be slightly exaggerated: others refer to 50 or 60lbs weight, although some would have been obliged to shoulder more equipment.

30 The claim by Napier that they covered 62 miles in 26 hours has been exploded. Jonathan Leach and George Simmons, who actually made the march, estimated

it as 'upward of 50 miles' and '52 miles' respectively, in 24 hours, while Samuel Pollock stated it was 66 miles in 30 hours. Fortescue suggested 45–50 miles in 25 hours; but 43 miles (69 kms) in 22 hours is more likely.

31 Soult made little attempt to follow up his thrust, and retraced his steps to Plasencia shortly after. Permission to strike west towards Abrantes had been refused by Joseph, while Ney had already been ordered back towards Salamanca, after a running fight with Robert Wilson's troops at the Puerto de Baños.

32 Writing from here on 13 August, Alexander Gordon referred to the bridge at Arzobispo as having been given up because 'the Spaniards will not fight, will not maintain a position, will do nothing, are the damnest set of Cowards.' And in the same letter: 'How different were the Portuguese: 'The difference between the two Countries is very great: the one assists you with everything they have, and does something towards the defence of their Country. The other treats you as Enemies rather than friends and at the sight of the French run away, in short do nothing but lie and deceive you.'

33 Of Alburquerque's cavalry and Bassecourt's infantry, 600 men and 400 horses were captured, and over 800 killed and wounded.

34 The docked tails of the British cavalry distinguished them, even at some distance, from the mounts of the enemy, and often opportunely.

35 Indeed, the heat was such that handling any metal that had been exposed to the sun for long – whether swords or even their hilts, bayonets, stirrup-irons, or buttons – was likely to blister one's fingers.

36 Wellesley had issued instructions that from 27 July, until further orders, the stoppage of sixpence-a-day for the supply of provisions to the troops should be reduced to threepence, and with justice; and it was not until 2 September, when regular provisions were again distributed, that this deduction reverted to the usual daily stoppage.

37 While in bivouacs, several hours would elapse between the slaughtering of bullocks and distributing rations to the men, but when the army was in movement, there was no time for the meat to be properly 'hung', and the diet would invariable be – as has been temptingly described – *bœuf à la rigor mortis*.

38 Probably a disease known as 'sand crack'.

39 Young Daniel Mackinnon (1791–1836), the future historian of the Coldstream Guards.

40 Cigar-smoking was also considered a panacea by some troops during the disastrous Walcheren Expedition, concurrently under way, for repelling the mosquitoes infesting that marshy area. In that ill-considered venture – an attempt to destroy the French fleet in the Scheldt estuary near Antwerp – Walcheren Fever, largely due to malaria, was to cause the death of some 60 officers and 3,900 rank-and-file, compared to hardly 106 killed in action. Thousands more fell sick with the disease, the remittent fever leaving many permanently debilitated or incapacitated, and unable to resume active service. Its after-effects were such that as late as March 1812 Wellington was complaining of the unhealthiness of troops sent out as reinforcements, who had served in the expedition.

5

September 1809 to July 1810: Recuperation, reorganization, and marking time

By the time Craufurd had crossed into Portugal, the main army was well along the highway via Mérida towards Badajoz on the Guadiana, where Wellesley called a halt on 3 September. Unfortunately, the swamps of the Guadiana valley were mosquito-ridden, and malaria was soon to cause decimating losses among the troops, already exhausted after their arduous withdrawal, having no provisions, no stores, no means of transport; being overloaded with sick; the horses of the cavalry being scarcely able to march, or those of the artillery to draw guns; and the officers and soldiers being worn down by want of food, and privations of every description.

Badajoz was to gain a reputation for sullen hostility – Ensign Aitchison, writing in December, stated that 'Nothing can equal the incivility of the inhabitants here' – but this was not yet so apparent.[1] Although there were no public places of amusement, according to Capt. Stothert, Doña Payna opened her house every night 'to the best society and the British Officers, who are received with the utmost politeness. Conversation, cards, the song and dance, succeed each other, and form what is called the tertullia, similar in most respects to a London rout.'[2] Schaumann had found himself billeted 'with a very decent family,' which gave him an opportunity of describing the Spaniards frugal way of living and feeding.

> They believe in plenty of vegetables and water, which, in so hot a climate is, at all events, very sensible. In the morning they have chocolate, toast and water. At midday they eat a stew or soup consisting of two kinds of meat, in which they also put a kind of small meat sausage (*salchichas*) strongly favoured with pepper and garlic, some bread and red pepper, or bread and water, oil, or, instead of that, the fat of fried bacon, and onions made into a sort of pulp. Or they eat a couple of eggs fried with

ham, poultry cooked with rice, rabbits, a good deal of pork and mutton (very rarely beef), salad, vegetables, small flat peas (*garbanzes*), dried beans, green cabbage leaves, and drink very little wine... The fact that we Englishmen ate so much meat, drank so much wine and so little water, were constantly on our legs, and never slept after the midday meal, and yet remained fresh and healthy withal, struck the Spaniards with horror and amazement, and was always a riddle with them. They always said they could not emulate us there. '*Son Demonios*!' ['They're devils!'] they exclaimed.

On 16 September Wellesley first signed his new name – Viscount Wellington of Talavera and Baron Douro – having been raised to the peerage on 4 September, on the news of his victory reaching London.[3] The battle of Talavera was a turning-point of the war in that until then the British, with their small army, had seen themselves as auxiliaries to their allies, assuming that the Spaniards would be taking the lead in ejecting the French from their country. It was now only too clear that the boot was on the other foot. The Spaniards might be left to hold Andalusia, but the campaign had brought home to Wellington the impossibility of relying on them: any formal military collaboration would jeopardise his army.

When explaining to London the reason for his retreat, Wellington emphasised: 'I lament as much as any man can the necessity for separating from the Spaniards, but I was compelled to go and I believe there was not an officer in the army who did not think I stayed too long. The fault I committed consisted in trusting at all to Spaniards, who I have since found were entirely unworthy of confidence;' and as he intimated to Beresford: 'My plan now is to remain on the defensive, and not to enter into any plan of co-operation of any description (unless ordered from England) till I shall see defined objects and corresponding means to effect them.' Elsewhere, he had commented that, as far as the Spanish commanders were concerned, 'nothing will answer excepting to fight great battles in plains, in which their defeat is as certain as the commencement of the battle.'

When discussing the conduct of Cuesta at Talavera, Napier quotes Wellington when affirming that

'the Spanish army, with very trifling exceptions, was not engaged – whole corps threw away their arms, and ran off, when they were neither attacked nor threatened with attack. In their flight from Talavera they plundered the baggage of the British army, which was, at the moment, bravely

> engaged in their cause'. For this reason, he would not, he said, again co-operate with the Spaniards. 'We are worse off than in a hostile country; never was an army so ill-used; – the Spaniards made all sorts of promises; – we had absolutely no assistance from the Spanish army; on the contrary, we were obliged to lay down our ammunition, to unload the treasure, and employ the cars in the removal of the sick and wounded. The common dictates of humanity have been disregarded by them ... I have fished in many troubled waters, but Spanish troubled waters I will never try again,' was his expression, when speaking of this campaign; and he kept his word.

Stothert was one of many officers writing in a similar vein: 'the mind sickens at the melancholy consequences of the imbecility of those chiefs, to whose guidance the Spanish armies are entrusted; who by their futile plans conceived without judgement, and attempted to be carried into execution without ability, disappointed alike the hopes of their country and the British leaders, who in vain looked forward to any co-operation which might produce a beneficial result ...'

Aitchison, writing home from Belém on 26 September confirming that his wound had healed, and that he would be returning to the army near Badajoz, refers to Wellington – who had been 'very ill with ague' – being expected daily in Lisbon. He would be surveying an area north of the capital, which it was his intention to defend at all costs, and his plan to do so was elaborated on 20 October in a *Memorandum* to Colonel Richard Fletcher, the commanding engineer there. It was vital to have a secure base from which the British army could continue the struggle; or, if the worst came to the worst, it could embark at leisure. He still had faith in the Portuguese will to resist,[4] but while the Spanish peasantry might carry on their desultory guerrilla warfare, his doubts as to whether their regular armies could do so for much longer were confirmed in the following month with news of their disastrous defeats at Ocaña, and also Alba de Tormes, where Del Parque's army – having shown some grit at Tamames six weeks earlier, inflicting comparatively heavier casualties on an inferior French force – was scattered by Kellerman's cavalry.[5]

The frontier fortress of Elvas, on a height some 8 miles west of insalubrious Badajoz, was chosen as a hospital base for the survivers of the retreat from Talavera. It was here that Sherer first came face to face with the realities of war: the sight of so many wounded in its streets: 'their contracted limbs supported by crutches, or their shattered arms lightly suspended in black silk handkerchiefs, were moving indolently ...' – may well have startled him. Many were suffering not only from malaria, which together with typhus and enteric fever, were among the scourges that afflicted the Peninsular army throughout the war. 4,000 men were buried at Elvas alone.[6]

On 4 October the 2nd Division was reviewed. On seeing Wellington for the first time, Sherer was 'much struck with his countenance; and, in his quick-glancing eye, prominent nose, and pressed lips, saw, very distinctly marked, the ready presence of mind, and imperturbable decision of character, so essential in a leader,' but next day he was himself laid low with fever. It was not until late March that he could rejoin his comrades near Portalegre, there learning that almost 300 of the regiment had died during his absence.

While the health of Wellington's troops gradually improved during the winter, he was obliged to draw his officers' attention to their responsibilities. The army's state of indiscipline was causing him serious concern; indeed, it might be described as 'infamous'. As he reported in January to the Earl of Liverpool, then secretary for war: 'They behave well generally when with their regiments and under the inspection of their officers; but when detached and coming up from hospitals, although invariably under the command of an officer and always well fed and taken care of, they commit every description of outrage. They have never brought up a convoy of money that they have not robbed the chest, nor of shoes or of any other article that could be of use to them ... that they do not steal ... At this moment there are three general courts-martial sitting in Portugal for the trial of soldiers guilty of wanton murders, robberies, thefts. I assure you that the military law is not sufficiently strong to keep them in order.'

Another major worry, and the burden of repeated letters of complaint, was the lack of specie, or dilitariness in its supply. A few weeks later he was reiterating to Liverpool: 'We are still much distressed for money, and I shall not be able to pay the troops on the 24th of this month [April 1810]. We owe for everything we have had lately from the country, as well as for the means of transport employed in moving our supplies from our own magazines.'[7] Too often, his men had to wait two months or more before getting paid; payment of the muleteers and drivers, upon whose services in keeping the army supplied the Commissariat so much depended, might be six months in arrears.[8] The safe shipment of bullion to the Peninsula was the responsibility of the Royal Navy, protecting numerous and regular convoys carrying supplies and equipment of all kinds, and at the same time transporting reinforcements; returning with the severely wounded, and escorting back prisoners of war. Without naval support, the war could not have lasted long, and their contribution to the eventual success of Wellington's Army is too often taken for granted.[9]

At Vila Viçosa, 18 miles west of Elvas, where survivors of the 23rd Light Dragoons were then stationed, its officers, while awaiting their return to England to recruit, engaged in any amount of horseplay and pranks 'to kill time and relieve their wanton spirits,' apart from ending their mess every night 'by all getting drunk and flinging the dinner service, and finally the chairs and table, out of the window;' while on one memorable morning Schaumann heard

> the trampling of feet in the street, and a crowd of people collecting ... an English bishop had arrived and was going to pass through the town ... [and] at that very moment the alleged bishop really did make an appearance, riding solemnly down the street on horseback, accompanied by all the officers ... bearing their helmets reverently in their hands. The bishop (a captain of the regiment) was clad in red velvet breeches, white gaiters trimmed with lace, a long skirted red velvet jacket, an English flannel dressing-gown trimmed with black, a large Spanish collar ... *à la* Van Dyck, with a clerical band, a wig, a moustache, an old-fashioned hat with a large tassel, and gauntlet gloves. In his left hand he carried a sceptre, on which a huge lemon was stuck, surmounted by a cross. With his right hand he blessed the people. And thus they marched in solemn silence through Vila Viçosa to Borba, at which place they intended to take luncheon. The whole town was in an uproar. Everyone wanted to get a glimpse of the English bishop. The extraordinary part of it was than no Portuguese would believe that it was only a joke. The whole crowd shouted: *'O Bispo Inglese! O Bispo Inglese! Tem visto O Bispo Inglese!'* I only wished that Lord Wellington might by chance have encountered this cavalcade; how quickly it would have dispersed!

Other officers, among them Major the Hon. Charles Somers Cocks (16th Light Dragoons), recuperating after the Talavera campaign, were less wild. On joining his regiment encamped at Vila Viçosa, he regretted only that he did not have his gun with him, for the walled chase of the Braganza palace pullulated with game. We find him asking his family to send out writing and sketching equipment, a 2-foot portable military telescope and compass from Messrs Dolland, Stockdale's largest map of the Peninsula laid on canvas and folded in a case, any good accounts of Moore's Spanish expedition being published, and evinced an interest in receiving recent works from the pen of Cobbett.[10]

Apparently, when a Scottish regiment had been stationed at neighbouring Borba, the tattoos 'carried out at night by eight pipers in old Highland costume ... struck the inhabitants ... dumb with astonishment.' It was not always easy living in the proximity of their Allies, but it had advantages and offered a variety of distractions. Capt. William Bragge, writing several months later, when the little town was 'terribly crowded with Infantry' marching in or out, confessed to one of its main attraction: 'You cannot conceive anything more grateful to the Taste of a Thirsty Man than the Borba Wine, which is the finest in Portugal and agrees better with the English Constitution than any other Liquor.'

Beresford was fully occupied training and disciplining the Portuguese regulars, of which by the following summer there were 25,000 effectives. A Portuguese militia was also being established – some 45 regiments containing up to 1,000 men each, which would play an important part in garrisoning fortifications and outposts.[11] Another significant force to be called out was the *Ordenança*, a 'Home Guard' of partially-armed peasantry, who knew every goat-track throughout the country. When the next French invasion took place, as was inevitable, they would be invaluable in harrassing the enemy and causing as much chaos as possible along their lines of supply and communication. They would also be employed in preventing marauding, and at the same time demolishing systematically any bridges, ferry-boats, mills, ovens, etc. of use to hostile forces; in breaking up roads; even destoying food and fodder that could not be carried away. It might be difficult to get the mercantile population of the few towns to carry out such instructions as radically as the peasantry, for they had much more to lose. This 'scorched earth policy' would be further implemented by the evacuation of the civilian population together with their cattle and livestock and all means of transport from a wide tract of land to behind the outer defensive lines of Lisbon – a series of fortifications in depth across the hills to the north of the capital on which militia regiments, together with several thousand artisans and labourers levied from both urban and rural areas, were already hard at work.

Within days of his defeat of the Austrians at Wagram, and even before he would have heard of the outcome of the battle of Talavera, Napoleon was selecting additional units to be marched into the Peninsula and, implying that he would return there in person to 'finish the business,' had instructed his brother Joseph to defer all offensive movements.[12] It was not until 27 April that it was announced that Marshal Masséna would command the 138,000-strong 'Army of Portugal', although he would not be given control of all French forces in Spain, for Napoleon preferred the system of divide and rule, and partitioned the country into several independent military governments, leaving Joseph little else but the 'Army of the Centre'. He was still under the delusion that he would thus retain a tight personal control, even over armies many hundreds of miles distant, with the inevitable result that by the time a dispatch reached any one of his marshals, their contents would have been rendered obsolete by a more recent turn of events.

In an attempt to keep their supply lines open along highways permanently threatened by *guerrilleros*, a corps of *gendarmes*, consisting of 20 squadrons of 200 veteran troopers, each with seven officers, had been formed. These bodies would shuttle between a series of strongpoints established at convenient positions along these arteries: fortified towers defending bridgeheads, strategically sited buildings appropriately strengthened, or specially constructed and palisaded wooden forts served as their bases.[13]

While these guerrilla bands or *partidas* frequently intercepted dispatches and fed Wellington with valuable information concerning enemy dispositions and movements, generally stirred up the natives to a more active resistance and opposition to the invader, and did their best to ensure that the number of Spaniards collaborating with the enemy was reduced to the minimum,[14] they could no more be relied on by Wellington than their nominal 'armies', and even groups controlled by such resourceful leaders as Espoz y Mina rarely carried out operations from which he was able to profit. Many were little better than bandits, preferring the undisciplined life, extorting food from their own countrymen, to being drilled (and starved) in their own regular forces. Their merciless depredations made them as unwelcome to a population under duress as the French, whose protection some sought as being the lesser of two evils.[15] As a result of their plundering proclivities, large areas of the country not under effective French occupation were as thoroughly pillaged and wasted as if they had been laid under contribution by the enemy, and chaos was come again. However, there is little doubt that the constant war of attritian practised by these partisans bled the French white, and their importance in contributing to the successful outcome of the war should not be slighted; nor the stubborn Spanish defense of besieged towns such as Gerona or Zaragoza, which had been able to keep French armies at bay for months at a time. Nevertheless, caution must be advised. Only very rarely can the figures of enemy losses, so recklessly circulated in support of guerrilla successes, be substantiated; the premise floated that the value of their participation in the struggle has been underestimated, is speculative.

Lord Londonderry came close to the truth in his *Narrative* when remarking: 'Much has been said of these guerillas, as well by the Spaniards themselves as by the historians of other countries, who have derived their information chiefly from Spanish sources; but all who have served in the Peninsula can attest that a less efficient and more mischievous body of marauders never infested any country. It is not denied that they cut off, from time to time, a small convoy, or an isolated detachment; but unfortunately they did not confine their operations to attacks upon the enemy. Whoever fell in their way, be he friend or foe, rarely escaped unplundered; and the inhabitants of the smaller villages everywhere dreaded their appearance as much as that of the French.'

Wellington was convinced that even if large parts of Portugal had to be given up to the French, as long as they were held at bay in the highly defensible area north of its capital, the contest could be continued;[16] but, should the worst happen, it would still be possible to evacuate the army to Cadiz and Gibraltar, and a new front might be opened in Andalusia. Portuguese forces could be saved by shipping them to Brazil. Adequate shipping must be at his disposal – both transports, and men-of-war to protect an embarkation – should such an emergency arise, while Admiral Berkeley's cooperation would be essential also to guard both ends of Wellington's land lines.

The wide estuary of the Tagus, in flood during the spring, in itself provided a stronger defence than any point in the rolling country further east. Although he considered it unlikely that the French would invade from the direction of Badajoz (held by Spanish troops), Wellington kept Hill's 2nd Division, supported by a Portuguese division and other units, on the Allied right in the vicinity of Elvas. The main body of the Anglo-Portuguese army had been withdrawn belatedly from the valley of the Guadiana and divided into two. Beresford, although occupied with increasing the numbers and potential of the Portuguese troops, commanded a powerful central force at Abrantes to defend the west (right) bank at that reach of the Tagus.

The road east from Abrantes via Vila Velha de Ródão to Castelo Branco and Coria – that by which the army had advanced to Talavera – was one which the French might use, although impracticable for wagons and artillery. A more likely approach, which Wellington himself would defend, would be by either of two roads much further north, along a corridor beyond the Serra da Estrela. These led south-west from

Ciudad Rodrigo (on the Agueda in Spain) to Almeida before descending to Celorico, from which one skirted the north flank of the Estrela range[17] towards the Ponte de Murcella (near the confluence of the Alva and Mondego), where defensive earthworks were raised; the other veered north-west to Viseu. Both converged later on Coimbra, no great distance north-east of which extended 'the damn long hill' of the Serra da Buçaco,[18] its southern extremity rising steeply from the Mondego and effectively obstructing an approach to the city from that direction.

Wellington ordered a lateral track immediately west of this hogsback ridge to be repaired: it might come in useful, for the *serra* provided an admirable defensive position. By making a stand there, he would delay the French army long enough to allow a considerable proportion of the Portuguese civilian population to retire behind the Lines, which by then should be ready and manned. To make it more likely that the invader would be lured towards the Busaco ridge, Wellington ordered the destruction of all alternative roads, among them that known as the 'Estrada Nova' – from Guarda to Castelo Branco via Covilha and then through the hills well above the right bank of the Tagus as far as Abrantes. Stretches of roads or tracks winding along the steep flanks of the *serras* could be blown up with ease. Several bridges over the rivers Côa, Mondego, Alva, and Zêzere were also demolished.

By mid January 1810 Wellington's Headquarters was at Viseu.[19] The infantry was spread out over a wide area further east towards the frontier, while part of his cavalry was stationed between Viseu and Santa Comba Dão, where there was green forage, and also between the coast and Coimbra, near which, at Tentúgal, where Schaumann was stationed,[20] there was plenty of poultry at hand; he appreciated the wild duck and snipe brought in by the peasants, and also the local lampreys. The cavalry horses, although apparently relishing the maize grown in the vicinity, remained very thin. 'At every inspection the generals would raise an outcry, and ascribed their condition, first to maize, then to insufficient food, and anon to the fact that the grass we gave them was too moist.' One day, Schaumann was talking to the local lay magistrate or *Juiz de Fora* about his troubles, who remarked with a smile: 'If your horses grow thin it means that the people in my district grow all the fatter, and surely that is a good thing!' On asking him to explain these cryptic words, he answered: 'Well, this is how it happens. Hardly have the dragoons drawn their corn than hundreds of old women appear on the scene with bottles of brandy or wine concealed in their aprons, with which they bargain with the men for the return of their corn. Your horses have hardly any corn, although they have probably had heaps of straw and grass.' Schaumann rode off to report his discovery to General Payne at Coimbra, adding, to rile him, that this sort of thing had never been heard of in the K.G.L. cavalry, whose mounts had remained in perfect condition. The result was a 'furious general order' being 'immediately issued and circulated, according to which, when the trumpet blew for feeding time, officers were to be present to superintend, and were not to go away until the horses had devoured the last grain of corn in their presence.' And so, before long, 'the horses grew fatter, and the poor townsfolk thinner.'

Schaumann's domestic bliss was interrupted on 29 April, when he was ordered up the Mondego valley to Seia,[21] below the flank of the Serra da Estrela, from which he would fetch snow for himself and his mess to cool their wine and make lemonade, while occupied in superintending foraging parties between there and Viseu.[22]

From Tomar, units commanded by Beresford had marched north to Fornos de Algodres, his new Headquarters not far west of Wellington's at Celorico.[23] Here they met to discuss how the British Commissariat might feed his Portuguese should their own commissariat fail entirely, for as D'Urban commented on 3 May:

> This is absolutely requisite or the Troops will often starve, for such is the poverty, imbecility, and total want of arrangement of the Portuguese Government, that any regular system of supply is not to be expected. In short from one or other or all of these causes or defects, the whole Civil Branch of the Army is in such a state of confusion that I hold it utterly impracticable to carry on operations with it for more than a week or two together, if even so long. The many Months of repose since the Spanish Campaign, the evils then experienced, the remonstrances of the Marshal [Beresford], have produced no effect whatever, and we are about to commence another Campaign destitute of everything that keeps an Army in motion. I have foreseen this, I have represented frequently that it would be so, the Marshal, I fear, hoped otherwise, the promises of this wretched Government have deceived him again for the 100th time.[24]

At least, within a week, according to D'Urban, an arrangement had been made 'to prevent a competition of demand for Carriages. The British require the *whole*, and afterwards give us *one third*. The necessary Orders, Routes, and Instructions for the next Convoy of Sick, [were] despatched to the Inspector-General of Hospitals, the Brigades and Regiments, their March arranged, Hospitals ordered, etc.'

Transport continued to be a problem, although by now the Commissariat had gradually assembled an adequate number of mules. The majority of them continued to be hired, although a proportion were known as 'public', or owned by the Commissariat, and their muleteers, usually one to every three beasts, were on their role of employees, and given the same ration as the troops. All supply mules were grouped in brigades of variable size, normally between 20 and 100 (averaging 50, but occasionally more) under the supervision of the head muleteer (*capataz*), responsible for its records, route, etc.[25] From the Autumn of 1810 the mules were appropriately branded on the neck or another conspicuous part, which while it made them more difficult to sell, and would distinguish the regiment to which they belonged, had the disadvantage in that it was less easy to switch them from one unit to another. With time, each regiment had more mules than carts,[26] although mules were a more costly form of transport (partly because in winter they had to carry their own fodder in addition to their load), while many more were used on depot or general transport duties. It was incumbent on those responsible to keep the mule transport occupied even when the troops were in quarters: one instruction to the Commissariat implied that the expense of their upkeep was such that, if kept idle for an length of time, their pay would almost cover the value of the supplies to be moved! But, as Tomkinson had emphasised, the maintenance of their service was essential: 'any disturbance with them would have deprived us of supplies and consequently crippled our operations, [particularly] in countries where there was nothing to be had, and where any other army without mules would not have remained.'

Already, in mid March, Wellington's much improved intelligence system had informed him that the French were massing in the vicinity of Salamanca.

On 19 July, the cavalry advanced north-east from Seia through Gouveia, Linhares, and Celorico, reaching Baraçal on the 30th. Meanwhile, the inhabitants of the Mondego valley had been removing all their portable property into the mountains, well away from the route of probable invasion.

Much earlier, in mid December, Crawfurd's Division had marched north-west across the Roman bridge of Vila Formosa to Ponte de Sor and over the Tagus to Tomar. On the 29th, having made a detour west via Leiria and Pombal to enter Coimbra, Leach 'could not but observe, that the crowd of students with which the streets swarmed, and the legions of idle young vagabonds coming under the head of *clericos*, with the crowns of their heads shaved, running all over the city after a host, might have been better employed … in training themselves to the use of arms …' Their march was then continued to Celorico, which became Headquarters of the 1st Division; the 2nd was based on Pinhel, the 4th at Guarda. The Light Brigade (now including Portuguese *Caçadores*), a regiment of K.G.L. hussars,[27] and Ross's battery of horse artillery were deployed not far west of the Agueda. The 95th were distributed further east, facing the frontier between the Douro and Almeida.

Major the Hon. Edward Cocks, although not having a very good opinion of the K.G.L. infantry, thought highly of 'the courage, skill, zeal, and marked good conduct of the cavalry … old Hussars, almost all Hannoverians, and many of them men of great respectability. These men are perfectly to be depended on and understand outpost duty better, and take more care of their horses, than British dragoons.' On 6 January, Leach, cantoned at Villar Torpim, described deep snow falling soon after taking up his new quarters, rendering the miserable villages 'still more forlorn. Coursing and shooting were our chief employments during the day, and at night we either whiffed away cigars over some Douro wine, and speculated on the campaign which was soon expected to commence, or danced boleros, fandangos, and waltzes, with the good-looking daughters of an Israelite, in whose house I was billeted ...'[28]

In the following month Leach moved to Mata de Lobos, no great distance north-east of Pinhel, where he

> passed many happy but bandit-like days … sitting at night over a brass pan of charcoal, and with my three jolly subalterns, reposing in the same diminutive den, rolled up in our cloaks, on some straw. Among our other amusements, whilst thus detached far in front of the army, we frequently got up foot-races (our horses being in but poor trim for such feats), played matches at foot-ball, and rackets against the tower of the church, had duck-hunted with dogs on a piece of water, and sometimes turned a pig loose, with his tail greased ... [which] became the lawful prize of the man who could catch him, which was no easy matter. Our gallant commander, Colonel Beckwith, was ever among the first to encourage those meetings, considering ... that to divert and amuse his men, and to allow them every possible indulgence compatible with the discipline of the battalion, whilst in the interval of quiet permitted it, was the surest way to make the soldiers follow him cheerfully through fire and water, when the day of trial came ...

Leach reminded his readers that while garrison towns in England and elsewhere might 'boast of excellent libraries, billiard-tables, whist clubs, and dinner clubs, independent garrison balls and garrison concerts, etc., the rascally villages between the Coa and Aguada, growing out, as it were, from amongst the huge blocks of granite, and peopled by the most wretched, idle, dirty, ignorant, priest-ridden peasantry any where to be found, afforded none of these resources.' The activities of some officers concentrated on supplying pipes of Port wine, silver plate, or even a flock of sheep, to relations at home.[29]

During the next few weeks, Craufurd's unit was involved in several skirmishes with troops attempting to penetrate his line of outposts. Such was the efficiency of his system that not once between March and June was the irregular 40-mile front he was guarding either surprised or pierced, except at a bridge over a defile near Barba del Puerco during the night of 19–20 March. Simmons recalled the night 'being dark and stormy, with rain occasionally, caused the river to make more noise in its passage over the rocky bed than usual, and completely prevented our advanced sentinels hearing the approach of the enemy,' some 600 strong. Although taken prisoner, the sentries had time to raise the alarm. The rest of the company raced to the scene and, directed by Captain Hare, commenced a galling fire. As Simmons described it, 'the moon for a few minutes shone brightly, then disappeared, and again at intervals let us see each other. We profited by this circumstance, as their belts were white and over their greatcoats, so that where they crossed upon the breast, combined with the glare of the breast-plate, they gave a grand mark for our rifles.' Before long, Colonel Beckwith brought forward three companies to their relief. As Leach remembered it: 'One blaze of fire on the head of their column, as soon as it could be distinguished, followed instantly by a cheer and a charge, sent the enemy headlong down the side of the mountain in the utmost confusion, and across the bridge, to which they were pursued by our men, pouring in a constant fire, and with good effect.' Costello described the outcome of the action as being at first doubtful, but 'after about half an hour's hard fighting, the enemy was obliged to retreat percipitately … under a close and murderous fire from us. This was, I believe, the first and last time the French ever attempted to surprise a rifle picket.' But as Leach remarked, '… until 24 July, we were stationed so close to the outposts of the French, as to render it necessary for the soldiers and officers to sleep fully accoutred, with their clothes on, ready to get under arms in an instant … the French cavalry were eternally in motion, in large bodies, towards our chain of posts, and we were as often under arms waiting for them.'

Although surrounded by the French on 26 April, it was not for another month that any siege operations commenced, both bad roads and rain throughout April and May delaying the forward movement of their artillery towards Ciudad Rodrigo, a fortress that they could not risk leaving in the rear. Any attempt by Wellington to disperse the besiegers would have been a hazardous operation, for he would very soon find himself greatly outnumbered, particularly by cavalry, within a few hours' march.

At this period, according to Simmons, 'Several Germans, Swiss, and Italians ... deserted from the French, and occasionally Frenchmen, who all speak with horror of prolonging the war in Spain, as they dare not individually leave their camp. The Spanish guerrillas lay in wait to destroy them, and have become so impudent of late, that they have even attacked convoys of considerable force.' Aitchison confirms that desertion was frequent, and that Wellington had adopted a policy which, 'without expense to the country encourages desertion. The dragoons who come over to us receive the value of their horses and appointments etc., which are disposed of by public sale and the produce paid in dollars. Even *Frenchmen* have deserted to us and some from their distinguished corps – the artillery.'[30]

And yet, it would seem that Wellington was anxious about the progress of the war, as he confided privately to General Graham on 3 May: 'I do not think the service in this country is likely to hold out a prospect of any thing very brilliant. I must maintain myself on the Peninsula till it is necessary to withdraw from it; and when it is necessary to withdraw, I must carry off the army without disgrace, and without loss, if possible.'

Meanwhile, Anglo-Portuguese troops further south had been ordered to proceed towards Wellington's main concentration in the Mondego valley. Leaving General Leite – one of the few Portuguese Commanders, together with Lecor and Fonseca, on whom Wellington could rely – to guard the frontier at Elvas, in mid July Hill's 'Corps' was instructed to cross the Tagus at Vila Velha and make their way north-west across country to join him. Sherer records his satisfaction on 'seeing, for the first time, a large division of Portuguese under arms. The men were remarkably fine, and, considering the short time that had elapsed since their organization, in very high order'.

The redoubtable Marshal Masséna, who had somewhat reluctantly accepted the command of the 'Army of Portugal', with orders 'to drive the leopard into the sea', entered Valladolid on 11 May en route for Salamanca. Ciudad Rodrigo would have to be occupied before invading

Portugal, but he left much of the detail of its investment and capture to his subordinates, among whom were Ney and Junot.[31] It was not until 24 June that he supervised operations in person from his headquarters at the neighbouring Caridad monastery. On 10 July, General Herrasti, the Spanish governor, having by then delayed the French for several weeks, capitulated after an honourable resistance.[32]

Meanwhile, their cavalry had been reconnoitering villages between there and the Portuguese fortress of Almeida, and in force. This had caused Craufurd's picquets to retire, but it was not until dawn on 21 July that Fort Conception,[33] guarding the frontier crossing, was blown up, the explosions making Simmons, sleeping soundly under a tree, to spring up and seize his sword. Three days later he saw action in the rocky valley of the Côa, not far south and south-west of Almeida, their picquets being driven in.

> The whole plain in our front was covered with horse and foot advancing towards us. The enemy's infantry formed line and, with an innumerable multitude of skirmishers, attacked us fiercely; we repulsed them; they came on again, yelling, with drums beating, frequently with drummers leading, often in front of the line, French officers, like mountebanks running forward and placing their hats upon their swords, and capering about like madmen, saying, as they turned to their men, 'Come on, children of our country. The first that advances, Napoleon will recompense him'. Numbers returned to the attack. We kept up a very brisk fire. Several guns began to play upon us, and as the force kept increasing every moment on our front, and columns of infantry were also moving upon our right flank, we were ordered to retire half the company.

But as Leach remarked, 'Those who have seen and know this narrow and difficult defile, need not be informed that, to keep back as many thousand infantry as Marshal Ney might think proper to send forward, whilst the road was choked with troops, baggage, and artillery, which it was absolutely necessary should be covered and protected, during a retreat of a mile or more, and until they had crossed the bridge in safety, was no easy matter.'

Allied casualties in a combat, which it had not been necessary for Craufurd to accept, were heavy; but those of Ney's Corps were substantially heavier, and at about 5 p.m. a flag of truce from the French brought the action to a conclusion.[34] But as Wellington wrote, when excusing Craufurd for having involved his outposts in such 'foolish affairs': 'I cannot accuse a man who I believe has meant well, and whose error was one of judgement, not of intention.' According to Burgoyne, Picton had ridden towards the spot, but then lost his way 'among the rocks at a distance from the field [of action].' He was *not* culpable, as Napier has insinuated, for not advancing his 3rd Division in support, saying that Crauford might get out of his own scrape; but he was obliged to evacuate Pinhel, to which the Light Division likewise retired.

Simmons, who had been shot though the thigh, remembered falling with great force:

> For a few moments I could not collect my ideas, and was feeling about my arms and body for a wound, until my eye caught the stream of blood rushing through the hole in my trousers, and my leg and thigh appeared so heavy that I could not move it. Captain Napier took off his neckerchief and gave it to a sergeant, who put it round my thigh and twisted it tight with a ramrod, to stop the bleeding. The firing was so severe that the sergeant, on finishing the job for me, fell with a shot through the head ... some men put me into a blanket and carried me off. [Some of the soldiers] had neglected to cover their wounds, which now became one frightful mass of maggots all over the surface; it really made me tremble to see them dressed. The flies and mosquitoes followed us like myriads. We had no means of keeping off the swarms of insects, and the slow pace the bullocks went, made us feel the vertical rays of the sun with redoubled force. We had some salt meat rations which, in the feverish state of our existence, we turned from with disgust.

Among the disabled was Costello, who with others, hobbled back to a village 'with the help of a couple of rifles that served as crutches.' He was then crammed with six others into a bullock cart. At daybreak, while refreshing his parched lips with some water, 'Lord Wellington and some of his staff galloped up. He glanced at us, and seeing our crowded condition ... ordered one of his aides-de-camp to obtain additional conveyances, bread and wine ... [and] rode off towards Almeida.' Although the sustenance promised never made its appearance, Costello and his companions, among them Simmons, reached Coimbra on 1 August, and from Figueras the survivors sailed to Lisbon, but several had died on the journey.

[1] Reputations stick. Michael Glover (the military historian), before visiting the town in the 1960s, was warned by Spaniards from other parts of the country

that he might not find them particularly agreeable, and his own experience 'did nothing to disprove the verdict.'

2 As Capt. John Burgoyne described it: 'A lady gives out there is a *tertullia* at her house every night, and, without further invitation, any one of her own class in society who chooses, calls in after nine in the evening, and sits down without ceremony … they talk politics, play at cards, sing, play, dance, tell stories or play at forfeits, &c. They break up about eleven or twelve. The owners of the house give nothing but candles and fire, but then there is no need of invitation, and every one comes and goes as he likes. The indelicate stories and conversation which pass before the most respectable women, and even to them, would not be believed in England; the ladies do not appear at all shocked by it, but on the contrary constantly join in the hearty laugh … They are passionately fond of smoking, and make cigars by rolling up tobacco in a small piece of white paper, which, when half smoked, they frequently give to their neighbour to finish.'

3 Among those who privately voiced their momentary disapproval was Thomas Graham, who felt it was undeserved, writing: 'The honor bestowed on Sir A.W. for the worst campaign ever made is too ludicrous and evinces a partiality the most disgraceful.'

4 As Aitchison had remarked: 'The Portuguese armed peasantry always accompanied us and did wonders, but in Spain I never saw one armed peasant and indeed not one person seemed to have the least interest in the cause we came to support. We are good mercenaries but we are not strong enough, nor is it to be expected we can transform the war – the Spaniards have shown *they will not fight* – and without their assistance we can do no good.'

5 These actions had taken place on 19 November (when 14,000 were taken prisoner and 50 guns captured), and on 28 November respectively.

6 Losses were serious, but could not be compare with those among British troops sent to the yellow-fever-riddled West Indies, where the service lost c. 80,000 men during the years 1793–6, including 40,000 dead, which later figure exceeded the total losses of Wellington's army from *all* causes, including desertion, during the whole of the Peninsular War. Nevertheless, Charles Boutflower, a surgeon of the 40th Regiment stationed at Elvas, noted in his Diary on 22 October: 'Sickness has constantly prevailed in the Army to an alarming extent, there being seldom less than 8000 sick on an average, of which the deaths have been most afflicting.' The precise cause of malaria was not yet known, and few hospitals had enough Peruvian or chinchona bark, producing quinine, which had proved to have an efficacious effect.

Aitchison had commented that there were 'men in charge of sick now who till they came here never prescribed in their lives, and there are others who have had no practice beyond answering a prescription in an apothecary shop in England. Such men are entrusted with the lives of soldiers, but it must always be the case in a great degree while the pay remains so small as to induce those only to enter the service who would starve at home. I have myself heard a surgeon say that he had no doubt that *two-thirds* of the deaths in this army were due to the inattention and ignorance of the medical officers.'

7 A network of commissariat depots was established, based on Lisbon and Oporto, which were extended or were emptied with the ebb and flow of the front during the course of the war. Occasionally, as at Condeixa, the rapidity of a retreat necessitated their partial destruction, but this was rare. In the southern

sector of the front, Abrantes, Portalegre, Elvas, were important depots, while others were set up further north after Masséna's expulsion from Portugal, and prior to the Vitoria campaign.

8 See also note 25.

9 See Christopher Hall's *Wellington's Navy* for an overview, notably Chapter 4, which gives some idea of the complexity of the organising of convoys, of the flow of prodigeous amounts of bullion, specie, and Treasury Bills from London to Lisbon and Cadiz, and also to several rebellious *juntas* along the Biscay coast from Corunna to Gijón – apart from the massive quantities of arms and munitions distributed to them.

10 Cocks was always very specific when itemising what dress and equipment should be brought out, and in recommending their suppliers, as is evident from the letter to his brother James, dated 2 February 1812: see Julia Page's *Intelligence Officer in the Peninsula*.

11 3,000 of them, commanded by General Leite, were to form half the garrison of Elvas.

12 It was only in mid December that reference to him leading a Spring offensive ceased. The cause of this volte-face was his impending divorce from Josephine and his marriage to the Archduchess Marie Louise of Austria, which, after protracted negotiations, took place in Vienna on 1 April 1810.

13 According to Henry Ross-Lewin (32nd), 'these blockhouses might contain from two to four hundred men, and some had eight guns mounted on them; they were entered by means of ladders, and were impregnable to the irregular Spanish troops.'

14 Those that did collaborate, largely confined to the wealthier and least religiously bigoted citizens in some of the larger towns, were known as *Afrancesados*.

15 They would not think twice before attacking lightly escorted convoys of wounded French troops, or isolated and unprotected French hospitals, massacring both doctors and wounded, and then boast about their perilous exploits.

16 Thankfully, he retained the confidence of a nucleus of his staff, among them D'Urban (although not in his immediate entourage), who in early April provided an objective opinion in his private *Journal*: 'The firmness of mind which Lord Wellington has continued to preserve since the Battle of Talavera, in spite of the despondency of almost every one about him, as well as all the people at home, and the perseverence with which he continued in a forward position ready for offensive operations yet fully prepared for defensive ones, has saved Portugal, and may, and probably will, be the Salvation of Spain. This admirable firmness proves him a Hero, if he had done nothing else to deserve the name.'

17 The peak of Torre, rising in this range not far north-west of Covilha, at 1,993m (6,538 ft) was the highest in Portugal.

18 Anglicised as either Busaco or Bussaco.

19 Already, as early as mid January, Wellington had reckoned that it would be from this direction that the French would be invading. On 14 January Capt. John Burgoyne received Wellington's order from Q.M.G. Murray to 'survey the course of the Cris, and to ascertain its course, by how many bridges and fords it is crossed, where the roads crossing it lead to, whether it fills in winter, and how long it remains full, and whether the destruction of the bridge between Mortagua and Santa Combadão, and the destruction of the road

leading to the bridge on the right of the river, would be a serious impediment to the use of the road from Viseu to Coimbra by Mortagua and Mealhada. Let him [the officer concerned] calculate the means of destroying that bridge and road. I should wish the same information regarding the Dão, which joins the Cris immediately below Santa Combadão. Also the same respecting the river about a league or a league and a half from Viseu.'

20 His private life there was pretty hectic: one of his several affairs was 'with an exquisite child called Joaquina Cavaleira', whose 'excellent mother brought her round to me every evening, decked out like a bride, and then fetched her in the morning.'

21 Seia or Cea, was also Headquarters in mid April, but for three days only, the explanation for which (according to Burgoyne) was that Wellington, 'having heard of a fine house there, occupied by a nobleman's family, the lady of which was very engaging, and the daughters handsome, musical, and entertaining, determined to remove there; but finding in the house not so good accommodation as he espected, owing to twenty-one children who were in it – the lady, from having had no less than twenty-five children, something the worse for wear, and the young ladies much secluded, in the old Portuguese style – his Lordship got immediately disgusted, and returned to Viseu.' The fidalgo's name was Luis Bernardo, a brother of the Bishop of Guarda, and his wife 'a fat little person', but the mother of only twenty-three children, as described by E.W. Buckham, who dined with the family in December 1812, when the party was 'served on massy plate … disinterred from its hiding-place in the garden.' By then, they lived in an rehabilitated conservatory adjoining their ruined palace.

22 At intermediate Mangualde he found Mr Hughes, one of his clerks, 'leading a fine life, and not only kept a girl, but also two horses, two hunting dogs, and a groom.'

23 Also a hospital base, on reaching which, John Cooper had a 'severe relapse of fever. The infection was dreadful: nearly all in the room where I was were at one time insensible, bawling out the most incoherent jabber. I had my turn of that also. Although there were about twelve of us in two small rooms, there was not a single chamber utensil. A blanket was spread on the floor instead. Some made use of a window for every purpose. I saw neither bason, soap, nor towel. Such was the place, and such our condition. While at Celorico I saw one of the 27th regiment hanged for robbery. On the same tree, a short time before, three of his comrades were hanged for a similar offense. However, having a good constitution, I soon recovered, and returned to Guarda.'

24 In Aitchinson's view, the resources of the country, if properly managed, were 'sufficient to pay all the troops they can raise, but the government both civil and military from top to bottom is the very essence of corruption …'

25 In Tomkinson's opinion, it was not for almost another two years that the system of supplying the army by means of mules was brought 'to the greatest perfection,' despite the cost. He felt that had it been possible to have paid the muleteers earlier than they were, more reasonable terms might have been agreed. As it was, a 'dollar per diem for each mule was an immense allowance.' In fact, the payment in arrears of muleteers was deliberate policy, not just because money was tight, which while it may have caused some discontent and occasional recalcitrance or theft, discouraged desertion, for in such circumstances they would lose the accumulating wages due to them.

[26] For example, by the Autumn of 1810 the 2nd Division possessed 769 mules but only 10 bullock carts. Carts were rarely used when troops were in the field. As noticed later by Major Augustus Frazer, the mules were frequently 'not merely sheared, but absolutely filigreed in the most whimsical manner [by] … people whose trade it is to shear and to cut their hides in the fantastical manner admired in this country,' which suggests that gypsies may have participated in plying their trade in the management of mules and mounts.

[27] Craufurd had the advantage of speaking German fluently.

[28] Many 'New Christian' or crypto-Sephardi Jewish families lingered in this part of the country after their expulsion from Spain in 1492.

[29] See Rory Muir (ed.), *At Wellington's Right Hand: the Letters of Lieut.-Colonel Sir Alexander Gordon*, pp. 111 and 113.

[30] This is corroborated by D'Urban, writing on 17 August: 'The Desertion of the Enemy increases and the Disgust of all Ranks of his Army at the War and its fatigues and privations is at a height that cannot fail of being very embarrassing to him,' while Cocks also refers to them coming in 'by handfuls,' between 40 and 50 passing through his post during the last month. Simmons described how one lone deserter wanted to come over when the river Agueda was running 'so furiously that he durst not cross it.' Some Spaniards hiding close by from the French, 'observed him, and did not know his wishes, but seeing this Frenchman without arms and unsupported, deliberately stoned him to death, several of us looking on without the power of doing the unfortunate man any service.' Leach, describing the same or a similar scene, refers to three Spanish shepherds, tending their sheep, as having 'intercepted him, and beat him to death with their clubs.'

[31] Junot had taken back to France with him a collection of maps and reports made previously, which covered central Portugal, but it would seem that Masséna chose not to demean himself either by referring to them or seeking the advice of Junot or anyone else (except perhaps Pelet) apropos the condition of alternative routes by which Lisbon might be best approached.

[32] His 4,000 strong garrison was marched away, prisoners. 100 guns, the majority being in a bad state or disabled, together with 7,000 muskets, fell into French hands, but it had cost them 180 killed and over 1,000 wounded; and their artillery having thrown 11,000 shells and 18,000 round shot into the place, Masséna was left short of ammunition, and with a much-impaired fortress to defend.

[33] The extensive and impressive fortifications of Fort Conception (Fuerte Concepción) still surviving, lie a few miles north of Fuentes de Oñoro. Throughout early June, John Bourgoyne had been both repairing the fort, and placing explosive charges, saucissons, etc. ready to blow it up, should that be necessary in the face of a overpowering French advance which, on Wellington's instructions, he was obliged to do on 21 July. As it would require a garrison of 1,000, and would be difficult to be relieved once surrounded, there was little alternative.

[34] Oman states that the total British loss was 333 (36 killed, 214 wounded, and 83 missing), including 28 officers, but many of the missing, if not taken prisoner, may have been killed.

6

August 1810 to March 1811: Masséna invades Portugal; Busaco; The Lines of Torres Vedras; and Barrosa

Almeida, which it was hoped might hold up the French advance by several weeks, was now left isolated, but although invested by Ney's Corps, they did not immediately attempt to break ground. Wellington concluded that it was possible that once the French had concentrated, they would by-pass it and 'make a dash at us, and endeavour to make our retreat as difficult as possible.' The stronghold, with its strong Vaubanesque fortifications, was commanded by Colonel William Cox.[1]

Major Charles Cocks, writing on 21 August, remarked that Masséna's 'ignorance and want of information is astonishing; in his first summons [before opening fire] he addressed Governor Cox as if he was a Portuguese. The major had already noticed

> increasing symptoms of neglect and dislike in the Portuguese peasantry towards us; they think we are retreating and deserting them and conceive this is a proper moment to show all the rancour which has long been brooding in their breasts. I do not blame them for disliking us, the contempt with which Englishmen treat them is a sufficient cause for it, but I despise the manner with which they have hitherto fawned on us and not dared to show their dislike till they think they are getting rid of us. Today [1 August], two of my patrols were attacked in two separate villages,[2] a man in each is badly wounded. I immediately visited each village with a party, seized some of the inhabitants whom I considered as culprits and have sent them onto General Cole at Guarda.

In the event, on the evening of 26th a catastrophe overwhelmed Almeida only a few hours after the French bombardment had commenced. There are conflicting accounts of what happened, but the most likely explanation is that a barrel, accidentally damaged while taken

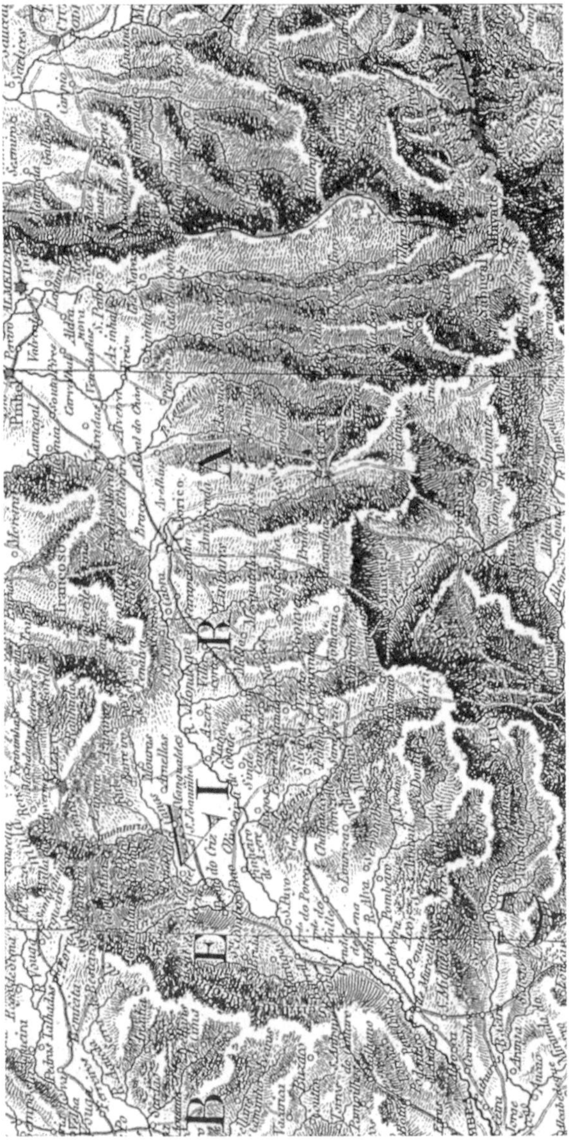

Detail from Jasper Nantiat's *A New Map of Spain and Portugal* (1810) of the area between Ciudad Rodrigo (top right) and Coimbra (bottom left). Compare with that opposite

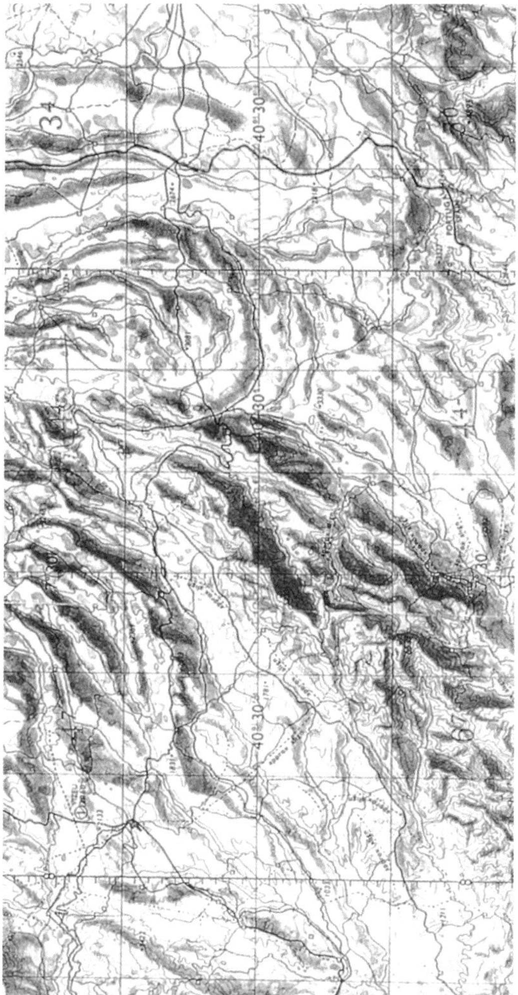

Part of an aeronautical map of the same area: Ciudad Rodrigo being just off right centre. The Busaço ridge is obvious to the north-east of Coimbra (lower left)

from the main powder magazine in the castle to guns manning the walls, had left a train of powder on the ground: ignited by a shell, it had burned back. Whatever the cause, the resulting explosion sheared off the tops of building throughout the town, leaving little more than the outer fortifications. Although well aware of the severe damage, Cox bravely endeavoured to gain time, for he still had a garrison of 4,000, even if stunned, although only 200 of his gunners had survived to man the 100 guns still serviceable. Several Portuguese officers then mutinied, compelling Cox, unable to prolong its defence, to capitulate prematurely.[3]

With both frontier fortresses in his hands, Masséna, at the head of almost 65,000 men, including 8,400 cavalry and 114 guns, could now turn his attention to disposing of the British Army, which had retired west down the Mondego valley. On 3 September, Sir Stapleton Cotton, his cavalry screening the retreat, was instructed to 'take care that the telegraphs are destroyed' once Celorico and Guarda had been evacuated. Three days later, Hill was ordered to withdraw gradually from his position at Sarzedas (west of Castelo Branco), make his way through very intricate hilly country in the region of Sertã, cross both the Zêzere and Mondego, and join the main Allied concentration on the eminently defencible ridge of the Serra de Busaço.

The progress of Masséna's veterans was harassed ceaselessly by the *Ordenança*, who, lacking any better ammunition, often peppered them with bird-shot – producing superficial wounds which festered, causing death. Nevertheless, as anticipated, rather than following the road leading south-west between the Mondego and the Serra da Estrela, the main bulk of the 'Army of Portugal', once they had descended to the valley floor, veered north-west along an execrable road towards Viseu, entered by its vanguard on 19 September.

Cocks, writing from the Ponte de Murcella,[4] refers to his 'most interesting duty' during the previous few days, watching the French from his position on the north flank of the Serra: 'The road of the enemy lay through a large plain, on one side of which is an immense mountain. On this mountain lay I, and very much at my ease counted the divisions which marched at the foot. Unfortunately their principal force did not take this route but I, one day, saw 5,000 infantry and 2,000 cavalry perfectly, with all their baggage and etcs.' Their advance had 'caused most horrible confusion' among the Portugese belatedly hurrying ahead of it, for they

> have such a dread of the French, they desert the villages for leagues on either side of their route. Though one must feel sorry for these unfortunate

> people, driven from their homes and their habits of indolence, into mountains and activity, yet sometimes in these gangs of fugitives one meets with such curious combinations and such extraordinary demonstrations of dread that it is impossible to help laughing. Fancy to yourself, but first recollect that the scene lies in a grove of pine trees, with firs and brambles about knee high. Fancy to yourself an elderly, fat woman in a flowered satin petticoat trudging away, in one hand a parasol, in the other a lapdog. Then two boys, knock-kneed and trembling, with countenances devoid of every colour but a pasty yellow; a footman, like an old English serving man, with his shoes in his hand, then two misses with fans, crying 'Jesu Maria'; three serving maids, with bundles, howling; two bullocks lowing; a car with wheels squeaking and a peasant in a cocked hat and a long gun, more frightened than the whole party. Fancy all this trudging through the firs taking *me* for a Frenchman and setting off in every direction.

On 23 September, the enemy vanguard, advancing south-west from Viseu, drove back Craufurd's picquets near the village of Mortágua, and two days later their whole force faced the steep heath-covered ridge of Busaco, up which curled a road from the hamlet of Moura.

Little did Masséna realise that almost the entire Anglo-Portuguese army – over 51,000 strong, together with 60 guns – lay in wait for him beyond the crest, deployed in positions chosen with great care; behind them extended a repaired track, along which troops could move rapidly to any section of the ridge requiring reinforcements.[5] Towards its northern end, within an extensive walled enclosure, stood a convent dating back to the 1630s, which served as Wellington's Headquarters, its cork-lined cells – except for those of the Abbot, and the Prior, Brother Antonio of the Angels, 'which nobody wanted, because it was found full of lumber, rags, and old iron' – being requisitioned by fifty officers, including Wellington's staff. The best room did not answer, having only one door; so another, with two, was placed at his disposal, first being sluiced out and dried by a cheering fire.[6]

Schaumann, peering down from the ridge on the afternoon of the 26th, could see 'three dark columns of a colossal army ... advancing under clouds of dust, and gleaming with the glint of arms.[7] Below, at the foot of the Serra and beyond a ravine, enemy pickets were already stationed. At last the huge mass seemed to break up into small regular clumps as the army went to bivouac. At some distance beyond ... one could see the huge bivouacs of their cavalry, and still further away ... a black mass, consisting of wagons, carts, mules, ambulances and the commissariat, could be divined.'

Sherer, on fording the Mondego with Hill's contingent, described the scene in more detail. [8] Their position

> extended nearly eight miles along this mountainous and rocky ridge, and the ground on which we formed inclining with a slope to our own rear, most admirably concealed both the disposition and the number of our force. My regiment had no sooner piled arms, than I walked to the verge of the mountain on which we lay, in the hope that I might discover something of the enemy. Little, however, was I prepared for the magnificent scene which burst on my astonished sight. Far as the eye could stretch, the glittering of steel, and clouds of dust raised by cavalry and artillery, proclaimed the march of a countless army; while, immediately below me, at the feet of those precipitous heights, on which I stood, their picquets were already posted: thousands of them were already halted in their bivouacks, and column too after column, arriving in quick succession, reposed upon the ground allotted to them, and swelled the black and enormous mass. The numbers of the enemy were, at the lowest calculation, seventy-five thousand,[9] and this host formed in three distinct and heavy columns; while to the rear of their left, at a more considerable distance, you might see a large encampment of their cavalry, and the whole country behind them seemed covered with their train, their ambulances, and their commissariat. This was the French army.

While Wellington had a very exact idea of Masséna's dispositions, he would not allow any fires to be lit that night, which might give away his own. As William Tomkinson (16th Light Dragoons) noted: 'Every one expected and wished for a general attack at daylight. The army is in most beautiful order, and the Portuguese as fine-looking men and as steady under arms as any in the world.'

Busaço

The Anglo-Portuguese army was under arms well before dawn on the 27th. Although there were sounds of movement, and then sporadic firing between the *tirailleurs* and riflemen, mist shrouded the valley floor. As this lifted, Wellington could discern a column ascending the steep hill-slope, the first of many which made the attempt, only to be disintegrated.

Typical was a later confrontation, when Ney's mounted a powerful attack towards the 1/52nd and 1/43rd of Craufurd's Division, which, within 25 yards of the crest, received a staggering volley at almost point-blank range, followed by a bayonet charge, while the two-deep lines of the flanking companies – eight on each side – delivered volleys into the columns they enveloped. Within minutes, the French turned about, panic-stricken, and streamed downhill, the riflemen briefly in pursuit. Leach described the effect of Crawfurd's charge as

> instantaneous and most decisive; and it is impossible to describe the confusion and carnage which … ensued in the enemy's ranks. It can be readily conceived, that so large a column, wedged close to a road of no great width, being once broken and forced back, those pressing on from the rear to support it were literally borne back down the mountain by the tide of fugitives … [while] the instant the attacking columns were turned back, they were exposed to the fire of our whole division; whilst our battalions and some caçadores were ordered to pursue, and to give them a flanking fire, and the horse artillery continued to pour on them a murderous fire of grape, as they were struggling through the narrow streets of Sula, and trampling each other to death in their great haste to escape.

A second attack by Ney found itself opposed by Pack's Portuguese in line, whose rate and accuracy of fire now equalled that of their Allies, which brought them to a halt. To Schaumann, they 'behaved just like the English troops, and, indeed, fought with such valour that the French believed them to be Englishmen disguised in Portuguese uniforms.' He was equally impressed by the little he saw of Wellington during the battle, remarking on his 'extraordinary circumspection, calm, coolness and presence of mind. His orders were communicated in a loud voice, [10] and were short and precise ... He wears no befeathered hat, no gold lace, no stars, no orders – simply a plain low hat, a white collar, a grey overcoat, and a light sword.'

Ney's troops found it impossible to break through in the face of this hail of fire. Turning on their heels and picking their way among their wounded strewn over the slope, they retreated as fast as they could towards their second brigade, which together with several battalions of Reynier's and Ney's Corps, never saw action.[11]

Masséna, un-dissuaded by the saner counsel of his subordinates, some of whom, from previous experience, were well aware of the hazards of making a frontal attack on Wellington when in such a position, had perversely insisted in sending forward his columns. Now he knew better, finding them repeatedly repulsed by the punishing reception he was evidently not expecting. Although with 20,000 fresh infantry at hand, Masséna had had enough. It was not yet midday, but no further attacks were made, although some minor skirmishing took place during the afternoon, which ceased towards the evening, when 'and a flag of truce came in, bringing General Simon's baggage, and with it a pretty little Spanish woman, part of his establishment.'[12]

During this cessation of hostilities, unarmed parties of both armies were employed in collecting their dead and wounded, while Leach himself 'went down into the village of Sula, and had some conversation with several French officers and soldiers. They acknowledged their loss to have been very severe; and one man assured me, that his company, which numbered one hundred men in the morning, could only muster twenty-two effective men after their repulse.' Sherer remarked also on the fraternisation taking place when our men descended to 'a small brook, which flowed between the opposing armies, for water; and the French and English soldiers might be seen drinking out of the same narrow stream, and even leaning over to shake hands with each other. One private, of my own regiment, actually exchanged forage-caps with a soldier of the enemy, as a token of regard and good-will.'

An unsuccessful attempt was made to occupy Sula the moment the truce was over, after which the French spent the remaining hours of daylight entrenching their areas of bivouac, the view of which that night, as far as Sherer was concerned, 'far exceeded in grandeur, its imposing aspect by day. Innumerable and brilliant fires illuminated all the country spread below us; while they yet flamed brightly, the shadowy figures of men and horses, and the glittering piles of arms, were all visible ... the view interrupted by a few dark patches of black fir, which by a gloomy contrast, heightened the effect of the picture.' Several deserters entered the Allied lines during the night and, according to Leach, all of them reckoned that Junot's Corps, not yet engaged, would storm their position next day; but in the event no such attack was made.

By the following afternoon if was obvious to Aitchison that from 'the smoke of villages and heath set on fire for that purpose,' which was to mask his movement, Masséna, 'having despaired of forcing us was endeavouring to turn us and Lord Wellington gave the necessary directions to prevent it. About 10 at night we, the 1st Division, were moved *by torchlight* with all the artillery on the hill, from it to the rear of the left centre, from whence we filed off to the road leading to Mealhada – this operation was very tedious and it was daylight before the rearguard was in motion.'

In his dilemma, Masséna had ordered General Ste Croix with two regiments of dragoons to reconnoitre and report on ways to circumvent the impeding ridge. Before long a track was found leading north-west from Mortágua via the hamlet of Pala to Boialvo, passing between its northern extremity and the Serra da Caramula, which determined Masséna to send his entire force on this circuitous cross-country route to meet the main Oporto–Coimbra highway, there swinging south. There was little resistance.[13] Although Masséna was thus able to turn the Allied flank, it did not deter Wellington: it was not part of his long-term strategy either to hold his position for long, or to descend from it to attack the French, already well trounced. He had a head start, and while his infantry evacuated their positions as planned and marched towards Coimbra, Wellington's cavalry converged on Mealhada, from which, as a rearguard, they retired, bickering with Masséna's cavalry throughout the 30th.[14]

John Kincaid had been among a reinforcement for the 95th Regiment, which, landing at Figuera da foz, had marched east towards Coimbra and crossed the Mondego. The first thing he noticed was that the civil authorities, 'in making their own hurried escape, had totally forgotten that they had left a gaol full of rogues unprovided for, and who, as we were passing near them, made the most hideous screaming for relief. Our quarter-master-general very humanely took some men, who broke open the doors, and the whole of them were soon seen howling along the bridge into the wide world, in the most delightful delirium, with the French dragoons at their heels.'

Schaumann had great difficulty fighting his way through Coimbra, the streets being crammed not only with infantry passing through, notably General Craufurd's division, but also

> artillery, the tail of the Portuguese army's baggage convoy, marauders, and the refugees from perhaps fifteen of the neighbouring villages. Old people, lame and sick people, women just risen from childbed, children, and whole families with all their belonging, packed either on bullock carts, mules, horses or donkeys, were to be seen mixed up with all kinds of beasts, among which pigs, owing to their unruliness and horrible cries, were most conspicuous. And this throng, marching to the wailing and lamentation of the fugitives ... presented a scene which I shall never forget ... Ladies who ... had perhaps never left their homes except to go to Mass, could be seen walking along ... wearing silk shoes and their heads and shoulders covered only with thin scarves. Monks and nuns ... in procession, not knowing whither they were going.

The fatiguing march towards the protection of fortifications constructed across the wide peninsula north of Lisbon – known as 'The Lines of Torres Vedras' – progressed without much interruption, although the rearguard was involved in intermittent skirmishing, notably at Alcoentre. Any immediate pressure the French might have exerted on the Allied troops was relieved by the fact that on entering Coimbra, they preferred to devote two days to sacking the place *en passant*.[15] This was after Masséna had driven his opponent south 'in full retreat' after what is still characteristically described by chauvenistic pens as 'a great victory' on his part. His wounded were left in Coimbra, but inadequately guarded.

Ten days after the battle, Trant, with 400 of his militia, made a daring raid, capturing the Mondego bridge, by which the remaining French might have escaped, and also two fortified hospitals,[16] including that installed in the convent of Santa Clara, whose garrison of some 200 infirm soldiers put up a stiff resistance; but by nightfall over 4,500 men – many of them sick and wounded, and 80 officers – were being conducted towards Oporto as prisoners.

The Allied army progressed south in three columns. Hill's 'Corps' and Hamilton's Portuguese forded the Mondego at Penacova and, joined by units on the Alva, marched via Espinhal towards Tomar.[17] Wellington's main force followed the highway through Leiria, Batalha,[18] and Rio Maior to Alenquer, while Picton's Division veered west through Alcobaça and Obidos,[19] to approach Torres Vedras.

Schaumann referred to the congestion at Condeixa, where 'a supply of victuals, shirts, boots and horseshoes was distributed among the troops marching through, and what was left was burned,' as confirmed by Kincaid, who remarked that 'the commissariat were destroying quantities of stores which they were unable to carry off. They handed out shoes and shirts to any one who would take them, and the streets were literally running ancle deep with rum, in which the soldiers were dipping their cups and helping themselves as the marched along.'[20] At Pombal, Schaumann 'found shelter in the house of the once famous minister named Pombal, which was now in ruins ... abandoned by its present tenants, and in it we found a number of things lying about, of which, as the saying goes, suited our taste,' among them a rug which later saw service as a tent.

At Leiria, 'quantities of spilt coffee, sugar, chocolate, corn and flour, still lay about in the streets, together with rags, broken crockery, and paper ... at the chemist's shop all the jars had been destroyed': yet another scene of desolation, in spite of Draconian orders imposed by Wellington to put a stop to plundering, which applied to both troops and civilians: several caught red-handed were promptly hung, including a soldier's wife, as Schaumann witnessed; while Kincaid, on entering the place, saw 'an English and a Portuguese soldier dangling by the bough of a tree – the first summary example I had ever seen of martial law.' His attention was also attracted to a group of officers on their knees in a street, encircling 'a pyramid of letters, the contents of a mail just arrived from England. Needless to say that I joined the kneelers, and was rewarded with a letter addressed to myself, the first that I ever received through the medium of a paving stone.' At Leiria too, knowing that the enemy were close behind and that convent doors would scarcely protect their tender inmates, troopers broke them down, and out came the nuns 'as thick as a flock of sheep and set off for Lisbon, some of them jumping up behind the dragoons, clasping their gallant deliverers tightly round their waists'; and just in time, for when William Grattan (88th) passed through the place some months later, he found it little more than 'a heap of ruins.' This had not been part of the 'scorched earth' policy which Wellington had ordered to be carried out over an extensive area north of the capital, whereby livestock had been driven into the hills away from the French line of march; and ovens and mills destroyed; likewise stores of grain, etc. The *Ordenança* would be an additional hazard to be faced by any French troops forced to stray from their bivouacs in their desperate search of food and forage.

The mass exodus of the population living north of the Lines involved some 200,000 people, which together with their cattle, were herded south into what was basically an entrenched camp over 500 square miles in area. It was not easy to convince the peasantry that they must leave their villages, but Wellington had no compunction about ordering his cavalry commanders to inform local magistrates that 'if any of them stay, or if any of the inhabitants have any communication with the enemy, they will be hanged.' The threat had its effect, and before long he was able to report that 'The people of Portugal are doing that which the Spaniards ought to have done. They are removing their women and properties out of the enemy's way, and taking arms in their own defence. The country is made a desert, and behind almost every stone wall the French will meet an enemy.'[21]

Leach, whose regiment had been making soup from the heads and offal of the cattle killed for the troops, which they then distributed to the starving masses passing by, remarked that he had 'a thousand times wished it were possible that every man, woman, and child, of all ranks, in England, could have been transported to this heart-rending scene only for five minutes; that by having had an insight into the various miseries to which the ill-fated inhabitants of the theatre of war are inevitably subjected, they might return satisfied, and bless their stars that an army of Frenchmen were not riding rough-shod over old England, and inflicting on its people similar miseries ...'

The nearer they got to Lisbon, the devastation seemed to increase, the roads being 'littered with smashed cases and boxes, broken wagons and carts, dead horses and exhausted men. Every division was accompanied by a body of refugees as great as itself, and rich and poor alike, either walking, or mounted on horses or donkeys, were to be seen, all higgledy-piggeldy ...' Any ladies such as Schaumann had seen tripping along delicately, were now 'wading in torn silk shoes or barefoot in the mud', for just as British columns started entering the Lines on the 8th of October, the first of the autumn rains came pelting down.[22] Providentially, on leaving Rio Maior, Schaumann's commissaries discovered 'several sacks full of new English boots' in an old church which had been used as an army store, which were forthwith loaded onto their mules. Sherer, bivouacking near Santarém, was certain that the inhabitants, until their arrival, were 'unwilling to believe that the enemy would be suffered to penetrate so far'; but now the bank of the Tagus below the town 'was crowded with fugitives, waiting to be transported across, and the most affecting groups of families sat weeping on the ground ...' At Alhandra, immediately in front of the eastern extremity of the Lines, Sherer found himself quartered in the spacious but gloomy sacristy of a church, from the walls of which the images of departed saints seemed to frown upon them; but 'they could not ... repress the mirth, frighten away the appetite, or scare the slumbers of men so cheerful, so hungry, and so tired as we were. Our cloaks ... and some of our blankets, were excessively damp ... [but] luckily ... the priests had left the drawers in the sacristy full of their vestments; and with gay and heavy pontificals spread beneath and over us, we slept as sound as any canon in the closes of York or Durham.'

Behind the Lines

By the 10th, leaving only a few cavalry patrols and the Light Division to hold off Masséna's vanguard, the Allies were deployed behind the Lines, already manned by the militia.[23] To Sherer, the 'posts and batteries' in the fortified heights to which they had now been moved 'were by no means in a perfectly serviceable condition; as in some, no guns were at the time mounted, and in others, the necessary ammunition had not been provided.' By the 13th, his regiment was marched to Bucelas, near which ran the second line of defence, and

> the post being considered highly important, six British battalions were stationed in it in reserve. The whole time we remained here our line was regularly under arms two hours before break of day every morning; and when the sun appeared above the horizon, we generally manoeuvred for an hour before we were dismissed. For a few days ... my friend and I pitched our tent in the market-place. Here I took my meals, but slept with my company in [another] church, in which about two hundred of our men were accommodated. The senior officer had the sacristy ... the rest of us made ourselves truly comfortable in the large organ-loft. I used often to lean out of this gallery, and contemplate the strange scene below me. How a sober citizen from St Paul's churchyard would have stared to see a serjeant of grenadiers writing his reports on the communion-table, a fifer lounging at his ease in the pulpit, and practising his favourite quick step, and the men dividing and calling off their rations of raw beef on tombs of polished marble. Such, however, is but too faithful a picture of an every-day occurrence on actual service.

As Schaumann remarked with surprise, when first approaching the Lines: 'As far as the eye could see there was nothing but gun embrasures. Earthworks on the hill and barricades made with wine casks, boxes and even trunks filled with earth and stones, formed the entrance to Villa Franca;[24] every means of access was blocked. A few 24-pounders frowned darkly upon the road. To the left on the Tagus lay a respectable-looking fleet of gun-boats manned by English sailors. All garden walls had been thrown down, and trenches ran to the very edge of the river.' Next morning he marched to Mafra, reached after having been soaked to the skin by the drenching rain.[25] Writing from there on the 11th, Tomkinson, when referring to its stables and cloisters being extensive enough to accommodate the whole brigade of cavalry, complained that from 'the constant fag on our retreat, the horses were in a low state, and the regiment much in want of shoeing and a little rest,'[26] which Cocks confirmed, remarking that as they had been 'almost constantly in the field without tents, for nearly four months, and our late, long marches had completely worn out our shoes. Two or three days more such would have ruined us by laming every horse ...' It was soon after that Schaumann was ordered to Torres Vedras itself,

> to clear the ground between us and the enemy of all victuals as quickly and as thoroughly as possible. Accordingly, I was given a detachment of hussars from time to time, with which I carried out raids. My people followed us with mules and empty sacks. When we reached a village we sent patrols to the left and right of it; then we would go forward, post sentries, and proceed to plunder the houses and barns which had long lain deserted by the inhabitants. As a rule, the owners had concealed their property badly; everywhere one would see from large damp patches on the walls that something had recently been walled up just there; or from hollow sounding places in the gardens that things had been buried. In all these matters my shoemaker, Joaquim, displayed the utmost virtuosity. We often found large supplies of corn, wheat, oil, flour, ham, pork, sausages, and vegetables; unfortunately, however, we also found clothes, beds, linen, and furniture, and I was not always able to prevent either my own people or the poor devils who had been left behind, from making off with these articles.

Exactly a year had passed since Wellington had had the foresight to investigate the viability of a project taking shape in his mind, which was to defend Lisbon by an extensive line of fortifications across intricate terrain some 20-30 miles north of the capital. Already, after Vimeiro, he had recognized the potential of its natural features, well-described by Oman as 'a ganglion of mountains rather than a well-marked chain.' Major Neves Costa of the Portuguese Engineers had made a survey of the area already, which, although unreliable, was of some utility; but the decision to build the Lines and the method of constructing them were entirely Wellington's, as outlined in his detailed *Memorandum* dated 20 October 1809. This was addressed to Colonel Richard Fletcher, commanding the Royal Engineers, who with Q.M.G. George Murray and Benjamin D'Urban, had accompanied him in a thorough reconnaissance of the whole district. Wellington re-visited the Lines four months later, by which time works had been well advanced, Fletcher having been ably assisted by Captain Jones.[27] Local peasant labour and the Lisbon militia had been supervised by Captain Mulcaster, together with some 150 N.C.Os. and 18 engineers. 21,000 palisades and 10,000 fascines had been fabricated; hills were scarped, glacis levelled, walls and earthworks raised, lateral roads laid out to facilitate communications, low-lying areas flooded to impede the enemy, the whole complex and arduous task being undertaken with as much secrecy as possible.[28]

The northerly of the two roughly parallel chains of batteries and forts, extended along a 26-mile front from Sizandro on the coast to

Alhandra on the Tagus, and the second line from just north of Mafra to meet the river near Póvoa de Santa Iria. At first, the Lines consisted of 126 redoubts holding 427 guns (shortly increased to 152 works and 534 pieces of ordnance).[29] Both flanks were protected by the Royal Navy, which had commandeered several shallow draught vessels, manned by some 800 sailors and each mounting one or two heavy guns, for it was quite possible that Masséna might construct rafts to float down the Tagus in an attempt to outflank Wellington. In the estuary itself, over 250 transports of varying size and quality were anchored under the protection of eleven ships of the line.[30] Nothing was left to chance. Lieut. Frederick Berkeley commanded the gun-boats, from which, on 12 October, General Ste-Croix was almost cut in two by a ricochetting roundshot.[31]

General Fane was sent across the Tagus with 1,500 Portuguese cavalry, together with a battalion of *Caçadores* and a few guns, where they were assisted by the local *Ordenança* in watching the river banks, and to prevent the enemy foraging in the Alentejo. Although Fane failed to set fire with his rockets to some enemy boats assembled at the dockyard below Santarém, these salvos served as a warning 'shots across their bows': any attempt to cross would be strongly opposed.

The 'Lines' themselves were garrisoned by 25,000 Portuguese militia and 11,000 *Ordenança,* 8,000 Spanish troops under La Romana,[32] and 2,500 British marines and artillerymen.[33] A system of semaphores had been prepared, by which a message could be transmitted from the Atlantic to the Tagus – a distance of 29 miles – in seven minutes, while from his Headquarters at Pero Negro (south-west of Sobral), a written order could be received by any unit within an hour.[34] Hill's 'Corps' was posted near the eastern flank, extended to the west by Craufurd's Light Division, while Picton and the 3rd Division were placed at first in the vicinity of Torres Vedras itself, in front of which, beyond the Sizandro, rose the formidable entrenched camp of São Vicente. The rest of the army was massed on either side of Pero Negro, near which Monte Socorro, rising to a height of 1,292 feet, provided a fine observation post.

In spite of the congestion, there seemed to be still plenty of room in which to maneouvre. Villages further south and in Lisbon itself seemed to absorb the influx of refugees, although many had crossed to the south bank of the Tagus also. Both civilians and the military were moderately well provisioned, and additional supplies could be ferried across the estuary with ease. In Sherer's opinion,

> Lisbon, after the first alarm, became as it were intoxicated by a strong feeling of security: there was never a period when this city was more crowded with objects of misery, or when provisions were more extravagantly dear; yet at no time had their theatres been better filled, their societies more gay and brilliant, than when seventy thousand vindictive enemies lay within sixteen miles of the city, panting for the plunder of it. It is but justice to add, that every thing which prudence and humanity could suggest was done by the inhabitants of Lisbon, to alleviate the public misfortune. The port was open to all vessels laden with provisions, the magazines were filled with them, charitable institutions were set on foot, and food daily distributed to such of the fugitives as were necessitous and helpless, while labour was provided for the others. The police, too … was most active; and whatever secret and treasonable spirit existed among the disaffected, was compelled to remain inactive and harmless.

Two probing attacks in the vicinity of Sobral by units of Junot's Corps had been repulsed on 14 October, when Masséna, attended by a large staff, was distinctly seen reconnoitring the area, a league behind which, according to Stothert, the 'principal part of the French infantry have hutted in a pine wood.' Masséna had just heard of Trant's exploit at Coimbra, in taking prisoner all his wounded, which had created 'a considerable sensation among the troops, whom the officers are endeavouring to persuade that the news is unfounded.' Junot himself – so close to the capital he had occupied three years earlier – was more preoccupied by the lack of food and forage, which confirmed Wellington's premonition, as expressed to his brother Henry on the 21st, that the French 'will lose the greatest part of their army if they attack us. They will starve if they stay much longer; and they will experience great difficulty in their retreat.'

Stothert confirmed that deserters 'continue to arrive, who affirm that the enemy's baggage is sent to the rear,[35] and that a considerable force, under Loison, has already fallen back' on Tomar to collect provisions, 'of which particularly bread, the troops are in great want. The accounts of deserters, however, are always to be received with extreme … caution.' Tomkinson admitted that desertion was not confined to the French: 'since we have been in the lines, many of our infantry have passed over. Whether they think the enemy will gain Lisbon, and that they shall have their share in the plunder, or what is the reason, scarcely any one knows. Seven from the Fuzileers went off in one night, and these from one of the best regiments in the service.'

In his dilemma, on 31 October, Masséna sent Foy, with an escort of 600 men, to Paris – not reached until 22 November – to report to Napoleon that the Lines were so strong that if his army attacked them, it would be seriously compromised, and requested further instructions.[36] The latter, brought back by Foy at the head of a straggling column of 1,800 men from Ciudad Rodrigo threading the tortuous Estrada Nova in appalling weather, and not received by Masséna until 5 February, were to hold out regardless until Mortier and Soult reinforced him: this was never to happen.[37]

According to William Grattan, during this period, the Connaught Rangers occupied themselves in such pursuits as each of them fancied.

> We had no unnecessary drilling, nor were we tormented with that greatest of *bores* to an officer at any time, but particularly on service, uniformity of dress. The consequence was that every duty was performed with cheerfulness; the army was in the highest state of discipline; and those gentlemen who had, or fancied they had, a taste for leading the fashion, had now a fine opportunity of bringing their talents into play.
>
> With such latitude it is not to be wondered at that our appearance was not *quite* as uniform as some general officers would approve of; but Lord Wellington was a most indulgent commander; he never harassed us with reviews, or petty annoyances, which so far from promoting discipline, or doing good in any way, have a contrary effect … Provided we brought our men into the field well appointed, and with sixty rounds of good ammunition each, he never looked to see whether their trousers were black, blue, or grey; and as to ourselves, we might be rigged out in all the colours of the rainbow if we fancied it. The consequence was, that scarcely two officers were dressed alike! Some with grey braided coats, others with brown; some again liked blue; while many from choice, or perhaps necessity, stuck to the 'old red rag.' Overalls, of all things, were in vogue, and the comical appearance of a number of infantry officers loaded with leather bottoms to their pantaloons, and huge chains suspended from the side buttons, like a parcel of troopers, was amusing enough. Quantities of hair, a regular brutus, a pair of mustachios, and screw brass spurs, were essential to a first-rate *Count*, for so were our dandies designated. The 'cut-down' hat, exactly a span in height, was another *rage*; this burlesque on a *chapeau* was usually out-topped by some extraordinary-looking feather; while, again, others wore their hats without any feather at all – and indeed this was the most rational thing they did. In a paroxysm of a wish to be singularly singular, a friend of mine shaved all the hair off the crown of his head, and *he* was decidedly

> the most *outré*-looking man amongst us, and consequently the happiest. I myself had a hankering to be a *Count* ... so I hit on the expedient of cutting my hat down a couple of inches lower than any one else.

Major Cocks complained of the lack of books, admittedly 'not very portable articles in a campaign', for 'we have plenty of leisure time upon our hands, the 130,000 men who are here assembled to fire and sabre at one another remaining all perfectly quiet and, except the generals, going on just as unconcerned as if the one party were in London and the other in Paris.' He continued: 'We live very well, having plenty of mutton, beef, fowls, turkey, coffee, butter, bread, potatoes and figs.[38] My cellar – alias pigskins – is stocked with sherry, Collares, an excellent wine of this country like claret but not so strong, and some draught wine. Perhaps I never told you that wine in this country is carried in pigskins, dried and stripped of their hair but retaining their original strength. The mouth is sewed up and the liquor generally drawn by one of the ears or a foot. The prudence of not putting *new wine into old skins* is exemplified for new wine sometimes ferments and then the skins, unless they are very strong, burst. Old skins are the best as they never give the wine taste, which unseasoned ones always do.'

In another letter, Cocks commented that Masséna was undoubtedly 'in the greatest of military difficulties. How far his abilities will get him out is now the question. A French officer, a prisoner, with whom I was conversing, said of him that he *had been* a good general but was now in his dotage ...' We also find Cocks writing to his long-suffering cousin Thomas on 22 December, requesting him to attend to several commissions – apart from sending out more note-paper and books – 'for the length of this campaign has made great havoc with my equippage:

> First, Egerton, the bookseller: Gilbert, bootmaker, Old Bond Street; and Cunningham, hosier, corner of St James's Street, Piccadilly; I should be much obliged to you to settle with.
>
> Second, would you order me a new hussar saddle with accountrements complete, from Whippy. There is a new hussar saddle at my father's in Cavendish Square; I should ask this to be also fitted up and sent out at the same time. I wish for pads for the valises to be made very large and fixed to the saddle. The saddle is to be strong, roomy and extremely high in the withers. Will you tell Whippy to remember that a saddle for service must not be made like one for a gingerbread field day but strong and calculated to save in every respect the horse's back and withers.

Third, would you order a new helmet from Hawkes. I wish it to be very light and very low. If he has forgot my measure then there is an old hat of mine at Cavendish Square.

Fourth, a new sabre and belt from Prosser. It should be roomy in the handle and not too heavy at the point. Will you be so good as to have it proved. My present sabre is a very bad one. It should not be *too broad* at the point. I have no particular liking to Prosser and if you know any cutler esteemed better it would perhaps be desirable to employ him. I do *not* like the handle roughed with fish skin.

Fifth, four pairs of new hussar boots, not open, from Gilbert, three pairs of laced boots with spurs to them all.

* * *

Masséna had sat down and waited, and his army dug in; but as the days passed, morale declined, and his position became increasingly desparate. As Leach remarked, when surveying the no-man's land dividing the picquets of the two armies, into which the French made frequent sorties for forage: 'after the first week, I do not believe as much provision could have been found for man or horse, in the whole valley, as would have rationed half a squadron of Lilliputian cuirassiers for twenty-four hours;' continuing:

Deserters were constantly coming over to us ... bringing all sorts of reports, vague and contradictory, but which, nevertheless, served us to speculate on. Thus, between constantly strengthing our position; endeavouring to keep off agues by dint of cigars, and of such fluids as were sometimes attainable from the sutlers who paid us a visit from Lisbon; reconnoitering our French neighbours with telescopes; trying to keep our horses, mules, and donkeys alive during the inclement weather, with chopped straw, or what little herbage the hills afforded, with, now and again, a very diminutive allowance of barley or Indian corn; and the occasional arrival of letters and newspapers from England, – we passed some five or six weeks, wondering whether Massena would attack us, or walk away from our front.

The 15th of November put a rest all surmises on this point. I happened to be on picket in front of Arruda on the night of the 14th; and looking, as usual, with all our eyes, in the twilight of the following morning, towards our opponents, the French sentries, we thought, could be discovered as heretofore: but when day broke thoroughly, we found that the cunning rogues had played us an old trick of theirs, by placing figures of straw

> upright, with a soldier's cap on each, and a pole by their side to represent a musket. Their whole army had retired, during the night, in the direction of Santarem; and we were sent in pursuit some hours afterwards.

Masséna withdraws

Allied units followed cautiously, for Masséna was very wily: it could be a feint to draw Wellington into the open; but Wellington had no wish to waste lives needlessly, observing: 'as this is the last army England has got, we must take care of it.'

Simmons found the houses in Alenquer 'entirely sacked, the windows and doors torn down and burnt, as well as most of the furniture; china, pier-glasses, and chandeliers all dashed to pieces with the objectless fury of savages. They had left many miserable fellows behind, who were too ill to march: these were, of course, put to death by the Portuguese whenever we happened to miss finding them out. We found several peasants whom the French had murdered and left upon the road ... It was a dreadful sight to see so many fine towns and villages sacked, and without a creature in them.' Schaumann described having passed

> spots where French cavalry piquets and bivouacs had stood, paths made by sentries, small entrenchments, huts, burnt-out watch fires, bones, rags, and broken utensils. Close to Alemquer we found a number of French soldiers lying in a trench. They were a party of sick men whose cart had broken down and they had been left behind by their comrades. The peasants had cut their throats. At Alemquer ... we entered a house in order to prepare breakfast with the provisions we had brought with us. Our host could not tell us enough about the desolation and misery of the French? At first they had lived in luxury, and wasted everything and trampled it under foot; but ultimately they had been reduced to eating their pack donkeys, then their sick or fallen cavalry horses, and finally dogs, cats and rats. Instead of vegetables, moreover, they had to eat cooked maize, fig and cactus leaves, and thistles ...

Masséna halted some 28 miles further north, taking up a strong position between hilltop Santarém and Rio Maior, but extending as far as Tomar. Here, he might survive longer, for not every peasant had followed Wellington's 'scorched earth' policy to the letter, nor was every district entirely stripped of produce and livestock; but the French suffered severely both from sickness and semi-starvation, apart from the reprisals by vengeful partisans whenever they extended their search for supplies further afield than any district occupied in force. In their desperate search for corn and any other food, fodder, and drink hidden from them, they would thrust their bayonets or ramrods into the earthen floors of peasant homes and, if this had no positive result, pour water onto the ground, which – first sinking into earth recently disturbed – would give away the whereabouts of hoards of provisions of all sorts. But wherever they foraged, they were likely to be taken prisoner by Allied cavalry units or picked off by bands of the *Ordenança*, who were also effectively manning the line of the Zêzere, further north-east, while the intricate, hilly, country near the Mondego was occupied by Trant's and Colonel John Wilson's troops.

Masséna had the intention of constructing a bridge over the Tagus, by which he could overrun the fertile Alentejo. To forestall this, on 17 November Wellington had ordered Hill, together with cavalry and artillery, to hold the river's left bank opposite Abrantes in addition to Fane's units already there, the crossing supervised by the naval contigent, whose armed flatboats were firing on Santarém by 12 November; and by chance some few Congreve rockets even exploded over the town.

One mid December day, French officers had approached the British. Tomkinson described the incident: they, 'having taken off their swords, … came down to speak to us, saying their object was only foraging, and that we need not put ourselves to any inconvenience, as they should soon withdraw. They complained much of the way they were going on, and hoped to put an end to the business one way or other … They invited us to a play at Santarem they had got up, and we them to horse-races, football, and dog-hunts. The communication was put a stop to by a general order.'

Costello likewise refers to such fraternisation, and that they frequently met the French 'bathing in the Rio Maior, and would often have swimming and jumping matches. In these games we mostly beat them,' and that, touched with pity at their distressed and half-starved condition, our men shared with them the ration biscuits. 'Tobacco was in great request. We used to carry some of ours to them, while they in return would bring us a little brandy.'

It was on 18 November that John Edgecombe Daniel, an officer in the Commissariat Department, among a fleet of reinforcement, sailed into the Tagus estuary, having weighed anchor at Falmouth on the 3rd. 'A Lisbon pilot now came on board, bringing us *all* the news – *how* that the whole population of the kingdom of Portugal had fled into Lisbon, where they had created the greatest scarcity and distress; – *how* every man capable of bearing arms was forthwith enrolled in the '*ordinanza*' or militia, and sent up to the *great English General*, who some folks thought would yet beat the *Francezes*, though for his own part (shrugging his shoulders), he dare say '*nada*' (nothing), – only that being an old man he had escaped the levy, and being very poor, he hoped that whatever party proved conqueror, he would not be molested in his useful occupation of pilot.'

The resilience of the French impressed Wellington. As he wrote to Lord Liverpool on 21 December:

> It is certainly astonishing that the enemy have been able to remain in this country so long; and it is an extraordinary instance of what a French army can do. It is positively a fact that they brought no provisions with them, and they have not received even a letter since they entered Portugal. With all our money, and having in our favour the good inclination of the country, I assure you that I could not maintain one division in the district in which they have maintained not less than 60,000 men and 20,000 animals for more than two months. This time last year I was obliged to move the British cavalry only from the district they now occupy with their whole army, because it could not be subsisted. But they take everything, and leave the unfortunate inhabitants to starve.[39]

Writing to Lord Aberdeen on 22 December, Alexander Gordon expressed his disgust at the British Press for criticising Wellington for not having 'utterly destroyed Masséna and his army'; and yet he had proved his capacity to defend Portugal and had reduced the enemy to the possession of merely 'the *ground they stand upon*.' If only the Government acted with vigor and sent out another 10,000 men, he would answer for the ultimate success of British arms; and he went on to thank God that Wellington was 'not a man to be moved by popular clamour, or to be raised or depressed by the false assertions and unfair and delusive ideas held out by the people of your infamous newspaper writers. Lord Wellington will act as he thinks fit and for *their Good* not to *please them*. Here there is no one but is perfectly confident of the result of his plans, his judgement.'

In a dispatch to Lord Liverpool, dated the 29th, Wellington summed up his perception of the state of affairs at the end of the year: 'Having such an enemy to contend with, and knowing (as I do) that there is no army in the Peninsula capable of contending with the enemy, excepting that under my command; that there are no means of replacing any large losses I might sustain; and that any success acquired by a large sacrifice of men would be followed by disastrous consequences to the cause of the allies, I have determined to persevere in the system which has hitherto saved all, and which will, I hope, end in the defeat of the enemy.'

This was, as he had stated earlier in the month: 'to confine them as much as possible, but to engage in no serious affair on ground on which the result can be at all doubtful.'

Barrosa

While Wellington watched and waited for Masséna's next move, a separate campaign was taking place in Andalusia, where Cadiz was still blockaded by Victor. Soult having marched north in late January 1811 with 20,000 men to besiege Badajoz, it was thought to be a propitious moment to make a landing in Victor's rear, who, in the event, had to detach 7,300 men from his investing force to counter this menace.

The expedition consisted of 5,200 men commanded by Sir Thomas Graham,[40] ferried out of Cadiz and reinforced by troops from Gibraltar. After assembling at Tarifa, they were met by some 9,600 Spaniards under General La Peña, and marched up the coast past Vejer. Unfortunately, Graham conceded overall command to La Peña, as disposing of the higher proportion of the combined force.

After a deal of indecisive and needless counter-marching, on approaching the San Petri river crossing on 5 March and finding it barred by a small French force under General Villatte, La Peña lost whatever nerve he had and proposed that the projected attack on Victor be called off. The army would be less exposed to the enemy if the security of the Isla de León could be regained, and this could be reached with ease by a bridge of boats, for its near end was still in the hands of Spanish units under Zayas. But first, Villatte's troops would have to be dispersed. Additional troops having joined La Peña, Zayas made a well-timed sortie from his position. Attacked in front and rear by superior numbers, Villatte then retired across a creek to the north-east. La Peña now instructed Graham to descend from the Cerro de Puerco, a small but defensible hog's-back height he had occupied near the Torre de Barrosa, a coastal watch-tower. Graham disputed the order as unreasonable, for the hill provided a secure base from which to attack Victor. La Peña acquiesced to the extent of ordering five infantry battalions and six squadrons of cavalry (under Colonel Stamford

Whittingham) there as a rear-guard. Graham, against his better judgement, after leaving one battalion under Colonel John Browne (28th) on the Cerro, where it settled down to rest after the gruelling marching of previous days, lead down the bulk of his men into the stone-pine woods which extended between the hill and La Peña's main force still stationed nearer the San Petri bridge.

Victor, advancing along the road from Chiclana, was aware of some of these unaccountable movements, but not all. Assuming that the Cerro was now unoccupied, he sent General Laval with 4,000 men to mount its south-eastern slope. General Ruffin, with 2,800, would ascend further west, each column accompanied by six guns, while two squadrons of Dragoons swung round to cut the coast road near the Torre de Barrosa. Graham's force had not long traversed the woods when a report reached him from a K.G.L. patrol that they were skirmishing with the vanguard of a strong enemy thrust. Graham's units faced about, and he rode back to find Browne already hard pressed. Robert Blakeney (28th), heard Captain Calvert, on seeing red uniforms ahead through the trees, cry out:

> 'That must be Colonel Browne's flank battalion,' and darting forward soon discovered his surmise to be fact. General Graham came forward instantly to meet us, saying 'Browne, did I not give you orders to defend Barrosa Hill?' 'Yes, sir,' said Browne; 'but you would not have me fight the whole French army with four hundred and seventy men?' 'Had you not,' replied the general, 'five Spanish battalions, together with artillery and cavalry?' 'Oh!' said Browne; 'they all ran away long before the enemy came within canon-shot.' The general cooly replied, 'It is a bad business, Browne;[41] you must instantly turn round and attack.' 'Very well,' said the colonel; 'am I to attack in extended order as flankers, or as a close battalion?' 'In open order,' was the reply, and the general returned to the troops in the wood.

Graham had some difficulty in extracting the brigades of Dilke and Wheatley from the wood, which together with Major Duncan's ten guns, six companies of riflemen ahead of them, then pressed uphill to Browne's support. The ensuing struggle was very fierce, the contenders suffering heavy losses. Leading the attack in the centre, Major Hugh Gough, commanding the 87th Regiment of Wheatley's Brigade, remembers the French waiting until they came within 25 paces of them, before they broke,

> and as they were in column when they did, they could not get away. It was therefore a scene of dreadful carnage ... They made, while we were amongst them (about a quarter of an hour), little or no opposition. We could have taken or destroyed the whole regiment, but at this moment the 47th French regiment came down on our right, and General Graham, who was, during the whole of the action, in the midst of it, pointed them out and begged I would call off my men ... With the greatest difficulty, by almost cutting them down, I got the right wing collected, with which we charged the 47th, but after firing until we came to within about 50 paces of them, they (for us, fortunately) broke and fled, for had they done their duty, fatigued as my men were, at that moment, they must have cut us to pieces.

The confused action ended with a squadron of K.G.L. hussars under Frederick Ponsonby charging the hesitating enemy rearguard, whose dispersion would have been complete had Whittingham's Spanish cavalry been with him, but together with their infantry, they were nowhere to be seen. Graham then retired to the Isla.

The pusillanimity of La Peña, who had kept his troops immobile within earshot of the battle and later had the audacity to claim the victory, was more than Graham could stomach.[42] When writing on 25 March to congratulate him on 'the promptitude and determination' of his attack, Wellington could only remark: 'The conduct of the Spaniards throughout this expedition is precisely the same as I have ever observed it to be. They march the troops night and day, without provisions or rest ... They reach the enemy in such a state as to be unable to make any exertion or execute any plan, even if any plan had been formed; and then, when the moment of action arrives, they are totally incapable of movement and they stand by to see their allies destroyed, and afterwards abuse them because they do not continue, unsupported, exertions to which human nature is not equal.'

1 Cox, a brigadier in the Portuguese service, was described by D'Urban as 'a most active, zealous, excellent officer but the Correspondence, and other sedentary duties ... have almost imperiously detained him from the more active and more important ones of being constantly amongst his Garrison and not only watching over their discipline, but training and fashioning their minds to the confidence necessary for what may perhaps be required of them.'

2 As confirmed by Tomkinson: both were first shot at; Williams at Marmeleiro, where he had remained tied to a tree all day, and Thompson at Rochoso, where he was found 'lying amongst the rocks dreadfully bruised with stones.'

3 Masséna then attempted to persuade his captives to join him in preference to being marched prisoner to France, an offer they accepted, ostensibly, only to make their escape to the Allied lines the moment an opportunity occurred.

4 Spanning the Alva not far south of its convergence with the Mondego.

5 The southern sector, comprising three fifths of the length of the ridge, was defended by Hill's 2nd Division and James Leith's 5th Division, about one third of the Allied force, but which saw little action. Further north stood Picton's 3rd Division, reinforced by Portuguese units, the line extended by three brigades of Spencer's 1st Division. The crucial sector near the main road crossing the ridge was entrusted to Pack's brigade, supported by Coleman's, together with Craufurd's Light Division. Lowry Cole's 4th Divison, together with von Löwe's K.G.L. brigade and Archibald Campbell's Portuguese brigade, were deployed further north.

6 Although Colonel Frazer of the Royal Engineers, later visiting the battlefield (on 22 April 1813), stated that he had 'just made his bed on the bedstead on which Lord Wellington slept the night before the action', some narratives suggest that he slept in the open among his troops wrapped in his cloak, which accords more with his character. Dr McGrigor, after inspecting the hospitals at Coimbra on his way to the front in January 1812, had likewise made the detour. He was escorted by one of the friars, who 'pointed out the main scenes of action, still evident by the remains of clothing – French and English – plumes, shoes, heaps of bones. The pious monk, pulling me by the sleeve to one spot, said this was the place where he found a wounded Frenchman whom he had put out of pain by knocking his brains out with a stone.'

Relics of the former convent are engulfed by a pseudo-Manueline royal palace, now a hotel, but the walled and well-wooded estate can have little changed, although the ridge of the Serra de Buçaco was then far less thickly wooded than it is today. Nearby is a small museum devoted to the battle.

7 As at Vimeiro, the sun's reflection on French bayonets gave away the direction of their advance, a point noticed by Wellington, whose troops, when in similar circumstances, were ordered to march with reversed arms.

8 So similar, that one wonders whether it had been read by Schaumann before he penned his reminiscences …

9 In fact 62,500 effectives.

10 As remarked on by Sherer, among others, who had 'distinctly overheard him' giving orders to Hill, and was 'particularly struck with the style of this order, so decided, so manly, and breathing no doubt as to the repulse of any attack ; it confirmed confidence … He has nothing of the truncheon about him; nothing full-mouthed, important, or fussy: his orders, on the field, are all short, quick, clear, and to the purpose.'

11 French casualties had already risen to 4,600, including 300 officers (among them one general killed and four wounded), a higher percentage of officers to men than was to occur in any other action during the war. Those of the Allies – 33,000 of whom had not even come up into the fighting line – were a mere 1,250, half of whom were Portuguese, of which total only 200 were killed.

12 General Simon, who had been wounded and taken prisoner, was not alone in having a companion. Masséna's current mistress, a certain Mme Henriette Leberton, attended him in the guise of a cavalry officer.

13 It would have been difficult for Trant's militia, who were in the vicinity, to have held them up for long; but apparently, according to Tomkinson, the

Heavy Brigade, guarding the left flank of the Allies position, had been pushed back along the Boialvo road 'in dreadful confusion', and mistaking 'some bushes for the enemy,' they had 'fired at them for half an hour.'

14 Wellington's Headquarters that night were at Condeixa, 6 miles south of the river.

15 British officers had already requisitioned any telescopes and mathematical instruments remaining in the University.

16 Within a few months their place would be taken by British sick and wounded, whom according to Surgeon Henry, lying in the long corridors, which contained double rows of beds, 'classified into wards according to the nature of the case ... and a sufficient number of orderlies to each', were given as much care as possible. Conditions seem to have been considerably better there than at Celorico, from which Wellington himself ordered that several hundred should be transferred to Coimbra that December. It may be mentioned here that, according to Samuel Broughton, the lack of knowledge of the Portuguese medical authorities 'almost exceeds belief,' and their surprise 'at the surgical apparatus of an English medical officer, and at the commonest operations, proved the lamentable state of the whole profession ... The people in general, as well as the medical practitioners, are in perpetual terror of infection, for they are wholly ignorant of its nature and the most common ways of preventing it.' They remained prejudiced 'against the use of mercury, in cases where we know of no other remedy to check the progress of disease,' and likewise against vaccination, although recently inoculation was 'performed gratuitously.'

17 The newly-formed depot at Espinhal was hurriedly broken up and its contents distributed to passing units, while several others in the area, some of them Portuguese, were also wasted; in one of them, 20,000 rations of corn were destroyed, together with 6 pipes of wine and 35 puncheons of rum.

18 In which, according to Burgoyne, the 'British regiments of this [3rd] division were quartered ... as well as the generals and many other officers,' followed by several other divisions, 'during which time a dinner was prepared at the convent for the whole of their officers,' before the community embarked at São Martinho do Porto 'with their plate and most valuable effects' in a ship held at their disposition.

19 Due to recent incidents when traversing deserted towns, Picton's men were ordered into fields rather than being quartered in the vacated houses of Alcobaça, which they would inevitably plunder. According to John Burgoyne, Picton always took 'the greatest pains ... to protect the inhabitants ... from any excesses of the soldiers; and when unavoidable irregularities have been committed, he has frequently given considerable sums out of his own pocket, to remedy he mischief done.'

20 Tomkinson noted that Trooper Foxall (16th Light Dragoons) had ingeniously packed a quantity of tea 'in a pair of nakeen small clothes, tying up the legs, and carrying them filled round his neck to bring it to the bivouac.'

21 Already, Wellington had written to Lord Liverpool requesting compensation for the unfortunate Portuguese, many of whom had lost all they ever had. The amount voted was later increased, and supplemented by several subscriptions for widows and orphans. But regrettably, as Burgoyne emphasised some months later, the 'large sums to their relief from England either arrive very late, or have fallen into bad hands, which is sure to be the case unless Englishmen, and not Portuguese, take a very active part in the distribution.'

22 Tomkinson described the deluge as 'the heaviest I ever experienced.'

23 Cocks was insensed by the fact that during several skirmishes the French had a way 'which must not be allowed. They cry for pardon but still keep galloping to the rear, or perhaps throw themselves on the ground, and it is impossible to get the prisoners off when you are certain of being attacked yourself by a superior force. We are obliged to cut down or shoot several who did this ...'

24 Villa Franca de Xira, just north of Alhandra.

25 Colonel Charles Colville, recently arrived in Lisbon, refers to 'the curious costume into which the officers ... had thrown themselves. Their precautions for keeping out the wet are more sensible and equally various in hat covers, shoe stirrups, pantaloons, clogs, great-coats and cloaks of oiled silk, cloth – plain and patterned – so that the only invention for the purpose which I have not yet seen adopted ... is the thatched coat and cap worn by the bullock drivers, an excellent covering, at least for people on foot, but which has the appearance of so many moving corn ricks.'

26 Tomkinson had commented also that although the French had retired through the town after the battle of Vimeiro, the building was uninjured, for which the monks said they were indebted to Loison, which is surprising. It was at Mafra, on 7 November, that Wellington 'gave a splendid entertainment' when investing Beresford with the Order of the Bath.

27 Later General Sir John Jones, and author of the *Memoranda Relative to the Lines thrown up to cover Lisbon in 1810*, included also in the 3rd (1846) edition of his comprehensive *Journal of the Sieges ... in Spain during the years 1811 to 1814.*

28 Apparently, Masséna was entirely ignorant of their construction. One can imagine his astonishment and frustration when brought up short by the unexpected sight of this formidable barrier. Expecting a walk-over, he had not bothered to bring any siege artillery with him.

29 A small area west of the capital, surrounding a beach east of the fort of São Julião, near Oeiras, on the north bank of the estuary west of the sand bar, had been fortified also, should it be necessary to embark the army; and likewise the south bank, should Soult's army approach from the east, although the frontier there was still held by the Spaniards at Badajoz and the Portuguese at Elvas.

30 Kincaid was much amused at seeing some naval officers riding up to the front 'on mules; with huge ships' spy-glasses, like six-pounders, strapped across the backs of their saddles. The first question invariable was, "Who is that fellow there?" pointing to the enemy's sentry, close to us, and, on being told that he was a Frenchman, "Then why the devil don't you shoot him!"' As Kincaid went on to remark: 'Repeated acts of civility passed between the French and us during this tacit suspension of hostilities. The greyhounds of an officer following a hare, on one occasion, ran into their lines, and they very politely returned them.'

31 Capt. Browne refers to the sailors being stationed at Alhandra, where 'Nothing could exceed the delight of our Jack Tars, on finding themselves thus called on for land service, and the fun they used to have in this forsaken village, as they sat in the streets, smoking their pipes, in venerable, velvet covered chairs, studded all over with brass nails ...'

32 Colville refers to them, posted behind the Lines, as being 'a perfect nuisance, and tho' for policy's sake Lord Wellington bedaubs them with praise in his Despatches, he cannot but wish he was without them.' When asked to clean

out their quarters, to prevent disease, their response was that 'the Spanish patriots were not made to become scavengers to the filthy Portuguese.'

33 Wellington had also received 6,500 reinforcements from England, supplemented by a number of Portuguese regulars who had not seen action at Busaco: he had now some 34,000 British and 24,500 Portuguese effectives to draw on.

34 This system had already proved useful near the front prior to Masséna's invasion, although bad weather tended to obscure visibility, and Wellington had received help from Admiral Berkeley's naval semaphore experts to establish a line of five stations at prominent points behind the Lines. A more elaborate system was established later, when investing Bayonne.

35 If so, this is surprising, as providing tempting prey to Trant's troops, among others.

36 General Gardanne, instructed en route by Foy to reinforce Masséna, marched from Ciudad Rodrigo on 20 November with 5,000 men, but encumbered by a convoy of supplies, his attempt to get through was brought to a halt by the flooded river Codes, north-east of Abrantes. Masséna, entirely isolated and without any reliable communication from France, had no idea that he was so close; while Gardanne, led to believe that not only was Masséna retiring via the Mondego valley but that Hill was near by and likely to fall on him with 10,000 men, had precipitately countermarched when within 18 miles – as the crow flies – from French outposts near Punhete.

37 General D'Erlon, descending the Mondego valley, had already reinforced Masséna in late December with some 8,000 men: more mouths to feed!

38 Colville refers to a 'good many of the British brigades have established kitchens and other modes for feeding such of the Portuguese poor as for want of other refuge have preferred remaining among the hedges or other cover in our cantonments. The fund of my own Brigade proceeds from the heads, feet and insides of our fresh beef, with the exception of tongues and heart. Purchases of Indian wheat, corn and rice by subscription among the officers already gives ample relief to 120 people of all ages, and would do more had we better convenience for cooking.'

39 The situation of the French near the Spanish frontier was not much better. Intercepted letters written from Ciudad Rodrigo by the Duchess d'Abrantes to her husband, dated mid December, complaining of being deprived of news, mention that she was unable to look out of her window 'without seeing cartfuls of dead bodies which they throw outside the town without taking the trouble to bury them'. More recently, deaths – not counting those among the inhabitants – had been nine a day from the small hospital there, while at Salamanca the numbers were in the region of forty a day.

40 Promoted Lieut-General in the previous year.

41 Surtees described John Frederick Browne as 'then a most wild and eccentric character,' who when at Tarifa (where the women went *tapada* or partly veiled into the street), not liking this habit of hiding their beauty, would stop and make them 'open the mantilla, that he might have a fair peep … to the great scandal of the good ladies of this still Moorish town, and which, had it been on any other occasion, might have been attended with unpleasant consequences to himself.' Apparently, Browne later mended his ways.

42 Graham losses were 1,238, of which 200 were killed; those of Victor were 2,060: 262 killed, 1,694 wounded, including Villatte, and Ruffin (mortally); 134 unwounded prisoners were taken, together with five guns and an eagle.

7

March to May 1811: Masséna pursued from Santarém to Sabugal, and at bay at Fuentes de Oñoro

There had been little change in Wellington's front. Masséna's endurance astonished him: entirely isolated, without receiving reinforcements or supplies of any sort – not a single dispatch had got through to him – he had been able to subsist for five weeks before retiring to a more defensible position at Santarém, which also gave him a wider area in which to forage.

There had been 'no news of consequence' of any military activity in Estremadura; nor elsewhere. Alexander Gordon, had remarked on 5 January that it was 'really shameful that notwithstanding the immense force of the enemy we have drawn upon us, that the Spaniards are doing nothing towards forming an army and are contented with a war of partisans which is all very well, but will not drive the French out of their country.'

Sherer had spent a February morning intently watching the French through his telescope from the far bank of the Tagus. He could pick out 'a troop of their dragoons exercising on the plain below the town; there a general officer riding out with his staff; here some field officer visiting his guards and picquets, and there several of their men washing and cleaning their arms and appointments on the very brink of the stream. You constantly heard the sound of their voices; and, on a still day, might readily distinguish what they said. We often, indeed, conversed courteously with their officers, until the prating imprudence of some individual caused such intercourse to be forbidden ...'

Even with a naked eye, he could discern 'their picquets posted, and their fatigue parties felling trees to form abbatis, digging entrenchments, or constructing breast-works; while ... forage parties, detachments, or orderlies, were constantly going out and returning.' Leach noticed that the 'extensive wood of olive which clothed the sides and summit of the hill [of Santarém] the year before ... on our route to

Talavera … [had been] cut down in less than forty-eight hours by the French, who constructed with them a double row of most formidable abattis across the whole of the ridge.' One night,[1] on reconnoitring the French position, Leach, with his companions, made themselves as comfortable as possible in a pinewood, but to escape from the heavy rain, they 'crept into an old water-course … [where] rolled up in our cloaks, and doubled up by wet and cold, we did contrive, nevertheless, to fall asleep. But it is impossible to forget being suddenly awoke, a short time afterwards, and feeling myself all at once buoyed up and floating down the little ravine, in the same plight as if I had been dragged under a ship from stem to stern. There was a general outcry from all the party … and a scramble to get on *terra firma* took place. Taking a few mouthfuls of rum and a cigar, the remainder of the night was spent at the foot of a fir-tree, smoking, shivering, and cursing our stupidity for having taken up so injudicious a position.'

Otherwise, Leach appeared to pass the time agreeably enough. The sportsmen of the division

> constantly had recourse to gun, pointer, and greyhound; and in the marshy plain between the Rio Maior and the Tagus we contrived to amuse ourselves very well, and often with success; hares, quails, snipes, and golden plovers, being abundant. In these pastimes the French cavalry pickets, posted on the marsh, never interfered with us, nor interrupted our sport … On the contrary, their conduct was courteous, and, if I may use the expression, gentlemanly to a degree ... One morning, in a thick fog, a small patrole of ours suddenly found themselves close to a superior force … and instantly retired; but, in the hurry, one of our dragoons dropped his cloak. Our patrole had ridden but a short distance to the rear, when it was called to by the French, one of whom riding up … dropped the captured cloak on the ground and rode away, making signals to the English dragoon who had lost it, to pick it up. This was carrying on the war as it should be; and it is but justice to add, that we rarely found them deficient on this point.

On another occasion they indulged in racing, with several 'half-starved devils, whose diet had for some months consisted principally of chopped straw and winter-grass, started, with gentlemen riders, for a sweepstakes. Before they had gone one hundred yards, the horse which was ridden by my friend T. of the 43rd regiment, came down heels over head, from sheer debility; and those in his wake, according to the nautical phrase, ran foul of him and his racer, who lay floundering on the earth. A greater burlesque on horse-racing never was witnessed: were I certain of seeing so amusing an exhibition at Newmarket, Epsom, or Doncaster, I verily believe I should seldom fail to attend their meetings.'

Not to be outdone by the French theatrical performances, 'the soldiers of a certain company in our battalion did make the attempt, having converted an old house, in which olive oil had formerly been made, into a theatre: the blankets and great-coats ... made capital side-scenes; and had not to much wine and grog found their way behind them, no doubt the piece would have gone off with great éclat. But, as the truth must be told, they all forgot their parts; and it was a toss-up whether our ... horse-racing or play-acting was the most perfectly ludicrous.'

* * *

On 19 February, in the absence of any sign of promised support, Masséna assembled a council of war at Golegã (not far north of Santarém), to decide what to do: their situation was becoming desperate. After hearing out conflicting proposals from Ney, Junot, and Reynier, he decided that withdrawal towards the lower Mondego valley, still comparatively undevastated and where they might subsist, would be the most expedient solution, and one to enforce promptly. There, with a shorter line of communication with Ciudad Rodrigo, provisions and reinforcements could reach them. Meanwhile, any equipment they would be unable to drag away with their remaining serviceable horses, was destroyed.[2]

From his post – 'a loop-holed chapel, a circular pig-stye, dignified with the name of a redoubt, and a few miserable hovels, formed the defences and cantonments of our little garrison, which consisted of two companies of infantry and twelve dragoons' – Sherer recalled: 'On the night of the 4th of March, as I was going my rounds, my ear caught some unusual noise on the French bank; and approaching to the edge of the water, and lying down, I distinctly heard the trampling of horses, the sound of wheels, and the cracking of whips. For three hours I lay perfectly still, listening to those truly grateful sounds. It was now evident that a second campaign was about to open; and that we should leave the narrow limits we had occupied since October, for some new and more interesting scenes. The next day our detachment quitted the island; and it was known that the enemy had broke up from Santarem, and was in full retreat.'

Wellington had been waiting impatiently for reinforcements to reach him. The first transports, carrying 6,000 men, sailed into the Tagus estuary on 1 March, but it was not until the 6th that all had disembarked. Until then, he would not have an adequate force at hand to put into action a plan he had formulated to bottle up the enemy or at least make their eventual retreat more hazardous. Nor was his Commissariat quite ready, for Wellington was well aware that the moment his divisions advanced, it would be into a virtual desert: they would have to carry all their food and supplies with them. Nevertheless, as Reynier's and Junot's units still appeared to be in their defensive positions, he hoped to intercept them before they moved off, as was very likely.

Masséna's Retreat

In the event, Masséna troops precipitatedly decamped during the night of 5-6 March, discreetly evacuating their positions while leaving their watchfires burning, and blowing up two bridges behind them. By the following day, three Corps of his emaciated and shrunken army were converging on Leiria, the vanguard a full march ahead of their pursuers: the opportunity of striking a swingeing blow had been missed. Few could have anticipated the suddenness of Masséna's withdrawal; for had Wellington attacked Masséna's rearguard early on the 5th with troops already in the vicinity, it would have been destroyed.

Reynier's units followed a separate road leading due north from Tomar past Ansião towards Espinhal: Nightingale's brigade of the 1st Division and a squadron of dragoons was detached to follow them. Loison, on whom Beresford, based on Abrantes, had been keeping a close watch, evacuated Punhete, burning both boats and bridges to thwart any interruption of his retreat.

At 3.0 A.M. on 8 March Beresford crossed the Tagus to confer with Wellington at Torres Novas, when orders were given to throw a bridge of boats across near Tancos to enable additional units to march to the relief of Badajoz. On that same day it was learned that Menacho, the gallant governor of that beleagured fortress, had destroyed several enemy works in a successful sortie on the 3rd, in which he had been killed.[3] The unexpected news that Imaz, replacing Menacho, had capitulated to Soult on the 10th,[4] did not reach Wellington until late on the 13th. Beresford's instruction to proceed had been countermanded already, due to false report that Masséna might turn and fight beyond Tomar, causing a brief delay; but now that haste was no longer essential,

Beresford progressed at a normal pace towards Badajoz via Ponte de Sor (18th), Portalegre, and Arronches, approaching Campo Mayor on the 25th with the 2nd and 4th Divisions and a Portuguese contingent, some 18,000 men. For the ensuing action, see p.201.

Few expected to encounter the harrowing scale of gratuitous destruction in the wake of the French retreat. Simmons described the streets of Santarém as 'strewn with household furniture half-burnt and destroyed, and many ... quite impassable with filth and rubbish, with an occasional man, horse, or donkey rotting and corrupting and filling the air with pestilential vapours.'[5] On reaching Pernes, he found the houses 'nearly all unroofed, and the people in a starving condition. Two young ladies had been brutally violated in a house that I entered, and were unable to rise from a mattress of straw.[6] On the line of march, comparing notes with other officers, I found that they all had some mournful story to tell of the savage French Vandals which had come under their immediate observation.' Even General Picton – 'not a man easily to be moved by sentiment,' in Oman's just opinion – had remarked that 'nothing can exceed the devastation and cruelties committed by the enemy during his retreat: he has set fire to all the villages and murdered all the peasantry for leagues on each flank of his march.' At Porto de Mós, not far south of Batalha, Donaldson (94th), was aghast by what he saw on entering a gutted convent,[7] for

> the finest furniture had been broken up for firewood; the very floors torn up, beds cut in pieces, with their contents thrown about, intermixed with kitchen utensils, broken mirrors, china, &c. &c. all in one heterogeneous mass of ruin, and not an inhabitant to be seen ...
>
> The mules with the stores had arrived, and the store-keeper looking for a place to put them in, when we joined him. At last he pitched on a chapel for the purpose. There was a large fire in the middle of the floor, on which was heaped broken pieces of the altar, wooden images, frames of picture; even the ornamental wood-work of the organ was broken up for the purpose.
>
> In searching for the cleanest place to set down the bags of biscuit, we found a door leading to some place apart from the chapel. As it was quite dark, I caught up a burning piece of wood to inspect the place – but what was my horror, when I entered and found the half-consumed skeletons of human beings on every side; some lying, others kneeling, and more of them standing upright against the walls. The floor was covered with ashes, in many places still red ... Such an appalling sight was never [before] witnessed.

Wellington was now closer on the heels of the retreating horde, with Ney, commanding the rearguard, being harassed repeatedly by the *Ordenança*, although his Commissariat found it hard keeping up with him, such was the increasing speed of the chase.[8] Tomkinson halted for a moment at Alcobaça, where the French had left the abbey a wreck: they 'had burnt what they could, and destroyed the remainder with an immense deal of trouble. The embalmed kings and queens were taken from out of their tombs, and I saw them lying in as great preservation as the day they were interred.[9] The fine tessellated pavement … was picked up, the facings to the stone pillars were destroyed nearly to the top, scaffolding having been erected for that purpose …[10] They either burn or destroy every town and village they pass through, and we daily see poor wretches of inhabitants in the most miserable state. They kill many, whose bodies we see in each day's march.' But Alcobaça was not alone in being sacked. Colonel Frazer (R.H.A.) was outraged by the state in which he found the noble Convento de Cristo at Tomar, it's canvases 'torn to pieces, and many carried away; the organ broken, and altars thrown down, fireplaces made in the cloisters, and everything broken and defaced ... in wanton barbarity.'

Meanwhile, the 6th Division was ordered forward to interrupt any attempt by Montbrun's cavalry, then west of Coimbra, to cross the Mondego, then in spate. Trant's troops defended the north bank opposite the bridge, two arches of which had been broken. To Capt. Browne, entering Coimbra on 16 March, it showed every appearance of being completely ransacked: 'Several of its beautiful Churches had been converted into Stables for Cavalry, and were filled with straw and dirt. The doors of the Vestries had been forced open ... Altars and Images were defaced, and the marks of pistol bullets shewed that they had been shot at, as a mark. Rich vestments, covered with gold or silver embroidery, were used as horse-clothes ... The splendid robes which the French had left ... we gathered up respectfully, and cut them into waistcoats and dressing gowns. On our days of halt and washing, it was not an unusual sight, to see Officers, whilst their shirts were drying, pacing to and fro, in front of a bivouac formed by branches of trees, in the bedizened garments of Catholic Priests and Bishops.'[11]

Several actions took place between Leiria and the Mondego, notably by cavalry at Pombal, and at the bridge over the Ancos at Redinha, across which Ney's rearguard were forced before his flank was turned some two miles beyond. Manoeuvred out of Condeixa, left in flames, they retreated east through intricate hilly country towards Miranda do Corvo, between Espinhal and the Ponte de Murcella. On the 13th, rather than risking a battle while astride the Mondego, Masséna extricated his army by veering north-east up the parallel valley of the Alva. Ney's Corps pressed east through Casal Novo, by-passing Masséna, who with Loison's Division had halted at Fonte Cuberta, two miles to the south. [12]

In thick fog at dawn on the 14th, although ordered to stick to Ney's heels only, Sir William Erskine,[13] commanding the vanguard, rashly chose to attack the French rearguard at Casal Novo. Had not Picton's Division been in their vicinity when the mist lifted, they would have found themselves in a tight spot. The Light Divison alone suffered 100 unnecessary casualties due to his mismanagement, by which Erskine lost any residual confidence Wellington may have had in him. Both William Napier and his brother George were wounded in this reckless action, the latter vividly describing Erskine's reaction when Colonel Ross warned him that the place was still occupied: 'He kept blustering and swearing it was all nonsense – that the captains of the pickets knew nothing about the matter, and that there was not a man in the village. Just as he spoke the dense fog began to clear, and bang came a shot from a twelve-pounder, which struck the head of our column and made a lane through it, killing and wounding many. Then came a regular cannonade, but the wise Sir William was sure it was a single gun and a picket supporting it, and desired Colonel Ross to send my company against its flank …'

It was between Casal Novo and Miranda do Corvo, further west, that more prisoners than usual were captured, mostly skirmishers and marauders: over one hundred on the 14th alone. Masséna decided that it was only by destroying all regimental and personal baggage that could not be carried on his surviving pack mules, together with all his wheeled transport except the minimum of caissons and gun-carriages, that he could keep ahead of his pursuers. Ney set the example by burning his own carriage. Even the sick and wounded were removed from waggons and placed on sound beasts of burden: all others were mercilessly hamstrung, for the sound of shooting them would give away their position. Grattan records that on the 15th their rearguard was surprised 'in the act of cooking … leaving several camp kettles full of meat behind them … As we approached the town [Miranda], the road leading to it was covered with a number of horses, mules, and asses, all maimed; but the most disgusting sight was about fifty of the asses floundering in the mud, some with their throats half cut, while others were barbarously houghed or otherwise injured. What the object of this proceeding meant I could never guess; the poor brutes could have been of no use to us ... I believe they were unable to have travelled another league. The meagre appearance of these creatures, with their back-bones and hips protruding through their hides ... produced a general feeling of disgust and commiseration.'

The same village was the home of one of the Portuguese *Caçadores*, who immediately rushed to his house, the door of which was open, only to find (as Costello recounted) 'stretched across the threshold ... the mangled bodies of his father and mother, their blood still warm and reeking from bayonet stabs. His only sister lay breathing her last, and exhibiting dreadful proofs of the brutality with which she had been violated. Frenzied with grief, the unhappy man staggered. He stared wildly around him, then rushed forth ... towards some French prisoners nearby, who were being guarded by some of our dragoons ...[and] attacked them with the fury of a madman. He shot one and wounded another, and would have sacrified a third had not the guard made him prisoner. On the circumstances being made known to the General, he was liberated.'

On crossing a range of hills in the mid afternoon of the 15th the Allies descended into the valley of the Ceira, spanned at Foz do Arouce by a long narrow bridge,[14] its near end defended by Ney's rearguard on an a low ridge, while several of Masséna's divisions were ranged along heights above the far bank. The Allied army was still numerically weaker than that of Masséna's, and Wellington remained cautious, unwilling to engage in any action unless confident of the result. Assuming that it was too late in the day to press ahead, Picton and Erskine, having thrown out their picquets, had already halted, ready to encamp, when Wellington rode up. A rapid survey of the enemy positions convinced him that an immediate strike would be effective. Simmons remarked that they were all hungry and tired: he was 'frying some beef and anxiously watching the savoury morsel, when an order was given by Lord Wellington himself to Colonel Beckwith: "Fall in your battalion and attack the enemy; drive in their skirmishers, and I will turn their flank with the 3rd and 1st Divisions".' As they advanced, Simmons saw Kincaid 'shot through his cap, which grazed the top of his head. He fell as if a sledge hammer had hit him. However, he came to himself and soon rallied again.' Meanwhile, a musket ball shattered the butt of Simmons' rifle, which luckily saved his right thigh, at which he 'laughed and pushed on.'

Engaged in a frontal fight, the French was surprised by several companies of the 95th which had approached the bridgehead by a hollow road. Hearing firing almost in their rear, a whole regiment, thinking their retreat cut, panicked and made for the bridge, already jammed with retiring cavalry. Fugitives plunged into a ford further downstream, only to find it deeper than expected: many were drowned and their regimental eagle lost.[15] Ney ordered a battalion to charge the 95th, which were driven back on their supports (the 52nd) long enough to enable the remaining French to defile across in some disorder under shellfire – both from Ross's and Bull's horse artillery batteries and from their own guns, failing to distinguish friend from foe in the twilight – before blowing up the bridge.[16] Simmons and his companions, on entering their camp, where fires remained lit, collected 'shoes and shirts of better quality than their own' from jettisoned knapsacks, and 'roasted some pork which the French had left, and had plenty of biscuit, took a glass of grog and a pipe, and talked over the business of the day,' before rolling himself in his blanket and nodding off. As they had been starved of bread for several days, the biscuits were a welcome windfall.

Little action took place on the 16th, for rain fell in torrents, and the Allies had again out-marched their supplies, although prior instructions had been given to ship them direct to Figueira da Foz, at the mouth of the Mondego.[17] Scouts sent across the Ceira to investigate, reported that the bulk of the French had marched north-east before dawn towards the Ponte de Murcella, and it was not until next evening that Wellington was again in touch with them.

Schaumann described the banks near the destroyed bridge at Foz do Arouce as 'still covered with dead bodies. A number of exhausted donkeys, horses and mules, which had not been able to wade across the large smooth stones of the roaring stream, and which the barbarians had made unfit for use by either hamstringing them or twisting their necks, were still writhing in the mud, half dead. Among them lay commissariat carts, dead soldiers, women and children, who had either died of cold, or through the explosion. Over the whole of this ghastly confusion of bodies, our cavalry now proceeded to march without mercy, until the whole was churned into a mess of blood and slush. Never during the whole of the war did I again see such a horrible sight.'

Schaumann may well have been confusing or conflating his description with what he had seen at Miranda, for the memory of such sickening scenes would be blurred by their too frequent recurrence, even if, occasionally, the gloom was brightened by some glitter, for while 'the French ... [were] compelled to abandon ... all the silver, gold, valuables, silks and velvets, costly ecclesiastical vestments, monstrances and crucifixes, which they had plundered ... and as the Portuguese peasants cut the throats of all the Frenchmen they encountered, the Light Division became the heirs to all their abandoned treasure.' The most appalling scenes of the Thirty Years' War, which Schaumann in particular would have known from historical descriptions, were 'nothing compared with the horrors, the misery and the devastation' he witnessed.[18]

Wellington halted briefly at neighbouring Lousã to write urgent dispatches, among them to Beresford, confirming that, even if it reduced his own numbers, he had Cole's 4th Division and De Grey's heavy dragoons at his disposal, not for the relief of Badajoz – news of its fall to Soult had just reached Headquarters – but to keep him at bay by defending both Campo Maior and Elvas. Their confident tenor confirm that Wellington considered the crisis as over: there was no longer any doubt that Masséna would evacuate Portugal, nor any urgent need to keep the Lines garrisoned. Both the Lisbon Militia and *Ordenança* were dismissed, the former on furlough. Units north of the middle Mondego, including Trant's and Wilson's brigades, were still to keep a close watch, should Masséna attempt to cross the bridge-less river; unlikely, as he had no pontoons, nor was it fordable at that season.

On reaching the Ponte de Murcella on the Alva, Ney's Corps made no attempt to make a stand, for although Wellington had thrown up defensive earthworks there during the previous summer,[19] they faced east, and were thus valueless to the French in retreat. Anyhow, it would have been hazardous measure, as Allied units were already fording the river near Pombeiro, further east towards Arganil.

On the 19th, from Sobreira, Simmons had crossed the Alva by a wooden bridge thrown over it, and bivouacked in a pinewood, while the cavalry 'followed the enemy rear-guard, and in crossing a plain took 800 prisoners. One was a Portuguese and aide-de-camp to Loison. He had a Spanish girl in hussar uniform as his companion. This fellow, on his arrival in Lisbon, will be put to death as a traitor to his country if he has not better luck than he deserves. (20th) Light Division moved through Galizes ... (21st) Two hundred more of the enemy taken by the cavalry. (22nd) Went into houses at Moimenta da Serra [near the larger town of Gouveia].' On the 26th they reached Celorico, where Simmons read a letter from Cadiz with news that 'the rascally Spaniards have deceived General Graham, but the English alone gave the French a terrible beating,' referring to Barrosa.[20]

The bulk of the 'Army of Portugal' continued their laborious progress along the rugged north flank of the Serra da Estrela towards high-lying Guarda, to be outflanked by Picton's 3rd Division, which had crossed directly 'by a mountain track from Manteigas' to Prados. D'Erlon's units, followed by the Light Division, then veered north past Almeida, into which he threw a garrison. Already, on 9 March, Masséna had again sent Foy to Paris with a dispatch explaining his predicament to Napoleon. Partly to save face, he reiterated his determination to keep a foothold in Portugal: rather than retire on Ciudad Rodrigo, from Guarda he would move south into the Tagus valley.[21]

Stothert describes the ensuing allied advance as being 'so skilfully combined, that the heads of several columns made their appearance on the heights of Guarda at the same moment, and the celerity and precision of their Maneouvres so intimidated the enemy, that without firing a gun, he immediately commenced his retreat towards the Côa, in the direction of Sabugal, pursued by the cavalry and light troops, who skirmished with the rear-guard and made about 300 prisoners.'

Simmons recalled that on the 28th he made a forced march east to Alverca da Beira, while a party of Rifles commanded by Colonel Sydney Beckworth pressed ahead to dislodge a body of the enemy busy grinding flour and baking bread near Freixada, which they did, making prisoners, before bearing south towards Guarda.[22] Passing through one village, Simmons found the mayor's wife had been murdered by placing 'upon her bosom a huge piece of granite taken from the market cross [or *pelhourinho*], so heavy that it took me and six men to remove it.[23] The blood was running from her ears and mouth. Her dress upwards was most respectable, but her lower habiliments had been dragged off her.' It was near here that Donaldson passed a convent, at the entrance of which lay an old man '... and a genteelly dressed Portuguese was standing beside him; he spoke to us as we passed, but we had no time then to pay attention to what he said. We learned after, from the men who were following us with the baggage, that he had been hung up by some of the French soldiers, because he would not, or could not, show them where he had hid his money. His old father who was lying at the door, had been shot, and his mother's throat cut. His sisters had been first violated by the monsters, and then cruelly used: one of them had her eyes blackened, and the other her arm broken. His life was saved by the French General, who came up just as he had been suspended, and ordered him to be cut down.'

Sabugal

The Allies' pushed south-east though Pega towards Sabugal (between Belmonte and the frontier),[24] occupied by Reynier 'in great force.' Here, on 3 April, Beckwith's Brigade, after fording the steep-sided Côa, up to their armpits in water, advanced over several low ridges to suddenly find their line of skirmishers face to face with no less than seven French columns: due to the morning fog, they had found themselves a mile below the place intended. Simmons's company had approached within twenty yards of one column before they could see it, when

> The most hideous yelling assailed ...[his] ears ... the French drumming, shaking their bayonets, and calling out 'Long life to the Emperor Napoleon.' Luckily the ground was thinly patched with stout [chestnut] trees, which afforded our men good shelter in retiring. Nothing could intimidate our brave fellows, retiring and keeping up a hot and destructive fire upon the enemy's close column so as to anoy them very materially ... We retired very steadily about fifty yards into a deep valley, the French firing from a great number of cannon, throwing grape and shells, which splintered the trees and naturally killed several men. Finding the enemy did not advance farther, the Colonel formed part of the 43rd Regiment, our little line of skirmishers moving up at the same time and making a desperate attack upon a gun that was keeping up a very destructive fire. Everyone near the gun was bayoneted or shot. We were driven back, attacked again, but were again obliged to retire, when luckily the other part of our Division moved up, and the guns were ours. Colonel Beckwith on the second attack, had his horse's side pierced by a grape-shot; a bullet hit him slightly on the eyebrow; as he wiped the blood away he called out, 'My brave lads, I am no worse; follow me.' General Picton's Division advancing now on our left, the enemy moved off in the greatest confusion.

Donaldson well remembered:

> As we advanced up the hill [beyond the river], we formed line. General Picton rode up in front of us, with his stick over his shoulder, exposed to the heavy fire of the enemy, as composedly as if he had been in perfect safety. 'Steady, my lads, steady!' said he; 'don't throw away your fire until I give you the word of command.' We were now close on them; the balls were whizzing about ours ears like hailstones. The man before me received a shot in the head, and fell. 'Why don't they let us give the rascals a volley,' said some of the men. The left of our brigade, which was nearest them, now opened a heavy fire; and by the time the line was all formed, the French had taken to their heels. At this moment a severe rain storm commenced, and darkened the air so much that we lost sight of them completely; when the sky cleared up, they were discovered about a mile

> forward, scrambling their way over hedge and ditch without any regularity. The ground which they had occupied now lay before us, strewed with the dead and wounded; and the Portuguese regiment belonging to our division were busy stripping them naked. In this barbarous action, however, they were joined by very few of the British. The [Light] division to our right and left [the 5th] had by this time succeeded in turning the flanks of the French army; and they were now retreating in great confusion.[25]
>
> After waiting under arms for some time, we were ordered to encamp on the ground we then occupied ... The night ... was uncommonly dark, and at intervals the rain fell in torrents; fires had been kindled in the hollow trunks of some large chestnut trees, which, burning up as high as the branches, illuminated them to the very top. The flickering lurid glare which these fiery columns threw on the naked bodies of the slain, the indistinct objects in the back ground, and the groups of soldiers which flitted around them, presented a scene at once sublime and picturesque; it looked like the midnight orgies of some supernatural beings.

Both Slade and Erskine had displayed their incapacity as cavalry commanders, and it was due to the crass incompetence of the latter that the opportunity was lost of taking Reynier's Corps in the rear, although admittedly the dense fog had also inhibited action. Erskine's reputation was such that, on hearing of his appointment to command the Light Division in Craufurd's absence, Wellington had commented to Torrens at the Horse Guards that he was 'generally understood ... to be a madman.' But he was not the only general posted to the front to receive such a scathing compliment,[26] for as Wellington had continued: 'Really, when I reflect on the characters and attainments of some ... on whom I am to rely ... I tremble; and as Lord Chesterfield said of the Generals of his day, "I only hope that when the enemy reads the list of their names he trembles as I do." ... I pray God and the Horse Guards to deliver me from General [Stafford] Lightburne and Colonel Sanders [? John Saunders].'

The Allied vanguard pressed east next day through Alfiaites and Aldeia da Ponte, crossing into Spain at La Alberguería de Argañán, with the Light Division entering Fuentes de Oñoro on 8 April, there forming a line of outposts facing east. The only body of enemy troops remaining on Portuguese soil was the garrison at Almeida, promptly invested by the 6th Division.

By 11 April, Masséna was back at his former headquarters at Salamanca, after an absence of almost ten months: the campaign had cost him dear.[27] His men were reclothed and shod, for many had been marching in 'rivlins' (moccasins cobbled from hides of cattle they had consumed), and supplied with food, forage, and new equipment from his depots.

On that same day (11 April) Tomkinson describes two regiments of dragoons being sent back and distributed among villages just west of the Côa, nearer their supplies, for they been on half-rations of bread and, having received no corn since the 4th, has been obliged to cut rye. He also refers to receiving mail from England, which says much for the efficiency of the military postal service.[28]

Ciudad Rodrigo still remained a strong bastion facing Wellington, would have to taken in due course, once a siege train had been landed and brought to the front. Meanwhile, he would concentrate his forces along the frontier, move his Headquarters to the village of Freineda, and there await developments. He was still wary of Masséna, unlikely to give up without a fight, and who was expecting reinforcements from General Bessières.

Beresford's contingent was already in position near Badajoz, from which, on hearing of Victor's defeat at Barrosa (5 March) Soult decided to return to Seville, leaving Mortier (recalled to Paris shortly after) with some 11,000 men to garrison the fortress.

Campo Maior

On 25 March, a minor action took place on the Allies' approach to Campo Maior (about 10 miles north-west of Badajoz), the outcome of which would have been more advantageous had not Long's 13th Light Dragoons run out of control in their pursuit of Latour-Mauburg's units, taken by surprise, and had suffered heavy losses as a result. The controvery and recrimination over the responsibility for the mishandling of this encounter was carried on for years between Long and Beresford, said to be partly due to Wellingon's characteristic refusal to withdraw his initial reprimand, although later changing his opinion over their conduct in the action.[29] Sherer remembered halting

> to let the cavalry pass to the front. They were about 2000 in number; they moved past us in file at a brisk trot: their cattle were in beautiful condition, and occasionally broke into a proud prancing canter.
>
> It is at such a moment, and in such a situation, that an infantry officer cannot altogether suppress a feeling of envy ... on this particular day I felt it very strongly: we knew that there was every probability of a handsome

> affair with the enemy, who would, of course, evacuate the town, and retire upon Badajos; but the nature of the ground was so favourable for the operations of horse, that it was also very likely the engagement would be confined entirely to that arm. Our suspicions were not ill-founded; the French were no sooner apprized of our advance, than they hastily formed behind the town. Four regiments of their cavalry presented a front to our people, while their infantry (a column of about 1200) commenced their retreat, carrying with it several pieces of artillery. A most brilliant charge was made upon the enemy's dragoons by the thirteenth light, supported by the Portuguese. Our people behaved with great intrepidity; but the affair was altogether conducted, on our part, with such a total absence of skill, that the French secured the retreat of their infantry and guns, sustaining indeed a loss, but a loss very little heavier than our own. Our fine brigade of heavy cavalry [commanded by Lumley, and being halted by Beresford] was never brought up to the enemy, and our columns of infantry followed slowly in the rear. At every half mile we met some mark of this ill-conducted contest, which was carried to the very gates of Badajos; near which, several of our men, who, consulting only their courage, had pursued without any order or regularity, and, indeed, with the main body of the French cavalry marching on in their rear, were captured …

The Allied armies were divided by 120 miles of rugged country, and the Tagus. To satisfy himself that all was well, Wellington, setting off from Villar Formoso on 15 April, made a flying visit to Beresford Headquarters.[30] After four days spent planning the siege of Badajoz, and leaving elaborate instructions as to what defensive measures should be taken in differing situations – for almost inevitably Soult would return in an attempt to relieve it – he started back north on the 25th, being met at Portalegre by a dispatch from Spencer, reporting that on the 22nd a French reconnoitering force had run into his picquets 5 miles west of Ciudad Rodrigo,[31] but had retired after a rough reception; and also that trustworthy intelligence had been received from an agent in Salamanca that Masséna was re-concentrating his forces there for a dash at Almeida.

Fuentes de Oñoro

Within a remarkably short space of time, Masséna had managed to re-equip the relic of his 'Army of Portugal' and, having scraping together all possible reinforcements, returned to the fray with the intent of redeeming his lost reputation if not re-gilding his tarnished laurels. On 2 May, with 42,200 infantry, 4,500 cavalry,[32] and 38 guns, Masséna marched out of Ciudad Rodrigo, but did not follow the direct road to Almeida, veering north-west past the frontier fortress of Fort Conception,[33] but directly west towards the village of Fuentes de Oñoro, straggling above the far bank of the Dos Casas rivulet and on a minor track leading west to Freineda. Some 2 miles west of Fuentes flowed the Tourões (or Turones), a minor tributory of the Aguada; while about 5 miles beyond, dominated by Castelo Bom, lay the rugged ravine of the Côa.

Wellington had placed his 23,000 British troops, 11,000 Portuguese, 1,850 cavalry, and 48 guns on a low ridge between the Dos Casas and Tourões, facing east. The bulk of his force: Picton's 3rd Division, Ashworth's Portuguese Brigade, and the Light Division (Craufurd, who had been on leave, only arrived on the evening of the 4th), stood immediately north-west of Fuentes de Oñoro, abutted by Spencer's 1st Division, while about a mile further south was Houston's 7th, which had recently joined the main army. The 6th, extended by Erskine's 5th, were deployed further north, straddling a low ridge behind the Dos Casas,[34] and it was towards the latter divisions, early on the morning of 3 May, that two columns were observed to be proceeding.[35] Wellington initial order to the Light Division to support the 5th and 6th was countermanded later when Masséna, with five divisions, appeared to be directing his main thrust towards Wellington's more powerful concentration at Fuentes. In the village, a maze of granite walls, and almost a fortress in itself, he had placed 28 of his light companies – some 2,260 men commanded by Colonel William Williams (60th).

At about 2.00 that afternoon, ten battalions impetuously attacked the village after fording the Dos Casas, but gained a brief foothold only. A second assault by over 4,000 men, although disordered by artillery fire, by sheer weight of numbers was able to push the defenders back onto higher ground, and Williams himself was seriously wounded. Wellington now sent in the 1/71st (led by Colonel Cadogan) and 1/79th, supported by the 2/24th, which after hard fighting was able to clear the place and, in spite of fresh battalions being brought forward by Masséna, still held the west bank of the dividing stream as night fell, when they were ordered to retire behind the village. Little fighting of any consequence had taken place elsewhere.

An informal truce was established next morning, after the mist had lifted, when Donaldson saw both sides 'busily employed burying the dead and bringing in the wounded; French and English promiscuously mixed, and assisted each other in that melancholy duty as if they had been intimate friends. So far did this friendship extend, that two of our lads who spoke French, went up that night after dark to the enemy's picquet, and having conversed and drank wine with them, returned unmolested to their company.'[36]

There was intermittent shooting only, but having seen enemy cavalry manoeuvering without any particular purpose south of the village, Wellington guessed intuitively that Masséna would attempt to turn his right flank on the following day, to counter which he could make two alternative deployments: either shift his whole line south, and thus uncover Almeida (threatened by the columns first seen), or swing his right flank at right-angles to Fuentes, and risk his communications with Malhada Sorda and Guarda being cut. Meanwhile, he moved the 7th Division to Poço Velho and his cavalry to Nave de Haver, further south, already held by Julian Sanchez's guerrillas.

It was the latter, surprised on the misty dawn of the 5th, who were first attacked and dispersed, while the British cavalry was forced back on Poco Velho, from which two battalions of the 7th Division were expelled and retired on the rest of the division further west, with French cavalry and infantry in pursuit.[37] This Division, together with two squadrons sent to protect them, would have found themselves in a hazadous situation in comparatively open country, with only occasional rock outcrops offering cover, had not the Light Division been ordered to shepherd them back towards the western extremity of what was becoming Wellington's new alignment, for he had re-deployed Picton's 3rd Division facing south immediately west of Fuentes, the hinge of his position. This wing was extended towards Freineda by Ashworth's Portuguese brigade, and Spencer's 1st Division, beyond which the 7th, somewhat shaken during its withdrawal, faced about.

Craufurd had been able to protect them from any convergence of artillery fire and infantry attack by the expedient of keeping his line battalions in mobile squares and his riflemen as small groups of skirmishers, which, whenever they found cover, had keep up a galling fire on the enemy infantry and cavalry. Whenever they were charged, they would sprint into a square. Meanwhile, Cotton's cavalry charged the French guns; and Bull's horse artillery, from positions they had taken up between each of Craufurd's squares, had kept up a fire on them. Leap-frogging back in this disciplined fashion and in almost perfect order, over two miles were thus covered, and with negligible casualties. At one moment Captain Norman Ramsay's two guns were entirely surrounded by their cavalry, at which he coolly limbered up, and both guns and caissons were escorted back to safety at a gallop, his mounted gunners, with drawn swords, slashing their way as they ran the gauntlet of the encircling mass.

By now, Masséna had some 22,000 men within artillery range of Wellington's south-facing line. Apart from where it was divided by a narrow cleft cut by the Tourões, the Allies were protected by the reverse slope of a slight intermediate ridge between two tributary rivulets of the Dos Casas, from which his artillery had a wide field of fire over the heads of a strong line of skirmishers. But no attack came in that sector, for while Craufurd was still withdrawing, Masséna, intending to break the hinge of the Allied position before anything else, had sent ten battalions to attack Fuentes itself, where after briefly forced uphill towards the church, the 1/71st and 1/79th rallied and, supported by the 2/24th, thrust them over the Dos Casas.[38] Again they attacked, and the pendulum of battle swung back, with the Allies giving way until reinforced by light companies of the 1st and 3rd Divisions and the 6th *Caçadores.*

Once more the French were ejected from the maze of granite-walled alleys, until Masséna ordered forward no less than eighteen fresh battalions, which, by sheer weight of numbers, were able to drive the Allies through the village. But Wellington, well aware of the importance of this pivot in his defence, had already ordered forward the 1/88th and the 74th of Mackinnon's brigade of Picton's Division, which, advancing in two columns abreast, counter-attacked, the already blood-soaked lanes becoming the hub of a horrid hand-to-hand struggle, with bayonets being driven home and volleys exchanged at point blank range, until the French staggered back towards their own lines. But here, joined by the last reserves of three divisions advancing on a wide front, they again returned to the attack – some units for the sixth time – but it was not pressed home. Neither was any offensive action taken by their remaining divisions further west, facing Ashworth's, Spencer's and Houston's units, although there was a sporadic artillery duel, until their guns were silenced by British numerical superiority. Their position would have been jeopardised if ordered forward while the village still remained in Allied hands. By 2.00 the battle was virtually over.[39]

On this rare occasion, Wellington ordered his troops to entrench part of their new front during the night between the bastion of Fuentes and the Tourões. Masséna cavalry attempted to find a gap in this line next morning, but it appeared almost impregnable. He would be ill-advised to mount another attack without suffering further losses he could ill afford, so having fed his men with food intended for Almeida, Masséna withdrew towards Ciudad Rodrigo. It was not long after that he was informed that the redoubtable Marshal Marmont would be replacing him.[40]

Meanwhile, he had smuggled a message into Almeida ordering Brennier to escape as best he could after destroying its surviving fortifications, which – much to Wellington's mortification – he did during the night of the 10th, crossing the unguarded bridge at Barba del Puerco with 900 of his garrison of 1,400. That he was able to do so was due largely to the negligence of Erskine and Colonel Charles Bevan (who afterwards shot himself).[41] As Wellington commented in a private letter to his brother: 'I begin to be of the opinion that there is nothing so stupid as "a gallant officer". They (the blockading force) had ... allowed the garrison to slip through their fingers and escape ... There they were, sleeping in their spurs even, but the French got off.'

Schaumann, entering Almeida soon after, described the state in which the French had left it, having

> thrown about 100 wagons into the moat, and … blown up the walls and ramparts to such an extent that the *débris*, by falling into the moat, had covered everything up. The carriages of the heavy guns lay smashed on the ramparts. A portion of the walls was still standing where the mines had failed to explode. The gates were shattered … most of the houses were lying in ashes, and shells and splinters of bombs strewed the streets. All guns had either been spiked, or shot had been fired at them and dented their sides, or else shot had been hammered into their muzzles. Vast stores of entrenching materials had been burnt or otherwise rendered useless, muskets had been broken in two, and, in fact, everything had been destroyed. Some men of the English Artificers' Corps, however, were already busy cutting out the damaged vent holes of the spiked guns in an ingenious fashion and, by means of a screw thread, fitting new ones to them. All the *débris* was still smoking, and as some of the mines had not exploded, it was dangerous to wander about among it.
>
> Before their evacuation the French had hidden live cannon and howitzer shells in the ashpits of all chimneys, baking ovens, and fireplaces of the bouses and barracks, so that the returning inhabitants or troops might be blown to pieces the moment they began to light fires!
>
> Here and there girls in their Sunday clothes could be seen peering from the windows, and endeavouring to attract our attention by frivolous gestures. After I had ordered a new cloth coat at a tailor's we had luncheon at what once had been a restaurant, the owners of which had gone off with the troops and left behind the most glorious jams, liqueurs and fruit preserved in brandy.

In early June, William Grattan, recuperating after having been wounded at Badajoz, revisited Fuentes, where

> Every house, I might almost say every face, was familiar ... The heaps of embanked earth, which denoted the places where many of our old companions had been interred, were covered with grass, which grew luxuriantly over the graves ... We traversed the churchyard where so many of the Imperial Guard and our Highlanders had fallen; and we marked well the street where three hundred of the former had been put to death by the 88th Regiment.[42] Many of the doors still retained the marks of the contest; and the chimneys, up which the Guard had sought shelter, bore the traces of what had taken place ... untouched, unmended.
>
> We walked on to the chapel wall, where the 79th had suffered so severely, and through which the French had forced their passage, under a torrent of shot, against the bayonets of the brave Highlanders. The chapel door was riddled through and through with bullets, and the walls bore the marks of the round shot fired by the French batteries.

* * *

Lisbon slowly reverted to a life of wartime normality, and those many thousands who had been obliged to settle within the Lines now returned to their homes, too often to find them destroyed or derelict. Although the capital remained the main port of supply and the base of army contractors until towards the closing stages of the war, it never experienced the physical destruction that so many other towns and villages had to suffer, nor was it again so close to the front. It thus continued to be the occasional retreat of both convalescents and officers on leave, who might there indulge in the most dissolute distractions. Any who stayed too long or showed too little inclination to rejoin their regiments were nicknamed 'Belemites', for the main cavalry depot and several other barracks were in the western suburb of Belém.

Elaborate instructions had been laid down regarding the proper behaviour of both officers and men when in Lisbon, where General Sir Warren Peacocke was for some time Commandant. According to Schaumann, as Peacocke was 'incapable of taking command in the field, [he] had been specially sent here by Lord Wellington, who knew his eccentric and harsh character, in order, by means of every kind of interference, to make the life of English officers in Lisbon as difficult and unhappy as possible.' Wellington, who invariable remained at the front, was intolerent of officers requesting leave to visit the capital, and it is recorded that he remarked on one occasion that if so-and-so insisted on going, he had told him that 'he may stay there forty-eight hours, which is as long as any reasonable man can wish to stay in bed with the same woman.'

Dr McGrigor,[43] disembarking there some months later, reported to Wellington that he had found both 'an immense number of sick and of medical officers at Lisbon, and also a very great number of either sick or reported sick and wounded officers,' stressing that the 'exceptional accumulation of officers, their ladies and the wives of soldiers at Lisbon,[44] … detained at the capital … a disproportionate part of the medical officers.'[45]

Several descriptions survive of the temptations and distractions of Lisbon to satisfy all tastes, whether of the fashionable gambling-house kept by a dignitary of the Church; the performances at the São Carlos opera-house, where there were 'a number of pretty ballet dancers in amazingly short skirts, all of whom were kept by various notabilities,' according to Schaumann, who confided that 'As soon as the ballet was over we would visit certain houses, of which there were plenty in those days, where girls both young and pretty were to be found.'[46] At an earlier stage, Sherer had attended a comedy 'not unlike our *Beggar's Opera* at a theatre in the Rua das Condes, followed by a ballet, in which 'Madame Brunet, a handsome woman, and a graceful dancer, formed the chief attraction,' before ending his day 'taking an ice at the Grotto, a very excellent coffee-room.'

Others preferred harder liquor. George Woodberry (18th Hussars) was 'much annoyed one day with a confounded headache: fancy I must have been a little groggy last night, Smith & Cotton were dam'd drunk, so was Rowlls. Cotton, in going home, fell off his mule, & it strayed away; was oblig'd to walk near three miles.' However, Woodberry also rode over to the palace at Queluz on another occasion, describing the apartments as 'very beautiful, particular those painted & decorated under the direction of Junot when here in 1808. The gardens are laid out with more taste than any I have seen in this country & the fountains are superior to any I ever saw in my life. Like all the palaces & beautiful buildings I have seen … this charming place is going fast to decay, every part of it neglected.'

Comparatively few officers had taken their wives with them to the Peninsula, but in several cases they were left at Lisbon rather than having to face the hazards of the front. Some seem to have taken it all in their stride. Taken prisoner at Olivenza in early May, 1811, Colonel Louis-François Lejeune, when in Elvas, described with an artist's eye the astonishing sight of a British captain, 'in his scarlet uniform, mounted on a beautiful horse, and carrying a large open parasol': that was extraordinary enough; but

> behind came his wife, elegantly dressed and wearing a very small straw hat. Seated on a donkey, she held up an umbrella and caressed a little black and tan King Charles spaniel on her knees, while she led gracefully by a blue ribbon a tame goat, which was meant to supply her with cream for her cups of tea night and morning.
>
> At Madame's side walked an Irish nurse, carrying slung across her shoulders a bassinet made of green silk, in which lay an infant, the hope of the family. Behind Madame's mount marched a huge grenadier, the captain's faithful servant, with his musket over his shoulder, urging on with a stick the lady's long-eared steed. Behind him again came a donkey laden with the voluminous baggage of the family, surmounted by a tea-kettle and a cage of canaries. A groom or jockey in livery brought up the rear, mounted on a sturdy English cob, with a hide gleaming like polished steel. The groom held a huge posting whip in one hand, the cracking of which made the donkey mind its pace, and at the same time kept order among the four or five hunting dogs – hounds, spaniels and greyhounds – which served as scouts to the captain during the march of his little cavalcade.

1 An adequate force was ready to counter any attempt on Masséna's part to cross the Tagus during the hours of darkness, which would be alerted by lighting beacons set up on its left bank.

2 The cavalry and artillery had lost over 5,000 mounts and draught horses since November, and some regiments had only a few surviving pack-mules to carry their slender rations and reserve ammunition: 51 caissons were burnt in Junot's Corps alone. Leach stated that their horses 'were kept alive latterly on the stalks of the vine, bruised and mixed with corn, when they were so fortunate as to procure any of the latter article.' By 15 March 1811, of the 62,500 present at Busaco, the 'Army of Portugal' had dwindled to 40,000.

3 Less than three weeks earlier, on 19 February, some 9,000 men under Mendizabal, deployed along a ridge west of the Gebora, a tributary of the Guadiana north of Badajoz, had been surprised by Soult's 4,500 infantry fording of the river during a foggy morning, during which their cavalry, circling north, outflanked the ridge and attacked the Spanish camp in their rear, near which the more numerous allied cavalry, abandoning the infantry, broke and fled. Mendizabal's infantry formed squares which soon disintegrated. Although 2,500 escaped into Badajoz, their casualties amounted to well over 800; 4,000 were taken prisoner, and 17 guns were captured. French losses totalled 400.

4 There was no excuse either for the Spanish having surrendered Alburquerque, north of Badajoz, on the 16th.

5 Lieut. William Bragge (3rd Dragoons), passing through Santarém six months

later, referred to eleven convents and eight churches having fallen victim to their 'wanton Mischief.'

[6] A diarist in Ney's Corps has recorded that rape was habitual, and had seen one foraging detachment returning to camp with peasant girls found in a half-deserted village, then selling them to their comrades for a couple of gold pieces or a pack-horse. Colonel John Wilson, writing to D'Urban, reported that on one such plundering excursion 'they murdered more than 100 persons and after making a desert of the Country, carried off many families and every female above 12 years old for the use of the Soldiery. This they do all around us ...'

[7] Oman, when visiting the building almost a century later, remembers being told by the locals that 200 people had been burned there 'in the time of the French.'

[8] The fact that Portuguese units had been integrated into British divisions put an additional strain on the British Commissariat, increasing by about a third the number to be fed. D'Urban had commented in January that the Portuguese had suffered at the hands of those responsible for feeding them, not only by the 'infamous neglect' of the administration, but also by 'the villainy of the Commissaries they employ. They make 9 Rations of Bread out of the same quantity of Flour that provides 15 to the British Bakers.'

[9] Among them would be those of Inês de Castro and Dom Pedro I, not Pedro the Cruel, as he had assumed.

[10] How different had it been when seen by Donaldson, quartered there a few months earlier, before retiring on the Lines, when 'a whole division of the army, consisting of not less than five thousand men were lodged in the galleries alone, without filling them.' Attached to it 'was a spacious chapel, the whole inside of which was decorated in the most superb style; and the walls covered with valuable paintings, and in it a magnificent organ ...' Before the last of the monks had driven off in their chaises – taking with them 'not a few boxes of doubloons' – they 'liberally supplied' the troops with whatever remained in their larders and kitchen, but staved in most of the 700 pipes of the choicest wines in their cellar to prevent them falling into the hands of the enemy. Had they not done so, the 94th Regiment might never have marched off through the pouring rain that same afternoon for Torres Vedras.

[11] Browne also referred to the enemy having turned out of their monasteries the monks, who 'covered the roads', not that he felt 'much sympathy for these fat and idle vagabonds. We furnished them however with rations, in order to secure their good opinion, and I believe they became no mean auxiliaries, in directing public feeling and vengeance, against every thing that was French.'

[12] Had they not mounted precipitately, Masséna and his staff would have been taken prisoner here, when a party of hussars, to their mutual surprise, stumbled upon them enjoying an alfresco meal.

[13] Temporarily replacing Craufurd, on leave in England.

[14] Often mis-spelled Foz de Aronce in later descriptions, largely due to the repetition of an uncorrected printer's error in Napier's *History*.

[15] This was recovered at low water and sent to London.

[16] Had Erskine attacked the rearguard – isolated by the bridge from the main enemy body – an hour earlier, Ney would have suffered far more casualties than the estimated 250. Wellington's losses were nine killed and 62 wounded only.

[17] Hence, supplies were unloaded at Foz-Dão, not far beyond Raiva (below

Penacova, at the southern end of the Busaco ridge), the valley there now being partly submerged by a reservoir. Seasonal variations in water level on both the Mondego and Douro determined to what extent they might serve as a means of transport.

18 And yet, according to Stothert, as soon as the French retired, the peasantry 'came with their implements of husbandry from their hiding places, and commenced their labours; in many places the vines were already trimmed, and the industrious farmer, busied in his fields, seemed anxious to repair the loss of time, and the devastation committed by the enemy.'

19 Burgoyne had recorded his supervision of the mining of several bridges in this area, notable at Val des Pinos, the Ponte de Murcella, Serpins, Foz de Arouce, and Góis.

20 Already, on the 20th, Pakenham had commented that Wellington had 'the option of disorganising his army by a close pursuit without supplies, which while it lasted must have been brilliant, or a temporary halt, forgoing the opportunity, not to return, but retaining his army in discipline, supply and efficiency. He chose the latter without hesitation.' Thus there was a brief lull in the pursuit.

21 Ney refused to accept such an order, with the incontestable argument that the army would be unable to subsist there, was deposed of his command for insubordination and sent to Paris, his 6th Corps passing to Loison. Junot, trudging south towards Belmonte, was soon reporting that he could advance no further without starving, and Reynier was begging Masséna to give up his plan, for the same reason. On 28 March, Masséna conceded, with reluctance, and ordered both their Corps to retire across the frontier towards Ciudad Rodrigo.

22 Where Simmons found the fortress-like cathedral 'had been converted into a stable and the organ sadly cut and hacked about in the most wanton manner (by Catholics).'

23 Kincaid says four men.

24 Tomkinson describes having driven off six regiments and a cavalry picquet from Pega, where they found a French infantryman caught by the peasants had been buried alive. Headquarters that night were at adjacent Marmeleiro.

25 Total French casualties at Sabugal were at least 760, including a higher proportion of officers than usual; the British, a mere 162, of which only two officers and fifteen men were killed. Enemy casualties would have been higher had not Reynier rapidly retired under cover of the violent hailstorm which had come on during the fighting.

It was when reconnoitring some distance from the field of action that John Waters – so enterprising at the Passage of the Douro – was captured by a French outpost. Refusing to give his parole, as a prisoner he was sent towards Salamanca with an escort; but better mounted than they, chosing his opportunity, he put spurs to his horse, evaded his pursuers, and two days later regained Headquarters, where Wellington had ordered his baggage to be brought, well knowing that any intelligence officer as astute and resolute as he would not be long absent. It was soon after this exploit that Waters was made brevet lieutenant-colonel.

26 Two of his generals were killed from falling from balconies in Lisbon during the war: whether it was cowardice or some other disgrace, or merely inebriation, which caused them to end their lives in this way, remained a matter of dispute.

[27] It has been estimated that his total losses, taking into account the reinforcements he had received, were 25,000 men, of which only 2,000 were killed in battle; 8,000 had been taken prisoner (including those in the hospitals of Coimbra); the rest had been picked off by Portuguese irregulars, had deserted, or died from malnutrition or actual starvation. In addition, Masséna had lost almost 6,000 horses of the 14,000 with which had entered Portugal, numerous guns, and virtually all his wagon train.

[28] Writing a year later, when referring to mule transport, and praising the postal system by then perfected, Tomkinson states that the advance from the Lines 'through a country completely exhausted, was most wonderful. The enemy were quite astonished how we got on.'

[29] Cavalry commanders were often the butt of criticism. We find Surgeon Boutflower writing that 'the incapacity, not to add, want of courage, of many ... has become so notorious, that there is scarcely a Dinner party, or assemblage ... where the Conduct of our Cavalry Generals is not spoken of with disgust & contempt.'

[30] Wellington had every reason to be preoccupied, for Alexander Gordon (when writing on 8 April from 'a dirty smoky hovel with hail and snow showering in' at Villar Formoso) stated: 'We have no later account of Beresford than the 1st of April when he was at Elvas and had not crossed the Guadiana. It is inconceivable his delay and bad management ... he appears to be like all the rest of the Generals, not worth anything. In short, if Lord Wellington is not on the spot everything goes wrong, and he can place little or no confidence in any of them.' However, he retracted his stricture a fortnight later, when in Elvas itself, for having 'seen things in their true light, it does appear that Beresford has done as well as he could do, and has not lost much time'; nevertheless, not believing that Marmont's threatened advance on the Aguada was serious, Gordon felt Wellington should have remained longer at Elvas, where 'his presence is most necessary, and where, in my opinion, he has much to fear from the talents of Soult.'

[31] The fortress had also been re-supplied by a large convoy, which Erskine had failed to intercept, although warned of its approach by Julian Sanchez's guerrillas.

[32] By no means was all Masséna's cavalry brought into action during the ensuing battle.

[33] This had been partly blown up by the Allies the previous July, but although semi-derelict, was still a formidable obstacle.

[34] Here it was a ravine, yet only knee-deep at Fuentes itself.

[35] Donaldson described the day as being 'uncommonly beautiful, the sun shone bright and warm, the various odoriferous shrubs, which were scattered profusely around, perfumed the air, and the woods rang with the songs of birds.'

[36] A lieutenant of the 79th records that when the bugles on both sides had sounded the cease fire on the evening of the 5th, a Frenchman had called out in good English to say that they would bring some of their wounded, followed by a cheer on the part of the Camerons, who then participated in the exchange. The same author remarked that the French had returned during the night and cut off the flesh from some forty horses which had been left on the battlefield, not the first time this practice had been noticed.

[37] Writing in March 1813, Larpent stated that Wellington had observed at dinner one day that he had 'committed a fault, by extending his right too much at

Poço Velho; and that, if the French had taken advantage of it, there might have been bad consequences, but that they permitted him to recover himself and change the front before their face.'

38 One member of the 71st recorded that he had fired 107 rounds that day, which had made his shoulder so bruised by the recoil that he could hardly touch his head with his right hand; two years later, at Vitoria, he was to fire 108 rounds!

39 Total French casualties at Fuentes de Oñoro were 2,844; those of the Allies, 1,804.

40 Already by 20 April, having formally reproved Ney for his insubordination (and for whom he had other plans), Napoleon had come to the decision that Masséna would have to be superceded by Marmont. Foy was sent back with an appropriate dispatch recalling him. This had been delivered at Salamanca on 10 May.

Many years later, in conversation with Stanhope, Wellington expressed the opinion that, of his adversaries, Masséna was the ablest of Napoleon's generals. He certainly had the highest opinion of his power of resistance, and related that when they met in Paris years later, Masséna was very much excited at seeing him, greeting the Duke cordially with the words: 'Ah Monsieur le Maréchal, que vous m'avez fait passer des mauvais moments! And he declared to me that I had not left him one black hair on his body; he had turned grey, he said, all over. I answered that I thought we had been pretty even – things nearly balanced between us. No, he said, how near you were taking me two or three times! – which I was.'

41 For Alexander Gordon, this was 'a further proof of the lamentable evil …that where he [Wellington] is not himself in person, he can never be sure of any military operation being carried on (whatever may have been his orders) according to his wishes; and still less according to any military idea of the subject.'

42 They had found themselves caught in a cul-de-sac, where one end of an alley had been previously barricaded, and appear to have been massacred rather than taken prisoner in the ensuing conflict.

43 Dr James McGrigor (1771–1858), appointed chief of the army Medical Department in the Peninsula, for which service he was knighted in 1814 and created a baronet in 1830.

44 Peacocke referred to the females as being 'the most insubordinate and troublesome part of his charge.'

45 His inspection had convinced him that Lisbon 'was so very agreeable a residence that many officers and soldiers would be slow to resume their duties in the field, and that it was a much more attractive station for the medical officers themselves than the divisions of the army … in an inclement season of the year,' as it then was. All that would soon change, with both malingerers and medical officers being ordered to the front.

46 In a letter to his brother James, who was sailing out to the Peninsula, suggesting that he bought his horses and mules on arrival in Lisbon (the latter preferably *macho* or he mules) he added: 'your horse and mule must be of the same sex or you will have great trouble,' Major Edward Cocks also went on to caution him: 'You can very well amuse yourself while you are making these purchases … [but] Bear in mind that the girls are very hot for anyone who does not know the town.'

8

May to December 1811: Albuera; the first siege of Badajoz; El Bodón, and Arroyomolinos

Meanwhile, Beresford's main preoccupation had been to cross the Guadiana and reinvest Badajoz: as long as it remained in enemy hands it threatened Wellington's southern flank. In the expectation that Soult would attempt to relieve the fortress, Beresford had been instructed to concentrate his forces, and to oppose him if certain of his strength – taking into consideration 'the relative numbers of both armies, and making a reasonable allowance for the number of Spanish troops which will co-operate with him.' If he felt that his resources were insufficient to risk engaging in a general action, he should retire.

According to Sherer, the work of investment 'proceeded but slowly from the great want of materials,' and

> rendered extremely difficult, from the heavy and sudden rises of the river, caused by the melting of the snows. A flying bridge was, however, at length established, and our army was transported to the Spanish bank in safety, and without opposition, on the night of the fifth of April.[1] On the sixth we moved about three miles, and took up our ground on a plain covered with Gumcistus; a small village, lying a little to the rear of our right, was occupied by the head-quarters and staff.[2] Here a most extraordinary accident occurred, for which it is difficult to account satisfactorily. A body of the enemy eluded the vigilance of some Portuguese outposts, and surprised a squadron of English dragoons, all of whom were captured. These dragoons had been, for twenty-four hours previous, on out-line picquet, and were desired to consider themselves released from duty, though they were still kept close to the line of picquets; an arrangement by which, combined with the utter want of caution in the outposts, they were taken. But this is not all: the enemy arrived at Marshal Beresford's quarter in the village, and the first alarm was given by the fire of a serjeant's guard, posted over the person of the marshal. They took several horses belonging to the

> staff from their stables; and if they had not been unnecessarily alarmed, to find that they had penetrated so far, they might have carried off the whole of the head-quarter staff, for they returned themselves unmolested.

D'Urban states that it was not until 9 April that the Allies were able to cross and assemble near the road to Olivenza (some 15 miles south-west of Badajoz), in the face of which enemy vedettes and more advanced units had retired. Leaving some troops at La Albuera,[3] Beresford pushed south-east towards Zafra, already evacuated by Mortier, near which, at Los Santos de Maimona, cavalry skirmished on the 16th. Olivenza, with a garrison of only 300, had surrendered by noon the previous day after a brief bombardment. On the 24th, the Guadiana again rose and carried away the temporary bridge, which cut communication with the Portuguese bank.

During the next three weeks, desultory demonstrations by Colborne were carried out further east near Llerena and along the northern flank of the Sierra Morena to keep Latour-Mauberg occupied. Meanwhile, the bridge was being replaced, and by May 5 – coinciding with the second day of battle at Fuentes de Oñoro – a more substantial pontoon bridge had been positioned further upstream, where the Caya entered the Guadiana. Fascines and gabions were being prepared, together with platforms for the artillery, which with their ammunition was ready to be brought forward to Badajoz from Elvas.

On 8 May, the first parallels were being dug at three points, not too successfully near Fort San Cristóbal, where picks and spades soon hit solid rock. Within the next three day, of Beresford's nine engineers, six had been either killed or wounded: hardly an encouraging start, while his artillery – if it could be so described – had already suffered: four out of five of Dickson's 24-pounders being damaged or dismounted on the 11th.[4] It was learned next day that Soult was marching from Seville with 23,000 men.[5] This number, in comparison with what he expected to have at hand,[6] made Beresford confident that any confrontation would turn out to his advantage, even if the speed of Soult's approach precipitated the immediate suspension of his operations; fascines and gabions being burned, and guns, ammunition, and stores withdrawn to Elvas.

La Albuera

By early evening on 15 May, units taken from the investment were converging on La Albuera and deployed over undulating ground west and south-west of the village – already 'uninhabited, and in ruins' – where between its river (the Nogales) and a tributary, both fordable, extended a low tree-covered ridge. Immediately north of their confluence stood a stone bridge bearing the road from Santa Marta. Sherer noticed that every inch of ground to the west of the river was 'favourable to the operations of cavalry – not a tree, not a ravine, to interrupt their movements.' Assuming that Soult would aim for the bridge, Beresford had posted Alten's K.G.L. Brigade to defend it, with Hamilton's Portuguese Division to the north, and Collins's Portuguese Brigade in support. Otway's Portuguese cavalry defended the left or northern flank. Sir William Stewart's 2nd Division stood on slightly higher ground west of the village in a two-deep line, behind which waited the bulk of the British cavalry. Blake's troops arrived at about midnight and encamped,[7] at dawn being deployed in two lines facing the westernmost brook to form the Allied southern flank, with Loy's cavalry on their extreme right. More Spanish infantry, together with Cole's 4th Division – not having received orders to march from Badajoz until midnight – only reached the field in the early hours of the 16th.[8]

By then, Soult, approaching from Santa Marta,[9] had occupied a wood some three-quarter of a mile east of the river, from which 3,800 infantry, accompanied by light cavalry and 12 guns, appeared to be advancing directly towards the bridge; in consequence, two Spanish battalions were sent to reinforce Alten. Behind this vanguard marched a second column – Werlé's brigade of 5,450 infantry, two brigades of cavalry and another 12 guns – which then unexpectedly veered south; but before Beresford realised what was happening – no skirmishers having been placed in advance to give prior warning – Loy's cavalry had been surprised and routed by the French cavalry, which had forded both streams, while in their wake no less than nineteen infantry battalions, emerging through the trees and re-forming, threatened to roll up the Allied southern flank, a menace encountered by Beresford ordering Blake to re-deploy his troops to face south, and sending Stewart's 2nd Division to their support. Sherer saw the greater part of the Spaniards 'hastily formed front to the right to meet the attack,' but 'after a short and gallant resistance, [they] were overpowered and driven from their ground. The enemy now commanded and raked our whole position: the fire of his artillery was heavy, but, fortunately for us, not very well directed. It now became imperiously necessary to retake the important post, unfortunately, not blameably, lost by the Spaniards.'

Blake, assuming the French would advance from the east, had sent only four of Zaya's battalions – a quarter of the force at his disposal – to take up this position near the crest of a low hill. They found themselves facing two French Divisions (over 8,400 men), the first of which – its core, 50 men broad and 45 deep, together with flanking battalions – was closely followed by 10 battalions in four columns. Until the first two columns merged, the breadth of the attack was about 400 yards and their total depth, 600 . Their left flank was protected by 3,500 cavalry with additional guns to those advancing with the infantry.

The Spanish withstood this massive thrust remarkably well, even bringing the first division to a standstill, while Blake's only battery also went into action. By now, Stewart's Division had reached their right flank, the leading brigade deployed in line to the south-west, the advance being described by Sherer as 'in double quick time, led by that General. The first, or right brigade, commanded by General Colborne, was precipitated into action under circumstances the most unfavourable: it deployed by corps as it arrived near the enemy, fired, and was in the act of gallantly charging with the bayonet on a heavy column of their infantry, when a body of Polish lancers, having galloped round upon its rear in this most unfortunate moment, (for a charge is often a movement of exulting confusion), overthrew it with a great and cruel slaughter.'

This counter-attack, with 2,000 muskets firing directly into the exposed French flank – against Beresford's specific orders, which were to form his three brigades into line behind the Spaniards – was made on Stewart's initiative, and would have been even more effective had not the weather, threatening since dawn, suddenly broken. The downpour put the majority of Colborne's muskets out of action moments before their undefended flank was charged by Polish lancers. Taken by surprise, unused to facing this arm and unable to fire, the first three of Colborne's battalions were massacred, not even the wounded being spared; only the 2/31st, which had time to form square, were able to resist the onslaught.[10] Some of the Poles passed through Zayas's line, and Beresford and his staff found themselves overrun. The burly marshal parried the thrust of one lancer and, seizing him by the neck, dashed him senseless to the ground. Havoc was caused also among a battery of the K.G.L., but apart from one howitzer dragged away, their other guns were recovered.

When the rain ceased, the firing increased amid clouds of acrid smoke, which further reduced visibilty and, in the confusion, Hoghton's brigade, firing at French cavalry, had also caused minor casualties among the Spaniards. Lumley then sent in two squadrons of the 4th Dragoons, which retired in the face of a renewed attack by enemy cavalry. Zayas's

Spaniards were replaced by Abercrombie's and Hoghton's brigades and the 2/31st of Colborne's, and these seven British battalions – some 3,700 men in a two-deep line – found themselves confronted by at least 7,800 French in a close-range fire-fight, extended round the flanks of a dense column of 200 men broad and 40 ranks deep, into which they discharged repeated volleys. But artillery was enfilading the flank of the British line with both grape and canister, which although inaccurate, caused carnage, notably among Hoghton's men.[11]

A Spanish brigade ordered to advance in their support, refused to do so. In their place, Beresford ordered forward both Hamilton's and Collins's Portuguese, although Cole's 4th Division were nearer, and Alten was sent to reinforce the right; but Hamilton never received his order. Cole now took the initiative. On rapidly consulting with both Colonel Henry Hardinge and Lumley (whose cavalry was to support him further west), he deployed the 4th Division in one long line of 4,000 men facing south-east, which bore down obliquely on the massed French, who countered by sending forward cavalry on their west flank, and fresh infantry units on their east. Cole's light companies formed squares, between which, to approach the British line, cavalry would have had to pass, but suffering severely by enfilading fire, they turned back before reaching sabre range. Cole's left then came under attack by Werlé's division, advancing in three columns, and by his artillery. While each battalion of William Myer's brigade facing them was outnumbered by three to one, they had the advantage in fire-power, and although their line was raked by grape, they held their ground, steadily firing into the dense columns.[12]

Meanwhile, the Lusitanian Legion had redeployed to extend Cole's line to the left, and with both his flanks swinging forward, the French found themselves in a destructive cross-fire from which there was no escape. Myers's brigade charged. The French opposing them wavered and turned tail, panic soon spreading throughout their divisions, which began to break up. Covered by their remaining artillery and a battalion of grenadiers (Soult's reserve), they made their way to the rear, now hard-pressed by the Portuguese brought forward by Beresford. Although the infantry had retreated to and formed a defensive line between the two streams, their cavalry swarmed menacingly; their artillery, although withdrawn, still kept up an effective fire. The downpour recommenced. By now the contending forces had been locked in battle for no less than four hours. The survivors were exhausted.[13] Yet several of Beresford's units had not seen action: his cavalry, ably commanded by Lumley, had suffered only 48 casualties.

The remaining hours and all next day were spent recovering the wounded. Those of Soult's army that could limp away, did so, having first 'destroyed the contents of many of their tumbrils and ammunition cars, to facilitate the conveyance of their wounded … followed, at a respectful distance, by our cavalry and light infantry.'[14] Beresford sent a flag of truce to Badajoz, urgently requesting medical assistance, clothing, etc. for the wounded French, as he had none to spare; although they had fed, dressed, and attended them, they could not also cover them or remove them. The answer was negative. On entering a small chapel on the 20th, Sherer found it still filled with their wounded, 'very great numbers of whom had suffered amputation, and who lay on the hard stones, without even straw, in a dirty, comfortless state ... for we had nothing to give them on the spot, and, owing to the want of conveyances, they had to wait till our own people had been carried to the rear.' Sherer 'again went down to that part of the field, which was covered with the slain; they lay ghastly and unburied: here and there ... a loose-made grave, where some soldier or officer had been to perform an act of private friendship.' He was struck by the fact that numbers of the British corpses had their hands 'clasped together in the attitude of prayer ... placed by the Spaniards in this manner they superstitiously imagine it important to lay out their dead,' a simple and touching proof of their attachment to their companions in arms, even if heretics.[15]

Surgeon George James Guthrie, now back in the Peninsula (he had been invalided home after the Talavera campaign), found himself in charge of a makeshift hospital at Valverde, ten miles to the west, but 'without conveyance, without stores, except those that the panniers of the regimental surgeons contained, and encumbered with near 3,000 wounded … The doctors all worked as no men ever worked before, the toil was incessant ...'[16]

Sherer's regiment was withdrawn to Elvas, its hospitals likewise full, where 'It was a strange thing to see, in the crowded wards … English and French soldiers lying helplessly side by side, or here and there performing little kind offices for each other, with a willing and cheerful air. Their wants and thoughts, I observed, they communicated to each other in phrases of Spanish, which language many of the French privates spoke fluently, and our men understood well enough for all common purposes.'

Wellington, on reaching La Albuera on the 21st, when commiserating with Beresford, who was distraught, confided: 'We must make up our minds to affairs of this kind sometimes, or give up the game'; while the story has been often told that on seeing rows of unburied dead of the 29th still lying in ranks where they had stood, and then visited the wounded survivors of the Worcester Regiment, he remarked: 'I am sorry to see so many of you here,' to which a veteran sergeant replied, 'If you had commanded us, My Lord, there wouldn't be so many of us here.' Nevertheless, as far as the British public were concerned, the battle had to be written up as a victory:[17] indeed, the French were the first to retire from the field and Badajoz remained unrelieved, although Soult later alleged that the Allies had admitted to their defeat.

Wellington could ill afford another Albuera, the most sanguinary of Peninsular War battles in proportion to the numbers engaged. However much his many sterling qualities were appreciated, Beresford was not given independent command during the remaining three years of the war; and with the excuse that his strong hand was essential to the further improvement of the Portuguese forces and their militia, he was posted to Lisbon,[18] and 'Daddy' Hill, who had landed there on the 24 May, resumed command of the 2nd Division.[19]

* * *

The French still held the vital border fortresses of Ciudad Rodrigo and Badajoz. Soult remained a potential threat, for he could still assemble an effective field army from forces dispersed throughout Andalusia. Marmont, who had inherited Masséna's 35,000 men, lingered in the vicinity of Ciudad Rodrigo, unlikely to renew hostilities so soon after their mauling at Fuentes de Oñoro. An additional 60,000 under Marshal Bessières were strung out further north-east, largely pinned down in keeping open communications along the great road to France, harrassed constantly in the guerrilla war of attrition, their troops being picked off whenever the opportunity offered.

Spencer, left in command in the northern sector, with instructions to avoid any serious action, was ordered to march sufficient reinforcements south to make up for Albuera's casualties. They would follow the familiar corridor between their separated forces, running south-west from near Fuentes de Oñoro via Penamacor and Castelo Branco to Vila Velha de Ródão on the Tagus,[20] and on via Nisa and Portalegre to Campo Maior or Elvas.

The first siege of Badajoz

The renewed siege went badly. Although ground had been broken on 29 May, Wellington still had no proper siege train – only antiquated Portuguese cannon,[21] which could not be relied on – nor sufficient equipment at his disposal; his engineers, while adapt at running up defences, had little practical knowledge of carrying out a formal siege, nor had he properly trained sappers.[22] He was also working against the clock, for it was essential to take the fortress before Marmont and Soult combined forces, as they well might. What guns he had at hand opened fire on 4 June, but they were not close enough to damage seriously either the castle or the transpontine fort of San Cristóbal, guarding the stone bridge over the Guadiana. 'It was against this Fort we are throwing up our [earth-] works,' wrote Private Wheeler. At night,

> as soon as the Enemy hear the pickaxes they give us light by throwing out a quantity of fire balls. This would be very accommodating on their part if they did not open as many guns as they can bring to bear on the place ... The other night we began to brake ground in a fresh place, they very politely gave us a light by sending out six beautiful fire balls, the word 'down' was given, but before we had time to stretch ourselves on mother earth they discharged a volley of round and grape shot. One of the round shot must have passed pretty near my cranium. I thought I was wounded, my head ached violently. I felt the pain for a long time and it was with difficulty that I could perform my duty. Had I been working in a place where there was no danger I certainly should have given up, but here I was ashamed to complain, lest my comrades should laugh at me.
>
> It is astonishing with what rapidity our works advances, in a short time we had four batteries ready. When off duty, in our camp we are exposed to the scorching heat of the sun, we have no tents, not a tree or bush to shelter us, we have to fetch every drop of water we use at a distance of three miles, we must be ready at a moments notice should the enemy sally. The other day an accident of an alarming nature occurred, a fire broke out in our camp, the ground being covered with a sort of thistle that was completely dried by the sun ... It was making rapid progress to the spot where the whole of the ammunition was deposited. Fortunately we subdued the fire before it caused any mischief.
>
> The day our Batteries opened on Fort San Cristoval I was on covering party and stationed in the trench in front of No. 4 Battery.

Fire from an enemy mortar had dismounted one gun. Another was soon mounted, but with difficulty, as they 'dapped another shell into the battery and wounded several men.' It was necessary to amputate an arm and both legs of one poor fellow. 'Dr Webster commenced the operation with a leg, this done the arm followed. It was thought proper that the man should rest awhile before the other limb should be cut off, but the man insisted that the Dr should proceed, observing 'it's no use to make two bites of a cherry, what use is it making so much fuss about a leg that will be of no service to me or any one else again.' It was soon off and he dropped into a deep sleep. Early the next morning the Dr visited him, he found him leaning on the only elbow he had left smoking a short black pipe, and was apparently as comfortable as if the amputations had taken place a month.'

On the night of the 6th, to divert the enemy's attention, 'all our guns were opened on the Fort, but the French Commandant was not to be duped, the sly old fox had anticipated our visit ... We advanced up the glacis close to the walls. Not a head was to be seen above the walls, and we began to think the enemy had retired into the town. We entered the trench and fixed our ladders, when sudden as a flash of lightening the whole place was in a blaze ... The top of this wall [was now] crowded with men hurling down shells and hand granades on the heads of them below, and when all these were expended they have each six or seven loaded firelocks which they discharged into the trench as quick as possible. Add to this some half dozen canon scouring the trench with grape ... Heaps of brave fellows killed and wounded, ladders shot to pieces, and falling together with the men down upon the living and the dead.' The ladders were then found to be too short. Those 'who had gained the top of the ladders could not reach the top of the wall with their firelocks', and seeing that there was with no hope of entering the place, the order was given to retire. 'Next morning our little party of 100 were reduced to between 20 or 30, a cessation of arms for two hours took place to remove the killed and wounded,' while more ladders were prepared. But a second attempt to storm the fort met with no better success, while casualties were too high a proportion of the comparatively few men involved in these attacks. On retreating down the glacis, Wheeler was cut off, but avoided being taken prisoner when the French sallied out.

> I threw myself down by a man who was shot through the head and daubed my white haversack with his blood. I shewed this to the enemy

> when they ordered me to get up and go into the fort. From the appearance of the blood they must have thought I had a very bad wound in the hip, so they left me – except one who searched my pockets, took off my shirt, boots and stockings ... Situated as I was this added fresh horrors to my view, the place was covered with dead and dying, the old black walls and breach looked terrible and seemed like an evil spirit frowning on the unfortunate victims ... As the moon ascended it grew much lighter and I began to fear I should not be able to effect my escape, for the enemy kept a sharp look out and if anyone endeavoured to escape they were sure to discharge a few muskets at him. I soon perceived that as often as our batterys fired they would hide behind the walls. I made the most of this by sliding down as often as I observed a flash from our works. By daybreak I had got to the plain below the fort. I had nothing to do but to run for it across to the No. 1 Battery. This plain, like our camp, was covered with small dry thistles. The enemy discharged two guns loaded with round shot, and several muskets at me. My comrades cheered me and I bounded across like a deer, the Devil take the thistles. I felt none of them until I was safe behind the Battery.
>
> Capt. Douglas gave me a drop out of his bottle, and I made for camp where I arrived just in time to have my name struck out of the killed and wounded list ... I had three shots pass through my cap, one of which carried away the rosehead and tuft, my firelock was damaged near the lock, and a ball had passed through the butt.

On 10 June, some iron guns just arrived from Lisbon were brought into action, and although the breach in the castle wall was soon 'practical', intelligence had been received that both Marmont and Soult, and also units under D'Erlon, were converging on Badajoz in strength. There was not enough time to make the assault *and* repair the defences: reluctantly, two days later, Wellington turned the siege into a blockade, withdrawing his guns and *matériel* to Elvas, and took up a defensive line running north-east through Campo Maior to the small fortress of Ouguela. This would be difficult to turn, while ancient watch-towers in the vicinity provided semaphore stations from which – as behind the Lines of Torres Vedras – orders could sent rapidly to any point.[23] Within a week, the whole army of 44,000 men had been withdrawn to the right bank of the Guadiana, where Wellington, his Headquarters at Elvas, waited, knowing that Spencer's units were on the march to Portalegre.

By 18 June, Soult and Marmont had concentrated some 60,000 near Mérida, and entered Badajoz two days later. On the 22–23rd they made a reconnaissance in force towards the Allied position, but both French marshals were wary of attacking. They had serious problems of logistics to resolve; to stay where they were for long would be impossible and, on a personal level, collaboration was irksome. On the 27th, after blowing up the defences of Olivenza, Soult turned his back and marched towards Seville, leaving Marmont, with 47,000 men, astride the Guadiana, to subsist as long as he could: the latter remained there, undecided, until decamping on 15 July.

With the immediate threat removed, Wellington took stock. As Badajoz had been re-garrisoned and well-supplied by the enemy, it would be more advantageous to seize Ciudad Rodrigo first. With this objective in view, on 18 July orders were sent to land the 'modern' siege train (so long expected from England) at Oporto.[24] During ensuing weeks, under the supervision of Alexander Dickson, some 160 river craft carried these heavy guns up the Douro to Peso de Régua, where they were transferred to over 1,000 creaking ox-carts, which hauled them along what Somers Cocks described as 'a superb *cabrazada*' or goat-track climbing in zig-zags up the precipitous south bank of the river to Lamego and then south-east across country to their temporary base at Vila da Ponte. From there, they would be dragged towards Almeida.

Having obtained a fortnight's leave, chosing to revisit Oporto, Cocks described the descent of the Douro from Peso de Régua as being rapid, 'especially in particular points where the falls of the river are very great. The vessels are guided by a large oar fixed to their stern in lieu of a rudder. In going down one of the falls we ran foul of a vessel coming up. This threw the head of our boat so completely out of its direction that it went against the rocks on the other side and we were obliged to be carried stern first almost down the fall.' On reaching his destination, he found 'nothing particularly worth seeing … at least I found nothing out,' but, as he admitted: 'Three years ago I should have seen all the churches and all the hospitals … but instead of solemn churches and musty tombs I came to Oporto to seek laughing dames and spritely lasses to enliven the dull campaign which had just closed. But I was unlucky in the time I chose, all the best families … were at the watering places and had not returned to the city for the winter? There were no balls, no concerts, no frolics, I dined sometimes with the English merchants who gave me a quantity of hot port, very good perhaps, but as strong as the port of England. I was not used to it and it got into my head, which I did not at all approve of.'

By now, Sir Rowland Hill, back in the Peninsula after a few months' absence due to illness, had replaced Beresford in the southern corridor;

1. George Landmann, 'Sir Arthur Wellesley's Quarters at Vimeiro'

2. Attributed to Henry Thomas Alken, 'Hussars at ease, being supplied with provisions'

3. Thomas St Clair, 'Fording the river Mondego'. Wellington and Beresford are mounted (21 September, 1810)

4. Thomas St Clair, 'Troops bivouacked near Vila Velha' (19 May 1811)

5. William Bradford, 'Crossing the Tagus near Vila Velha'

6. Depiction of a mine exploding during the storming of the main breach at Ciudad Rodrigo

7. Thomas St Clair, 'Distant view of Ciudad Rodrigo with guerrillas in the foreground'

8. Thomas St Clair, 'Working parties opening a parallel at Badajoz in June 1811'

9. View across the Guadiana of Badajoz, seen from near Fort San Cristóbal (published by Edward Orme)

10. View of Elvas with the Forte da Graça (foreground), and right, the Amoreira aqueduct (published by Edward Orme)

11. San Sebastian: Allied artillery firing from the summit of Monte Ulia (published by Edward Orme)

12. 1779 plan of the Bidasoa estuary at low tide, showing the sand flats across which troops waded on 7 October 1813

13. 'Camping,' from 'Military Discoveries or the Miseries of Campaigning'

14. Bayonne from the sandhills to the west, near the position of the bridge of boats (published by Edward Orme)

Map 1: Physical map of the Iberian Peninsula and area guide for the following maps

8
7
Bayonne
Orthez
Toulouse
San Sebastian
Tarbes
Carcassonne
Vitoria
Pamplona
Perpignan
Gerona
Soria
Zaragoza
Lerida
Barcelona
Tarragona
Teruel
Valencia
Albacete
Alicante
Murcia
Cartagena

Map 2: The Vimeiro campaign; and the Lines of Torres Vedras

Map 3: Moore's campaign; and the Oporto and Talavera campaigns

Map 4: Masséna's advance to Busaco, and his retreat from the Lines; Fuentes de Oñoro

Map 5: The Ciudad Rodrigo – Badajoz corridor; La Albuera

Map 6: From Salamanca to Madrid and Burgos and back; and the Vitoria campaign

Map 7: The Battles of the Pyrenees, Nivelle, Nive and St Pierre. Compare with that on page 368

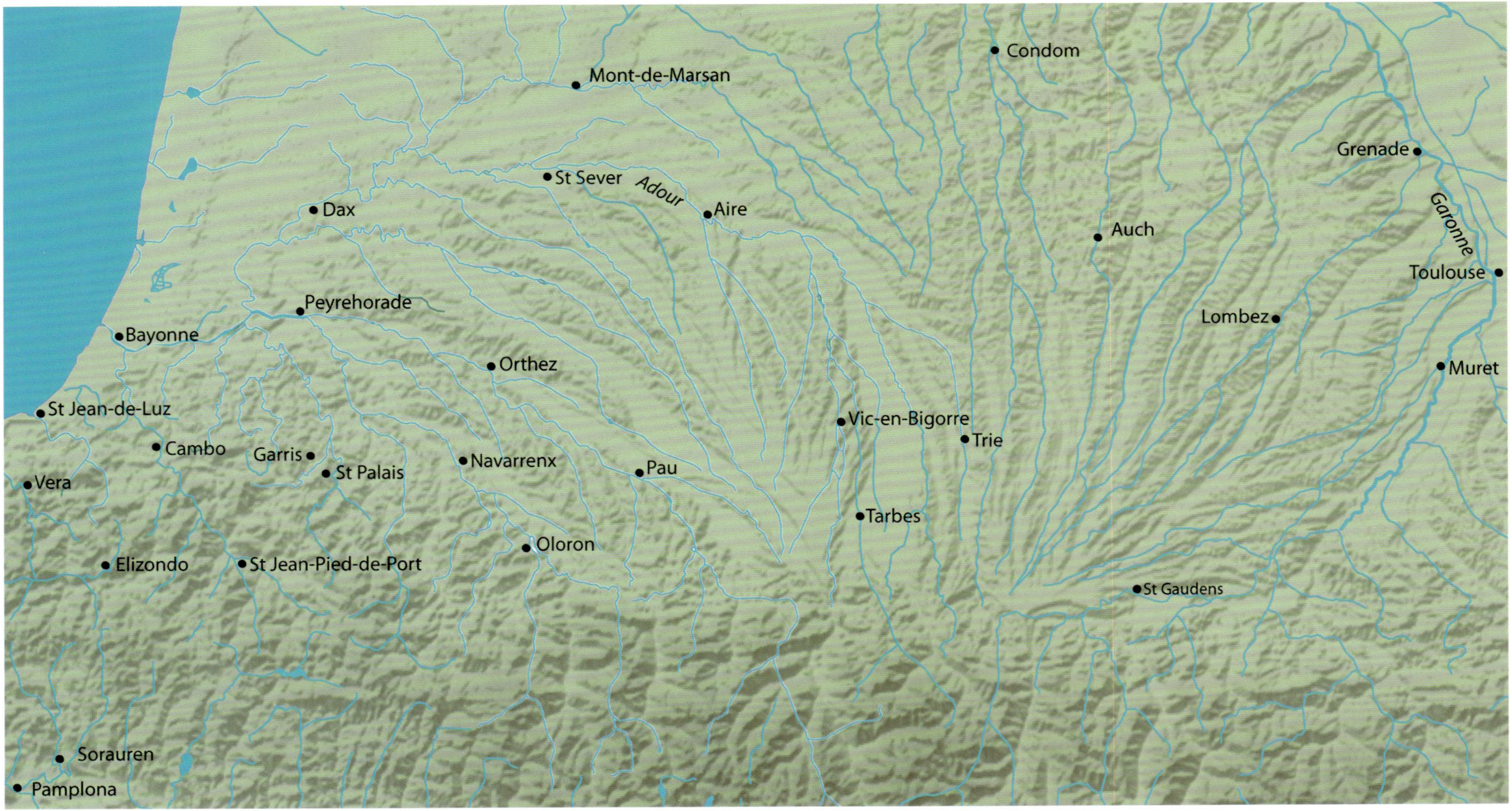

Map 8: The final campaign in France: Bayonne to Orthez, Tarbes and Toulouse

Graham replaced Spencer, who went home on sick leave, to Wellington's relief.[25] Wellington himself rode north early in August to establish Headquarters at Fuenteguinaldo, south-west of Ciudad Rodrigo, which was blockaded, leaving the bulk of his troops – amounting to some 46,000 – in cantonments along his lateral communications.

Lieut John Cooke, with the 43rd, recently landed in the Peninsula, when near Arronches had met the Light Division marching north. He described them defiling past, displaying

> wide and patched trousers of various colours, and threadbare jackets. Their brawny necks were loosened from their stocks and their brown-barrelled arms were slung over their shoulders, or carelessly held in their hand. A joyous buzz ran through the cross-belted ranks, as their soldier-like faces glanced towards us to greet many of their old comrades, now about to join in their arduous toils after a long separation. A cloud of dust marked their further progress as they receded from our view. Following in succession, we brought up the rear.
>
> At the expiration of an hour's march, we entered a wood and formed column; the roll was called and the whole Division was dismissed. Then, a multitude of voices, the tearing and cutting down of branches of trees, the crackling of fires, rattling of canteens, shooting of bullocks through the head, the hurrying of parties of soldiers for rum and biscuit rations, and the neighing of horses, braying asses and rampant mules, resounded throughout the forest ... Groups of officers stood in circles and every countenance was decked in smiles; a hearty welcome greeted us from all hands.

In their wake had followed 'a few hardy women ... mounted on strong and weak asses; Portuguese boys and officers' milch goats; drivers, purveyors and medicine chests; and sometimes a few sutlers, headed by a man better known as Tick, owing to his giving credit to officers in precarious times. This person would lay on an enormous percentage for small articles of luxury, disposing of bread at 9 shillings a 4lb loaf, with tea, sugar, and brandy in a proportionate ration.'

Lines of supply had to be set up or re-established. There were several routes from Oporto other than riverine, although some vessels continued up the Douro to Barco de Alva, beyond the left flank of the front facing Ciudad Rodrigo. Among them were one from Vila da Ponte to Pinhel and Almeida, and another ascending the Mondego valley from Coimbra to Celorico and Almeida.[26] Further south, both Santarém and Abrantes were bases, while from Nisa, the Tagus was crossed at Vila Velha for Castelo Branco (and later, for Coria), or the road followed south-east to Portalegre,[27] for Elvas. On 3 September an intercepted dispatch confirmed that Marmont and Dorsenne (replacing Bessières) were converging with almost 60,000 men in the vicinity of Salamanca intent on relieving Ciudad Rodrigo, but Wellington did not intend to be caught at a disadvantage in open country, and on the 23rd the blockade was lifted.

El Bodón

Two days later, a desperate action was fought at El Bodón (some nine miles south-west of Ciudad Rodrigo) between 1,000 Allied infantry, 500 cavalry and two batteries of artillery against 2,500 French cavalry supported by one battery. Donaldson (with the 94th, part of Colville's Brigade) describes being turned out of the village at 2 o'clock that morning to occupy a ridge crossed by the road from Ciudad Rodrigo to Fuenteguinaldo. Six hours later, enemy columns were seen approaching their precariously exposed position, separated by six miles from the rest of the army. Hardly had their main post been reinforced, than

> the advanced squadrons of the enemy's cavalry and artillery made a furious attack ... and succeeded in taking two pieces of Portuguese artillery. The Portuguese artillery behaved bravely, having stood until actually cut down at their guns, which were posted on a rising ground to our right.[28] The 5th regiment was now ordered to charge, and they succeeded in retaking the guns. While this was going on ... we were attacked by another body of cavalry in front, which was met and repulsed with determined bravery by the 77th regiment [also part of Colville's Brigade]. Our cavalry was warmly engaged, and charged different bodies of the enemy which ascended on the left. Here we kept our post gallantly, surrounded by about two thousand cavalry – until at last the French infantry being brought up, we were ordered to retreat in squares on Fuente Guinaldo, supported only by the small body of cavalry already mentioned. The French cavalry seeing us prepared for retreat, rushed furiously on, and the various squares were now successively charged by powerful masses of their cavalry, one in particular on three faces of the square, but they halted, and repulsed them with the utmost steadiness. The French in those charges suffered severely, having a tremendous fire poured in on them each time. As they rushed on with impetuosity, when they were

> brought to a dead stop by the points of our bayonets, they were thrown into the greatest confusion, and were brought down by our shot in numbers. The whole now proceeded to retreat in excellent order, at an ordinary pace, keeping exact distances, ready to form up in the event of a charge being made.
>
> We were much annoyed by shot and shell from the heights where the French artillery were posted, some of which falling in the squares did great mischief, killing and wounding several of our men, and blowing up our ammunition. We had about six miles to retreat in this manner ... with the French cavalry hanging on our flanks and rear ... At length we came in sight of the rest of our army, and the main body of the French hung back, but we were escorted into the very lines by their advanced guard. Here, however, they met with a warm reception from some squadrons of our cavalry, which made them retreat. We halted in rear of Fuente Guinaldo, where an entrenched camp had been formed, and remained here that night and next day, during which the French, having brought forward their infantry, took post on a hill opposite, and we expected an engagement; but Lord Wellington ... deemed it more prudent to retire. When night came, we were ordered to rekindle a great number of fires, for the purpose of making the French believe we still remained in our encampment. Two hours after, we commenced our retreat, and marched all night.

Wellington had ridden up to the front early in the action, just as Charles Colville was posting his units, and as Colville admitted, at a 'most fortunate moment for in that space of time he had perceived the enemy were moving off to their right and he [Wellington], after giving directions for the 77th and one Portuguese regiment to follow and join the 5th, galloped off at full speed.' He was much relieved that Wellington had been 'at hand to direct, as he did, the general movements which his uncommon quickness and experience enables him to do with such happy effect, and by his presence authorising measures of defence and of partial offence when without such authority retreat alone would have been justified.'[29]

'By universal and uncontradicted accounts the affair was most brilliant,' declared Cocks, when describing the action: 'We had a brigade of Portuguese artillery – 9 p[ounde]rs. The French cavalry charged it and were in possession of most of the guns. The 5th Regiment was lying down a little distance in the rear. The commanding officer would not allow them to get up till the enemy was close to them. At the distance of a few yards this little Regiment poured a volley into the enemy and, dashing on thro' the smoke with the bayonet, charged the French cavalry, drove them and retook the guns.' It was the first time Tomkinson had ever heard of infantry charging cavalry, with 2,000 muskets firing directly into the exposed French flank;[30] nor had he ever seen 'an affair in which a small force retired more regularly, and kept the eight squadrons from pressing on them ...'[31]

Not long after this action, Donaldson commented on how very different were the sentiments of those who were in direct contact with their opponents and many of his countrymen at home, 'whose ideas of the French character were drawn from servile newspapers and pamphlets, or even from so low a source as the caricatures in print shops; but I myself must confess, in common with many others, that I was astonished when I came in contact with French soldiers, to find them, instead of pigmy spider-shanked wretches, who fed on nothing but frogs and beef tea, stout, handsome looking fellows, who understand the principles of good living, as well as any Englishman amongst us; and whatever may be said to the contrary, remarkably brave soldiers.'

Wellington took up a defensive stance near Fuenteguinaldo next day while awaiting the Light Division.[32] Then, having concentrated his forces, he retired to a stronger position further west, nearer the Côa, to await developements. In the event, Marmont did not attack, but cautiously pulled back to the north-east, allowing Ciudad Rodrigo to be again isolated by the Allies.[33]

A brigade of cavalry commanded by General John Gaspard Le Marchant had recently landed at Lisbon (together with a pack of foxhounds), among them the 3rd Dragoons, in which served Capt. William Bragge, who, writing to his father, reported that news from the front was sparse; indeed

> We hear little or nothing of Ld Wellington, who keeps not only the Portuguese but the Officers of his Staff in the dark with regard to his Intentions, and I understand at his own Table he rattles away to the General Officers etc., and fills them full of Humbug Accounts which they have scarce Time to repeat to their confidential Friends before an order arrives for the Brigades to march without Delay at least 20 Points of the Compass from the one expected. I saw a Letter from the Brigade Major of the Royals which says the Horses have been 6 days without corn and other Regiments 13 Days, both were consequently obliged to fall back. He likewise mentions that the 11th Regt having lost two Picquets and an odd file or two, which has so enraged Ld W. that he is determined to exchange the Officers immediately for the Purpose of bringing them to a Court Martial.

While in Lisbon, Bragge had been astonished by the way the Portuguese would shoe their horses, for 'the whole Foot is rendered insensible by the Practice of cutting out the Frog and hammering the Shoe on with immense nails all round the toe, notwithstanding which they have few lame Horses or Broken Knees.' Among other surprises was the way 'the Ladies and Gentlemen bathe together and our watching them is considered a high compliment, and as few of them can read, write, work or draw, the Gentleman amuses himself with a few hours sleep in the day Time, whilst his Wife and Daughters sit in the Parlour Windows and amuse themselves with searching each others Heads, a Chase which seldom fails affording considerable sport to its Amateurs.' Bragge himself was not alone in complaining of the 'Race of Fleas more venemous and hungry than any to be met with in England', which had forced him to 'sleep on an old Chest about 4 feet long and make up a Bed with Two Blankets and a Cloak.' Before long, he described having 'accomplished a Bedstead on the principle of a Camp Stool, which stands nearly 2 feet from the Ground, is quite Firm and only weighs about 30 lbs.' [34]

Not all cavalry officers were as informed and resourceful as Bragge. Cocks had commented on

> the deplorable ignorance and want of spirit which pervades our Cavalry officers on their first arrival from England. Can you conceive a Gentleman reporting officially 'that the French army has gone to *Castile*', which he conceived must be a *very large town* though he 'could not find it *in the map*, for it held the whole army.' An Englishman by national character is so vain and so much accustomed to underrate the military profession that he thinks if he knows a few maneouvres he is fully qualified to perform his duty. His own courage he never doubts; till when at length placed in situations of responsibility he finds to his cost that the intrepidity which enables a man to use the powers of his mind in danger is but a rare gift of nature and usually requires an habitual acquaintance with an enemy not to be acquired in the heath of Newmarket and the Purlieus of Covent Garden, nor even Jackson's School [of pugilism].[35]

From his headquarters at Fundão, Le Marchant rode over to Freineda, which he was surprised to find so spartan. To him, these frontier villages were

> the most melancholy desolated places that can possibly be imagined ... my quarters ... seldom watertight, always without windows, and with

> not an article of furniture, whether beds, tables, chairs, etc. I mention this to show the dilapidated state of the country which has the misfortune to be the theatre of war … Chestnuts are now coming in, the woods for miles in extent are mostly of that description … loaded with fruit, which is allowed to drop off, and is gathered by the poor who are employed by the proprietors at an allowance of 2d per day. When all are collected that can be found, the pigs are turned into the woods, one of the causes of the pork being in such estimation. The chestnut I do not think better than you find it in England. The poor live principally in the winter on this food, which is eaten in different ways, they make bread of it, which I do not find good.

When later writing to his daughter, Le Marchant mentions the woods at the foot of the Serra da Estrela being also 'frequented by wild boars … wolves and foxes, as well as a small tiger.'[36]

Arroyomolinos

Hill had been ordered to clear General Girard's troops from the vicinity of Cáceres, to enable Morillo's Spaniards to forage there, and on 23 October he advanced discreetly north-west from Alburquerque towards Cáceres, which Girard abandoned on the 26th, allowing the Spaniards to re-possess it next day. A forced march in appalling weather brought Hill by dusk to Alcuéscar, immediately west of Arroyomolinos, below the Sierra de Montánchez, where, as Sherer remembered,

> We lay upon our arms, without fires, about six hours; and at two in the morning of the 28th, we moved forward, in profound silence, by a narrow bad road, upon Arroyo de Molinos, near which town we halted, at half-past six, on ground highly favourable both to our formation and concealment. We were divided into three columns. The first brigade was directed straight forwards on the town; our own, with one of Portuguese, made a rapid circuitous march to the right of it, and arrived, under cover of fog and rain, within a few yards of the road, by which alone the enemy could retire, and on which they were then forming, preparatory to their march, in profound ignorance of our approach: our cavalry moved in the centre, ready to act as occasion might require.
>
> The cheers of the first brigade, which entered the town charging, and bayonetted, drove, or captured his rearguard … our cavalry galloped forwards, dispersed, sabred, and made prisoner his few horse, who,

> after attempting some formation to the left of the infantry, which stood for a moment in a posture of defence, fled in great confusion. About two hundred yards behind the spot, where the enemies columns were formed on the plain, rose the rocky and precipitous Sierra de Montanches, and to this … they ran with unresisting panic. We followed them closely, and scrambling among the rocks, quite mixed with them, and made prisoners at every step …

'One thing in our success at Arroyo de Molinos gratified our division highly,' Sherer stressed: 'it was a triumph for our general, a triumph *all his own*.'[37] Blakeney described their silent approach, and how

> The enemy, driven out of the place, formed in two columns on the plain outside, under the base of Montanchez, protected by their cavalry. Casting a glance to the north, they perceived the 50th Regiment with the guns advancing. The fire from the 71st Light Infantry, issuing from the gardens, disturbed their close formation; and in the meantime the 92nd … filed through the streets and formed line on the enemy's flank, who, upon the double assault, commenced a rapid retreat … At this junction the Spanish cavalry … rode into the plain and separated the enemy's horsemen from their infantry … The British cavalry having at length come up, accompanied by the German Hussars, the affair became more serious … Their infantry still pushed forward with uncommon rapidity, yet in perfect order, fancying without doubt that all their danger was left behind. But as they approached the eastern horn of the crescent range … they were met directly in front by our right column, headed by light companies of the 28th, 34th and 39th … Becoming desparate, and arriving at where the mountains began to dip, they made a rush at the broad and high stone wall which ran along its base, and tearing open a breach, the head of their column, led by General Gerard [sic], entered the opening at the very moment that the light company topped the rising ground and saw them. Thus Gerard made his escape …

This brilliant operation caused more than a flutter among the French dovecôtes,[38] and was partly responsible for a number of redeployments of their armies – among them, the transference of Montbrun's contingent of Marmont's army to aid Suchet on the Mediterranean coast – which took some pressure off Wellington's position near Ciudad Rodrigo.

General Renouard,[39] the fortress Governor, had been captured while attempting to recover a herd of cattle grazing on the glacis, seized by Julian Sánchez's band. Referring to Renouard, Bragge remarked that

He is considered a clever Man and is certainly delighted with the Idea of seeing England, for which purpose I believe he became a Prisoner. He was taken by the Spanish Guerillas, a Cohort who carry on the most destructive War against the French and rarely pass a Day without killing some of them. The General says they have no communication with the Spaniards and dare not go out Foraging without a Brigade of Infantry and Regt of Cavalry, that he has himself been three Years in the Country without news from any of his Friends in France, and that a *Moniteur* [the official newspaper] is never seen by any Officer except some of the leading People who, for their own sakes, keep the Events of the Time a profound secret. I know a Frenchman will say anything but at the same time believe a good deal of this Intelligence.

Among several contemporaries describing the activities of guerrilla bands, or *partidas*, was Charles O'Neil, who also alluded to Don Julian's exploits.

These were principally, at first, Spanish peasants, who, unable to present any efficient force against the French, and unwilling to submit to them, threw themselves into the mountains, and, being well acquainted with all the passes and hiding-places, did the French much damage, by cutting off their communications, robbing their stores, and murdering every one who dared to stray from the main army. As the war proceeded, their numbers were enlarged by all those who were weary of the restraints of law; – every robber that feared a jail, or could break from one, every smuggler whose trade had been interrupted, – and there were thousands of these, as they still are, in Spain; every one who was weary of the restraits of his life, and sought for excitement; and all idlers who preferred the wild and reckless daring of those troops to the drill and watch of the army, were found either as associate or chief in these bands. They soon became regularly organized, chose their chiefs, and had watchwords, by which they could obtain a safe pass all over the country. They were professedly our allies, but they were almost as much a terror to us as to our foes. They proved, however, invaluable to our army, as a means of communication with each other, and as spies on the movements of our enemies. It was impossible for the French to communicate with each other at all, except by sending strong escorts, and these were often cut off; while, on our side, news could be sent with almost the rapidity of telegraph, and this undoubtedly was a great advantage to us. The chiefs of these bands were often obliged to procure subsistence and treasure for themselves, by robbing their own countrymen; and, indeed, one of the principal causes of the sudden growth of these bands was the hope of intercepting the public and private plate, which was being carried from all parts of Spain to be coined into money. Yet, though most of these bands were worthless characters, there were some among them of more noble spirit. Some were actuated by revenge – some by a gallant, enterprising spirit – and a few by an honest ambition to serve their country.

Our troops often met with many adventures with these foes [sic]; and many were the weary hours, in our toilsome marches, that were beguiled by the recital of their hair-breadth escapes, or of their own wonderful adventures.

Cocks was of the opinion that the guerrillas were particularly useful,

because they oblige the enemy to form so many detachments in order to secure his communications and command in some measure the resources of the country. There will never be any want of these guerrillas, a Spaniard is very vain and fond of an irregular plundering life, he does not care for hardship the least, but cannot bear continual labour. This is just the character for a guerrilla …

As for the rest of the inhabitants, the landowners, the great farmers and the towns people, they are heartily tired of the war and would be very glad to put an end to it in any way. The Spaniards do not possess the inexhaustible patience of the Portuguese. This nation, which in personal appearance and manners is very inferior to the Castilians, in essential qualities is much the superior.

With winter approaching, the opposing armies withdrew into cantonments, leaving their outposts to keep wary eyes on possible offensive movements. Londonderry described the billets as being 'for the most part, extremely small and incommodious.[40] The rain, which fell in torrents, soon penetrated the thin roofs of the cottages ... and even the larger mansions ... of which the general and staff officers were put in possession, ceased, at last, to resist a deluge so incessant.' Meanwhile, 'every disposition was made to pay attention to the sick, of which the numbers became every day more alarming ... [having] swelled to the enormous amount of sixteen thousand men ... till scarcely a regiment could muster upon parade two-thirds of its numerical strength; and the medical attendants almost sank beneath the fatigues which they were condemned to endure.'[41]

The idea had been floated several months earlier by Commissary-General Kennedy that future operations would be facilitated if the army had their own Commissariat Wagon Train, which would enable them to be independent of invariably inadequate hired local wheeled transport, and also relieve the inhabitants from having their bullock-carts requisitioned. Commissary Daniel records that Colonel Sturgeon and his artificers were employed constructing them after a pattern approved by Wellington. Models had also been provided for British contractors to copy, and 400 or more were built and shipped out to Lisbon during ensuing month.[42] They were 'drawn by four oxen purchased for the purpose, and were made capable of bearing eight hundred pounds weight,' their wheels revolving on iron axle-trees. They were placed under the supervision of commissariat officers, 'with conductors, artificers and other subordinates, and were to prove invaluable when transporting heavy ammunition in readiness for forthcoming sieges and in forming supply depots.[43] Daniel calculated that apart from wheeled transport – and not including those for Hill's 'Corps' in his figures (probably another 3,000) – some 12,000 mules followed the army in their Spring offensive, carrying forward food and equipment for each Division, together with ammunition, entrenching tools, regimental books, medical supplies, forges for shoeing the cavalry,[44] officers' baggage, not to forget candles, etc.

Sturgeon was also busily supervising the building of a long bridge over the Agueda near the Marialva ford (south-east of Gallegos), essential for future operations against Ciudad Rodrigo. The immense amount of material necessary, not only timber but axle-trees and any other old iron was requested from Almeida for the construction of a pile engine, etc., while from the 3rd, 4th, 5th, and 6th Divisions, carpenters, sawyers, wheelwrights, blacksmiths and other artificers were mustered to expedite the completion of the structure by the year's end. [45]

In October, Wellington transferred his Headquarters from Fuenteguinaldo to Freineda,[46] a granite-built village no distance west of Fuentes de Oñoro and south of Castelo Bom, which remained his base for two successive winters. Schaumann was impressed by the quiet and unostentatious life there; no one would have known that the Commander-in-Chief was at hand: there was 'no throng of scented staff officers with plumed hats, orders and stars, no main guard, no crowd of contractors, actors, valets, cooks, mistresses, equipages, horses, dogs, forage and baggage wagons ... Just a few aides-de-camp, who went about the streets alone and in their overcoats, a few guides, and a small staff guard; that was all!' According to Tomkinson, Wellington himself usually rose 'at six every morning, and employs himself to nine (breakfast hour) in writing. After breakfast, he sees the heads of departments, viz.: Quarter-Master [-General] and Adjutant-General, Commissary-General, Commander of artillery, and any other officers coming to him on business. This occupies [him] until 2 or 3 p.m., and sometimes longer, when he gets on his horse and rides to near six – this, of course, is interfered with when the troops are before the enemy. At nine he retires to write again, or employs himself until twelve, when he retires for the night. His correspondence with England, and the Spanish and Portuguese governments, is very extensive.'

When not so close to Headquarters, the monotony of the days and long winter evenings was enlivened by a variety of harmless amusements, if the troops were not actively occupied.[47] On obtaining a brief leave of absence, Leach, with some of his comrades, set out early in January to Robledillo de Gata, in the snow-bound sierra south-east of El Bodón, where he had made the acquaintance of a Spanish family in the previous autumn, taking with them a mule loaded with a change of clothes, tea, sugar, cigars, meat, etc. Once arrived, having collected the village belles and a fiddler or two, they danced with great glee before inviting their partners back to their billets for supper. Some young clerics included in the invitation were jealous of the preference given by the local lasses to 'heretical Englishmen', and had showed it. After the girls had been escorted home, it was decided that the 'clericos', still hanging about the street, should be taught a lesson for their discourtesy by battering them from head to foot with a volley of snow-balls, which sent them scuttling for shelter. After which frolic, Leach and his chums floundered back through the snow next day to rejoin their battalion.

The district abounded in game, and Ensign Frederick Mainwaring (51st) indulged in coursing and shooting:

> In the evenings there was always a party at some one's quarters, where cigars, egg wine [egg-nog?], and good humour generally sent half of us tipsy to bed; three times a week a division club, established by the German Light Brigade in an empty convent, added to our amusements and brought us all together – here was music, dancing, and cards – a pharo bank for those who were disposed to lose their money – two military bands for the youngsters to dance to – and a sutler's room, where was every species of refreshment at most moderate prices. Many a wild mad scene have I been witness, and perhaps partaker of, at this club, but all was in perfect good humour, no arguments or strife, nothing but the ebullition of health and youth; our Generals and superior officers joined in and added to all our pleasures and hardships.

Wheeler, writing from Penamacor on 28 December, described having spent

> Christmas as comfortable as our situation would permit. The weather is very cold and we have had so much snow – the oldest people say they do not remember such a great fall.
>
> The house I am quartered in is neither built for comfort or convenience ...The ground floor, as is the case with all the houses here, is set apart for Horses, mules etc. The two next stories are for the accommodation of the inmates, the garrets of cocklofts (for there are no ceilings) is set apart for the servants, in one of these garrets the cooking is performed. A broad thick stone is placed in the corner on which the fire is made, no chimney to convey away the smoke, the only chance it has to escape is through a hole in the corner made by removing a couple of tiles. Generally, the place is so full of smoke you cannot see across the room, and as the fires are made of wood this is very disagreeable to the eyes.
>
> This fire was always occupied by the female part of the family. The mistress, an old shrivelled hag who had been smoke dried some sixty winters and would be a fit character for one of the witches in *Macbeth*, places herself on the right. Next to her are seated her three lovely daughters, real brunettes, with eyes as black as sloes. Then the servants, one of whom seems to be the sister of the old wi[th]ered hag in the opposite corner, and three others about the same age as the young ladies, but far from disagreeable, complete the group. Thus huddled together, each having their string of beads and crosses to charm the devil from them, they relate some horrid tale of a slaughtered friend by the enemy, or of some headless ghost, till their fears are worked up to such a pitch that the least noise frightens them. Then they count their beads, crosses themselves and repeat their Avi Maria till their fears are lulled to rest.
>
> On one of these occasions I forced myself into their company. Their remarks soon convinced me I was an unwelcome guest. I was a heretic, and they began to consign me body and soul to the Devil. I began to rake the embers for a cinder to light my pipe, but this was not my real intention. I had prepared a Devil with the powder of three cartridges and had placed it unperceived on the hearth. My comrade had got another in the other room, ready to start if wanted. I applied the fire to mine, up jumped the party, calling on Jesu, Maria and Joseph and all the Holy saints they could think up. The Devil burnt beautifully, it was a complete Mount Etna in Miniature. Away went the women into the other room as we had anticipated. There they found another Devil ready to receive them. From this they retreated down stairs, leaving the place strewed

> with beads crosses and slippers. Every night after this we were left in full possession of the fire, the ladies having provided themselves with charcoal fires in their own apartments.
>
> It is astonishing how the term 'heretic' sticks to the English. No good office can wipe out the foul stain, if you wish to come on terms of friendship you must pass for an Irishman. You then are considered as one of themselves, a good Christian.

In less wintery weather, pony, mule, and donkey races and point-to-points were organised; there were Regimental Dinners to attend; theatricals were held in buildings converted for the occasion. Schaumann remembered a large barn being 'transformed into a theatre, in which the officers acted, and the regimental bands provided the orchestra.'[48] 'In addition to Shakespeare's plays, many favourite English comedies were given. Many of the officers acted extremely well, and I saw one infantry subaltern in particular who as regards costume, mimicry, dancing and singing, impersonating a *prima donna* with such inimitable skill and comicality that he might without fear have appeared on any stage. All infantry brigades had their own messes. But if one happened to be invited to dinner with any one of them, the difficulties were two-fold: first of all, the long distances one had to go to reach them, and secondly, the return home in the dark when one was drunk. On the home journeys one either lost one's way, or plunged into an abyss or swamp, or else was scared by a wolf.'

At Covilhã, some distance further south-west, when headquarters of Sir Stapleton Cotton's Cavalry, 'barbarously brilliant' balls were held, the local females being passionately addicted to dancing. Schaumann, who obviously had an eye for the girls, commented ungallantly that as regards morals he had never come across 'such a Sodom and Gomorrrah as that place was. The girls and the women of the higher as well as the lower classes were practically all disreputable. Pure virgins were rare ...'

Inexplicably, on the first occasion that a Ball was proposed,[49] all the well-bred ladies in the vicinity had declined the invitions. During Junot's time, troops briefly occupying the place had given a dance to ingratiate themselves. To avoid any trouble being caused by refusing to attend, the wives of the local gentry had sent instead 'their chambermaids and other working-class girls ... decked in their mistresses' fine clothes and jewels'. Someone had revealed the ruse and, to avenge the affront, the French officers had arranged that at a blast of a trumpet the moment the quadrille was over, they 'would fall upon the women and overpower them – a plan which was actually carried out, amid the most terrifying shrieks.' Naturally, the genteel ladies of Covilhã suspected another such outrage, until reassured that the British would behave themselves, when they relented and tripped along to the ball, which was a great success. [50]

Once the band had struck up, and wine, punch and grog distributed, there was no holding them.

> Spanish, English and German dances were executed amid the most appalling tumult. The ladies were besides themselves with joy. Some of them, in order to facilitate their movements, had pinned up their dresses tightly in front of them, so as to outline their figures very sharply behind, while others had pinned them behind, producing the reverse effect. Everyone was extremely lively. Even our general, Sir Stapleton Cotton, our Quartermaster-General, Colonel Elley,[51] and our old Lieut.-Colonel v. Arentschildt, laid aside their gravity and danced *sarabandes* and *fandangoes* with the rest.
>
> While the whole throng were whirling round the ball-room, or looking on in open-mouthed wonder at the splendid scene, the servants and the children swarmed like locusts round the buffet, and, after stuffing themselves with all they could, actually began filling their pockets.

1 Already, in late March, Capt. Squire had reported on measures which might be taken to cross the Guadiana at Juromenha, dominating the river south-west of Elvas, where for lack of pontoons and boats – although seven flat-boats, transported on ox-drawn carriages, were en route from Abrantes, 84 miles distant – a trestle bridge was soon under construction. Troops were ready to cross, when the river rose, overturning the trestles. Oman refers to it as being a 'cask-bridge', perhaps floated on barrels?

2 This was probably that of Villarreal.

3 Wellington himself, when briefly visiting Beresford a fortnight later, thought that this village – some 15 miles south-east of Badajoz and close enough to prevent the entry of any material relief – would be 'the most central and advantageous place' to assemble his units when opposing any attempt by Soult to relieve the fortress. There were few defensive positions in this area of low-lying hills with the characteristics he would have preferred.

4 The British Army had not been supplied with any battering-train or heavy siege guns, nor would it be until that autumn. Several of those in the siege were brass 24-pounders dating back to the 17th century, taken from the walls of Elvas; nor were his gunners experienced. No two had the same bore, nor shot the same size, so shot had to be selected from a miscellaneous pile which might fit each gun!

5 Not far from the real numbers, which were 23,000 men: some 18,300 infantry and about 3,760 cavalry.

6 Beresford's army included 8,740 British and 9,100 Portuguese infantry, 1,150

British and 850 Portuguese cavalry, and 36 guns. He was joined by 13,900 Spaniards, among them 1,700 cavalry, commanded by Blake and Castaños, and 2 batteries of artillery: a total of some 30,000 infantry and 3,700 cavalry.

7 D'Urban states that on arrival, 'in spite of all instructions [they] took up wrong ground in the dark;' and it was not until 7.00 that they were properly deployed, due to 'their total want of all system of movement, and consequent unwieldiness.'

8 John Cooper mentioned that his companions were already 'weary and jaded ... with being on piquet duty near the city walls for thirty-six hours ... every one complaining of want of rest and sleep.'

9 Regrettably, Long had retreated precipitately in the face of Soult's advancing cavalry when attacked by them near Santa Marta – 'of a piece with his conduct upon more than one previous occasion,' in D'Urban's view – for which Beresford relieved him of his command, and placed the Allied cavalry in General Lumley's competent hands.

10 58 of their 80 officers and 1,190 of their 1,568 men were casualties or taken prisoner, with a high proportion killed to wounded; among the Buffs – the 1/3rd – 212 were slain, and 234 wounded. The enemy cavalry lost 200 out of 880.

11 56 of the 95 officers and 971 of the 1,556 men present in Hoghton's Brigade were either killed or wounded, notably among the 1/57th.

12 Myers himself was killed, and 1,045 of his 2,015 officers and men were casualties in this action. It is hard to estimate what proportion were likely to succumb to their wounds, but it should not be minimized.

13 Despite the appalling losses sustained by the brigades of Colborne, Hoghton, and Myers, Sherer was of the opinion that with the belated arrival of Kemmis's, Beresford could have pressed the counter-attack, and had Wellington commanded, 'he would have altogether destroyed the army of Soult, and captured the whole of his matériel.'

14 French casualties have been estimated at between 7,000 and 8,000 men. Almost 100 prisoners were made in a skilful cavalry action at Usagre (north-west of Llerena) a week later, when Soult's rearguard was attacked by Lumley.

Allied losses totalled about 5,900, of which a disproportionate number – over 4,000 – were suffered by the 8,300 British infantry taking part in the battle. Compared to the slight Portuguese losses, casualties among the Spanish troops – referred to by D'Urban as having 'behaved gallantly but [which] were so devoid of discipline that they stood in the way and did more harm than good' – were heavy. Wellington, writing to his brother Henry on 22 May, commented that while the Spaniards may have behaved admirably, from what he had understood, they had also stood like 'stocks, both parties at times firing upon them, [being] quite immoveable, and this is the great cause of all our losses ... [They] can do nothing but stand still, and we consider ourselves fortunate if they do not run away.'

As Graham sarcastically remarked when writing to Lord Liverpool on 27 May: 'The news of the victory ... has filled the minds of the people ... with the most determined belief of the superiority of the Spanish army, which now in the public opinion neither admits of nor requires improvement, being already perfect. Without being a witness to this unfortunate national egoism ... it is not to be believed, nor would anyone image it possible that people of all ranks should be so ready to deceive themselves and others. Instead of a grateful and generous feeling of sympathy for the loss of the British troops at Albuera, the people here universally believe that it is purposely exaggerated … and that at all events the safety of the British and Portuguese was entirely owing to the intrepidity of the Spanish soldiers, and the activity and judgement of their leaders,' as one Spanish 'Gazette' had the audacity to claim.

15 Some four months later, Sherer happened to pass through the village to rejoin his regiment at Zafra, by which time, 'Not a vestige of that memorable battle remained ... the grass grew thick and strong, and wild flowers were springing from the turf'; while scrawled on the chapel wall were the words: 'La Guerre en Espagne est la Fortune des Généraux, l'Ennui des Officiers, et le Tombeau des Soldats.'

However, in the following April, Wheeler, when encamped nearby, remarked that it still presented traces of the battle: 'In some places large fires had been made, no doubt to burn the dead, again in other places are long ridges or Burrows [barrows] where some have been buried – of this there can be no doubt for here and there is visible an arm or leg projecting out of the earth. The place is completely strewed with broken shells, breast plates, pouches, scabbards and caps, both of French and English.'

16 Guthrie deserves more recognition for his services, having designed a new type of splint, innovated surgical methods to reduce the need for amputation, and improved techniques for controlling haemorrhages; but, as he later recalled, 'It was only at the last battle of Toulouse that the surgery of the British army approached perfection. There were even there one or two mistakes. Another campaign in the south of France would have made us perfect.'

17 Writing to his brother William on 2 July, Wellington had remarked: 'The battle of Albuera was a strange concern. They were never determined to fight it; they did it to occupy the ground as they ought; they were ready to run away at every moment from the time it commenced till the French retired; and if it had not been for me, who am now suffering from the loss and disorganization occasioned by the battle, they would have written a whining report upon it, which would have driven the people of England mad. However, I prevented that.'

18 This was also partly to recuperate from his traumatic experience at La Albuera, but Wellington still relied on him not only to keep the Portuguese up to the mark in training, but also to bring some order into the state of their Commissariat and Financial Departments.

19 Beresford's deployment of troops and the apparent lack of unified command during the contest were subjects of controversy and recrimination for decades, notably after the publication of the third volume in Napier's *History*, although it might perhaps be emphasised that its author, who had a personal grudge against Beresford, had neither taken part in the battle nor visited the battlefield.

20 It was not until July that a contingent provided by Admiral Berkeley had floated up several flat-boats up the Tagus from Abrantes and then dragged laboriously over rapids, that any provisional bridge was in place at the Vila Velha crossing, later replaced by pontoons.

21 From repeated firing and subsequent overheating, the muzzles of the old brass guns soon started drooping, 'unbushing' or the blowing out of the vent or touch-hole, through which the propellant charge within the gun was fired.

22 It should be emphasised that the Ordnance Department had virtually no

experience of conducting a siege since the campaign of 1793, when investing Dunkirk; neither had Wellington been provided with any trained engineers to supervise the necessary sapping and mining.

23 The position was strong, but unpleasant, as described by Schaumann: 'All day long we were infested by snakes, blowflies, and other vermin, while our water came from a dirty stream known as the river Caya, in which the whole army bathed, the cattle went to drink, and dirty clothes were washed. At night we were plagued by scorpions, mosquitoes, and a piercingly cold wind.'

24 This consisted of thirty-four 24-pounders, and four 18-punders; eight 10-inch mortars, and ten 5½-inch mortars; two 8-inch howitzers, and twenty 5½-inch howitzers.

25 On one occasion, Marmont, by making a feint, had imposed on Spencer to the extent of causing him to destroy supplies and blow up some of Almeida's partly restored defences.

26 At a later date, Viseu, São João de Pesqueira, and Santa Comba Dão are also referred to as depots between the Mondego and Douro.

27 John Daniel, stopping at a wayside house en route to Portalegre, records a not uncommon experience, when enquiring for shelter, of it being refused 'under the plea of there being a doente or sick person in the house with an infectious fever; but we were too much accustomed to hear this excuse to be alarmed, and after a little altercation with the old woman we were admitted, and the four of us slept upon the floor in the kitchen, in our blankets or boat-cloaks.'

28 John Cooke, later visiting the site, remarked that the ground near their position was 'so steep that the Portuguese, while throwing balls into the valley, could not see the advance of the French cavalry until they were upon them. Not that I wish to detract from the deserts of the Portuguese but, as it has been stated that they stood to their guns to the last, I only wish to demonstrate how it happened.

...The whole of the dead French soldiers lying in the valley were stripped and in a perfect state of preservation, blanched like parchment by the alternate rain and sunshine. Their skins had become so hard that the bodies, on being touched, sounded like a drum. The vultures had picked the bones of the horses perfectly clean, but had left the soldiers untouched. Although four months had elapsed since they had fallen, their features were as perfect as on the day they were killed. Some of these soldiers were gracefully proportioned, and extended in every possible attitude.'

29 According to Alexander Gordon, if it had not been for him, Wellington might have been taken prisoner during this action. Apparently, although Wellington admitted to this in public, he seems to have overlooked thanking Gordon himself, which provoked the petulent comment that Wellington had 'no idea of gratitude, favour, or affection, and cares not for anyone however much he may owe to him or find him useful.' It was certainly not in his character to be demonstrative; and yet when writing to Lord Aberdeen after his death at Waterloo, Wellington was the first to acknowledge that Gordon had served him zealously for many years and on many trying occasions.'

30 Tomkinson later noted in his Diary that 'on burying an officer of the Fuzileer Brigade, there was no Prayer-Book to read the service from. Lieutenant George Brown, of the 23rd Regiment, stepped forward and repeated the service from recollection, and with exactness.'

31 During this action, Colonel Felton Hervey, who had lost an arm at Oporto, was about to be cut down by a French cavalry officer, but immediately perceiving

that his antagonist had one arm, brought up his sword in the usual salute and rode past, one of many examples of chivalrous conduct still displayed between the combatants.

32 It is said that when Craufurd – who had not made a night march as expected – reported his belated arrival, Wellington remarked with some asperity, 'I am glad to see you safe,' to which Craufurd nonchalantly replied, 'Oh! I was in no danger, I assure you.' When Wellington rejoined: 'But I was, from your conduct,' Craufurd was heard to mutter, 'He's damned crusty today.'

33 Writing on 14 September, Borgoyne confirmed that he was then busily occupied 'training 200 men of different regiments to the duties required in a siege, which, to our disgrace and misfortune, we have no regular establishment equal to, notwithstanding the repeated experience of the absolute necessity of such a corps to act under the Engineers in a campaign.' In view of 'our bad success in our last,' it would be hazardous indeed to undertake the siege of Ciudad Rodrigo without appropriate preparation.

34 When en route to the front, Bragge was quartered briefly at Abrantes, where, not yet acclimatised, nor used to drinking wine, he described the troops as having been 'extremely ill and I'm sorry to say still continue falling sick of the Flux, but many have been completely cured by our giving them Dr Moncrieffe's Proscription [sic] and I'm going to purchase all the Tinct[ture]. of Rhubarb in the Town, which will scarcely fill a Half Pint Bottle.'

35 'Gentleman Jackson' or John Jackson (1769–1845), champion of England in 1795–1803, had opened a boxing-school in Bond Street.

36 The Spanish lynx or *Gato montés*. But as he added: 'I have bought a skin of the latter which I will send you as a curiosity. I saw none of these animals; but in very cold weather, when they are pinched for food, they descend from their haunts to the great annoyance of the villagers, and carry off cattle, and any domestic animals that have the misfortune to be within their reach ...'

37 Almost 1,300 prisoners were taken, together with all their baggage, three guns, and 5,000 dollars levied at Cáceres only days before. Hill's casualties were minimal (64 wounded and 7 killed), while those of Penne Villamur, commanding Spanish cavalry, were about 30.

38 Bragge, reporting the event from Castelo Branco on 1 November, wrote: 'We yesterday heard of General Hill's success but till within these 3 days never knew of his having left Portalegre, although we halted for 2 Days a short distance from it. The Officer who went through Castelo Branco had himself counted 1,000 Prisoners, amongst whom were a German Prince (I believe, Darenburgh) and also one General Officer [Bron].' It was Blakeney who was later to escort D'Arenberg to Lisbon.

39 Renouard, who was Swiss, had a brother who was Vice Master of Trinity College, Cambridge.

40 Billets were by no means always available. Lieut. James Hope recorded that at one period, during the 181 days a campaign had lasted, he had only slept thirteen nights under a roof. But very often there was not a solitary habitation nor even a single goat to be seen. And, wherever it might be, one would have to keep a look-out for scorpions or the occasional snake; while at certain seasons, apart from being infested by ants and fleas, among other insects, one was likely to be teased by clouds of gnats and midges or – particularly near the lazily flowing Guadiana – attacked by mosquitoes.

41 One of the main general hospitals was then at Celorico, down in the Mondego valley north-west of Guarda, but with overcrowded buildings and a staff overwhelmed with work, mortality was high. Cornet Francis Hall (14th Light Dragoons) was not far wrong when stating: 'It is at a hospital station and not on a field of battle that the calamities of war are best estimated', for during that Autumn at Celorico alone, 'from 50 to 100 men were buried daily', and even after he arrived there in the winter, 'from ten to twenty corpses were carried daily through the streets ... and flung into a hole, which constituted a common receptacle without the town.'

42 Daniel suggest that over 600 carts were constructed at Lisbon, Oporto, and Almeida, but in this figure he may well have been including those imported from England.

43 By the beginning of 1812 there were 87 commissaries and 255 clerks employed by the Commissary-General in the Peninsula, not taking any account of storekeepers, conductors, bakers, coopers, blacksmiths and farriers, carpenters and wheelwrights, et al, and these numbers would increase during the next next two years.

44 Surtees, writing several months later, remarked that greater losses among mounts were suffered by the 'want of farriers or horse-shoers in the regiments, than from almost any other cause,' but he was referring to those of officers in infantry regiments, implying that the staff and general officers employed most of the 'good shoers.'

45 It was dismantled after Ciudad Rodrigo had fallen, and stored at Almeida, as described in Chapter 7 of *Inside Wellington's Peninsular Army*.

46 With occasional intervals, Freineda remained Wellington's winter Headquarters from 2 October 1811 until 5 March 1812, and again from 22 November 1812 until 22 May 1813.

47 Daniel describe the troops in the villages nearest to Ciudad Rodrigo being 'employed in making facines and gabions, for which they received a small gratuity.'

48 Burgoyne refers to officers of the Light Division acting plays in a chapel at Gallegos, which 'contrary to the predictions of the old priest there, did not fall down on their heads, and crush them to death.'

49 Getting up a dance, whether a local hop or a more substantial affair, would appear to have been a regular form of entertainment. John Mills, writing from Los Santos, near Zafra, on 25 March 1812, refers to having 'had balls every night since we have been here. The Spaniards, though very anxious to come to them, are so afraid that the French on their return should know they favoured us with their company, that instead of an invitation we give them an order, or in other words, embargo them.'

50 On another occasion (in 1813), an anonymous writer, after describing a race meeting held by the 7th Division, mentions that 'the officers all sat down to a handsome dinner and then attended a grand ball, for which the local ladies had, strange to relate, been specially provided with shoes and stockings.'

51 In fact Lieut-Colonel Sir John Elley of the Adjutant-General's Department, but attached to the Cavalry.

9

January to April 1812: The fall of Ciudad Rodrigo, and Badajoz

On 8 January, with the ruse of widely publicising the fact that 'field sports' would be taking place on that day at Fuenteguinaldo, the 2,000 strong French garrison of Ciudad Rodrigo were surprised to find themselves tightly re-invested. Although surrounded by massive masonry walls and substantial outworks, these could not resist artillery for long, and Wellington's siege-train was now at hand.

The fortress occupied the entire flat summit of a hill on which an ancient castle dominated a bridge of Roman foundation spanning the Agueda, crossed here by the former highway from Salamanca to Almeida. Its main weakness was the proximity of two connected heights some 700 yards north of the enceinte; the more distant Greater Teson rising 14 feet higher than the walls. In the summer of 1810, when the stronghold had resisted the French for twenty-five days, they had placed batteries both there and on the closer Lesser Teson. These had breached the walls, and the counterscarp had been blown in by a mine. Once in their hands, they had repaired the walls, filled in the parallels excavated between the Tesons, and constructed a strong redoubt on the Greater. Masséna's siege train, together with abundant ammunition, remained within the fortress.

Wellington's aim was to occupy the Greater Teson first, and on the night of the 8th it was attacked by ten companies of the Light Division under Colborne, which approached to within 50 yards before their presence was discovered. Encircling the works, and lying prone on the glacis, four companies fired on any head showing above the wall. Four more descended into the ditch, set their ladders against the inner wall and clambered in, while the last two burst through the rear palisade.[1]

Trenches, to a large extent following the lines of those dug by the French, were then excavated in the frozen earth despite heavy fire from the walls. Working parties, 180 rank and file from the 3rd Division, who had received some training as sappers and miners, did duty in three shifts. Donaldson, taking his turn, remembered the frost being 'so excessive that we were almost completely benumbed, and nothing but hard working, I believe, kept us from perishing with the cold; indeed, it is said that some Portuguese soldiers actually died from its effects.'[2] Already, in mid December, Burgoyne had been supervising the preparation of gabions, fascines, stakes for forming palisades, and cutting planks for platforms, which were loaded onto cars. Bags stuffed with hay were also supplied: they provided a painless landing to those jumping into deep defensive ditches.

On the afternoon of the 13th, Allied guns opened fire, and in fierce night fighting the French were evicted from the outlying convent of Santa Cruz, immediately west of the walls. Donaldson continued:

> On the 14th, the batteries in the first parallel were formed, and commenced firing from twenty-two pieces of cannon; that same night the fourth division carried all the remaining outworks, and we were established in the second parallel, one hundred and fifty yards from the town, on the 15th ... The French kept up a very destructive fire on us during the whole of our operations, and ... they threw out some fire balls to enable them to see where we were working, that they might send their shot in that direction; one of them fell very near where a party were working, and by its light completely exposed them to the view of the enemy; a sergeant belonging to our regiment, of the name of Frazer, seeing the danger ... seized a spade, and jumping out of the trench, regardless of the enemy's fire, ran forward to where it was burning, and having dug a hole, tumbled it in and covered it with earth.

The garrison made a brief sortie that day, while the Allies bombarded the convent of San Francisco in the northern suburbs, which was then abandoned. A thick fog descended on the town on the 16th, allowing further progress to be made in digging a second parallel, which more closely approached the walls. Pits were also dug, from which marksmen could pick off enemy gunners more effectively.

By the 19th,[3] two breaches had been made: the larger where the masonry had been weakened previously; the smaller some 250 yards further east.[4] Both appeared practicable, although the approaches to them were steeper than one might wish. The plan of assault, to take place that night, was as follows:

Picton's 3rd Division would attack the main breach, preceded by two subordinate attacks. Colonel O'Toole's 2nd *Caçadores* and the Light

Company of the 2/83rd would cross the Agueda bridge, escalade the outworks in front of the castle, and take the two guns enfilading the main wall facing west. The 2/5th of Campbell's Brigade would advance from behind the Santa Cruz convent towards the river, where they would scale the outer wall there, enter the main ditch, and sweep north towards the breach, while the 94th would attack outworks further north and turn north, clearing the outer ditch and overpowering any troops occupying ravelins bearing on the breach. The remaining nine companies of the 2/83rd, manning the western section of the second parallel, would fire on the main walls, while Henry Mackinnon's Brigade stormed the breach from the eastern section, their place being taken by Power's Portuguese. Mackinnon would be supported by three companies of riflemen to his left, who would keep up a brisk fire on the walls at close range after clearing neighbouring ravelins.

The Lesser Breach would be stormed by Vandeleur's Brigade of the Light Division, advancing from behind the San Francisco convent, closely supported by Barnard's Brigade, while Pack's Portuguese would cause a diversion by attacking the wall to the south-east, which, if successful, could be pressed home.

At 6.50 on the evening of the 19th, O'Toole's men crossed the Agueda and soon attained their objectives, while the 2/5th – accompanied in error by the 77th (which should have remained in reserve) – did likewise, on reaching the breach being joined by the 94th. Donaldson described his regiment,

> having formed behind the walls of an old convent, each section being provided with a pick-axe and rope ... advanced rank entire under a heavy fire from the garrison, to the brink of the trench, where planting the one end of the pick-axe firmly in the ground, we threw the noose of the rope over the other, and then descended by it into the ditch. After descending, we moved along towards the breach. Our orders were to remain there, and protect the right brigade; but our colonel finding no obstacle in the way, pushed up the breach, leading his regiment to the attack; the 5th regiment, which also belonged to the covering party, joined us as we ascended, and together we succeeded in establishing ourselves on the ramparts, in spite of the obstinate resistance ....

In the event, these units of Campbell's Brigade scrambled up the debris before Mackinnon's men, but both brigades were stopped short at the summit, for the French had cut two 10-foot wide and 10-foot deep trenches across the masonry terreplein behind, thus isolating the breach. The Allied position was precarious, for among unexpected hazards they found themselves facing were breast-works constructed at right-angles to the trenches, each mounting a howitzer, from which a sharp fire was kept up. To reach this newly-erected interior semi-circular wall, a 16-foot drop into the main ditch, paved with sundry sharp obstacles, had to be first negotiated.

The survivors of the 'forlorn hope' of the 88th had got this far, having silenced the howitzers,[5] when a mine placed directly below the breach was exploded, with disastrous effect, blowing up substantial numbers of the 3rd Division now entering it, including Mackinnon himself. But the mine had been too powerful, for it not only killed many of the defenders, but further weakened and widened the breach, allowing the remainder of the two brigades involved in the storm to advance directly into the fortress and along its walls.

Meanwhile, the Light Division had stormed the Lesser Breach comparatively unscathed, although both Vandeleur and Craufurd were wounded, the latter fatally and, having cleared the walls in its vicinity, they forced its defenders back into the town. By now, other sectors had been entered by Pack's and O'Toole's men, and the garrison surrendered without much further fighting.[6]

Regrettably, many of those who had taken part in the storming, then ran amok: several buildings were set alight, and it was some time before discipline was restored among the more intoxicated and insubordinate. According to Donaldson, among the prisoners taken 'were eighteen deserters ... who were subsequently tried and shot. The town was partially plundered by those who had straggled from their regiments, but the different columns remained formed on the ramparts until day-light, when a party from each regiment were sent to bury the dead, and collect the wounded ...'

Bragge, writing home on the 20th from Aldeia da Ponte (14 miles south-west), described having distinctly heard the bombardment; but almost immediately after the fall of the fortress, due to the shortage of forage, the cavalry was marched west, and within four days Bragge found himself 'detached with a Newgate Crew to a Village ... absolutely buried amidst the Mountains of Estrêla.'[7]

Partly due to the scarcity of forage, Bragge was obliged to make a long and circuitous ride south, during which, as he remarked, 'the variety of Lodgings I get into on a March is really amusing; at Sabugal My Bed was composed of a Pillow, a Rug, *two dirty Petticoats* and Two large Towels ... I got some Lice of course ...'

By mid March, he had reached Borba, a small town,

> more delightfully *clean* and neat than any thing we see in England, every House and Cottage nicely Whitewashed within and without, all the Churches and Public Buildings standing detatched, the Streets very wide and not a Bit of Filth to be seen, whilst the Pots and Pans, highly polished and arranged in order over a good Fire Place, render every Cottage in the Alentejo a more desirable Residence than the most sumptuous Houses North of the Tagus. Estremoz is the only Town of considerable Note we had to pass through … a most beautiful place, although surrounded with a Nest of Massive Walls and ditches. I saw there 16 Twenty Four Pounders on their Road to Badajoz, which together with as many more of the same Calibre form only a Part of the immense Train destined for the Reduction of that Place …
>
> Genl. Le Marchant has his whole Brigade within reach of him and has therefore begun playing Soldiers in order to prove the efficiency of some miserable awkward Manoeuvres which he has himself been coining.[8] I have no doubt they all occurred to Sir David but were rejected for others infinitely superior.[9] Be that as it may, our Schoolmaster had the three Regts out yesterday and would I have no doubt treat us with more Field Days should opportunities offer themselves.

While Ciudad Rodrigo's breaches were being repaired, trenches filled, the place re-victualled and an adequate Spanish garrison installed, the main Allied army proceeded south towards Badajoz. Beresford took the opportunity to make a brief visit to Lisbon, where, in D'Urban's words, 'His appearance was indispensably necessary, for many arrangements with the Government, and to ascertain the actual proportion of our Means to our Expenditure; an investigation, which strange to say, has never been fully entered into hitherto, and which now becomes imperiously necessary, for the Machine, after many expedients to keep it going, at length defies them altogether, as might well be forseen, and threatening to stop altogether. Pay, Provisions, Transport, all wanting – all in ruins.'

Second siege of Badajoz

Wellington now turned his concentrated attention on Badajoz, predictably a harder nut to crack, for its defences were more formidable, and it had a larger garrison – some 4,500 effectives – commanded by the resourceful General Phillipon. Iron guns were ordered forward to Elvas, together with recently arrived reinforcements from Lisbon and additional Portuguese troops under Beresford. By 26 February the majority of the Allied units at Ciudad Rodrigo, with the exception of the 5th Division and the K.G.L., were proceeding south along familiar roads;[10] but, to confuse the enemy, Wellington himself did not follow them until the 6th of March, by which time he had almost 60,000 men in the southern corridor. Of this number, 19,000 under Graham advanced towards D'Erlon, commanding much weaker units in the area, who in the face of this concentration, retired south, leaving Badajoz to its own devices. Graham would also be keeping a weather eye on Soult, while Hill, with 14,000 men, pushed east towards Mérida, should Marmont approach from that direction.

Daniel remembers seeing the 4th Division marching out of Elvas at break of day on the 16th March 'in grand procession towards Badajoz, the baggage, ammunition, facines, gabions, entrenching-tools, and all the apparatus for a siege following the troops through the plain. The scene was so interesting that hundreds of spectators had assembled ...on the ramparts ...' The fortress was reinvested next day.

Since the previous June, the French had connected the southern outwork of Pardaleras with the town walls, and also reinforced those between that fort and the river; to the south-east, the Rivillas (a minor tributary of the Guadiana) had been dammed to form an inundation, beyond which Fort Picurina had been strengthened. A French sapper sergeant deserting to the Allies had brought plans indicating the position of recently placed mines, which partly decided Wellington to attack the fortress from the south-east, between the Santa María and Trinidad bastions, which lay behind the Picurina outwork. It was near this, supervised by Colonel Fletcher, that working parties began to dig a parallel and communication trenches. On one occasion, when a sortie interrupted their excavations, William Lawrence killed a French sergeant.

> I was in the trenches and he came on the top. Like me, he had exhausted his fire and so made a thrust at me with his bayonet. He overbalanced and fell, and I pinioned him to the ground with mine. The poor fellow expired. I was sorry afterwards and wished I had tried to take him prisoner, but with the fighting going on all around there had been no time to think, and he had been a powerful-looking man ... If I had allowed him to gain his feet, I might have suffered for it, so perhaps what I did was for the best? At such times it is a matter of kill or be killed.
>
> In case of another attack, a large number of men afterwards formed a covering party for the 800 of us who were busy in the trenches every

night. And it still rained. The trenches were so muddy that our shoes were covered. It poured down so fast that, in places, balers had to be employed.

One night ... just as the guard was about to be relieved, a shell from the town fell amongst us and exploded, killing and wounding about 30 men. The next morning a terrible scene presented itself to us, for the remains of our mangled comrades strewed the ground in all directions. I never saw a worse sight of its kind. Some of them had their arms and legs – and what is worse, their heads – completely severed from the bodies.

To counter these operations, Phillipon extended earthworks eastwards from Fort San Cristóbal, on the right bank of the river, from which the Allied parallel could be enfiladed, but these were abandoned once Leith's 5th Division had invested that fort on the 22nd, on which afternoon a storm flooded the Allies' trenches and their pontoon bridge was swept away, temporarily separating several units.[11] The weather had cleared sufficiently by the 25th to allow 28 heavy guns to open fire,[12] largely against the Picurina, which was stormed by a detachment of the 3rd Division. Kincaid describes a string of Portuguese militia, reaching almost from Elvas to Badajoz, each man carrying a 24-pound shot, and 'cursing all the way and back again.'

Surgeon Walter Henry, en route to join the 66th Foot at Mérida, on reaching Alburquerque, then the site of a depot supplying Hill's troops, noticed that 'all the world was out on the walls of the castle (situated on a high hill) to witness the exciting spectacle' of the cannonading of Badajoz, for 'although twenty miles distant, every shot could be heard distinctly; and at first, before a broad pall of smoke covered besiegers and besieged, every thing going on could be seen with a glass. When I mounted to the castle, after breakfast, I found a great crowd of well dressed spectators with many ladies. Deep interest was painted on every countenance; and no wonder, for many of those now assembled were inhabitants of Badajoz, and had obtained permission ... to quit the city when it was first invested; leaving their homes, and some their husbands and families, behind.'

By the 30th there were 38 guns battering the walls.[13] Meanwhile, Henry had been ordered to take charge of a batch of wounded from Mérida into Portugal, making a detour to the north of Badajoz.

The convoy consisted of one hundred and twenty sick, thirty or forty of whom were so ill or had continued or remittent fevers, that it was necessary too tie them on the mules' backs, lest they should fall off

> through weakness. Others were supported by men of the escort sitting behind them; but by the end of the second day's march these enfeebled subjects would ride by themselves bravely and vigorously, and call out lustily for rations. I am convinced that the lives of several amongst them were saved by this march, and the recovery of the rest was materially accelerated. To be sure ours was a march cheered by the most exciting military music all the way; and the sound of the twenty-four pounder salvos, with the occasional glimpse of the smoke-wreathed city, formed a cordial more tonic and stimulating and restorative than all the elixirs in the world.
>
> On the 6th of April, the last day of our march, the cannonade was much louder and closer than usual, and as I rode along I became more and more convinced that a crisis was approaching. On our arrival in the evening, at Campo Mayor, we found the whole population in a state of intense excitement and anxiety. It was known generally that Badajoz was to be stormed during the night; and as we were only seven miles distant, even the pattering of the musketry could be distinctly heard in the calm of the evening, between the heavy reports of the battering artillery.

The three breaches made between the Santa María and Trinidad bastions were now practicable As time was running out – for intelligence had also reached Wellington to the effect that Marmont was threatening Ciudad Rodrigo – he determined on assaulting the place at 10.00 that same evening.

The Light and 4th Divisions would storm the two outer breaches; Picton's 3rd would escalade the castle, while Leith's 5th would assault the San Vicente bastion on the west side of the fortress, abutting the river. Major Wilson with the 1/48th would make a feint attack on the San Roche lunette protecting the dam forming the flooded area north of the Picurina fort, while Portuguese units attacked the bridgehead on the right bank of the Guadiana. The advance of the Light and 4th Divisions, approaching the breaches from the south, was soon revealed by the glare of fire-balls, exposing them to a hail of bullets, grenades, and other combustables, while their guns swept the ditches. Having run that gauntlet, they found that the debris knocked down from the breaches into the water-filled ditch had been cleared away, and that the breaches themselves were protected by an elaborate *chevaux-de-frise* constructed with sharpened bayonets and sword-blades chained to the ground and to heavy beams bristling with spikes. A hail of bullets cut swathes among the compact masses struggling up the steep ascent and vainly attempting to force their way past through these obstructions.

The ramparts were lined with live shells and barrels of powder, cart wheels, and other projectiles in readiness to hurl down into the ditch. Another encumbrance was the mounting heaps of dead, dying and wounded, for the carnage was horrific.

The author has no wish to welter in gore, enough being provided in the more literate descriptions of the storm penned by surviving participants: among them was John Cooper, with Bowes's Brigade (4th Div.), who recalled receiving orders at 9.00 that evening to

> 'Pile knapsacks by companies,' 'fall in, and move off silently.' The night was dark, the town was still, while our batteries kept thundering away at the breach.
>
> When our men had approached within 300 yards of the ditch, up went a fire ball. This showed the crowded state of the ramparts, and the bright arms of our approaching columns. Those men who carried grass bags to fill up the ditch, and ladders for escalading the walls,[14] were now hurried forward. Instantly the rampart was in a blaze; mortars, canon, and muskets, roared and rattled unceasingly. Mines ever and anon blew up with a horrid noise. To add to this horrible din, there were the soundings of bugles, the rattling of drums, and the shouting of the combatants. Through a tremendous fire our men rushed to the top of the glacis, down the ladders, and up the breach. The entrance was impossible, for across the horrid gap the enemy had placed, in spite of our fire, a strong beam full of sword blades, etc., forming a chevaux de frise, behind which, intrenched, stood many ranks of soldiers, whose fire swept the breach from end to end.[15] Besides, the top of the parapet was covered with shells, stones, sand bags, and logs of wood, etc., ready to throw down into the ditch. As the breaches could not be forced, and as our men kept pouring down the ladders, the whole ditch was soon filled with a dense mass which could neither advance or retreat. Upon these the enemy threw the missiles from the parapet, with a continuous fire of musketry and round shot. My comrade was killed while descending a ladder. Some men went further to the right, and jumped into that part of the ditch that was filled with water, and were drowned.

William Lawrence, with Kemmis's Brigade, and one of the ladder party, remembered when

> at the breach, a French sentry on the wall cried out three times, 'Who comes there?' No answer being given, a shower of shot, canister and grape, together with fire-balls, was hurled amongst us … and I received

two small slug shots in my left knee and a musket shot in my side. Despite my wounds, I stuck to my ladder and got into the entrenchment. By now, many had fallen, but on the cry of 'Come on, my lads!' from our commanders, we hastened to the breach. There, to our dismay, we encountered a *cheval de frise* and a deep entrenchment, from behind which the garrison opened a deadly fire on us. The *cheval de frise*, was a fearful obstacle and although attempts were made to remove it – my left hand was dreadfully cut by one of the blades – we had no success. We were forced to retire for a time and remained in the breach weary with our efforts to pass it.

My wounds were bleeding and I began to feel weak. My comrades persuaded me to go to the rear, but it was difficult because, when I arrived at the ladders, they were filled with the dead and wounded. Some were hanging where they had fallen, with their feet caught in the rounds [rungs], and all around I could hear the implorings of the wounded. I hove down three lots of ladders, and on coming to the fourth, I found it completely smothered with dead bodies. I drew myself up over them as best I could and arrived at the top. There I almost wished myself back again, for what greeted me was an even worse sight – nothing but dead lying all around, and the cries of the wounded mingled with the incessant firing from the fort.

I was so weak I could hardly walk; on my hands and knees I crawled out of reach of the enemy's musketry. I hadn't gone far when I encountered Lord Wellington and his staff. He wanted to know the extent of my wounds and what regiment I belonged to.

'The Fortieth,' I said, and told him I had been one of the forlorn hope. He enquired whether any of our troops had got into the town. I told him no, and that I did not think they ever would ... One of his staff bound my leg with a silk handkerchief and, pointing to a hill, told me that behind it I would find a doctor to dress my wounds. I was lucky – the musket shot in my side would have been fatal had it not penetrated my canteen first, making a hole going in and coming out.

After I arrived, Lieutenant Elland was brought in by a man called Charles Filer, who had found him at the breach, lying wounded with a ball in his thigh. The lieutenant had asked to be conveyed from the breach so Filer had raised him onto his shoulders. The night was dark, and the clamour of cannon and musketry and the cries of the wounded so noisy, that Filer did not notice when a cannon-ball took the lieutenant's head off, so he was astonished when the surgeon asked why he had brought in a headless trunk? Filer declared that the lieutenant had had a head on when he had found him, for how else could he have asked to be taken from the breach?

Donaldson, with the 3rd Division, recalled that

> not a single star shewed its head; the air was still, not a sound could be heard but the noise of the field cricket, and the croaking of frogs; every word of command was given in a whisper, and the strictest silence enjoined, which I believe was unnecessary; few felt inclined to speak. At last the order was given to advance, and with palpitating hearts we commenced our march – slow and silent, a dead-weight hanging on every mind; had we been brought hurriedly into action, it would have been different, but it is inconsistent with the nature of man not to feel as I have described, in such a situation ... Yet this feeling was not the result of want of courage; for I never witnessed any thing like the calm intrepidity displayed in the advance, after we came within range of the enemy's cannon. ... we reached a sort of moat about fifty feet wide, formed by the inundation of the river; here we had to pass, rank entire, the passage being only capable of admitting one at a time. On this place the enemy had brought their guns to bear, and the kept up such a fire of grape and musketry on it, that it was a miracle any of us escaped. When we reached the other side we formed again, and advanced up the glacis, forcing our way through the pallisades, and got down into the ditch. The ladders by which we had to escalade the castle were not yet brought up, and the men were huddled on one another in such a manner that we could not move; we were now ordered to fix bayonets. When we first entered the trench, we considered ourselves comparatively safe, thinking we were out of range of their shot, but we were soon convinced of our mistake, for they opened several guns from angles which commanded the trench, and poured in grape shot upon us from each side, every shot of which took effect, and every volley of which was succeeded by the dying groans of those who fell. Our situation at this time was truly appalling. The attack had commenced at the breaches towards our left, and the cannon and musketry which played upon our troops from every quarter of the town attacked, kept up a continuous roll of thunder, and their incessant flash one quivering sheet of lightning; to add to the awfulness of the scene, a mine was sprung at the breach, which carried up in its dreadful blaze the mangled limbs and bodies of many of our comrades.
>
> When the ladders were placed, each eager to mount, crowded them in such a way that many of them broke, and the poor fellows who had nearly reached the top, were precipitated a height of thirty or forty feet, and impaled on the bayonets of their comrades below; other ladders were pushed aside by the enemy on the walls, and fell with a crash on those in the ditch; while those who got to the top without accident were

> shot on reaching the parapet, and tumbling headlong, brought down those beneath them. This continued for some time, until at length a few having made a landing good on the ramparts, at the expense of their lives, enabled a greater number to follow. When about a company had thus got collected together, we formed and charged round the ramparts, bayoneting the French artillery at their guns. In the direction taken by the party I was with, they had drawn out a howitzer loaded to the very muzzle, pointed it towards us, and a gunner had the match ready to fire, when he was brought down by one of our party; in this direction we charged until we reached the sally-port communicating with the town. In a short time the whole division were established in possession of the castle …

The survivors of the two divisions taking part in the assault were now retired and reformed for a second assault, made by clambering over the bodies of the fallen; but this time they were able to penetrate the breach without much opposition, partly due to secondary attacks proving effective. Blakeney recalled catching sight of Wellington and his staff 'behind a rising mound', which although within range of shells, screened them from direct fire. 'One of his staff sat down by his side with a candle to enable the general to read and write all his communications and orders relative to the passing events. I stood not far from his lordship. But due respect prevented any of us bystanders from approaching so near as to enable us to ascertain the import of reports which he was continually receiving; yet it was very evident that the information which they conveyed was far from flattering; and the recall on the bugles was again and again repeated. But about half-past eleven o'clock an officer rode up at full speed on a horse covered with foam, and announced the joyful tidings that General Picton had made a lodgement within the castle by escalade …' [16]

The 3rd Division had suffered heavily – Picton himself was wounded – and in the confusion they had fired momentarily on the 5th which, although meeting desparate resistance, had broken into the town belatedly from the far side after escalading the bastion of San Vicente. Those defending the breaches, finding themselves attacked from the rear, surrendered. Phillipon, with the remainder of the garrison, retreated across the Guadiana bridge to Fort San Cristóbal: a few cavalry only escaped, to take news of the disaster to Soult.

Phillipon, who had hoped at one point that he might hold out within the castle for some time, capitulated next day. For this reason, all the live cattle of the garrison had already been driven within the enceinte, which soon added to the tumult and pandemonium which now broke out as the frenzied troops commenced their rampage. Long ringing in Blakeney's ears was the sound of

> the howling of dogs, the crowing of cocks, the penetrating cackle of geese, the mournful bleating of sheep, the furious bellowing of wounded oxen maddened by being continually goaded and shot at and ferociously charging through the streets, were mixed with accompaniments loudly trumpeted forth by mules and donkeys and always by the deep and hollow baying of the large Spanish half-wolves, half-bloodhounds which guarded the whole. Add to this the shrill screaming of affrightened children, the piercing shrieks of frantic women, the groans of the wounded, the savage and discordant yells of drunkards firing at everything and in all directions, and the continuous roll of musketry kept up in error on the shattered gateway; and you may imagine an uproar such as one would think could issue only from the regions of Pluto; and this din was maintained throughout the night.

The scene of bedlam grew worse when, as described by Lieut. Ernest von Hodenberg (K.G.L.), 'a couple of hundred ... women [the soldier's wives] from the camp poured also into the place, when it was barely taken, to have their share of the plunder. They were, if possible, worse than the men. Gracious God! Such tigresses in the shape of women! I sickened when I saw them coolly step over the dying, indifferent to their cries for a drop of water, and deliberately search the pockets of the dead for money, or even divest them of their bloody coats.'

Lieut. Neville (with the 5th Division), limping from the frightful scene, chanced to meet his servant – 'his haversack already well filled with plunder'[17] Neville had also been

> hit on the head, but in the excitement of the escalade had not minded it, nor [as he recalled] had I felt a slight wound in my leg: but, as I began to be rather weak, I took his advice, and he assisted me on. In passing what appeared to be a religious house I saw two soldiers dragging out an unfortunate nun, her clothes all torn: in her agony she knelt and held up a cross. Remorse seized one of the men, who appeared more sober than the other, and he swore she should not be outraged. The other soldier drew back a step and shot his comrade dead. At this moment we found ourselves surrounded by several Portuguese: they ordered us to halt, and presented their muskets at us. I said to my servant, 'throw them some of your plunder:' he instantly took off his haversack and threw it

among them: some dollars and other silver coin rolled out. They then let us pass – had he not done so they would have shot us – as they did several others. We got safe to the bastion, and my servant carried me on his back to the camp.

Surtees, several of whose companions had been killed, recalled seeing an officer coming out of the town 'with a frail fair one leaning on his arm, and carrying in her other hand a cage with a bird in it; and she tripped it over the bodies of the dead and dying with all the ease and indifference of a person moving in a ball-room, – no more concern being evinced by either of them ... It is really lamentable to see such utter absence of all right feeling. Soon after this, the men began to come out with their plunder. Some of them had dressed themselves in priests' or friars' garments – some appeared in female dress, as nuns, &c ... reeling ... for by this time they were nearly all drunk ... scenes were witnessed in the streets as baffle description.'

An unnamed captain told Buckham that he had been

induced to enter a house, in consequence of hearing the dreadful shrieks of females; and here he found two soldiers of his own regiment, and a mother and daughter on their knees before them, supplicating for mercy. It was the utmost he could do to prevail on them to leave the house; for all military subordination was dissolved in the uncontrolled licentiousness which is regarded as the just reward of successful valour. Every place which was supposed to contain spirits was speedily broken into ... It was no uncommon sight to find, next morning, two British soldiers lying dead in the streets, pierced through with each other's bayonet, while the keg or bottle, the fatal cause of such mutual massacre, was lying between them.

When the fury of the sack had somewhat abated ... the ludicrous succeeded to the terrible. British soldiers were seen issuing from the gates of the fallen fortress, bigirt with all the ample foldings of Spanish *togery*, and bringing away every thing that was either portable or driveable. One fellow had made capture of a calf; the animal refusing to be either led or driven, the Connaught hero, unwilling to relinquish his prize, brought it away in triumph, like another Milo, on his shoulders. It was purchased by the messman of the regiment for a bottle of rum!

Dr McGrigor met Phillipon being escorted out of Badajoz,[18] hand in hand with his daughters, 'all three with their hair dishevelled, and with them were two British officers, each holding one of the ladies by the arm, and with their drawn swords making thrusts occasionally at soldiers who attempted to drag the ladies away. I am glad to say that these two British officers succeeded in conveying the governor and his two daughters safely ... to the camp'. One 14-year-old, whose earrings had been torn from her, was lucky enough to be protected from the drunken mob by a young officer in the 95th, Harry Smith, who later married the girl.[19] Some officers, when attempting to restrain them from the worst excesses, were shot by their own men, inflamed by drink, for the violence was indiscriminate, forty-eight hours elapsing before any semblance of discipline could be restored among the frenzied, rampaging, survivors of the storm. Donaldson stressed that 'in justice to the army', in most cases the atrocities had been 'perpetrated by cold blooded villains, who were backward enough in the attack. Many risked their lives in defending helpless females, and although it was rather a dangerous place for an officer to appear, I saw many of them running as much risk to prevent inhumanity, as they did the preceding night in storming the town.'[20]

Grattan records that to put a stop to such an appalling scene,

> it was necessary to use some forbearance, as likewise a portion of severity. In the first instance, parties from those regiments that had least participated in the combat were ordered into the town to collect the hordes of stragglers that filled its streets with crimes too horrible to detail; but the evil had spread to an extent that this measure was inadequate ... At length a brigade of troops was marched into the city, and were directed to stand by their arms while any of the marauders remained; the Provost Marshals attached to each division were directed to use that authority with which they are of necessity invested. Gibbets and triangles were in consequence erected, and many men were flogged, but, although the contrary has been said, none were hanged – yet hundreds deserved it.
>
> A few hours more were sufficient to purge the town of the infamous gang of robbers that still lurked about the streets, and those ruffians – chiefly Spaniards or Portuguese, not in any way attached to the army – were infinitely more dangerous to our fellows, bad as they were. Murder – except indeed in a paroxysm of drunkedness, and in many cases, I regret to say, it did occur in this way – never entered their thoughts, but the miscreants here referred to would commit the foulest deed for less than a dollar.

On the morning after the storm, Wellington had wept openly on seeing the dead and wounded choking the blood-soaked breaches.[21] He could ill afford losing men at this rate, and as reiterated when writing to the Secretary of War, he hoped that he would 'never again be the instrument of putting them to such a test as they were put to.' At the same time he earnestly requested that a corps of sappers and miners be formed without delay, for such 'great losses could be avoided ... and time gained in every siege, if we had properly trained men to carry them on ...'

Surgeon Henry recollected that during that long night the churches at Campo Maior had been 'filled with people praying with extreme fervency – weeping, sobbing, exclaiming – enquiring wildly and anxiously for intelligence, or listening intently to the loud and confused sound of mortal strife.' Day dawned, 'and with it an ominous calm and lull', until at length a horseman was seen

> galloping full speed along the road. The agony of suspense then became almost intolerable: but when he approached nearer and was seen to stop suddenly, stand up in his stirrups and wave his hat repeatedly round and round his head – a shout of ten thousand '*Vivas!*' rent the air, prolonged and reiterated along the fortifications until lost in the overwhelming peeling of all the bells in the city.
>
> My military dress procured me two or three score of warm embraces – the pale countenences of the women brightened up and their dark eyes beamed out brilliantly. Never were fair ladies so condescending and so affectionate, and I believe, if I had chosen, I might have kissed half Campo Mayor. 'Viva os Inglezez!' was in every mouth. At length getting satiated with the numerous accolades, and remembering that my last day's march was a short one, I delayed the starting of my sick convoy for a couple of hours, and determined to gallop over to Badajoz.
>
> I reached the bridge over the Guadiana in three quarters of an hour, but my surprise was great; instead of finding every thing quiet, and every body occupied in attentions to the wounded and preparations for burying the dead, as I had expected, I beheld a scene of the most dreadful drunkenness, violence and confusion ... Joining some of the medical officers who were assisting the most urgent cases, and amputating limbs shattered by roundshot, I remained during the morning and forenoon; then hastily eating a biscuit, partially blackened by gunpowder, and taking a mouthful of wine from a soldier's wooden canteen, I returned to my charge at Campo Mayor. The bells were still ringing merrily at intervals, and every body was rejoicing – rejoicing! after what I had just witnessed!
>
> I hastened to get my party in motion, and with many bitter reflections on the calamities of war, proceeded on the march.

> When we had advanced about a league … towards Elvas, we saw at a distance a large body of men approaching. It was the French garrison of Badajoz, about three thousand five hundred in number, on their route to embark for England. There was a striking difference in the appearance and bearing of the veterans from that of the young soldiers. The former had a bold and self-confident look, that said '*N'importe – c'est la fortune de guerre – notre temps viendra.*' The poor young conscripts, of whom there appeared a fourth-part, on the contrary, looked completely *abuttus*; and their furtive, timid glances, betrayed the fear of discovering a loaded gun or a Portuguese knife in every object around them.

Henry found no difficulty in obtaining permission to carry on his profession in the crowded hospitals at Elvas, and he also revisited Badajoz. It was the general opinion that 'although the British and Portuguese troops – but chiefly the former – bore then, and still bear the principal share of the odium, the lower classes of the inhabitants were also chief performers in the horrid tragedy. The rascally mob – the disgrace of all large cities – as soon as the magazine of brandy in the cathedral was opened, joined, when they became half-drunk, in all the brutalities of the time. Having superior local knowledge, they conducted the English and Portuguese strangers to the houses of the principal and richest inhabitants, and when the doors were burst open, shared in the spoil and the crime.'

On the third day, when the troops were exhausted by their own excesses, the tumult rather subsided than was quelled. Even before the attack on Badajoz had begun, feelings against the fortress were running high, for, according to Grattan (wounded in the assault, and later moved to Elvas), 'Badajoz had ever been looked upon by them as unfriendly to our troops, and they contemplated with delight the prospect of having it in their power ...' Many felt likewise.[22]

From Castelo Bom, Dr McGrigor had reached Elvas early in March, where on arrival he was inundated with complaints of the inadequacy of the means which the medical department had at their disposal, writing on the 14th that 'To this day the Commissariat had not found conveyance for the purveyor for any bedding, stores or even medicines to Elvas or any of the new stations,' nor was there 'a single spring wagon in the Alentejo.'

This is not surprising, for on first entering Headquarters some weeks earlier, he had found that his predecessor had sailed to England with most of the essential office books and papers (the immediate return of which was then demanded by a 'very wroth' Wellington), while among other matters which had required immediate attention had been the checking of both the apothecary's and purveyor's expenditures.[23]

As at Ciudad Rodrigo, Badajoz was re-garrisoned by Spanish troops, and on 11 April Wellington's army started their march north to interrupt Marmont's brief incursion at the head of 20,000 men, who by 12 April had advanced as far as Castelo Branco, but after two days there, on hearing of the fall of Badajoz, he made a precipitate retreat. The Allied vanguard re-entered Castelo Branco on the 17th.[24] Nevertheless, the raid had the effect of delaying an urgently needed convoy of provisions for Ciudad Rodrigo, but little else other than dispersing Trant's militia at Guarda, and by chance capturing Colquhoun Grant, one of Wellington's more resourceful intelligence officers (who later made his escape, in itself a dramatic story).

John Cooper, becoming ill on reaching Aronches, was left behind in charge of six other sick men, with orders to escort them to Portalegre. 'How was this to be done? They were sitting on the road unable to walk. Much baggage was passing; but not one of the Spanish muleteers would take up my poor feverish men. I grew desperate. An empty car came up; I ordered my men to get into it, but the driver would not stop. I threw their knapsacks into the car; he threw them out again. Enraged, I drew my bayonet, took it by the small end, and swinging round, gave him such a blow on the mouth with the heavy end as stunned him. Then I got them on the car, and he drove on, holding his mouth as if he had got the tic.'

Donaldson, likewise struck down by 'fever and ague', and unable to keep up with his regiment, eventually reached the general hospital forming at Castelo Branco, there being 'provided with a mattress and bed-clothes.' His criticism of the medical profession was unduly harsh, considering the conditions in which they worked, commenting that wounded men were often left unattended for as much as 'three days after an engagement before it came to their turn to be dressed, and it may be safely calculated that one-half of those men were thus lost to the service;' and that 'many a time I have heard the sick crying for drink and assistance during the whole night, without receiving it.' He was under the strong impression that many of the medical men were little less that 'apothecaries' boys, who, 'having studied a session or two, were thrust into the army as a huge dissecting room, where they might mangle with impunity, until they were drilled into an ordinary knowledge of their business'; and who in the field, in 'cutting down upon a ball for the purpose of extracting it, ten chances to one but they severed an artery they knew not how to stem; but this gave no concern to these enterprising fellows, for clapping a piece of lint or bandage, or a piece of adhesive plaster on the wound, they would walk off very composedly to mangle some other poor wretch, leaving the former to his fate.' However, as he had to admit, 'in justice to the whole … the duties of a surgeon in the Peninsula, were fatiguing and arduous in the extreme.'[25]

Surgeon Boutflower commented that the Army was 'far from healthy, or rather that part of it employed in the late Siege; the dreadful weather, aided by the horrid intemperence that took place, is making a melancholy ravage amongst the men; till drunkenness becomes a punishable crime, a British Army in the Peninsula never can be properly effective.'

Llerena

Several cavalry actions were also taking place at this time, both south-east of Zafra, the first on 26 March, when the 3rd Dragoons converged with Slade's cavalry brigade at Bienvenida, and which together with 10,000 infantry under Graham, intended to surprise an enemy force quartered at Llerena. In Bragge's opinion the progress of the former expedition beggared all description, for

> we marched on without any advance guard except Sir T. Graham, Sir S. Cotton and numerous Staff who were met about 3 in the Morning by a small Patrole of the Enemy who immediately fired and Galloped back. This circumstance alarmed our noble Leaders who faced about and at Speed dashed amongst the Infantry. The Night was dark and the Brunswick Oels Infantry in front, who, supposing themselves attacked by the French Cavalry, sans Ceremonie wheeled into Line and fired a Volley, seconded by the 51st, but having fortunately faced the wrong way the whole of their Balls flew across the column of Cavalry and another Column of Infantry marching in a Parallel direction. This Circumstance put all the Cavalry to Flight and for about half an Hour created the greatest Confusion, not to mention the Alarm given to the Enemy, the Death of two Officers and some Privates who thus fell Victims to the unsteadiness of our Noble Staff. We arrived at Llerena at Day Break but not before the Enemy had retired in the greatest Order.

D'Urban, when referring to the raid, had noted that it was bound to fail, and that their escape, 'but not with such *complete impunity* would in all probability have been effected, for in spite of all precautions, their Intelligence was so perfect … they were aware of what we were about before 12 o'clock at night, and were under arms accordingly. A proportion of the People of this Province have become so entirely French that the Enemy would not have more willing or more efficient Spies in France itself!!! Memorandum. – Even British Troops must never be permitted to Load for a Night Attack.'

Tomkinson, writing on the 9th and 10th of April, describes a function and ball he attended to celebrate (prematurely) the news of General Ballesteros's imminent triumph, for it had been reported that he had 'entered Seville', although 'not a word was said of our success against Badajoz,' as he wryly remarked.[26]

> At Zafra they said they would give us a bull-fight, and talked of it with so much assurance that we all expected it. All the windows round the grand square (Plassa) [*sic*] were filled with the ladies of the town. The men congratulated them[selves] on Ballesteros' success, telling us we were to see how they would drive the French out of the South, stating at the same time that we had nothing like bull-fights in England, and that it was right to show us one. After waiting for more than two hours, we learnt there was no bull to be had; indeed, they had never the least idea where to get one. Some officers then asked our commissary to lend a poor foot-sore bullock, which was driven into the Plassa. He had marched several leagues that morning, and had more the appearance of dying than coming to grace so gay a scene. We had now a bull, but no matadors. The poor animal stood in the middle of the square without moving, when one of our farriers, coming past, took off his apron, and began to plague him by throwing it in his face. He was soon joined by two or three dragoons, who, by dint of pushing the animal and other means, made him move about a little. Both parties were soon tired of their sport. The bullock was sent back to the commissary, killed and eaten the same night, and so ended our bull-fight.

Villagarcía

On 11 April a successful cavalry action took place at Villagarcía,[27] the first at which General Le Marchant, with his Heavy Brigade, was present. Tomkinson remembered seeing the enemy formed quarter of a mile away, beyond a stone wall. 'We came down the hill in a trot, took the wall in line, and were in the act of charging when the 5th Dragoon Guards came down on our right, charged, and completely upset the left flank of the enemy, and the 12th, 14th, and 16th advancing at the same moment, the success was complete. The view of the enemy from the top of the hill, the quickness of the advance … with the spirit of the men in leaping the wall, and the charge immediately afterwards, was one of the finest things I ever saw.'

Bragge was not so impressed, writing:

> The Big Wigs choose to consider this Affair a great Feather in Sir Stapleton's Cap but when the superiority in Numbers and Horses is so much in our Favour together with the Ground, we ought not to think much in taking 4 officers, 140 Men and 114 of the worst Horses you ever beheld. The Loss of the 5th Dragoon Guards was 12 killed, 2 missing, 1 Officer and 35 Men wounded, and 24 Horses missing.[28] It is worthy of remark that scarcely one Frenchman died of his wounds, although dreadfully chopped, whereas 12 English Dragoons were killed on the Spot and others dangerously wounded by thrusts. If our men had used their Swords so, three Times the Number of French would have been killed. We had six Regts in the Field.

On 11 June units commanded by Slade charged and routed enemy cavalry at Llerena and then ineptly pursued them towards Maguilla, to the north-east, taking 120 prisoners. They were then attacked diagonally by a small force held in reserve by the French: the tables were turned, and in a body the brigade of dragoons wheeled round and rode off as rapidly as they could, regardless of all the exertions of the officers to halt them.[29] On learning of the minor disaster, Wellington had commented to Hill: 'I have never been more annoyed than by Slade's affair, and I entirely concur with you in the necessity of enquiring into it. It is occasioned entirely by the trick our officers of cavalry have acquired, of galloping at everything – and then galloping *back* as fast as they galloped *on* the enemy. They never consider their situation, never think of manoeuvring before an enemy – so little that one would think they cannot maneouvre except on Wimbledon Common: and when they use their arm as it ought to be used, viz. offensively, they never keep or provide a reserve.'

[1] The garrison of 60 was overwhelmed at the cost of 26 British casualties.

[2] Snow had fallen on the 2nd of January, and five men had died two days later in the bitter weather.

[3] It was on the previous day that Wellington received bona fide news regarding Napoleon's disastrous defeat in Russia.

[4] Alexander Dickson's had noted that 2,754 rounds of 24-pounder shot were fired during 2½ days of the siege. As a mule could carry only 8 rounds of that calibre, this would amount to almost 360 mule-loads: but see also footnote 13.

[5] Apparently, Wellington was not at first convinced of the value of howitzers firing shrapnel, and it was not until the end of May that we find him writing from Fuenteguinaldo to Alexander Dickson: 'We *must* have in this part of the country immediately the 6 howitzers, and as many spherical case (principally) as you can carry.' His losses would have been lighter at his sieges had he taken advantage of the high-angle fire of mortars and howitzers to silence enemy guns.

[6] French casualties were some 530, while the garrison, some 1,937 men commanded by General Barrie were marched off as prisoners, leaving behind their siege train, which included 150 heavy guns. Allied casualties amounted to about 1,100, 568 of them in the storming, of which 125 were killed. The most serious individual losses were Robert Craufurd, the idiosyncratic commander of the Light Division who, shot through the lungs, died 48 hours later and was buried in the Lesser Breach, where he had fallen; and Henry Mackinnon, who was carried by a sergeant's party to neighbouring Espeja, where he was buried with full military honours in the village market-place. Ensign Stepney had previously cut off a lock of his hair to send to his widow.

[7] This was Folques, just east of Arganil, itself some distance north-east of Lousã.

[8] A reference to his training activities at the Royal Military College at High Wycombe.

[9] Referring to Gen. Sir David Dundas (1735–1820), whose drill books and Rules and Regulations dated back to the 1780s.

[10] According to Daniel, four Divisions passed throguh Abrantes en route to obtain 'their new clothes and other articles of equipment which had come up the Tagus.'

[11] An additional hazard to the bridges were the trees and large beams floated down river by the French.

[12] It should be stressed that Wellington never intended to bombard the town, which would inevitably cause heavy casualities among its Spanish citizens (as he had witnessed at Copenhagen in 1807), and so high-angle fire from mortars and howitzers had been forbidden. The additional amount of ammunition consumed, had this been ordered, would have also thrown an even greater strain on the already meagre transport available.

[13] Alexander Dickson – not taking account of grape and case-shot or 5½ howitzer shells – estimated that the total consumption of solid shot during the siege was 18,832 rounds for the 24-pounders and 13,029 for the 18-pounders, which was some 3,590 mule-loads, in addition to having expended 2,523 barrels of powder, each weighing 90 pounds, a further 1,200 mule-loads. In 1999 Philip Haythornthwaite estimated that 'the total weight of the munitions expended amounted to over 437 tons', all of which had to be transported to the besiegers. This substantial figure was exceeded at San Sebastian some seventeen months

later, when over 900 tons of shot plus 224 tons of powder might have been expended, much of it having been landed at adjacent Pasajes.

As Richard Glover has emphasised, every mule required a daily ration of 7 to 13 pounds of hay, 9 to 16 pounds of oats, and some 8 pounds of straw, all of which put a great strain on the exiguous transport. Such figures may give some idea of the prodigious amount of *materiél* and forage to be carried forward to the front when conducting a siege. Nor do these figures account for the regular provision of food and drink for the besiegers; of scaling-ladders, mule- or waggon-loads of picks and shovels with which to dig parallels or erect protective cover for artillery, let alone brushwood, osiers, etc. to manufacture gabions and fascines, planks for laying out gun emplacements, sandbags innumerable, and timber for revetting trenches and saps once they had been excavated, axes, bill-hooks, and what not. It may be mentioned here that the heavy English entrenching equipment was jettisoned and replaced by lighter-weight but more portable tools whenever they were found, which enabled the mules to carry a larger quanity.

14 Capt. James MacCarthy, wounded during the assault, stated that the heavy ladders were made with chestnut wood.

15 William Grattan was astonished by 'the vast quantity of combustible matter which out-topped this stupendous defence [the castle walls, which] was in a blaze, and the flames … lighted not only the ramparts and the ditch, but the plain that intervened between them and the Rivillas. A host of veterans crowned the walls … each man had beside him eight loaded firelocks; while at intervals, and proportionately distributed, were pikes of an enormous length, with crooks attached to them, for the purpose of grappling with the ladders. The top of the wall was covered with rocks of ponderous size, only requiring a slight push to hurl them upon the heads of our soldiers, and there was a sufficiency of hand-grenades and small shells at the disposal of the men that defended this point to have destroyed the entire of the besieging army …'

16 Dr McGrigor, who happened to be close to Wellington for some time prior to him receiving this news, unnerved by the repeated failure of all attempts to break in, described the scene: 'At this moment I cast my eyes on … Lord Wellington, lit up by the glare of the torch held by Lord March; I shall never forget it … The jaw had fallen and the face was of unusual length, while the torchlight gave his countenance a lurid aspect, but still, the expression of the face was firm. Suddenly, turning to me and putting his hand on my arm, he said, "Go over immediately to Picton and tell him he must try if he cannot succeed on the castle." I replied, "My Lord, I have not my horse, but I will walk as fast as I can and I think I can find my way. I know part of the road is swampy." "No, no," he replied, "I beg your pardon, I thought it was Delancey." I repeated my offer … but he said "No." In this very uncomfortable state of mind Lord Wellington had remained but a few minutes when we heard a noise …[of] a horseman approaching. Immediately after this, a voice called out harshly and loudly, "Where is Lord Wellington?" We all five exclaimed, "Here! Here!" "My Lord," continued the officer, "the castle is your own," and on being further questioned he said he believed that Sir Thomas Picton and the whole division were in possession.'

17 Simmons states that many were later 'made to throw away a quantity of things, and to prevent them secreting any of the articles, their packs were examined, and the plunder that had not been made away with was collected into heaps

and burnt.' He was convinced too that many men of the rank and file who had previously behaved well, had been entirely demoralised by taking part in such a siege.

Some officers also seem to have indulged in the looting. Buckham, recently disembarking at Oporto, had noticed several officers arriving there from Badajoz 'to dispose of some odd articles of plunder,' including a captain from a distinguished regiments of the 3rd Division ... carrying 'two or three massy silver chalices, as his hard-earned share of the spoil.' Although horrified to hear the gruesome details of the storm as recounted by his acquaintance, Buckham does not seem to have been shocked or surprised to find the captain absent from the front.

18 Least it be assumed that it was only the Allies who engaged in plunder, it should be noted that as recently as the 3rd of April, having received complaints daily that his garrison had been looting both houses and churches, Phillipon had ordered out patrols to prevent it and bring in any men caught doing so, who would be summarily shot.

19 In the late 1840s, when Govenor of the Cape of Good Hope as General Sir Harry Smith, Ladysmith was named in her honour.

20 Capt. Browne states that 'it was reported ... that the Adjutant of a Regiment lost his ...[when on ordering a soldier] out of a house which he was plundering, & the Soldier replied by running him thro' the body with his bayonet. Old men have been hurled from window ... & children have been thrown after them ... Gallows were erected ...& soldiers were hung from them, but all in vain.'

21 In the storming alone, there had been 3,713 casualties (of which 744 were killed), among them 929 and 925 respectively in the Light and 4th Divisions, and a high proportion had been among officers and N.C.Os. The total Allied casualties during the whole siege were c. 4,670.

22 Another officer, on duty there in May 1810, had been 'hissed and abused by the rabble of the place ...' Tomkinson felt its inhabitants 'had always been very uncivil to the British, and from our passing things over [turning the other cheek?], they thought they could do what they pleased. It could not have happened to fall upon people who deserved it more, though it would have been as well had it not gone so far.'

23 'The stores of the apothecary include medicine, surgical materials and surgical instruments, while those of the purveyor or hospital commissary include hospital clothing and bedding, wines, articles of comfort for the sick, materials for repair, hospital tents, marquees, &c. Various reports were prevalent ... of the immense and improvident expenditure of the stores, particularly of the purveyor's, and it was whispered that some of the departmental clerks ... had been carrying on a system of peculation.' Wellington had asked McGrigor 'to keep a vigilant eye on those gentlemen and put some anonymous letters, addressed to him, into my [McGrigor's] hand.'

24 Marmont could no longer 'maintain an offensive posture', as ordered by Napoleon in his dispatch dated 9 May, being then still unaware of the fall of Badajoz. John Daniel refers to Wellington leaving Nisa on the 17th, but the troops, including the brigade of German heavy dragoons, 'a remarkable fine body of men, just arrived from England,' were delayed for two hours by heavy rain from crossing the Tagus at Vila Velha. The village itself was an 'entire mass of ruins and plundered huts, and even these were crowded with sick soldiers,' but Daniel and his companions eventually found shelter in a cluster

of miserable huts among nearby cloud-enveloped rock heights, where they managed to light a fire, dry their clothes, and cook their rations.

[25] During ensuing months, McGrigor did everything possible to improve the state of the hospitals, confirming, when writing of Celerico's, that those with 'sloughing sores were placed in an airy hospital by themselves … The utmost attention to ventilation, fumigation and cleanliness and, above all, strict attention to the comfort and nourishment of enfeebled patients … the utmost cleanliness of the wards and bedding and especially of the persons and linen of the patients have now been rigidly enforced. We regard cleanliness and ventilation not only as a means of cure and of comfort but as essentially requisite to prevent contagion.'

[26] In fact Ballesteros, at the head of 10,000 men and 800 horse, had swerved away from the vicinity of Seville on the 4th, withdrawing into the mountains, although his threatening advance on the city, combined with those of Penne Villemur and Morillo, had caused the governor to send an appeal to Soult for support, which had the effect Wellington had desired. But, as Tomkinson emphasised, such rejoicings for the occupation of Seville by Ballesteros 'were very characteristic of Spanish patriotism and exertion to save their country … Ballesteros marched with a miserable detachment to occupy a town which a couple of French battalions would in half an hour have dispossessed him of. He never made any haste in his march to effect the purpose of it, yet, when he set out from Zafra … the inhabitants rejoiced as if the south of Spain had been freed by the movement.'

[27] Villagarcia de la Torre, north-west of Llerena.

[28] In fact, British casualties amounted to 58.

[29] Slade casualties were 22 killed, 26 wounded, and no less than 2 officers and 116 taken prisoner, many being wounded. Twenty of the latter were recovered two days later while their captors were away foraging, and the 50 dragoons Slade had sent on this mission had surprised and mauled the enemy on their return.

10

May to August 1812: Almaraz; the Salamanca campaign, and occupation of Madrid

With both Ciudad Rodrigo and Badajoz in his hands, the time was ripe to take the offensive, but Wellington was seriously inhibited from doing so by the shortage of ready cash, a perennial preoccupation. Oman devotes several pages to this problem, and it's causes.[1] As he wrote: 'Officers and men had grown to regard it as normal that their pay should be four to six months in arrears …', largely due to the lack of metallic currency: there was a scarcity of both gold and silver, to the extent that 'the Jews of Portsmouth used to board every home-coming transport, to offer convalescents or sailors 27 shillings, or even more, in paper for every guinea that they had on them.' Already, when corresponding with Lord Liverpool on 26 May, Wellington had reiterated: '… I cannot reflect without shuddering upon the probability that we shall be distressed, nor upon the consequences which may result from our wanting money in the interior of Spain.' The accumulation of debts could only damage their credit, on which he could not depend indefinitely. He would be obliged to rely on receiving supplies from the large magazines in his rear, although the well-cultivated corn country through which he intended to march should enable the cavalry to subsist, allowing some of their supply mules to be re-allocated to provision infantry regiments.[2]

Wellington was also preoccupied by the shortage of men, after the heavy losses of recent months, and although in principle opposed to such a project, he now agreed, reluctantly, to allow Spanish volunteers, up to 100 per regiment, to be incorporated into British line regiments; and they would be armed, clothed, fed, and paid in the same manner. There were certain conditions: they should be over 5 foot 6 inches in height, between 19 and 27 years of age, and fit. They would not be required to fight elsewhere than in the Peninsula, and when discharged would receive a month's full pay. It would appear that recruiting parties were not too successful, but those few hundred that did enlist – some in preference to joining Julian Sanchez's mob – seem to have fought with courage even if they had to be restrained from killing in revenge.[3]

Before advancing, Wellington had also to consolidate his position of advantage along the frontier by improving his communications with Lisbon and Oporto by both road and river. To facilitate troop movements, it was as essential that the Roman bridge at Alcántara, spanning the Tagus some distance east of his usual crossing at Vila Velha, be repaired;[4] also imperative was the destruction of the strategically important pontoon bridge on the Tagus at Almaraz: this would sever communications between Soult and Marmont, or at least make them precarious.

Almaraz

On 7 May Wellington sent orders to Hill at Almendralejo (south of Mérida) confirming that he should now proceed unobtrusively north-east to Almaraz, known through intercepted dispatches deciphered by Capt. Scovell to be sparsely defended. Hill set off with three brigades, and a regiment of cavalry, some 6,000 men; the rest of his Corps would remain where they were, should D'Erlon make any offensive move. At Merida he was joined by Portuguese cavalry, some heavy artillery (plus six 24-pound howitzers), a pontoon train and 30-foot ladders, under the supervision of Colonel Alexander Dickson, ever resourceful. By the 15th they had reached Trujillo, there leaving the baggage-train, and proceeded discreetly by night past Jaraicejo with one mule per company to carry camp-kettles.

Hill's intention was to divide his force into three detachments, the first to demonstrate against an ancient hill-top castle and outlying forts commanding the Pass of Miravete, beyond which the Madrid highway descended steeply towards the Tagus; the second would veer to the left to surprise and storm the castle from its rear; the third would thread a bridle path to the right, which wound down to the river, to attack the forts defending the bridge. In the event, both flanking columns found that the ground through which they were filing to be far steeper than expected, while a daylight reconnassance confirmed that the castle's outworks were too strongly sited to be seized without a proper siege. A day was wasted in finding other ways by which the Mirabete defences might be neutralised, during which the presence of his troops may well have been noticed, and the alarm given to those at the bridge: and it was essential to destroy the bridge before units stationed at Talavera advanced to support them. Local guerrillas pointed out that the Tagus might be reached also by a circuitous track over the Pass of La Cuerva, some distance further east: they could provide a guide through what was rough and intricate terrain, described by Capt. MacCarthy as 'mazy sheep-walks in the brushwood.' Once this alternative approach was decided on, Kenneth Howard's brigade, together with a Portuguese contingent, set off on their hazardous expedition. It was agreed that when in the immediate vicinity of their objective, the artillery (unable to advance further than the upper pass), together with units left there under General Tilson-Chowne, would mount a false attack on the inaccessible castle, a demonstration which might distract those by the river.[5]

The pontoon bridge, which stood west of the old stone bridge (nearer the village of Almaraz), previously broken by Cuesta,[6] was defended by Fort Napoleon, on rising ground near the south bank and connected to bridgehead fortifications; Fort Ragusa stood on the opposite bank, the whole complex being garrisoned by about 700 men, many of them from foreign corps. After sawing their unwieldy ladders into two to enable them to be carried during their night-long descent, often in Indian file, it was not until after 6.00 on that May morning that the vanguard of 900 had assembled behind thickets within a short run of Fort Napoleon. The French were not entirely taken by surprise, and when Hill's men, in three columns behind their ladder parties, rushed simultaneously towards the fort, they were immediately fired on. Ladders were rapidly spliced together and mounted to reach the wide berm of the rampart – some men even climbing on each others shoulders; and by re-laying them against the inner parapet, a foothold was gained within the fort. Part of the garrison surrendered; but the majority retreated towards the bridgehead works (its guns unable to fire on their pursuers without hitting their own men), and swarmed onto the pontoons, the central link of which then gave way.[7] Four Highlanders of the 92nd plunged into the river to recover the pontoon, collected craft moored to the far bank, and a bridge of sorts was soon in place. By the time the tail of Hill's party had reached the scene, fighting was virtually over. Fortifications on both banks, and all provisions, powder, ammunition, and equipment assembled there was destroyed during the next few hours, including 20 pontoons.[8]

By the 21st, having picked up his men at Mirabete, Hill was already west of Trujillo. Hill might have bombarded the castle[9] en route had he not meanwhile received false intelligence from Erskine that D'Erlon and Soult were crossing the Sierra Morena to intercept him. This expedition, in which losses had been minimal,[10] was referred to at the time by D'Urban as 'of infinite importance both real and moral, and is indeed the most advantageous Coup of the Second Class during the War.'[11]

On 24 May, Colonel Sturgeon, together with 17 cartloads of *matériel*, was sent from Elvas to Alcántara, where a form of suspension bridge was constructed across the 30 yards of its destroyed arch, rising some 140 feet above the swirling river. Capstans could adjust the tension of the cables stretched across this section, over which double rows of planks were laid. Should it be necessary, the whole could be dismantled or replaced within a few hours.[12] Within a few days this new span was taking the weight of heavy artillery.

* * *

At this time there were five French armies in Spain: Suchet had 60,000 men on the Levante coast; in the north and centre were two forces – 48,000 under Caffarelli, and 52,000 commanded by Marmont. Soult – watched by Hill (with 18,000 men, cavalry and artillery) – controlled 54,000 in Andalusia, while in the vicinity of Madrid were another 18,000, nominally under Joseph and Jourdan. While there may have been over 230,000 enemy troops under arms, a figure not including many thousand sick and wounded, many units were dispersed, pinned down by guerrilla bands, now more active and numerous than ever. Opposing them were Wellington's 60,000 regulars.

Napoleon himself still attempted to retain overall control of troop movements, which, at such distances – for dispatches might take three to five weeks to reach his marshals – was distinctly counterproductive. Wellington was also corresponding with several Spanish commanders, encouraging them to take the initiative by making offensive movements (but avoiding direct confrontations) which would divert the French from concentrating against him, while Lord William Cavendish Bentinck had been sent with an expeditionary force from Sicily to threaten Suchet.

On 4 June, having ridden from Oporto, on entering Fuenteguinaldo, then Wellington's Headquarters, Buckham expressed his surprise, perhaps natural to a novice, for he had imagined the flower of the army collected around the commander – 'gallant men and stately steeds … all the pomp and circumstance of war …'

> The reality soon chased away the illusion, for the village presented the veriest piece of still-life, not to be quite dead, that I ever saw. In the market-place were some half dozen Spanish women, sitting in a row, selling eggs and cabbages, and half a dozen soldiers in their undress were the buyers; now and then an officer in a plain blue coat would cross the plaza, on foot or horse-back; and this was all that met the eye. The place, however, was full, I may say crammed, and had it not been for a friend to whom I brought a letter of introduction, I must have bivouacked for the night; as it was, he gave me up a part of his quarter, which consisted of one room about twelve feet square. Lord Wellington with his personal staff occupied a low-roofed farm-house. The rest of the houses were taken up by officers of the departments of the quarter-master, adjutant, and commissary-generals. These, at the time of my arrival, were all employed in their respective offices, and as everyone at head-quarters has sufficient employment, the mystery of this apparent desolation soon became intelligible. I received instructions on the following day to station myself at Almeida, and with a 'hei mihi!' reached my post a few hours afterwards.

And there Buckham remained for several months, already complaining on 30 July that his life was 'now but a stupid chronicle of breakfasts, and dinners, and sleep'; nor could he 'express half the vexation' he felt 'at being immured in this vile garrison, while our troops, by all accounts, are in full march upon Madrid.'

* * *

Before advancing on Salamanca, Wellington set in motion a cavalry thrust along the north bank of the Duero with the intention of preventing enemy units crossing to the south and reinforcing Marmont; but by the time this force of 800 sabres commanded temporarily by D'Urban had set out from Braganza on 22 June, they had already done so. D'Urban therefore decided to create a diversion and threaten their communications. His three regiments crossed the Esla on the 26th, circled north of Zamora and forded the Duero at Fresno de la Ribera two days later. Having penetrated to La Bóveda de Toro, he crossed back to the north bank and quartered his brigade at Castronuevo, forced to do so for want of bread. On 3 July he received instructions from Beresford to report to Wellington on the condition of the Duero fords. By the 8th, he was nearing Valladolid, but was obliged to retire to avoid being cut off, as units commanded by Bonnet and Foy were in the vicinity. Ordered to rejoin the main army on the 15th, D'Urban re-crossed to the south bank. On the 19th he took up a position at Parada de Rubiales (some 17 miles north-east of Salamanca) in conjunction with Le Marchant. For the battle of Salamanca three days later, see below.

* * *

Already, early in June, seven infantry divisions, Pack's and Bradford's Portuguese brigades, four cavalry brigades, and 9 batteries – a total of 48,500 men, including 4,000 cavalry and 60 guns – had been assembled on the Agueda. On the 12th Wellington reviewed his cavalry, but as Tomkinson commented: 'Sir Stapleton [Cotton] put them through some movements, contrary to the desire of Lord Wellington, who said he had no wish of the kind. After doing one or two things, the affair got confused, the Peer rode off in the midst of it, expressing what he thought, "What the devil is he about now".'

At dawn next day, the Allied army proceeded in three columns towards Salamanca,[13] entered early on the 17th, where Tomkinson found the 6th Division formed up in the immense Plaza Mayor, 'filled with inhabitants, expressing their joy in the most enthusiastic manner. The women were the most violent, many coming up to Lord Wellington and embracing him. He was writing orders on his sabretash, and was interrupted three or four times by them.'

On seeing the sights, Simmons conceded that the cathedral was 'a handsome building, and possesses a good organ of large dimensions', but had little good to say of the religious community, few of whom could have contributed in any way to the prosecution of the war. For him, Salamanca had

> a very priest-ridden appearance, and makes one sympathise with the unfortunate people of such a country who are, partly by coercion, but more through the tenets imbibed from their earliest years, the dupes of superstition and bigotry. They fancy it necessary towards their eternal salvation to aid in supporting these fat-sided and sleek-faced rascals, who, under the pretended semblance of soul-savers, congregate in large bodies, gourmandising the richest viands and drinking the best wine, and have frequently been known to live in every species of vice and idleness. Such men are decidely drones in the industrious hive. [And yet] I have often seen the poor peasants handcuffed and taken from his little field ... called a *volunteer*, and entered upon the book of a regiment.

And yet many of the clergy were happy to help their heretical Allies. Tomkinson referred to Alejo Guillén, whom he met, as one 'who was much with Lord Wellington, and had sent him nearly all the information he received from Salamanca' without the French – with whom he had been on apparent good terms – suspecting him;[14] indeed, Tomkinson thought that in general the Spaniards were 'very good in obtaining and forwarding information – as in the instance of this priest – he ascertains all the detachments in the country, the strength of any large assemblage of troops, by either having persons to count them as they enter the towns, or from returns made by the alcaldes for provisions. These, when obtained, are sent by foot-messenger, who will march ten leagues a day, and if requisite, they can be forwarded from place to place by priests or alcaldes, who can be trusted, finding messengers at each place. They frequently go night and day.'

During the next fortnight, three conventual dependencies in its western suburbs, previously fortified and manned by the French, were besieged by the 6th Division under General Clinton,[15] who would appear to have been a martinet, according to George Bingham, having previously kept 'teasing us with squad drills, and first principles, and harasses both officers and soldiers?' Unfortunately, that Division had no experience of sieges, and having only two engineer officers and nine artificers to instruct the men, progress was slow. And resistance was strong: it was not until 27 June that the last of the forts capitulated when set alight by red-hot shot from a howitzer battery and some 6-pounders.[16]

Bragge, writing on the following day, likewise records having been impressed by the architecture of Salamanca.[17] He had also found its citizens 'certainly more zealous of the cause' that those in the South, and described their latest reinforcement:

> Dons Julian [Sánchez] and Carlos [de España], the great Guerilla Leaders,[18] joined our Army with their Myrmidons and a more verminous looking set of fellows you never beheld. The Infantry [are] in English Clothing and the Cavalry, both Horse and Man, completely armed and equipped in the Spoils of the Enemy, so that it is impossible to distinguish Friend from Foe. The Don himself wears a Pelisse like the 16th Dragoons with an immense Hussar Cap and the Eagle of Napoleon reversed. In this dress, accompanied by aides de camp equally *genteel* in Appearance, Twelve Lancers, a Trumpeter in scarlet on a grey Horse and three led Horses I saw the renowned Chieftain enter Salamanca amidst the acclamations of the Multitude who received him with every mark of Respect.

The Dammage we have done the Inhabitants by Feeding our Cattle of every Description on Green Wheat is incalculable, but they appear to bear it with the greatest Patience, being perfectly satisfied that Lord Wellington will drive the French out of Spain.

Writing on the 30th from Fuentelapeña (between Salamanca and Toro),[19] Le Marchant described the army as having been constantly on the march since the 1st of the month:

It was in that day I left Crato in the Alentejo; but on our marching to Salamanca, Marmont retired across the Tormes, as we supposed towards Zamora, leaving a garrison in the forts of Salamanca, which covers the only bridge on the river, the fords being very uncertain. To our surprise he returned; and then we took up a position [at San Cristóbal], on the right bank of the Tormes, commanding the heights that cover the town, and fronting towards Zamora. Marmont placed his army at the foot of our position, and so near that the two armies were within half a range of a six-pounder, and perfectly in view of each other, there not being a tree or a single impediment to obstruct it. The outposts were in constant communication. As you may suppose, we entertained no doubt of a sanguinary conflict. On the first day [21 June] that he took up his ground, I had thirteen horses killed in two of my regiments from a cannonade without a man having suffered. The singularity of the case leads me to mention it.

The forts of Salamanca, contrary to all expectation, held out. Marmont on the second day of his return retired his left flank. It is nonsense to give you the names of villages, as none of the maps contain them.

On the day succeeding he made a movement to our right, which, had he not failed, would have given him a complete view of our disposition, and facilitated his attack. The affair that followed was short but sharp. We lost some valuable officers.

Before daybreak both armies were constantly ranged in order of battle opposite each other; the bands and trumpets of the enemy playing; ours preserved a solemn silence.

On the third day, when the morning set in, we found to our astonishment that Marmont had retired during the night; and upon pursuit we traced him to a position two leagues on our right, appuyé on the Tormes.

Wheeler described the ensuing action:

On the descent from the ridge, the Light companeys of the Guards were engaged with the enemy Skirmishers. We had brought our light guns

> with us, a few rounds from them and the sight of us caused the enemy to fall back and establish their pickets. Our Regt. then extended to our right along the ridge for the night. In the morning we were relieved by the Portuguese, we then fell back some distance, piled our arms, and was cleaning our firelocks etc. In about an hour the Rum was brought, but in the midst of serving it Sir Thomas Graham rode down and ordered us to fall in, and advance. We were soon on the move, and soon under fire. I was not best pleased for I had not got my rum.
>
> As we advanced the shot whistled brisker, Sir Thomas was in front, he wheeled round his horse, and ordered us to deploy on the first Division. Sir Thomas sat with his back to the enemy shading his eyes with his cocked hat, watching the companys deploy.[20] He expressed his satisfaction at the manner we had performed the movement. As our line passed him he said 'my lads you shall give them a taste of your steel directly.' Sir Thomas then gave the word double quick, in a moment thirty buglars was sounding the charge and off we dashed in double quick with three cheers, and away went the enemy to the right about. We had now gained the ridge without discharging a single musket, our buglars sounded the 'halt' and 'fire'. Two of our guns, on our right, opened on them, at the same time about a dozen of our Cavalry shewed themselves. The sight of the Cavalry induced the enemy to form square, what a glorious opportunity this gave us to pepper them. There they were about 150 yards from us in a cluster like bees descending the hill. What between our fire and the fire of our guns they were knocked about like nine pins. ... In this affair Major [Samuel] Rice's favourite Pye Bald Tom was shot under him. We are all sorry for poor Tom, as he was the Major's pet ... Tom was as fat as a mole. The Chassueurs [sic] had stripped every bit of flesh off his bones.[21] The Major had Tom's hoofs taken off, they are to be converted into snuff boxes.

Le Marchant narration's continued: 'The next day he [Marmont] began to cross considerable bodies of troops by a ford, compelling Lord Wellington to leave his position and fall back to protect his line of operation, his resources being mostly drawn from Ciudad Rodrigo. In proportion as Marmont detached, Lord Wellington did the same.'[22]

The weather had been very variable, at first being stiflingly hot,[23] and then bitterly cold and windy during these days of jockeying for position – Wellington later mentioned to Stanhope that he had 'never suffered more from cold than during the manoeuvres of the days preceding the battle of Salamanca.' Bragge, after witnessing some skirmishing near the Duero fords, had been ordered back to Nava del

Rey, and 'once more got into decent Houses and good Beds', only to be 'roused at 2 o'Clock, eat an enormous Breakfast'; but finding it to be a false alarm, he again retired to his 'downy Couch'. During the heat of the day, as described by Surgeon Boutflower, it was 'not uncommon to see five hundred of the enemy, and as many of our men, bathing together in the Douro in the most perfect good humour possible, at the same time that the cavalry of the two rival armies come down on their respective sides of the river to water, it being perfectly understood that neither party shall ever approach the river armed. Any infringement of the agreement is noticed by firing on any armed cavalry or infantry on either side.' John Mills, encamped near Medina del Campo, remarked on the inhabitants coming out in droves, having not seen British troops before; but although they were 'uncommonly kind,' they made us pay 'enormously for everything' they brought with them. This was not too easy, for not only where the Commissariat short of money; the men were 'nearly four and the Staff five months in arrears,' while the peasants were not used to paper money, only hard cash. It would appear that as long as it was metal, it was acceptable.[24]

There was a lull in the actual fighting until 16 July, when further complex movements took place, intended by Marmont to force the Allies back towards Ciudad Rodrigo, but each was countered by Wellington.

He had learned meanwhile that the diversions he had instigated elsewhere in Spain were keeping the separate French armies occupied, with the exception of some 13,000 under Joseph, which had set off to reinforce Marmont, although the latter was apparently ignorant of the fact. Writing to Graham, Wellington succinctly summarised the position: 'Marmont will not risk an action unless he should have an advantage; and I shall certainly not risk one unless I should have an advantage; and matters therefore do not appear likely to be brought to that criterion very soon.'[25]

On the 18th the contending armies found themselves moving parallel to each other, but apart from occasional 'sharp cannonading from both sides', no fighting took place; nor did it throughout the 21st, during which they both made a gruelling march of over 20 miles under a blistering sun. By that evening the Allies were back in their former position at San Cristóbal, while Marmont was near Huerta, a village on a right-angle bend of the Tormes some 10 miles due east of Salamanca.

Somers Cocks, writing light-heartedly on the 19th, refers to having done 'plenty of marching lately, very little fighting but a good deal of chess-playing with the enemy. I expect the next fortnight will bring us to hard blows. The two armies are close to each other today, we get plenty of lemon ice-cream and I received yesterday a strong reinforcement of claret but am still badly off for champagne. Very little game or poultry is stirring. At Medina del Campo we were encamped eight days, we had a ball every evening ... PS: 23rd: Beat the enemy yesterday ...'

Salamanca

It would be invidious for the present author to describe in any detail the ensuing battle, one which has been masterfully reconstructed by Rory Muir,[26] who has emphasised that while the progress of the main events might be sufficiently clear, there was a deal of contradictory evidence as to the precise chronological sequence of specific movements and actions on separate parts of the field, and also many inconsistencies in earlier expositions.

The French had crossed the Tormes early on the 21st – there were then two fords in the vicinity of Huerta – and thus threatened the Allies' lines of communication, but Wellington had already taken the precaution of sending baggage, unessential supplies and ammunition, towards Portugal, should he be obliged to retreat,[27] for the French infantry, travelling lighter, could march slightly faster, giving them the capacity of turning his flank. By nightfall the bulk of both armies were over the Tormes and occupying parallel positions within its wide bend south-east of Salamanca, with the French vanguard occupying the village of Calvarrasa de Arriba, on the road to Alba de Tormes.

The terrain here is largely rolling open country, with slight elevations and troughs, while nearer Alba extended tracts of cork-oaks and olive-groves, more wooded than at present. The only prominent hills in the area were the characteristically steep-sided but flat-topped Lesser Arapile and, some 800 yards further south, the Greater Arapile, beyond which a slight ridge merged with more undulating country further west. West of the two hills lay the village of Los Arapiles.

During the night of Tuesday the 21st the armies were drenched by a violent thunderstorm, the deafening claps of thunder and lightening flashes terrifying the horses, many of which broke loose from their picquet ropes and stampeded,[28] while torrents of rain deepened the fords traversed only hours before.

The parallel march in a south-westerly direction continued throughout the morning, with Wellington closely observing every movement of Marmont's eight divisions, the torrid July sun beating down as it had at Talavera almost exactly three years earlier. On approaching the Arapiles, the Allies was able to occupy the nearer and lower of the two, the French seizing the Greater. Desultry fighting took place for some time in the vicinity of a chapel-crowned knoll west of Calvarrasa de Arriba.

Most of the Allied troops were concentrated, half-hidden, behind a slight elevation – the hill of San Miguel – extending west not far north of Los Arapiles,[29] with the exception of the Light and 1st Divisions, facing south-east towards Calvarrasa, and the 3rd Division, temporarily commanded by Pakenham (as the wound Picton had received at Badajoz had re-opened earlier in the campaign), together with D'Urban's cavalry, which had crossed the bridge at Salamanca earlier that morning, and was moving rapidly towards of the village of Aldea Tejada (some distance north-west of Los Arapiles) to protect the Allied right flank.

Wellington then redeployed his right, bringing Leith's 5th Division (with Stapleton Cotton's cavalry, Le Marchant's Brigade leading, to its right) and Cole's 4th (supported by Clinton's 6th) into a line running east and west just north of Los Arapiles. Hope's 7th Division was withdrawn from its position north of the Lesser Arapile to one behind the 5th Division.

After gazing for some time from the summit of the Lesser Arapile towards Marmont on the Greater, Wellington got bored watching the enemy columns marching and countermarching with no apparent objective in view, and pondered on the possibility that he might have to order his army to retire. Instructing his staff officers to report immediately any significant change in enemy dispositions taking place, he rode off to have a scratch lunch, doubtless interrupting it every so often to turn his telescope on them, if only to satisfy himself that their deployments were not threatening.

Marmont had already finished *his* meal and, on resuming his scrutiny of visible Allied units, noticed clouds of dust drifting west from the direction of Salamanca. If these were British troops, he intended to hasten their retreat, for although some red-coats stood opposite him, he did not anticipate they would be rash enough to attack. To put them in their place, Maucune's 5th Division advanced on the straggling village of Los Arapiles under an artillery barrage. His *tirailleurs* briefly occupied its southern edge, where the light companies of the Guards found themselves outnumbered until reinforced; but once expulsed, the French did not return to the attack. Thomières's 7th Division, which was intended to support Maucune's, bypassed it, and continued to march west along the low ridge of Monte de Azán, pushing well beyond what was assumed to be the Allied right flank.[30]

By the early afternoon it was evident to Wellington was Marmont's foremost divisions were indeed over-extending themselves most imprudently along the exposed ridge, presumably with the intention of cutting both the road from Salamanca to Tamames and the highway to Ciudad Rodrigo. This was the opportune moment to attack and scatter the French rather than making a fighting withdrawal. Another glance through his glass was enough to convince him. Immediately despatching A.D.Cs to specific units ordering them to advance, Wellington galloped west towards Leith's and Pakenham's men.

Very concisely, the progress of the battle was as follows: The 3rd Division, together with D'Urban's and Arentschild's cavalry, were ordered to ascend the ridge in their front and drive all before them in an oblique charge against the head of Thomières's foremost column, while Leith Division, lying down to protect themselves from the long range artillery dual which had commenced, would advance in echelon and his cavalry to charge the French immediately after the 3rd had struck.[31] Cole was to send forward two brigades once Leith's attack was well under way, while Pack's Brigade would storm the Greater Arapile.[32]

At some time between 3.30 and 3.45 Marmont, from his position on the Greater Arapile, now aware of what was happening on his left flank, was issuing orders for its reinforcement when an exploding shell severely wounded his right arm and side, putting him out of action. The messenger sent to his second-in-command, found that Clausel, hit in the heel, had gone to the rear to have it dressed, so command devolved on Bonnet, who was incapacitated soon after; but by then Clausel, not disabled by his wound, was back in the saddle and took control. (Thomières had been killed while attempting to rally his demoralised troops.) Thus, for at least an hour, and the most critical one, the French had no effective commander.

Leith's strong 5th Division, deployed in line, now entered the battle, Greville's brigade leading, followed by Pringle's (in the rear of which waited the 7th Division), which moved directly towards Maucune's position under a heavy cannonade. During the advance, Wheeler found some water, 'but it was so bad we could not drink it, however it served to rince our mouths and wash the dust off our faces, this refreshed us much.' Not long after,

> Lord Wellington rode up to us, and entered into conversation with Colonel Mitchell. He waited some time looking anxiously towards the

> hill, as the enemy's fire was very brisk. Colonel M – said to Lord W – that he should like to advance and drive them from the hill, but his Lordship looked as serious as a Judge going to pass sentence of death, shook his head and said it is not time yet. At length he called out '7th Division, Advance'; spurred his horse, rode to our left and in a few minutes was lost in dust and smoke. We had not advanced far before the fire slackened and then ceased altogether.
>
> We afterwards learnt that the hill had been charged by the heavy Cavalry, the whole of the enemy was in full retreat. We kept advancing but could not keep up with them. About 9 we halted for the night and every thing seemed quiet, but at 10 o'clock a smart fire of musketry was heard, it continued about a quarter of an hour then all was quiet for the night. Having examined a few dead Frenchmen for money etc. we collected what dead bodies were near and made a kind of wall with them. We did this to break the wind which was very cutting as we were very damp with sweat. Under this shelter we slept very sound until morning.

At about 3.45 the 3rd Division advanced in two columns, which, once seen by the enemy, taken entirely by surprise, became the target of their guns, but Pakenham's artillery was soon replying in kind. Le Marchant's dragoons, who had been advancing to the right of Leith, quickened their pace, and wheeled to the left on reaching the summit of the low ridge Thomières had occupied, formed in two lines, and swept down obliquely on Maucune's left flank. The impact was terrific, their heavy 35-inch-blade sabres causing havoc among the first two battalions in their path, and as they thundered on, another three virtually disintegrated.

Le Marchant then drew rein and regrouped, for Taupin's Division was approaching rapidly to offer what cover it could to Macaune's shattered units. Although able to form square across Le Marchant's front, they held their fire too long, broke in the face of the impetuous cavalry charge, and fled south-east closely pursued towards a wooded area. It was here that Le Marchant himself was shot through the spine.[33]

Meanwhile, D'Urban's and Arentschildt's cavalry, having made a wide sweep west of Miranda de Azán, came up behind the French left, which had no time to form square before they were attacked and scattered, the bulk of their infantry unable to re-align properly to face heavy fire from Wallace's three battalions of the 3rd Division in line; and although the 1/5th of James Campbell's battalions suffered in Curto's cavalry attack, this was soon driven off.

Shortly after ordering his troops to charge, Leith himself was seriously wounded, but the formation into dense squares adopted by

Maucune's first line was unable to withstand the British fire: they were penetrated and broken, their confusion perhaps increased by Thomières's men retreating upon them.

Wellington had already ordered Cole's 4th Division, to Leith's left, to advance in a single two-deep line against Clausel's 2nd Division, and in the ensuing intense musketry duel, Cole was wounded; his men, suffering severely from artillery enfilading their flanks, were forced back in some disorder by Clausel's counter-attack mounted by his second brigade together with Bonnet's 8th Division, which had advanced from behind the Greater Arapile and fallen on Cole's left flank.

The situation in the Allied centre could have been a hazardous had not Wellington, instinctively sensing the danger, meanwhile brought forward in person the two British brigades of Clinton's 6th Division, and deployed them into a two-deep line extending diagonally south-west from the Lesser Arapile, while Beresford (wounded soon after) redeployed Spry's comparatively unhurt Portuguese Brigade (of Leith's Divison) to threaten the flank of the French attack, already under fire from Sympher's battery on the Teso de San Miguel, and raked also from the Lesser Arapile. Clinton's line pressed forward, meeting Bonnet's column near the middle of the intervening valley, where the fire-fight became increasingly ferocious, until the French broke, leaving Clausel's position untenable: before long his men were joining the mass of fugitives retreating past the Greater Arapile, with Clinton's Division their wake.

Ferey had meanwhile been instructed to defend the main avenue of retreat along the Alba de Tormes road, and his seven battalions in a three-deep line, each flank buttressed by a battalion in squares, briefly resisted Clinton. Wellington now brought the fresh batteries of the 1st and Light Divisions into action, firing obliquely towards this line, which crumbled soon after Ferey himself had been cut in two by a round shot. By itself, Foy's single Division – still near Calvarrasa, facing the Light Division – was incapable of making any stand against the onslaught of which he was witness. The battle was over as darkness fell, illuminated by the long grass which – as at Talavera – had caught fire, indiscriminately burning to death many of the wounded.

Lemonnier-Delafosse described the rout as 'a shapeless mass of soldiery rolling down the road like a torrent – infantry, cavalry, artillery, waggons, carts, baggage-mules, the reserve park of the artillery drawn by oxen, were all mixed up. The men, shouting, swearing, running, were out of all order, each one looking after himself alone – a complete stampede. The panic was inexplicable to one who, coming from the extreme rear, knew that there was no pursuit by the enemy to justify the terror shown. I had to stand off far from the road, for if I had got near it, I should have been swept off by the torrent in spite of myself.'

The Allies were too exhausted to press vigorously on the enemy, who should find themselves trapped, unable to cross the Tormes at Alba. It was only later that Stapleton Cotton's cavalry, sent to investigate, reported back that contrary to specific orders, Carlos de España, instructed to hold the bridge at all costs, had withdrawn his troops, allowing the fugitives to escape: an example of Spanish irresponsibility.

Next morning,[34] Commissary Daniel was reassured to see many females, having 'prepared a great quantity of lint and rags for the use of the wounded,' setting out for the battlefield, carrying with them 'tea, coffee, and such other refreshments as they thought might be most acceptable: and here might be seen the interesting spectacle of Spanish girls supporting from the field such of our wounded as were able to walk, carrying for them their knapsacks and muskets.' At one corner of the field, 'about two hundred wounded men had crept or been collected together, and were waiting very patiently to be removed: each man wrapped in a blanket, by which they might be distinguished from the dead lying about. Some waggons of the royal waggon train and some country waggons and mules supplied by the Commissariat, were moving over the field taking up the wounded: but it is to be feared many poor fellows concealed amongst the corn must have perished before they were found.'[35]

Lieut. Robert Knowles, slightly wounded and then laid low with fever, had intended to ride out to the battlefield, and later described the condition in which wounded officers had been left as as being 'extremely ill off, not having a farthing to purchase the comforts which are necessary to men reduced to skeletons by wounds and sickness. The Army is only paid up to 24th March, but they had the generosity to give to each wounded officer 20 dollars a few days after our arrival in this town. The sum (to a few who nursed it well) has supply'd the necessarys of life; others have sold their horses, asses, or mules; others their epaulettes, watches, rings, etc., and, to the disgrace of John Bull, others have perished from want.'[36]

Bock's and Anson's cavalry brigades came up with the French rearguard that afternoon near the village of Garcia Hernández, north-east of Alba, where a spirited action took place, in which the K.G.L. charged and broke three enemy squares. According to Bragge, Wellington was 'a Spectator and declares he never saw so gallant an Affair.'[37] Any close pursuit of the rapidly retreating army was given up soon after, except by some light cavalry.

Joseph Bonaparte had reached Blascosancho (between Avila and Arévalo) on the 25th, but on hearing of the defeat from both Marmont and Clausel, and that the latter was in no state to put up a further fight for some time,[38] he retired on Madrid via Segovia. Wellington advanced on Arévalo and veered due north towards Olmedo (on the Valladolid road), where he gave a celebratory ball. Their progress next morning presented 'a droll sight' to Lieut. John Cooke, '… the officers, after the fatigues of the previous night, sleeping as they rode along, still dressed in their ball attire. Wearing crimson, light blue, or white trousers, richly embroidered with gold and silver, and velvet and silk waistcoats of all colours, decorated in a similar manner, they seemed dandies ready alike for the dance or the fight. Most of them had received a wound, and others more. None of the officers present at this time, including the senior officer, had reached 25 years of age.'

Salamanca had been Wellington's most brilliant offensive battle to date, as Foy himself – who rarely conceded credit to his adversaries – candidly admitted: not only did it greatly enhance Wellington's reputation; it encouraged the Spaniards to maintain their resistance.

Clausel, having retreated north-west beyond Valladolid, entered briefly by the Allies on the 30th, appeared to have been knocked out of the ring temporarily, leaving Wellington in a quandary whether or not to advance further, for although he had cut the direct road between Madrid and France, if Joseph marched north-west from Segovia,[39] this could menace his communications with Portugal. It would be advantageous politically to capture Madrid, the most important military depot and hub of communications in French-occupied Spain. If entered now, he could join forces with Hill, approaching from the south-west: together they could combine against any possible convergence of Soult's and Joseph's forces. In the event, the bulk of the Allied army marched south via Cuellar (where a depot was established),[40] there leaving Clinton's weak 6th Division, while Anson's cavalry brigade and two division of Galicians remained at Valladolid to watch the line of the Duero.[41]

The Occupation of Madrid

Madrid was entered on the 12 August, the garrison of 2,500 surrendering after only token resistance,[42] but the Allies' tenure of the capital – where over 180 brass guns, 20,000 muskets, 14,000 suits of clothing,

40,000 pairs of shoes, saddles, equipment or all sorts, quantities of powder and other *matériel*, and provisions were captured – was to be short-lived. The Madrileños in general, who by then had endured almost three years of French occupation, welcomed them ecstatically.[43] Wheeler 'never before witnessed such a scene. At the distance of five miles from the gates we were met by the inhabitants, each had brought something, viz. laurel, flowers, bread, wine, grapes, lemonade, aquedente,[44] tobacco, sweetmeats, etc.,' but he found it hard to submit to a custom 'so unenglish ... to be kissed by the men. What made it still worse, their breath was so highly seasoned with garlic, then their huge moustaches well stiffened with sweat, dust and snuff, it was like having a hair broom pushed into one's face that had been daubed in a dirty gutter.'

Handsome young Somers Cocks admitted that he had 'never been kissed by so many pretty girls in a day in all his life, nor did he ever expect to be again.' Nor was he, for the 79th were sent to El Escorial, where he was quartered for ten days, which 'would have angered old Philip could he have risen from the grave and seen 20,000 British and Portuguese – the two nations he most hated – at least latterly, coolly in possession of his favourite grid-iron palace.' Some days later Cocks was complaining that he had not yet

> … obtained a Sight of Valladolid, which I very much regret as I wish to render this Campaign as much like a Tour of Pleasure as possible and by seeing as much as other People to prevent being humbugged hereafter. The Cathedral and Castle at Segovia were well worth seeing, as well as the magnificent Aqueduct built by Trajan. About two leagues from thence we halted in a very Picturesque Valley amidst the Mountains of the Sierra Guadarrama, over which there is only one Pass but that so admirably contrived you may trot the whole way if your Horses are good enough …
>
> The Inhabitants [of Madrid] testified their Joy by hanging all their Curtains, Tapestry etc. out of the Windows, which had a very pretty effect and was greatly encreased for 3 Nights by a splendid Illumination with Immense Wax Candles. On the third Night they gave a Ball to the Army, which afforded me an opportunity of seeing more splendid Cloathes than I ever saw before. The Women are beautiful, very fond of the English and all – What d'ye call 'ems in England? Therefore you may suppose we rather regret leaving Madrid, although going to a Pallace.

This was that of San Ildefonso,[45] on the north flank of the Guadarrama range, where Bragge was also quartered for 'a delightful Week, ... being constantly in the Company of a very Gentlemanly and entertaining Patron who was Vicar of the Place and had a very accomplished Niece living with him, as good natured as she was pretty, therefore ... I was what the Spaniards call 'muy contento' with my situation.' While in the capital, Bragge had got acquainted with several English, among them 'a most curious Trio: an Irish Friar, formerly confessor to the Queen, a Scotch Saddler and a mad Widow, all of whom have resided there upwards of 20 years.' On reaching Valladolid in early September, he commented: 'Claret is here 3d a Bottle. At Madrid the English drank up a stock for 6 *Months* in 3 Nights.' On 8 September Bragge received 'a Fortnight's pay', which allowed him to 'buy some Cloathes as every thing I have is worn out, and my new Boots are at Abrantes, where – I suppose – they will stay until the War is over. We have lately been in a state of Beggary but I trust we shall now get Money more regularly.' He hoped that the present campaign would be 'Lord Wellington's last,' for he was 'quite weary of Service. You cannot conceive half the Misery of it – we are quite wretched. What think ye of having choice of Quarters (in a Village where the People were half of them absolutely dying) after 5 Generals and their Staffs [were already installed]? This happened to my Squadron the other Night and the consequence was that I slept in the same House with two other Officers, two Portuguese Boys, the Patron and his wife and 9 Guerillas. I wish some of our gay young Men in England could have changed Beds for the Night. I forgot to observe there were *no Doors* in this elegant Hovel but plenty of Fleas.'

Among several others who had been much impressed by Madrid was Donaldson: 'the delightful walks of the Prado, the gardens breathing perfume – the beautiful fountains – the extensive and picturesque view from the Segovia gate – the cool and delicious shades on the banks of the Manzanares – their women – their music and nightly serenades ... our troops were allowed free access to the museum, in the street Alcala, nearly opposite our barracks. In it there was a very valuable collection of natural history, particularly a lump of native gold brought from South America, which weighed many pounds, some enormous boa constrictors,[46] and the entire skeleton of a mammoth ... [and] we were admitted, gratis, to see the bull fights ...'

Donaldson admits to having 'only witnessed the sight once. Lord Wellington was present, and sat in a box on the right of the king's, the royal box being empty', and after describing the performance, commented that he

> ... did not believe that many of our men were much captivated with this amusement; it was rather considered a cruel and disgusting one. I cannot understand how it is so much encouraged in Spain, unless it be to serve the same purpose that we pay boxers to murder each other, namely, to keep up the national courage.
>
> I have known some of those 'bruising' fellows in the army, – indeed every regiment has its 'bully;' but although there were always forward enough to abuse and tyrannize over their fellow-soldiers, who were not of the 'fancy,' I never knew one of them that displayed even ordinary courage on the field; and it was invariably by fellows of this description that outrages, such as those perpetrated at Badajoz, were committed.

Alexander Gordon had been provided with luxurious quarters in the Royal Palace (in the meadows below which, according to Daniel, upwards of 14,000 troops were encamped), from where he wrote to Lord Aberdeen on the 25th August: 'You cannot conceive how happy the people are with us here. You would be delighted to see the fine collection of Pictures both here, and in private houses, I scarce do anything else; and am now become well acquainted with the style of every master. There are Good Pictures to be bought, and I think if I can procure one or two very good Murillos I shall buy them for you, but I shall not go further than from £50 to £100. I shall confine myself to this master as one cannot be mistaken in his paintings, and I certainly think him the best of the Painters of his day. There is one however who has painted much here who I also think delightful, and is not known in England, Mengs.' He continued at some length: 'There are a number of Titians & Rubens to be seen, and procured here, but I cannot say I esteem generally the works of the latter ... Velasquez is certainly the first Portrait painter of the Spanish style ... You might if you were here pick up a number of fine things as almost everything is to be sold,[47] I understand there are some fine Greek & Roman Antiques & statues to be had,' etc.

Meanwhile, during the two weeks Wellington remained in the capital, being fêted and obliged to entertain, much of the time was occupied in attempting to revitalise the local politicians and military, having distributed large amounts of captured equipment to them, but it was a thankless task. He remarked at the time how extraordinary it was that the revolution in Spain 'should *not have produced one man* with any knowledge of the real situation; it really appears as if they were all drunk thinking and *talking* of any object but Spain: how it will end, God knows!,' the next day expressing the view that the only way 'to get them to do anything on any subject is to *frighten* them.'

Writing from Almeida on 30 July, Buckham reported that the French prisoners 'are pouring down upon us. The Spaniards have treated them, by all accounts, with a most revolting cruelty during the march from Salamanca, and the joy of the poor fellows was unbounded when they were delivered into the custody of the Portuguese. A French officer told me, and I had it confirmed in various ways, that if any of the prisoners through fatigue lagged behind in the route, they were immediately bayoneted. This spirit of retaliation is the damning spot of the Peninsular warfare. The lives of ten thousand, or twice ten thousand lost in a hard-fought field, excites not half the emotion which the mind feels at the cold-blooded massacre of a few defenceless beings.'

At least the Portuguese troops were disciplined: the French could not expect much sympathy from their peasants.

* * *

As far as Spanish appreciation of the importance of the battle of Salamanca is concerned, it is worth recording the remarks of two later visitors to the site, among them, Richard Ford, who on 2 June 1832 rode into the university city, after traversing the battlefield, where corn waved thickly 'over soil fertilised by the blood of brave Britons who died for ungrateful Iberia.'[48] Ford had found himself escorted round by the identical guide who had attended Wellington, for Francisco Sánchez – better known as '*El Cojo*' (the Limper), having lost a leg in the action – who still lived at Los Arapiles. Indifferent and incurious, few if any Spaniards, even those officers garrisoned at Salamanca, ever bothered to make the brief excursion there.

A month later Lieut.-Colonel Sir Benjamin Badcock (a Captain in the 14th Light Dragoons at the time of the battle), briefed to investigate discreetly the military situation on the Portuguese frontier at the commencement of the civil war fermented by Dom Miguel against his brother, found himself in Salamanca, and likewise visited the site, where, calcined by the sun, bones were still to be seen; but on attending a grand parade in the city to celebrate the anniversary of the battle, such was Spanish suspicion, that he was requested not to do so in future: they did not care to be 'officially observed.' On another day, when enquiring why one section of the town lay in ruins, certainly in a more derelict state than he remembered it, was told that the French had left a large deposit of gunpowder there, and that the Spanish garrison at the time 'could find no better place to smoke in than the apertures of the place': naturally, the consequent explosion was blamed on the British.

Badcock had several encounters with people who recognized him after the twenty years which had passed. Near Castillejos de Dos Casas (north of Fuentes de Oñoro, where he had been wounded) a woman – now with four children, but retaining her good looks and the cheerful disposition he remembered – rushed to embrace him, exclaiming excitedly; 'Oh, you are the officer that was quartered in my house, and was the last to piquet there.' A muleteer formerly in the British service asked whether they were coming again, remembering their former treatment and pay: many still received British pensions, including '*El Cojo*', 'grown enormously fat' on his. Pensions were also received by some ladies who had been attached to British officers, the nearly obliterated names of whom they tenderly preserved on scraps of paper. 'The peasantry ... inquired most particularly after the Señor Lorde (the Duke of Wellington). One female, of the name of Leonora, seemed still to sigh for some former attachment.' The state of the road at the Puerto de Baños was exactly the same as he recollected it, rutted by the wheels of the heavy artillery dragged across the pass, for the peasants could not afford to keep it in repair.

When taking a *paseo* round the ramparts at Ciudad Rodrigo, Badcock was summarily arrested and charged with making drawings, but on commenting to the governor how well he knew the fortress, was released with a growl. At Badajoz, he was condescendingly allowed, if escorted, to visit the Great Breach, which appeared to have remained untouched, except that the large stone placed where so many of his gallant countrymen had been buried, had been broken to pieces, a sad reflection on the honour due to them.

1 Notably in volume IV of his *History*, pp. 65-69, and volume V, pp. 349-52.

2 Daniel provides a detailed summary of the numbers of horses and mules assembled for the forthcoming advance: seven infantry divisions required almost 4,000 mules; and the ten cavalry regiments and the Horse-artillery, with 5,060 horses, required almost 3,000 mules. In addition there were mules 'transporting ammunition (about 800), and those appropriated to the conveyance of intrenching tools, regimental books, medicines, forges,' etc.: in total 'scarcely less than 10,000 public mules were perpetually following the army, besides the crowd of baggage animals belonging to officers ...', say another 2,000; and this did not include those of Hill's Corps, which was followed by a train which 'could not fall far short of 3,000 animals.' Thus the total number of mules accompanying the advance was in the region of 15,000, apart from the cavalry, mounts for the staff, draughts animals and immense herds of cattle 'on the hoof.' It is of interest that Aitchison, writing on 27 May from Castelo de Vide, while returning to the front, remarked: 'We have the

prospect of being well fed (which we were not then [in 1809]); *our commissariat seems admirably arranged*; we have now always full rations of meat, biscuits and spirits, the men are remarkably healthy – there is an appearance of a better vintage than there has been for five years – so say the natives.' Regrettably, due to the lack of any firewood with which to cook – the enemy having already burned all doors, window-frames, and any other combustible material they could find – vines were sometimes cut for that purpose.

It is of some interest to learn that George Bingham, writing from Castelo de Vide three weeks earlier, refers to an outbreak of smallpox there, which had attacked a number of children and Portuguese women ,'who have attached themselves to our men,' but the soldiers themselves, 'who have been all vaccinated have stood it, without taking the infection. Gareth Glover noted that, in the numerous narratives of the period perused, this was the only statement substantiating the fact that British troops were apparently routinely innoculated for smallpox before going abroad, a comment I endorse.

3 The reader is referred to Robert Burham's informative chapter, Filling the Ranks, in *Inside Wellington's Peninsular Army*; likewise concerning Wellington's ungoing wrangle with the Duke of York over the matter of Provisional Battalions.

4 Had this been done earlier, when marching his men north from Badajoz, a contingent could have crossed there, taken Marmont in the rear and cut off his retreat entirely.

5 Those involved were to approach close to the rock-bound fortress during the night. When their presence was noted, they were met by a murderous fire from the defenders, which had the intended diversionary effect, but they were only able to slip from their cover without serious loss by the peak being enveloped in a dense cloud, providentially obscuring their withdrawal.

6 Twenty years were to pass before the stone bridge was repaired, travellers being forced meanwhile to use an unwieldy ferry.

7 Various explanations have been given: that it was not a proper pontoon bridge, but one in which a river boat served as a central link, which could be removed when the bridge was not in use, and this had collapsed under the weight; others have suggested that the first units across cut the cables holding it in place, or that it had been sunk by a shot from Fort Ragusa. This had soon came under fire from those guns on Fort Napoleon which had been turned on it, and its garrison had likewise then fled.

8 Capt. Webber R.A., visiting the site four months later, was surprised to see how thoroughly the forts had been dismantled, and noticed several brass 12-pounders, which had been spiked, lying in a ditch.

9 The garrison was relieved by Foy on the 23rd.

10 189, including 35 killed. French casualties have been estimated at at least 400.

11 A toast to the success was in order, the more so because Wellington had recently been sent 1,000 bottles of claret, and his officers 1,000 more, the spoil of a raid near Vitoria by Longa's guerrillas..

12 For its construction, see Leith Hay's *Narrative of the Peninsular War* and, for greater detail, Roberts Burnham's chapter on Bridge Building in *Inside Wellington's Peninsular Army.*

13 John Burgoyne, who had been sent on 23 May by Wellington to inspect and report on the latest state of the Douro as a means of communication, returned on 15 June to Headquarters at Aldehuela de la Bóveda. Sadly, his *Journal* for that period was omitted from his published *Life.*

[14] Another very reliable informant was Dr Patrick Curtis (1740–1832), professor of Astronomy and Natural History, and rector of the Irish College, who was inducted archbishop of Armagh in 1819, quid pro quo.

[15] Burgoyne mentions that although they had been informed about their existence and provided with 'a confused sketch' by a spy who was not a military man, they had not expected them to have been fortified 'with ingenious nicety.'

[16] The battering-train brought forward by Wellington was inadequate for the task in hand, having as yet only four 19-pounders and as they soon ran out of shot, there was a brief lull in the bombardment between the 21st and 26th, when more amunition reached Salamanca. The Allies casualties in capturing these fortified convents, which included General Bowes, was heavy: 430, while those of the defenders was only 200, although almost 600 prisoners were taken. Cocks described 'Red-hot shot' being fired, Major Henry Sturgeon having the idea of using bellows to heat the balls in a furness, from which they were carried to the 6-pounder guns or howitzers 'in iron crab claws ... some good wads of turf [were then] placed between them and the powder. In less than an hour the convent was partially on fire...'

[17] As had many others, among them George Hennell, who, the morning before leaving the city, was woken by his window being blown in by an explosion, 'and stones falling on the roof.' He assumed the French had returned, but found it had been caused by a Spanish sentinel smoking close to a store of ammunition, which 'dashed to the ground all the houses within 100 yards circumference and buried the whole of their inhabitants ... I went and saw the ruins, saw several dug out, they were in bed when it happened (½ past 6 in the morning). I suppose it killed 40 or 50 men women & children.' In fact, only a few soldiers and about 20 civilians were killed, and several houses wrecked.

[18] Gen. Carlos de España (1775–1839), was a regular army officer of French royalist origin, born d'Espaigne or Espinac. He later became a ruthless Governor of Catalonia, where he was assassinated.

[19] Daniel described the farmers here being 'busily occupied in cutting their barley, which (and even rye sometimes) from the scarcity of oats, being used by us as forage corn, they thrash out immediately ... the grain being thinly spread over a stone threshing floor ...a sledge drawn by two oxen is passed over it, which not only beats out the corn but also cuts the straw.'

[20] An early reference to the fact that Graham's eyes were starting to give him such trouble that Wellington had agreed that he should leave for England to seek professional advice, which he did on 4 July.

[21] The Chasseurs Britanniques, forming part of the brigade; but see page 212, note 36.

[22] Some days later, on hearing that the forts at Salamanca had surrendered, Marmont retired north-east, with the Allies at his heels.

[23] Writing on 5 July from Medina del Campo, John Mills describes the sun as intense and that he was 'quite burnt up,' there being no trees within miles to shade their march (apart from six poplars, which they cut down in order to cook their dinner), and mentioned that Wellington had ordered the troops 'to be put into the towns during the day and moved out at night,' when mosquitos were 'extremely troublesome.' Burgoyne stated that the object of moving in the night was 'to conceal our movements as much as possible.' It was was not always easy to find shelter. Mills refers to a barrack at Medina capable of

holding 6,000 cavalry, being entirely unroofed by the French for the timber.

John Cooke described the heat as such that one soldier 'put up a blanket to keep the rays from him', and the bivouac near Cabrerizos (immediately east of Salamanca) soon 'presented a droll appearance as the whole Division had hoisted blankets in a similar manner. Agueda, a Spanish *muchacha* with sandy hair from the *pueblo* of Fuenteguinaldo, preferred the sound of the bugle-horn to her domestic occupations. She was the sole female to be seen amid the sunburnt soldiers and the brilliant masses that now covered hill and dale, ready at a moment to deploy in battle array.'

24 Mills had sat on a Brigade Court Martial on some men who had been passing counterfeit dollars. These had been made 'out of buttons and they are very well executed.' These coiners had found that the regimental badge on their easily flattened brass buttons gave them the appearance of minted money. Anything that looked like a coin seems to have passed muster. Richard Ford, when in Seville twenty years later, would find an extraordinary variety in the small change received when making minor purchases, even Roman coins occasionally.

25 One wonders when it was, and what was said, when Wellington gave 'some of his Laconic speeches previous to the Battle [of Salamanca]' referred to later by Captain Bragge as 'although not the Language of the Marlboroughs and Peterboroughs ... very much in 'this modern Hero's style of addressing his Generals and ... found to answer equally well.'

26 In *Salamanca 1812* he succinctly explains the manifold problems faced when attempting to describe the complex confrontation, and provides an analysis which would be hard to emulate. I subscribe to the proposition that the volume should be made compulsory reading to any author – amateur or professional – with pretensions to being a military historian.

27 Wellington did not anticipate that he would be able to hold his ground should Joseph's army join Marmont's, as was expected.

28 According to Bragge, the mounts of 'the whole Brigade broke from their moorings and dashed over the Men, wounding about 50 ... only conceive our confusion. We recovered all our Nags but the 5th lost 18 Horses.'

29 The name by which the battle of Salamanca is known to both the French and the Spanish.

30 The French divisions were now approximately in line from west to east, with Thomières's in the van, followed by Maucune's 5th, Taupin's 6th, Clausel's 2nd; further east were Bonnet's 8th and Sarrut's 4th. Ferey's 3rd and Foy's 1st Divisions were still north-east of the Greater Arapile.

31 However effective they might have been, the Allied guns were outnumbered by 78 to 54.

32 In the event, after ascending the lower slope of the Greater Arapile and clambering up the steep last few yards before reaching the crest, they were thrown back by the 120th Ligne firing at them at close quarters.

33 He was one of only two British cavalry officers killed in the battle.

34 Burgoyne had met 'at ten at night, all the medical men of the city coming out by torchlight, with jackasses loaded with bandages, &c., to dress the wounded,' while 'the most respectable Inhabitants carried the Soldiers [back into the city] on their Backs,' according to Bragge.

35 Notable is the description of Captain Barralier's plight, as recorded in Rory Muir's *Tactics and the Experience of Battle*, pp. 259-61.

36 In the same letter, he remarked that while the Spaniards seem to be actively employed recruiting, their general outcry had been 'Let us have British officers and we will fight like British soldiers.'

37 The Allies lost 127 of the 770 present at this action; French casualties, including prisoners taken, were in the region of 1,100. In the maneouvring before Salamanca and in the battle itself, the Allies had suffered 5,200 casualties, some 850 being mortal; French losses were approximately 12,400 – including 4,100 wounded, the rest being either killed, missing or captured, of which there were many. For a detailed breakdown, see Muir's *Salamanca*. They had also left 20 guns on the field.

38 Clausel, writing to Joseph Bonaparte from Arévalo shortly after the battle, admitted to have been able to rally only 22,000 men, although numerous stragglers must have caught up with him later.

39 To forestall this, a detachment under D'Urban had entered Segovia on 4 August. In his wake, the army ascended the only road, a paved one curling up the north flank of the Guadarrama range to the Navacerrada pass, then down to the Escorial, reached on the 9th by D'Urban, who had then pushed ahead cautiously south-east towards Madrid. Wellington entered Segovia on the 7th, and made his Headquarters at San Ildefonso. The gardens (in which a display of water-works was given) and palace greatly impressed Commissary Daniel.

Regrettably, on the afternoon of the 11th, the Portuguese cavalry let him down badly at Majadahonda, only 7 miles north-west of the capital, when caught unawares and attacked by a strong enemy force making an eleventh hour attempt to stem the Allied advance. They were outnumbered by three to one, admittedly, and supported by K.G.L. dragoons belatedly, but they would not rally after their first discomforture, allowing three horse-artillery guns to be captured, temporarily. 15 officers and 182 men were casualties in this unfortunate affair.

40 Grattan records that as the triumphal army traversed any village on their advance, whether on Valladolid or Segovia, the inhabitants would meet them with 'wine, fruit, bread, and vegetables, which were all bought up by the soldiers,' and at the end of each day's march, their bivouacs were invaded by young girls and men with similar provisions, the evenings being 'wound up by boleros and fandangos.'

41 Five of Clinton's battalions had only just arrived from England, some still feverish, having taken part in the ill-fated Walcheren expedition three years' earlier. Although they had yet to acclimatise themselves to the heat of a Spanish summer, they brought up the strength of his division to 7,000. Wellington had stationed them at Cuellar as a precautionary measure, should Foy, who had then moved east to Aranda, attempt to push south.

42 As the Spaniards had reported that the garrison in the Retiro were 'to protect their sick only', Burgoyne with six dragoons had been sent in to summon the place, but being fired at from that direction, he entered the town elsewhere. Early next morning, he and Wellington reconnoitred the Retiro fort, which capitulated on the following day.

43 Excepting several thousand who had taken up the French cause – the so-called *Afrancesados* – together with the numerous minor officials and hangers-on, not daring to face the ferocity of their more patriotic fellow citizens, panicked, making off by all possible means with their portable valuables, some forming a chaotic caravan trailing south to Aranjuez.

[44] *aguardiente*, spirits, often an inferior brandy.

[45] Also known as La Granja. According to Bragge's patron, an eye-witness to the event, in the previous May a band of 800 guerrillas had descended on the place, 'at that Time garrisoned by eighty of the Imperial Guard and two officers. 300 entered the Town and 500 surrounded the Place about Noon, but in less than two Hours the Eighty French drove them out ... killing and taking numbers, to the great satisfaction of the Inhabitants who have a greater dread of these Villains than they have of the French.'

[46] Richard Ford, the future author of the great *Hand-Book for Travellers in Spain*, referred to two of these reptiles having escape during a fire in the menagerie and taken up their quarters in the botanic gardens, where they had remained until 1844, when one, 22 feet long, was shot, and where 'one of the old ones still remains, and there are several young ones ...[which] feed on the rabbits and on any unfortunate cat or dog who unwittingly stray in to study botany.'

[47] A few weeks later, Gordon 'picked up a very fine Grecian Coin of Syracuse of Dionysius, very perfect about the size of half a crown in brass.'

[48] Only quite recently, a rumpus was caused at Salamanca apropos placing a plaque in the Plaza Mayor to commemorate Wellington, which some deemed to be a gratuitous effront to Spanish honour and entirely unwarranted.

11

September to November 1812: Frustration at Burgos; withdrawal to Portugal

While his system of intelligence kept Wellington fully informed of events and enemy troop movements throughout the Peninsula, from a strategic point of view it was not easy to decide what move to make next.

On 14 August Clausel, with the recuperated 'Army of Portugal', re-entered Valladolid, precipitately abandoned by Santocildes's Galicians, who left 400 French convalescents there together with quantities of small arms collected previously from prisoners.[1] Foy had rescued the garrisons of Toro and Zamora, further west, although Astorga had fallen to Spanish irregulars. Joseph was some distance to the south-east of Madrid, but could no longer be regarded as a serious threat. Soult, ignoring Joseph's orders to abandon Andalusia, was still besieging Cadiz, but should he move north, Hill's 'Corps' could defend the capital. Nevertheless, the Allies would be greatly outnumbered if Clausel, together with Soult and Joseph, combine against him; and it was almost certain that once Napoleon had knocked Russia out of the ring, he would again concentrate against the British in the Peninsula. Would not the present be as good an opportunity as any, and before they received reinforcements, to push French troops north of the Duero, further towards if not over the Pyrenees.

And yet, as Wellington wrote dejectedly and with some presentiment to his brother Henry on 23 August: '... though I still hope to be able to maintain our position in Castile, and even to improve our advantages, I shudder when I reflect on the enormity of the task which I have undertaken, with inadequate powers myself to do anything, and without assistance of any kind from the Spaniards ... I am apprehensive that all this may turn out ill for the Spanish cause. If by any cause I should be overwhelmed, or should I be obliged to retire, what will the world say? What will the people of England say? What will those in Spain say?'

Wellington himself left Madrid on 31st August, having sent ahead the 1st, 5th, and 7th Divisions, Pack's and Bradford's Portuguese Brigades, and those of Bock's and Ponsonby's cavalry, a total of some 23,000, which crossed the Duero unopposed on 6th September. Clausel retired, keeping his distance. Wellington followed him north-west through and past Burgos, invested on 19 September.

A depot was established at Arévalo,[2] from which cattle on the hoof and provisions could be distributed to both parts of the field army, now divided between Burgos and Madrid, with a forward depot being set up near El Escorial. Hill's 'Corps', which had previously marched up the Tagus valley, evacuated by the French, to occupy a position between Toledo and Aranjuez, were supplied by the valley road. Wellington had just received intelligence that Soult, on hearing of the fall of Madrid, had given up the siege of Cadiz on 24 August after a parting bombardment and the destruction of remaining *matériel*. General John Skerrett had then occupied Seville, abandoned by Soult on the 27th.[3]

Hill's troops, entering Toledo on 30 September 'amid the loud and continuous acclamations of a patriotic multitudes – were most cordially welcomed, and billeted in the best houses.' Sherer's host was 'a rosy-looking canon,' who lodged him superbly and treated him most courteously. After 'taking a goblet of delicious white wine,' he sallied forth into its 'steep, narrow, inconvenient streets' to see all he could before sunset, for at dawn next day the march was to continue. He passed three hours in the cathedral, from which many of the best paintings had been removed, but noticed several by Bayeu surviving in the cloisters. The organ was excellent, the singing good, although he had expected more impressive ceremonial. Then to the imposing Alcázar, 'now dirty, deserted, and silent,' before dining with a friend, seeing 'a broad, ridiculous farce' at the theatre, and attending a spirited ball given at the Archbishop's palace. Sherer recalled the occasion:

> It was very late when I returned to my billet, but I had all the luxury of a short, deep slumber in a capital bed, with sheets of the finest linen, and trimmed with broad muslin borders. In two hours the bugle roused me; in my anti-chamber, neatly laid out on a marble slab, I found chocolate, fruit, and sweet biscuits; and my good canon already up, and waiting to take leave of me. I drank his chocolate, shook him cordially by the hand, mounted, and rode off; and found myself before midday, in a vile, open, unsheltered bivouack, with very little, and very bad water, and not a breath of air stirring around. Such were the varieties, which not

> infrequently presented themselves during our marches in the peninsula. The next day, again brought us into excellent quarters in the small town of Yepes, where we halted for three weeks …

The vintage was taking place, with 'the finest red wine from Val de Peñas, in La Mancha' being found in the market. Excursions were made across the parched plain to Aranjuez, 'on the very edge of a green valley, filled with groves, and parks, and gardens,' enchanting, even if the palace itself was 'not a magnificent building', while he was 'fatigued and restless with gazing on the dazzling splendour' of the so-called 'Casa del Labrador.'

Burgos besieged

The stronghold of Burgos was garrisoned by 2,200 well-armed and provisioned men commanded by General Dubreton. On surveying the citadel, dominating the town, Wellington found it more substantial than expected, perhaps unaware that four years earlier Napoleon himself had inspected its dilapidated defences and left instructions that they should be substantially restored and improved, an order only partly carried out. Nevertheless, its reduction was vital before he could advance further north-east; while it would provide a defensive bastion also against any future enemy incursions into Castile from that direction. Clausel might be enticed to fight in an attempt to relieve it.

Some 500 yards north-east of the citadel rose the redoubt of San Miguel, defended by part of the garrison. Using the same tactics as those that had succeeded at the Greater Teson at Ciudad Rodrigo, this outlying fort, known as the Hornwork, was seized on the evening of 20 September, but casualties were high, for which Bragge blamed Wellington for 'having employed a Division not used to the noble science of storming … as it was the Troops advanced to the Glacis and there stood to be shot at without endeavouring to gain the Fort …', adding that he understood that it was intended 'to take the Castle by Sap, which is – I believe – a rather tedious process, but as Lord Wellington in all his military Career never missed taking a Fort, I do not imagine he is going to be outdone at Burgos.'

Although a few field guns were found in the Hornwork, there were no siege train to hand, only three 18-pounders. At an earlier stage in the campaign, Pakenham had suggested using the ordnance found at Madrid, but the idea had been turned down; Wellington had assumed that the reduction of Burgos would be a walk-over. It would take weeks for any sufficiently heavy guns to be brought forward, either from Salamanca or landed at Santander and hauled up and across the intermediate ranges; nor had he sufficient ammunition. On 26 September, a dispatch was sent to Commodore Sir Home Popham, lying off the coast, ordering up barrels of powder from Santander, which reached Burgos on 5 October, followed by other convoys. The two 24-pounders, belatedly requested, on leaving the coast on 9 October, had taken nine days to reach Reinosa, still 50 miles north of Burgos, and were then sent back.[4] Whether their presence at Burgos would have sufficed to sway the balance, is unlikely.

As at Badajoz, Wellington was short of adequately trained sappers and miners.[5] After several ineffectual attacks in the face of determined sorties, the outer walls of the castle eventually fell, but it was not until the afternoon of 18 October that the main assault took place, and that failed. Capt. George Bowles (Coldstream Guards) was of the opinion, with which several other officers concurred,[6] that although this was 'one of the longest jobs the noble Marquis has had in hand for some time, and, much as I *revere* him, I must say that in this case he has shown rather more of a quality nearly allied to obstinacy than is to be wished. The fact is that he was repeatedly told by those whom he consulted previous to commencing operations, his means (three eighteen-pounders, four howitzers) were totally insufficient.'

The whole undertaking had gone badly. Bragge, writing home on the 25th, was of the opinion that it would 'cost the British Army dearer than Ciudad Rodrigo' to take, and he was right.[7] Among the too many lives being lost was Somers Cocks, killed in Dubreton's sortie on the 8th of October. Tomkinson described 'Lord Wellington, Sir Stapleton Cotton, Generals Pack and Anson, with the whole of their staff, and the officers of the 16th Light Dragoon and 79th Regiment, attended him to his grave [in their camp ground]. He is regretted by the whole army, and in those regiments in which he has been not a man can lament a brother more than they do him. I took upon myself the arrangement of his affairs, and the disposal of what I thought should be sold the day after his funeral. It is usual on these occasions to sell his appointments, etc. In this instance I took upon myself to give most of them to his friends. The sword he had in his hand when he fell I keep myself.'

Colonel Ponsonby, Bragge's commander, had received a barbed comment in his letter of the 25th, as being

> ... no great Genl. He was ordered the other Day to advance until he was stopped, which he did by moving our Regt down an Avenue with a Front of Threes and no advanced Guard until the Enemy thought proper to Fire a Gun, which enfiladed the Road and might have killed 30 Men had it been pointed properly. Another shot took two Light Dragoons Heads off and the next passed under my Mare's legs and the covering Sergts' horses without doing either any Injury.
>
> Burgos is one of the worst large Towns I have seen in Spain and the Country round it extremely dreary although abounding in Corn. The People [are] horridly ugly and what is rather remarkable for Spaniards excessively dirty, therefore I have no wish to go farther North, except to embark.
>
> I still continue well, but most of our Officers are complaining and some of them very ill with Fevers and Agues which cannot be wondered at as we have only been under a Roof two Nights since we left Valladolid.

Additionally, 'All the Troops, both English and French, are considerably weakened by Sickness; our sick amount to 20,000, in which are included men taking Medicine whether with or away from their Regiments, and the Army under Soult are so weakened by it, that he is striving to the utmost to keep out of Genl Hill's Road.' Among sentences worth quoting from his next letter, written just prior to breaking up their camp, one refers to the Spaniards, who 'according to their own accounts have been doing wonders lately [starving the French out of Astorga], but I am incredulous enough not to believe a single Syllable of their Dispatches.' As another confirmed: 'With the Assistance of borrowed Money and some deceased Officers' Kits, I have been enabled to rigg myself again tolerably well but was a few weeks since almost naked.' While, talking of uniforms, did his Father not agree with him in thinking it 'very bad Policy to send Life Guardsmen on service and to keep Hussars in London, who are in no respect half so well calculated to keep Cockneys in order as the Old London Troops?' and, apropos the Prince of Wales's sartorial obsessions: 'I begin to think with the Editor of the *Examiner* that some Princes were born for Tailors.' [8]

Several changes had taken place in French dispositions during the siege. Clausel had been superceded by General Souham in command of the 'Army of Portugal', now numbering 42,000; and this might be reinforced by 11,000 under Caffarelli, which had been occupied dispersing guerrilla packs further north. On 19 September Wellington received intelligence from Hill (with some 28,000 Anglo-Portuguese plus 8,000

Spaniards on the Tagus south of Madrid), that the junction of Soult's, Joseph's, and Suchet's armies had taken place ten days earlier and that the combined forces of the first two, certainly outnumbering his own, were marching on the capital, even if only at a Spanish pace.

Retreat

In the face of these growing enemy concentrations – on 20 October two of Souham's divisions had attempted to test the strength of the Allies, only to retire, smarting – Wellington reluctantly decided to relinquish the siege. After dark on the 21st he pulled back his field army, joined unobtrusively by the besieging units, which by next morning was already several miles south-west of Burgos on the Valladolid road. As he confessed to McGrigor: 'We cannot keep Madrid. Hill is obliged by an overwhelming force to quit his position; he is in fact on the march towards us and I must leave this place tonight.' After agreeing to McGrigor's arrangements for the removal of wounded, he added: 'but be most careful not to let a syllable of my intention of moving escape you.'

As the rearguard of Stapleton Cotton's 1,300 cavalry were soon finding themselves hard-pressed by 6,000 French cavalry,[9] Wellington ordered a battery of horse artillery and two battalions of K.G.L. to reinforce them. On the 23rd there was a sharp engagement at a minor river crossing at Venta del Pozo (north-east of Villodrigo), caused by Anson's Light Horse reforming on the wrong flank after crossing, thus masking the guns and allowing the bridge to be taken. Another rearguard action was fought on the 26th at Villamuriel, south of Palencia, near the confluence of the Carrión and Pisuerga, which Wellington crossed next day at Cabezon before traversing Valladolid.[10]

Both here and elsewhere, too many of his dispirited troops, their rearguard continually harrassed, got beastly drunk on the new wine. Foy then swung round and got a toe-hold on the south bank of the Duero at Tordesillas, while the rest of the Allied army crossed further east, destroying bridges in its wake. Souham now called off the chase, while Caffarelli's was again distracted by the activity of guerrilla groups springing up behind him like dragon's teeth.

Wellington determined to hold the line of the Duero as long as possible before retiring on Arévalo, where Hill was ordered to join him. George Burrough's recalled bivouacking near the river-bank, where they 'began to cook their provisions, and send our baggage animals for forage. The woods soon began to ring with the sturdy strokes of the axe, and the crackling blaze of the fires of the olive leaf illuminated the camp. The lofty clamours of the Portuguese; the nasal murmurs of the Spaniards; mingled with the neighing of horses, the lowing of cows, and the braying of asses, could not fail of reminding one of the medley scenes and discordant sounds of Saint Bartholomew's fair.'

Torrential Autumn rains then commenced; the roads, such as they were, becoming quagmires. Morale was low, the troops were short of rations, and lax discipline deteriorated further as the troops plodded on, chagrined at the indignity of having to retreat in the face of an enemy they had so severely trounced only three months before.

After crossing the Duero at Boecillo (due south of Valladolid) the Headquarters staff followed a route south-west towards Salamanca which ran parallel to the highway, passing through Rueda, Torrecilla de la Orden, and Pitiegua.[11] It was in a dispatch from Rueda dated 31 October, that Wellington admitted to having 'got clear in a handsome manner of the worst scrape I ever was in.'[12] It was here also that Judge-Advocate-General Larpent, just reaching the front from Lisbon, had his first interview with Wellington to discuss his future duties, when he was informed that he would be sent some 'fifty cases against officers, to examine, in order to ascertain whether any can be made out on evidence,' which apparently was the 'great difficulty.' Larpent soon adjusted to the daily tenor of life at Headquarters, rising at 5.00 in the morning of 7 November to see for the first time 'what it was to put seventy thousand men in motion, about ten thousand public, and a greater number of private mules, horses, &c.,' as the army trudged south-west, shortly to converge with Hill's 'Corps'.

* * *

Soult's and Joseph's troops had commenced their progress north-west towards Madrid in mid October: by the 27th, the former were nearing the Tagus at Aranjuez. Although the Allies held the north bank, and several bridges had been broken, the river was still fordable at several places. It was hazardous for Hill to remain, for his position might be turned by Joseph, approaching from the east.

On the 29th, Hill received Wellington's dispatch instructing him to join him north of the Guadarrama range. The withdrawal commenced at once, although some units disgraced themselves at Valdemoro, where hundreds of drunken stragglers were captured by French cavalry. Donaldson remembered passing

> pontoons burning on the road side ... set on fire to prevent them falling into the hands of the enemy ... We supposed at first that we would again occupy Madrid, but when we came in sight of it the Retiro was in flames, and we could hear the report of cannon, which preceeded from the brass guns in the fort being turned on each other for the purpose of rendering them useless ... the stores of provision and clothing which we had previously taken were also burned, and every preparation made for evacuating the place. The staff officers were galloping about giving directions to the different divisions concerning their route; the inhabitants whom we met on the road were in evident consternation, and every thing indicated an unexpected and hurried retreat: instead, therefore, of entering the city, we passed to the left [west] of it.

Although contrary to orders, while skirting the capital, Sherer could not resist riding into it very briefly, time to have a coffee in the Plaza Mayor, where one of many gentlemen congregated there, with tears in his eyes, reproached him: 'I know the English are brave, and loyal – I know this retreat is a measure of necessity; but why, why did you come hither, if you could not calculate on maintaining possession?' Nevertheless, 'though dreadfully dejected, [they] shewed no signs of anger or indignation, but were respectful and friendly to the last. I left the city, encountered no General to put me under an arrest, a punishment ... I deserved, and reached the camp highly delighted at having seen Madrid; for, after all, is it not possible to see in half an hour a scene of interest which may be remembered for ever?' Sherer had to be content with a telescopic view of the distant Escorial before making the ascent to the Puerto de Guadarrama by a fine road – that traversed by Napoleon four years earlier – 'so admirably laid down, that your cannon meet with no obstacle, which an additional pair of horses, or a drag-rope cannot overcome.' Having shepherded his 'Corps' across the range, Hill was nearing Villacastín when another dispatch arrived, ordering him to veer west via Avila and Alba de Tormes rather than marching on Arévalo.[13]

By 8 November the entire Allied force, numbering 52,000 Anglo-Portuguese plus 18,000 Spaniards, were concentrated east of Salamanca, along a 20-mile front running south from San Cristóbal to Alba. Within a week Wellington found himself facing 90,000 French, for the forces of Joseph and Jourdan, Souham,[14] and Soult had meanwhile converged not far east of the Tormes, north of Alba. Although a minor action took place nearby on 10-11 November, in which Soult's units were unsuccessful in their attempt to force the river crossing, little occurred during the next few days as Wellington awaited an attack which never materialised, enemy cavalry merely reconnoitering their line. Sherer anticipated – nay, hoped for – a general engagement, as Hill's units 'had not been present at the glorious victory at Salamanca, and longed eagerly for the battle ...', but it was not to be, although early on the 15th Soult's army was in motion across the fords of the Tormes at Galisancho, and cautiously extending to the west.[15] Wellington redeployed his troops, bringing all those north of the river to the south bank, where they took up positions facing south and south-east, very close to those occupied less than four months earlier.

Soult seemed intent on severing Wellington's communications with Portugal, which could not be risked. In the early afternoon of the 15th, just as another downpour commenced, the Allied army was ordered to retreat west, and fast. Before long, the whole area became one huge swamp, through which, as darkness fell, the dejected infantry columns splashed. Having covered some 10 miles, and as no more had been seen of the French that day, they were permitted to bivouac as best they could. Meanwhile, the Commissariat had broken down. Plentiful supplies of biscuit and other provisions had been sent back into Portugal, but by another route, one inaccessible to those responsible for distributing them.[16] All that most battalions were lucky enough to get that evening was beef, as 'tough as a shoe sole' to Simmons, who had taken a slice from one of many half-starved bullocks 'lying dead in the mud ... yoked to carts laden with baggage;' while Sherer described how those still on the hoof 'were slaughtered daily, as we halted, and putting your miserable ration on a stick, or on the point of your sword, you broiled it on wood-ashes, and ate it greedily, half-smoked, half-raw, without knife, fork, or any conveniences, the whole of our baggage having, of course, preceded us.'

Daniel recalled that the road was almost impassable in places, and that while the troops had 'to wade, for a considerable distance, through water above their knees ... Wellington passed by, attended by about fifteen staff-officers and a few orderly dragoons: he wore an oil-skin cloak, and looked extremely ill, which is not to be wondered at considering the anxiety of mind and fatigue of the body which he was enduring ... [he then] took shelter in a cottage, and many officers of rank were obliged to lie down in their cloaks under hovels near their horses ... We had but little to eat, and nothing to drink; and it was impossible to light a fire ...' Larpent was lucky enough to find dry quarters at Aldehuela de la Bóveda, where three Spanish officers burst in during the night and, despite his vigilance, either they or his hosts stole not only his pistols but also purloined the bread and rum of his servants … but as he reflected, 'Honesty is not a Spanish virtue. We all of us lose things daily.'

The weather further deteriorated as the army tramped south-west, fatigued, hungry, and harassed by cavalry hovering on their flanks like hyenas: some 600 stragglers were taken, and another 1,000 seized next day, among them Sir Edward Paget, commanding the 1st Division: having lost an arm at Oporto, he was unable to defend himself when attacked by three dragoons. Soult's artillery came into play intermittently, although with shot and shell falling into the sodden earth, it did little harm. On the 16th, Sherer's regiment, posted above the hamlet of Matilla de los Caños del Río, were surprised at the sight of

> two squadrons of our German Hussars retiring before a large body of the enemy's horse. As we had piled arms in columns at quarter distance, we were instantaneously formed, and the enemy halted about a musket-shot from us. We stood, for about fifteen minutes, calmly looking at each other. They were about two thousand in number, all covered with large white cloaks, and looked remarkably well … They suffered us to retire through the village, and across the plain to the wood, where our division lay, unmolested; for as they had no guns, it would have been a ticklish affair to attempt any thing against a steady battalion of infantry; but they pushed down about six squadrons to the left … and had a trifling brush with some of our cavalry, who came up hastily from their camp, after which they retired …

The Light Division were in action briefly near the Huebra bridge at San Muñoz, a village half-way to Ciudad Rodrigo, but casualties were slight. The most southerly column seems largely to have avoided enemy attention and, not having to defend themselves, spent the time getting sodden with wine and spirits when not plundering peasants and slaughtering herds of swine among the oakwoods;[17] some men were reduced to eating acorns, while their mounts 'plucked away at the leaves ... the only food they had for four days.' Wheeler entered a forest of oaks, which

> swarmed with pigs feeding on the acorns. The work of destruction soon commenced … so we were soon stocked with pork. But we had neither salt or bread. We soon found the acorns were a good substitute for when roasted they eat much like chestnuts. It must be observed that they were highly seasoned with hunger, that you know is the best sauce. The acorns were very large together with the oaks, are a different sort from any I had ever seen in England.

This day [16 November], some of the enemy's cavalry flanked us, and made sad havock amongst our baggage. Much was destroyed and many men and women were made prisoners. However I had the good fortune to escape, somehow I was overlooked in all this bustle. Seeing the Dragoons returning the way they came, I began to congratulate myself on my good fortune and was returning in order to get nearer my Regiment ... when I espied six Dragoons, galloping towards us. There were eight of us in the Company, each having a loaded musket, so we determined to try our strength, and to reserve our fire until they came so close that each of us could not miss our mark. They had arrived within twenty yards, when some shots from the wood dropped four horses, another moment and we fired. This settled the business, there was not one left to return and tell the tale. We found that the party in the wood, like ourselves, had been overlooked and had resolved to remain under cover of the brushwood until they found all safe, and to fire upon any stragglers of the enemy that should come within reach. We joined them, then went to inspect our prey. We found a rich booty, six hundred and thirty two dollars. This being distributed amongst us gave each thirty five dollars there being eighteen of us. In a quarter of an hour we were on the march again. The women were returned to our army the next day. After this, the enemy gave us no more trouble. On the 20th November we arrived and encamped under the walls of Ciudad Rodrigo. The enemy returned to Salamanca and we proceeded to Moimento [? Moimenta da Serra, near Gouveia], which is the Head quarters of our division.

Thus ended a campaign that opened on the 2nd January, and closed the latter end of November.

Writing home several months later, Lieut. Robert Fernyhough described being laid low not long after the battle of Salamanca by 'a violent fever and ague' and, while being escorted back with the sick and wounded towards the Portuguese frontier during their retreat, had fallen into the hands of a French Hussar regiment, who had treated him vilely:

They knocked the cart from under me, sabred the men, and dragged me into the middle of the road, stripped me, tearing my clothes to shreds, and turning me over with their sabres, plundered me of what little I had remaining, tore a gold ring from my finger, and then left me naked, to perish with cold and hunger.

I lay in this miserable state two days and nights, with no mortals near me, except dead ones; one of which lay with his head upon my legs,

> having died in that position during the night proceding, and I was too weak to remove the body; I could not raise myself, I was so reduced.
>
> In this suffering state I continued to exist, which I attribute to some rum, of which I drank a considerable quantity from a Frenchman's canteen, who was humane enough to let me do so, when I explained to him that I was a British officer … The day following an escort of French dragoons came up, with a number of prisoners … among them a soldier of the ninety-fifth, belonging to the same company as myself; he recognized me, and begged of the Frenchmen to allow him and three others to remove me to a village … I was conveyed on their shoulders in a blanket, almost in a state of insensibility, except when roused by the inhumanity of the three soldiers, who several times tumbled me into the mud, in the most unfeeling manner, swearing I was dead.

Fernyhough was left in 'an old un-roofed barn', where the Spaniards returning to their village carried him, and where another English soldier, having escaped from the enemy, took shelter.

> The poor fellow found me in a state of starvation, and took me upon his back … to the village, and craved food for me from door to door; but the inhuman Spaniards shut their doors in our faces, refusing both shelter and food, at the same time they were baking bread for the French. However, my fellow sufferer … found a dead horse, and he supplied me with this food and acorns, which at the time, I thought very dainty … [but] in justice to the Spanish women; two girls … notwithstanding the threat of punishment to those who should relieve me, absolutely did, two or three times, bring me a little food, saved from their own meals.
>
> In this miserable state I lay, when Colonel [Alexander] Gordon, one of Lord Wellington's aides-de-camp, found me, on his return to Rodrigo, from the French head quarters, where he had been with a flag of truce respecting General Sir Edward Paget, who had been made prisoner during the retreat.
>
> He gave me a gold piece (three dollars) to buy bread with, and assisted my escape to Rodrigo, from whence I was conveyed to the light division in a cart, a mere skeleton, and covered with all kinds of flith and vermin.

Chaos had reigned briefly on the 18th November, when Generals Clinton, Dalhousie, and Stewart, assuming they knew better on receipt of their marching orders, by following alternative routes, led their divisions into an area clogged by Spanish troops; but by the following evening the whole Allied army were safe if not entirely sound; rations were abundant; and they were under cover in cantonments. 'A handful of Indian corn being issued to each man,' and as described by Sherer, 'they all immediately began pounding it between large stones, which strange hand-mills then passed from one to another, keeping up such a noise throughout the whole night, that no one in camp could possibly have closed his eyes. Such were the little additions to our annoyance and misery.'

Few would ever disagree with Donaldson when he commented that 'Retreating before the enemy at any time was a grievous business,' and that

> ... in such weather it was doubly so; the rain, now pouring down in torrents, drenched us to the skin, and the road, composed of clay soil, stuck to our shoes so fast, that they were torn off our feet. The night was dismally dark, the cold wind blew in heavy gusts, and the roads became gradually worse. After marching in this state for several hours, we halted in a field on the road side, and having piled our arms, were allowed to dispose ourselves to rest as best we could. The moon was now up, and wading through the dense masses of clouds, she sometimes threw a momentary gleam on the miserable beings who were huddled together in every variety of posture, endeavouring to rest or screen themselves from the cold. Some were lying stretched on the wet ground rolled up in still wetter blankets, more having placed their knapsacks on a stone, or their wooden canteen, had seated themselves on it with their blankets wrapped about them, their head reclining on their knees, and their teeth chattering with cold; while others more resolute and wise, were walking briskly about. Few words were spoken, and as if ashamed to complain of the hardships we suffered, execrating the retreat, and blaming Lord Wellington for not having sufficient confidence in us to hazard a battle with the enemy, under any circumstances, were the only topics discussed.[18]
>
> A savage sort of desperation had taken possession of our minds, and those who had lived on the most friendly terms in happier times, now quarrelled with each other, using the most frightful imprecations on the slightest offence. All former feelings of friendship were stifled, and a misanthropic spirit took possession of every bosom. The streams which fell from the hills were swelled into rivers, which we had to wade, and vast numbers fell out, among whom were officers, who, having been subject to the same privations, were reduced to the most abject misery.
>
> It was piteous to see some of the men, who had dragged their limbs

> after them with determined spirit until their strength failed, fall down amongst the mud, unable to proceed further; and as they were sure of being taken prisoner, if they escaped being trampled to death by the enemy's cavalry, the despairing farewell look that the poor fellows gave us when they saw us pass on, would have pierced our hearts at any other time; but our feelings were steeled, and so helpless had we become, that we had no power to assist, even had we felt the inclination to do so.
>
> [A day later] we halted sooner than usual, and the weather being clearer, we got fires kindled, – still no rations; but we were encamped among oak trees, and greedily devoured the acorns which grew upon them, although nauseous in the extreme, the junior officer commanding the brigade and our colonel joining in the repast. In many respects the officers were in a worse situation than the men, not having any thing to change themselves, as their luggage had been sent on before us.
>
> If any thing could have given us comfort in our miserable situation, it was having a kind and sympathizing commanding officer: he made many of the weakly men throw away their knapsacks, and by every means in his power he endavoured to infuse comfort and courage into their sinking hearts, braving every difficulty in common with the meanest individual, and even rejecting the superior accommodation which his rank afforded, when he saw the men suffering.

Capt. Browne, almost immediately on reaching Ciudad Rodrigo, was ordered by Wellington himself – who 'was in a terrible ill-humour, & his countenance was full of anger & vexation'–[19] to bring in as many stragglers as possible and report back to him. Collecting a dozen long waggons, a dozen soldiers from the guard and a doctor, he set off , not turning back until reaching Sancti-Spiritus. 'As the Sun broke out, I never can forget the sight of horrors that was exposed to my view. Groupes of women & children & drum boys lay perishing with cold – some had already died in a sort of rolled up posture – others were not yet dead, but convulsed with a sort of hysterical laugh which sometimes precedes death … [We] carried such as were unable to move to the road, there placing them in the waggons under the care of the Doctor, who administered the biscuit & wine that we had brought … I took back to the waggons 120 men, & collected together about a hundred more who were able to walk after having received some refreshment.'

These were taken to the General Hospital established in Ciudad Rodrigo, where, as he later heard, several 'became ideots' [sic]. Browne then reported to Wellington, who thanked him and invited him to dinner. Referring later to the painful events he had witnessed, Browne made an acute observation which may be appropriately quoted here:

> I began to remark the different effects of a continued war-fare like that of the Peninsula on the character of the Officers & common Soldiers. The latter appeared to me, to become daily more ferocious & less fit for return to the duties of citizens, & I sometimes apprehended that when they should be disbanded in England after the restoration of peace, the country would be over-run, with pilferers & marauders of every description. The Officers on the contrary seemed to become more thoughtful & humane, & more anxious to exert themselves in softening the misery with which they were surrounded …
>
> In all the cold & rain of the last three days of the Burgos retreat, Ld. Wellington was on horse-back with the troops from sun-rise to sun-set, sharing all their privations & encouraging them by his presence to proceed cheerfully on their march. It had the happiest possible effect both on Officers & men, & some were heard to exclaim, 'Never mind this ugly weather, we shall soon be back again, & that's the fellow as will shew us how to lick the French.'

Meanwhile, on 28 November, the different regiments of Hill's 'Corps' started their march south, to be 'distributed in mountain villages, south of the Sierra de Francia, and here we halted for eight days. Here, too, we were restored to our baggage, and under cover. Miserable as were the hovels in which we were quartered, our gaiety in these chimney-corners, where we sat roasting chesnuts, and boiling potatoes, would not a little have surprised our friends at home, could they by magic have been transported from their curtained and carpeted drawing rooms to these mountain-cots, and have seen the accommodation we thought ourselves so fortunate in procuring.'

And there, and in the vicinity of Coria, they remained until the following May.

1 On the 18th, Clausel sent a probing force across the Duero, the river line being watched by Anson's dragoons, but they retired to the north bank two days later.

2 Arévalo, lying half way between Tordesillas and Avila, would have been topped up from Almeida and Ciudad Rodrigo, from which depots almost 2,000 carts were then continually shuttling, an indication of the magnitude of the Commissariat's engagement to supply adequately any forces advanced so far from their habitual bases.

3 Skerrett later joined Hill with 4,000 men. In the event, it was not until 16 September that Soult, reluctant to leave Andalusia, marched leaisurely north-east from Granada with his combined forces (including D'Erlon's units which had united with him at Cordoba) to converge with those of Joseph near Almanza, well out of the way, although this did not take place until 2 October.

4 As Wellington later explained to the Prime Minister: 'In regard to means, there were ample means both at Madrid and at Santander for the siege of the strongest fortress. That which was wanting at both places was the means of transporting ordnance and military stores to the places where it was desirable to use them. The people of England, so happy as they are in every respect, so rich in resources of every description, having the use of excellent roads etc will not readily believe that important results here frequently depend upon 50 or 60 mules more or less, or a few bundles of straw to feed them; but the fact is so.'

5 Burgoyne, by then a Lieut.-Colonel, whose description of the siege is invaluable, attests that troops sent to work at the saps refused to do so, although gabions and fascines had been laid out to protect them. However, some men who had been coal miners in civil life came forward from the ranks when called for to assist in this arduous work.

6 There was an unusual amount of discontent shown, while some officers took advantage of the situation by requesting leave of absence. McGrigor was in the room when two entered, one a captain in the engineers who had received letters from home informing him that his wife was dangerously ill, to which Wellington had replied that he could not spare him at that moment; the other, a general of noble family, who complained of suffering from rheumatism, was given short shrift, Wellington interrupting his request with 'and you must go to England to be cured of it. By all means. Go there immediately.'

On 25 October, Tomkinson referred in his Diary to 'Several officers had their notions fixed on England, and … Captain MacIntosh (raised from the ranks), went before a medical board and got sick leave … He was much better than myself *after* he had passed the board. I should never have shown my face again with the regiment had I applied for such leave.'

7 Total Allied losses at the former siege had been slightly over 1,100, of which less than 200 were killed; at Burgos the figures were over 2,000 (a quarter of them killed), compared to the garrison's 623.

8 As Bragge remarked two months later: '… if at any Time you can inform me that a London Mob have stoned the Hussars out of Piccadilly and made the Prince recall his Life Guards, I shall have additional Satisfaction in receiving your Letter.'

9 Already, according to Lieut. William Smith (11th Light Dragoons) with the rearguard, the debris of retreat was only too evident: broken carts and casks, scattered provisions, numbers of men lying in the mud, drunk or dead, apart from the carcasses of horses, mules, and oxen littering the road.

10 Again, the problem arose about the transport of the wounded. When McGrigor reported that he had be laying hands on all available carts and mules to convey them back to Salamanca, Wellington had rounded on him: 'And you have made Salamanca chock full. I cannot stop there,' before being reassured that they were already in movement on Ciudad Rodrigo and then towards Oporto, should it be necessary to embark them. When Wellington expressed his approbation, McGrigor could not help reminding him that he had been blamed on a previous occasion for issuing a similar instruction without consulting

him, to which Wellington had replied: 'It is all right, as it has turned out, but I recommend you still to have my orders for what you do.'

11 It was in May 1837, when dining on bacon and eggs with the amiable old priest of Pitiegua, that George Borrow, as recorded in *The Bible in Spain*, was informed that he was seated where Wellington and Craufurd had once sat 'after they had beat the French at Arapiles', an understandable mistake – for Craufurd had been killed six months prior to the battle – but his reputation as commander of the Light Division, even among Spaniards, long outlived him.

12 On that same day, Burgoyne had noted: 'Cold weather, with heavy dews at night. It is astonishing how our men can stand it. Their clothing is very old, and having no covering but a single blanket or a great coat; the ground is wet; no tents or wood near enough to make huts.'

13 Hill had ordered Deputy Commissary-General Routh either to get the stores previously accumulated in the Tagus valley at Talavera and Trujillo taken back to Badajoz, or have it destroyed.

14 Within days, Souham was superseded by D'Erlon in command of the 'Army of Portugal'.

15 It is recorded that, while crossing the former battlefield, still littered with unburied and decomposing Frenchmen, horses hoofs would frequently send their skulls rolling.

16 Colonel James Willoughby-Gordon, serving as Quartermaster-General since August 1811, was responsible for this deplorable bungle, which deprived the army of food for three days. He was sent home in January and, much to Wellington's relief, replaced, as requested, by the dependable George Murray, who had served in that responsible position earlier.

17 'One day,' wrote Dr MacGrigor, 'I saw five hundred men at least in a state of beastly intoxication. All subordination was gone, all alike – English, Scots and Irish – were equally the slaves of drunkenness ... Had the enemy come upon us at the time we should have been an easy prey to him.'

18 It is of interest that D'Urban, in his annotated copy of Jones's *Account of the War*, affirmed that the retreat 'was conducted with singular coolness and ability. Lord Wellington was always master of his movements; he marched when (and only when) he thought proper, and halted to rest the troops whenever he found it expedient.'

19 As confirmed by McGrigor, who described him as 'in a very bad humour' when cross-questioning him regarding the state of the wounded, and 'adverted in bitter language to the disorder of the retreat and indicated especially some divisions ...and ... some officers in particular ... and read to me a severe order, which he said he would issue to the army.' He had also remarked: 'I never knew till now, nor believed, how unjustly poor Moore had been dealt with in the outcry raised against him in England about his retreat. I consider him the worst used man that ever lived. Nothing is so unmanageable as a British army in retreat, or when foiled.'

12

December 1812 to May 1813: Rehabilitation; offensive preparations

By 19 November the Allies were back in their former cantonments in Portugal, while the French, suffering equally from the appalling weather, dispersed to find what food and forage they could, and shelter in the way of winter quarters.

Looking back on the year, Wellington had some reasons to congratulate himself and his army, in spite of their present sorry condition.[1] Foy well expressed the state of play: 'Lord Wellington has retired unconquered, with the glory of the laurels of Arapiles, having restored to the Spaniards the country south of the Tagus, and made us destroy our magazines, our fortifications – in a word all that we have gained by our conquest, and all that could assure the maintainance of it.' Certainly, the whole of Andalusia had been liberated; almost 20,000 prisoners had been shipped back to England; huge quantities of enemy *matériel* had been captured; their prestige had been shattered, and their confidence severely undermined.

Early in December, Private Wheeler made a computation of the distance he had covered since the advance on Ciudad Rodrigo eleven months before: 'The number of miles marched over in this time, if averaged at eight miles per diem, 2328. This is not over-rating it. Portugal had been walked over from north to south and back again, three times. Spain, from Baddajoz to within two or three days march of Truxillo and back to Baddajoz again. Then from Rodrigo to Salamanca and on to Madrid, and from Madrid to Validolid, Burgos and Monistaro, and lastly from Monistaro [Monisterio de Rodilla] down to Ciudad Rodrigo. Besides the counter marching, when near the enemy. If I had avaraged ten miles per diem I think I should not have over rated it.'

Although there had been rumours that Napoleon's Russian campaign had met with disaster, it was not until 18 January 1813 that formal confirmation reached Wellington's Headquarters, which naturally influenced his future strategy. Newspapers were soon arriving, containing awesome details, the reading of which gave a further boost to morale.[2] Nor could such disheartening news be kept from the French troops for long, which, throughout the winter, had remained the object of unremitting guerrilla activity carried out by the now more confident and better-armed Spanish partisans. These had also been supplying Wellington with valuable information concerning enemy dispositions in addition to that received from his own intelligence officers. He was almost as well aware of the situation behind their front as the French were themselves. It was not long before news reached him that both Caffarelli and Soult had returned to France,[3] taking with them large bodies of troops.

Wellington's divisions were now dispersed over a wide area, the 1st in the upper Mondego valley, between Guarda and Viseu, with the 3rd further north; the 4th were cantoned near the south bank of the Douro near São João da Pesqueira, while the 5th were placed further west, in the vicinity of Lamego. The 6th and 7th lay near Seia, on the northern flank of the Serra da Estrela, while the Light Division, together with Alten's brigade of cavalry, remained between Guarda and their familiar billets in villages near the frontier. Pack's and Bradford's Portuguese were placed north of the Douro, between Penafiel and Vila Real, and most of the remaining cavalry, apart from D'Urban's units near Braganza, were sent as far west as the coastal plain.[4] Hill had his headquarters at Coria, with brigades of the 2nd Division spread among the mountain villages in the vicinity, while his cavalry was based at Brozas, not far south-east of Alcántara.

The Allied army had not distinguished itself during the last few weeks, and their commander, frustrated, and partly to blame for the fiasco at Burgos, was in an irritable and censorious mood. He had lost some 3,000 men on the retreat, mostly from exposure or by their straggling and, in his view, a high proportion of these casualties could have been avoided if all those responsible to him had carried out their duties scrupulously. On 28 November Wellington distributed a confidential memorandum to his general officers, which soon became public knowledge, causing ill-feeling among many, whether or not the cap fitted. The content of this withering, and indiscriminate, condemnation may be exemplified adequately by one or two paragraphs:

> It must be obvious to every officer, that from the moment the Troops commenced their retreat from the neighbourhood of Burgos on the one hand, and from Madrid on the other, the Officers lost all command over

their men. Irregularities and outrages of all descriptions were committed with impunity, and losses have been sustained which never ought to have occurred.

Yet the necessity for retreat existing, none was ever made on which the troops had such short marches; none on which they made such long and repeated halts; and none on which the retreating armies were so little pressed on their rear by the enemy.

I have no hesitation in attributing these evils to the habitual inattention of the Officers of the Regiments to their duty as prescribed by the regulations of the service and by the orders of the Army.

[and later] ... and they must endeavour to inspire the Non-commissioned Officers with a sense of their situation and authority: and the Non-commissioned Officers must be forced to do their duty by being constantly under the view and superintendence of their Officers; by these means the frequent and discreditable recourse to the authority of the Provost and to Punishments by the sentence of Court-Martials will be prevented, and the soldiers will not dare to commit offences and outrages of which there are too many complaints ...

Not surprisingly, the sweeping reprimand was immediately leaked to the press. Writing home in early February, Bragge had commented:

I was very sorry to see Lord Wellington's Letter to his Generals ... at full length in the rascally London Newspapers with suitable remarks by the Editors, one of whom cooly observes [that] the Army was in a state of Mutiny and the Retreat more dreadful than that of the French through Russia. My own opinion is that Lord Wellington never wished or intended the aforesaid Letter to be published, nor was it, I believe, in many instances read to the Troops but to the Officers only. It was perhaps rather too violent and never would have been necessary had his Lordship proper General Officers under him or Men of his own choosing. At present the Ministers or Duke of York order out a batch of Generals, who in general have neither Talent or Experience. Some blunder is committed, Lord Wellington speaks his mind, the Great Man is offended or probably sulky at being crossed, and never bothers to exert himself or act upon his own Judgement again. Here I think commences a slackness which is quickly felt throughout the whole Machine, occasions incalculable Mischief and has induced Lord Wellington to call this 'God Almighty's Army' a thousand times.

Except General Hill there is scarcely a General Officer in this Army of any Talent and very few of any Activity except Sir. S. Cotton and I

> suppose no commander ever had so few clever Men on his Staff almost all of them being coxcomical or Old Women, amongst the latter I include Col. Gordon, the Quarter-master General, who – I believe – has returned to England after doing considerable Mischief instead of saving several Millions a Year, for which purpose he was sent out.[5]

The disreputable behaviour, or worse, of some of the British rank and file – notably when in retreat or in the wake a storming – was incited usually by the criminal element, the delinquents, bruisers, and unruly spirits among Wellington's troops, which he has been criticised speciously for calling 'the very scum of the earth.' It was in conversation with Stanhope in November 1831,[6] that he thus reiterated an opinion aired only days earlier, when making the comparison:

> The French soldiers are more under control than ours. It was quite shocking what excesses ours committed when once let loose. I remember once at Badajoz, when we stormed the town, entering a cellar and seeing some soldiers lying on the floor so dead drunk that the wine was actually flowing from their mouths! Yet others were coming in not at all disgusted at seeing them, and going to do the same. Our soldiers could not resist wine ... People talk of their enlisting from their fine military feeling – all stuff – no such thing. Some of our men enlist from having got bastard children – some for minor offences – many more for drink; but you can hardly conceive such a set brought together, and it is really wonderful that we should have made them the fine fellows they are. I have never known officers raised from the ranks turn out well, nor the system answer; they cannot stand drink.

The Duke was referring to Badajoz as one of the more flagrant incidents only among all those which had been brought to his attention. And how many had not! Should it be imagined that his strictures were excessively reactionary and elitist, unprejudiced evidence is found in several contemporary narratives, not only in that of Donaldson, with whom one can well sympathise, when he recounted that

> There were few ... with whom I could associate that had an idea beyond the situation they were in: those who had were afraid to show they possessed any more knowledge than their comrades, for fear of being laughed at by fellows who, in other circumstances they would have despised ... If a man, when accused by his superiors of which he was not guilty, ventured to speak in his own defence, he was called a *lawyer*, and

desired to give no reply. If he said that he thought it was hard that he should be condemned without a hearing, the answer was, 'Be silent, sir! *you have no right to think*; there are people paid for thinking for you – do what you are ordered, sir, right or wrong.'

If he did not join with his neighbours in their ribald obscenity and nonsense, he was a Methodist, – if he did not curse and swear, he was a Quaker – and if he did not drink the most of his pay, he was called a miser, a mean scrub, and the generality of his comrades would join in execrating him.

In such a society it was a hard matter for a man of any superior information or intellect to keep his ground; for he had few to converse with ... and to try to inform his comrades was a vain, and by them considered a presumptuous attempt. Thus many men of ability and information were, I may say, forced from the intellectual height which they had attained, down to the level of those with whom they were obliged to associate; and every thing conspired to sink them to that point where they became best fitted for *tractable beasts of burden*.

Blackguardism was fashionable, and even the youngest were led into scenes of low debauchery and drunkenness, by men advanced in years. Many of the officers, who, at least, *ought* to have been men of superior talents and education, seemed to be little better, if we were allowed to judge from the abominable oaths and scurrility which they used to those under their command, and the vexatious and overbearing tyranny of their conduct, which was too often imitated by those beneath them.

Not a pretty picture, but not far off the mark. It would appear that, due to the influence of the Duke of York, when commander-in-chief, officers of an older generation which had fought in Flanders in the mid 1790s had ceased to pride themselves on their drinking capacities. Private Wheeler commented that although Wellington's strictures were severe, yet he could not say they were uncalled for.

The conduct of some men would have disgraced savages, drunkenness had prevaled to such a frightful extent that I have often wondered how it was that a great part of our army were not cut off. It was no unfrequent thing to see a long string of mules carrying drunken soldiers to prevent them falling into the hands of the enemy. It would not be fair to me to mention any particular Corps, all partook in some degree a share of the disgrace ... But there is some excuse, from Burgos to Salamanca is chiefly a wine country and as there had been a good harvest, and the new wine was in tanks particularly about Valladolid the soldiers ran

> mad. I remember seeing a soldier fully accoutred with his knapsack on in a large tank, he had either fell in or had been pushed in by his comrades, there he lay dead. A saw a Dragoon fire his pistol into a large vat containing several thousands of gallons, in a few minutes we were up to our knees in wine fighting like tigers for it.

During that campaign, as Stapleton Cotton recalled,[7] such was the army's state of intoxication that the egregious General Erskine 'was never to be seen after a certain hour, however urgent the necessity for his presence; while at headquarters the officers and staff were generally assisted to bed at night by attendants nearly as tipsy as themselves.'[8] The majority of officers conducted themselves in an exemplary fashion, such as Lieut.-Colonel Thomas Lloyd,[9] whose qualities were eulogised by his friend Napier, and described by Donaldson, close to him during the recent retreat, as blending the qualities 'of a brave, active, intelligent officer with those of the gentleman and scholar,' and whose system of discipline was not coercive:

> He endeavoured to encourage, not to terrify – if there was a single spark of pride or honour in the bosom, he would fan it into a flame. His aim was to prevent crime rather than to punish it, and he rarely resorted to corporal punishment. When he did so, it was only in the case of hardened ill-doers, with whom no lenient measures would succeed; even then, he never punished to the tenth part of the sentence awarded; and if the culprit sued for pardon, promising not to be guilty again, he would say, 'I take you at your word, and forgive you, but remember your promise.'
>
> The men's interests formed his chief study, and complaint of the meanest individual was heard and investigated with the strictest impartiality, without respect to persons. By the measures he took, he made every individual interested in his own honour and that of the regiment [the 94th]; and I believe that every man in it loved and honoured him. So successful were his efforts, that he brought the regiment into a state of order, cleanliness, and discipline, which could never have been attained by any other means.

In exenuation, it should be realised that both the officers and rank and file had not only suffered physically during that Autumn: so had their pockets. The financial state of the army was at its nadir, and not until mid November did the situation improve slightly with increasing shipments of specie from England, including £100,000 in guineas, the first of several consignments of gold, which was transported directly to Headquarters for Wellington to channel its distribution in person.[10] By that September the army's pay was in arrears by six months, with bat and forage money owing for even longer; the Commissariat Department, constantly plagued by lack of ready cash, was owed for ten months, and a proportion of the muleteers had not been paid for as long as fifteen, while unpaid drafts had increased to a staggering figure of almost 5,000,000 dollars, these figures being supplied by Commissary-General Kennedy when complaining to London in the middle of the following February. To enter into any explanation of the expedients put into operation to keep the Army afloat financially, would be far beyond the scope of this book. Wellington felt that speculation on the value of commissariat drafts by unscrupulous British merchants in Lisbon – referring to them as 'sharks' in correspondence with Bathurst – and the shady transactions of some Portuguese contractors,[11] were partly to blame for their penurious plight. Although the profit motive cannot be discounted, in most cases the successful prosecution of the war came uppermost, as wrote one trader when scouting any such allegation: 'Deplorable indeed would it be if ... a narrow system of Finance should by leaving him destitute of money unnerve Lord Wellington's aim.'[12]

Capt. Browne referred to 'The man who lived in the greatest style & luxury at Head Quarters was the Commissary ... Like many others of the same department, he joined the army on a mule, & as poor as Job, but in the course of a couple of years contrived to amass considerable wealth.' When such an occurrence was brought to Wellington's notice, his politic reply was that 'the only control which he had over them was that in which the provisioning of the army was concerned, & that if they did their duty in that respect he required no more – that the Treasury at home had decided on the mode in which their accounts were to be kept, & had sent out Commissaries of accounts whose duty it was to see that these forms were rigidly attended to, & that whether they made money or lost it was no concern of his.'[13]

There were ways of making money, which some junior Commissaries found difficult to resist. One was when buying corn, for which they required a certificate from the local *alcalde* stating the market price they were paying (or at least giving a voucher for). Most village *alcaldes* 'would sign anything for a dollar, & therefore his certificate was usually just what the Commissary might choose to dictate to him.' Another way was when dealing with muleteers, 'many of whom were owners of ten to twenty mules' and were paid 'a dollar a day for each

Mule, & likewise furnished with a ration for themselves & their animals.' As this payment was quite frequently several months in arrears, in despair some of them eventually deserted, taking their mules. 'Thus all their arrears of pay were forfeited, but these arrears were drawn by the Commissary when the day for payment came, & remained in his own pocket.' Often, when specie was scarce, both suppliers and *capatazes* would be paid 'by bills on the Treasury. They knew not what to do with these pieces of paper, which they were unable even to read, & willingly offered them for half their value to those who had money to purchase them. Pay-Masters and Commissaries alone had the means of taking advantage of this state of things.' Inevitably, there were a number of instances of misappropriation, defalcation, peculation, etc. by the staff, but in general the Commissariat Department managed remarkably well when considering the range of problems with which they had to contend.[14]

An additional preoccupation had been caused by the outbreak of the war with America, which had occurred in June 1812, for if their export of flour to Portugal was stopped, this would seriously jeopardize Allied operations; but in the event this did not happen, for the Yankees preferred to supply Wellington's units in the Peninsula and get paid for it, realising that should they be forced to withdraw, being starved of flour, it was more than likely that these troops would be sent across the Atlantic to fight against them (as in fact did happen not long after the battle of Toulouse); and so the profitable trade had been allowed to continue.[15]

* * *

It did not take long for Wellington's army to recuperate after the fatigue and exposure it had experienced during the retreat; being well fed, re-clothed, re-shod,[16] and sheltered, their morale was soon restored. Throughout the winter they were drilled rigorously and underwent extensive training in readiness for the Spring offensive planned by Wellington.[17] He kept details of this close to his chest, for rumours were too frequently leaked to the British Press and other bodies by his less discreet officers – referred to as 'croakers' – either directly or in correspondence with their families.

The army was also receiving considerable reinforcements, both Portuguese and from England, apart from new equipment of all sorts,[18] in addition to improved carts. A corps of military police was formed to deal with delinquents.[19] In general, the troops were in a more disciplined and healthier state than ever before.[20]

During the long winter nights, holed up or snowed up in desolate village houses, Leach and his mess-mates 'wiffed away cigars over some Douro wine, and speculated on the campaign which was soon expected to commence', when not, as on former occasions, assembling the local girls, with whom they 'frequently danced half through the night', nor were they 'at all averse to hot punch between the boleros and fandangos.' Leach described how the Light Division had established a theatre at Gallegos, to which Wellington and his staff rode over from Freineda to attend performances of Sheridan's *The Rivals*, with Lydia Languish and Julia impersonated by young men 'dressed uncommonly well, and [although] looking somewhat feminine on stage,' would be 'drinking punch and smoking cigars behind the scenes, at a furious rate, between the acts.'[21] Another day it was the turn of *She Stoops to Conquer* to be vociferously applauded. The play-bills were run off on the printing-press at Freineda.[22]

Sherer found the winter at Coria as 'mild as an English spring; our tables were well supplied with game and wine: we had books and newspapers; these last contained long details of the Russian campaign, and were therefore highly interesting': such news must have given morale a considerably lift. Meanwhile, 'Every effort had been made, during our long halt, to render the various corps efficient in discipline, field exercise, and equipment. An order of Lord Wellington's directed, that three tents per company should be carried for the men, on the bat mules, hitherto appropriated to the conveyance of the large iron camp kettles, the use of which was discontinued, and small ones substituted, to be carried by the soldiers themselves.'[23]

Coursing and woodcock-shooting took up much of the time, while Wellington's pack of fox-hounds, kennelled at Headquarters, was often out, baying over the hills.[24] But Freineda was too small to accommodate all its ramifications: the Commissary-General and the Medical Department were quartered at Castelo Bom,[25] while the officers in command of the artillery and the Royal Engineers were housed at Malhada Sorda, to the south, as was Judge-Advocate Larpent. Not yet inured to military life, Larpent went to bed at seven to keep himself warm in a room 'opening to the street, without ceiling, only with loose pantiles, with holes to let out the smoke of a fireplace without a chimney; a window tinned up by last year's occupiers, except for four small panes, two of which are broken;[26] there is a hole in the floor to look through at my five animals and three servants, who all sleep on the straw below me ... Here are no books, no women but ladies of a certain description ... '

It was not long before he was offered new quarters at Freineda, where he soon adjusted to working with Wellington, referred to as 'the Peer', whom he found 'very ready, and decisive, and civil', even he felt like a boy going to school when taking in his charges and papers concerning Courts-martial for instructions. Some officers were apparently 'much afraid of him.' Before long, Wellington left Larpent to make his own decisions, remarking: 'If your friends knew what was going on here, they would think you had no sinecure ... how do you suppose I was plagued when I had to do nearly all myself?' On one occasion, he got angry over the leniency of the Courts-martial, protesting to Larpent: 'How can you expect a Court to find an officer guilty of neglect of duty, when it is composed of members who are all more or less guilty of the same?'

Following the routine established the previous year, Wellington would receive his principal officers immediately after breakfast in an inner apartment,[27] among them Dr McGrigor, reporting 'on the number of sick and wounded with all the details of their movements,'[28] followed by the Adjutant-general, Quartermaster-general, Commissary-general; and less frequently, the Paymaster-general, and the head of intelligence.

On alternate days, when he was not out hunting, Wellington would work 'until about four o'clock, and then, for an hour or two, parades with any one whom he wants to talk to, up and down the little square at Freineda (amidst all the chattering Portuguese) in his grey great coat.'

One officer recorded that they never gamed nor did he remember seeing a pack of cards at Headquarters. Capt. Browne, who dined there occasionally, refers to Wellington only drinking the best French wines, supplied by guerrilla chiefs whenever they captured a convoy. At other times a couple of mules might be dispatched as far afield as Coimbra to collect wine, cigars, and such creature comforts, while at Christmas 1812 his guests shared two turkeys and some tins of mincemeat sent up from Lisbon. To one embarrassed young staff officer invited to dine, excusing himself as having already engaged to do so with General Hill, Wellington rejoined: 'Go by all means. You will get a much better feed than here', adding 'As you are a stranger, I will give you some useful information. Cole gives the best dinners in the army;[29] Hill the next best; mine are no great things; Beresford's and Picton's are very bad indeed!'[30]

Any general officer fresh to the Peninsula, when invited to dine at Headquarters, as was customary, soon learned to keep his place when it came to venturing an unsolicited opinion on the military situation. One who did so, demonstrating on the tablecloth what he thought should be done if the French move in this direction, and then that, as inevitably they might try to, and having the presumption to ask what Wellington would do in the such circumstances, received short shrift: 'Give them the most infernal thrashing they've had for some time.'

According to Larpent, one day the Commissary-General – presumably referring to Willoughby Gordon – told Wellington that the army 'had eaten nearly all the oxen in the country, that the cultivation of the lands of Portugal could not go on for the want of them, and that he scarcely knew where to turn for a supply of beef, as there was this year no reserve store near Lisbon. Lord Wellington said, "Well, then, we must now set about eating all the sheep, and when they are gone, I suppose we must go".'

There was no lack of vituals at Freineda, where three women suttlers held sway, among whom, as described by Browne, was the formidable Antonia, 'a stout lusty person of rather a jolly countenance, dirty enough ...', who 'amassed a considerable fortune by her attendance at Head-Quarters, to which she was attached for ... several years, her goods becoming worse & her prices more exhorbitant each succeeding campaign.'[31]

Apparently, the Commander-in-Chief swore like a trooper at any thing that displeased him; he was also 'remarkably fond of the Portuguese & listens to any complaint made to him against the English [by them] but never any made by the English against them.'

The cheerfulness or gloom at table depended to a large extent on the news received from divisional commanders, or from England. Wellington himself was often the most playful of the party.[32] When he wished the company to retire, he would call for coffee and leave the room a little while later, when it was expected that his guests would likewise disperse to their respective quarters. As Browne recorded: 'He would then read or write in his bed-room for about an hour, & then go to bed.' 'He had a small portmanteau iron bed-stead, covered with Russian leather with one pillow of the same material'; but if he suspected any movement by the enemy, 'he used to lie down on his bed-stead in his clothes, with his boots near him, ready to put on, & his cloak thrown around him. His horse, & that of his orderly dragoon were always ready saddled ...' Browne himself made do with a sort of hay-loft, and had difficulty keeping out the excessive cold for, as he remembered, 'the hail used to get under the tiles & fall on my bed as I slept. To remedy this as well as I could I borrowed tar-paulins from the

Commissary, & slung them over the spot ... The Crevices in the walls I stopped up with clay, & at last made a sort of fire place which was a great comfort.'

Landing at Lisbon after some months in England recuperating from the incapacitating wound in his thigh received at the final storming of Badajoz, in which he also lost the upper joint of his third finger, by 21 January Charles Colville had rejoined the 3rd Division, then cantoned at Moimenta da Beira, south-east of Lamego. Together with his nephew as A.D.C., four horses and seven mules, they had traversed Coimbra, beyond which curiosity led him, as had many others, to spend a night at the convent at Busaco; but as he wrote, apart from 'occasional bad stabling and forage and the villainy of the road, frequently as dangerous for a horse to move upon as a broken flight of steps would be, I brought up my stud without accident and in very tolerable condition. As for myself, I bore the journey particularly well, seldom sitting down after my ride of 16 or 20 miles until the setting in of darkness obliged me to return from the walk I usually took to see my surroundings.'

In March, Coville found time to visit Oporto briefly by taking one of the huge Douro wine boats floating downstream from Regua, the river-port below Lamego. He described its progress in more detail than had Somers Cocks several months earlier, partly to explain the immense difficulties surmounted by the Commissariat when keeping the troops provisioned from the coast with both food and *materiél.*[33]

> The distance of 14 leagues (of four miles each) we did in twelve hours, without a sail but occasionally using our oars, or rather sweeps, which are as large as would be required for a frigate. Our rudder was a machine about thirty foot long poised on a pivot, having but two or three feet immersed in the water; it was worked by occasionally one, and at other times, six men on a high stage elevated nearly amidships. The management of this unwieldy machine was very dextrous when going down the narrow rapids which we freqently met with in the first four or five leagues. When towing the craft upstream in those parts of the river where the banks do not admit of towing paths, you will see twelve or sixteen men in a row, bare footed, skipping with their tow ropes from rock to rock in a way only to be matched by so many monkeys. The work these men do shows the Portuguese of this part of the country in a very favourable light as regards industry and perseverence.
>
> The scenery ... is very good the whole way ... In the neighbourhood of Regua, where the best wine is made, the vines are in terraces up to the summit of lofty mountains.

Writing on 21 April, Burgoyne refers to 'The four companies of Royal Sappers and Miners, with four sub-lieutenants (about 200 in all) move to headquarters and 100 mule-loads of stores, including 1000 entrenching tools, and other stores in proportion;' while a brigade 'of six iron eighteen-pounders on travelling carriages is to move with the army, and has been, or is to be well equipped with horses and bullocks. It is at present at Covilhão, and has some 150 rounds per gun. It is ordered to be completed to 700 per gun. Five millions of rations are ordered to be collected at Barco d'Alva, at the mouth of the Agueda, by means of the Douro boats, which is partly effected; and a very large number of rations (probably from the same stores) are now being put into Ciudad Rodrigo. About 100 bullock-carts a day, enter that place with biscuit and corn.'

Among other reinforcements reaching the front during this period were the 18th Hussars, to whom Schaumann had been transferred, only to find that 'the dear old troubles with the forage started afresh.'

> Every day we commissaries were called before Sir Colquhoun Grant to be reprimanded,[34] and to listen to peremptory orders and threats. Our protests and proposals, based upon the experience of many years, were as good as useless. He imagined that everything would be the same here as in England, and thought it exceedingly strange that we should dare to contradict so great a man as he thought himself to be. Was he not six feet high, and had he not a huge black moustache and black whiskers? Had he not in a dashing fancy hussar uniform, carried out the most brilliant cavalry parades on Blackheath? And was he not in addition, aide-de-camp, equerry and favourite of the Prince Regent? His whole manner bore the stamp of unbounded pride and the crassest ignorance, and he tried to conceal the latter beneath positive assertions which he did not suffer to be contradicted. We all came away from such interviews swollen with rage and righteous indignation.
>
> We were comforted by the conciousness of having done our duty to the best of our ability, and the knowledge that Lord Wellington, who was better acquainted with what could be demanded of the commissariat in this country, would be the first to put him in his place if he should venture to complain about us ... I did not get the smallest help from the regiment. The whole crowd were like fledglings; they only knew how to open their mouths to be fed. If anything was lacking the officers knew no other remedy than to exclaim to one's face in a cold and stately fashion: 'I shall report it!' How different things were in the 1st German Hussars!
>
> As Lord Wellington wanted to inspect our brigade, we marched out on the 18th May ... It was a wonderful sight to behold these three

regiments maneouvering with their magnificent horses. The 10th, the King's Own, were all mounted on half-blood horses worth from thirty to forty guineas apiece, while the officers' chargers were animals of a nobler breed and all thoroughbred horses worth 100 to 150 guineas and more. Moreover, the 10th regiment wore scarlet shakos. Lord Wellington appeared with a brilliant staff. During the maneouvres poor Colquhoun Grant had to gallop himself almost to death, racing *ventre-à-terre* with his brigade adjutant, Lieut. Charles Jones, who was also adjutant to the 10th King's Hussars. The latter was a small man with fox-red hair, a red moustache and red whiskers, and he also wore a red shako. It was very funny to see him galloping behind the tall black-whiskered general, who wore an enormous three-cornered hat with a long fluttering feather; and from that day those two were never spoken of in the brigade except as the black giant and his red dwarf.

At this parade proud Sir Colquhoun Grant, who as the Prince Regent's favourite and equerry, expected to be most highly honoured by Lord Wellington and thanked in the most flattering terms, was to suffer his first humiliation; for the Commander-in-Chief hated these puffed-up favourites who were sent out to him from England. At the end of the function, therefore, Lord Wellington turned his horse round sharply, and putting his hand to his hat merely galloped past Sir Colquhoun, shouting as he went in sonorous and very precise tones: 'Grant! If you will dine with me, I dine at six o'clock!'

Never shall I forget Sir Colquhoun's face when he heard this laconic invitation. It was pitiable! – quite crestfallen! Even the Prince Regent had never dismissed him as haughtily as that! Out of respect for the Commander-in-Chief he could not decline the invitation, and he was therefore obliged to ride over to headquarters at Villar Formosa and back, a matter of at least four leaguas, despite the fatigue occasioned by the parade. A good job, too! Silently shaking his head, he looked sadly at Lord Wellington's back, and then gesticulating violently, he rode away with his red dwarf. '*Traga la, perro!*' ['Swallow that, you dog!'] thought I.

The 15th Hussars had also returned to the Peninsula after an absence of four years, riding to the front via Tomar, and Seia,[35] where on 8 May, a cold and windy day, Major Edwin Griffith was lucky enough to find himself

… in great comfort in sitting over a brassiere of charcoal, which the senhoritas at my billet sent me, & not only that, but hearing that I had a friend to dine with me, they made an excellent pudding of rice, eggs, milk, & nutmeg with their own fair hands … The general desire of the different people we were quartered upon all the way is to be civil, & accommodate as far as laid in the power, often surprised me. I really don't think there is another nation upon earth who after having been harassed for five years by foreign troops, & a constant succession of strangers in their houses, would not only give you a good room, fire (if wanted), lights, a comfortable bed, clean sheets, towels, table cloth, &c &c, but also receive you with the utmost good humour, & at the same time in the most respectful manner.

It was essential to accumulate a deal of first-hand topographical information before routes could be issued to the various units which were to advance to their forward assembly areas prior to the planned Spring offensive. Q.M.G. Sir George Murray' staff, among them several officers from the three cavalry brigades were dispatched to the districts through which this would take place, four of them to examine the passages of the Douro. Capt. Thomas Mitchell explored the area – partly within Spain – west of the Esla,[36] which entered the main stream not far east of Miranda; Capt. Philip Bainbrigge investigated the region further west, between the Douro and the Sabor; while Major Charles Broke reported on tracts between the Sabor and Tua. Within five weeks, maps had been drawn at a scale of 4 miles to one inch for most of central and north-eastern Portugal.[37] Naturally, they were unable to compile them for areas further east or north-east through which it was intended the advance would take them.

At McGrigor's suggestion, Wellington had requested prefabricated wooden huts, together with carpenters, to be shipped from England, and on arrival a number of these portable sheds were erected in the vicinity of Castelo Rodrigo, not far north of Almeida, to serve as temporary hospital for some 4,000 wounded and convalescents.[38] Meanwhile, Commissariat depots were established at Bragança, Mirandela, and Miranda do Douro.

The situation behind the French front, intelligence concerning which was being received regularly by Wellington, partly due to Scovell's assiduity in deciphering coded messages, was unexceptional. Their morale was low, and wherever they bivouacked or went into cantonments they remained the target of Spanish partisans, more confident and better armed, who continued unremittingly their guerrilla war.

To prevent any concentration against him, Wellington had planned a diversion to keep Marshal Suchet occupied, for he still commanded some 60 or 70,000 men – the largest single French force in Spain – even if a high proportion of it was penned up in garrisoning captured fortresses near or inland from the east coast. Several changes of commanders had taken place during recent months, and although Wellington may not have chosen General Sir John Murray to lead the units put at his disposal, he acquiesced to the appointment, and Murray duly landed the heterogeneous force on the Mediterranean shore.[39] In early June, after a creditable action at Castalla (north-west of Alicante) on 13 April, his 15,000 Anglo-Sicilians were transported up the coast to besiege Tarragona, but the operation was a complete fiasco, for which Murray was later court-martialled. Nevertheless, it had the effect of engaging Suchet's attention to the extent that not a single man was sent to support Joseph and Jourdan.

By now, even if he had serious reservations about their reliability, Wellington had been given (nominal) command of both regular and irregular Spanish forces, despite indignant opposition in some quarters. This gave him additional troops of varying quality to dispose of whenever expedient, as long as they scrupulously avoided confronting French armies by themselves, the fatal penchant of too many Spanish generals. However, there were one or two of them – Pedro Girón, for example – and perhaps Longa and Espoz y Mina, who might be trusted to obey orders when the time came to make his long-planned push towards the Pyrenees.

The army closest to the Portuguese frontier was then commanded by General Gazan (temporarily replacing Soult, who had been recalled to Paris); D'Erlon's stood further east nearer Segovia; part of Reille's remained in the vicinity of Palencia. Together, they comprised from 80 to 100,000 men, although large contingents from Reille's had been ordered by Napoleon to reinforce Clausel, who, with another 30,000, was still attempting to keep open communications with France, for the whole area between Burgos and the border was now in a state of turmoil.

The three first-mentioned were planning to concentrate just north of the Guadarrama range in the expectation that Wellington would approach from the west, but they were confused by conflicting reports concerning the movements of Hill's 'Corps' and Morillo's Spaniards, further south.

Hill's men were in fine fettle. Hill himself hunted once or twice a week with his pack of hounds, until they were broken up by a singularly unfortunate accident, as recorded by Surgeon Henry, for

> One very fine day there was a strong field – we found and had a splendid run of nearly two hours, with only a short check – every body well up.

> At last Mr Reynard, being hard pressed, made for his earth in a steep bank of the Allagon, but feeling somewhat flurried by the long chase, the animal, wise as he was, forgot his topographical marks, and, instead of descending his hole obliquely, he went sheer down a perpendicular bank, one hundred and fifty feet high, and was followed by five couple and a half of the best of the dogs. They were all killed instantly, and Sir R. Hill, the huntsman and two or three of the leading horsemen had a narrow escape; for the bank was most treacherous, giving no indication of danger until almost too late.

The Allied field army now totalled some 81,000 effectives. Of this combined strength, the British contributed about 52,500, including Cotton's 7,400 cavalry and the Portuguese, 28,800 infantry plus 900 cavalry. 106 pieces of field artillery were also in readiness.

George Woodberry recorded that while the cavalry advanced towards their forward positions, they were gathering whatever green forage they could find from fields near and far from their route which had not already been consumed. This had left the women and children in adjacent villages, who had suffered privations enough, little on which to subsist. Nor were they safe from the pillaging proclivities of bad characters among drafts of reinforcements being marched from depots to their regiments, often escorted by officers from other units, and thus ignorant of their presence in the detachment they temporarily commanded. An officer in the Cameron Highlanders emphasised the difference between campaign-hardened troops and those of recently recruited reinforcements, however well they may have looked when on parade in England, observing that on their first long march, one hundred had 'dropped down and were left on the road', while not one veteran was missing when the roll-call was made after it.[40] Several roads on the line of march – notable that from Abrantes to Nisa and beyond – had been infested during recent months by banditti, often deserters from the Allied armies, and a number of robberies and murders had taken place.

On 12 May, Larpent observed that at Freineda there were indications of an impending move, 'such as the packing of Lord Wellington's claret, etc.' Eight days later, after a delay caused by heavy rain, the Light Division, three cavalry brigades, and contingents of Spanish troops, set out from Ciudad Rodrigo.[41] Before re-entering Salamanca, they had a running fight with a French division and two cavalry brigades, which suffered 500 casualties, while all their baggage, *matériel*, and accumulated supplies in the city were captured. By the evening of the 26th, Wellington, by now reinforced by Hill's Corps marching from Béjar,[42] had aligned his troops in their former position between San Cristóbal and Alba de Tormes. He very deliberately flaunted his presence,[43] hoping that by doing so the French would get the impression that the entire Allied field army faced them: in fact, it was a mere 30 per cent of the total. After the skirmishing at Aldealengua, just east of Salamanca, Colonel Frazer counted some eighty dead of the enemy. He then followed Wellington into the city, where they were met with some 'vivas', 'and some ladies rushed out of the crowd and seized his lordship's hand': but there was less expression of joy than he had expected, although there was 'an illumination' that evening, which Frazer did not attend, having retired to bed early and, as he wrote: 'not without some sorrowful ideas at the sight I had witnessed. There was not even the false emotion of honour where there was no danger, and to slaughter flying enemies, though duty requires it, is nevertheless shocking. I spoke to many of the wounded: none uttered a complaint.'[44]

Three months earlier, on 10 February, Wellington had written to Bathurst in London requesting that the ordnance and stores listed in his dispatch of that date be embarked in transports to Corunna, to be at his disposal whenever required, for it was likely that the campaign he was preparing would require a deal of *matériel* with which to undertake a siege or two in the north of Spain. He did not wish to be caught unprepared, as he had been at Burgos, and emphasised that 'twice the quantity of each article listed' should be in readiness to be shipped from England the moment he reported that they were necessary at a destination he would then specify.

It was not always easy dealing with bureaucrats in London. One may quote from a letter sent to the gentlemen of the Foreign Office several months earlier, in which Wellington was constrained to answer an officious demand:

> We have enumerated our saddles, bridles, tents, and tent poles, and all manner of sundry items for which His Majesty's Government hold me accountable. I have dispatched reports on the character, wit and spleen of every officer. Each item and every farthing has been accounted for, with two regrettable exceptions for which I beg your indulgence.
>
> Unfortunately the sum of one shilling and ninepence remains unaccounted for in one infantry battalion's petty cash, and there has been a hideous confusion as to the number of jars of rasperry jam issued to one cavalry regiment during a sandstorm in western Spain. This reprehensible carelessness may be related to the pressure of circumstances, since we

are at war with France, a fact which may come as a bit of a surprise to you gentlemen in Whitehall.

This brings me to my present purpose, which is to request elucidation of my instructions from His Majesty's Government, so that I may better understand why I am dragging an army over these barren plains. I construe that perforce it must be one of two alternative duties, but I cannot do both:

1. To train an army of uniformed British clerks in Spain for the benefit of the accountant and copy boys in London; or, perchance,
2. To see to it that the forces of Napoleon are driven out of Spain.

I have the honour, etc.

Wellington

In the middle of 1812 Bathurst had accepted the position of Secretary of War in Liverpool's administration. Both supported Wellington to the best of their ability, even if, during ensuing campaigns, he had received some extraordinary inept projects from them, 'thrown out for consideration'. One of these, suggested by Colonel Henry Bunbury, under-secretary at the War Department, was that once the French had been evicted from Spain, the bulk of the army should be moved to either Italy or northern Germany, a hair-brained scheme which he rejected out of hand.[45] It was not until after his victory at Vitoria that Wellington was given virtually complete discretion in the conduct of military operations, and his advice on a variety of other pertinent problems was sought and accepted.

1 The December 'morning states' record that thirteen Allied regiments had more 'sick' than 'effectives': no less than 18,000 men were in hospital and, among British battalions, there were only some 30,400 men present with the colours.

2 Normally, postal communications with England were maintained by a weekly packet sailing from Falmouth to Lisbon (and at a later date to Pasajes, provisionally), where the mail was handled by a Packet Agent. This might be delayed by bad weather. On arrival, a Postmaster or two attached to the Quartermaster-General's Department would arrange the distribution, at first by the main civilian postal routes and by April 1810, as Headquarters and the front moved progressively further from Lisbon, these were extended and operated by the Commissariat Department, while the frequency increased to a daily service, the mail being carried by letter-parties consisting of half a dozen men detached from cavalry regiments and an NCO placed at fixed points or convenient intervals between formations. It was not until mid August 1811 that Major George Scovell, ordered to superintend military communications in general, established a Corps of Mounted Guides in an attempt to improve both

the efficiency of the postal service and also the routine transmission of orders and reports between Headquarters and commanders of distant units, notably with Hill's 'Corps'.

3 Writing in late March, Bragge remarked: 'I sincerely hope the latter will not return, as he is beyond Doubt one of the First Generals in the French Army and better able to cope with his Lordship than any other.' In the event, Soult was not sent back, to take command at the western Pyrenean front, until mid July 1813.

4 Although large stocks of hay were collected at Celorico and elsewhere behind the frontier during the winter, it was the duty of individual cavalry regiments to search for forage, a constant fag throughout that severe season, for which purpose it had been recommended by Wellington that the horses of both cavalry and artillery brigades be dispersed into groups of twenty or thirty in each village.

5 Willoughby Gordon had not only displayed gross incompetence but, unscrupulously, had been also in correspondence behind Wellington's back to Lord Grey and members of the Whig Opposition, not only leaking the contents of confidential dispatches to them. He was replaced, much to Wellington's satisfaction, by General George Murray, but it was not until 18 March that Murray reached Headquarters at Freineda.

6 As Richard Glover observed in *Peninsular Preparation* (1963), 'these drunken thugs were tough with a ruggedness unknown and scarcely conceivable in the decorous modern England of today' [sic]. These brutes could only be brought to heel by flogging, the commonest form of punishment, which was some deterrent to other than the incorrigible and thick-skinned; and while 'nothing is easier than to denounce so barbarous a punishment as this, yet it baffled the wit of the authorities to devise a milder punishment that could control the appalling thugs of whom the rank and file of the British Army was largely composed.' And yet, as Glover reiterated, 'by and large, flogging was effective in maintaining an adequate degree of subordination, even in an army where many soldiers were criminals, is evident from Wellington's repeated observation that, while atrocious crimes were all too frequently committed by soldiers in isolated detachments, his men were usually well behaved while serving with their own unit. When separated from their units, the men had too sporting a chance to 'get away with' robbery or murder; under the eye of their own officers and N.C.O.'s detection was too certain and punishment too severe for the same temptation to exist.'

7 When, several years later, the Cabinet asked who in his opinion should be sent to command an expedition to Burma, Wellington had replied: 'Send Lord Combermere'. 'But we have always understood that your Grace thought Lord Combermere a fool?' 'So he is a fool, and a d … d fool; but he can take Rangoon.' – G.W.E. Russell's *Collections and Recollections.*

8 Erskine had ended his life by jumping from a high window either in Lisbon (as stated in one source) or at Brozas, which relieved Wellington of at least one of the more incapable commander imposed on him by the Horse Guards at Whitehall.

9 Killed at the Nivelle on 10 November 1813.

10 During the following eight months approximately £1,150,000 in gold reached Lisbon; after that date shipments of specie was made via ports on the north coast to Wellington's Headquarters on either side of the frontier with France.

[11] Larpent refers to one agent at present at Headquarters as 'a sly, money-making man, who has realized about £25,000 during the war, [who] said the news was so good, that he now hoped to get a peace, and that the Portuguese would get rid of the "beefs," meaning the English.'

The family of Henrique Teixeira de Sampaio (1774-1843, later Conde da Póvoa), who had been educated in England, were among the more substantial and relaible contractors, able to supply the base depots of the Commissariat with immense quantities of provisions throughout the war. Commissary Schaumann refers to seeing Sampaio at Talavera, which would confirm that he was not office-bound, and would have had experience of the army's requirements at first-hand.

[12] But as late as December 1813 we find Wellington protesting: 'It is in vain to expect to be able to continue to carry on our operations through the winter unless we should be supplied with money from England …'

[13] Indeed, as Wellington himself had previously put it concerning members of what was part of the Civil Administration of the army, and not an officer: 'the prejudices of society against a Commissary almost prevent him from receiving the common respect due to the character of a gentleman.'

[14] Writing on 17 April, Larpent refers to a Mr. M —, a clerk who 'had been guilty of fraud and embezzlement of stores (some pork, rice, and milk) … sold out of the store at Galigas [Gallegos],' who when accused had shot himself, realising that 'prosecution was inevitable. By the Mutiny Act he was liable to transportation for life, fine, imprisonment, or pillory: and he could not stand the disgrace. He partly admitted the charges, but pleaded sickness and distress. It was unfortunate that the discovery fell on such a subject, for it was, I believe, the first falling off from general good conduct.'

[15] From 220,000 barrels in 1810, this had risen to 940,000 in 1812, and it was not until the end of the following year, by which time supplies were available from northern Europe, that the British government stopped issuing licences. Meanwhile, alternative sources of supply were being sought, notably from North Africa. The interruption by American privateers of convoys from Britain to the Peninsula was negligible.

[16] Writing in January, McGrigor emphasised that the lack of great coats at that season, and of shoes and stockings, had contributed greatly to the men's state of excessive fatigue, mentioning also that the 79th (Cameron Highlanders), who were in rags, suffered additionally because wearing kilts, 'a cause of rheumatism, sore legs, etc.' Some regiments were luckier than others. Larpent refers to men of the 50th having been given 'a pair of pantaloons each, and several days' double rations of spirits, and some other presents' by the inhabitants of Bejar, where there was a cloth trade, to thank them for having driven away the French. John Cooke states that 'In his knapsack, each man was provided with a reasonable supply of necessaries, including three pairs of shoes and an extra pair of soles and heels.' It is of some interest that Cooke had previously commented on the fact that 'The French infantry wore broad-toed shoes, studded with nails.'

[17] D'Urban, writing in January apropos the disciplining of his Portuguese cavalry (and perhaps still smarting over their disgrace at Majadahonda), refers to 'Drills, Riding-school, and strict attention to Grooming and Economy were rapidly enforced … and I succeeded at length in overthrowing the villainy of the Commissariat so far as to effect good subsistence for the Men and Horses.'

[18] John Cooper, stationed at São João da Pesqueira during the winter, described the arrival of several fresh regiments from England, among them 'some troops of the Life Guards and Horse Guards Blue, with tents and blankets for all the army,' and commented that although every man's kit was now completed, 'The government should also have sent us new backbones to bear the extra weight.'

[19] On 30th March, Larpent had suggested that Wellington 'insert a passage in general orders … to be read every day until we march, to let them know that a new police corps was established to catch them, and to tell them that seven officers [in a Court-martial] would be sufficient now to hang them, and that Courts would be held always ready in every division. He said he would think about it …'

[20] This, although he had observed to Larpent on 4 April that they were 'now all so round-shouldered and slouching in their gait, that he was sure, if his regiment here was in its present state to pass in review on Wimbledon Common, the whole would be sent to drill immediately, and declared quite unfit for service. Indeed, he added, that the men had now got into such a way of doing everything in the easiest manner, that he was often quite ashamed of the sentries before his own quarters … He also laughed at our notions in England about the supply of the army, saying that some corporate body or society in England had once made him an offer of twenty bullocks for the army, which would last head-quarters only about a week. General M — said it must have been a mistake – the offer must have been for his table only; not for the army.'

[21] Notable performers were Capt. Samuel Hobkirk, Lieut the Honble Charles Gore, and Lieut Edward Freer (all 43rd Regiment), playing Mrs Malaprop, Lydia Languish, and Lucy respectively, and Lieut Lord Charles Spencer (95th) as Julia.

[22] One each had been supplied in the previous Summer for the Military Secretary, the Adjutant-General, and the Commissary-General.

[23] The heavy cast-iron camp kettles were jettisoned and replaced by those of light sheet-metal, enabling smaller groups to cook at short notice. These, according to Burgoyne, were put 'in a bag, and carried by the men, at the rate of one for each six men, who on march will carry it alternately … All the soldiers besides have their little semi-circular tin saucepan, with its soup-plate in it.' Even scythes had been ordered from England, to facilitate hay-making. Rather than being hampered by having to carry their heavy great-coats, they were provided with blankets, being more portable. When comparing the equipment of the contending armies, John Cooke had observed that the sleeves of the lighter-weight French greatcoats were 'slashed at the cuff to enable them to handle their arms and to prime and load with facility;' but he also remarked on the fact that 'Their flints were excellent but the powder of their cartridges was coarse; that of the British army was remarkably fine, but their flints were indifferent.' In March the infantry were issued with Trotter's bell-tents, large enough to accommodate 25 men, and providing drier cover than if bivouacking. 'The Infantry are to have Three Tents per Company and the Officers of Cavalry one each – a Regulation which will probably save the Lives of Thousands of the former,' wrote Bragge.

Profiting from experience gained during the American War, by 1794 John Trotter (1757–1833), an enterprising army contractor, was supplying most

British regiments, also with tentage – later bell-tents rather than ridge-pole tents – for the Ordnance corps; by 1807 he had 109 storage depots throughout England warehousing a variety of military stores, including saddlery and medical equipment. In the following year the ramifications of his business were integrated into the Storekeeper-General's Department, and his nephew appointed to the new post.

24 Under the aegis of Tom Crane, a former private in the Coldstreams, and Welligton's huntsman. Henegan, whose memory may have been at fault, refers to a Tom Marsden as holding this post.

25 Dr McGrigor had been assigned the best house in the place, no window of which was glazed, which he shared with John Gunning, the surgeon at Headquarters, his staff , servants, and muleteers.

26 By no means usual. In the following May, Sir Augustus Frazer had found himself sharing a village house near Salamanca 'consisting of four rooms, [which] had literally no windows … no uncommon thing here. The rooms are whitewashed, and while the sun shines and the door is open, one manages to see without a candle, which in a dark day must be at all times necessary.'

27 George Woodberry (18th Hussars) described Wellington's residence as wretched, the ceiling of his main room being so low that Colonel Colquhoun Grant ('the Black Giant') could hardly stand upright in it.

28 Also 'the total in each hospital station … the number of dead; the number fit to be marched to their regiments or convalescent; the cases of diseases, with the causes of these,' etc. Among other subjects discussed would be the state of the hospitals and the cost of their repair, purveyor's estimates for the purchase of provisions, wine, and so on. When, on one occasion, McGrigor had suggested that each brigade should be provided with conveyances for the wounded, Wellington, while agreeing that the idea was excellent had it been practicable, 'because it was lamentable to see so many men slightly ill or wounded sent constantly to the rear, and thus diminishing the force of the army in a greater proportion than the reinforcements from England were adding to it,' he was adamant in his response: 'I cannot risk encumbering the army and impeding its movements, either in advancing or retiring,' and for the time being the matter dropped.

29 Cole had to keep up his reputation.; see page 386

30 The manager of Picton's household was a Welshman named Tyler, whose bulk testified to his recipes, but perhaps more to the quantity supplied than their quality. The reputation of some amphytrions, among them Major Victor von Arentscholdt, was such that Schaumann vowed he would never dine with him again, nor did any other officers invited go a second time.

31 In Larpent's opinion, there was 'a shocking set of servants at head-quarters; idle, drunken English servants and soldiers, almost all bad, and the Portuguese are every day running off with something or other …' In the same letter he commented that there had been 'no chaplain here for these last eight or nine months, or any notice taken in any manner of Sunday! It used to be, I hear, a very regular and imposing thing to attend divine service performed out of doors with hats off, but the people must now think we have no religion at all …'

32 Many accounts refer to his affability, although George Eastlake, when dining with him at Lesaca in September 1813, records that on that occasion, when perhaps he was preoccupied, he carried himself 'with much dignity at table and is treated with profound respect when addressed. Indeed it seemed impossible to take a liberty with him. He drank wine with no one …'

[33] A deal of dredging and blasting of rock, etc. had taken place to facilitate the movement of vessels further upstream, where the river ran through gorges.

[34] (1764–1836), not to confused with Wellington's intelligence office with the same name.

[35] Griffith had also noticed the magnificent ruin of the palace there: see p.157, note 21.

[36] After the war, Thomas Livingston Mitchell (1792–1855) remained in the Peninsula at Murray's request to complete the sketches of battlefields, the compilation of which, when eventually published in 1841, became known as '*Wyld's Atlas*', the 'elephant folio' being issued by James Wyld. Mitchell was knighted in 1839 for his services in exploring the interior of Australia and surveying much of that continent.

[37] A topographical survey of most of central Portugal had been made prior to Busaco after the issue earlier in 1810 of a manual entitled *Instructions for the officers in the department of the Quartermaster-General*, to which a report on the condition of the road between Trujillo and Merida had been annexed as a model.

[38] It was possibly these, or a later consignment, which were to serve as a hospital at Santander.

[39] As Oman had commented: 'perhaps he thought that here at least was a general who would take no risks, and have no dangerous inspirations of initiative.'

[40] Writing to Colonel Torrens at the Horse Guards on 2 February 1813, Wellington reiterated: 'I am of the opinion, from long experience, that it is better for the service here to have one soldier or officer, whether of cavalry or infantry, who has served one or two campaigns, than it is to have two or even three who have not. Not only the new soldiers can perform no service, but by filling the hospitals they are a burthen to us. For this reason, I am unwilling to part with the men whom I have formed into the provisional regiments; and I never will part with them as long as it is left to my discretion.'

Cavalry regiments formerly returning to England had been obliged to leave their acclimatised mounts in Portugal, for not only were remounts of quality difficult to find, but losses among pampered and newly arrived horses was heavy, and it took time for them to get used to the often green fodder available to them.

[41] Writing from Malhada Sorda (adjacent to Freineda) on the 7th, Colonel Frazer, commanding the horse artillery, refers to 'the battering guns passed us yesterday, and the pontoons will today or tomorrow.' Curiously, only two days earlier, while remarking that while the rains may have caused a delay in taking the field, he was under the impression that the main reason was the 'deficiency in transport', and that 900 mules were 'wanting in the Artillery Department alone, and I believe, 3000 or 4000 in that of the Commissariat.' Perhaps he was not yet aware of precisely what movements were in progress. He also mentions that there was 'at last a regular corps of sappers and miners', and that the former were 'busy practising both double and single sap.'

The Spanish Fourth Army (general Girón), with some 25,000 men took their place under Wellington's command during the advance, together with an additional 17,000 under the Conde de Abispal joining later, making a total of approximately 46,000 regular troops. This does not include Carlos de España's division, left in Castile, or any of Espoz y Mina's irregulars.

[42] In the face of Hill's approach, General Villatte had withdrawn a detachment from Ledesma, but, by retiring to a new defensive position not far east of Salamanca, where he prudently waited developments, he had lost any direct communication with General Daricau at Zamora on the Douro.

[43] Noticeably, by holding a splendid dinner at Freineda in honour of Beresford, which took place on 16 May, the second anniversary of Albuera, where a large tent was set up, with most of the guests arrived wearing medals, and were entertained by Joe Kelly, a well-known singer serving in the Life Guards. Next morning, according to Larpent, 'all the fashionables were at the review … near Espeja, and a very fine sight it was.' But he thought Wellington looked 'a little fagged and anxious.'

Among other regiments, the 28th, en route from the vicinity of Coria, also celebrated the anniversary by giving a dinner to Hill and the staff of the 2nd Division. Charles Cadell described the deficiency of tables and chairs being ingeniously made up as follow: a nice piece of turf having been selected, Lieut. Irwin 'marked out the length and breadth of a mess table, for 100 covers. The sward was carefully lifted, and a trench dug round large enough to accommodate the party; the sods and mould were then carefully placed in the centre, and levelled; this centrepiece was excavated sufficiently to give room for our legs underneath; when the mass was raised to a proper height, the sward was carefully laid on, so that we had a beautiful green table … and every guest brought his knife, fork, and plate. The wine of the country being excellent, we all enjoyed ourselves much; so much so, that some of us bivoucked under the table for the night.'

[44] He did have a chance next morning to ascend the tower of the cathedral – 'one of the most beautiful buildings I have ever seen' – before examining the convents 'fortified by the French, and destroyed by us after their surrender.'

[45] This was in July 1813.

13

May and June 1813: The Vitoria campaign

Now took place one of the more spectacular movements of the entire war. With remarkable circumspection and secretiveness, Wellington had ordered his pontoons on the Tagus at Vila Velha de Ródão to be shifted north across country to the Douro, where at Barco de Alva (north of Almeida) they were to form two substantial bridges. Augustus Frazer, commanding the Horse Artillery, writing from Malhada Sorda early in May, confirmed that the pontoons were expected daily; on the 15th he was at Sabugal discussing with Fletcher how they might be transported more expeditiously, for the carts carrying them broke down repeatedly.[1] Wellington was getting impatient: on inspecting them the previous afternoon, had ordered one 'to be burnt, and vanished in the smoke!' It was thus decided to place them on horse-drawn carriages, using axles and wheels borrowed from the artillery, rather than relying on lumbering ox-transport, which enabled the complex operation to be completed within four weeks.[2]

From mid-May, well before Wellington advanced on Salamanca, 70 per cent of the Allied army – some 60,000 men – were converging on the rugged high-lying north-eastern province of Trás-os-Montes. Commanded by Graham, these columns, forming the Left Wing of the army, crossed the Douro by ferries and pontoon over a period of two days before continuing their cross-country march to positions of assembly in the vicinity of Miranda do Douro to await further orders. The Civil Department (including Larpent, 'Hunter, the Paymaster-general, and Mr Whitter and nine other clerks ... and the military chest, &, and two or three commissariat parties'), received their route on the 20th, and from Almeida, 'daily roused at five o'clock,' they rode west towards Marialva, passing the Douro at the 'Barco de Pocinho' below Vila Nova de Foz Côa to approach Torre de Moncorvo.[3] Larpent was impressed by the sight of 'about eighty cars drawn up to pass with ammunition, boards, planks, and beams, for the repair of bridges,' waiting to cross the river.[4]

Already, on 29 April, several cavalry brigades, riding from their winter cantonments, once they were across the river at Oporto, had turned east near Braga to reach Braganza by 22 May. According to Bragge, they were

> ... in as good order as could be expected after having crossed the Province of Tras os Montes by a Route never before attempted by British Cavalry and which never ought to have been marched. We were two Hours getting up one Hill, and for three Days never got the Regiment out of single Files, scrambling over Rocks, Mountains, and Precipices for 8 Hours every Day. We halt here Tomorrow and on the 25th move on towards Benavente ...[5]
>
> The French have divided their Force, and do not appear to be aware of this deep laid Scheme but have their Eyes soley turned on Lord Wellington ... [and] will probably cross the Douro in double quick Time as soon as they know of our Column being on their Flank. ... the current Opinion is that they will immediately Fall Back towards Dueñas and Burgos and should they *not feel* themselves equal to a General Action on that Ground they must retire across the Ebro ... I am sanguine enough to expect as Brilliant a Victory as we gained the last Year on the Plains of Salamanca ... [but] Few people, however, are so sanguine in the Expectation as I am, which I am sorry for, as a croaking Officer dispirits the Men.

Wheeler recalled that during their progress the infantry were 'continually starting hares', and 'being provided with some good greyhounds, the fatigue of marching was much enlivened. So great was the quantity of game ... that it was no uncommon thing to have half a dozen up at once, some of which would be running through the intervals of our column.' On 24 May, he encamped near Miranda. The Spaniards were lost in admiration at the sight:

> I know of nothing more surprizing to the eye of a stranger than to see our canvas towns rise up in a moment ... one day I was at some distance from our camp talking to some Spaniards that inhabited a small village near us. We were in full view of our division but the tents were not pitched. I heard the bugle sound to stand by the tents. I managed to draw the people's attention into the opposite direction ... till the bugle sounded again. ... I then pointed to the camp [where a] minute before nothing

> was to be seen but the soldiers, now the whole camp was studded with several hundred bell tents as white as snow and as regularly placed as if it had been the work of much labour and time. To a people so naturally superstitious ... it must appear like magic ... for they expressed their astonishment in a volley of 'Caravos [*carajos*],' then devoutly crossed themselves exclaiming 'Jesu Maria – these English are the Devil.'

Graham now entered Spain, setting up temporary headquarters at Carbajales de Alba, north-west of Zamora, between the Aliste and the right bank of the Esla, tributaries of the Duero.[6]

Villate had retired due east in the face of Hill's approach to Salamanca with apparently a much superior force. Hill halted there until advised that Graham had turned the line of the Douro, although his cavalry patrolled both north towards that river and north-east in the direction of Medina del Campo. Hill's presence here should be enough to suggest to the French that the Allied advance could be parried to advantage by attacking its flank from the east as it marched on Valladolid.

At dawn on 28 May, Wellington himself, barely attended, set out from Salamanca, by dusk reaching the gorge of the Douro opposite Miranda, 50 miles north-west, where he and his party were slung individually across the swirling river in 'a kind of hammock' suspended by ropes and worked by a windlass,[7] to meet Graham at Carbajales next day. Here, he inspected the bulk of the Allied army and supervised their passage of the Esla, then swollen by melting snow. At daybreak on the 30th, a force of cavalry and infantry forded the icy torrent, but it was soon obvious to Wheeler that

> we had either missed the [Almendra] ford or that the water was risen by the rain. Which ever was the cause, we soon found the water was too deep and the stream so rapid that in a very short time the whole of the infantry was upset. Some sank to the bottom borne down by the weight of the firelock and knapsack, to say nothing of the pouch containing sixty rounds of ball cartridges. This proved to be the awkwardest companion … the pouch would slip off the knapsack and hang suspended round the neck … itself sufficient to drown a man without the other encumbrance. But for the Hussars I should not be alive to tell the tale, they flew to our assistance and picked up as many as the could … There were three regiments of Cavalry and two of Infantry plunging about in it and so dark we could scarcely see each other, besides expecting every moment to receive a volley from the enemy.

> The manner in which we crossed after order was in a measure restored was as follows ... A Serjeant of the 15th Hussars conveyed two of us across in the following manner. I held hold of the [downstream] stirrup, the other man held fast by the horses tail, the Serjeant carrying each of our firelocks.

A small enemy picquet in a village beyond the far bank was surprised and dispersed by the Hussars: the infantry would have been vulnerable, for 'there was not a single round of ball cartridge but was sodden with wet, so we began searching for wood to make fires to dry ourselves so as to be ready to advance as soon as we could get our pouches renewed with fresh ammunition. We picked up many prisoners in the village, some in bed, others half dressed. In a house I with two of my comrades found an officer and a Spanish woman in bed. It was laughable to see him rub his eyes and stare at our red Jackets.'

Once a foothold was gained, pontoons were placed in position and, by the evening of the 30th, three infantry divisions, together with cavalry and artillery, were across the Esla, although several mounts, men and some equipment had been lost: indeed, the river was blamed for any subsequent appointments, etc. mislaid by the troopers, the invariable excuse given at later inspections causing one commanding officer to exclaim: 'Bless me! That Esla must be choked up with camp equipage ...' Wheeler described the bridge-building process:

> Large flat bottomed iron boats were launched, their heads anchored towards the current, their sterns also made fast by anchors. A sufficient number of boats are placed side by side at a short distance from each other and strongly secured by cables and chains to the banks. Planks being laid on the boats, the bridge is ready and capable to bear cavalry, infantry, guns, etc.
>
> You might form some notion with what dispatch such bridges are completed when I inform you that the whole of our army, baggage and stores were transported across, the bridge broken up and placed on the Waggons by four o'clock in the afternoon. I have called the vehicles waggons because in their construction they resemble timber carriages, these carriages are drawn by from eight to sixteen bullocks according to the nature of the roads.[8]

Daricau's cavalry, stationed at Zamora, had made a sweep to the west of the Esla less than ten days before and, seeing no sign of movement, had reported that the coast was clear: there was no reason to suspect any attack from that quarter. Taken by surprise, the French lining the Duero, rolled back by this huge outflanking thrust, had no alternative but to retreat precipitately east through Toro, already approached by the vanguard of Hill's Corps.[9] Larpent described how the liberated citizens 'entertained Lord Wellington and his staff with a concert, lemonade, and ices, &c. [but that] the former did not admire the time lost in singing psalms for him, as he said.'

Schaumann observed that although 'he was welcomed with long speeches and a sumptuous luncheon,

> these hollow ceremonies seemed to be boring and painful to Lord Wellingon, for he was not over pleased with the Spanish nation, and he had gathered that the French had not been at all unwelcome to the inhabitants of Zamora and Toro. He was very grave, talked only to General Graham, and did not touch any of the delicacies he was offered. The Spaniards, accustomed to their own and the French generals, who affected a sort of oriental pomp in their uniforms covered with gold lace, embroidery and stars, and always appeared surrounded by locust swarms of pretentious, dandified and voracious aides-de-camp, could not understand Lord Wellington's simplicity. 'Is that Lord Wellington?' they exclaimed; 'the man who is sitting there so meekly in a grey coat, has only one officer at his side, and will not eat or drink anything? Good God!'

Meanwhile Hill, on receiving his expected orders on 2 June, together with his four divisions, by forced marches had advanced directly on Toro via Fuentesauco, infantry crossing the Duero by a makeshift structure replacing the damaged arch of its bridge,[10] and artillery and cavalry at a neighbouring ford. According to Surgeon Henry, the water was 'inconveniently deep for the smaller baggage animals, and several poor donkies got out of their depth and were lost. One of our soldier's wives, mounted on a good stout ass, swam her animal gallantly a quarter of a mile down the river, directing its course to a shelving bank on the proper side, which she reached in safety amidst a volley of cheers from the Division.'

By noon on the 4th, virtually the entire Allied army was established north of the river, leaving only Julián Sánchez's cavalry to mop up along its south bank towards Tordesillas, and a Spanish division to garrison Salamanca. '...in every town we passed through', Henry continued, 'the inhabitants received us joyfully, standing at the doors of their houses with pitchers of cool and delicious water in their hands, which they distributed to the thirsty men, and accompanying this kind attention with looks and expressions of cordial friendship, '*Viva los Inglezez!*' rang in our ears all the way.'[11]

Sherer, on crossing at Toro, bivouacked in a pine wood

> ... near the village of Morales, and close to the ground where the day previous our hussars had had a very brilliant affair with a superior body of French heavy dragoons, sabring great numbers, and taking about two hundred prisoners.[12] We continued our march across the fertile plains of the province of Valladolid; on the sixth we saw that city ... but I had no opportunity of visiting it; on the eighth we took up our ground near a ruined village; out of two hundred houses, only ten remained habitable. There was a church ... which had been most curiously and ingeniously fortified ... as a post for a detachment; platforms were constructed here for all their sentries, so raised and protected, as to secure them from surprise: such was the state of watchfulness and preparation, which, even amid the plains occupied by their armies, traversed by their columns, and scoured by the cavalry, all the small detachments of the enemy were compelled most strictly to observe.

From Toro, Surtees advanced through La Mudarra (north-west of Valladolid) and Ampudia towards Palencia,[13] traversing 'one continued plain of waving corn, mostly wheat of the very finest description. There are no hedges or dikes ... only landmarks to divide the different fields, so that its appearance is like an immense sea ... the long corn undulating in the wind as the waves in the ocean.' Broughton remarked on the 'concourse of mules, carrying the baggage of the army, and the various camp followers, [which] occupied more than treble the space of the army itself, and presented a moving scene so far as the eye could reach on all sides.'

Out-manoeuvred by Wellington's advance, which they were powerless to stop, Joseph and Jourdan, after attempting to concentrate at Valladolid, could only retreat on Burgos, followed by Gazan, withdrawing from Arévalo, and Leval from Madrid.[14] By 2 June, no French troops of consequence remained south of the Duero: they were streaming north-east along the highway in disorder, hampered by a vast train of baggage and plunder, and the carriages of numerous fleeing *Afrancesados*. Wellington, with the central of three columns, with Hill's 'Corps' to his right, pressed hard on their heels, having no intention of allowing them time to unite with Clausel's army, reported to be in the upper Ebro valley or further north in Navarre, for he would then be outnumbered.

During the next eighteen days the French were repeatedly outflanked, as Wellington's columns thrust resolutely across the rolling Castilian *meseta.* Roughly parallel to them were Giron's Galicians, protecting the left flank. Some idea of the direction of this broad sweep may be gauged by plotting the route recorded in Browne's *Journal,* and outlined in a map in volume VI of Oman's *History*.[15]

Leaving Toro on 2 June, Headquarters proceeded north-east across country via Mota del Marqués, Castromonte, Ampudia, Palencia, Amusco, Melgar de Fernamental, and Castrojeriz, reached on the 11th, there waiting for supplies to catch up.[16] From Melgar, west of Burgos, a dispatch was sent to Colonel Bourke at Corunna, instructing him to order the transports anchored there, carrying heavy artillery, ammunition, biscuit and flour, to sail to Santander, off which, protected by a naval convoy, they were to wait until the the French had evacuated the port.

On 9 June, Tomkinson's *Diary* confirms that since passing the Esla, their march had been through 'one continued corn-field. The villages are but thinly scattered ... so that it appears a difficulty to find hands to cultivate the crops ... It is generally wheat, with a fair proportion of barley, and now and then a crop of vetches or clover. The horses fed on green barley nearly the whole march, and got fat. The army has trampled down twenty yards of corn on each side the road (forty in all) by which the several columns have passed. In many places much more, from the baggage going to the side of the columns, and so spreading further into the wheat.'

Graham's column, on Wellington's left, swung round from Villafrades de Campos to Becerril de Campos, while the right-hand column skirted Torrelobatón, with its imposing castle, and Cigales to reach the Pisuerga at Dueñas, there following Joseph up the great road. On 13 June, alarmed by what was only an Allied reconnaissance, the French retired precipitately from Burgos after blowing up its fortifications. The previous evening, when it had been pouring with rain, Sherer, commanding a picquet on a height near their riverside encampment to the west of the city, recorded that, to add to their discomfort, they had 'nothing to eat, and on these bare hills there was no food for firing. The morning, however, brought with it consolation; for at early dawn, while gazing with my glass at the distant castle of Burgos, I had the satisfaction to see it suddenly enveloped in thick white smoke, and the sound of a tremendous explosion announced to me that the enemy had blown up,[17] and would of course abandon it. In ten minutes a second explosion followed, and, in about a quarter of an hour, I could distinctly see the yawning ruin.'

Leaving Spanish cavalry to mop up along the great road, Wellington wheeled to the north into more mountainous country through Villadiego and Masa, where it was learnt that Joseph had given up any idea of defending the line of the Ebro. This was crossed west of Frias by the Allied columns veering north-west to Medina de Pomar,[18] there swinging east via Quincoces de Yuso towards Berberana.[19] A sharp action took place at San Millán, when the Light Division stumbled on an enemy division. Wellington happened to be at hand and, taking command, extricated them from a tight spot, in which encounter the French suffered 400 casualties, and lost most of their baggage and equipment. He then rode north to meet Graham's column at Osma, where a further action took place, and numbers from Reille's Division were captured. Interrogated, they had no idea of the whereabouts of those units sent to reinforce Clausel, which was reassuring.[20] It was now obvious also that any thoughts Joseph might have entertained of leading his army down to Bilbao could be discounted. Graham's troops were now working their way round behind a line of hills to the north-west of Vitoria, while Giron's Spaniards were in movement still further north, nearer the Biscay coast.

At dawn on the 19th, the Light and 4th Divisions, after turning east at Espejo, were ordered into line, supported by Hill's entire 'Corps', for three French divisions were holding a strong position in the Bayas valley to cover the retreat of the rest of their army. It was cold and raining. Graham's column had not yet circled east as planned, although the 6th Division was approaching from the vicinity of Medina de Pomar,[21] but belatedly. The converging columns had to move with caution, particularly as the lateral tracks were hardly convenient for the passage of artillery. In Surgeon Henry's words:

Some little affairs had taken place, and a couple of French Divisions getting entangled in the intricate country to our left, had come into collision with our Light Division; but had effected their escape with trifling loss. All classes cheered us as we passed; and though, from the long march the men's shoes were worn out, and blistered feet among the soldiers, and sore backs among the horses and mules had become more numerous than was agreeable – the whole army was in the highest spirits. Scientific combinations had been carried into effect in distant, but harmonious movements of different Corps and Divisions … without any disturbing impediment – all had been inspired with the confidence, and almost the certainty of success under their great leader …

After further skirmishing, Wellington's set up Headquarters at Subijana. His army totalled almost 79,000 men, including 8,300 cavalry, and 90 guns, but their precise position was hidden from the French by the convoluted terrain. Several transverse mountain ridges lay between the Bayas valley and that of the wider Zadorra, itself enclosed by high hills except to the east. To the north-west and north the Sierra de Arrato was prominent; to the south rose the Heights of La Puebla, while through a gap in the hills to the south-west, by which the Zadorra entered the valley, Wellington allowed the French to debouch without interruption: they would find themselves a cul-de-sac of their own making, the exits from the valley being obstructed by an immense accumulation of carts and carriages, which would take days to clear. Unless prepared to abandon the lot, they would be forced to fight.

Demoralised by the rapidity of their retreat, induced by the relentless pressure exerted by the outflanking Allied columns, on approaching Vitoria the French army was brought to a halt.[22] Evidently, as confirmed by reconnaissance, Joseph and Jourdan expected to be attacked head-on from the west, and by the evening of 20th June, four and a half infantry divisions commanded by Gazan were deployed on rising ground east of the Zadorra, supported by artillery, as their first line of defense. His left flank rested on the northern slopes of the Heights of La Puebla. Behind him, astride the great road, D'Erlon's two divisions were bivouacked, although some units were placed near the pass of Salinas, not far north-east of Vitoria itself: others guarded Joseph in person. A third line, immediately west of the town, was formed by Reille's three infantry divisions. Maucune's division was to set out next morning to escort the convoy along the *chaussée* or highway to France, but although this may have disencumbered the future battlefield to a minimal extent, it also reduced Joseph's strength. Foy, having collected isolated garrisons along the coast to reinforce his division, while making the steep ascent from Bilbao to Vitoria, had veered towards France to avoid interception by Graham: there was still no sign of Clausel.[23]

Vitoria

On the 21st, anticipating a serious engagement, Surgeon Henry was up before day-light. At first, 'nothing could be seen but the dense vapour – after another hour the mist was clearing away – the men were striking the tents and getting under arms – in half an hour more the whole was in motion towards the village of Puebla, where there was a bridge over the Zadorra ... about two leagues from Vittoria.' It was on this right or southern flank that the action commenced, with Hill's 'Corps' traversing the La Puebla defile, having sent Morillo's Spaniards (supported by Cadogan's Brigade and additional light companies) up and over the shoulder of hills to his right to attack Gazan's flank.

Wellington, personally commanding two columns, approached the Zadorra valley from west of Nanclares, where, posted on a hillock,[24] he could observe most of the battlefield, including the Heights of La Puebla. He delayed any further advance until he *heard* firing from the north-east, confirming that Graham's wing was engaged.[25] Sight of this area was masked by the Arinez knoll,[26] rising at a central position in the valley floor, round which the Zadorra, fordable at that time of year, coiled diagonally across the French front.

Once firing from that quarter *was* heard, Wellington unleashed his units in a vigorous attack. The right-hand column (Cole's 4th and the Light Division, together with four brigades of cavalry) would push through Nanclares, from which the French expected the main advance. From some distance to their left, Picton's 3rd and Dalhousie's 7th, supported by cavalry and artillery, would attack both the right and rear of Gazan's line from the north-west. Together, the southern and two central columns would be outnumbering Gazan force by 50,000 to 35,000.

By 8.30, Hill's men found themselves engaged in a spirited action against units sent to intercept them by Gazan.[27] The combat in this sector continued sporadically until almost noon, as described by Sherer, who with O'Callaghan's brigade

> … marched upon the village of Subijana de Alava, in front of the line, and had orders to carry it with the bayonet. The enemy opened upon us with fourteen pieces of artillery, from their position, as we moved down, but with little effect. I could never resign myself that they would resign so important a post … without a struggle; and when we got close to it, and began to find the ground difficult and intersected with walls and banks, I expected every moment to be saluted with a murderous discharge of musquetry, and to see them issue forth; and I had prepared my men to look for, and disregard such an attack. Not a soul, however, was in the village, but a wood a few hundred yards to the left, and the ravines above it, were filled with French light infantry. I, with my company, was soon engaged in smart skirmishing among the ravines, and lost about eleven men, killed and wounded, out of thirty-eight. The English do not skirmish so well as the Germans or the French; and it really is hard work to make them preserve their proper extended order, cover themselves, and not throw away their fire; and in the performance of this duty, an

> officer is, I think, far more exposed than in line-fighting. I enjoyed, however, from my elevated post, a very fine view of the field. Below me, it was really dreadful to see how the other regiments, which skirmished opposite the wood, suffered from the fire of the French voltigeurs.

It was during the advance that Surgeon Henry first caught sight of

> the whole French army posted on a range of heights about two miles off, in order of battle, with Vittoria in the centre. The position appeared to be nearly four miles in length – the greater part of the troops were in column – some in line, and the Artillery was disposed in batteries on the most commanding points. Numbers of mounted officers were moving about slowly from one part of the field to another.
>
> This was the first time I had seen a powerful army prepared for battle; and the sensation was exciting, exhilerating and intoxicating. I was young and ardent, and felt strong emotions in anticipating the approaching combat and the probably discomforture of those imposing masses. I longed to join in the struggle and 'throw physic to the dogs.'
>
> When our Division had advanced along the high road to Vittoria, within long cannon-range of the enemy's position, we were ordered into a field to the right, and then halted. The word was then given, 'With ball-cartridge prime and load!' In the meantime Sir Rowland Hill and a large staff, including the staff-surgeon and myself, rode forward to a small height whence there was a better view; but the crowd of mounted officers having attracted a shot from one of the enemy's nearest batteries, the greater part of us was ordered away …
>
> The contrast between the aspect of the two armies at this part of the field was striking enough. On one side the dark and formidable masses were prepared at all points to repel the meditated attack – the infantry in column with loaded arms, or ambushed thickly in the low woods at the base of their position – the cavalry in lines with drawn swords – and the artillery frowning from the eminences with lighted matches. While on our side all was quietness and repose. The chiefs were making their observations, and the men walking about in groups, amidst the piled arms – chatting and laughing, and gazing; and apparently not caring a pin for the fierce hostile array in their front.

Before long, Henry was ordered to the assistance of O'Callaghan's Brigade, which were suffering severely. 'We collected the wounded in a little hollow, out of the direct line of fire, but within half musket-shot – unpacked our panniers and proceeded to our work. This Brigade had, I believe, four or five hundred men put *hors de combat* in the course of an hour; so, we were fully employed. A stray cannon-shot from a distant battery would drop among us occasionally, by way of a hint to inculcate expeditious surgery. Spring wagons were in attendance, in which we placed our patients and sent them to Puebla ... where Dr McGrigor ... had made the most judicious arrangements for their reception and comfort.' It was not for some hours that Henry was able to ride ahead to regain his own division.

Longa's Spaniards had been sent ahead by Graham. By 10.00 the great road was under fire; by noon or shortly after, it had been cut, and the rest of Graham's force became engaged along a wide front north of the Zadorra.[28] Unaccountably, two bridges spanning it opposite Wellington's advancing columns had been left un-destroyed: that at Tres Puentes was neither defended, nor was the approach to it in view of the French, being masked by a hillock within the sharp bend of the river here, a fact revealed to Wellington by a peasant at about noon. Kempt's Brigade, ordered to skirt the near bank and cross, rapidly took up a position on a slight elevation further east, and in their wake followed the 15th Hussars.

By then, Picton's Division had emerged from the hills, taking a more southerly path than had Dalhousie's 7th, which, traversing rougher country, had not yet appeared. One of Wellington's A.D.Cs rode up with an order for Dalhousie to attack the Mendoza bridge, with the 4th and 6th to support him. This was more than Picton could stomach. He told the astonished aide to inform Wellington that 'the 3rd Division, under my command, shall in less than ten minutes attack the bridge and carry it, and the 4th and 6th may support if they choose'. Within moments, Picton was leading his men towards the bridge, encouraging them with the words 'Come on, ye rascals! – Come on, ye fighting villains!' The idea that he was guilty of grave insubordination never seems to have entered his head: or was it a risk he was prepared to take. Luckily for him, Kempt's rifles in skirmish order were able to take in flank the guns facing Picton, which after firing a few salvos at long range, limbered up and retired, leaving the rest of the Light Brigade and the 4th to pour across the Zadorra, as did D'Urban's Portuguese dragoons near Nanclares. Picton advanced towards the knoll of Ariñez, rolling up the flank of a French division en route. While Gazan was re-deploying them astride the hill, facing north, Wellington had galloped up to take command of the proceedings. There was now no holding the 3rd Division, Kempt's Brigade, and Grant's advance brigade of Dalhousie's 7th, which had come up. Both the knoll and the hamlet of Ariñez was soon in their hands. John Cooper remembered how

> the cannonading was tremendous and continuous, so that the musketry, which was also incessant, was lost in the horrid din caused by perhaps 200 pieces of artillery. The smoke, the hissing of balls and shells, and the rush of cavalry and flying artillery, with occasional hurrahs, formed an indescribable uproar. We debouched from the wood, and formed line in front of the light brigade, among whom I saw my brother, about fifty yards behind me. We nodded; and while doing so, a ball ploughed up the earth before him. On my right a ball tore a man's knapsack from his back, but did not kill him. Through a fine field of ripe wheat we advanced in line covered by a squadron of the Life Guards, and began to surround the French centre. Here the smoke was so dense that we could hardly distinguish friends from foes. After passing a fence, an officer galloped past our company and shouted, 'We have taken forty pieces of artillery down there'. This quickened our steps and pulses. A minute or two pass and Wellington with his staff gallops to a hill in our front and orders up six pieces of artillery, which instantly began blazing away at the enemy who were now in full and hasty retreat, Wellington in the meantime glassing the total route of the foe with great earnestness.
>
> The uproar of battle now ceased as by magic, for the left wing of the army, perhaps two miles distant, had driven in the enemy's right upon their centre, and taken possession of the great high road leading to France.

Cooper soon found himself amidst the wreck of the enemy's stores: 'I came upon a sack of meal or flour lying on the road. Out of this I filled my haversack, and ran on with my scarlet jacket well powdered. Further on a bag of leaf tobacco came my way. Of this, I tied up about two pounds in my sash. On we swept, and took possession of some hundreds of bullocks and sheep which the enemy had abandoned, after hamstringing some of the poor animals.'

Several enemy units, supported by 80 guns in perhaps the heaviest artillery duel during the entire war, had been redepoyed in an attempt to consolidate their line in the face of Picton's thrust, but this, now reinforced by Cole's comparatively fresh 4th Division, inexorably drove a wedge between D'Erlon and Gazan's exhausted troops, breaking the French centre. Gazan's men – some in action for over eight hours – retreated south-east: D'Erlon's were pushed north-east. Reille's two divisions, which during three hard-fought hours had successfully defended their bank of the Zadorra against Graham, gave way also once aware that the centre had collapsed.

Already decomposed into milling groups, panic ensued once it was realised that their main route of retreat had been cut and, virtually disintegrating, the whole army streamed due east, flinging away encumbering packs and even muskets to hasten their flight. All but two of their 153 guns were abandoned, together with 415 caissons.

Any laden with loot were soon relieved of it, but only a mere 2,000 were taken prisoner: there was far more valuable booty to be picked up, which was found irresistible. Apart from vast quantities of military equipment, an immense park of vehicles of every type waited to be plundered: splendid horses, hundreds of carriages and baggage-waggons weighed down with plate and specie, packed with paintings and valuable property, largely the spoils of war, together with a profusion of food and drink, had been left by the French in their wake. The contents of their Military Chest, partly pillaged by their own cavalry, was soon dispersed. State Papers, cases of maps, Jourdan's baton, and Joseph's silver chamber-pot were among the pickings of the spoil in what had become a free-for-all. Joseph himself had only just avoided capture.

The sun was already setting by the time Surgeon Henry reached the extraordinary scene. Although most of the baggage had already fallen to the victors, according to him,

> there was still one large convoy, escorted by some Cavalry, that appeared to have a fair prospect of escaping in the approaching darkness. A troop of Horse Artillery, commanded, I think, by Captain Bull, galloped up and unlimbered within range on a rising ground near the road, whilst we stopped to see the result. The convoy was at this time entering a small defile … when the Captain pointed the first gun, exclaiming – 'Now for the first carriage.' He made a beautiful shot, for the ball killed the two front mules in the leading carriage, and thus stopped the whole; and before the impediment could be removed our Dragoons were up, and the whole convoy captured.'
>
> After such a day's work there was a great deal of confusion at nightfall – soldiers and officers straggling about, unable to find their Corps. The Staff-Surgeon, a Mr Frith, Chaplain to the Forces,[29] and myself, strayed about the country three hours after dark, fruitlessly endeavouring to find the Second Division. Regiments, Brigades and even Divisions, became intermingled; and it was at least mid-day after the battle before this confusion was remedied. In the course of our wandering that eventful evening *we* also got our humble share of the plunder; for we picked up a sheep, a keg of cognac brandy, and I stumble over a piece of superfine cloth that made me afterwards a pair of inexpressibles, of which I was sorely in need.
>
> After wandering till midnight to no purpose, we fell in with some stragglers of the Buffs and 57th, who kindled a fire, skinned and dressed

> our sheep, and broiled us a chop upon the coals. They divided their biscuit with us, and we gave them a share of our cognac. After this we wrapped ourselves in our cloaks and slept profoundly ...

Schaumann had entered a hotel, 'crammed with English officers ... about 150 ... of all ranks and regiments,' seated around a table already set for the French, and were devouring everything placed before them and quaffing a variety of French wines out of huge tumblers. 'Everyone was shouting: 'Taste this one, taste that one!' And we tasted so often that not one of us remained sober. At last, overcome by sleep, we ached for beds, and the landlord and his men were obliged to bring every available mattress, cushion and blanket down into the dining-rooms, where they spread them all along the walls. Upon these extempore couches we dropped pell-mell, with our spurs and everything on. A few officers who were completely drunk remained lolling on their chairs, or fell under the table, while others who could find no beds lay on the table itself. At five o'clock everybody got up hurriedly and hastened away. '

In the pandemonium, numerous French officers' wives and children (including Gazan's, soon returned to him), and a promiscuous assortment of camp-followers forming what has been unambiguously described as 'un bordel ambulant', were left in the lurch. Schaumann had commented that 'the unmarried ladies belonging to the French army, most of whom were young and good-looking Spanish women, dressed in fancy hussar uniforms and mounted on pretty ponies, or else conveyed in carriages, were first robbed of their mounts, their carriages and their jewels, and then most ungallantly allowed to go. But, as all they wanted was protection and a new lover, both of which they soon obtained, they were to be had for the asking.'

Not surprisingly, the battle terminated in an orgy of celebration, in which the local girls, reported to be 'very pretty and condescending,' were said to be in fear of mass ravishment. According to Capt. Browne, the regular soldiers' wives – thoroughly professional in searching for their share of the prize, 'were seen for weeks after the action in muslins, three or four gowns one over the other, trimmed with fine lace, several pairs of earrings dangling from their ears, reticules, watches & fans as part of their costume. The contrast of these decorations with their brazen tanned faces and brawny arms was ludicrous enough. I have heard that upward of 500 Spanish Damsels passed into the civil Branches of the service, who had followed the victors in time to rob them of their spoil.'[30]

Wandering among this chaotic shouting and screaming throng were hundreds of abandoned mules and oxen: the tumultuous scene beggared description. What could not be carried away from the battlefield or consumed on the spot was then put up for auction in what became a vast impromptu market-place. The camp of the infantry, according to Tomkinson, was 'turned into a fair – it was lighted – the cars, etc. made into stands, where the things taken were exposed for sale, and many of the soldiers, by way of adding to the absurdity of the scene, dressed themselves up in the uniforms found in the chests,' while the citizens of Vitoria amply repaid themselves for the sums extracted by French contributions.

Cooper halted in a nearby village, where, after driving a herd of sheep and goats into an enclosure for the night '… all set to work with coats off and sleeves up: the furniture of the house we occupied was smashed, and fires were lighted both inside and out of doors. Some killed sheep, while others made fat dumplings. A party here was frying chops; another party there smoking tobacco: all happy as princes. At a distance, in a house, a selfish few, who had found or stolen a cask of rum, were drinking copiously. This speedily put them to sleep. Being orderly serjeant, I went not near them. But I was not idle: I killed three sheep as my share, and made and baked, or rather burnt, several loaves, after which I milked some goats and had a splendid supper.' In the midst of all this 'the belley [sic] was not forgotten,' confirmed Wheeler,

> An hundred fires were occupied in preparing food, all our campkettles were in requisition and loads of cooking utensils that had been taken from the enemy. The cooking reminds me of seeing one of our men walk into camp having a large table cloth tied by the four corners, it contained dishes, tureens, plates, knives and silver forks. He found it ready laid. The guests were not there so he bundled it up together and walked away with it. While we were regaling ourselves Major Roberts paid us a visit,[31] he said 'Now my lads you see I am no false prophet, did I not tell you yesterday we should have plenty.' He told us to make ourselves merry, but above all things to keep sober, for the moment was not known but we might move.
>
> What a contrast between this night and the last. Twenty four hours before we had not enough in the regiment to bait a mouse trap, this night we could scarce move without trampling on all kinds of provisions. Suffice it to say that after eating and drinking, singing and smoking we dropped off asleep, marched the next morning loaded like donkeys, leaving as much provisions in the camp that would serve for a month.

Rain now descended in torrents, making roads impassable, and the cavalry, which should have carried on the pursuit, were called off after skirmishing with a slender rearguard. Any idea of capturing Joseph's army *en masse* was given up. Sherer recalled that

On the morning of the 22nd, the army marched forward, leaving a captain's detachment from every regiment at Vittoria. I was sent on this unpleasant duty. The streets of the town, as may be imagined, were all bustle and confusion: here, cars, filled indiscriminately with French, English, and Portuguese wounded, were conveying their groaning burthens to the convents allotted for their hospitals. There, officers, wounded and pale, their uniforms all bloodstained and dirty, were riding towards their billets at a slow pace; their servants leading the animals by the bridle, and often supporting their drooping and suffering masters, to whom the agony of motions appeared intolerable. Here, a few groups of French prisoners stood, eagerly looking out of the door of the church where they were confined; there, our detachments lay halted in the streets, waiting for orders; while long trains of commissariat mules laden with biscuit, were filing past us to follow the army. From the gate, Spanish troops were marching in to garrison Vittoria, while astonishment was painted on the features of the inhabitants; to whom, having been so long under the dominion of the French, their present situation appeared novel, and their liberation almost incredible.

For two or three days, I was employed with strong fatigue parties, collecting the guns and caissons scattered on the roads, and among the field to the north of the town. We dragged into park 174 cannon; of these, ninety were field pieces, all foul mouthed from recent use. The ground, for nearly a square league, was covered with the wreck of carriages, cars, chests, and baggage; and, here and there, whole fields were literally white with thickly scattered papers. In their search for money and valuables, the soldiers had ransacked every thing; they had torn out the linings of the carriages, and cut open the padding; they had broken all the correspondence chests of the various military and civil offices, and had strewn out papers, returns, and official documents, that had been, for years, perhaps, accumulating. You saw the finest military books and maps trod under foot, and utterly spoiled by the rain … in one part, very near a half destroyed barouche, I found a very interesting and beautiful letter, written in English, and addressed to his wife from Naples, by a Monsieur Thiebault; who, it appeared, had been treasurer to Joseph Buonaparte. With a little trouble, I discovered no less than twenty written by the same person … I gathered them up … In the evening I went to a café, and seeing there several of the French officers taken, I asked one of them, if he knew a Monsieur Thiebault ... ; he replied, extremely well, that he had been killed by a chance shot among the baggage on the 21st; that his son was a prisoner, and quite disconsolate; and that his wife, a most sweet woman, and a native of Scotland, had left Vittoria for Bayonne on the 20th, and was still ignorant of her irreparable loss.[32]

Writing home on the 24th from Urdiain (half way between Vitoria and Pamplona), Bragge related that he had 'had a View of the whole Battle from Morning to Night', in which 'our Cavalry had little to do ... except support the Infantry.' The French, in his opinion, had fallen back 'in admirable order, taking advantage of the numerous Villages, Woods and Inclusures, and keeping up a tremendous Cannonade on our Troops who continued advancing ... until they reached Vitoria ... but the Ground was so intersected with Woods and Inclusures that the Cavalry could not act against their Infantry, and their Cavalry took care to keep out of the Way, which accounts for our not having taken more Prisoners ... [During] the last Hour the Horse Artillery were serving them with Grape and Cannister Shot at 80 and 100 Yards distance, so you may suppose their killed and wounded were pretty numerous.'

Indeed they were. Larpent, visiting the general hospital set up in Vitoria, was horrified by what he saw: 'Seventeen or eighteen hundred men, without legs or arms, or with dreadful wounds, and having nothing to eat for two or three days, their misery extreme, and having not nearly hands sufficient to dress or take care of the men – English, Portuguese, Spaniards, and French together ... Half the wounded have been scattered around the villages in the neighbourhood: and there are still many to come in, who arrive hourly, and are lying in all the passages and spare place around the hospital.'

Wellington himself, although well pleased by the outcome of the battle, had every reason to be critical of the ensuing indiscipline, which had caused serious inroads in the number of his effectives. Writing to Bathurst on 2 July, he first made the notorious stricture, frequently repeated out of context: 'We have in the service the very scum of the earth as common soldiers,' but which referred more specifically to those few who had chosen to ignore the wounded they had been instructed to attend, preferring to join in the indiscriminate pillage. He continued: 'The loss of British rank and file in the battle was 3164 ... from irregularities, straggling, &c., since, for plunder, 2733. The loss of Portuguese rank and file in the battle was 1022 ... and their diminution from the same causes is 1423.'[33]

French losses must have exceeded 8,000. The survivors of Joseph's crippled army, about 55,000 of them, rampaging vindictively and running the gauntlet of partisans,[34] filtered back to France through the intricate mountainous terrain of the Pyrenean foothills, but were ineffectually pursued, for the Allied army was in no condition – exhausted as it was by a pitched battle after advancing 300 miles in less than thirty days, let alone the orgy of celebration – to follow up what was certainly their most materially profitable victory.[35]

Graham's column proceeded steadily north-east along the highway, dislodging any residual resistance en route, notably at Tolosa, to approach San Sebastian,[36] blockaded on the 28th, two days later reaching the estuary of the Bidasoa, here marking the frontier.[37]

Clausel's army, on hearing of the débâcle, managed to escape interception by Mina. Wellington had sent the 4th and Light Divisions in pursuit, followed by the 3rd and 7th, but on 29 June gave up at Cáseda what had become a wild-goose chase.[38] The 18th Hussars of the K.G.L. bivouacked here and held a jumble sale of plunder, in which Schaumann participated. They had already rifled the royal kitchen-wagon of delicacies after the battle, when every officer 'got a hermetically-sealed tin which when opened disclosed a wonderful roast joint or fowl in aspic, perfectly fresh and delicious to the taste. Some of these tins contained preserved fruit or jam. Every evening some of these tins were opened, and we enjoyed them immensely'.[39] Schaumann himself

> purchased a whole sackful of candlesticks, teapots, silver ingots bearing the treasury mark, plates, knives and forks for half their value; also a chamberlain's coat of blue velvet and gold lace. Some infantry officers showed me some priceless sporting guns which had belonged to King Joseph, and a good deal of personal underclothing consisting of superfine shirts and silk stockings. The later had 'J' embroidered on them in red silk, surmounted by a crown, which proved they were the property of the King. What astonished us most, however, was the vast number of military and court uniforms, belonging either to the King, his marshals, or to other dignitaries and officials of his entourage, made either of fine cloth, or brown, blue and scarlet velvet, and covered with gold lace. We had jackets and forage caps made out of them. Nearly every officer in our brigade had one of them. Watches, crosses of the Legion of Honour, and gold stripes were to be had by the score. The crosses ... were bought up at any price by our vindictive Spanish muleteers, and slung on their mules' tails with a view of casting scorn and mockery on the French.

Apparently a good time was had by all at Olite, where Schaumann had 'plenty of affairs', one with the local organist's wife, 'who always availed herself of her husband's duties in the church' to visit him. Such gallant activity was hazardous, as he explained:

> The plain in which the town lay was dusty, the heat terrific, and the inhabitants gloomy and ill-natured. This was particularly true of the agricultural labourers, who used to walk through the streets at night in gangs, and carried carbines under their cloaks. They were so jealous that no hussar was safe whom they saw joking with a girl. They actually killed two men of the 10th Hussars close to the gate of the town, and tore their eyes out. The eyes were found afterwards about twenty feet away from their bodies. They used to shoot from the street at the window of my chief muleteer, when he was quietly lying in his room at night, and the bullets almost grazed his ear. When our adjutant, Duperrier,[40] and the officers of the brigade were returning home at night, after a grog party at my house or elsewhere, they frequently had to fight their way through this mob with their swords and compel their respect.

On 7 July Henry Somerset, Marquess of Worcester, a lieutenant, gave his second ball, for which he had engaged the band of the 18th to play. As they did not turn up, he sent an NCO in search of them, who eventually 'found the whole in a room [elsewhere] dancing, completely naked, except having their pelices across their shoulders.' According to Woodberry, the Fandango was the rage: 'the women danced them, and many behaved in a very immodest manner,' but he was uncertain whether 'they were stripp'd or not,' having left early, as had the more respectable women, leaving others, unabashed, to carry on the hop, the character of which would 'beggar all attempts at description.' [41]

While at Olite, the expected severe reprimand from Wellington reached the 18th Hussars on account of their plundering proclivities.[42] Schaumann refers to the officers having

> hatched all kinds of plots against their chief, Colonel Quentin,[43] whom, as a foreigner and a favourite equerry of the King, they heartily loathed, and the whole brigade accused Sir Colquhoun Grant, our commander, of untruthfulness, and of having maligned them to Lord Wellington, the result was that Sir Colquhuon in the first place received a sharp rebuke from the Marshal for all these irregularities, and then fell into disgrace. And this so deeply humbled his pride that he went about like a whipped dog ... In order to complete his misery the officers of the 10th made a

> caricature of him, in which he was ludicrously represented on horseback with his adjutant, Captain Jones, galloping along behind him, and under the drawing they wrote the description 'The Black Giant and his Red Dwarf.' Then they stuck this up on the public notice board of the town on which the mayor exhibited his official orders.

Broughton, stationed at Logroño, west of Olite, was of the opinion that the Spanish rather regretted the absence of their French, in spite of the fact that the inhabitants and the English who were in temporary occupation

> interchanged civilities with each other, and balls and other parties have been mutually given and received. These entertainments… do not afford me any high idea of Spanish society. The men are for the most part vulgar, vehement and noisy, and the women deficient in delicacy and manners. Before a party has been long assembled segars are introduced, the smoak of which fills the room and creates an odour, that … is not very agreeable to those unaccustomed to such practices; to which may be added the constant effluvia proceeding alike from both sexes. I have not yet observed, that the Spaniards possess a greater degree of intelligence, or information than their despised neighbours the Portuguese, nor could I discover any really good grounds upon which they can rest their boasted superiority.

* * *

It has been argued that Wellington should have followed up his victory by pressing on the rear of the main French army rather than turning on Clausel, whose force was of secondary importance, but Wellington had outmarched his transport, and was living off the land provisionally, for although some supply bases were being established on the Biscay coast, they were not yet equal to the demands made on them;[44] and by now he was running short of ammunition.

There were also political implications, should he intend to push into France itself. Following the signing of the Armistice of Pleiswitz on 4 June, there was the possibility that Napoleon might make peace with the Russians and Prussians, which Britain would not accept. But should this happen, the Emperor could well lead his armies in person against Wellington.[45] He would meanwhile deploy his divisions as near the Pyrenean frontier as possible, ready to invade when the time was ripe.

On 4 July, leaving Pamplona to be invested by Spanish troops, Hill, with 22,000 men, advanced due north from Pamplona past Sorauren, beyond the Puerto de Velate entering the Baztan valley, from which any lingering French units were expelled after 'a good deal of desultory fighting' on the 6th, according to Surgeon Henry, who attended to the wounded amongst the light troops engaged ...

> One poor fellow [whose arm he had amputated] had good reason for his indignation; for it appeared that the Light Company of the 50th had surrounded a farmhouse in which about a score of the French had sheltered themselves. Finding they could not escape, they held up a white handkerchief from a window, as a signal of surrender – the firing ceased on both sides; but when the first of the English, who happened to be my patient – entered the door, a rascal discharged his musket at him – shattering his hand which he threw up instinctively to save his head. The remainder then made a rush out, and in the surprise of the moment most of them escaped.
>
> Next day we advanced to Maya ... As the evening advanced, the French retired to the top of the Pass, there was literally an engagement in the clouds; both parties being enveloped, and a bickering musketry fire kept up amidst their picturesque and voluminous folds. There were not many casualties; but staff surgeon Wasdell and myself, thought it necessary to sit up all night in the Church of Maya, to dress any wounded that might be brought in. At sunrise the next morning, Lord Wellington passed through the village to the front; and in riding past the church, he sent for one of the surgeons. I went out, and for the first time, had the honour of a short conversation with his Lordship. He was pleased to hear that so few men had been hit, and that their wounds were, for the most part, slight. He then rode on, saying courteously – 'Good morning – go on with your duties.'

By the 15th, Wellington had forced them from Vera, on the Bidasoa between the Baztan and Irún. In Spain, only Pamplona and San Sebastian (and inconsequential Santoña, near Santander) now remained in the Allied rear, while of enemy armies, only Suchet's was still operating, but in distant Catalonia.

The Basque peasantry, among whom the army were to dwell during the next few months, dressed entirely differently from those of other provinces. They were frequently employed as guides, and paid a dollar a day, for they 'were well acquainted with every inch of ground or by-paths for leagues around their habitations. They knew the various fords across rivers and tributary streams', etc. The females, as portrayed by John Cooke, then stationed at Vera, possessed

> very fair complexions and are extremely beautiful ... Their hair is combed back without any curls, and plaited into a long tail, which hangs down below the hips. Their jackets are of blue or brown cloth, and pinned exceedingly tight across the breast ... The woollen and only petticoat ... is of a light or mixed colour, reaching to the middle of the calf ... They are remarkably nimble of foot, and always carry their little merchandise on the top of the head. They seldom wear shoes or stockings, except on Sundays and saints' days.
>
> The men go bare-necked and wear a blue cap or bonnet, similar to those worn in the highlands of Scotland, with bushy hair hanging in ringlets on their shoulders. They are gaunt, sinewy, and remarkably alive race of men, of sallow complexion. Their limbs are admirably proportioned, and they are as upright as a dart. With long and rapid strides, or at times breaking into a short run, they traverse the steep acclivities with their shoes and stockings frequently slung on a long pole,[46] which they carry sloped over their shoulders, or grasped in the middle like a javelin. They use it to assist them in scaling or descending the crags, or frightful precipices. Their waistcoats are double-breasted, without a collar. The breeches are of brown cloth or velveteen, fitting tight over the hips, without braces, and reaching to the cap of the knee ... A red sash is twisted round the loins. In hot weather they usually carry the short blue or brown jacket slung over the left shoulder.

But while Cooke and his colleagues may have been thus musing on what female company they might get to know better, storm clouds were gathering ominously, for on the afternoon of 11 July Marshal Soult's carriage rattled in Bayonne.

1 Writing to Bathurst on 11 May, Wellington complained that although 'quite new,' he understood that the construction of the carriages was 'shamefully bad.' As he added: 'The truth is, that English tradesmen, particularly contractors, are become so dishonest, that no reliance can be placed on any work, particularly in iron, done by contract.'

2 For a detailed description of the problems in constructing, transporting, and the laying of pontoons, from the arrival in Lisbon of the first consignment in the Summer of 1811 until the end of the war, see 'The Pontoon Train' in Robert Burnham's chapter on Bridge Building Operations in *Inside Wellington's Peninsular Army*.

[3] Although Major Edwin Griffith slept here in comparative luxury, having two apartments to himself, 'with matted floors, silken hung walls, glazed windows, and a carved ceiling ... from the centre of which was suspendid a cut glass chandelier,' the following night was spent at Fornos, 18 miles east, 'squeezed into a loft', the roof of which 'barely kept out the sunbeams ... the ragged walls hung with cobwebs & filthy garments ... & we all turned in with our clothes on by the dim & cheerless ray of a stinking oil lamp, which had no sooner burned out, than a whole host of rats, attracted by the savoury smell of our canteens invaded the apartment, & continued squeaking & racing, round & over us the night through.'

[4] Working parties had been improving several tracks descending to the banks of the Douro during previous weeks.

[5] Not in fact Benavente, but further south, nearer Zamora.

[6] Both rivers are now broader and deeper, the latter being dammed to form a reservoir.

[7] The only other description I remember reading of this contraption is that by Buckham, in a letter written some four months earlier, when attending a fair at Miranda. The traversal of the river was 'effected by three ropes which play upon each other through running blocks secured to a scaffolding, and worked by a wheel ... The men twist their heels over the rope, having their waists secured to it by a cord, and holding on by their hands. The women contrive to sit in a sling, and in this way are drawn across with surprising expedition. It was amusing to see a party consisting of half a dozen men and women, two or three cows, and some noisy pigs, all brought over at the same time.'

[8] When, in the previous Autumn, crossing a similar bridge for the first time – that over the Tagus at Almaraz – Sherer had described it as 'very unpleasant; you stagger, as at sea, and feel quite giddy.' Woodberry noted that the pontoon he crossed was made of '9 Boats with Boards &c across them.'

[9] Lieut. John Cooke encamped 'among some luxuriant, well-watered vegetable gardens, the sight of which proved very refreshing after a long, sultry, and weary march. It was most gratifying to observe with what relish the officers and soldiers devoured the raw cabbages, onions and melons.'

[10] The stone bridge had been destoyed in the previous year by the Allies, while the French had burned the wooden beams with which they had repaired it. The crossing was made by dropping long ladders into the stream from each pier, and then placing planks from one set of rungs to the other, which were then crossed in Indian file, the guns and baggage being dragged over a ford. Badcock, passing through both Toro and Zamora twenty years later, remarked that nei ther of the bridge had yet been repaired, except by a temporary wooden structures.

[11] On traversing Torrelobatón, 'where we were well put up & got plenty of bread & wine,' but where nothing else could be procured for love or money, Major Edwin Griffith had noticed that although 'we were cheered & welcomed into all the towns & villages we passed ... [it was] not with the same enthusiasm with which we were received when advancing through the same country in the winter of 1808 & 9.'

[12] According to Woodberry, the Hussar Brigade captured 239 men and 181 mounts, with only 16 casualties. Cooke refers to 'The whole of the captured, raw-boned horses ... bore evident marks of bad provender, escort duties, marches, and counter-marches. Nearly all had the most horrible sore backs,

almost frying in the sun. Innumerable flies settled on and irritated the poor animals. A number of English medical officers were busily employed dressing the wounds of the French cavalry, some of which were of a most shocking description from sabre cuts on their heads and faces.'

13 A depot was established here soon after. Being in a wheat belt, quantities of bread was baked there and then sent forward.

14 Leval had only received orders to evacuate the capital on 26 May.

15 The abnormal speed with which the advance was made, caused a severe strain on the Commissariat. As S.G.P.Ward has emphasised, once a bullock-cart was loaded from a depot, it rarely travelled faster than 12 miles a day. This was no great problem as long as the Infantry marched at its usual pace of about 15 miles a day, with occasional halts, for the divisional mules could catch up with them, but sustained marches of 20 miles or more a day stretched the system beyond its limits. This occurred on 16 June, five days before the battle of Vitoria, by which time three weeks had passed since the start of the advance, and the troops, having outrun their supplies, were obliged to subsisted as well as they could off the country, a situation which accounts to some extent for their fatigued state, and the slowness of the ensuing pursuit. Already, on the 15th, they were evidently fagged, as Woodberry noted: 'My heart aches for the unfortunate Infantry who I saw this day on the march such numbers laying on the Roadside unable to stir a step further, it is impossible for the poor fellows to march 35 to 40 miles two days running ...'

16 Woodberry also commented that when the mail from England reached Headquarters on the 4th, Wellington had only allowed the letters to be distributed to his officers, 'reserving the newspapers till a future time thinking if the officers got them now they would be reading the news instead of attending to their duties...'

17 The force of the explosion, detonated prematurely, had killed over one hundred of their own men, apart from citizens, and blew out the cathedral's glass.

18 Major Griffith described the descent into the Ebro valley from the Puerto de la Mazorra, although being very beautiful, 'the base & sides thickly wooded with magnificent oaks & chestnuts,' was 'down two miles of road cut through solid rock & steeper than any I had ever attempted to lead a horse down before ...'

19 Commissariat depots were shortly set up at both Medina de Pomar, and adjacent Villarcayo, and also at Reinosa, further west on the main road from Burgos to coastal Santander. It is probable that Wellesley's reason for placing them there, at least provisionally, was in the event that he might be unable to push back the French into France as intended; in which case he would keep a strong hold on the mountainous country west of Vitoria, and receive his supplies with ease from Santander. A small vessel had entered that port late in June with a consignment of flour, shortly loaded onto mules dispatched from the front, but it was only during the first week of July that shipments arrived regularly; and it was not long before they were being sent forward, with transports converging on both Bilbao and Pasajes (immediately east of San Sebastian), closer to the front.

20 Wellington had been informed that Clausel was still in the vicinity of Pamplona on the 16th; it was unlikely that he could reach Joseph for another few days, and it was thus vital to bring about a general action before he did so. From Burgos, on the 9th, it had taken six days for a courier, protected by 2,500

men, to take Joseph's dispatch ordering Clausel to join him: no answer ever got through!

21 It was near here, on crossing the Ebro, that Surtees commented on having met with, for the first time, *manteca de vaca* ('cow butter'), for want of which they had only *manteca de puerco* (hog's-lard') previously. This was sold by 'very stout-made' women wearing a quite different dress from what he'd seen, who long followed them 'with loads of butter, wine, cheese, etc. ... so pleased they were with the excellent prices their merchandise brought,' carrying it on their backs 'as the fish-wives of Newcastle carry theirs ... by passing a broad leather belt across the forehead and over the shoulders ...'

22 Their force amounted to 66,000 men, 13,000 less infantry than the Allies, but in cavalry and guns – 11,300 and 138 respectively – outnumbering them.

23 In the event, Wellington was made aware on the 20th that Clausel was within a day's march by the arrival that evening of a loyal innkeeper, who had ridden some 40 miles to provide him with that important intelligence, which may well have decided him to engage with the French forthwith.

24 As Major James Hughes (18th Hussars) noted: 'All the infantry movements were like clockwork, nothing could be more beautiful. I had an opportunity of being near Lord W. at the middle of the day, we were halted near a hill from [which] he directed the operations, he was dressed in a grey frock and gave his orders with so much coolness watching all the movements with the sangfroid of an indifferent spectator.'

25 Graham commanded the 1st and 5th Divisions, Pack's and Bradford's Portuguese brigades, and Longa's Spaniards. These 20,000 men, cautiously working their way east behind the Sierra de Arrato, would not only be surprising the French by outflanking them entirely, but would also cut their main line of retreat.

26 The elevation was known also as 'Inglesmendi', the Hill of the English, for it was here in 1367 that a battle was fought by troops commanded by Sir John Felton, supporting Pedro the Cruel against Enrique de Trastámara..

27 The 1/71st suffered heavily (Cadogan receiving a fatal wound), but the 1/50th and 1/92nd were able to hold their position dominating the enemy flank.

28 Joseph had assumed this was a feint, and had sent an infantry division and two of cavalry along the Logroño road, leading south from Vitoria, in the expectation that he would be attacked from the opposite direction. By the time the cavalry had come trotting back, the battle was virtually over.

29 The Revd Edward Cockayne Frith, attached to the 2nd Division, who has been referred to as 'the fighting parson,' being one of the few clerics who felt it was his duty to accompany the troops into action, and about whom several anecdotes have been recorded.

30 According to Browne, 'These fair ladies were speedily reconciled to this change of position, caused by the fortunes of war, & remained with their new masters until the army passed the Pyrenees, when the vast increase of baggage which had been occasioned by such recruits, calling for Ld Wellington's interference, he issued an order before we entered France, that they should be sent home ... [but some] contrived to absent themselves for a few days and then reappeared ... attired in every sort of dress that can be conceived, some in jackets above & petticoats below, others as hussars, some again in habits, others in muslin with large straw bonnets. They were found laughing and singing along the whole line of march, perched for the most part on the panniers that were slung over

the mules … Ld Wellington himself, angry as he was to see such an increase of baggage, could not help smiling as he passed them to their loud "Viva Wellington" …'

31 David Roberts of the 51st Foot.

32 These letters were returned to the son. Sherer went on to record that a bookseller there had assured him that in the fortnight after the battle he had sold more books to the British than he disposed of in two years to the French, who had been constantly passing through the place, 'and expressed great surprise that among our officers so many reading men should be found.'

33 Total Allied casualties, including Spaniards (comparatively few: Girón's Galicians, arriving in the wake of Graham's column, were never engaged), have been estimated at 5,150, of which 840 were killed. Oman – whose casting up of figures was not always accurate – calculates differently, for naturally a proportion of the wounded died, some stragglers returned to the ranks, and there are always several imponderables to be taken in consideration when scrutinising such 'official' returns.

34 George Hennell (43rd), on taking possession of one of the better houses in a village on the approach to Pamplona, found it rifled by the French: 'Every chest & drawers was broken open & the clothes they did not chose to take away were strewed knee-deep on the floor. They demanded of the richest man in the town (a priest) all his shirts, and they even stripped him of his boots. He gave them some excellent wine & because he neither would nor could give them more they cut out his tongue & stabbed him. Some of our officers saw him dead.'

35 Larpent remarked that the army was 'already terribly harassed and out of sorts,' and that '… in marching, our men have no chance at all with the French. The latter beat them hollow; principally, I believe, owing to their being a more intelligent set of beings, seeing consequences more, and feeling them. This makes them sober and orderly whenever it becomes material, and on a pinch their exertions and individual activity are astonishing. Our men get sulky and desperate, drink excessively, and become daily more weak and unable to proceed, principally from their own conduct. They eat voraciously when opportunity offers, after having had short fare. This brings on fluxes, etc. In every respect, except courage, they are very inferior soldiers to the French and Germans. When the two divisions, the fourth and light, passed through Taffalla the day before yesterday, the more soldierlike appearance and conduct of the foreigners, though in person naturally inferior, was very mortifying. Lord Wellington feels it much, and is much hurt. The 23rd and 11th Portuguese regiments, who behaved on the field on the 23rd as well as any British did or could do, are on the march, though smaller animals, most superior. They were cheerful, orderly, and steady. The English troops were fagged, half tipsy, weak, disorderly, and unsoldierlike; and yet the Portuguese suffer greater hardships, for they have no tents, and only bivouac, and have a worse commissariat.' He had also noticed that on the 28th Wellington himself 'seemed knocked up … he ate little or nothing, looking anxious, and slept nearly all the time of sitting after dinner.'

36 Foy had thrown in a garrison before pulling back into France.

37 Bragge refers to Graham as the 'old veteran … about 66 Years of Age and beats all his Aides de Camp by dint of hard Riding.' Others found him less vigorous than previously, and he was having serious problems with his vision.

[38] This lay on the river Aragón some 6 miles south-west of Sangüesa, the furthest east reached by Headquarters. Surtees mentions having entered Murillo el Fruto, further south near the monastery of La Oliva, before returning north through Sangüesa.

Clausel eventually crossed the Pyrenees by the Somport pass, north of Jaca. Meanwhile, Pamplona, with a French garrison, was blockaded by Hill.

[39] Such delicacies fell to comparatively few units. John Duffy (43rd) confirms that due to a serious logistical breakdown, it was only on the 27th that the Light Division had their first full delivery of bread for eight days, during which period, 'by receiving it 5 & 6 Ounces at a time in all it has not amounted to more than two pounds per man of Bread & Biscuit – We have had a little flour & the Soldiers have been allowed to collect beans from the Fields …'

[40] Henry Duperier or Du Pré.

[41] Many were more decorous. One given at Artajona in early September by Major Griffith, was held at his house, 'being the best, & the people the first in the village. The display of beauty was very good, & we generally mustered from ten to twenty couples every night. The Spanish country dance is much prettier than ours; instead of scampering up & down the middle of a set, pulling & jostling everybody about as the English do with great exertion, the figures of their dances possess both meaning & elegance, they dance in excellent time & particularly easy & gracefully. Between the country dances waltzes were performed; & two or three times boleros & fandagos in the true Castilian style & spirit.'

[42] Already, on 29 June, when informing Bathurst of the result of the battle, and also referring to the unexceptable indiscipline of the newly arrived regiments as being 'as usual, the worst of all', Wellington had specifically indicted the 18th Hussars: 'a disgrace to the name of a soldier, in action as well as elsewhere; and I propose to draft their horses from them, and send the men to England, if I cannot get the better of them in any other manner.'

[43] George Augustus Quentin (1760–1852), known as 'The German Officer', whose court-martial in 1814 excited much controversy.

[44] The allied army's average *daily* consumption at this time was 100,000 lb. of biscuit, 200,000 lb. of forage corn, and 300 head of cattle, which may give some slight idea of the scale of the Commissariat's activity.

[45] In the event, when the Armistice ended on 11 August, Austria declared war on the side of the Allies, although due to bad weather in the Bay of Biscay, Wellington did not receive this welcome news until 7 September. Indeed, the resounding Allied triumph at Vitoria had significant political repercussions, causing the coalition against Napoleon to harden, not only in distant Vienna, where Beethoven had composed a martial piece in its honour, replete with rolling cannon-fire and musketry.

[46] This defensive weapon, provided with a sharp spike, is known as a *makhila*.

14

July and August 1813: 'Fair bludgeon work' in the Pyrenees: Roncesvalles, Maya, and Sorauren

On 12 July Wellington rode over from Lesaka to visit Graham, commanding on the coast at San Sebastian, blockaded by land since 28 June, and now invested by the 5th Division and Bradford's Portuguese Brigade. Richard Fletcher, on whom Wellington had long relied as Chief Engineer, was preparing to besiege the stronghold, and he approved his plan of placing the guns facing north along the isthmus and on the sandhills to the east,[1] writing to Bathurst that same day: 'I hope we shall soon have San Sebastian; and if we get well settled in the Pyrenees, it will take a good reinforcement to the French army to drive us from thence.' Three days later, he received confirmation of rumours that Soult had replaced Joseph and Jourdan as commander in the Western Pyrenees, and had entered Bayonne on the 11th.[2] Soult had promised his master that once his scattered units had been re-assembled, re-equipped, and their ranks filled, he would mount a counter-offensive against 'the motley levies' barring his way, and, by relieving beleaguered Pamplona, instil renewed enthusiasm into his reconstituted force.[3]

San Sebastian, with a population approaching 10,000, predominantly Basques, but said to be pro-French, was entirely dominated by Monte Urgull, a rocky outcrop, with a fortress surmounting its then bald summit. The compact town itself, defended by walls and Vaubanesque outworks, lay across an isthmus bounded to the west by a harbour and land-locked bay in which lay the island of Santa Clara. South of the narrows of the isthmus – on either side of which extended beaches – rose the hill of Ayete, where stood the fortified Convent of San Bartolomé. To the east flowed the tidal Urumea, while beyond an expanse of sandhills reared the ridge of Monte Ulia, prolonged towards the land-locked harbour of Pasajes, where siege ordnance began to be landed early in July; and thence hauled into position. This ridge-line was continued by that of Jaizkibel, descending towards Fuenterrabía, an ancient frontier fortress guarding the left bank of the Bidasoa estuary.

It was not easy to stop San Sebastian's strong garrison, commanded by General Rey, from receiving both reinforcements and supplies, or evacuating his sick and wounded at night, despite naval patrols. Such support had been inadequate in Wellington's opinion.[4] He complained to the Admiralty that his soldiers were obliged to unload transports at Pasajes,[5] because not enough seamen were at hand, and he had to rely on the local women to land ordnance, ammunition, and stores by means of their harbour boats.[6]

On 17 July, San Bartolomé was successfully stormed, from which parallels approaching the town walls were completed by the 23rd. Batteries were positioned and breaches soon effected, and a mine was exploded in the already severed water main entering the town, blowing down the counterscarp of the western flank of the hornwork, but no preparation had been made to take advantage of this contingency. The whole operation had been carried out far too hurriedly, and the 5th Division, together with Henry Bradford's brigade, failed in the assault which took place on the 25th. They had not expected to find a second ditch and wall, which Rey had run up behind the first.

Wellington had remained at Lesaka, but as Larpent noticed, he was 'very figetty [on the 24th] ... when I went to him about two poor fellows who are to be hung for robbing Lord Aylmer's tent; and today he came out to the churchyard [the terrace of San Martín], where we were listening, about eight o'clock, to judge from the noise of the guns whether our batteries had ceased, and what the firing was. He has been once over [to San Sebastián] himself, but appeared to wish to leave it to Graham, and not directly to interfere. At eleven this morning, however, Colonel [de] Burgh came over with an account of our attempt having failed ... Lord Wellington has ordered his horse, and is going over immediately.'

Allied casualties amounted to 571, while among the prisoners was Harry Jones, who recorded that some of the French had behaved despicably. When wounded and lying helpless, a soldier next to him had exclaimed 'Oh, they are murdering us all!' On looking up, Jones 'perceived a number of French grenadiers, under a heavy fire of grape, sword in hand, stepping over the dead, and stabbing the wounded; my companion was treated in the same manner: the sword withdrawn from his body, and reeking with blood, was raised to give me the *coup de grâce*, when fortunately the uplifted arm was arrested by a smart

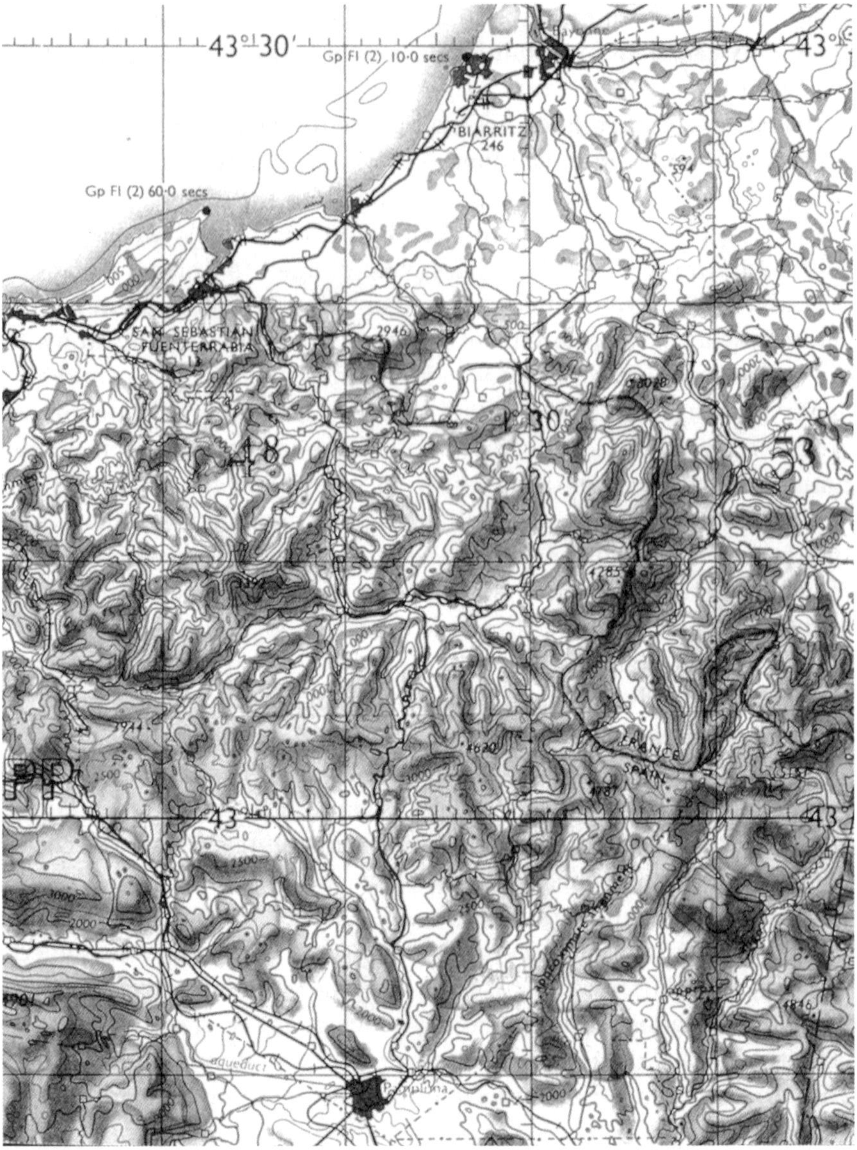

From Pamplona to Bayonne: detail of an aeronautical map, reproduced to emphasize the intricate terrain of the western Pyrenees. See map 7 in the colour section, which does not indicate contour, for place-names.

little man, a serjeant, who cried out, 'Oh mon Colonel, êtes-vous blessé!' (the serjeant must have mistaken my rank, from seeing a large gold bullion epaulette on my right shoulder, and the blue uniform, rendering it more conspicuous) and immediately ordered some of his men to remove me into the town.'

* * *

Already, by 23 July, within a fortnight of his arrival at Bayonne, Soult's columns were on the march, but with only four days' rations in hand. The advance he had planned was risky unless results were rapid and decisive, for it would be impossible to live off the land in the inhospitable country being traversed; both food and ammunition would run short if there was delay en route. Soult was confident that his superior force could ascend and cross the watershed far faster than Wellington could muster and move sufficient troops across country to offer substantial resistance, while any flank march on their part would be threatened by D'Erlon's thrust to the pass above Maya, and descent into the Baztan valley.

The rapidity with which Soult was able to re-structure and mobilise his army certainly took Wellington by surprise, even if loath to admit it except in faint praise, as when later remarking to Stanhope that, in his opinion Soult was not equal to Masséna: 'He did not quite understand a field of battle: he knew very well how to bring his troops on to the field, but not so well how to use them when he had brought them up.'[7]

The ensuing campaign, the 'Battles of the Pyrenees' took place within the mountainous triangle between San Sebastian, St Jean Pied-de-Port, and Pamplona. The foothills of the main range could be entered more easily from the north, which gave the French an advantage, for although steeper, the ascents between the wooded spurs to the summit of transverse ridges and passes were much shorter than on the Spanish side, where the jumble of rounded peaks, separated by deep valleys and tumbling watercourses, was far more confusing, and extended much further, while cross-tracks between valleys were few and tortuous.

As it would be impossible to defend a front of over 40 miles with the 60,000 troops at his disposal, Wellington placed limited numbers in depth at the three principal avenues by which the enemy was most likely to penetrate in force, and kept the rest in reserve to reinforce whichever part was so threatened. Until just prior to the battle of Vitoria, he had not found himself in anything like such rugged country since defending the 'damn long hill' at Busaco: his lines defending Lisbon lay along comparatively low hills. How very different would be a cross-country ride here, when compared to a canter over the rolling plains west of Salamanca! There would be unfamiliar problems of communication to resolve in such labyrinthine terrain, in which it was easy to loose one's way, especially with frequent mist and low clouds blowing in from the sea and obscuring the heights.[8]

The coastal sector was commanded by Graham with the 1st Division; the 5th still faced San Sebastian. Hill, with the majority of the 2nd Division, together with Pack's Portuguese brigade and a Portuguese Division (now commanded by Silveira), remained in the Baztan valley. Between the two, defending the left bank of the Bidasoa, were Longa's Division and additional Spanish troops. The Light Division was posted at Vera, and Dalhousie's 7th at Echalar, further south-east, while Wellington's Headquarters was at Lesaka, at a mid-point behind the last two villages. The right flank of the Allies' irregular and discontinuous line was defended by Morillo's Spaniards, supported by John Byng's Brigade of the 2nd Division, deployed across the pass at Roncesvalles, with units of Cole's 4th Division just below them on the Pamplona road. Picton's 3rd Division was stationed at Olague (south of the Puerto de Velate); the 6th placed near San Esteban, at a bend of the Bidasoa north-west of that pass and west of the Baztan valley, from where it could support either sector.

Wellington had been receiving intelligence of enemy infantry concentrations both near inland St Jean Pied-de-Port and behind the right bank of the lower Bidasoa, where pontoons and flying bridges were being assembled. Instructions were sent to Morillo, Byng, and Cole to 'maintain the passes in front of Roncesvalles to the utmost but to disregard any wider turning movement to the Allies right,' and also to report daily to Headquarters. In fact, the initial movement noticed was the replacement of Reille's troops near the coast by four brigades of Villatte's reserves, as the former marched east to reinforce Clausel's.[9]

Although Wellington was aware that French units were moving east, he assumed it was a feint on Soult's part; he still expected that their main thrust would be towards San Sebastian. He was preoccupied by the situation there, for the siege was not going to plan. On the 25th, realising that the scheduled assault had failed, he had set off north-west from Lesaka, unaware that on that same morning D'Erlon's Corps (21,000 men) were ascending towards the Col de Maya. Murray was unable to tell him until his return to Lesaka late in the evening that heavy gunfire from that direction had been audible throughout the afternoon. It was not until 10.00 that night that a dispatch arrived from Stewart at Maya, confirmed by Hill, that his units had been obliged to fall back towards Elizondo after an action which had commenced eleven hours earlier and only 20 mountainous miles away (as the crow flies): see below.

Roncesvalles

Simultaneously on the 25th, almost 34,500 infantry under Clausel and Reille, with two cavalry divisions and Soult in person, were climbing up long spurs on either side of the Val Carlos, the more easterly by an ancient track mounting towards the Ibañeta pass. No intelligence of either of these sudden advances could have reached Wellington beforehand: that they coincided with his cross-country ride in the opposite direction was indeed unfortunate. As he admitted later to Larpent, 'In truth, I suspected that all Soult's plan was merely by manoeuvres to get me out of the hills, and to relieve one or both of the besieged places ... and I expected him to turn short round towards St Sebastian accordingly. I had then no notion that with an army so lately beaten he had serious thoughts, as I am now sure he had, of driving us behind the Ebro.'

On either side of the Ibañeta pass rose two heights: the Linduz and the Altobiscar. Reille's three division were making their way up a path ascending along the eastern flank of the western spur. Before dawn, Clausel's three divisions started their ascent up the more easterly track past the fort of Château Pignon and towards the Col de Bentarte. The track then swung round the Altobiscar before reaching the pass itself and descending to the hamlet of Roncesvalles on the southern slope.[10] On Clausel's approach, Cole's pickets retired to warn Byng. Three light companies, another from the 5/60th Rifles, and a company of Spanish infantry – together some 500 men – were able to keep the *voltigeurs* of three divisions at bay for 4 hours, inflicting disproportionately heavy casualties. After a lull, the French were able to force Byng's men back towards an even stronger position on the slope of the Altobiscar, where they remained holding the pass, although their right flank was turned by units veering east towards the foundry of Orbaitzeta, until brought to a halt by Morillo's Spaniards.

Ross's Brigade was ordered forward and deployed to the west on a narrow front near the summit of the spur up which Reille's troops were approaching, and below the partly wooded Linduz. Further west, the upper end of the Baigorry valley (also known as the Aldudes) was defended by Archibald Campbell's Portuguese. In the early afternoon a brisk action took place between the contending forces, with the 1/7th taking over from the 1/20th when the latter's ammunition was exhausted. The whole area then became enveloped in dense low cloud, reducing visibility to 20 yards and bringing fighting to a standstill. All the opposing troops could do was to bivouac, which they did within sound of each other.

Cole was in a quandary, for he had only 13,000 men at hand. Although ordered to hold on at all costs, he was in a hazardous position, and judged it wiser to retire gradually in the face of what were certainly overwhelming numbers, which could well encircle him in the fog. Although Cole had sent a dispatch to Headquarters at 1 o'clock, reporting that he was facing a major offensive, this was not received by Wellington until late that evening, and it was not until 8 o'clock the following evening that a second dispatch from Linzoain reached him at Almandoz, on the northern flank of the Puerto de Velate, to confirm that Cole was in retreat towards the Arga valley. South of the Puerto de Velate lay the valley of the Ulzama, between which and that of the Arga were several transverse ridges. In Cole's wake followed Clausel's and Reille's divisions, but their progress was slow, as they were forced to follow each other down the tortuous old road: it was quite impossible to march in parallel columns through such intricate country.

Maya

We must put the clock back to dawn on the 25th, with D'Erlon's Corps ascending from Urdax towards the Puerto de Otxondo, not far down the south side of which, in the Baztan valley, stood the village of Maya. The old road from Bayonne to Pamplona climbed steeply between two spurs to approach the summit, there turning west along a broad grassy saddle before bearing south downhill along the flank of the Alcorrunz. Roughly parallel but east of this ran the 'Chemin des Anglais', a track mounted beyond the intervening spur to a point west of another height (the Gorospil or Anchestegui), before crossing the watershed and descending directly to Maya. From that point, the 'Chemin des Anglais' bore west along the wide summit of the main pass (with the lower wooded height of Goizamendi rising to the south) before continuing west across the mountains towards Echalar and Vera.

This sector was defended by William Stewart with John Cameron's and William Pringle's brigades of the 2nd Division – Pringle himself had joined the brigade only a few hours before – together with three battalions of the 7th Division. Although it was not his responsibility, Stewart had ridden south to investigate the firing heard between Campbell's Portuguese and Reille's units, and was not at hand when the head of a French division reached the Gorospil.[11] Sherer, on relieving a picquet on the ridge above Maya at 7 o'clock that Sunday morning,

> learned from the captain of it, that he had seen a group of horse and a column of troops, pass along the face of a distant hill, at dawn, and disappear. I requested him to make a special report of this when he reached the camp, which he did. A *deputy quartermaster-general* came up soon after; rode a little to the front, said, that there was, indeed, a small column discerniable about three miles off in a vale, but that it was only a change of bivouack, or som trifling movement of no consequence.
>
> I thought otherwise, and the event proved I was not mistaken. The light companies were, indeed, ordered up by this officer, as a measure of precaution; how very weak and insufficient a one, will be seen. In less that two hours, my picquet and the light companies were heavily engaged with the enemy's advance, which was composed entirely of voltigueur companies, unincumbered by knapsacks, and led by a chosen officer. These fellows fought with ardour, but we disputed the ground with them handsomely, and caused them severe loss; nor had we lost the position itself, though driven from the advances of it, when joined by the hastily arriving groups of the right corps of our brigade, (my own regiment).
>
> The enemy's numbers now, however, increased every moment; they covered the country immediately in front of, and around, us. The sinuosities of the mountains, the ravines, the water-courses, were filled with their advancing and overwhelming force.
>
> The contest now, if contest it could be called, was very unequal; and, of course, short and bloody. I saw two-thirds of my picquet, and *numbers*, both of the light companies and my own regiment, destroyed. Among other brave victims, our captain of grenadiers nobly fell, covered with wounds; our colonel desperately wounded, and many others; and surviving this carnage, was myself made prisoner.[12]

Sherer was conducted to D'Erlon, 'who was on horseback, on a commanding height near, surrounded by a large group of staff officers', but on being introduced to him as an English captain, the general 'took off his hat instantly, and spoke ... in a manner the most delicate, and the most flattering, asking no questions, but complimenting highly the brave resistance which had been offered to him. It was a strange scene – French faces and uniforms all around me; and two columns of his reserve halted just behind him ... Their clothing was nearly new, their appointments excellent, and their whole appearance clean, steady, and soldier-like.'

Meanwhile, Surgeon Henry, finding himself the only commissioned officer left at Maya, 'mounted his horse and rode towards the top of the Pass, where the Brigade was encamped,' on the way meeting the batmen of Cameron's Brigade on their mules, going to the rear for forage. On continuing his ascent, he

> heard a shot or two from the top of the mountain, which in a few minutes thickened into a sharp fire of musketry. The piquets, I found, had been attacked and driven in; and when I reached the top I met the troops in motion to support them. It soon became plain that the enemy were in great force – pushing strong columns up the hill, preceded by a swarm of light troops.
>
> It was the Count D'Erlon who commanded here, and the business had been managed skilfully by the feint at Los Alduides – this being the real point of attack. Nothwithstanding a gallant resistance, the Count established himself with fourteen or fifteen thousand men at the summit of the mountain, to the right of the Pass; and in two hours from the time I had left Maya, the camp of the First Brigade, (whose mules had gone to forage) tents and contents – the town of Maya, – the Head Quarter Baggage – the Commissariat and Hospital Stores, &c., &c., lay below him absolutely at his mercy.
>
> It was very plain that without energetic measures I should lose my own goods and chattels with the rest: so 'Self-love and social here the same,' I galloped down the mountain to Maya, at some risk of my neck. None of the staff had yet returned, and the servants were in great confusion and alarm. I immediately directed every thing to be packed up and sent to the rear with the greatest expedition; and took upon myself the whole responsibility. I also hurried away the Commissariat bullocks and biscuit, but had no mercy on the rum, as the mules employed in removing it would be wanted to carry the wounded, that were now beginning to drop in. Accordingly, the Commissariat Conductor set to work staving the casks, and we had soon a stream of old Jamaica running down the steep street into the rivulet at the bottom, fit to turn a mill. I wonder how the little fishes liked their grog.
>
> The wounded now began to arrive fast. Many had been dressed by their own medical officers, but a large proportion required instant

> attention, which was paid them as far as the time and my ability permitted – the slighter cases being sent away on foot, and the more serious ones on mules. The enemy allowed us longer time than I expected in these operations; so that when a few of his sharpshooters began to make their appearance close to one end of the long straggling street – the Governor – my humble self – with the last of the convoy, was moving leisurely, and without any confusion, out at the other.
>
> Dire was the consternation of the poor inhabitants when they saw us retreating through the beautiful valley of the Bastan, which had been the scene of such gratulation and triumph on our advance three weeks before.

The four companies ordered up from their camp in support, found themselves attacked by a line of 700 *tirailleurs* ascending in advance of D'Erlon's columns. The 350 British held them at bay for forty minutes, but losses were heavy. Pringle sent forward three battalions, but in a piecemeal fashion; the first two, failing to contain the French, were pushed back downhill. The 1/28th, entering the fray slightly further west nearer the Goizamendi, reinforced by Cameron's 1/50th, approached in line from the west, but were likewise driven back by the superior numbers.

Pringle, taking command of both brigades, sent half a battalion of the Gordon Highlanders (1/92nd) in a two-deep line against the advancing masses. Extending over both sides of the 'Chemin des Anglais', for the next twenty minutes they fired continuous volleys into the French, unable to return their fire effectively, but were slowly forced back as additional forces reached the front.

Four battalions now opposed three divisions, but the French were unable to put their numerical superiority to any great advantage in such a constricted area, although by 4.30 they had overrun Cameron's camp – 'plundering ... cutting down the tents, strewing about the officers' linen, and tearing open their portmanteaux' – and were turning south downhill along the main road. Stewart arrived belatedly with the 1/82nd from Grant's Brigade of the 7th Division in an attempt to stem the tide, taking up a position just east of the Alcorrunz, where the unequal struggle continued. At about 6 o'clock, two battalions of Barnes's Brigade (7th Division), advancing rapidly along the 'Chemin des Anglais' from the west, together with survivors of the 1/92nd, charged the French flank. Before long, the balance had swung against the enemy, who, although retaining the actual pass, were held there as night fell. By the time Hill had arrived, the fighting was over.[13]

Stewart and Barnes then retired down the Baztan to Elizondo without D'Erlon being aware of it until next morning. By 4.00 a.m. on the 26th, Wellington had received Hill's dispatch at Lesaka. Taking stock of the changed situation – although still in ignorance of Cole's position – orders were distributed to several commanders, while Graham was warned to prepare for a French thrust towards San Sebastian and instructed to embark his siege *matériel* at Pasajes, just in case. The Light and 7th Divisions were ordered south-east to support Hill; Pack was sent south; and Picton north-east from Pamplona. Wellington himself rode up the Bidasoa valley to meet Hill, whose units were by now in a strong position near Irurita, south-west of Elizondo. From Almandoz, where he received Cole's belated dispatch at about 8.00 that evening, instructions were sent to both Cole and Picton to contain the French for as long as possible at Zubiri, where the road from Roncesvalles entered the Arga valley.

Sorauren

By 10.00 on the 27th Wellington had entered Olague, south of the Puerto de Velate and almost 7 miles – as the crow flies – west of Zubiri, on the far side of a mountainous ridge, only to learn that Cole, together with Picton, was already over 12 miles south-west of Zubiri. Spurring south with Fitzroy Somerset, Wellington reined up on reaching the bridge at Sorauren. From here, he could see his troops on a transverse ridge to the south-east – later known as 'Cole's' – facing a nearer parallel ridge along which Clausel's men were already forming.

The events of the next few minutes were later graphically described by Wellington:

> Why, at one time it was rather alarming, certainly, and it was a close run thing. When I came to the bridge at Sorauren, I saw French on the hills, on one side, and it was clear that we could make a stand on the other hills in our position of the 28th; but I found that we could not keep Sorauren, as it was exposed to their fire and not to ours. I determined to take the position, but was obliged to write my orders accordingly at Sorauren, to be sent back instantly, for had they not been dispatched back directly by the way I had come, I must have sent [them] four leagues round in a quarter of an hour later. I stopped, therefore, to write accordingly, people saying to me all the time, 'The French are coming !' 'The French are coming !' I looked pretty sharp after them, however, every now and then, until I had completed my orders, and then set off, and I saw them

> just near one end of the village as I went out at the other end: and then we took our ground.

Somerset galloped back north with a hastily written 13-line instruction to Q.M.G. Murray, still at Olague, to re-route Pack's 6th Division by a track over the Arraiz pass west of the Puerto de Velate and via Lizaso.

As Wellington ascended Cole's Ridge, his familiar silhouette – wearing his 'grey frock coat, buttoned close up to the chin, with his little cocked hat covered with oilskin' – was immediately recognised by a line of Portuguese skirmishers. Shouts of 'Douro!' resounded, and within minutes the cheering was taken up by the 4th Division further along the line. John Bainbrigge could 'never forget the joy that beamed in every countenance when his Lordship's presence became known. It diffused a feeling of confidence throughout all ranks. No more dispiriting murmurs on the awkwardness of our situation: now we began to talk of driving the French over the frontier as a matter of course.'

The Allies were formed along the mile-long ridge, its west flank descending steeply from a pilgrimage chapel into the Ulzama valley; while on the ridge to the east was a slight dip, north of which lay a 300-yard wide saddle or land bridge, but at a lower level, connecting Cole's with 'Clausel's ridge'; further east, the ridge descended steeply to the hamlet of Zabaldica in the Arga valley.

The Ulzama turned east behind the mountain extending south of Cole's position, and – together with the roads descending both the valley of the Ulzama and that of the Arga – then passed through a gap in another, but much lower, ridge to flow into the Arga on approaching Pamplona itself. This latter ridge was held by O'Donnell's Spanish Division, with Picton's Division further east, together with some British cavalry, while facing the gap stood Morillo's Spaniards.

The main Allied force disposed along 'Cole's Ridge' consisted of five brigades: Ross's, and Campbell's, with Anson's further forward along the land bridge, and those of Byng and Stubbs in reserve. The separate hill dominating Zabaldica was held by Spaniards, with Anson's 1/40th in support.[14]

Having studied the French dispositions, and glimpsed Soult himself through his telescope, Wellington considered it unlikely that any offensive movement would take place that day. Clausel was unsuccessful in persuading Soult to attack without procrastination: the Marshal merely scanned his maps, had a snack and then a nap, leaving Clausel beating his head against a tree muttering 'Who could go to sleep at such a moment!'. Soult cautiously waited until more troops, other than those milling about behind his position, had come up. The thunderstorm which threatened, and broke later that afternoon,[15] would have made offensive action ineffectual.

Although the Allies were under arms before dawn on the 28th – coincidentally the fourth anniversary of the battle of Talavera – no immediate French attack took place: Foy, with an infantry division and two of cavalry, merely making a demonstration in Picton's front. By 10.00, Wellington was relieved to see Pack's 6th Division, which had been delayed by the storm, approaching the Ulzama valley – two brigades crossing to the east bank south of Sorauren, while one remained on the west. Pack then turned north, where he was attacked by Conroux's division, but the latter soon found themselves fired on from both flanks: by the Portuguese brigade from across the river, and Cole's skirmishers descending towards them. They broke and fled through the village of Sorauren.

Before long, five French divisions were advancing, outnumbering by two to one those defending 'Cole's Ridge'. Five brigades were stumbling down the opposite slope of the valley before clambering up towards the Allied left flank; one division was approaching the Spanish-held hill on their right, while a second – four battalions one behind another – was pressing across the land bridge. Having comparatively little climbing to do, this attack was the first to be met, by two of Anson's battalions (the 3/27th and 1/48th) in a two-deep line. The musketry advantage was 1,200 to 300, in the face of which the French disintegrated. The Allies were not at first so successful on their left flank, the 7th *Caçadores* being unable to hold their position, while both Ross's and Campbell's brigades were outnumbered by almost three to one. Wellington himself, leaving the 1/40th to hold the 'bridge', sent Anson's other two brigades in a diagonal charge, firing downhill, but with bayonets ready, against the mounting infantry, with orders not to descend too far. This counter-attack was supported by bringing forward the brigades of Byng and Stubbs, while Ross and Campbell returned to the fray. This onslaught was enough to defeat the French, whom, stumbling back down and across the valley, made for the safety of their own ridge.

Initially, their simultaneous attack on the Spanish-held hill had been more successful, although Morillo's troops held them from the summit; but when driving them into the Arga valley, they followed too far, and were unable to reform in time to withstand a second assault, which broke them. But on reaching the hilltop, the French were met by the 1/40th, a volley from which was enough to bring them to a halt. In spite of suffering heavy casualties themselves, the battalion continued firing at close range for several minutes, until the French turned and fled.

Although four hours of daylight remained, Soult did not return to the attack. He may have suffered as many as 4,000 casualties; but Allied losses were also heavy: 2,652.[16] Soult was in a dangerous situation. He had run out of rations, and there was no food at hand in those hostile mountains. Although it would be sensible to retreat by the way he had come, political advantage might be gained by forcing his way north-west to the relief of San Sebastian. While both armies attended to their wounded on the 29th,[17] and Soult was making up his mind, orders were sent to Hill and Dalhousie to withdraw their units from the Baztan, move south and take up a position at Lizaso, which, weary and drenched, they entered on the afternoon of the 28th. Should they require support, the Light Division was advanced towards Irurtzun.[18] Wellington was encouraged to learn that an attempt by the enemy to cross the Bidasoa meanwhile, had failed. Meanwhile, more ammunition had been received, which, with the artillery, was hauled up to the summit of 'Cole's Ridge' and placed south of the land bridge and near the western extremity of the ridge. Shortage of ammunition had been a preoccupation. John Cooper recalled the time when his colonel put his hands on his shoulders, saying:

> 'Serjeant Cooper, go up the hill and tell the brigade-major to send down ammunition immediately, or we must retire.' This was necessary, as our men were taking cartridges out of the wounded men's pouches. I scrambled up the slope ... [and] dragged a Spaniard with his mule laden with ball cartridge down to my company. The poor fellow was terribly frightened at the whizzing of the balls about him, and kept exclaiming 'Jesous, Marea! Jesous, Marea!' However? I pushed him forward to my former station. Having unladen his beast, he disappeared in an instant.
>
> Throwing off my knapsack, I smashed the casks, and served out the cartridges as fast as possible, while my comrades blazed away. Close to me, a serjeant named Tom Simpson sat, pale as death, on his pack, holding his breast. 'Tom,' said I, 'are you wounded?' Tom spoke not. He had just received a shot in his left side.
>
> Hardly had I served out the ammunition and thrown down my knapsack, before a swarm of the enemy suddenly rushed over the brow of the hill, and swept our much reduced company down the craggy steep behind. Some of them seized the captain of the 9th company, and attempted to pull off his epaulets, but he resented this by a blow of his left fist. However, he was led off a prisoner.

By jumping down among the rocks my dress cap fell off, having my forage cap in it, and thus I was left bareheaded under a blazing sun. However, whatever number of balls followed me, they all missed, and I had the pleasure of seeing a fresh body of red jackets coming in haste to our relief; and by them the enemy were swept off the hill in their turn …

On calling the roll I found my company had lost twenty men. One of them, named Malony, that I had returned as missing, soon after made his appearance. I said, 'Malony, where have you been?' 'Fighting, sure,' said Pat. 'You have been skulking.' 'Have I! Look there!' said he, ripping open his jacket and showing me his blackened breast. A ball had struck his breast plate. I could say no more; but I felt sorry for being so hasty.

Pack, wounded in the Ulzama valley, was replaced by Pakenham, who now led the 6th Division across the valley to outflank Sorauren, while Picton was alerted to advance at short notice. With Dalhousie's 7th extending the line of the 6th to the north-west, and Hill ready to hold D'Erlon at bay, Wellington was confident that he could return to the offensive the moment Soult made a move next morning, as he must: indeed, his cavalry and artillery was already retreating along the Roncesvalles road.

Ominous sounds of movement were heard before dawn on the 30th. As day broke, men could be seen hurrying up both the Arga and Ulzama valleys, although some units were also advancing on Sorauren itself. In what is sometimes referred to as the Second battle of Sorauren, Wellington's artillery opened fire on these targets, and also towards 'Clausel's Ridge'. After a vigorous bombardment, the coordinated attack was implemented by Picton advancing up the Arga, Pakenham converging on Sorauren – Dalhousie in support to the north-west – and Cole impetuously crossing the intervening valley and storming the opposite ridge. Although the French were still superior in numbers, their morale had plummeted.

Capt. Arthur Kennedy (18th Dragoons), traversing the battlefield three days' later, described it as 'incredibly horrid',[19] for the ground

was literally strewed with dead and dying French, who have been lying there for three days without any food or any sort of medical aid. The poor wretches abandoned by their General and his surgeons crawled down the hills and collected as well as the could in groups, some without arms or legs, others dying every moment and hundreds among them lying dead under a scorching sun which had the most extraordinary effect of completely roasting the body the moment it expired. All the dead were

> completely black and swollen with the heat most enormously although not more than five minutes dead ... The numbers of our men wounded has been so great that we were not able to collect those of the enemy till yesterday evening. To-day the spring wagons are at work collecting as many as they can but hundreds have died for want of care ...

Maucune's Division were effectively wiped out in the vicinity of Sorauren; Foy's, at Zabaldica, although still in some kind of order, was caught between Cole and Picton. Finding his road of retreat towards Roncesvalles cut, Foy had no alternative but set off across trackless mountains to the north-east, joined en route by other isolated units. Eventually, some 10,000 men percolated back into France with him, but in a state of destitution. The only troops able to retreat comparatively unscathed were those retiring up the Ulzama valley by the Maya road, although many stragglers were taken in their rear.

As Colville recorded:

> All the fighting from the 27th to the 30th took place on the left of the position while the right, which was the post of the 3rd Division, was never seriously attacked ... The enemy contented themselves with demonstrations which, when pushed too far, we made them repent with our Artillery ...
>
> On the 30th we had the mortification to see them move regularly off from ground where we could not incommode them, while they formed their junction with their main body. We, however, had shortly after orders to follow but with caution, as at first his Lordship could not be certain whether their retreat was real or a feint with intent to turn his left. The confusion and evident consternation among the enemy soon showed the former to be the case and we hemmed them in by a parallel march, principally on the high road, while the 4th and 6th Divisions pressed their rear and left flank so that at times they were perfectly bandied about.

In his letter of 3 August, Bragge mentions that there were '200 wounded Frenchmen in every Village for Miles. A Flag of Truce went into Pamplona Yesterday for medical Assistance and 3 Surgeons were immediately sent out.' He was disappointed at not having taken part in the contest, the excuse being that 'Nothing but a Man, a Mule or Goat can Travel up the Field of Battle, therefore the Cavalry on both sides were kept completely in the Back Ground and our Infantry alone entitled to their hard earned Laurels. We still remain in a miserable Village near the Position and about one League from Pamplona, which is still rather watched than Blockaded, as the Garrison are making Daily Excursions and reaping all the Wheat round the Walls.'

At one time during his retreat, Soult had the intention of breaking through to the north-west past Lizaso towards Tolosa and separating the Allied units near Sorauren from those further north, and it was between the villages of Gorrontz-Olano and Artegui (south-east of Lizaso) that Hill, with four brigades, was in action on the 30th against D'Erlon's three divisions, which outnumbered him by 18,000 to 8,000, and had to give ground until reinforced by the 7th Division followed by Archibald Campbell's Portuguese brigade and Morillo's Spaniards approaching from the south-east. Headquarters on the night of the 30th was in a wood near Lanz, north-east of Lizaso.

As Picton, pressing north parallel to and east of the Maya road, had cut any practicable cross-tracks towards the Roncesvalles route, and Cole had reached that bearing north-east into the Baztan and towards Maya,[20] Soult's forces merged with D'Erlon's, and their 35,000 men, instead of forcing their way over the Puerto de Velate into the Baztan, were obliged to retreat across country towards the Doña María passes – those over the Puerto de Arraiz and two others further west – before descending towards Santesteban, at the elbow of the Bidasoa valley and some 7 miles due west of Irurita, south-west of Elizondo. In their wake followed Hill and Dalhousie.

By the 31st, Headquarters was at Irurita, from which D'Erlon, by then at Santesteban, taken by surprise by a sudden onslaught by Cole's 4th Division, fled precipitately down the narrow, steep-sided Bidasoa valley, jettisoning supplies and baggage. The pursuit through Sumbilla and the Ventas de Yanci continued throughout 1 August, with the enemy sustaining mounting casualties and loosing numbers of prisoners.

Unfortunately, the Light Division, working their way east as fast as was possibly over the mountains, reached the bridge at Yanci too late to cut off their retreat. As John Cooke vividly recorded:

> At twilight [on the 31st], from the summit of a tremendous precipice, we overlooked the enemy within a stone's throw. The river separated us. The French were wedged in a narrow road, with inaccessible rocks enclosing them on one side, and the river on the other. Such confusion took place amongst them as is impossible to describe. The wounded were thrown down during the rush, and trampled upon. Their cavalry drew their swords, and endeavoured to charge up the pass of Echalar, the only opening on their right flank, but the infantry beat them back. Several of them,

> horse and all, were precipitated into the river; others fired vertically at us, whilst the wounded called out for quarter. They pointed to their numerous soldiers in bearers, supported on the shoulders of their comrades. The bearers were composed of branches of trees, to which were suspended greatcoats, clotted with gore, or bloodstained sheets, taken from various habitations, to carry off their wounded, on whom we did not fire.

Surtees refers to the enemy sending

> a pretty strong corps of light troops across, which got engaged with our people; but we soon drove down through the woods again towards the bridge. At length, we got two companies posted just over the bridge, in front of which all the rear of the French column had to pass. Poor creatures! they became so alarmed, that they instantly began to cut away, and cast off, all the loads of baggage, and both cavalry and infantry, &c. to make the best of their way. But the mountain on their right was inaccessible; consequently they had all, as it were, to run the gauntlet. Great was the execution done amongst the enemy at this bridge, and many were the schemes they tried to avoid passing. At length they got a battalion up behind a stone wall above the road, on the opposite side, from whose fire we received some damage...

He went on to remark that the enemy, to save themselves, 'were compelled to adopt the cruel alternative of either throwing their wounded men down to perish, or run the risk of being shot or taken themselves. I believe the former, shocking as it seems, was generally adopted; and I have reason to believe that the greater part of them were thrown into the river; for, from the point where we first came in view of them to near where this affair took place, the Bidassoa was literally filled with the dead bodies of Frenchmen, and they could have come into it in no other way.'

While many escaped up the road to Echalar, the surviving wounded, non-combatants, and stragglers were taken prisoner, amounting to about 1,000. The Light Division did not pursued those that had got away; they could not have stirred another step,[21] while the 4th Division, now coming up, was hardly less weary.

Blakeney described how, on the morning of the 2nd, Wellington had 'hurried to Echallar to reconnoitre the enemy and consult his maps, taking a party of the 43rd ... as a guard; but the enemy unobserved, discovering the party sent a detachment to cut them off. A Sergeant Blood of the 43rd with some men, being in front, perceived the enemy coming on at speed; and ... dashed down from rock to rock roaring out the alarm. [Wellington] instantly mounted and galloped off; the French came up, but only in time to fire a volley after him.'

After Soult's fruitless nine-day offensive, the survivors of his army entered Vera and dispersed to take up defensive positions in the hills above the right bank of the Bidasoa between there and Echalar, to the south-east; but Dalhousie's 7th, having cut across country from Sumbilla to Echalar in pursuit of Clausel, surprised them. The leading troops of Barnes's Brigade – 1,800 men or less – charged uphill with such speed and vigour that the 3,000 survivors of Conroux's Division turned and fled at the first volley, causing confusion among units sent to reinforce them, the whole then retreating precipitately over the Col de Lizarrieta, south of the fog-bound Pic d'Ibantelli towards Sare. D'Erlon's troops, not engaged, made their back into France through the hills further east.[22]

By 3 August, Wellington was again at Lesaka.[23] Next day, on approaching the village, Larpent got caught up in 'the baggage of head-quarters (three divisions) eight miles extent of loaded mules in a string,' and in trying to pass them, had to lead his horse 'along some very dangerous places, where if he had slipped, he must have fallen down into the river (and four or five mules actually did so).' He then reached the site of captured baggage, where 'For nearly two miles there were scattered along the road, papers, old rugs, blankets, pack-saddles, old bridles, girths, private letters, lint, bandages, one or two hundred empty and broken boxes; quantities of intrenching tools, rags, French clothes, dead mules, dead soldiers and peasants, farriers' tools, officers' boots, linen, &c.'[24]

Two or three weeks later, Surtees, when skirting the Bidasoa, described its banks as still revealing numerous remains of bodies which had been thrown into the stream,[25] although this did not deter either him nor Jonathan Leach from fishing there, where they caught 'some uncommonly fine trout'!

The possession of San Sebastian, which had successfully resisted one assault, was Wellington's next objective. He could not consider pushing into France before that was accomplished.

Blakeney, at Maya, records that there was often little in the way of demarcation between their advanced lines of sentries, as they faced each other during the ensuing lull in the fighting, and

> yet so well was civilised warfare understood that they never interfered with each other and scarcely ever spoke. The usual words, 'All's well', were

never cried out...[being] superseded by 'stone chatters' – white polished stones, about two pounds' weight, were placed on the spot where each sentry was usually posted at night, and he struck them against each other twice in slow time. This was repeated along the chain of sentries. Should any sentry neglect this for more than five minutes, the next sentry instantly struck the stones three times and quickly; this rapidly passed along the line, and a visit from the piquet immediately followed. By these means we were sure that a sentry could not sleep nor be negligent on his post for more than five minutes at a time. It was rather remarkable that whatever signal our sentries made was immediately repeated by those of the enemy.

Although not tolerated officially, a limited amount of circumspect fraternisation went on, notably when exchanges of wine, brandy, tea, salt, tobacco, etc. were taking place.

Lesaka had meanwhile 'grown very unwholesome, like an old poultry-yard,' and was inevitably crowded with fugitives, stragglers, with 'wounded and prisoners passing, with mules and muleteers innumerable.' General Longa was also there, 'looking like an English butcher in a handsome hussar dress,' but as for his troops, nothing was 'safe at all from their fingers – from a horse or mule to a bit of biscuit.' Larpent described the general pandemonium:

Noises of all sorts, threshing all going on in the rooms up stairs; the corn then made into bread and sold in one corner; aguardente [spirits of almost any sort, mostly brandy] being cried all about; lemonade (that is, dirty water and dark-brown sugar) the same; here is a large pig being killed in the street, with its usual music on such occasions; another near it with a straw fire singeing it, and then a number of women cutting up and selling pieces of other pigs killed a few hours before. Suttlers and natives with their Don Quixote wineskins all about, large pigskins, and small ditto, and middling ditto, all pouring out wine to our half-boozy, weary soldiers; bad apples and pears, gourds for soup, sour plums, etc., all offered for sale at the same moment. Perpetual quarrels take place about payment for these things between the soldiers of the three allied nations and the avaricious and unreasonable civilian natives; mostly, however, between Spaniards and Spaniards. The animals eating green Indian corn almost against every house here and in the churchyard, which contains four tents, from the want of stables and quarters. Not the least curious or noisy in this confusion, are about fifteen men and women with fresh butter 4s. the pound, who are come from near St Andero and beyond it – a stout race dressed in a curious, peculiar manner, who contrive to bring

> butter on their heads in baskets for above a fortnight together, and sell it at last in a state that I am very glad to eat it for breakfast for ten days after it arrives. It forms a sort of very mild cream cheese, in fact.

Wellington 'could scarcely rise from the lumbago; but was in good humour and good spirits'; Cole was 'quite knocked up'; while Picton, 'attacked again with a violent bowel complaint ...[had] fallen to the rear.' One day, Larpent, dining with Cole, who had the reputation of living very comfortably, remarked that even at this juncture he had travelling with him 'about ten or twelve goats for milk, a cow, and about thirty-six sheep at least, with a shepherd, who always march, feed on the road side, on the mountains, etc., and encamp with him. When you think of this, that wine and everything is to be carried about, from salt and pepper and tea-cups to sauce-pans, boilers, dishes, chairs, and tables, on mules, you may guess the trouble and expense of a good establishment here.'

1 Regrettably, Fletcher was killed on 31 August by a musket ball only minutes before the commencement of the successful storming. He was succeded in command of the Engineers by Lieut-Col. Howard Elphinstone, although Wellington had far more confidence in Burgoyne.

2 Soult had been recalled to Paris that March, where he had remained at Napoleon's disposition, for he had well served the Emperor, in whose view he had 'the only military brain in the Peninsula', and who had sufficient confidence in his abilities to entrust him with the immense task of reorganising and revitalising the army. Both Joseph and Jourdan were retired to their estates.

3 These amounted to approximately 72,650 infantry and 7,150 cavalry. Gazan remained chief of staff. Reille (Lieutenancy of the Right), Clausel (Left), and D'Erlon (Centre) commanded three infantry divisions and a light cavalry regiment each – Corps in all but name – leaving Villatte with a reserve of 17,250.

4 As he acidly commented: 'If the navy of Great Britain cannot afford more than one frigate and a few brigs and cutters ... to co-operate in the siege of a maritime place, I must be satisfied, and do the best I can without its assistance.'

5 Within a few weeks, Pasajes had become a general emporium, as did San Jean de Luz later. Broughton described 'British goods of every description' being 'profusely vended, at an immense price … and the natives seem most cordially to unite with the English, who have come hither for profit, in imposing to the greatest possible extent upon the officers and men of the army. An excellent market is held twice a week, where game, poultry, meat, vegetables, fruits &c. are well supplied, but at such prices as can seldom admit of the two first articles being indulged in. What do you think of an hare for three dollars, and a lean tough old fowl for nine shillings; the worst tea, three dollars a pound; butter and cheese, three shillings and sixpence? And so on in proportion.'

6 Colonel Frazer was at his 'wits end, or nearly so, with the ladies here ... they do every thing ... row, unload vessels, bring shot to shore, yet I have been a week begging, praying, and urging in vain, that they should receive rations, and some remuneration. Lord Wellington has ordered it, and a commissary is said to be coming, but he does not come, and I have to make all manner of excuses to them.'

7 As Oman has rightly observed, 'it is certain that none of the other marshals would have played such a creditable losing game on the Pyrenees and the plains of Southern France against such an adversary as Wellington.'

8 As the present author has himself experienced!

9 Why they were not sent to take the place of D'Erlon's below Maya, and D'Erlon's units shifted east to join Clausel's, is a mystery, for this would have saved Reille two-thirds of a long haul. In the event, he was delayed by torrential rain on the 20th, which broke the bridge at intermediate Cambo, and it was not until the 24th that he and Clausel were in position, but still some distance below Roncesvalles.

10 The present main road winds up the Val Carlos, lying between the two ridges.

11 As confirmed by Henry at Maya: 'whilst everything appeared quiet in our immediate front' earlier that day, 'on hearing a report that the enemy had appeared in force near Los Alduides, a post in the mountains, three leagues to our right ... Sir Rowland Hill, Sir William Stewart, and the whole of their staff rode off to the right; and the day being fine, almost every body in Maya followed in the same direction ...' This is not altogether surprising, for Wellington's opinion of Stewart, as previously expressed to Colonel Torrens, was that 'With the utmost zeal, and good intentions and abilities, he cannot obey an order,' and should always be placed 'under the particular charge of somebody.'

12 Apart from Sherer, some 140 men were taken prisoner: the other 260 were almost all killed or wounded.

13 In the sanguinary action, which had lasting some ten hours altogether, the Allies had 1,500 casualties (including 800 of the 1,900 present in Cameron's Brigade): the French must have lost about 2,100.

14 Wellington's forces at the ensuing battle amounted to approximately 18,000 men; the French numbered about 30,000.

15 Bragge, stationed near the invested town, recorded in a letter written a few days later that as night came on he 'could plainly perceive that Pamplona was illuminated and I since understand that the Gates were opened and a superb Entertainment provided for Soult and his Staff, who unfortunately was detained that Evening by a Prior Engagement.'

16 1,358 British, 1,102 Portuguese, and 192 Spaniards.

17 George Bingham refers to a French officer having requested permission, which was given, to remove the bodies of their slain, 'as they said for burial,' after which it was discovered that this was merely a ruse to collect the muskets they had thrown down in their retreat the previous day. 'The truce was immediately broken off. The next morning when we advanced, these arms and several others were found near the advanced guard, regularly piled up, and in no inconsiderable quantities.'

18 Allied wounded were also passing through Irurtzun on their way to the main hospital base, still at Vitoria.

[19] Additionally so because the peasants, on returning to their homes after seeking refuge during the battle, as the ground was hard and the bodies offensive, had not attempted to bury them, but merely covered them with straw and boughs, which set alight, by half roasting them only, had rendered them still more disgusting.

The French had also pillaged their humble dwellings; and Edwin Griffith, surprised by their reactions, commented that the Spanish and Portuguese were 'a strange race, at least to Englishmen,' for not long after 'crying, tearing their hair, & clasping their hands in agony', and invoking every saint in the calendar, one would see them 'beginning to examine into their losses & put things right again; before night they appear to have quite recovered their spirits; and the next day laugh, sing & bustle about again as if nothing had happened! What a happy disposition this, compared with the surly, discontented one of *John Bull*, who if his yields [are] somewhat less than he expected, or the tax gatherer calls for the pittance he is forced to pay towards the securing for *himself* blessings inestimable; grumbles & growls at the hardships imposed upon him & inveighs with bitterness against his sovereign, his minister, and everybody in the country who has the rank of gentleman.'

[20] A convoy from Bayonne, escorted by 1,000 men, was surprised and taken in the Baztan by Byng's Brigade, to whom fell a welcome supply of brandy, pork and biscuit. The escort, confident that they would have an uninterrupted march to Pamplona, were entirely ignorant of the disaster which had overtaken Soult.

[21] Surtees claimed that, when considering that each man carried a weight of between 40 and 50 lbs, and some much more, 'probably never troops made such a march over such a country before. We travelled at least thirty-two miles over mountains ... where you were sometimes nearly obliged to scramble upon your hands and knees. The day was exceedingly hot, and occasionally there was a great want of water ... I heard of one poor fellow, who, when he came to water and had drunk, lost his senses, fell to the ground, and shortly after expired.'

[22] Casualties were high in the nine-day 'Battles of the Pyrenees': Wellington's were some 7,000 of the 40,000 engaged; Soult's some 13,500 of the 53,000 men in action. Some 8 to 10,000 stragglers may have eventually rejoined their units, but their loss of his recently-assembled *matériel* was immense.

[23] Headquarters remained at Lesaka until moving to Vera on 10 October.

[24] Edward Hawke Locker, traversing the valley several weeks later, described it as still scattered with 'fragments of tumbrils, arms, and baggage,' while at 'a turn of the road, a heavy English gun had fallen over the precipice; and on looking down, we saw it lying amidst the artillery drivers and horses, who were dashed to pieces in the fall.'

[25] It was near here too, on 25 August – the anniversary of the regiment's formation – that seventy-three officers from the three battalions had a celebratory dinner, watched by the amazed French sentinels above the far bank, who, according to Leach, 'were too civil and well-behaved to disturb the harmony of so jovial a set of fellows,' for 'Neither vocal or instrumental music was wanting after the feast; and with the aid of cigars and black strap, we enjoyed the most extraordinary *fête champêtre* I ever witnessed.'

15

September 1813 to January 1814: San Sebastian stormed; Nivelle; Nive and St Pierre

By 19 August, the first of three additional consignments of siege artillery had landed at Pasajes,[1] although shot and powder for the guns did not arrive until the next convoy sailed in five days later!

Earlier-sited batteries facing San Sebastian were replaced, and new ones established, some guns being dragged up to a dominating position on the western extremity of Monte Ulia. These opened fire on the 26th, and a false assault was delivered three days later in the hope that Rey would explode prematurely the mines he was known to have placed in front of the breaches, but he did not take the bait. Enemy guns along the eastern wall overlooking the Urumea and those defending the castle were silenced before long, and a stretch of the wall itself had crumbled. To the north was a smaller breach, while the demi-bastion at the south-east angle of the town was destroyed also. It was known that Rey had been busy widening and deepening the interior ditch previously constructed, strengthening the secondary wall, raising fortifications in the streets, and preparing positions along the outer wall for his field guns.

The main attack was scheduled at noon on 31st, at low tide.[2] A heavy preliminary bombardment of the walls was lifted and partly concentrated on the castle at 11.00, as the storming columns started across the sand-hills and the exposed banks of the Urumea. The same troops that had made the first unsuccessful assault were reinforced by 750 volunteers from the 1st and Light Divisions. Their target was as before. The lesser breach, further north, would be assaulted some 35 minutes later by 800 Portuguese.[3]

As soon as the bombardment was lifted, both French musketry from the secondary wall running parallel to the east wall, and their artillery fire – from guns which only appeared after the British salvos had ceased – became heavy and accurate, and the Allies, assailed by a variety of combustibles and missiles as they climbed, then found themselves faced by a 20-foot deep dry moat. Their situation was as hazardous as it had been at Badajoz: they retired to the foot of the outer wall. Meanwhile, The Portuguese, wading through 3 feet of water at the double – several of those wounded, being drowned – had gained a lodgement in the lesser breach, from where they were able to enfilade the defenders behind the main one, but could not force their way further. Seeing the impetus of the attack slacken, Graham gave an unusual order from his position with a forward battery and by semaphore to others (some of which were as far as 1,200 yards away), which was to resume fire on the French defending the walls even if it was immediately over the heads of the storming units.[4] A few minutes later a terrific explosion occurred, for the mine placed below the main breach had been touched off by a mortar shell. It blew up 300 of the garrison, clearing the way for the storming party for whom it had been intended. Once the smoke and dust had partly cleared, they sprang over the dilapidated parapet, carried the ramparts and poured into the town past several houses which had caught alight close to the ditch. Tenacious street fighting continued for some time, until the survivors of the garrison – now little more than 1,000 – retired to the hilltop fortress. Any attempt to extinguish the flames, which spread rapidly from house to house in those narrow lanes, had long been given up: by now the frenzied troops were on the rampage, which their officers were powerless to control.

Naturally, the Spanish blamed the holocaust on the British, who, being jealous of the town's economic prosperity, had had started the fire deliberately, a calumny firmly denied by Wellington in his dispatch of 9 October: 'Every thing was done that was in my power to suggest to save the town. Several persons urged me, in the strongest manner, to allow it to be bombarded, as the most certain mode of forcing the enemy to give it up. This I positively would not allow for the same reason as I did not allow Ciudad Rodrigo or Badajoz to be bombarded; and yet if I had harboured as infamous a wish as to destroy this town from motives of commercial revenge, or any other, I could not have adopted a more certain method than to allow it to be bombarded.'

Apparently, the storming was watched from Monte Ulia by a large audience of men on a day's leave from the front together with non-combatants and hundreds from neighbouring villages intent on seeing the show and dressed to kill. Cooke of the 43rd, seated between two spritely young girls sucking sweets, which they shared with him, records that they kept ejaculating 'poor St Sebastian!', but when he suggested that they should rather say 'poor soldiers', they did deign to reply: 'Oh, si, si! Pobres soldados también.' Everyone rose with a burst of applause when the stormers finally broke into the town. Little did they realise that casualties had been so heavy as they were: over 2,300 on that day alone, with a notably high proportion of killed to wounded, largely caused by having to face grape fired at point-blank range.

Rey still commanded a garrison of about 1,300, but he was now encumbered by 450 wounded and almost 350 prisoners, which had to find what shelter they could in the open, where, not surprisingly, they suffered further casualties in the continuing bombardment. Rey refused a demand to surrender on the 3rd September, but retaining eleven only of his original 31 guns, he was unable to resist for long the 61 guns and mortars moved into position meanwhile to pound him on the 8th and, after two hours, his remaining defences having been levelled to the ground, and fearing that his magazine in the castle vaults might explode, hoisted a white flag. The garrison descended, laid down their arms, and were shipped off as prisoners of war to England.

Schaumann, with a party of officers from Pasajes, visited the charred ruins shortly after.

> All the roofs were off the convents, summer-houses and other buildings. The doors, windows, staircases and floors of the houses had been used as fuel, the walls were perforated by the cannon-balls from the castle, the gardens were devastated, and the whole place was deserted. From the distance the fortifications did not seem to have suffered much. But when we reached the gate of the town things looked different. The drawbridge had fallen into the moat, and it was not safe to cross it. The massive gates of the fortress had been torn from their supports, and one half lay flat on the ground, while the other stood leaning against the wall. In the town itself, nothing but the *débris* … showed where the high street had been; while of the fine houses, five stories high, both stately and massive in style, only the walls and fronts remained, and they were blackened with dust and smoke. The roads were blocked with *débris*, broken furniture, heaps of rags, crushed shakos, bandoleers, cartridge boxes, broken weapons, shells, fragments of bombs, and corpses already in an advanced state of decomposition; and a pestilential stench hung over the ruins. Apart from a few survivors among the inhabitants who, with faces grown wild and haggard from hunger, anxiety and sorrow, were groping about among the ruins of their houses, there was nobody to be seen. At

the breaches the sight was even worse, for they were literally covered with decomposed carcases, the smell of which poisoned the air.

The Spanish army had been ordered to occupy the town and fortress … after its fall, to bury the dead, and to clear away the *débris;* but in keeping with its excellent traditions, it had done nothing of the sort. There was not a single Spanish soldier in the place. After we had satisfied our curiosity we rode out of the town, and halting upon a height from which we could have another good view of the picturesque country round St Sebastian, we had lunch and rode back to Passages.

On these excursions I used to pass through various infantry cantonments, where it was most interesting to see the way in which our officers installed themselves and made themselves comfortable. They were quartered chiefly in deserted villages and buildings; They spent their day either hunting or fishing, and as there were heaps of trout in the rivers, the latter sport was the most productive. In the evening, after changing their clothes, they would feast in the mess, and then drink grog and smoke cigars by the side of a comfortable fire. Even Lord Wellington amused himself by hunting, and I often used to meet him with his entourage and a magnificent pack of English hounds riding out to a fox hunt. On these occasions he is said to have been in the best of spirits, genial, and *sans cérémonie;* in fact, just like a genuine country squire and fox-hunter. No one would have supected at such moments that he was the Field-Marshal of three nations.

San Marcial

It is convenient to describe here the action which took place soon after dawn on 31st August, only hours before the final storm, when Soult had attempted to relieve San Sebastian by a show of force at two points on the frontier. There were several fords across the Bidasoa at Behobie.[5] The south bank was not easy to defend, but some distance behind it rose the ridge of San Marcial, along which Wellington had placed General Freire's three Spanish divisions in line, with Longa's units to their right and as far as the narrows of the river further inland, where it ran through a rocky gorge for several miles.[6] In their rear stood the 1st Division and Aylmer's Brigade.

In dense morning mist, three French divisions under Reille forded the river below the village of Biriatou and, before the third column had yet crossed, two columns started to ascend towards the ridge behind their *tirailleurs.*

The Spaniards were beyond the effective range of their supporting artillery and veiled by bad visibility. Freire's troops descended to meet the enemy, who had broken their formations in climbing and, after delivering a volley at the range of 100 yards, charged. The French were not expecting such a vigorous attack, and after severe hand to hand fighting, retreated downhill. At noon, their third division advanced and gained a foothold on the western end of the ridge. Wellington, watching from the neighbouring Peñas de Haya (or Crown Mountain), declined Freire urgent request for help, sending a message to the effect that they had shown already their capacity to defeat the enemy, and could do so again, for the French, being unsupported, could not hold 300 yards of the crest. Thus encouraged, the Spaniards counter-attacked, driving them back down and over the Bidasoa.[7] As Wellington later remarked to Stanhope, when asked why he had not sent in any British units to assist his Allies: 'Oh, poor devils, they never won a battle. I made them win one though at San Marcial ... the French finding my troops at hand ... were beginning of their own accord to withdraw ... Well, I said, if I send you the English troops you ask for, they will win the battle; but as the French are already in retreat, you may as well win it for yourselves. So they accordingly did; and now I see that in their accounts this is represented as one of their greatest battles – as a feat that does them the highest honour.'

Soult's second thrust had been made before dawn in the vicinity of Vera, but Wellington had already given Dalhousie orders that, while San Sebastian was being stormed, he should demonstrate from near Maya against the flank and rear of the attack he was expecting might be made in this area.

Three of Clausel's four divisions crossed the Bidasoa with the intention of circling west behind the spurs of the Peñas de Haya, which would force the Spanish to relinquish the San Marcial ridge, but the only fighting which took place, and in a desultory manner, was between two of these divisions and Inglis's Brigade of the 7th Division and Miller's Portuguese brigade of the 4th.

Another French division faced the Light Division, which Wellington had placed above Vera, but they were wary of making much movement, for meanwhile Dalhousie had exceeded his instructions by allowing Portuguese units to advance and seize Zugarramurdi and attack Ainhoa (where they were repulsed), which threatened their rear. However, these operations had the effect of worrying Soult to the extent of ordering Foy's Division from the lower reaches of the Bidasoa to the support of D'Erlon's, then at Maya.

Clausel's troops recrossed the river under cover of darkness during drenching rain, which caused the fords he had used that morning to be flooded by 6 feet of water. On attempting to retire over the only bridge in the area, at Vera, they found it held by 80 riflemen of the 95th commanded by Capt. Cadoux, which, against enormous odds, were able to delay their retreat for two hours and inflict 200 casualties, General Vandermaesen among them, although Cadoux and many of his men were killed. Eventually, the French in this sector withdrew into France, having lost at least 1,300 men during the day's fighting, compared to 850 casualties among the Allies.

Reconnoitring enemy pickets and making demonstrations had their hazards. One morning Colville's nephew followed him from their encampment above Maya towards the village of Urdax.

> A company of Light Infantry were ordered out as an escort. The mountain side down which we descended was very beautiful, being rather smooth and open, with fine forest trees scattered about, as well as groups of thicket here and there ... After getting a little way down, the Light Company extended and threading the thickets, and examining carefully any rough ground they met with, gave the descent of the General the appearance of a grand battue in search of game. When we arrived at the foot of the mountain, none of the enemy appearing, the excort was halted and the General and Staff proceeded towards the village.
>
> I happened to be riding in front, and looking down off the road perceived about two hundred yards distant a picket of eight or ten men seated around a fire ... I galloped back to the General making signs to him to halt. On explaining to him what I had seen, the escort was again ordered to the front and the French picket retired quietly.
>
> The General moved on to a clump of trees on a rising ground near the village, a spot convenient for making observations ... Before we had been many minutes there the enemy opened a fire of musketry on us from the houses in the village, the balls rattling among the trees ... On the noise of the firing, a company of the 11th appeared ... commanded by a subaltern ... He was ordered to dislodge the enemy ... [but] was shot dead before he had advanced many paces ... All this time my uncle remained among the trees looking out with his field glasses. Near the clump there was a hut of a French officer, very neatly constructed as they always were, and tied to his bed post was a fine poodle, which I let loose and off he ran to the village as hard as he could go, running on scent like a hound after his master.

It is strange that a number of British troops deserted at this period. Writing on 25 August, Larpent confirmed that several men caught in the act of defecting had been shot. He also refers to Thomas Heaphy, the artist, then at Headquarters, who, 'nearly being involved in my scrape,'[8] in consequence of such risks had increased his price for a half-length water-colour portrait from 40 to 50 guineas: nevertheless, he had now painted twenty-six, 'and some excessively like.'

Little fighting took place in September, during which Soult was reorganizing his army and establishing field fortifications and gun emplacements in every defensible site available along and above the right bank of the Bidasoa as far as Vera, and then east along a line of steep-flanked hills. By the end of that month their garrison at Pamplona, having slaughtered their mounts and mules, turned next on the canine and feline population. Facing starvation, they surrendered unconditionally on 25 October and were marched away as prisoners. Both that fortress and San Sebastian were now garrisoned by Spaniards, leaving Hill's 'Corps' free to join Wellington's main field army, although most of the Allied cavalry remained just south of the mountains.

* * *

Schaumann, with the disreputable 18th Hussars, was stationed not far north of Sorauren, at the village of Ostiz, where the inhabitants spoke only Basque. 'The girls were pretty, and wore their hair in two long plaits, the tails of which were bound with pale blue silk ribbon. We were not so lucky with these Basque girls as we had been with the Spanish women; for they were shy, and we did not understand their language. But we consoled ourselves with the beauties among the soldiers' wives, whom we courted in the fragrent woods and with whom we dallied on the grass and among the flowers.' Suddenly, on 1 November, marching orders were received, and the regiment ascended towards the Donamaría passes. 'Never shall I forget it', enthused Schaumann:

> The roar of the mountain streams, mingled with the cry of the eagles, the sound of our horses' hoofs and the singing of the hussars, made a curious melody. Now and again we would meet a Biscay peasant, looking blooming and robust, with his blue baretta [beret] on the side of his head, and his cloak carried on his mountaineer's stick; and as he leapt lightly and boldly past us across the rocks in his sandals [*alpagatas*], he

> would greet us affably. Higher up we came upon a number of peasants employed and paid by Lord Wellington's general staff, who were levelling some of the more dangerous portions of the road with bundles of wood and logs and making them practicable for artillery. Very often the road ran alongside a precipice, down which, if a horse slipped or shied, both horse and rider plunged and perished. Here and there we came across some snow. When we came to a sudden sharp turning on the ridge of the mountains, a magnificent panorama presented itself to our view, reaching as far as the Bay of Biscay, and we even fancied we could discern the fields of France.

At this time, Wellington had a variety of problems with which to contend, largely provoked by the contemptible behaviour of the Spanish Government, who expected the British not only to clothe and arm, but also to feed and pay Spanish troops, while at the same time issuing orders to their commanders behind Wellington's back, although they had agreed that he should be in overall control. At least, he could rely on such men as Longa, Morillo, and Mina to accept his instructions rather than those of their devious politicians, although he was reluctant, and justifiably, to lead too many Spanish troops into France, knowing that, inevitably, they would plunder and take their revenge whenever they could get away with it, and thus set the whole country against them, a situation to be avoided at all costs. Their authorities were interfering behind the lines also, confirming their reputation for duplicity and total unreliability. At Pasajes, their customs inspectors had the audacity to hold up the landing of essential supplies with the excuse that they were checking whether contraband was hidden in powder barrels and flour sacks; they refused to provide warehouse space for stores when there were empty buildings in plenty; they stripped every convenience from a requisitioned hospital at Fuenterrabía, even burning the plank-beds and tables before handing it over to British medical services; and, at Bilbao, due to bureaucratic inefficiency or worse, wounded men were left to starve in a ropewalk. But inefficiency was evident also in the British Navy, capable of sending transports into Santoña while the small port was still in enemy hands; of unloading uniform coats at Pasajes but knapsacks and cross-belts at Corunna; and – with the excuse that ships lacked a convoy – a supply of greatcoats left at Oporto in May did not reach the front by November, by which time the weather there was freezing.

Members of the Portuguese Regency – no longer under the threat of French occupation – were also making unrealistic demands, and

Beresford was dispatched briefly to Lisbon to put them in their place, which did not endear him in their eyes, then or later.

However, news from northern Europe was improving. Russia, Prussia, and Austria had turned on the French, and Napoleon had plenty to occupy him; it was an opportune moment for the Allies to invade France itself. Local Spanish Basque shrimpers had pointed out to Wellington the precise position of a fordable expanse of the Bidasoa estuary, lying nearer its mouth than where the French had crossed. As the next low tide was not expected to occur until 7 October, Wellington had time to make all essential preparations for his main thrust at this point, where it would be unexpected. Although defended by earthwork, Soult's right flank was less heavily manned than his centre and left, ever since recent Allied demonstrations, for on 30 September, when riding over to inspect outposts at Roncesvalles, Wellington had ordered Campbell's Portuguese brigade to make a raid, which had put Soult on the alert.

It was essential to occupy the dominating feature of the western extremity of the Pyrenees, the bald 900m high summit of La Rhune. Descending south from it were two spurs. A minor road from Vera climbed up that known as the 'Hog's back', while further west, pointing almost directly at Vera, rose the 'Bayonette' ridge, crossed by a lateral ridge, and at their intersection stood the 'Star redoubt', one of several earthworks and forts in the vicinity. To take La Rhune, Wellington deployed the Light Division, its flanks supported by Longa's and Giron's Spaniards, to the left and right respectively.

To mount the seaward attack, three brigades of the 5th Division were concealed behind the fortifications of Fuenterrabía in readiness to traverse the wide estuary. The 1st Division waited further upstream near the fords used by the French a month earlier; in their support were Aylmer's British brigade, Freire's Spaniards and Bradford's and Wilson's Portuguese.

Just before 8.00 on 7 October, as the morning mist was lifting, batteries in front of Irún opened fire on French fortifications on the far bank of the Bidasoa, as men of the 5th Division – 'holding their firelocks and cartouche-boxes over their heads to keep them dry', according to George Gleig, a subaltern in the 85th – were cautiously guided across the estuary, to wade ashore unnoticed by enemy picquets. The 1st Division were also half-way across the river before they were observed. The supporting Spaniards ran into stiff opposition, although Bradford's men encountered comparatively little.

The 5th Division, after taking the village of Hendaye, then spread out: Robinson's Brigade setting off along the coast to reach some ruined fortifications half-way to St Jean-de-Luz; the others pushed ahead to capture earthworks and their garrisons, taken entirely unawares near the Croix de Bouquets.

The 1st Division were held up briefly at Behobie, but once the French found their right flank threatened, they retreated towards their fortified camp at Urrugne, on the road to St Jean. Wellington ordered his troops not to pursue any further, although it was only 11.30 when the fighting ceased. Casualties on both sides had been minimal, between 400 and 450, but the French lost all their forward artillery, most of their baggage, the huts of their cantonments, and were thoroughly demoralised by the speed and surprise of the Allied attack.

Gleig described this camp as 'exceedingly exposed ... stretching along the ridge of a bleak hill ... the only fuel now within our reach, consisted of furze, the green and prickly parts of which we chopped up and gave as forage to our horses, while the stems and smaller branches supplied us with very indifferent material for our fires.' Shortly, 'crowds of sutlers, and other camp-followers, began to pour in ... taking possession of such of the enemy's huts as had escaped the violence of our soldiers, opened their shops ... and soon gave to the spot ... the appearance of a settled village during the season of a fair ...'

The French put up more resistance opposite Vera, although a feint thrust by the 6th Division nearer Maya had briefly taken them off their guard as two brigades of the Light Division commenced their long stiff climb up the Bayonette, with Colborne's on the left and Kempt's to his right, about one mile apart. Between them, and west of Colborne, were Longa's Spaniards. The French were cleared from their fieldworks lower down the spur without too much trouble, but it took Colborne's entire brigade to force them out of the 'Star redoubt' while ascending towards the main ridge. Although the French were in earthworks and supported by artillery; they gave way under the impetus of this attack, and slid down its northern slope of the ridge. The 3/95th of Kempt's brigade, once it had occupied the Hog's Back, fanned out behind a line of skirmishers, with two battalions of the 43rd to its left, extended by two of the 17th Portuguese Line, overran a line of fieldworks stretching along the crest towards the summit of La Rhune, and joined forces with Colborne's men. Some 300 prisoners were taken, cut off in the intervening valley between the two ascending brigades. Girón's force was heavily engaged in their ascent, but the summit, being outflanked, was occupied next day, which enabled Wellington to dominate the enemy front. Allied casualties in this action were slightly over 800; those of the French must have been double.

Although ousted from them, they still appeared to have faith in the idea of defending themselves by manning a line of static defenses, rather than establishing lateral communications in their rear,[9] which would have provided flexibility. The front now extended from the coast near St Jean-de-Luz to Maya, some 16 miles as the crow flies. The chances of any French movement further south-east could be discounted, snow having already fallen at Roncesvalles. Donaldson, at Maya, was ordered one day to take a letter to Hill at Roncesvalles, but felt distinctly nervous:

> Judging from the proud and haughty bearing of some of our ensigns, in coming into the presence of the general second in command of the British army, I expected to be annihilated by his look, and I was ushered into the mess room to deliver my message with a palpitating heart; but I no sooner saw the humane and benevolent-looking countenance of the general, than my apprehensions vanished. Having read the letter, he questioned me concerning the health of the commanding officer, and asked me questions concerning our regiment (of which he was colonel), in the kindliest and most unaffected manner; then calling one of his servants, he ordered him to provide me liberally in meat and drink. Some time after, seeing me standing outside the tent, he called me, and asked whether the servants had paid attention to me. Next morning, on giving me a letter for my commanding officer, 'I did not intend,' said he, 'that you should have returned so soon, but we are going to remove down to the valley, and as it would be only taking you out of your road, it will be as well for you to proceed; but there is no necessity that you should go farther than the small village two leagues from this. I will give directions to my orderly dragoon to procure you a billet there, and tomorrow you can join your regiment.' He then ordered his servant to fill my haversack with provision; and when I was going away, he said, 'Remember now what I have told you, – don't go farther than the village; and here is something for you to get yourself a refreshment when you arrive there.'
>
> These circumstances have no particular interest in themselves ... only that they serve to shew the amiable disposition of a general, whose character for bravery and skill is too well known to the public to need any eulogium of mine. It was this feeling and humane disposition, and attention to their interests, that caused him to be much beloved by the troops under his command, and gained for him the appellation of father, – 'Daddy Hill' being the name he was called by his division.

La Rhune provided a superb view-point, from which – on clear days – Soult (now with Bayonne as his base of operations), could be kept under surveyance by Wellington while planning his next move. As he observed to Colborne, who had doubted that the French could be expelled from their entrenched positions with ease: '... with your local knowledge only you are perfectly right: it appears difficult. But the enemy have not enough to man all those works and lines they occupy. I can pour a greater force on certain points than they can concentrate to resist me.' John Cooper recalled that once the French had been dislodged from this summit, his company had encamped, but

> The ridge on which we pitched our tents was not more than thirty yards across, and its sides were very steep, especially on the French side. In this high and exposed situation the wind sometimes blew down our tents. This was the case one dark wet night: while a storm was raging, the top of the tent pole burst through the rotten cap, and down came the dripping tent upon us [all naked], with all the firelocks, belts, pouches, caps, etc. in glorious confusion.
>
> October 31st, our regiment was sent to the top of the highest spur of La Rhune, and our company was ordered to descend the other side and reconnoitre. This movement drew the whole French force in front of their numerous camps. We piled arms and walked about, while the French skirmishers below kept firing at us through a hedge. This was not pleasant, as we had no orders to return the compliment.
>
> From the top of La Rhune a complete view of the redoubts and camp of the French could be obtained. A regiment of Spaniards occupied this elevated spot, and had to burrow like rabbits among the rocks. Report said that some of them were frozen to death.
>
> To the eastward of our position the mountains had a splendid appearance: pile rose on pile, till they were lost in the clouds. Many were covered with snow, which was in some places fourteen or fifteen feet deep.
>
> In the valley behind our camp was a wood of chestnut trees. The fruit was plentiful, and when boiled made a good substitute for potatoes.

The main French positions along the short seaward sector – one-third of the total length of their defensive line – ran through Urrugne to Ascain, south-east of St Jean-de-Luz and on the south bank of the Nivelle, a river of no great consequence in itself. Soult, who had received reinforcements, deployed three divisions here (with at least another three or four in reserve), supported by artillery placed in extensive field-works: in all some 23,000 men. Along the other two-thirds, which extended south-east through Sare and Ainhoa to the flank of the Pic de Mondarrain (rising south-west of Itxassou on the Nive), were deployed another five divisions. This more rugged area was thus less strongly held than the coastal sector, indeed inadequately so.

Below the north-east flank of La Rhune rose the Lesser Rhune, which, with its several earth and masonry works, remained a key forward bastion still in French hands.[10] They would find if difficult to hold their line, should Wellington decide to break through here, but any such thrust would require careful planning. Harry Smith later described Wellington, after surveying the future field of battle, being in earnest conversation with generals Alten, Kempt, and Colborne. This was continued with Sir George Murray, who, extracting writing materials from his sabretache, began noting down the plan of attack. So clearly had he understood the Duke, that on reading back what was written, Wellington, his eye glued to his telescope, and face displaying great concentration, could only smile and say, 'Ah, Murray, this will put us in possession of the fellows' lines. Shall we be ready tomorrow?' 'I fear not, my lord, but the next day,' was the reply.[11] This says much for the confidence the C.-in-C. had in his Q.M.G., but by then they had worked closely together for several years. Allied troops in the coastal sector, now commanded by Sir John Hope (in Graham's absence on leave to seek relief from an eye complaint), were to drive in outposts, cannonade, and make similar demonstrations, but not to commit themselves to any serious action.

The bulk of the Allied army was divided into two 'Corps': one commanded by Beresford (back from Lisbon, with whom Wellington remained throughout the subsequent engagement), with the 3rd (Colville replacing Picton, on leave), 4th, 7th (under the Portuguese General Le Cor, Dalhousie being on leave also), the Light Divisions, and Longa's and Giron's Spaniards. Hill commanded the other, with the addition of the 6th Division (Clinton) and Hamilton's Independent Portuguese brigade. Totalling some 55,000 men, they would make a concerted attack between Ascain and the Pic de Mondarrain, a line defended by only 40,000.

Nivelle

The massive thrust took place at dawn on 10 November.[12] The Light Division (after taking some sustenance at 2.0 a.m.) together with three 3-pounder 'mountain' guns, had silently approached the outlying French picquets before lying down muffled in their blankets to await the signal to fall on the enemy. They had the hazardous task of taking the Lesser Rhune, first descending into a ravine between the two and from its western extremity attacking successively the defensive works along its crest. After a determined resistance, by 8.00 the French were forced out, and also from a strong 'star' redoubt on a neighbouring height known as the Mouiz.

Beresford's and Hill's 'Corps' had been advancing also, along the specific routes alloted to each unit, with Morillo's Spaniards on the far right wing, which were to threaten but not attack the Pic de Mondarrain. By 9.00, the fortified village of Sare was entered by the 4th Division, while the bridge at Amotz (on the road to St Pée) – providing an important lateral communication over the Nivelle between the French left and right – was in the possession of the 3rd Division by 11.00. The 6th Division advanced along the east bank of the river, and by noon the village of Ainhoa was occupied by Hamilton's Portuguese. However elaborate were their system of defenses, the French could not stem the tide of overwhelming numbers: with their left flank seriously threatened,[13] they abandoned their fortifications and withdrew rapidly towards Bayonne.

After a brief respite, the Light Division forged ahead to take additional redoubts, the commander of one surrendering when threatened that if he didn't capitulate at once, any survivors of his garrison would be handed over to the Spaniards, with consequences he foresaw! By mid afternoon, Hill and Beresford had taken all their objectives, while Hope's troops, having demonstrated effectively enough to ensure that those opposing them remained within their positions, occupied Urrugne and approached Ascain without great losses.

The church at Urrugne presented a curious spectacle that night, for the arms of Gleig's companions were piled along the side aisles, 'while the men themselves occupied the centre aisle. In the pulpit was placed the large drum and other musical instruments, while a party of officers took possession of a gallery erected at the lower extremity of the building.' Finding space by the altar, lighted by tapers, they spread out their cold salt beef, brown bread, cheese, and grog, and ate and drank 'in that state of excited feeling which attends every man who has gone safely through the perils of such a day,' before sinking to sleep on the paved floor, wrapped in their cloaks. Commissary Daniel spent that night 'upon the green of St Pe: the 3rd division were at bivouac in the woods near that place, with the 7th and 4th divisions on their left and the 6th on their right. Thus ended the battle of the Nivelle, which (if not the most sounding of Lord Wellington's victories) was at least one of the boldest and most interesting operations of the Peninsular war,[14] as the enemy occupied a tract of country not only exceedingly strong by nature, but fortified in a most extraordinary manner, every hill being crowned by a redoubt.'

The Allies paused for breath. Although the success of their advance had been very satisfactory, they were now faced by a particularly hard nut to crack, for Bayonne was the most powerful military base in south-west France, surrounded by a complex of Vaubanesque fortifications, and containing a substantial garrison, which could be reinforced and re-supplied by roads from Pau and Bordeaux converging at the suburban village of St Etienne; that of St Esprit stood on the north bank of the wide Adour, dominated to the west by a strongly bastioned citadel. Bayonne also straddled both banks of the Nive, a more serious obstacle than the Nivelle. Its flow was unpredictable: although fordable in certain places, the level could rise rapidly after heavy rains or melting snow in its upper reaches beyond St Jean Pied-de-Port in the Pyrenean foothills below Roncesvalles. The French front now extended east across a triangle of land, its apex just west of Bayonne. From south of what was then the sea-side hamlet of Biarritz, it ran through the village of Arcangues to Villefranque on the Nive.

Wellington was faced by an additional problem: the Spaniards. The unmitigated bad faith of their government had decided him to resign his theoretical command of Spanish troops, although he intended to retain Morillo's units, on which he could rely. Longa's troops, on entering Ascain, had plundered and committed atrocities. Writing to Bathurst from St Jean-de-Luz on 21 November, while admitting that while it was 'really hardly fair to expect that they [the Spaniards] will refrain from plundering a beautiful country, into which they enter as conquerers, particularly adverting to the miseries which their own country has suffered from its invaders,' if they continued to do so, 'they will ruin us all.' Wellington could not rely on them to desist, nor could he afford to provoke the civilian population to any form of 'guerrilla war' against his own troops. Preferring to sacrifice his then numerical superiority to Soult's army, the majority of the Spaniards were sent back across the frontier, where, cantoned in their own country, they would be the entire responsibility of their own miserable government. He had enough problems keeping the British regiments in check.

Schaumann remembered seeing

> the body of one Spanish muleteer, who had entered a house to steal apples, hanging from the window of that house as a warning to all marauders. In his mouth, which had fallen open in the process of

> strangulation, they had stuck an apple, to show what he had coveted! On the other hand, Lord Wellington frequently showed himself merciful towards regiments of which he was fond. On one occasion, for instance, during this period he came upon the 1st German Hussars, who were just about to enter bivouac, and as he was standing talking to Lieut.-Colonel Arentschildt and the other officers, one of the men of the regiment came riding up with a bleating sheep which he had stolen. The moment Lord Wellington saw the man, however, he only smiled, and turning his back on him, pretended not to have noticed anything, although the officers at his side were shuddering with fear.

Wellington still had some 63,000 infantry with him: 36,000 British, 23,000 Portuguese, and Morillo's 4,500 veterans. With these, he would continue offensive operations as soon as the rain ceased, for it was his intention to cross the Nive between Bayonne and Cambo, although it was defended by three French divisions, supported by cavalry and artillery; other units, approximating to a division, commanded by General Paris, stood further south-east. Soult had about 54,500 infantry at hand, not counting the sedentary garrison of Bayonne, another 8,800 men.

Headquarters remained at St Jean-de-Luz from late November until late February. Capt. Batty had remarked that the place 'had rather a gloomy appearance when the troops first went into cantonments', but shops had reopened soon after, once the inhabitants realised that their property would be respected. There was also a considerable influx of Spaniards bringing in provisions: even from distant Santander, women, wearing 'very singular and gaudy' costumes, 'brought, in truck-baskets slung over their shoulders, butter, chocolate, honey, &c.' On 3 December, their confidence increasing, some 3,000 Frenchwomen with their children crossed the Allied outposts facing Bayonne to return to their villages, and Batty records that 'Many young men were amongst these, disguised as women, to avoid being detained by the French authorities for the new conscription. Their fears were ludicrous when detected ... apprehending that they would be sent back ... or treated as spies.' Although many able-bodied men had been detained by Soult, this stock of females added considerably to the 700 Portuguese and 400 Spanish already in St Jean and its environs, acting 'as suttlers, *vivanderas*, washerwomen, &c.' While this influx reduced the number of hungry mouths to feed in Bayonne, it increased the problems of the Allied Commissariat.

Larpent described the daily scene in St Jean, where the British officers could be seen 'wearing their morning great coats; Lord Wellington in his plain blue coat, and round hat, or perhaps in his sky-blue Salisbury hunting dress,' while the streets were 'full of Spanish mules, with supplies, and muleteers, &c., all running against you, and splashing you as you walk; every shop crowded with eatables – wines, sauces, pickles, hams, tongues, butter, and sardines. The quay is always a busy scene, covered with some rum casks, and flower casks, and suttler stores ... The prices are still enormous, and of course the activity is the result. The French peasants are always on the road between this place and Bayonne, bringing in poultry, and smuggling out sugar in sacks on their heads.'

This, in spite of a proclamation having been issued, in which the peasantry was forbidden 'to supply the English with provisions or forage, on pain of death.' According to Capt. Rees Gronow (1st Guards), it stated that 'we were savages, and, as proof of this, our horses were born with short tails. I saw this absurd proclamation, which was published in French and the Basque languages, and distributed all over the country.' Other leaflets, printed in English, with Spanish on the verso, were stuck on sticks near the advanced posts, attempted to encite desertion, announcing that they would be 'paid for the arms and for the horses they bring with' [sic]; that 'none of them is obliged to serve; pass-ports are delivered to them to return to their native country, if they chuse, or to go to inner parts of France where they may freely exercise their professions; they are moreover treated with all sorts of regard. They are also warned that the whole French Nation is armed, and that in the case the English, Spaniard and Portugese [sic] armys should tread his [sic] territory, they would not find any where but death and destruction.'

Buckham, before being appointed to Beresford's staff at St Jean, had lodged in a 'miserable garret' at Ustaritz,[15] where a Commissariat depot was later established, from which he could see the French 'every morning at parade.' Here, 'Our sentries and theirs can talk to each other with perfect ease; no kind of molestation being offered on either side. They come down to water their horses, and their women to wash the linen of the regiment, and we do the same. The French soldiers often endeavour to entice our fellows to desert, by sticking a piece of beef on the point of a bayonet, or by holding out a canteen, accompanying their action with 'I say, come here! Here is ver good ros-bif; here is ver good brandy.'

Nive

At dawn on 9 December Hill's 'Corps' waded across three fords near Cambo, after which Morillo's Spaniards, a regiment of cavalry and a battery of artillery turned south-east as a flank guard against

Paris's troops. The rest of Hill's units veered north towards the Adour. Meanwhile, the 3rd and 6th Divisions, under Beresford, had crossed the Nive further downstream on pontoons laid during the night, one to a island in the river, from which they could then wade. With four Allied divisions now advancing on a front of 5 miles, the three opposing them retired on Bayonne.

Buckham was awakened by the sound of a train of artillery passing his quarters, and 'hastily got a cup of coffee'; but before he had time to reach the river bank, the light troops

> had already driven back the enemy's skirmishers. The engineers laid down the pontoon bridge with admirable expedition, and I passed over it in the rear of the third division about nine o'clock. The French showed themselves in good force several times on the heights, but always retired in a few minutes, leaving skirmishers to contend with our light troops. At ten o'clock a heavy firing commenced upon our left, and became, as the fog disperses, dictinctly visible. The first division soon became warmly engaged, when the intention of Lord Wellington was, that it should only have made a demonstration. The third division remaining under arms on the height which we had first gained on ascending the Neve, I went forward with the sixth division. In a little time it was understood upon the field that General Hill had succeeded in turning the enemy's left. This was at about twelve o'clock. A pause now ensued, the sixth division standing to their arms. I took this opportunity to enter a peasant's cottage by the road side. A little boy was the only member of the family who could speak French; the rest, consisting of an old woman, some girls, and two aged men, spoke nothing but the Basque, which is nearly the same as that which is used in Biscay. Their joy was so unbounded at the partial defeat which their countrymen had already sustained, that they capered about the room like a parcel of merry Andrews. One of the aged men personated a French soldier, and with an agility beyond his years, ran a few yards from the door, in order to convey the idea of a flying enemy; then distending his cheeks, he discharged a *bomb!* And fell to the ground, as if he had been killed by a ball.

Hope, ordered to make a reconnaissance in force, advanced between the coast and the Nive, and halted out of range of Soult's batteries in the heavily fortified camp of Beyris for several hours before pulling back, having left a line of outposts. John Burgoyne pushed through the pinewoods nearer the shore to survey the banks of the Adour. Behind Hope's outposts, and further east near Arcangues, stood the

Light Division, with Portuguese brigades to its left. The 5th Division remained in reserve, but the 1st Division and Aylmer's Brigade were sent as far back as St Jean-de-Luz, too far behind the front, should Soult make a counter-attack.

This was precisely what was impending, with Hope's picquets being assaulted early on the 10th near the two highways leading south from Bayonne through an area of scattered woods and bogs. The more easterly ran through Arcangues towards St Pée, off which a branch led to Ustaritz, on the Nive; the other – the Great Road – veered towards the coast and St Jean-de-Luz. The Light Division, finding themselves opposed by four divisions, retired on Arcangues, taking up a position behind a ridge between its château and church, both of which were hastily fortified. The latter was ideal for defence, containing – as do many Basque churches – two tiers of interior balconies, lit by windows. As the churchyard wall was at a lower level, the 1/43rd, which had taken possession, had four levels from which to pepper the exposed French artillery at long range – some 400 yards – causing their guns to fire inaccurately, until they were abandoned.

Further east, the 7th Division was able to bring the French advance to a stand; but near the Great Road, Bradford's Brigade and Campbell's Portuguese were hard pressed when defending the Château Barrouillet farm and dependencies against two and then three French divisions, until the 5th Division, with Hope in person, belatedly reached the field, followed by Aylmer's Brigade, forming line without halting, which tilted the precarious balance in the Allies' favour. The action, partly taking place in woods, was confusing, but the French were pushed back eventually.[16] On the 12th, Hill 'Corps' approached closer to Bayonne to take up a semicircular position between the Nive and Adour.

St Pierre

Wellington realised that Soult had deliberately withdrawn within his ring of entrenched camps,[17] as from there, with bridges spanning the Nive, he could attack the Allies on either side in force while holding them at the other. But Wellington could transfer his troops across the Nive at the bridge of Ustaritz; he had the foresight also to order up a pontoon bridge to span the stream at Villefranque, nearer Hill's front, which was in position by midday on the 11th, defended by the 3rd Division (as that at Ustaritz was by the 6th). The 4th and 7th were still west of the river.

During the night of the 12th, ominous sounds were clearly heard in Hill's camp, as Soult's artillery crossed Bayonne's bridges, and his subordinate commanders were alerted to expect an attack next day. The 3 mile-long position was divided into three by two narrow mill-ponds. A road ascending from Bayonne, on passing through the village of Haut St Pierre,[18] traversed the central, wider, sector and the low hill of Horlopo before continuing south-east. In the right-hand sector – closer to the Adour – a byroad climbed a ridge on which lay the village of Vieux Mouguerre. The left-hand sector was low-lying and wooded, crossed by a track towards Villefranque passing near the solitary hilltop Château Larraldia, occupied by Pringle's Brigade of the 2nd Division, of which Byng's Brigade held positions in front of the Croix de Mouguerre and between that and the village. The central sector was manned in depth by Barnes's Brigade and Ashworth's Portuguese, supported by artillery, while Le Cor's Portuguese were held in reserve behind the hill of Horlopo.

Dense masses of infantry were seen advancing from Bayonne early on the 13th. The leading division approached Hill's central sector by the main road; another veered south towards Pringle, and a brigade was heading towards Byng. Inopportunely, during the night, a sudden rise in level of the Nive had caused the pontoon bridge at Villefranque to give way. Wellington was advised immediately, for with that communication cut, Hill would have to hold out for four hours before reinforcements reached him. Although Pringle's 1,800 were opposed by 5,000, he was able to keep them at arms' length, inflicting some 450 casualties and suffering only 130. The château was attacked, but was never in danger of being taken.

Fighting on Hill's right flank was more hazardous. Although Colonel William Bunbury, heavily outnumbered, could have resisted longer, he ordered the 1/3rd (Buffs) to retire towards the rest of Byng's battalions, which were slowly forced down from their hill.

It was Hill's centre, with Stewart in local command, which was the most strongly attacked, by a numerous line of *tirailleurs* in advance of two columns. These were met by light companies, including the entire 6th *Caçadores,* while artillery was brought into action on both sides, two batteries being trained on those ascending the main road. As his skirmishers retired, Ashworth's four line battalions commenced a heavy fire, bringing the the columns to a halt. Although the French made some headway, by feeding in units from Barnes's Brigade, held in reserve – as Stewart had done with Pringle's at Maya – they were held well below the crest for three hours. There was a precarious moment, when Colonel Peacock lost his nerve and ordered back the 1/71st; but the situation was saved by Hill leading them forward again, and in person, leaving Peacock in the rear, beating forward Portuguese ammunition-carriers.[19]

The centre was then reinforced by bringing forward seven companies of the 1/92nd, Le Cor's Portuguese, and transferring the 1/57th and another battalion from Byng's sector. The struggle was becoming critical, but Hill, by then aware that the pontoon bridge had been replaced, that the 3rd Division was well on its way, and that the 6th was approaching from Ustaritz, was ordering a general counter-attack when Wellington himself rode up.[20]

With the help of a battalion of *Caçadores*, Pringle was able to press well back those in his front; and repulse others in the centre; but it was only by redeploying units borrowed from Byng, and a brigade of Le Cor's, with which to attack the area near Vieux Mouguerre, supported by artillery fire, that the tide of battle was turned in that quarter. Resistence crumbled, although Foy still held the hill of Croix de Mouguerre with a division and a half; but this too was forced back in fighting at long range.

1 According to Napier, Wellington's complement of guns now consisted of no less than 'fourteen iron 24-pounders, six 8-inch brass howitzers, four 68-pound iron carronades, and four iron 10-inch mortars. To these were added six 24-pounders lent by the ships of war, and six 18-pounders which had been moved with the army from Portugal, making altogether forty pieces commanded by Colonel Dickson.' They were accompanied by 'one hundred sappers and miners, now for the first time used in the sieges of the Peninsula ...'

2 Here, there was a mean difference of some 16 ft in height between tides.

3 A ford which approached the breach had been investigated in person late the previous night by a Major Kenneth Snodgrass, when the water had reached to his waist. Eluding the vigilance of a sentinel, he had clambered up the breach itself and even looked down into the town.

4 The margin of error was less than 40 feet vertically, but such was the accuracy of the new guns, that the only Allied casualties were from flying fragments and ricochets.

5 These lay near the former International bridge, now largely superceded by the motorway bridge further upstream.

6 Further south, the valley briefly opens out near Vera.

7 Spanish casualties in this action approached 1,700; those of the French were about 2,500. It had certainly been a desparately-fought contest: Wheeler, traversing the site later, saw 'several pairs with the bayonet in each other.'

8 Only a few days before, when incautiously wandering too near the front, Larpent had found himself being taken prisoner, although exchanged three weeks later.

[9] As had Wellington at Busaco, and behind the Lines of Torres Vedras.

[10] There would appear to be some confusion as to the position of the Lesser or 'La Petit Rhune'. The French I.G.N. map shows it as being due *west* of La Rhune, beyond the Col Zizkouitz, while both Oman's maps indicate it as being the height denominated Altxanga, the steep south flank of which is now skirted by the rack-railway ascending La Rhune from the Col de St Ignace. The maps in Batty, Jones, and Napier all depict it as being north-east rather that west of the summit of La Rhune.

[11] Although it required a day or so to prepare the orders in question, the timing of the advance was made contingent on the fall of Pamplona, which in the event did not take place for another 18 days.

[12] Edwin Griffith, stationed near Donamaria (south of Sanesteban, at the south end of the narrow Bidasoa valley, and some 14 miles as the crow flies from the front), had heard 'a tremendous cannonade' commence soon after daylight, but the 15th Hussars were not called into action as he expected, and they rode south a few days later to spend the following month cantoned in villages south-west of Pamplona, from which they were not ordered forward until mid December.

[13] Foy, on their far left wing, on hearing gunfire, had moved south-west – contrary to orders from D'Erlon, which were to join him – and although he did some damage in Hill's rear, was brought to a halt by Spanish units, and later retreated to Cambo to avoid being cut off.

[14] Undeservedly, it remains in the shadow of the more spectacular battles of Salamanca and Vitoria. In the day's fighting, Anglo-Portuguese casualties were about 2,450; those of the Spaniards, some 800. French losses were 4,350 (2,900 among Clausel's three divisions alone, including 1,200 prisoners), while less than 500 were lost in the seaward sector. 59 pieces of artillery were also abandoned by them. On both sides, the ratio of officers to other ranks killed was unusually heavy: 1 to 11.

[15] It was at Ustaritz that a Commissariat depot was soon to be established.

[16] In this 'Battle of the Nive', casualties on both sides were between 1,700 and 2,000. Partly due to Hope's unwise dispersal of his troops, the Allies lost more prisoners that day – some 500, largely from the overrun picquet lines – than in any other of the war; but on the same evening three battalions of the 2nd Nassau Regiment in the French service deserted, together with their officers, arms, and baggage. Fighting recommenced on this front during the next two days, but with an indecisive result, both sides suffering some 800 additional casualties.

[17] Those of Beyris, Marracq, and Mousserolles, the latter between Bayonne and the village of St Pierre, further east.

[18] Now the hamlet of Marichorry; the present St Pierre-d'Irube is closer to Bayonne.

[19] Lieut.-Colonel Sir Nathaniel Peacock, newly-arrived to replace Cadogan, was later cashiered, while Bunbury was allowed to resign his commission.

[20] He may not have taken the 'risk' of making the decisive counter-attack had he not known that strong reinforcements were at hand, but by doing so Hill won the battle of St Pierre virtually unaided and against heavy odds. While his losses (1,775) were light if compared to those of Soult's, some 3,300, it had been a near run thing.

16

February to July 1814: From Orthez to Toulouse; the sortie from Bayonne, and dispersal

Wellington's army was divided into two: Hope's 'Corps' of 18,000, together with several thousand Spaniards,[1] remained south of Bayonne, ready to cross the Adour and tighten the blockade. Four Allied divisions, together with Hill's 'Corps', Picton's 3rd Division, and some cavalry units forming the Allied right flank,[2] commenced their eastward advance by 14 February, to meet stiff opposition on reaching the Bidouze. Next day, Hill approached the village of Garris, where the French had taken up a strong defensive position. Surgeon Henry recorded that they had arrived there,

> after a long march, near sunset, and every body expected that the attack would be deferred till the next morning: but Lord Wellington at that time came up; and being apprehensive that Artillery would be mounted on this formidable height next day – ordered it to be assailed immediately.
>
> Four Columns then dashed into the ravine and up the steep side of the hill, which was one blaze of fire from the enemy's skirmishers behind the trees on its face, and the main body along the top. This was, for the greater part, as harmless as common fireworks – the balls going over our fellows' heads; but as it became dusk the effect was strikingly beautiful. Our troops soon reached the summit – scattering the French Division and taking a few hundred prisoners. Fifty or sixty unfortunate wretches concealed themselves in a house at the top until the affair was all over, and our men had piled their arms and were kindling their night fires; when they sallied out in a body, and attempted to escape down the hill. At the first rush our soldiers seized their arms, which were loaded – pursued them with a loud cheer, and shot or knocked down almost every man.
>
> This was altogether as shewy a little piece of fighting as I ever witnessed. The brilliant musketry along the side, and from the crest of the hill – the cheering of our men as they mounted – the continuous advance

> of numerous bugles – the roar of our Artillery reverberating in long echoes from one side to another of the deep ravine at the bottom – all very fine and grand.

The bridge at neighbouring St Palais was repaired and crossed on the 16th, thereby virtually isolating the garrison at St Jean Pied-de-Port, which Mina's Spaniards invested. The Allied advance was resumed on the 23rd, with Hill crossing the Saison and, leaving Morillo's troops to hold off the small garrison of Navarrenx on the Gave d'Oloron, veering north to approach the Gave de Pau at Orthez. Headquarters moved from Hasparren to Sauveterre.

Meanwhile, the weather on the coast had improved sufficiently for Wellington to commence operations enabling Hope to cross the Adour near its mouth by a substantial bridge of boats.[3] The coasting vessels with which to lay this, collected during recent weeks, entered the estuary on 24 February. Within two days, both men and *matériel*, supported by artillery and Congreve rockets, had crossed and established themselves on the far bank. A minor action was fought in the suburban village of St Etienne next day, but by that evening Bayonne, with its garrison of 14,000, including General Abbé's division, was isolated. Although batteries were constructed and trenches dug, it was to remain blockaded rather than besieged, and remained so for the following seven weeks.

Orthez

On the 26th, Beresford with the 4th and 7th Divisions, crossed the Gave de Pau near Peyrehorade and marched east along its right bank, followed by a pontoon train. Picton had seized a bridge further east, 4 miles below Orthez, and crossed with the 3rd Division. Wellington's main force, some 31,000 men,[4] were now north of the river, leaving Hill with the 2nd and Le Cor's Divisions plus some light cavalry (some 13,000 in all) on the south bank.

Four divisions of Soult's army – those of Taupin, Rouget, D'Armagnac, and Foy – were deployed from west to east along a road surmounting an L-shaped ridge north of the Gave de Pau. At its western extremity stood the church of the village of St Boès, which lay further east. On a hillock to the south were remains of a Roman camp. Three spurs descended from the ridge, the intervening valleys of which were waterlogged and impassable for artillery, the easternmost leading down towards the small town of Orthez itself,[5] behind which Harispe's division was posted, while further north stood Villatte's reserve division. Soult, commanding about 36,000 men, and with 48 guns, was opposing an army with a superiority in numbers of almost 7,000, and with 54 guns.

The ground was too broken up for the cavalry to act with effect, but William Verner, at the head of his squadron, described the appearance of the infantry, as they advanced in line, as 'more like a review ... the colours flying in the centre, and the bands playing, [but] it was not long before we received a salute from the enemy, which soon let us know that we had music of a different kind to attend to.'

The western end of the ridge was attacked by the 4th Division, the 7th in support, with Ross's brigade clearing the churchyard of St Boès of a battalion, but due to concentrated fire, he was unable to enter the village itself, even when supported by *Caçadores* sent across from the Roman camp, now occupied by the Light Division, and from which Wellington directed operations. Meanwhile, the 3rd and 6th Divisions ascended the two parallel spurs further east, but they were halted before they came within range of artillery fire. There was now a lull in the fighting while the 7th Division replaced the 4th and went to the support of Brisbane's brigade of the 3rd, which had ascended the spur nearest Orthez, at the head of which stood Foy's Division. At 11.30, all three attacks were reactivated, and the 1/52nd of the Light Division ordered forward to take in flank the French opposing the 7th near St Boès, where the fighting was particularly severe. In the face of these co-ordinated thrusts, Soult's units disintegrated to such an extent that three of his divisions could not be rallied; his cavalry, charging along the ridge towards St Boès, was cut to pieces or taken prisoner.

At 11.00 Hill commenced his crossing of the Gave de Pau some 2 miles upstream from Orthez, at the ford of Souars, defended by a French brigade. Surgeon Henry described the action:

> Immediately all was in motion. We soon reached the ford, which was covered by some of the enemy's light troops in a thicket on the opposite bank. A couple of guns galloped down, opened on them with grape and soon dislodged them – the grape whistling through the covert like duck-shot. The Division then rushed into the ford – five or six shells dropped amongst us in crossing; but, I believe every one was extinguished in the water without doing any mischief; and in the course of an hour the whole formed on the right bank and ready to advance.

We moved on very imposingly round their flank; and at length discovered that they had abandoned their position, and were making off at great spead; which the appearance of our Column tended materially to quicken. At the village of Montbrun we joined the Cavalry and the advance of other English Divisions in pursuit: at the time the whole French Army, despairing of effecting their retreat, if they preserved their formation, had broken irrecoverably, and the face of the country to a great extent was covered with a dense mass of fugitives. All arms were mingled – Artillerymen without their guns – Cavalry without their horses, and Infantry without their arms – were flying pell-mell, – helter-skelter – whilst our Light Artillery were pouring Shrapnell shells amongst them, and thus increasing the general terror and confusion.

We followed the rout till dark: a little before dusk they got into some degree of order, and made a stand at a village [Sault-de-Navailles] on a strong hill, with a small river in front; and opened with two or three guns. ... a shot from one of the enemy's guns ... struck the ground, rose again and knocked over one of the soldiers' wives, who always managed to keep up with the regiment. I ran to her immediately, but found there was only a graze, and slight contusion on the shoulder. At first she was sadly frightened; but when I assured her there was no harm done, she was so delighted that she pulled a fowl out of one enormous pocket, and half a yard of black pudding out of the other, of which she begged me acceptance. I cannot say I pocketted the fee; but we regaled on it at our bivouack that evening.

Although Soult had brought forward his reserve division, any attempt to form a defensive line was bound to fail; by nightfall the demoralized army had precipitately retreated to the north-east, leaving the Allies to bivouac on the heights above Sallespisse.

Writing to Colville three weeks later, John Keane provided a précis of the hard-fought battle:

The morning of the 27th set in fine, but very few thought the enemy would stand. The Lord had reconnoitred and each corps was in place by nine o'clock and moved forward as follows; 3rd on the right, Light in the Centre and 4th on the left. The 6th supported the right, the 7th the left. The enemy's position was well chosen for defence, keeping also a good eye to retreat as each ridge they occupied was connected with the great Bordeaux road. Once in motion we were soon under fire, and for two hours it was furious. The ground was certainly well contested ...

> Heath was our only shelter and we got well pounded ... Poor Parker was cut in two by a cannon shot close to the God of War. Taylor was wounded in the neck but is up again. Greenwell severely, Carr ditto – ball entered the chin and lodged in the roots of his tongue. It has been cut out and he is doing well. Elliott severely in the belly, but also doing well. Poor Nugent dangerously in two places, but there are some hopes. Baldwin severely, right arm broken. Capt. McDermot, 88th, only joined the day before, with his Vitoria wound open, was killed.

Wellington established Headquarters at Sault-de-Navailles, where he rested, briefly incapacitated by serious bruising caused by a projectile driving his sword-hilt against his hip and thigh.[6] Had this not happened, he may well have been able to turn the French retreat into a rout, had he sufficient confidence in his cavalry – once the bit was between their teeth – to allow them to pursue.[7]

By midday on the 28th, Soult's army was over the Adour, followed slowly by the Allies – depending on their Commissariat for supplies – via Hagetmau and St Sever, where Wellington likewise crossed the river, sending the Light Division ahead to capture magazines at Mont-de-Marsan.

Wellington now received a communication from the Mayor of Bordeaux to the effect that, if supported by Allies troops, he would declare against Napoleon. Forthwith, Beresford hastened north with the 4th Division and Dalhousie's 7th, and entered the city unopposed on 12 March. Dalhousie remained there until the cessation of hostilities,[8] while Beresford rejoined the main army with the 4th Division on the 18th.

Soult, on receiving additional reinforcements, rather than attacking Wellington, who had forced him back in an action at Aire-sur-l'Adour on 2 March, circled south-east along the right bank of the river, which he re-crossed at Maubourguet. Wellington, now reinforced by Morillo's units from Navarrenx and Freire's Spaniards from Bayonne to make up for the absence of the 7th Division, divided his army into three 'Corps', with the intention of pinning Soult against the Pyrenees near Tarbes.

By the 20th, Beresford's force on the left wing marched east, swinging round more rapidly than Wellington's in the centre (Headquarters moving via the villages of St Mont and Viella to Maubourget) and Hill's on the right wing (pushing south towards Lembeye), had cut two of Soult's roads of retreat. Spirited rearguard actions took place at Vic-Bigorre (in which Colonel Sturgeon of the Engineers, was killed), and on the 24th at Orleix (north-east of Tarbes),[9] but Soult's main force escaped the trap intended for it, and headed uphill through Tournay and across the high-lying plateau de Lannemezan to St Gaudens before veering north-east down the Garonne valley towards Toulouse.

Keane, described the former action to Colville:

> Lord Wellington was up, and reconnoitred; found them strong and the country stronger, for both sides of the road produced nothing but nearly impenetrable vineyards. The enemy's whole force was there, and Count d'Erlon with two divisions was charged with the defence of the road. The 3rd, supported by the 6th, was the leading column, my Brigade forming the advanced guard. From 12 to 2 a great deal of cannon and spitting on both sides. Sir Tho[ma]s [Picton] then looked vexed and decided to attack, tho' positively contrary to Lord W's directions. Accordingly we were at them and ably countenanced on the right by my friend Power [with his Portuguese brigade] the road was ours in 15 minutes and in the 10 following they were driven from a number of scattered houses by a brilliant charge of the 83rd, 87th, and 94th in two columns, one headed by the knight and the other by your humble servant. Here Arbuthnot was wounded (arm) and I hope not dangerously; and here two thousand *tirailleurs* flew before our little band ... There now only remained the vineyards, which certainly presented divers obstacles. However we walked at them and what between firing, roaring and bugling we chased Drouet and his frogs from one to the other into the town [Vic], then charged them through it, making a few prisoners. The rascals would not stand or they all would have been taken. Our great Lord had a very commanding view and honoured us by saying that he never saw a more gallant attack in his life [a phrase not infrequently on his lips!], and the execution spoke for itself.

Tarbes was entered without resistance, indeed with acclamation, but as it was expected that Soult (who had married a lady from there), would put up a strong defence of the river crossing there, but as the Allied columns approached the ridge east of the town, Soult retreated at 'such a quick pace until dark that we never neared him. There was great maneouvring on both sides; indeed the Lord's dispositions were monstrous fine.'

The Allies continued the pursuit in three columns, but the going was slow along deeply-rutted tracks, as pontoon trains and 18-pounder siege guns were dragged across country up and over steep ridges fanning out from the Pyrenees, taking seven days to cover a distance Soult had marched in four. Headquarters moved east and then north-east via Galan, Boulogne-sur-Gesse, L'Isle-en-Dordon, Samatan, and St

Lys, where, on the 26th, contact was regained with Soult's rearguard, but where, according to Larpent, a halt was made, 'which most of the army is in very much need of ... [and] to enable Lord Wellington to make arrangements and reconnoitre, &c.'

On ascending the church tower at St Lys, Toulouse could be made out distinctly through Larpent's telescope, as it was a fine day; but recent rains had caused the roads – perhaps 'as bad as any we have ever passed with artillery' – to be churned up, along which the troops 'splashed up to their caps, and hundreds were walking barefoot in the clay up to the calves of their legs for about five miles ... ' Wellington's barouche, in which sat General Alava, with a badly bruised hip – he had been standing next to Wellington at Orthez – was stuck fast in the mud for three hours.

At least 8,000 of Soult's army had also been shambling shoeless through the mire, while his cavalry were busily occupied shepherding forward another 5,000 stragglers. Hill's 'Corps' followed in their wake via St Martory, Cazères, and down the Garonne valley to Muret, near which the majority of his units went into cantonments. Meanwhile, Beresford's 'Corps' had been trudging north-east via Puymaurin and Lombez.

Wellington's first attempt to cross the Garonne was made at Portet, south of Toulouse. One reason for preferring to approach the city from this direction was the fact that the Royal Canal circled round both its north and east sides,[10] providing an additional obstacle to overcome, while to the west the transpontine suburb of St Cyprien was strongly defended, although the walls there could be battered once artillery had been placed close enough. Between the canal and the river Hers, east of the centre, rose the Calvinet ridge, also known as Mont Rave, the possession of which would be decisive if intending to invest the place.

Soon after dusk on the 27th, Allied units were marched south to the position chosen to lay the two pontoon bridges, but it was then found that even when placed end to end, they were some 80 feet short.[11] No form of extension could be rigged up fast enough to allow a sufficient number of troops to cross and form a bridgehead strong enough to withstand a counter-attack. Wellington, furious, had no alternative but to call off the operation. However, three nights later, the Garonne was spanned successfully further upstream at Pinsaguel, nearer Muret, and above its junction with the tributary Ariège. Hill, with 13,000 men, were soon passed over, but the few units which pushed ahead across the Ariège then found that there were no roads suitable for artillery approaching Toulouse from that direction. Wellington rode over to inspect the district himself, and could only concur with Hill that it was impracticable to attack from there in force. It was one of the few occasions in which Wellington – with little chance of reconnoitering earlier, admittedly – had found himself thwarted by lack of adequate topographical information.

Both troops and pontoons returned to the west bank of the Garonne, and were moved north, for the engineers had meanwhile found another site downstream, where the river narrowed, and where a bridge might be placed, although only by spacing the pontoons further apart than normally. On the evening of 4 April they were re-laid across the Garonne east of Merville, and Beresford, together with 19,000 men, including cavalry and artillery, was across by the following morning; but within hours the bridge was broken by the river in flood,[12] temporarily isolating this force. Guns were placed along its left bank to enfilade any advance of Soult's troops against them, but no such movement was made. Instead, the French had strongly fortified the Calvinet ridge, and the city walls had been lined with their heavier artillery.

By the 8th, with the exception of Hill's 'Corps' (left to invest and demonstrate against St Cyprien), the whole army had crossed the Garonne and was marching south, the Hers, a minor stream, protecting its left flank. The pontoon bridge was then re-established closer to Toulouse, should it be necessary to reinforce Hill during the concentric attack on the city which Wellington, having reconnoitered the area, planned to take place on the 9th, but then deferred to dawn next day, Easter Sunday. He was preoccupied by the fact that Suchet, still with some 14,000 troops concentrated in the vicinity of Figueras, might possibly be marching to Soult's support;[13] and it was vital to take Toulouse beforehand.

While Picton's 3rd and Alten's Light Divisions were to menace the 2 mile front formed by the canal between the Garonne and the Albi road, the main attack would be made further east against the northern extremity of the Calvinet by General Manuel Freire's two Spanish divisions supported by Portuguese artillery, and by Beresford's 4th and 6th Divisions (forming the left flank), which, with their guns, would press on south between the ridge and the Hers, and then circle round to ascend its south-east slope. Freire was to delay his attack until Beresford's troops were ready to assault the Calvinet simultaneously. In the event, Picton, contrary to orders, attempted to gain the Ponts-Jumeaux bridgehead south of the canal, but was forced back with loss, while Freire sent his troops forward prematurely, probably assuming that gunfire from Beresford's artillery – bogged down near the banks of the Hers – was the signal to attack. The Spaniards advanced – two brigades in line, another in direct support, and a fourth in reserve – in the face of artillery fire from both the Calvinet and the city walls, and then from musketry. On reaching the apparent protection of a road cutting between the hamlets of Les Argouletes and Périole, and within 60 yards of their objective, they were raked by grape and, on climbing the far bank, volleys from units emerging from defensive earthworks. Finding both their right flank and rear under attack, they broke and fled in disorder.

On observing this premature assault – one bound to fail – Wellington instructed Beresford to wheel right and ascend the Calvinet wherever he might be, rather than stick to the original plan of storming it from further south. By the time the order had been received, Beresford had already pushed ahead and, deploying both divisions in line, turned up the ridge; but on approaching the summit, he was met by two French brigades in columns. In the ensuing action, General Taupin lost his life and his division, its survivors seeking the safety of the Sypière redoubt further west, nearer the canal. Beresford was now in possession of the southern half of the Calvinet, where the 6th Division remained, facing north-west, awaiting their artillery to be dragged up the slippery slope, while the 4th bore downhill to reform along the east bank of the canal. By mid afternoon, after a brief lull, the Allies were in a position to press their attack, but the 6th Division suffered heavily from artillery firing over the heads of the entrenched infantry and from those units themselves, Colonel Macara having insisted on redeploying his battalions while under fire; but eventually the Augustin redoubt, the main bastion facing them, was taken.[14]

Meanwhile, Freire's Spaniards were rallied, and kept those troops occupied, which might otherwise have turned on the 6th Division. Brisbane's Brigade of the 3rd Division had made another fruitless attack on the canal, in which Brisbane was killed. After another lull, Wellington sent Freire's men forward again, supported by the Light Brigade. By now, most of Soult's units had retired behind the canal, where several of his positions came within range of Beresford's guns on the Calvinet, but the fighting petered out as dusk fell. Next morning, those troops not occupied attending to their wounded and burying the dead, were realigned; supplies and ammunition were brought across the Garonne, and siegeworks erected in expectation of Soult's counter-attack, while cavalry attempted to cut the road to Carcassonne, should he retreat in that direction, as was likely.

During the following night, rather than find himself confined within Toulouse, Soult abandoned the city and hastened south-east, leaving behind all non-transportable wounded, but carrying off as many guns of position as he could, together with their caissons. He was followed by Hill and Beresford as far as Villefranche-de-Lauragais.[15]

The Toulousains greeted Wellington as their deliverer; Royalist sympathisers invading the Allied camps. Daniel related that when invited into the city by the deputy-mayor and other dignitaries, Wellington was 'rendered very conspicuous by the restiveness of his horse, which on entering the square reared on its hind legs and literally danced over the ground. His Lordship carried his hat in his hand the whole of the time, and bowed to the people until the procession had entered the court yard of the "Capitole".'

During the late afternoon, Wellington was informed by emissaries from Paris that Napoleon had abdicated. They were sent on to Soult, who would only agree to capitulate on receiving formal confirmation from Berthier, Napoleon's Chief of Staff, but a specific order to do so did not reach him until the 17th. By then another bloody action had taken place, at Bayonne: see below.

Toulouse remained *en fête* fore several weeks. On the 26th, on the arrival of the Duc d'Angoulême, met by Wellington and his entourage, among them General Clausel, the animated scene as the procession crossed the Garonne bridge reminded Larpent of London streets at Lord Nelson's funeral: from every window hung 'Sheets, table-cloths, towels, &c., covered with green paper fleurs-de-lys ... The women, and some of the old men, were quite mad with joy, and screamed, *Vive le Roi et vivent les Anglais!* till they were stopped by absolute exhaustion, or some by tears of joy.'

One day, Larpent entered the former church of the Jacobins, to find it had been fitted up by the French as a cavalry barrack stable, for it could hold 700 mounts; on another, he attended a *soireé* given by Angoulême, at which Marshal Suchet put in an appearance: 'His head and cheeks and chin all overgrown with hair, like a wild man of the woods: and his dress more splendid than the drum-major of our Guards' bands on a birth-day.' Gradually, the enthusiasm and the euphoria of victory evaporated. Few disturbances took place, as 'our officers seem all to have behaved with considerable propriety'; nevertheless, Larpent had the feeling that 'the inhabitants dread our departure, and the return of their own people. They say that all order ceases, and all security, the moment our side of the line of demarcation is passed.'

The Light Division was quartered to the north-west, between

Grisolles and Castelsarrazin, where Leach, with the 52nd, 'spent five or six weeks very pleasantly, receiving the greatest kindness and hospitality from the inhabitants. Dances, fêtes champêtres on the banks of the Garonne, horse-races, and various gaieties, filled up our time ...' One day, curious to see them being reviewed by the Duc d'Angoulême, he rode over to Montauban, where Soult's army was then stationed, together with some of Suchet's units. Their general appearance was 'fine and soldierlike. The Spanish sun had left its mark on their countenances, which were for the most part lively and animated, without the smallest appearance of despondency or disappointment at the late change, or at the loss of their imperial master. Marshal Soult alone appeared sullen and dejected. But this possibly was his natural manner.' In the event, Soult was dismissed, being superseded by Suchet in command of their united armies.

By late May, Toulouse had become progressively deserted by the British troops, most of which had by then embarked at Bordeaux.

The Sortie from Bayonne

At Bayonne, Thouvenot, who still commanded a garrison of some 12,000 (to which it had been reduced by sickness and desertion), had stubbornly continued to hold out. Hope's troops still encircled the town. A line of outposts and picquets of the 1st Division stood on the right bank of the Adour; on the left, or south bank, were those of the 5th Division. They were supported by an additional four brigades, one of which was cavalry. Gleig, stationed with a mortar battery in the suburb of St Etienne, within view of the citadel, found himself the target of 'an incessant fire of round shot, shells, grape, and occasionally of musketry ...' from their walls, armed with 'a number of long swivel guns, which they could elevate or depress, or turn in any direction, at will ... These threw, with great force, iron balls of about a quarter of a pound weight,' and every so often 'a nine-inch shell would tumble through the roof, and burst sometimes before we had time to escape into another apartment – Then the crashing of the cannon-balls as they rushed through the partitions – the ... rattle of grape and cannister, which came pouring in by the windows ... produced a species of feeling, of which no words can convey an adequate notion to him who has not experienced it.'

At midnight on the 11 April, a messenger arrived with the news that Napoleon had abdicated. Under a flag of truce, Hope passed on this extrordinary intelligence to Thouvenot, who refused to credit it, having not been so-advised by Soult, his superior, and who answered that the Allies would be hearing further from him on the subject shortly.

Hope was warned by a deserter of a possible sortie, and while not entirely surprised when it took place, he did not expect it to be in such strength. At 3.00 on the morning of 14 April a feint was made from the southern line of fortifications, but the main sortie of 3,000 men in two columns burst out from the citadel on the north bank, broke through the encircling line of picquets, and attacked St Etienne, where General Andrew Hay was killed.[16] The fighting, much of it with bayonets, was very confused, and Stopford's 1st and Maitland's 2nd Guards Brigades suffered severely, Stopford himself being wounded. Hope was wounded also, and being pinned under his horse, was briefly taken prisoner.[17] His subordinates, out of touch with each other, were not at first aware what had happened. Although command devolved temporarily on Colville, it was not until General Hinuber, with the K.G.L., stationed near the riverside suburb of St Esprit, had rallied the unnerved units around the church of St Etienne and lead the main counter-attack, that a serious situation was resolved. Meanwhile, the 1st Guards had repulsed the westernmost column.

Thouvenot now ordered his troops to retire to the citadel, and a flag of truce was run up, enabling both parties to attend to their wounded and collect their dead. As Edmund Wheatley well recollected: 'The French poured out of the town, unarmed, and a singular scene ensued – they picking up their dead and we ours.[18] I went under the French batteries and had a long chat with some French Officers who gave me some snuff. And as the French soldiers passed us with their dead comrades, we reflected on the miserable trade of war.'

Dispersal

The next few weeks were occupied in the dispersal of the Allied troops. Some regretted having to leave France, where they were largely accepted as deliverers rather than conquerors, for both food and wine was both good and cheap. It was not always easy to disengage after such a long war, although one Commissary whose duty it was to pay off public and private debts and claims as promptly as possible, found it 'a thankless and disgusting task,' due to 'the various attempts at fraud and imposition' taken by some of the French, for 'Enormous demands were made (but very properly rejected) even for marks left by encampments, whereas in almost every instance, and always when possible, the troops encamped on heaths and uncultivated ground,' and so many 'were enriched in every direction we moved.'

Among those regretting the end of the British occupation would be the tradesmen of Bordeaux, of whom Larpent – who bought a 'cello for himself when there – wrote in mid July: 'They had made a famous time of it these last three months, for the army has in that time received six months' pay, and most of it had found its way into the pockets of the ... restaurateurs, the hotels, &c. Bordeaux has had its full share of the spoils of the *milords*. Nor have the inhabitants suffered ... except the little inconvenience of giving up a room or two ... as quarters for the officers.' Any depredations made by the troops were largely confined to helping themselves from local allotments, although this had been exaggerated, much of it being done 'by the French peasantry and country servants, who, if a soldier takes six cabbages, immediately take a dozen more themselves, sell them in the camp, and swear to the owners that the soldiers are the culprits,' while those with vineyards have 'their full revenge in the price of their wines, which was immediately doubled, by the arrival of the troops ... it is fortunate for the inhabitants that we shall be off before the grapes begin to ripen, and for our own soldiers likewise ... [for] the temptations would be irresistable ...'

The situation of the 'Soldier's wives', unless they were formally married, was less happy. Surtees described the scene at Bazas (southeast of Bordeaux), where the Portuguese and Spanish women and their children were separated from their 'husbands' and sent home, 'unless their protectors were to consent to marry them. Some adopted the latter alternative, having had children by them.' An officer in the Portuguese service later described to him how the women had 'formed a column of 800 or 900 strong; that they were told off in regular companies; and that the commanding-officer, a major, and all the captains, were married men, who had their families with them – all excellent arrangements; but that they were the most unmanageable set of animals that ever marched across a country. The officers had to draw rations for them all the way; but many of them ... left the column and went wherever they pleased. Few reached Portugal in the order in which they started.'

Portuguese troops remained with the British 'until the Commissaries can part entirely with the mule transport. They then separate, taking all the mules and muleteers with them attached to different regiments for rations, &c., and set out through Spain for Portugal, a good three months' trip.' Indeed, 'many were the heavy hearts in both armies on this occasion, for it is not easy to conceive how the circumstances of passing through scenes of hardship, trial, and danger together, endeared the soldiers of the two armies to each other.'

Remaining Spanish units had already been ordered back across the Pyrenees. Some Portuguese infantry were marched to Bordeaux and embarked for Lisbon. The majority of the British infantry likewise sailed home, although a battalion each from several regiments were unlucky enough to be sent to America. The cavalry made their way at a leisurely pace towards Calais, not always hospitably received en route. The Guards, among other units remaining at Bayonne, were the last to leave, once all stores had been loaded on transports and the wounded were repatriated. Among the disabled was Private Wheeler. Writing on 14 June from the General Hospital at Fuenterrabía, he described his wound as having got infected:

> I had every attendance that could possibly be given and all the remedies applied to prevent mortification, at length my leg and thigh were reduced so small that I could span it with my hand, but the wounded part and foot were swollen to an enormous size, and the wound was as large over as a tea saucer. It was at length agreed to amputate my leg, this I joyfully agreed to being heartily tired of such a frightful troublesome member. Twice were I removed to the surgery to undergo the operation, but each time the little Spanish Doctor, who had charge of me, overruled it and I was taken back to my bed, I understood my Doctor wished to try something else, then if that failed the leg was to come off. He brought from his home a small bottled filled with some thing like pepper and salt mixed, with this he covered the wound on which he put lint, bandaged it up, crossed himself, muttered something to himself and left me. Several times that day he visited me and my answers to his questions seemed to perplex him much. The next morning my answers seemed to please him, he took off the bandage in good spirits – when all the sluff excepting two spots, one about the size of a sixpence, the other smaller, came off with the lint. My wound now was changed from a nasty sickly whitebrown colour to a bright red. He capered about like a mad fellow, called the other doctors who all seemed surprised, he put some more stuff out of the bottle on the spots and the next morning I was removed downstairs [from the incurable ward].

Conditions were grim. The bed next to his had been occupied by six different soldiers, of whom five died;[19] nor had there been any 'minister of religion to cheer the dying sinner.'

> The people of England think little how her soldiers are neglected spiritual aid, or I believe it would not be so. If they could but hear or see the agony of the dying, their prayers, their despair and the horrid oaths uttered by some in their exit from this world, I am sure this most of wants would be attended to. It is true there are chaplains with the army who sometimes perform divine service, but of what use are they, the service they perform has no effect, for their mode of living do not agree with the doctrine they preach. I have often heard the remark 'That a Chaplain is of no more use to the army than a town pump without a handle.' If these Reverend Gentlemen were stationed at the sick depots and made to attend to the hospitals, they would be much more usefully employed than following the army with their brace of dogs and gun, running down hares and shooting partridges etc. In winter quarters these men once on a Sunday (weather permitting), perform divine service, but when the campaign opens ... few trouble themselves about days or anything else.

Wheeler, described his discharge from the hospital in early July, once his wound has healed:

> I am daily gaining strength, but my heel is much contracted and it is a question if ever I shall be able to walk again without the help of a stick, at present I hops about with a crutch and stick. The Convalescent Hospital is situated about a mile from Fontarabia on the main road to Irun. This is a delightful place, the grounds belonging to the convent are pleasantly laid out in shady walks, the gardens abound with grapes etc. so that we are compensated in a measure from the fatigues we have endured. The weather is beautiful, and having nothing to do we enjoy ourselves by stolling about the gardens talking to the Good Old Fathers of the Convent, who are very kind to us, or by taking a walk into town, to feast our eyes by gazing on the sweet faces of the pretty dark eyed maids of Fontarabia.

On 9 September Wheeler embarked at Pasajes for Portsmouth, 'sailing that same evening with about an hundred other ships conveying troops and laden with stores,' the fleet escorted by two sloops of war. Few could imagine that before many months were to pass so many would be called upon to fight the French yet again, and die, at Waterloo.

* * *

The immediate aftermath of the Peninsular War was possibly even more calamitous to Spain than the ravages of the conflict itself. Fernando VII, on his return from captivity at Valençay – where he had scant idea of the sufferings of his subjects under the French occupation – neglected the opportunity of exploiting their enthusiasm and good-will in putting his wasted kingdom back on its feet. Repressive absolutism was reinstated, with deplorable results.

In 1823, Fernando invited another French army – 100,000 men, commanded by the Duc d'Angoulême – to support his tottering regime. Michael Quin, an English journalist in Madrid at the time, remarked that the inhabitants could hardly believe that their neighbours had the temerity to cross the Pyrenees yet again, in the face of the heroic Spanish people, who, only a decade earlier, had 'destroyed the flower of their veteran army.' It was sad, but true, that whilst they were thus vaingloriously reassuring themselves, whenever the Spaniards alluded to the events of their War of Independence, 'the British army was never mentioned,[20] or thought of, no more than if such a force had never been in the Peninsula.'

And yet, in the resounding words of William Napier, the first great historian of the war – if not then making sufficient reference to the Portuguese contribution to the final success of Allied arms – it was this inconsequential army, never exceeding more than 40,000 British troops, which had 'fought and won nineteen pitched battles and innumerable combats; had made or sustained ten sieges, and taken four great fortresses; had twice expelled the French from Portugal, and once from Spain; had penetrated France, and killed, wounded, or captured two hundred thousand enemies, leaving of their own number forty thousand dead, whose bones whiten the plains and mountains of the Peninsula.'

These figures are largely confirmed by Wellington himself when in conversation with Stanhope on 10 October 1836, he stated: 'I made a computation of all the men I lost in Spain – killed, prisoners, deserters, everything – it amounted to 36,000 men in six years.[21] It would have been infinitely greater, but for the attention to regular subsistence. The French armies were made to take their chance and to live as they could, and their loss was immense. It is very singular that in relating Napoleon's campaigns this has never been clearly shown in anything like its full extent.'

It was after choosing my title that on re-reading several passages of S.G.P. Ward's indispensable *Wellington's Headquarters*, I came across the following sentences (my italics), which may likewise close this volume: 'Without the *presence* of Wellington the whole complex fabric of administration would have broken down. The absence of a commander cannot but lead to some dislocation; but Wellington and his decisions were so essential a part of the command that his absence, had it lasted for no more than a few weeks, and, on occasion, even a few minutes, must almost inevitably have led to failure … All depended on Wellington's *presence*, and the remarkable fact is that he was always there.'

[1] It was Colville's opinion that the Spanish contingent, reluctantly allowed back into France and now commanded by O'Donnell, would be sufficient, although he had his misgivings, for there was 'so much intrigue and ill disposition among that people that it is the common talk that we shall have to thrash them into a proper sense of their insignificance before we embark.' Wellington could still call on additional Spanish units remaining near their side of the frontier: they might be useful in blockading Bayonne as long as they could be restrained from plundering. But he would have to feed them, an additional drain on his magazines. Eventually, Hope had 16,000 Spaniards at hand.

[2] Wellington's heavy cavalry brigades, remaining south of the Pyrenees during the winter, did not join the main army for another fortnight.

[3] Its preparation and construction, and the actually crossing, has been described briefly in my study entitled *Wellington Invades France*, and in greater detail by Robert Burnham in *Inside Wellington's Peninsular Army* (pp.246-262). Although as many as 40 men may have lost their lives when several vessels were wrecked when attempting to pass the sand bar at the mouth of the estuary, Wellington was the first to admit, in a letter to Bathurst, that the naval officers concerned in the difficult operation had effected it 'with a degree of gallantry and skill seldom equalled.'

[4] Wellington had also ordered up Freire with 7,500 men from Bayonne, but they were unable to catch up with the field army until 4 March.

[5] Hill was instructed to demonstrate against the transpontine suburb of Orthez, the river here spanned by an imposing medieval bridge, the passage below the tower of which had been blocked; if all appeared to be going well, he should cross further to the east and turn the French left flank.

[6] Presumably Dr John Robert Hume, his personal surgeon and physician, was at hand, of whom there is little mention in the literature of the war, regrettably.

[7] French losses were over 4,000, not including a division of conscripts, belatedly approaching the field, dispersed in the general panic. Allied casualties were 2,174, of which 367 were killed.

[8] On 7 April a minor action was fought at Etauliers, north-east of Blaye, when Dalhousie defeated a force marching south in an attempt to recapture Bordeaux. Meanwhile, Admiral Penrose's squadron had entered the Gironde estuary on 27 March and proceeded to sweep it of hostile men-of-war and to wreck defensive batteries along its banks. Marines and seaman landed at Fort de Grave, on the southern shore of the estuary, at its mouth, and destroyed or

removed 22 pieces of heavy ordnance, while the guns of several forts along the right bank were put out of action without loss. Only Fort Blaye itself, despite bombardment, resisted until hostilities were suspended.

9 For a detailed description of the action here, the reader is referred to Michael Ayrton's revisionary exposition, correcting all previous accounts: see Bibliography.

10 Now the Canal du Midi.

11 When still at St Jean-de-Luz, Lieut-Colonel Howard Elphinstone, then commanding the Engineers, had warned Wellington that, should he need to span a large river, he would require additional pontoons to those already en route, but his objection had been overruled.

12 One of the pontoons, swept there by the force of the current, had to be recovered from a sandbank 5 miles downstream and replaced in position.

13 Wellington may not have been aware of the fact that Suchet had a strong personal aversion for Soult, and had already made several plausible excuses for not being able to come to the aid his superior, who had suggested repeatedly that he should abandon Catalonia, cross the eastern extremity of the Pyrenees, and by approaching from the direction of Quillan (south of Carcassonne), fall on the Allied flank.

14 The 1/42nd and 1/79th of Pack's Brigade suffered 414 and 214 casualties respectively out of the 750 and 484 present.

15 French casualties at Toulouse had been some 3,200; those of the Allies 4,568, of which at least 1,900 were among Freire's Spanish contingent.

16 Hay's death was not universally regretted: Gen. Frederick Robinson had referred to him as a fool, an arrant coward, and 'a paltry, plundering old wretch,' no officer, and who 'ought not to be a General'; but the same might be said of several others whose presence Wellington had to suffer over the years.

17 It was not the first occasion that Hope had endangered his life needlessly – at Barrouillet he had received three musket balls through his hat, when Wellington had reported confidentially to Torrens at the Horse Guards: 'We shall lose him if he continues to expose himself to fire as he did ... indeed his escape has been wonderful. He places himself among the sharp-shooters, without (as they do) sheltering himself from the enemy's fire. This will not answer; and I hope that his friends will give him a hint on the subject. But it is a delicate subject.' As Oman remarked of his rash behaviour: '... the whole mentality of this gallant officer ... makes one ponder on what would have happened if Wellington had fallen sick, and the command of the whole Allied forces had devolved on him.'

18 The Allies suffered some 600 casualties, and the French some 900 in the pointless sortie, which had no military justification, and for which Thouvenot was entirely responsible. He did not surrender until the 26th April, after Gazan had sent him Soult's copy of the armistice of the 17th.

19 Neil Cantlie has estimated that between January 1811 and May 1814 – during which the mean strength of the British forces was about 66,750 – there were some 35,525 deaths. Of these, about 9,950 died in battle or of related wounds. Among the chief causes of death for over 25,000 men were dysentery, fevers, typhus, and hospital gangrene: this, in spite of the belated but very considerable improvements in medical services activated by Dr James McGrigor, who had landed at Lisbon in January 1812.

[20] This was a very general feeling, and an observation made by many, among them Edwin Griffith, writing in his Journal towards the close of the war: 'I do not think gratitude forms any part of the characteristic *virtues* of a Spaniards. Oppressed by their enemies they receive us with open arms & open houses; but the *danger passed*, they, like all the rest of the world, too soon forget their benefactors. They certainly are a poor, and oppressed people, and with the prospect of starving before them, it is not to be expected that they would give a portion of the little they possessed with a good grace, but then they should not have forgotten that what we took and paid for, the French would have taken without paying for. In answer to this, which I have occasionally taken the liberty to remind them of, they would reply, "yes, but we cannot eat your money, & if there is no corn what is the use of money?"'.

One might add that any admission of gratitude towards the Portuguese for their substantial contribution towards the final eviction of the French from the Peninsula would have been considered by them as infra dig!

[21] Presumably, the Duke was not including Moore's losses in this total. Nor is there any mention here of the survivors. Kincaid, when referring characteristically to an inspection of officers commanding companies of the 95th on their return from the Peninsula, describes 'Beckwith with a cork leg – [Andrew] Pemberton and [Henry] Manners with a shot each in the knee, making them as stiff as the other's tree one – Loftus Gray with a gash in the lip, and minus a portion of one heel, which made him march to the tune of dot and go one – [Thomas] Smith with a shot in the ankle – [Charles] Eeles minus a thumb – [William] Johnstone, in addition to other shot holes, a stiff elbow, which deprived him of the power of disturbing friends as a scratcher of Scotch reels upon the violin – [James] Percival with a shot through his lungs. [John] Hope with a grape-shot lacerated leg – and George Simmons with his riddled body held together by a pair of stays...'

Selective Bibliography

The formidable body of books devoted to Wellington and his Peninsular campaigns makes selectivity essential in compiling what may seem to be an idiosyncratic choice. The author is the first to admit to having not seen nor read every title listed, but he believes that almost all of them are of some interest or value. Inevitably, he will be admonished for overlooking some which may have deserved inclusion: those he has found of particular help or relevance are prefixed by an asterisk; those known to him as having been reprinted in recent decades are prefixed by §, but there may well be others of which he is unaware.

Already in 1912, Sir Charles Oman had recorded over one hundred Peninsular narratives in the third Appendix to his *Wellington's Army*. Since then, many more manuscript journals, etc. have been discovered, edited – some perfunctorily so, others more generously and judiciously – the majority being listed in Paddy Griffith's 'Bibliography of Peninsular War Books since Oman' in the misleadingly entitled supplementary volume IX (1999) to the Greenhill reprint of Oman's *History*.

A number contain an informative Introduction: but too many preambles are little less than 'platitudinous', in Paddy's discriminating opinion. A few titles describing the Peninsula at an earlier period, even if not of military interest specifically, should not be overlooked, any more than Southey's narrative, condemned by Sir George Napier as one which, 'under the name of a *history* of the Spanish war', was 'totally destitute of all pretension to truth: and, as a history of *war*, I defy any man to find a military idea in the whole work except where he gives an extract from a despatch.'

No attempt has been made to list any of the material to be unearthed in specialist military Journals, notably that of the Society for Army Historical Research, while several other periodicals, among them the *English Historical Review*, contain valuable material, such as, in the latter – to mention one article only – T.J. Andrew's *Massena's Lines of March in Portugal and French Routes in Northern Spain* (pp. 472-97 in vol. XVI, 1901).

The Bibliographical Essays in Rory Muir's *Britain and the Defeat of Napoleon* and *Tactics and the Experience of War* are admirable. While readers are grateful to several military book publishers, among others, for having made a number of rare volumes again available (even if the text only of many have been reprinted facsimile), some of them would have been of more value if discreetly edited. Notable is the series of monographs being edited by Gareth Glover. 'British Memoirs of the Napoleonic Wars', the Appendix to *Inside Wellington's Peninsular Army*, compiled by Robert Burnham, further updates the lists contained in Oman's *Wellington's Army.*

The years of first publication, unless otherwise described, are shown in round brackets; the number of the author's regiment is printed within square brackets.

Abell, Francis, *Prisoners of War in Britain, 1756 to 1815* (1914)
*§Aitchison, John (ed. W.F.K. Thompson), *An Ensign in the Peninsular War: The Letters of J. Aitchison* (1981) [3rd Foot Guards]
§Anglesey, George, 7th Marquess of, *One-Leg, the Life and Letters of Henry William Paget* (1961)
Anon.; *see* Howell
§Anton, James, *Retrospect of a Military Life* (1841) [42nd]
Aspinall-Oglander, Cecil, *Freshly Remembered: The Story of Thomas Graham, Lord Lyndoch* (1956)
Ayrton, Michael and John Taylor, *The Sharpest Fight: the 95th Rifles at Tarbes* (2007)
Bacler D'Albe, Albert-Louis, *Campagne d'Espagne, Souvenirs Pittoresque*, tome II (1824), for its lithographs.
Badcock, Sir Lovell Benjamin, *Rough Leaves from a Journal kept in Spain and Portugal during the years 1832, 1833,and 1834* (1835) [formerly Lieut. in 14th Light Dragoons]
§Baretti, Joseph, *A Journey from London to Genoa through England, Portugal, Spain, and France* (1770); reprinted with an Intro. by Ian Robertson (1970)
*§Batty, Robert, *Campaign of the Left Wing of the Allied Army, in the Western Pyrenees and South of France in the Years 1813 and 1814 …* (1823), also well illustrated.[1st Foot Guards]
§Beamish, North Ludlow, *History of The King's German Legion* (1832; 1837)
Beatson, F.C, §*Wellington in the Pyrenees ... the Operations between ... July 25 to August 2 1813* (1914), §*Wellington: Crossing the Gaves and Battle of Orthez* (1925), and §*Wellington: The Bidassoa and Nivelle* (1931)
§Bell, Sir George, *Rough Notes of an Old Soldier, being Reminiscences of ...* (1867) [34th]; ed. Brian Stuart and retitled *Soldier's Glory, being 'Rough Notes of an Old Soldier'* (1991)
Belmas, Jacques Vital, *Journaux des Siéges dans la Péninsule … de 1807 à 1814* (1836–37)
Beresford; *see* Vichness
Bingham, George; *see* Glover, Gareth
Blackmore, Howard, *British Military Firearms,1650–1850* (1961)
§Blakeney, R. (ed. Julian Sturgis), *A Boy in the Peninsular War: the Services, Adventures, and Experiences of Robert Blakeney* (1899) [28th]
Blakiston, John, *Twelve Years' Military Adventure ...* (1829) [17th Port.]
Blanco, R.L., *Wellington's Surgeon General: Sir James McGrigor* (1974)
Blanco White, Joseph, *Letters from Spain* (2nd edition, 1825)
Bond, Gordon. C., *The Grand Expedition* [Walcheren] (1979)
Boothby, Charles, *A Prisoner of France* (1898) [R.E.]
Bourgoing, Jean-François, *Travels in Spain* (1789) *Modern State of Spain* (1808) *Travels of the Duke de Chatelet, in Portugal* (1809)
§Boutflower, Charles, *The Journal of an Army Surgeon during the Peninsular War ...* (1912); with an Intro. by Christopher Ticehurst (1997) [surgeon]
Bradford, Revd William, *Sketches … in Portugal and Spain, 1808–9* (1810), mainly for its plates.
*Bragge (ed. Simon A.C. Cassels), *Peninsular Portrait, 1811–14: The Letters of Captain William Bragge* (1963) [3rd (King's Own) Dragoons]

*§Brett-James, Antony, *Life in Wellington's Army* (1972) *General Graham, Lord Lynedoch* (1959); *see also* Costello and Wilson

Bridgeman; *see* Glover, Gareth

Brotherton, T. (ed. Bryan Perrett), *A Hawk at War. The Peninsular Reminiscences of General Sir Thomas Brotherton* (1986) [14th Light Dragoons]

*§Broughton, Samuel Daniel, *Letters from Portugal, Spain, & France … during the Campaigns of 1812, 1813, & 1814* (1815)

Brown, William, *The Autobiography, or Narrative of a Soldier* (1829) [45th]

*Browne, T. (ed. Roger N. Buckley), *The Napoleonic Journal of Captain Thomas Henry Browne* (1987) [HQ staff]

Bryant, Arthur, *The Great Duke: or, the Invincible General* (1971)

*§[Buckham, E.W.], *Personal Narrative of Adventures… during the War in 1812–1813* (1827) [Commissary General's Department; not Cavalry staff corps]

Bunbury, Thomas, *Reminiscences of a Veteran ...* (1861) [20th Port.]

Burghersh, Lord, *Memoir of the Early Campaigns of the Duke of Wellington in Spain and Portugal* (1820)

*Burgoyne (ed. Hon. George Wrottesley), *The Life and Correspondence of F.M. Sir John Burgoyne, Bart.* (1873) [R.E.]

Burnham, Robert; see *Inside Wellington's Peninsular Army*

Burroughs, G.F., *A Narrative of the Retreat of the British Army from Burgos* (1814)

Butler, L., *Annals of the King's Royal Rifle Corps*, vol. 2 (1923), on the 5th Battalion in the Peninsula.

Cadell, Charles, *Narrative of the Campaigns of the Twenty-Eighth Regiment ...* (1835)

Caldwell, George, and Robert Cooper, *Rifle Green in the Peninsula* (1998/2007; vol. 3 forthcoming) [95th], vividly illustrated by James Dann

Campbell, Colin; *see* Shadwell

Cantlie, Sir Neil, *A History of the Army Medical Department*, vol. 1 (1974)

Carter, John; *see* Glover, Gareth

Cassidy, Martin, *Marching with Wellington: with the Inniskillings …* (2003), containing the Diary of Lt Charles Crowe.

§Chambers, G.L., *Bussaco* (1910)

Christiansen, Eric, *The Origins of Military Power in Spain, 1800–1854* (1967)

Clarke, Edward, *Letters concerning the Spanish Nation* (1763)

Clode, Charles Matthew, *Military Forces of the Crown* (1869)

*[Cocks], Page, Julia, *Intelligence Officer in the Peninsula* (1986), devoted to Major the Hon. Edward Charles Cocks [16th Light Dragoons; and 79th]

Colborne (ed. G.C. Moore-Smith), *The Life of Sir John Colborne ...* (1903) [52nd]

§Cole, L. (ed. Maud Lowry Cole and Stephen Gwynn), *Memoirs of Sir [Galbraith] Lowry Cole* (1934)

Colville, John, *Portrait of a General* [Charles Colville] (1980)

Cooke, John, *Memoirs of the Late War: … the Personal Narrative of Capt. J.H. Cooke, 43rd Regiment …*(1831) *A Narrative of Events in the South of France ...* [and America] *in 1814–1815* (1835). The first volume of an edition of John Henry Cooke's *Memoirs* by Eileen Hathaway was re-titled * *A True Soldier Gentleman* (2000); the second, *Drums Beat Up Again*, is not yet published.

Cookson, J.E., *The British Armed Nation, 1793–1815* (1997)

§Cooper, John Spencer, *Rough Notes of Seven Campaigns ... 1809–1815* (1869) [7th]; with an Intro. by Ian Fletcher (1996)

Cooper, Robert, *see* Caldwell

Cope, Sir William H., Bart., *The History of the Rifle Brigade ...* (1877)

Corrigan, Gordon, *Wellington: a Military Life* (2001)
§Costello, Edward, *Adventures of a Soldier; written by himself* (1841; 2nd ed. 1852) [95th]; ed. by Antony Brett-James as *The Peninsular and Waterloo Campaigns* (1967); notably, ed. by Eileen Hathaway as **Costello. The True Story of a Peninsular War Rifleman* (1997)
§Cowell, Sir John Stepney, *Leaves from the Diary of an Officer in the Guards* (1854) [2nd Foot Guards]
Croker, Richard, *Travels through several provinces of Spain and Portugal* (1799)
Crowe, Charles; *see* Cassidy
*Crumplin, Michael, *Men of Steel: Surgery in the Napoleonic Wars* (2007), a clinically described exposition.
Dallas, Alexander, *Autobiography of, including his service in the Peninsula in the Commissariat Department* (1870) *Felix Alvarez; or, Manners in Spain … Accounts of … Events in the Late Peninsular War* (1818) [Commissariat]
Dalrymple, William, *Travels through Spain and Portugal in 1774* (1777)
*§[Daniel, John Edgecombe], *Journal of an Officer in the Commissariat ...* (1820)
Davies, D.W., *Sir John Moore's Peninsular Campaign, 1808–1809* (1974)
Davies, G., *Wellington and his Army* (1958)
Delavoye, Alex. M., *Life of Thomas Graham Lord Lynedoch* (1880)
*Dempsey, Guy, *Albuera 1811: the Bloodiest Battle of the Peninsular War* (2008)
§Dickson, Sir Alexander (ed. John H. Leslie), *The Dickson Manuscripts ...* (1908–12) [R.A.]
§Dobbs, John, *Recollections of an old 52nd Man* (2nd ed. 1863)
*§Donaldson, Joseph, *Recollections of the Eventful Life of a Soldier* (1825; new ed. 1852) [94th]
Douglas, Sir Howard, Bart., *An Essay on the Principles and Construction of Military Bridges, and the Passage of Rivers in Military Operations* (1816; 2nd ed. 1832)
§Douglas, John (ed. S. Monick), *Douglas's Tale of the Peninsula and Waterloo* (1997) [1st Royal Scots]
Duffy, Christopher, *The Military Experience in the Age of Reason* (1987)
Dumouriez, Charles-François, *An Account of Portugal, as it appeared in 1775 …* (1797)
Duncan, Francis, *History of the Royal Regiment of Artillery* (1872)
*§D'Urban, B. (ed. I.J. Rousseau), *Peninsular Journal of Major-Gen. Sir Benjamin D'Urban,1808–1817* (1930, reprinted 1988)
Dyneley, T. (ed. F.A. Whinyates), *Letters Written by Lieut.-General Thomas Dyneley ...* (1895; in book form, 1984) [R.A.]
Eadie, Robert, *Recollections of the 79th* (1829)
*Eliot, William Granville, *Treatise on the Defence of Portugal* (3rd ed., 1811) [R.A.]
Esdaile, Charles J., *The Spanish Army in the Peninsular War* (1988) *The Duke of Wellington and the Command of the Spanish Army* (1990) *The Peninsular War: a New History* (2002), *Fighting Napoleon: Guerrillas, Bandits and adventurers in Spain 1808–1814* (2004), *Napoleon's Wars: an International History 1803–1815* (2007), *Peninsular Eyewitnesses: the Experience of War in Spain 1808–1813*, forthcoming.
Espinalt y Garcia, Bernardo, *Guia General de Postas* (1804)
Evêque, Henri L', *Campaigns of the British Army in Portugal* (1812), for its illustrations
§Farmer, George (ed. G.R. Gleig), *The Light Dragoon* (1844) [11th Light Dragoons]
§Ferneyhough, Robert (ed. Philip J. Haythornthwaite), *Military Memoirs of Four Brothers* (2002) [95th]
Fischer, Christian August, *Travels in Spain in 1797 and 1798* (1802)
Fletcher, Ian, *Galloping at everything: British cavalry in the Peninsular War* (1999)

& with R. Poulter, *Gentlemen's Sons: The Foot Guards in the Peninsula and at Waterloo* (1992), *see also* Keep, and Knowles.

Forbes, Maj.-Gen. A, *History of the Ordnance Services* (1929)

§Ford, Richard, *A Hand-Book for Travellers in Spain* (1845, reprinted 1966 with an Introduction by Ian Robertson)

§Fortescue, the Hon. Sir John, *A History of the British Army* (1899–1930), volumes VI–X and corresponding map volumes, *see also* Harris

Fortescue and R.H. Beadon, *The Royal Army Service Corps, a History of Transport and Supply in the British Army* (1930–32); from 1794 to 1918, the first volume covering the Peninsular War period.

§Foy, Maximilien, *History of the War in the Peninsula ...* (1827) *Vie Militaire du Général Foy,* by Maurice Girod de l'Ain (1900), containing extracts from Foy's diaries.

Franklin, Carl, *British Rockets of the Napoleonic and Colonial Wars, 1805–1901* (2005)

Fraser, Ronald, *Napoleon's Cursed War: Spanish Popular Resistance in the Peninsular War,* (2008)

*§Frazer (ed. Edward Sabine), *Letters of Col. Sir Augustus Simon Frazer... commanding the Royal Horse Artillery ...* (1859)

Freer (ed. Norman Scarfe), *Letters from the Peninsula: the Freer Family Correspondence, 1807–1814* (1853) [43rd]

§Gardyne, C. Greenhill, *The Life of a Regiment* [92nd: Gordon Highlanders] (1901)

Garwood, F.S., *The Royal Staff Corps, 1800–1837* (Royal Engineer Journal, vol. 57; 1943)

Gash, Norman (ed.), *Wellington: Studies in the Military and Political Career of the First Duke of Wellington* (1990)

Gates, David, *The British Light Infantry Arm, c. 1790 –1815* (1987); *The Spanish Ulcer: a history of the Peninsular War* (1986)

Girod de l'Ain; *see* Foy

Glasse, Francis, *Ned Clinton; or, The Commissary: comprising Adventures and Events during the Peninsular War* (1825)

*§Gleig, George Robert, *The Subaltern* (1825) [85th]; ed. and with an Intro. by Ian Robertson (2001) *See* also Farmer, and Landscheit.

Glover, Gareth (ed.) **From Corunna to Waterloo: The Letters and Journals of Two ... Hussars, 1808–1816* (2007), being those of Major Edwin Griffiths and Captain Frederick Philips [15th Hussars], but they were not in the Peninsula between Feb. 1809 and Feb. 1813. *

(ed.) *Wellington's Lieutenant, Napoleon's Gaoler: the Peninsula Letters and St Helen Diaries of Sir George Ridout Bingham,1809–21* (2005) [53rd]

(ed.) *The Corunna Journal of Captain Charles Alphonse Pierrepoint AQMG* (2005) [20th]

(ed.) *Hellish Business: The Letters of Captain Charles Kinloch, 52nd Foot, 1806–16* (2007)

(ed.) *The Peninsular Diary of Ensign John V. Carter* (2007) [30th]

(ed.) *A Young Gentleman at War: The Letters of Captain the Hon. Orlando Bridgeman, in the Peninsula and at Waterloo,1812–15* (2007) [1st Foot Guards]

Glover, Michael, *Wellington as Military Commander* (1968) *The Peninsular War, 1807–1814: a Concise History* (1974) *A Very Slippery Fellow: The Life of Sir Robert Wilson, 1777–1849* (1978) *See also* Hennell

*§Glover, Richard, *Peninsular Preparation: The Reform of the British Army, 1795–1809* (1963)

§Gomm (ed. Francis Culling Carr-Gomm), *Letters and Journals of F.-M. Sir William Maynard Gomm ...* (1888) [Staff]
§Gordon, Alexander (ed. H. Wylly), *A Cavalry Officer in the Corunna Campaign* (1913) [15th Hussars]
*Gordon (ed. Rory Muir), *At Wellington's Right Hand: The Letters of Lt-Col. Sir Alexander Gordon,1808–1815* (2003) [Staff]
Gough, Hugh (ed. Robert S. Rait), *The Life and Campaigns of Hugh, first Viscount Gough* (1903) [87th]
Graham, William, *Travels through Portugal, Spain and France 1812–14* (1820), [48th]
Graham, Thomas; *see* Aspinal-Oglander, Brett-James, and Delavoye
Grant, Colquhoun; *see* Haswell
*§Grattan, William, *Adventures with the Connaught Rangers,1809–14* (1847; 1853); ed. Sir Charles Oman (1902) [88th]
Graves, Donald E., *Fix Bayonets! A Royal Welch Fusilier at War, 1796–1815,* (2006)
§Green, John, *The Vicissitudes of a Soldier's Life ... from 1806 to 1815* (1827) [68th]
Griffith, Edwin; *see* Glover, Gareth
Griffith, Paddy, *Wellington – Commander: The Iron Duke's Generalship* (1985) *The Art of War of Revolutionary France,1789–1802* (1989)
*(ed.) *Modern Studies of the War in Spain and Portugal, 1808–1814* (1999), the complementary vol. IX to a reprint of Oman's *History*, containing pertinent essays, and a bibliography of works published since 1930, etc.
Guthrie, George J., *Commentaries on the surgery of the War* (1855)
Hall, Basil, *Fragments of Voyages and Travels* (1831)
Hall, Christopher D., *British Strategy in the Napoleonic Wars, 1803–1815* (1992) *Wellington's Navy: Sea Power and the Peninsular War, 1807–1814* (2004)
Hall, John A., *The Biographical Dictionary of British Officers Killed and Wounded, 1808–1814, together with non-combat casualties* (1998), the complementary vol. VIII to the reprint of Oman's *History.*
Halliday, Andrew, *Observations on the Present State of the Portuguese Army* (1811)
Hamilton, H.B., *Historical Record of the 14th (King's) Hussars ...* (1901)
Hamilton, Thomas, revised and augmented by Frederick Hardman, *Annals of the Peninsular Campaigns* (1849)
§Harris, Benjamin Randall (ed. Henry Curling), *Recollections of Rifleman Harris* (1848); with Introduction by Sir John Fortescue (1928); ed. by Christopher Hibbert (1970); and ed. by Eileen Hathaway as *A Dorset Rifleman: The Recollections of Benjamin Harris* (1995) [95th]
Haswell, Jock, *The First Respectable Spy – The life and times of Colquhoun Grant* (1969)
Hathaway, Eileen; *see* Cooke, Costello, Harris, and Lawrence
§Hawker, Peter, *Journal of a Regimental Officer during the Recent Campaigns* (1810) [14th Light Dragoons]
Hay, Sir Andrew Leith, *A Narrative of the Peninsular War* (3rd ed., 1829) [29th and Staff]
§Hay, Capt. William, *Reminiscences under Wellington* (1901) [52nd, and 16th Light Dragoons]
Hayman, Peter, *Soult: Napoleon's Maligned Marshal* (1990)
Hayter, Alethea (ed.), *The Backbone: Diaries of a Military Family in the Napoleonic Wars* (1993) [RA], containing that of John Henry Slessor.
Haythornthwaite, Philip J., *Weapons and Equipment of the Napoleonic Wars* (1979) *The Armies of Wellington* (1994), *see also* Fernyhough, Rocca, Sherer, and Smith.

Head, Sir George, *A Home Tour through the Manufacturing Districts of England ... in 1835* (1840)

Heer, Richard, *The Eighteenth-Century Revolution in Spain* (1958), for late 18th Century background.

§Hennegan, Sir Richard D., *Seven Years' Campaigning in the Peninsula ...* (1846) [Field train]

*Hennell, George (ed. Michael Glover), *A Gentleman Volunteer: The Letters of ... from the Peninsula,1812–13* (1979) [43rd]

*§Henry, Walter, *Events of a Military Life ...* (1843); ed. by Pat Hayward, & entitled *Surgeon Henry's Trifles ...* (1970) [66th] Hill, Rowland; *see* Teffeteller

§Hibbert, Christopher, *Corunna* (1961); *see also* Harris , Howell, and Wheatley.

*Holland, Elizabeth, Lady (ed. The Earl of Ilchester), *The Spanish Journal of ...* (1910)

§Hope, *The Iberian and Waterloo Campaigns: The Letters of Lt James Hope 1811–1815* (2000) [92nd]

Horward, Donald D., *The Battle of Bussaco: Masséna versus Wellington* (1965) *Napoleon and Iberia – the twin sieges of Ciudad Rodrigo and Almeida, 1810* (1984)

§Houlding, J.A., *Fit for Service: The Training of the British Army, 1715–1795* (1981)

*Howard, Martin, *Wellington's Doctors* (2002) *Napoleon's Doctors* (2006)

§[Howell, Thomas], *Journal of T.S., a Soldier of the 71st Highland Light Infantry ...1806 to 1815* (1819), or as *Vicissitudes in the Life of a Scottish Soldier* (1828); attrib. to Thomas Pococke, and ed. Christopher Hibbert (1975), and to James Todd.

§Hughes, B.P., *Firepower. Weapons' Effectiveness on the Battlefield, 1630–1850* (1974)

Hughes, James; *see* Hunt, Eric

*Hunt, Eric E., *Charging against Napoleon: Diaries & Letters of three Hussars* [James Hughes, Arthur Kennedy, and George Woodberry; but also Loftus Otway et al] (2001) [18th Hussars]

**Inside Wellington's Peninsular Army ...*, by Robert Burnham, Ron McGuigan, Howie Muir, & Rory Muir (2006)

Jackson, Robert, *A Systematic View of the Formation, Discipline, and Economy of Armies* (1804) [surgeon & 71st]

Jacob, William, *Travels in the South of Spain* (1811)

Jardine, Alexander, *Letters from Barbary, France, Spain, Portugal, etc.* (1788)

*§Jones, John Thomas (later Major-General Sir John Jones, Bart.), *Journals of Sieges ... in Spain, ... 1811 to 1814* (1814; but preferable is the 3rd ed., ed. Harry D. Jones, 1846), including the *Memoranda Relative to the Lines thrown up to cover Lisbon in 1810* [R.E.] *Account of the War in Spain and Portugal, and in the South of France ...* (1818)

§Jones, Rice (ed. the Hon. Henry Shore), *An Engineer Officer under Wellington in the Peninsula: The Diary and War Correspondence of Lieut. Rice Jones* (1986)

Keep (ed. Ian Fletcher), *In the Service of the King: The Letters of William Thornton Keep ...* (1997) [77th/28th]

Kennedy, Arthur; *see* Hunt, Eric

Kennedy, Robert Hugh, *Detailed Instructions to Commissariat Accountants ...* (1812)

§Kincaid, Sir John, *Adventures in the Rifle Brigade ...* (1830) [95th] §*Random Shots from a Rifleman* (1835) [95th]

Kinloch, Charles; *see* Glover, Gareth

§Knowles (ed. Sir Lees Knowles), *The War in the Peninsula: Some Letters of Lieutenant Robert Knowles* (1913); with an Intro. by Ian Fletcher (2004) [7th]

Laborde, Alexander de, *A View of Spain; comprising a Descriptive Itinerary ... and General Statistical Account of the Country,* in 5 volumes (1809)

§Landmann, George Thomas, *Recollections of My Military Life* (1854) [R.E.], *Historical, Military, and Picturesque Observations on Portugal* (1818)
§Landscheit (ed. G.R. Gleig), *The Hussar: the story of Sergeant Norbert Landscheit ...* (1837) [20th Light Dragoons]
*§Larpent, Francis Seymour (ed. Sir George Larpent, Bart.), *The Private Journal of Judge-Advocate Larpent ...* (3rd ed. 1854); reprinted with an Intro. by Ian Robertson (2000) [Staff]
Lawford, J.P.; *see* Young
§Lawrence (ed. George Nugent Bankes), *The Autobiography of Sergeant William Lawrence ...* (1886); ed. by Eileen Hathaway as *A Dorset Soldier: The Autobiography of Sgt William Lawrence, 1790–1869* (1993) [40th]
*§Leach, Jonathan, *Rough Sketches of the Life of an Old Soldier ...* (1831) [95th] *Rambles on the Banks of Styx* (1847)
Lejeune, Baron Louis-François, *Mémoires du Général Lejeune ...* (1869; trans. Mrs Arthur Bell; 1897)
§Le Marchant, General John Gaspard, *Memoirs* (1841), reprinted with an Intro. by David Chandler (1997)
Leslie of Balquhain, Charles, *Military Journal of Colonel Leslie ... in the Peninsula ...* (1887) [29th]
Leslie, John H., *The Services of the Royal Regiment of Artillery in the Peninsular War* (1912)
Lever, Charles, *Charles O'Malley* (1841), fiction, but largely based on anecdotes heard from old soldiers of the 88th.
Levinge, Sir Richard George Augustus, *Historical Records of the 43rd Regiment ...* (1868)
Lewis, Michael, *Napoleon and his British Captives* (1962)
Link, Heinrich Friedrich, *Travels in Portugal* (1801)
Lloyd, Clive, *A History of Napoleonic and American Prisoners of War, 1756–1816: Hulk, Depot and Parole* (2007) *The Arts and Crafts of American and Napoleonic Prisoners of War, 1756–1816* (2007)
Locker, Edward Hawke, *Views in Spain* (1824), mainly for its lithographs.
§Londonderry, Marquess of, *Narrative of the Peninsular War* (1828)
Long, R. (ed. T.H. McGuffie), *A Peninsula Cavalry General, 1811–13: The Correspondence of ... Robert Ballard Long* (1951)
Longford, Elizabeth, *Wellington: The Years of the Sword* (1969)
McGrigor, J., *The Autobiography and Services of Sir James McGrigor, late Dir.-Gen. of the Army Medical Dept.* (1861) (ed. Mary McGrigor), *The Scalpel and the Sword* (2000) *See* Blanco
McGuigan, Ron; see *Inside Wellington's Peninsular Army*
§Mackinnon, H., *A Journal of the Campaign in Portugal and Spain ... from the Year 1809 to 1811* (1812)
Mainwaring, Frederick, *Four Years of a Soldier's Life* (Colburn's United Service Magazine, 1844) [51st]
§Malcolm, John, *Reminiscences of the Campaign in the Pyrenees and the South of France in 1813–14* (1828) [42nd]
Malet, Harold, *The Historical Memoirs of the XVIIIth Hussars* (1907)
Malmesbury, 3rd Earl (ed.), *A Series of Letter of the First Earl* (1870), vol 2 largely concerns the Peninsular War.
Mampel, Johann Christian, *The Adventures of a Young Rifleman ... from 1806 to 1816* (1826)

Marshall-Cornwall, James, *Marshal Masséna* (1965)
Mallinson, Howard, *Send it by Semaphore – the old telegraphs during the wars with France* (2005)
Masséna; *see* Marshall-Cornwall
*§Maxwell, William Hamilton (ed.), *Peninsular Sketches, by Actors on the Scene* (1845)
§Mayne, R. and J.W. Lillie, *A Narrative of the Campaigns of the Loyal Lusitanian Legion, 1809–11* (1812)
Milburne, Henry, *A Narrative of Circumstances Attending the Retreat … of Sir John Moore* (1809)
Mills (ed. Ian Fletcher), *For King and Country: The Letters … of John Mills, Coldstream Guards, 1811–1814* (1995)
Mitchell, T. Livingstone; *see* Wyld
*Mollo, John, *The Prince's Dolls: Scandals, Skirmishes and Splendours of the first British Hussars, 1793–1815* (1997)
Moore, James (ed.), *A Narrative of the Campaign … commanded by … Sir John Moore* (1809)
Moore, Sir John (ed. J. Maurice), *The Diary of* (1904) *See* Oman, Carola
Moorsom, William Scarth, *Historical Record of the 52nd Regiment ...* (1860)
§Morley, Stephen, *Memoirs of a Sergeant of the 5th Regt. of Foot* (1842)
§Morris, T. (ed. J. Selby), *Thomas Morris: The Napoleonic Wars* (1967)
Muir, Howie; see *Inside Wellington's Peninsular Army*
Muir, Rory J.B., **Britain and the Defeat of Napoleon, 1807–1815* (1996) **Tactics and the Experience of Battle in the Age of Napoleon* (1998) **Salamanca, 1812* (2001) See also *Inside Wellington's Peninsular Army*
Munster, George FitzClarence, later Earl of, *An Account of the British Campaign of 1809 …* (1831).
Murray, George; *see* Wyld
Myatt, Frederick, *British Sieges of the Peninsular War* (1987) *Peninsular General, Sir Thomas Picton 1758–1815* (1980)
Napier, Sir Charles (ed. Sir William Napier), *The Life and Opinions of General Sir Charles James Napier* [50th] (1857)
Napier (ed. W.C. Napier), *Passages in the Early Military Life of Gen. Sir George T. Napier* [43rd] (1886)
§Napier, Sir William, **History of the War in the Peninsula and the South of France* (1828–40) §*English Battles and Sieges in the Péninsula* (1852)
*Neale, Adam, *Letters from Portugal and Spain comprising an Account of the Operations of the Armies … from Mondego Bay to the Battle of Corunna* (1809) [surgeon]
Nichols, Alistair, *Wellington's Mongrel Regiment: A History of the Chasseurs Britanniques Regiment 1801–1814* (2005)
Nicol, Daniel, *Sergeant Nicol: The Experiences of a Gordon Highlander during the Napoleonic Wars* (2007)
Nosworthy, Brent, *Battle Tactics of Napoleon and his Enemies* (1995)
Oman, Carola, *Sir John Moore* (1953)
§Oman, Sir Charles William Chadwick, **Wellington's Army, 1809–14* (1912) *§*History of the Peninsular War*, 7 vols (1902–30); if only it had a proper index !
Ompteda, Baron Christian, *A Hanovarian-English Officer a Hundred Years Ago ...*, trans. by John Hill (1892); reissued as §*In the King's German Legion: Memoirs of Baron Ompteda ...* (1894)
§O'Neil, *The Military Adventures of Charles O'Neil …* (1851); with an Intro. by Bernard Cornwell (1997)

Ormsby, James Wilmot, *An Account of the Operations of the British Army ... during ... 1808 and 1809* (1809)
Otway, Loftus; *see* Hunt, Eric.
Page, F.C.G., *Following the Drum: Women in Wellington's Wars* (1986)
Page, Julia; *see* Cocks
Pakenham, Sir Edward (ed. 5th Earl of Longford), *The Pakenham Letters, 1800–1815* (1913/14)
Patterson, *The Adventures of Captain John Patterson ...* (1837) [50th]
Pelet, Jean-Jacques (ed. Donald D. Horward), *The French Campaign in Spain and Portugal, 1810–1811* (1973)
Peyron, Jean-François, *Essays on Spain* (1789)
Philips; *see* Glover, G
Picton (ed. Heaton B. Robinson), *Memoirs of ... Sir Thomas Picton* (1835) [Staff] *See* Myatt
Pierrepoint, Charles; *see* Glover, Gareth
Porter, Sir Robert Ker, *Letters from Portugal and Spain ...* (1809) [Staff]
Quentin, *The Trial of Colonel Quentin of the 10th Hussars* (1814)
Quin, Michael Joseph, *A Visit to Spain* (1823)
Rawson, Andrew, *The Peninsular War: a Battlefield Guide,* forthcoming
Redgrave, T.M.O., *Wellington's Logistical Arrangements in the Peninsular War, 1809–14* (unpublished Uni. of London PhD thesis, 1988),
Riley, Jonathan P., *Napoleon and the World War of 1813* (2001)
Roberts, David, *The Military Adventures of Johnny Newcome* (1815), with 15 plates by Rowlandson
Robertson, Ian C., *Wellington at War in the Peninsula, 1808–1814: an Overview and Guide* (2000) *Wellington invades France: the Final Phase of the Peninsular War, 1813–1814* (2003) *See* Baretti, Gleig, Larpent, and Weller
§Rocca, Albert Jean-Michel de, *Memoirs of the War of the French in Spain* (1815); with an Intro. by Philip J.Haythornthwaite, entitled *In the Peninsula with a French Hussar* (1990).
Rogers, H.C.B., *Wellington's Army* (1979)
§Ross-Lewin, Harry, *Life of a Soldier, a narrative of 27 years' service ...* (1834), or (ed. John Wardrell), *With the 32nd in the Peninsula ...* (1904)
Rothenberg, Gunther E., *The Art of Warfare in the Age of Napoleon* (1977)
Rous, John Edward Cornwallis (ed. Ian Fletcher), *A Guards Officer in the Peninsula. The ... Letters of ..., Coldstream Guards, 1812–14* (1992)
Routh, Sir Randolph Isham, *Observations on Commissariat Field Service and Home Defences* (1852)
Royal Military Calender, The (3rd ed., 5 vols, 1820): brief biographies of officers of the rank of Major and above.
*§Schaumann, August Ludolf Friedrich (trans. and ed. Anthony M. Ludovici), *On the Road with Wellington. The Diary of a War Commissary ...* (1924); with an Intro. by Bernard Cornwell (1999) [K.G.L. and Commissariat]
Scovell; *see* Urban
Semple, Robert, *Observations on a Journey through Spain and to Naples* (1807)
Second Journey in Spain (1809)
? Shadwell, Laurence, *Life of Colin Campbell, Lord Clyde* (1881)
*§[Sherer, G. Moyle], *Recollections of the Peninsula* (1824) [34th]; with an Intro. by Philip J. Haythornthwaite (1996)
Sherwig, John M., *Guineas and Gunpowder: British Foreign Aid in the Wars with*

France, 1793–1815 (1969)
*§Simmons, G. (ed. Willoughby Verner), *A British Rifle Man. The Journals and Correspondence of Major George Simmons ...* (1899) [95th]
Slessor, John; *see* Hayter
§Smith, Henry George Wakelyn (ed. G.C. Moore Smith), *Autobiography of Sir Harry Smith, 1787–1819* (1 vol. ed., 1910) [95th]; with an Intro. by Philip J. Haythornthwaite (1999)
Soult; *see* Hayman
Southey, Robert, *History of the Peninsular War* (1823–32) *Letters written during a Journey in Spain ...* (1808)
§Stanhope, Philip Henry, 5th Earl, *Notes of Conversations with the Duke of Wellington, 1831–1851* (1888)
*§Stothert, William, *A Narrative of the Principal Events ... in Spain and Portugal* (1812) [3rd Foot Guards]
*§Surtees, William, *Twenty-Five Years in the Rifle Brigade* (1833) [56th, and 95th]
§Swabey, William (ed. F.A. Whinyates), *Diary of Campaigns in the Peninsula ... 1811–1813* (1895) [R.A.]
Swinburne, Henry, *Travels through Spain in the years 1775 and 1776* (1779)
§[Tale, Sgt-Major W.], *Jottings from my Sabretache, by a Chelsea Pensioner* (1847) [15th Light Dragoons]
Taylor, John; *see* Ayrton
Teffeteller, Gordon L., *The Surpriser: The Life of Rowland, Lord Hill* (1983)
§Thackwell (ed. H.C. Wylly), *The Military Memoirs of Lieut-Gen. Sir Joseph Thackwell* (1908) [15th Hussars]
Thompson, Mark S., *The Fatal Hill: The Allied Campaign under Beresford in Southern Spain in 1811* (2002)
Thornton, James (ed. Elizabeth Longford), *Your Most Obedient Servant: Cook to the Duke of Wellington* (1985)
*§Tomkinson, William (ed. James Tomkinson), *The Diary of a Cavalry Officer ... 1809–1815* (1894) [16th Light Dragoons]; with an Intro. by the 7th Marquess of Anglesey (1999)
Townsend, Joseph, *Journey through Spain in the years 1786 and 1787* (1791)
Twiss, Richard, *Travels through Spain and Portugal* (1775)
Uffindell, Andrew (ed.), *The National Army Museum Book of Wellington's Armies: Britains Campaigns in the Peninisula and at Waterloo 1808–1815* (2003), containing numerous quotations from letters in that museum's archive.
Urban, Mark, *The Man who Broke Napoleon's Codes. The Story of George Scovell* (2001), with reservations, and despite some inadequacies.
Vane; *see* Londonderry
Vaughan, Charles Richard, *Narrative of the Siege of Zaragoza* (1809)
Verner, William (ed. R.W. Verner), *Reminiscences of William Verner(1782–1871) 7th Hussars* (JSAHR, 1965)
§Verner, Willoughby, *History & Campaigns of the Rifle Brigade, 1800–1813* (1912; 1919)
Vichness, Samuel E., *Marshal of Portugal: The Military Career of William Carr Beresford, 1785–1814* (Unpublished PhD thesis, Florida State University, 1976)
§Vivian, Richard Hussey (ed. The Hon. Claud Vivian), *Memoir and Letters* (1897) [7th Hussars & 54th]
*Ward, Stephen George Peregrine, *Wellington's Headquarters: A Study of the Administrative Problems ...* (1957), *Wellington* (1963)

§Warre, Sir William (ed. E. Warre), *Letters from the Peninsula, 1808–1812* (1909) [Portuguese Staff]

Webber, William (ed. R.H. Woollocombe), *With the Guns in the Peninsula … the Peninsular War Journal …* (1991) [R.A.]

Webster, C.K., *The Foreign Policy of Castlereagh, 1812–1815* (1931).

§Weller, Jac [John Allen Claude] (ed. Ian Robertson), *Wellington in the Peninsula, 1808–1814* (1962) (ed. Andrew Uffindell), *On Wellington: The Duke and his Art of War* (1998)

[Wellington, 1st Duke of] (ed. John Gurwood), *General Orders of ... Wellington* (1839) *Selections from the Dispatches and General Orders …* (1841)
(ed. John Gurwood), *The Dispatches of … Wellington* (1834–9; 1844; 1852)
(ed. 2nd Duke), *Supplementary Dispatches, Correspondence and Memoranda of … Wellington* (1858–72)

*Wheatley, Edmund (ed. Christopher Hibbert), *The Wheatley Diary ...* (1964) [K.G.L.]

§Wheeler, William (ed. Basil H. Liddell-Hart), *The Letters of Private Wheeler, 1809–1828* (1951) [51st]

Wildman, (ed. Michael Birks), *The Young Hussar; the Peninsular War Journal of Colonel Thomas Wildman ...* (2007) [7th Dragoons]

§Wilson, Sir Robert, *General Wilson's Journal, 1812–14* (1861), new edition by Antony Brett-James (1964); *see* Glover

§Wood, George, *The Subaltern Officer ...* (1825) [82nd]

Woodberry, George, *Journal of Lieut Woodberry in the Campaigns of 1813–15* (Paris 1896) [18th Hussars] *See* Hunt, Eric

Wyld, James, cartographer and publisher of an *Atlas Showing the Principal Movements, Battles, and Sieges … during the War from 1808 to 1814 ...* (1841), largely compiled by Thomas Livingston Mitchell, together with the *Memoir* by Sir George Murray annexed.

Young, Peter, and J.P. Lawford, *Wellington's Masterpiece: The Battle and Campaign of Salamanca* (1973)

Addendum

Among recent Dissertations and Theses of interest, as yet unpublished, are:

Bamford, Andrew, *The Performance of the British Army in Moore's Corunna Campaign* (Leeds, M.A., 2006), and *The British Army on Campaign 1808–1815: Manpower, Cohesion and Effectiveness* (forthcoming Leeds PhD. thesis)

Davies, Huw J., *British Military Intelligence in the Peninsular War* (Exeter PhD. thesis, 2006)

Linch, Kevin B., *The Recruitment of the British Army 1807–1815* (Leeds PhD. thesis, 2001)

McMillan, Bryan, *British Military Justice 1803–15: the Myth and Reality* (Leeds M.A., 2006)

Moore, Zeta, *Army Recruitment and the Uncertainties of the 'Fiscal-Military' State in Britain, 1793–1815* (London PhD. thesis, 2006)

Romans, Mark, *Professionalism and the Development of Military Intelligence in Wellington's Army, 1809–1814* (Southampton PhD. thesis, 2005)

Thompson, Mark S., *The rise of the Scientific Soldier as seen through the performance of the Corps of Royal Engineers during the early 19th Century* (Sunderland PhD. thesis)

Index

The author had intended this to have been even wider-ranging, including such recurrent topics as torrential rain, the scorching heats of six summers and freezing snows of six winters, but his enthusiasm soon melted. Thus, in a book so dense with references to a great diversity of subjects – many described more *en passant* than in detail – rather than compiling an intimidatingly elaborate and exhaustive index, he has preferred it to be selective if not idiosyncratic, yet adequate enough to direct one to matters of particular interest, even if, inevitably, some peripheral aspects are overlooked; nor, by any means, has every thread been taken up in the intricate fabric of war.

References to prisoners, for instance, are not included, nor several other matters referred to virtually passim: among them, the transport of ammunition, artillery, equipment, provisions, and supplies by bullock-carts or mule-back; or carters, drivers and muleteers; nor to constant looting, plundering and pillaging.

Apart from the headings British, French, Portuguese, and Spanish, several analogous themes will be found under cavalry; clothing and footwear; imposing discipline; insects and vermin; medical department; shelter; sports, pastimes and pranks; women; and wounded.